Pierre Bélanger ist Landschaftsarchitekt und Professor, der zurzeit an der Harvard Universität, Graduate School of Design lehrt. Im Jahr 2001 gründete er das Landscape Infrastructure Lab, das fachübergreifend und kooperativ Wissen, Medien, Design und Strategien für öffentliche Bauprojekte produziert. In seinen Schriften beschäftigt er sich mit der Konvergenz von Landschaft, Infrastruktur und Ökologie: Landscape Infrastructures DVD (Canadian National Research Council, 2009), „Regionalisation" (JOLA, 2010), „Power Perestroika" (New Geographies, 2009) Redefining Infrastructure (Ecological Urbanism, 2010), „Landscape as Infrastructure" (Landscape Journal, 2009) und „Landscapes of Disassembly" (Topos, 2007). Er ist ein von der Regierung ernanntes Mitglied des Ontario Food Terminal Board und wurde mit dem Professional Prix de Rome vom Kanadischen Ministerium für Kunst ausgezeichnet.

Jane Bennett ist Professorin für Politikwissenschaft an der Johns Hopkins Universität, wo sie politische Theorie und politisches Denken in Amerika lehrt. Zu ihren jüngsten Publikationen zählen *Vibrant Matter. A Political Ecology of Things* (Duke, 2010), Essays über den vom Dichter Walt Whitman geprägten Begriff „solar judgment" und über Michel Serres' Auffassung von Zeit, sowie das Buch *The Enchantment of Modern Life* (Princeton, 2001). Sie ist ein Gründungsmitglied der Zeitschrift *theory&event* und arbeitet derzeit an einem Projekt, das sich mit übermäßigem Verbrauch und Praktiken des Hortens beschäftigt.

Ila Berman ist Professorin und Direktorin für Architektur am California College of the Arts und Direktorin von Studio Matrixx. Sie ist eine Architektin und Architekturtheoretikerin mit einem Ph.D. der Harvard Universität, Graduate School of Design. Zu Bermans Arbeiten und Veröffentlichungen zählen das Buch *URBANbuild local global* (Stout, 2009), der Essay „Amphibious Territories" im zuletzt erschienenen *AD Territory: Architecture Beyond Environment*, *New Orleans: Strategies for a City in Soft Land* und die Ausstellung „Urban Mappings für eine Stadt der Zukunft" bei der 10. Internationalen Architekturbiennale in Venedig.

Raoul Bunschoten, Leiter von CHORA Architektur und Städtebau, ist Professor für Systematik des Städtebaus an der Fachhochschule in Düsseldorf und Berater des deutschen Ministeriums für Bau- und Stadtentwicklung in Fragen der nachhaltigen Stadtplanung und Energieeffizienz im Stadtentwurf. CHORA Architektur und Städtebau ist ein Planungs- und Architekturbüro, das im Jahre 1994 gegründet wurde. Es hat eine Reihe von Preisen für städtebauliche Projekte gewonnen, unter anderem den Ideenwettbewerb Tempelhof in Berlin, den Wettbewerb für einen neuen Stadtteil in Kopenhagen, die Hafenfront Århus, Dänemark, und ist Gewinner des Wettbewerbs für den öffentlichen Raum Schuytgraaf.

Michel Desvigne ist Architekt, der Gastprofessor an der Eidgenössischen Technischen Hochschule Lausanne, am Institut für Architektur in Genf und an der Harvard Universität, Graduate School of Design war. Er studierte Botanik und Geologie an der Universität der Wissenschaften in Lyon-II, bevor er an der École Nationale Superieure von Versailles einen Abschluss in Landschaftsarchitektur DPLG erwarb. Im Jahr 1988 gründete er das Büro Desvigne

Pierre Bélanger is a landscape architect and associate professor currently teaching at Harvard University, Graduate School of Design. In 2001, he founded the Landscape Infrastructure Lab, which produces cross-disciplinary and collaborative knowledge, media, design, and strategies for public works projects. His writings focus on the convergence of landscape, infrastructure, and ecology: Landscape Infrastructures DVD (Canadian National Research Council, 2009), "Regionalisation" (JOLA, 2010), "Power Perestroika" (New Geographies, 2009), "Redefining Infrastructure" (Ecological Urbanism, 2010), "Landscape as Infrastructure" (Landscape Journal, 2009), and "Landscapes of Disassembly" (Topos, 2007). He is a government-appointed member of the Ontario Food Terminal Board and recipient of the Professional Prix de Rome awarded by the Canada Council for the Arts.

Jane Bennett is a professor of political science at Johns Hopkins University, where she teaches political theory and American political thought. Her recent publications include *Vibrant Matter: A Political Ecology of Things* (Duke, 2010), essays on the poet Walt Whitman's notion of "solar judgment" and on Michel Serres's notion of time, and *The Enchantment of Modern Life* (Princeton, 2001). She is a founding member of the journal *theory&event* and is currently working on a project on over-consumption and practices of hoarding.

Ila Berman is professor and director of architecture at the California College of the Arts and principal of Studio Matrixx. She is an architect and architectural theorist with a PhD from Harvard University, Graduate School of Design. Berman's work and publications include the book *URBANbuild local global* (Stout, 2009), "Amphibious Territories" in the recent *AD* entitled *Territory: Architecture Beyond Environment*, the book *New Orleans: Strategies for a City in Soft Land* (Harvard, 2005), and the "Urban Mappings for a Future City" exhibition at the 10th International Architectural Biennale in Venice.

Raoul Bunschoten, principal of CHORA architecture and urbanism, is a professor of urban systematics at the University of Applied Sciences in Düsseldorf and advisor to the German Federal Ministry of Transport, Building and Urban Development on issues related to sustainable city planning and energy efficiency in city design. CHORA architecture and urbanism is a master-planning and architecture office that was established in 1994. It has won a range of prizes for large-scale urban projects, for instance in the Tempelhof urban ideas competition in Berlin, the New Suburb competition in Copenhagen, the Århus harbor front competition in Denmark, and the winning entry for the Schuytgraaf public space competition in the Netherlands.

Michel Desvigne is an architect who has been a visiting professor at the Federal Polytechnic Schools of Lausanne, at the Institute of Architecture in Geneva, and at Harvard University, Graduate School of Design. He graduated in botany and geology at the University of the Sciences of Lyon-II before continuing his studies at the École Nationale Supérieure du Paysage de Versailles, where he earned a degree in landscape architecture (DPLG). In 1988 he established the office Desvigne & Dalnoky and has collaborated with Renzo Piano, Richard Rogers, Herzog & de Meuron, Rem Koolhaas, and Norman Foster. In 2000, Desvigne & Dalnoky received the medal of the Academy of Architecture.

Ana Jeinić is an assistant professor at the Institute of Architectural Theory, History of Art and Cultural Studies at Graz University of Technology. She grew up in Banja Luka (in former Yugoslavia) and studied architecture in Graz, Venice, and Delft. In 2009 she graduated with a diploma thesis titled "LANDSCHAFT FINDET STADT: Auf dem Weg zu einem Landschaftsbegriff für urbane politische Ökologie."

Jeffrey Kastner is a New York-based critic and journalist and the senior editor of *Cabinet* magazine. Kastner's essays have been published in numerous books including, most recently, *Land, Art: A Cultural Ecology Handbook* (Royal Society, 2006) and *Experimental Geography* (Melville House, 2008). He is editor of *Land and Environmental Art* (Phaidon, 1998) and co-editor of *Odd Lots: Revisiting Gordon Matta-Clark's Fake Estates* (Cabinet Books, 2005), and has lectured widely on contemporary art and writing practice. He has served on the faculty of both the School of Visual Arts in New York and the Center for Curatorial Studies at Bard College in Annandale-on-Hudson, New York.

Nina Valerie Kolowratnik studied architecture at Graz University of Technology and Aalto University in Helsinki. Since 2008 she has been collaborating with Alessandro Petti, Sandi Hilal, and Eyal Weizman on the project "Decolonizing Architecture" in Bethlehem and London. Several sections of her diploma thesis "KAFR 'INAN—Images of Presence for a Landscape of Absence: A spatial re-reading of the Palestinian refugee question" have been published in magazines and exhibitions in Israel and Europe. Kolowratnik currently collaborates with Studio Miessen in Berlin. For 2011/12 she is a Fulbright candidate for postgraduate studies in the USA.

Bernhard König studied architecture and city planning in Weimar, Oxford, and Zurich and has collaborated with Herzog & de Meuron in Basel, the Office for Urban Projects in Leipzig, and the Bauhaus Dessau. He is research assistant at the Institute of Architecture and Landscape at Graz University of Technology and responsible for the research project "Integrated Regional INTEGRAL—Energy Landscapes" .

& Dalnoky und arbeitete mit Renzo Piano, Richard Rogers, Herzog & de Meuron, Rem Koolhaas und Norman Foster zusammen. Im Jahr 2000 erhielten Desvigne und Dalnoky die Medaille der Akademie der Architektur.

Ana Jeinić ist wissenschaftliche Assistentin am Institut für Architekturtheorie, Kunst- und Kulturwissenschaften an der Technischen Universität Graz. Sie wuchs in Banja Luka (im ehemaligen Jugoslawien) auf und studierte Architektur in Graz, Venedig und Delft. Im Jahr 2009 schloss sie ihr Studium mit der Diplomarbeit „Landschaft findet Stadt: Auf dem Weg zu einem Landschaftsbegriff für urbane politische Ökologie" ab.

Jeffrey Kastner ist ein in New York ansässiger Kritiker und Journalist und leitender Redakteur des Magazins *Cabinet*. Kastners Essays sind in zahlreichen Büchern erschienen, zuletzt in *Land, Art: A Cultural Ecology Handbook* (Royal Society, 2006) und *Experimental Geography* (Melville House, 2008). Er ist Herausgeber von *Land and Environmental Art* (Phaidon, 1998) und Mitherausgeber von *Odd Lots: Revisiting Gordon Matta-Clark's Fake Estates* (Cabinet Books, 2005) und lehrte über zeitgenössische Kunst und Schreibpraktiken; er hat an der Fakultät der School of Visual Arts in New York und dem Zentrum für kuratorische Studien am Bard College in Annandale-on-Hudson, New York, unterrichtet.

Nina Valerie Kolowratnik studierte Architektur an der Technischen Universität in Graz und an der Aalto Universität in Helsinki. Seit 2008 arbeitete sie mit Alessandro Petti, Sandi Hilal und Eyal Weizman am Projekt „Decolonizing Architecture" in Bethlehem und London. Mehrere Teile ihrer Diplomarbeit „KAFR 'INAN – Bilder der Präsenz für eine Landschaft der Abwesenheit. Ein räumliches Wiederlesen der palästinensischen Flüchtlingsfrage" wurden in Magazinen und Ausstellungen in Israel und Europa gezeigt. Kolowratnik arbeitet derzeit bei Studio Miessen in Berlin. 2011/12 ist sie Fulbright-Kandidatin für ein postgraduales Studium in den USA.

Bernhard König ist wissenschaftlicher Assistent am Institut für Architektur und Landschaft der TU Graz und für das Forschungsprojekt „INTEGRAL – Integrierte Regionale Energielandschaften" zuständig. Er studierte Architektur und Stadtplanung in Weimar, Oxford und Zürich und war unter anderem bei Herzog & de Meuron in Basel, dem Büro für Urbane Projekte in Leipzig und der Stiftung Bauhaus Dessau tätig.

Byron Kuth hat Architektur und bildende Kunst an der Rhode Island School of Design studiert und ist Architekt seit 1992. Gemeinsam mit seiner Partnerin Elizabeth Ranieri gründete er KUTH | RANIERI Architekts im Jahr 1990. Ranieri und er gründeten 2003 die Deep Green Design Alliance, einen multidisziplinären Think Tank für nachhaltige Strategien in Architektur und Städtebau. Zusätzlich zu seiner Praxis hat er am California College of the Arts unterrichtet, war Gastdozent an der Harvard Universität, Graduate School of Design, und nahm an den Friedman Professor Master Studios am College of Environmental Design an der UC Berkeley teil. Princeton Architectural Press mit der Graham Foundation veröffentlichte die Monografie *KUTH | RANIERI Architects* im Jahr 2010.

Byron Kuth holds degrees in architecture and fine arts from the Rhode Island School of Design and has been an architect since 1992. Together with his partner, Elizabeth Ranieri, he established KUTH | RANIERI Architects in 1990. He and Ranieri launched the Deep Green Design Alliance in 2003, a multidisciplinary think tank for sustainable strategies in architecture and urban design. In conjunction with his practice, he has taught at the California College of the Arts, was a visiting instructor at the Harvard Graduate School of Design, and participated in the Howard A. Friedman Visiting Professorship program at the College of Environmental Design at UC Berkeley. Princeton Architectural Press, together with the Graham Foundation, published the monograph *KUTH | RANIERI Architects*, released in 2010.

Klaus K. Loenhart was appointed professor and head of the Institute for Architecture and Landscape at Graz University of Technology in 2006. He studied architecture at the Munich University of Applied Sciences, as well as landscape architecture and architectural theory at Harvard University, Graduate School of Design. His multidisciplinary scope of interest developed through his practice at the office of Herzog & de Meuron and through his studies and teaching at Harvard University. After returning from the USA, he established the office partnership terrain:loenhart&mayr architects and landscape architects in Munich in 2003. At Graz University of Technology, he founded and now runs LANDLAB, a teaching lab and transdisciplinary exploration platform.

Timothy Morton is a professor of English (literature and the environment) at the University of California, Davis. He is the author of *The Ecological Thought* (Harvard UP, 2010), *Ecology without Nature* (Harvard UP, 2007), seven other books and over sixty essays on philosophy, ecology, literature, food, and music. He blogs regularly at http://ecologywithoutnature.blogspot.com.

Philipp Oswalt has been a professor at the University of Kassel since 2006 and director of the Foundation Bauhaus Dessau since 2009. He studied architecture at the Technical University of Berlin and the Berlin University of the Arts. He was editor of the architecture magazine *Arch+* and an architect at the Office for Metropolitan Architecture/Rem Koolhaas, Rotterdam. Establishing his own offices in 1998, he won the competition for the former women's concentration camp Ravensbrück. Oswalt has been visiting professor at the Brandenburg University of Technology in Cottbus, co-head of the European research project "Urban Catalyst," and head of the project "Shrinking Cities" of the German Federal Cultural Foundation.

Martin Prominski has been a professor for the design of urban landscapes at Leibniz University Hanover since 2009.

He studied landscape planning at the Technical University of Berlin and received a master's degree in landscape architecture from Harvard University, Graduate School of Design, with the support of a DAAD scholarship. He has a PhD from the TU Berlin, published in 2004 as *Landschaft Entwerfen*. He is a founder and (through 2010) editor of the *Journal of Landscape Architecture* (*JoLA*). Since 2008, he has been a member of the STUDIO URBANE LANDSCHAFTEN, an interdisciplinary platform concerned with research, practice, and teaching on urban landscapes. His current research focuses on theoretical issues of design, landscape, and ecology.

Philippe Rahm studied at the Federal Polytechnic Schools of Lausanne and Zurich. He obtained his architectural degree in 1993. In 2002, he was chosen to represent Switzerland at the 8th Architecture Biennale in Venice and was one of the twenty-five manifesto's architects of Aaron Betsky's 2008 Architectural Venice Biennale. He has participated in a number of exhibitions worldwide (Archilab 2000, SF-MoMA 2001, CCA Kitakyushu 2004, Frac Centre, Orléans, Centre Pompidou, Beaubourg 2003–2006 and 2007, Manifesta 7, 2008, Louisiana Museum, Denmark, 2009). Rahm was head-master of Diploma Unit 13 at the AA School in London in 2005–2006, visiting professor at the Mendrisio Academy of Architecture in Switzerland in 2004–2005 as well as at the ETH Lausanne in 2006–2007, and guest professor at the Royal School of Architecture of Copenhagen in 2009–2010. He is currently a visiting lecturer at Princeton, USA.

Elizabeth Ranieri earned degrees in architecture and fine arts from the Rhode Island School of Design. She and her partner, Byron Kuth, established KUTH | RANIERI in 1990. She is professor of architecture at the California College of the Arts, has taught at Harvard University, Graduate School of Design, and has participated in the Howard A. Friedman Visiting Professorship program at the College of Environmental Design at UC Berkeley. KUTH | RANIERI has won numerous AIA awards. The firm's installation, *The Body in Repose*, was part of the multimedia show entitled "Fabrications" exhibited at SFMOMA, New York, the MoMA, and the Wexner Center for the Arts. Princeton Architectural Press, together with the Graham Foundation, published the monograph, *KUTH | RANIERI Architects*, released in 2010. Ranieri's most recent article "Without A Trace" appears in ArcCA on faith and loss.

Rietveld Landscape was founded by landscape architect Ronald Rietveld after he won the Prix de Rome for Architecture 2006. In 2003 he graduated from the Amsterdam Academy of Architecture. Many of Rietveld Landscape's projects deal with current developments such as floods, increasing urbanization, extreme rainfall and drought, ecology and sustainability,

Klaus K. Loenhart ist Professor und Leiter des Instituts für Architektur und Landschaft an der Technischen Universität in Graz seit 2006. Er studierte Architektur an der Münchner Hochschule für Angewandte Wissenschaften, und Landschaftsarchitektur und Architekturtheorie an der Harvard Universität, Graduate School of Design. Sein interdisziplinäres Interessensgebiet hat er im Büro von Herzog & de Meuron und dem Studium und der Lehre an der Harvard Universität entwickelt. Nach der Rückkehr aus den USA gründete er 2003 die Büropartnerschaft terrain: loenhart&mayr Architekten und Landschaftsarchitekten in München. An der Technischen Universität Graz gründete er das LANDLAB, als Teaching-Lab und transdisziplinäre Forschungsplattform.

Timothy Morton ist Professor für Englisch (Literatur und Umwelt) an der University of California, Davis. Er ist Autor von *The Ecological Thought* (Harvard UP, 2010), *Ecology without Nature* (Harvard UP, 2007), sieben weiteren Büchern und mehr als sechzig Essays über Philosophie, Ökologie, Literatur, Nahrung und Musik. Er schreibt regelmäßig im Blog: http://ecologywithoutnature.blogspot.com.

Philipp Oswalt ist Professor an der Universität Kassel seit 2006 und Direktor der Stiftung Bauhaus Dessau seit 2009. Er studierte Architektur an der Technischen Universität Berlin und der Universität der Künste Berlin. Er war Redakteur der Architekturzeitschrift *Arch+* und Architekt im Office for Metropolitan Architecture/Rem Koolhaas, Rotterdam. Nach der Gründung seines eigenen Büros im Jahre 1998 gewann er den Wettbewerb für das ehemalige Frauen-KZ Ravensbrück. Oswalt war Gastprofessor an der Brandenburgischen Technischen Universität Cottbus, Co-Leiter des europäischen Forschungsprojektes Urban Catalyst und Leiter des Projekts Schrumpfende Städte der Kulturstiftung des Bundes.

Martin Prominski ist seit 2009 Professor für Urbane Landschaftsentwicklung an der Leibniz Universität Hannover. Er studierte Landschaftsplanung an der Technischen Universität Berlin und erhielt einen Master in Landschaftsarchitektur an der Harvard Universität, Graduate School of Design mit Unterstützung eines DAAD-Stipendiums. Er hat ein Ph.D. der TU Berlin, das im Jahr 2004 als *Landschaft Entwerfen* veröffentlicht wurde. Er ist Gründer und bis 2010 Herausgeber von *Journal of Landscape Architecture* (*JoLA*). Seit 2008 ist er Mitglied des STUDIO URBANE LANDSCHAFTEN, einer interdisziplinären Plattform für Forschung, Praxis und Lehre über urbane Landschaften. Seine aktuelle Forschung konzentriert sich auf theoretische Fragen der Gestaltung, Landschaft und Ökologie.

Philippe Rahm hat an der Eidgenössischen Technischen Hochschule Lausanne und Zürich studiert. Er erhielt seinen Abschluss in Architektur 1993. Im Jahr 2002 wurde er ausgewählt, um die Schweiz auf der 8. Architekturbiennale in Venedig zu vertreten und war einer der 25 Architekten von Aaron Betskys Manifest der Architektur Biennale in Venedig 2008. Er hat an einer Reihe internationaler Ausstellungen teilgenommen (Archilab 2000, SF-MoMA 2001, CCA Kitakyushu 2004, Frac Centre, Orléans, Centre Pompidou, Beaubourg 2003–2006 und 2007, der Manifesta 7, 2008, Louisiana Museum, Dänemark, 2009). Rahm war Leiter des Diplom Unit 13 an der

AA School in London 2005–2006, Gastprofessor in Mendrisio Academy of Architecture in der Schweiz 2004 und 2005, an der ETH Lausanne im Jahre 2006 und 2007, Gastprofessor an der Royal School Architektur von Kopenhagen in den Jahren 2009–2010. Derzeit ist er Gastdozent in Princeton, USA.

Elizabeth Ranieri hat Architektur und Bildende Kunst an der Rhode Island School of Design abgeschlossen. Sie und ihr Partner Byron Kuth etablierten KUTH I RANIERI im Jahr 1990. Sie ist Professorin für Architektur am California College of the Arts, lehrte an der Harvard Universität, Graduate School of Design und als Friedman Professorin für Master Studios am College of Environmental Design an der UC Berkeley. KUTH I RANIERI hat zahlreiche AIA Preise gewonnen. Die Installation The Body in Repose wurde Teil der Multimedia-Show „Fabrications" und am SF-MoMA, am New Yorker MoMA und am Wexner Center ausgestellt. Princeton Architectural Press mit der Graham Foundation hat die Monografie *KUTH I RANIERI Architects* im Jahr 2010 veröffentlicht. Ranieris jüngster Artikel „Without A Trace" erscheint in *ArcCA* über Vertrauen und Verlust.

Rietveld Landscape wurde vom Landschaftsarchitekten Ronald Rietveld gegründet, nachdem er den Prix de Rome für Architektur 2006 gewann. Im Jahr 2003 graduierte er an der Akademie für Architektur in Amsterdam. Viele Projekte befassen sich mit aktuellen Entwicklungen, wie Überschwemmungen, zunehmender Verstädterung, extremen Regenfällen und Dürren, Ökologie und Nachhaltigkeit, Infrastruktur und die sich verändernde Bedeutung des öffentlichen Raumes. Von Beginn an gehörte der Ökonom und Philosoph Erik Rietveld (Harvard Universität) zum Kernteam des Studios. Rietveld Landscape hat den niederländischen Pavillon für die 12. Architekturbiennale in Venedig kuratiert.

Curtis Roth ist ein Architekturstudent am Massachusetts Institute of Technology. Seine Interessen liegen in der historischen Verwendung der natürlichen Ressourcen, Landschaften und Architekturen als diskrete und oft schleichende Formen der politischen Macht. Seine Forschung konzentriert sich auf die Landschaften der landwirtschaftlichen Produktion, den geografischen Fallout der amerikanischen militärisch-industriellen Wirtschaft, die Bestandserhaltung als eine Form der kulturellen Amnesie und die Politik des globalen Emissionshandels.

Anne Sauvagnargues ist Professorin an der Universität Paris Ouest Nanterre La Défense, eine Spezialistin für zeitgenössische französische Philosophie (Deleuze, Guattari) und die Philosophie der Kunst. Sie arbeitet auf dem Gebiet der Formulierung einer Erkenntnistheorie des Kunstdiskurses, von der Philosophie zur Kunstgeschichte (Wölfflin, Riegl, Worringer) und der Entwicklung einer Philosophie der Gegenwart. Sie hat mehrere Bücher und Artikel über Deleuze und Foucault veröffentlicht: *Deleuze et l'art* (PUF, 2005) und *Deleuze: transcendantal L'empiricism* (PUF, 2010). Seit 2005 arbeitet sie gemeinsam mit Fabienne Brugère an der Serie *Ligne d'art* (Presses Universitaires de France) mit drei Publikationen pro Jahr.

Anne Schmidt ist Architektin und verfolgt derzeit als Stipendiatin ein postgraduales Studium an der Harvard Universität. Zuvor war sie als wissen-

infrastructure, and the shifting meaning of public space. From the outset, economist and philosopher Erik Rietveld (Harvard University) has been part of the studio's core team. Rietveld Landscape was curator of the Dutch Pavilion for the 12th Venice Architecture Biennale.

Curtis Roth is a graduate student and design researcher enrolled in the Master of Architecture Program at the Massachusetts Institute of Technology. His interests lie in the historic appropriations of natural resources, landscapes, and architectures as discreet and often surreptitious forms of political power. His research focuses on landscapes of agricultural production, the geographic fallout of the American military-industrial economy, preservation as a form of cultural amnesia and the politics of global emissions trading.

Anne Sauvagnargues is a professor at the University of Paris Ouest Nanterre La Défense as well as specialist in contemporary French philosophy (Deleuze, Guattari) and in philosophy of art. She works both in the formulation of an epistemology of art discourses, from philosophy to art history (Wölfflin, Riegl, Worringer), and in developing a philosophy of the present. She has published several books and articles on Deleuze and Foucault, including *Deleuze et l'art* (PUF, 2005) and *Deleuze: transcendantal L'empiricism* (PUF, 2010). Since 2005 she has been editing, with Fabienne Brugère, the series *Ligne d'art* (Presses Universitaires de France) with three publications per year.

Anne Schmidt is an architect and is currently pursuing a grant for postgraduate studies at Harvard University. Previously, she worked as a research assistant at the ETH Studio Basel, as a freelancer at the Foundation Bauhaus Dessau (2009–2010), and also as a scientific assistant for the project "Shrinking Cities" (2007–2009). She co-founded the project "Exposing New Orleans" (since 2005), and she most recently (in 2010) developed and exhibited with Philipp Oswalt a scenario of climate change for IBA Urban Redevelopment Saxony-Anhalt.

Lola Sheppard and **Mason White** founded Lateral Office in 2002. Sheppard is a professor of architecture at the University of Waterloo with a bachelor's degree from McGill University and a master's of architecture from the Harvard Graduate School of Design. White is a professor of architecture at the University of Toronto with a bachelor's degree from Virginia Tech and a master's of architecture from the Harvard Graduate School of Design. Sheppard and White are also co-directors of InfraNet Lab (2008), a research collective probing the spatial byproducts of contemporary resource logistics. InfraNet Lab is an editor of the journal *Bracket: Architecture, Environment, Digital Culture*. Lateral Office won an Emerging Voices

award from the Architecture League of New York in 2011 and the 2010 Professional Prix de Rome from the Canada Council for the Arts. Lateral Office/InfraNet Lab were also awarded the *Pamphlet Architecture 30* titled *COUPLING: Strategies for Infrastructural Opportunism* (Princeton Architectural Press, 2011).

Katrina Stoll is an architect, urban designer, and educator. She is currently a teaching fellow at North Carolina State University College of Design. She received a bachelor's degree in cultural anthropology at Cornell University and a master's of architecture from Columbia University. She taught architecture and theory at Syracuse University and directed the Master of Advanced Studies in Urban Design program at the ETH Zürich. Along with Scott Lloyd and Room 11, Stoll developed the "IP2100" project, which was featured at the Australian Pavilion for the 12th Venice Biennale. She has edited *Infrastructure as Architecture: Designing Composite Networks* (Jovis, 2011) and contributed to *Cities of Change: Addis Ababa* (Birkhäuser, 2009).

Pavan Sukhdev is special advisor and head of UNEP's Green Economy Initiative and leader of an Economics of Ecosystems and Biodiversity (TEEB) study, whilst still working full-time at Deutsche Bank. Sukhdev pursues long-standing interests in environmental economics and nature conservation through his work with the Green Indian States Trust (GIST). He is also chairperson of the World Economic Forum's Global Agenda Council on Biodiversity and was a speaker at Davos 2010.

Erik Swyngedouw is a professor of geography at Manchester University. He previously held appointments at the University of Oxford and the University of Leuven. He works on urban politics and governance, political ecology, and spatial political economy. He is author of *Social Power and the Urbanization of Water* (Oxford University Press, 2004) and co-edited *In the Nature of Cities* (Routledge, 2006).

John Thackara is a writer, educator, and design producer. He is the author of *In The Bubble: Designing In A Complex World* (MIT Press, 2005). As director of "Doors of Perception," Thackara organizes festivals around the world in which communities imagine sustainable futures—and take practical steps to realize them. Thackara is a fellow of The Young Foundation. He sits on the advisory boards of the Pixelache Festival in Helsinki and the Pecha Kucha Foundation in Tokyo. He is also a member of the UK Parliament's Standing Commission on Design. He authors a widely-read blog at http://designobserver.com.

Charles Waldheim is professor and chair of the Department of Landscape Architecture at Harvard University, Graduate School of Design. Waldheim coined the term "landscape urban-

schaftliche Assistentin am ETH Studio Basel und als freie Mitarbeiterin an der Stiftung Bauhaus Dessau tätig (2009–2010), sowie als wissenschaftliche Mitarbeiterin des Projekts Schrumpfende Städte (2007–2009). Sie ist Mitbegründerin des Projekts Exposing New Orleans (seit 2005) und hat zuletzt für die IBA Stadtumbau Sachsen-Anhalt 2010 gemeinsam mit Philipp Oswalt ein Szenario zum Klimawandel entwickelt und ausgestellt.

Lola Sheppard und **Mason White** gründeten Lateral Office im Jahr 2002. Sheppard ist Professorin für Architektur an der University of Waterloo. Sie hat einen Bachelor von der McGill Universität und einen Master für Architektur von der Harvard Universität, Graduate School of Design. White ist Professor für Architektur an der University of Toronto. Er hat einen Bachelor von der Virginia Tech und einen Master für Architektur von der Harvard Universität, Graduate School of Design. Sheppard und White sind auch Co-Direktoren der InfraNet Lab (2008), einer Forschungsgemeinschaft, die die räumlichen Nebenprodukte der zeitgenössischen Ressourcenlogistik untersucht. InfraNet Lab ist Herausgeber der Zeitschrift *Bracket: Architecture, Environment, Digital Culture*. Lateral Office wurde Emerging Voices von der Architektur-League in New York im Jahr 2011 verliehen und 2010 mit dem Professional Prix de Rome vom Kanadischen Ministerium für Kunst ausgezeichnet. Lateral Office/InfraNet Lab wurde das Pamphlet *Architecture 30* gewidmet mit dem Titel *COUPLING: Strategies for Infrastructural Opportunism* (Princeton Architectural Press, 2011).

Katrina Stoll ist Architektin, Stadtplanerin und Pädagogin. Sie ist derzeit Lehrbeauftragte am North Carolina State University College of Design. Sie erhielt einen Bachelor Abschluss in Kulturanthropologie an der Cornell Universität und einen Master der Architektur an der Columbia Universität. Sie lehrte Architektur und Theorie an der Syracuse Universität und leitete dasMaster of Advanced Studies in Urban Design Programm an der ETH Zürich. Zusammen mit Scott Lloyd und Room 11 entwickelte Stoll das Projekt IP2100, das im australischen Pavillon der 12. Biennale in Venedig vorgestellt wurde. Sie ist Herausgeberin von *Infrastructure as Architecture: Designing Composite Networks* (Jovis, 2011) und Autorin eines Beitrags in *Cities of Change: Addis Ababa* (Birkhäuser, 2009).

Pavan Sukhdev ist Special Advisor und Leiter des UNEP Green Economy Initiative und Leiter der Studie über Ökonomie der Ökosysteme und biologische Vielfalt (TEEB), während er noch Vollzeit bei der Deutschen Bank arbeitete. Sukhdevs Interesse an ökologischer Ökonomie und Naturschutz zeigt sich auch in seiner Arbeit mit dem Green Indian States Trust (GIST). Er ist Vorsitzender des Global Agenda Council des World Economic Forum über die biologische Vielfalt und war Sprecher in Davos 2010.

Erik Swyngedouw ist Professor für Geografie an der Universität Manchester. Zuvor war er an der Universität in Oxford und der Universität Leuven tätig. Er arbeitet über urbane Politik und Verwaltung, politische Ökologie und räumliche politische Ökonomie. Er ist Autor von *Social Power and the Urbanization of Water* (Oxford University Press, 2004) und Mitherausgeber von *In the Nature of Cities* (Routledgc, 2006).

John Thackara ist Schriftsteller, Pädagoge und Design Produzent. Er ist Autor von *In The Bubble: Designing In A Complex World* (MIT Press, 2005). Als Direktor der Doors of Perception organisiert Thackara Festivals auf der ganzen Welt, bei denen die Gemeinden nachhaltige Zukunftskonzepte entwickeln – und praktische Schritte unternehmen, um sie zu realisieren. Thackara ist ein Fellow der The Young Foundation. Er ist Mitglied im Beirat des Pixelache Festival in Helsinki und der Pecha Kucha Foundation in Tokio. Er ist auch Mitglied der Standing Commission on Design des britischen Parlaments und Autor des viel gelesenen Blogs: http://designobserver.com.

Charles Waldheim ist Professor und Leiter des Lehrstuhls für Landschaftsarchitektur an der Harvard Universität, Graduate School of Design. Waldheim prägte den Begriff „Landscape Urbanism", um neue Praktiken der Landschaftsgestaltung im Rahmen des nordamerikanischen Urbanismus zu beschreiben. Er hat ausführlich über das Thema publiziert und ist Herausgeber von *The Landscape Urbanism Reader* (Princeton Architectural Press, 2006). Mit Bezugnahme auf die Stadt Detroit als lesbares Beispiel für die städtisch-industrielle Wirtschaft in Nordamerika ist Waldheim Herausgeber von *CASE: Lafayette Park Detroit* (Prestel/Harvard Design School, 2004). Derzeit schreibt er das erste Buch über die Geschichte von Chicagos International Airport: *Chicago O'Hare: A Natural and Cultural History*.

Slavoj Žižek, marxistischer Philosoph und Psychoanalytiker nach Lacan, ist Senior Researcher an der School of Law, Birkbeck College, University of London, und am Institut für Soziologie, Universität Ljubljana, Slowenien. Er studierte an der Universität Paris und promovierte in Ljubljana über Psychoanalyse. Er war Gastprofessor an einer Reihe von amerikanischen Universitäten (Columbia, Princeton, New School for Social Research, New York University, University of Michigan). Žižek ist Autor zahlreicher Bücher und Essays, wie *The Sublime Object of Ideology* (Verso, 1989), *The Indivisible Remainder: Essays on Schelling and Related Matters* (Verso, 1996), *First as a Tragedy, Then as a Farce* (Verso, 2009) und *Living in the End Times* (Verso, 2010). Er ist Mitherausgeber (mit Clayton Crockett und Creston Davis) von *Hegel and the Infinite: Religion, Politics, and the Dialectic* (Columbia University Press, 2011).

ism" to describe emerging landscape design practices in the context of North American urbanism. He has written extensively on the topic and edited *The Landscape Urbanism Reader* (Princeton Architectural Press, 2006). Citing the city of Detroit as the most legible example of urban industrial economy in North America, Waldheim is editor of *CASE: Lafayette Park Detroit* (Prestel/Harvard Design School, 2004). He is currently writing the first book-length history of Chicago's International Airport, entitled *Chicago O'Hare: A Natural and Cultural History*.

Slavoj Žižek, Marxist philosopher and Lacanian psychoanalyst, is Senior Researcher at the School of Law, Birkbeck College, University of London, and at the Institute of Sociology, University of Ljubljana, Slovenia. He studied at the University of Paris and obtained his PhD in philosophy in Ljubljana studying psychoanalysis. He has been a visiting professor at a number of American Universities (Columbia, Princeton, New School for Social Research, New York University, University of Michigan). Žižek has authored numerous books and essays, including *The Sublime Object of Ideology* (Verso, 1989), *The Indivisible Remainder: Essays on Schelling and Related Matters* (Verso, 1996), *First as a Tragedy, Then as a Farce* (Verso, 2009), and *Living in the End Times* (Verso, 2010). He is co-editor (with Clayton Crockett and Creston Davis) of *Hegel and the Infinite: Religion, Politics, and the Dialectic* (Columbia University Press, 2011).

Zero Landscape

Unfolding Active Agencies of Landscape

BUILDING DESIGN CULTURE ART THEORY HISTORY LANDSCAPE PRACTICE ECOLOGY PLANNING TECHNOLOGY MEDIA

Why Zero? Es ist mit bloßem Auge erkennbar: Mit zunehmender Geschwindigkeit und Intensität besetzen und verändern wir die Lebensräume und Habitate, die uns auf unserem Planeten „zur Verfügung" stehen. Bei dieser Betrachtung sind es nicht nur die Architekturen der Stadt oder Agglomerationen, sondern unsere Gesellschaft an sich, welche auf der Oberfläche unseres Planeten agiert. Landschaft als Raum, aber auch als Idee, so ist aus dieser Perspektive erkennbar, wird in ihrer vielfältigen Handlungsmacht bedrängt, reduziert und oft marginalisiert.

Why Zero? It is visible to the naked eye: with increasing speed and intensity we are occupying and changing the living spaces and habitats that have been placed "at our disposal" on our planet. From this perspective, not only urban architectures or agglomerations are operating on the Earth's surface, but our societies as such. Apparent within this observation is that landscape—not only as space, but as idea as well—is being besieged, reduced, and often marginalized in its multifaceted agency.

KLAUS K. LOENHART

Doch im Augenblick, in dem der moderne Mythos von ungebremstem Wachstum und Erfolg sichtbare Risse zeigt, eröffnen sich andere Blickwinkel auf Landschaft und Umwelt. Auf dem Weg zur ökologischen Gestaltung der Zukunft befinden wir uns in einer Zeit, in der Kontroversen zwischen Gesellschaft und Umwelt sichtbar werden und zur Handlung rufen – ein Erkenntnisweg von „*matter of fact to matter of concern*". Aus dem vermeintlichen Hintergrund der Ökologisierung unserer Gesellschaft tritt Landschaft in Folge in ihrer umkämpften umweltlichen Bezüglichkeit hervor. Ein richtungsweisender Moment erfordert unsere besondere Aufmerksamkeit: *Zero* beschreibt die notwendige Neupositionierung zur Betrachtung des künftigen Handlungsraums von Landschaft – den Moment des Blicks „durch das Auge des (modernen) Hurrikans".

GAM.07 ortet und erkundet somit einen Nullpunkt der besonderen Art: Bis in die letzten Winkel unseres Planeten sind anthropogene Einwirkungen nachweisbar. Erstmals im Laufe der menschlichen Evolution scheint es möglich davon zu sprechen, dass es keine Natur mehr gibt, wie wir sie bisher gedacht haben – sondern nur noch kontinuierliche Landschaft als „evolutionäres" Produkt unserer Zivilisation – *Zero Landscape*.

Damit werden Umwelt und Landschaft kurzum zu Protagonisten erhoben – denn nicht nur die Stadt, die als vorrangiger Lebensraum des 21. Jahrhunderts prognostiziert wird, verändert die Lebensräume und Habitate dieses Planeten. Anzeichen für künftige Handlungsräume der Protagonistin Landschaft zeichnen sich nicht zuletzt ab, indem „die Dimensionen der anstehenden Aufgaben durch die verschiedenen ökologischen Krisen fantastisch vergrößert worden sind" und sich ein gemeinschaftliches Bewusstsein entwickelt, „was es bedeutet zu handeln".[1]

Landschaft entsteht immer in einem Geflecht von Bezüglichkeiten: Mit einem auf das Spektrum ihrer *agency* gerichtenen Fokus soll das schöpferisch-generative Potenzial von Landschaft als Ort simultaner Praktiken erkundet werden.

So befinden wir uns auf dem Weg zu einem Handlungsraum, in dem der Klimawandel – im Zusammenspiel mit der Bereitstellung von Nahrungsmitteln und Rohstoffen – wie auch der immense Bedarf an erneuerbaren Energien gravierend auf die Gestaltung künftiger Gesellschaften einwirken werden.

Mit der Versammlung und gemeinsamen Behandlung ökologischer, gesellschaftlicher und politischer Ereignisse treten die *agencies* (Handlungsmächte, Vitalkräfte) von Landschaft, deren Ökologie und Materialität als formende Akteure unserer kulturellen Entwicklung deutlich in Erscheinung.

1 Bruno Latour, „Ein vorsichtiger Prometheus", in: Mark Jongen, Sjoerd van Tuinen, Koenraad Hemelsoet (Hg.), *Die Vermessung des Ungeheuren*. München 2009, S. 360.

Yet in the same moment where the modern myth of unlimited growth and success exhibits visible ruptures, other vantage points on landscape and the environment emerge. On the path to an ecological shaping of the future, we are experiencing a time in which controversies between society and the environment are becoming visible and call for action—a cognitive path from "matter of fact to matter of concern." As a result of its embattled environmental referentiality, landscape is emerging from the supposed background of this ecologization of our society. This moment in time, a turning point, requires our attentive focus: *Zero* describes the repositioning necessary to ascertain landscape's future scope of action—a moment of looking "through the eye of the (modern) hurricane."

With this in mind, **GAM.07** locates and explores a special kind of zero point: anthropogenic influences are traceable to the most remote corners of our planet. For the first time in the course of human evolution it appears possible to assert that there is no such thing as nature as we once believed—only continuous landscape as an "evolutionary" product of our civilization: *Zero Landscape*.

From this understanding, environment and landscape become elevated to the rank of protagonists, for it is not only the city—forecast to be the predominant anthroposphere of the 21st century—that transforms the living spaces and habitats of this planet. Indications of future scopes of action for the protagonist "landscape" are not lastly becoming apparent in that "the dimensions of the tasks at hand have been fantastically amplified by the various ecological crises" and that a collective awareness is developing for "what it means to act."[1]

Now we are pursuing a scope of action in which climate change—in conjunction with the provision of food and natural resources—as well as the immense need for renewable energy will have a powerful influence on the configuration of future societies.

With the confluence and shared handling of ecological, social, and political circumstances, the agencies of landscape—its ecology and materiality—are clearly manifesting as formative players in the development of our culture.

Landscape always originates with a network of referentialities: explored within this publication—and with a focus on the spectrum of its agency—is the creative, generative potential of landscape as a site of simultaneous practices. The transdisciplinary character of this discourse on landscape is arranged in three sections, enabling the involved projects and texts to establish their references without being bound by categories.

1 Bruno Latour, "A Cautious Prometheus: A Few Steps Toward a Philosophy of Design (with Special Attention to Peter Sloterdijk)," http://www.bruno-latour.fr/articles/2008.html, p. 3.

After the predicted "end of nature," it becomes obvious that not only the human being but ecology as well is a "political animal." The question thus arises as to which extent landscape—its ecology and dynamics, and also the way we consciously approach these—may possibly become an integral part of our society-related ambitions and decisions. Possible practices and variations of ecology are therefore closely reviewed in the first **GAM.07** section, ***Contested Ecologies***. One of the related questions probes the extent to which cultural ecology can or should penetrate our societal practices, or whether the "ecologization" of society would follow more along the lines of a purely political, technocratic economy.

The projects and texts in the second section, ***Agency and Matter***, demonstrate how our conception of landscape as a product of society is shifting to an acknowledgment of its active role in chains of activities that generate culture. Landscape in its materiality and as a complementary and autopoietic system constitutes the discursive basis for coevolution: a cultural amalgam of society and ecology. Thus, we direct our attention to a development in which the landscape surrounding us—both natural as well as tainted by human activity—itself becomes a generative place, a medium, and a discourse and is recognizable as an "active agent."

Distortions of political, ecological, economic, and energetic landscapes are put up for discussion in the third section, ***Uneven Topographies***. Common to all of these projects and texts is their discursive nature, so that they may be considered as probing explorations. This repositioning of how we view landscape is, after all, tied to the hope of contributing to the recognition of the "agency of landscape" and of promoting the development of ecologically inductive thought.

Landschaft entsteht immer in einem Geflecht von Bezüglichkeiten: Mit einem auf das Spektrum ihrer *agency* gerichteten Fokus soll das schöpferisch-generative Potenzial von Landschaft als Ort simultaner Praktiken erkundet werden. In der Ordnung von drei Kapiteln bildet sich der transdisziplinäre Charakter dieses Landschaftsdiskurses ab, so dass die folgenden Projekte und Texte ihre Bezüge über die Kategorisierung hinweg knüpfen.

Nach dem postulierten „Ende der Natur" wird deutlich: Nicht nur der Mensch, auch die Ökologie ist ein „politisches Tier". So stellt sich die Frage, inwiefern Landschaft, deren Ökologie und Dynamik sowie unser Verständnis des Umgangs mit ihnen, womöglich zu einem integralen Teil unserer gesellschaftlichen Ambitionen und Entscheidungen werden können. In der ersten Gruppierung von **GAM.07**, ***Contested Ecologies***, stehen deshalb mögliche Praktiken und Varianten von Ökologie auf dem Prüfstand. Dazu stellt sich unter anderem die Frage, inwieweit eine kulturelle Ökologie die Praxis unserer Gesellschaft durchdringen kann oder soll, oder ob die „Ökologisierung" unserer Gesellschaft doch eher einer rein politisch-technokratischen Ökonomie folgen wird.

Wie sich unsere Auffassung von Landschaft als gesellschaftliches Produkt hin zur Erkenntnis ihrer aktiveren Rolle in Handlungsketten verlagert welche Kultur erzeugen, zeigen die Projekte und Texte in der zweiten Gruppierung ***Agency and Matter***. Landschaft in ihrer Materialität legt als komplementäres und autopoietisches System dabei die diskursive Grundlage für eine Co-Evolution: ein kulturelles Amalgam zwischen Gesellschaft und Ökologie. So legen wir unser Augenmerk auf eine Entwicklung, in der die uns umgebende Landschaft – natürlicher wie anthropogener Prägung – selbst zum generativen Ort, Medium und Diskurs wird und als *active agent* erkannt werden kann.

In der dritten Gruppierung, ***Uneven Topographies***, werden schließlich Verwerfungen politischer, ökologischer, ökonomischer und energetischer Landschaften zur Diskussion gestellt. Gemeinsam ist diesen Projekten und Texten, dass sie allesamt diskursiver Natur und somit als Versuchsanordnung zu verstehen sind. Mit dieser Neu-Positionierung in der Betrachtung von Landschaft verbindet sich schließlich die Hoffnung, zur Erkenntnis der *agency of landscape* beizutragen und die Entstehung von ökologisch induktivem Denken zu befördern.

Vibrant Matter—Zero Landscape

Interview with Jane Bennett by Klaus K. Loenhart

Dynamische Materie und Zero Landscape
Ein Interview mit Jane Bennett von Klaus K. Loenhart

Klaus K. Loenhart (KKL)*: For the* **Zero Landscape** *edition of* ***GAM.07****, landscape and the environment, often perceived as the seemingly passive background to our cultural endeavors, are elevated to the status of a protagonist. In your own work "on the seemingly passive," how have you found your position and its protagonists of a political ecology of things and its matter?*

Jane Bennett (JB): Prior to reading GAM's call for papers, I had not focused on the sensibility-shaping powers of the category "landscape." But of course "landscape" (like "environment") has presented the world as naturally divided into active bodies (life) and passive contexts (matter). I think many people now find this picture implausible. For us, landscape is better understood as an "assemblage" or working set of vibrant materialities. In *Vibrant Matter*[1] I inflected Deleuze and Guattari's notion of assemblage in this way:

1 Jane Bennett, *Vibrant Matter: A Political Ecology of Things*. Durham 2010.

Klaus K. Loenhart (KKL)*: In der Ausgabe* **Zero Landscape** *von* ***GAM.07*** *werden Landschaft und Umwelt, welche oft als scheinbar passiver Hintergrund für unsere kulturellen Bemühungen wahrgenommen werden, nun umgekehrt zu Protagonisten erhoben. Wie haben Sie bei Ihren eigenen Untersuchungen zum „scheinbar Passiven" Ihre Position und Protagonisten bezüglich einer politischen Ökologie der Dinge und deren Materialitäten entwickelt?*

Jane Bennett (JB): Ehe ich den cfp von GAM lesen konnte, hatte ich mich nicht näher mit den Kräften auseinandergesetzt, mit denen die Kategorie „Landschaft" unser Empfindungsvermögen formt. Selbstverständlich wurde durch den Begriff „Landschaft" (genauso wie durch den Begriff „Umwelt") eine Welt dargestellt, welche von Natur aus einerseits in aktive Körper (das Leben) und andererseits in passive Kontexte (die Ma-

terie) zerfällt. Ich bin der Ansicht, dass gegenwärtig viele Menschen eine solche Darstellung als unglaubwürdig empfinden. Für uns wird Landschaft weit besser als eine „Assemblage" oder als ein Arbeitsbereich dynamischer Materialitäten verständlich. In *Vibrant Matter*[1] habe ich mich an Deleuze und Guattaris Vorstellung von Assemblage auf folgende Weise angenähert: „Assemblagen sind lebendige und pulsierende Verbindungen, welche trotz der beständigen Gegenwart von Kräften funktionieren, die von Innen heraus Unordnung erzeugen. Sie verfügen über ungleichmäßige Topografien, da einige der Überschneidungspunkte, an denen sich die verschiedenen Affekte und Körper kreuzen, stärker frequentiert sind als andere [...] Jedes Teil einer Assemblage verfügt über eine bestimmte vitale Kraft, dennoch gibt es eine Wirksamkeit, die der Gruppierung als solcher eigentümlich ist: eine *agency* der Assemblage selbst." Ohne Zweifel besitzt eine Landschaft eine eigene Wirkungsmacht, eine Lebendigkeit, welche sich mit einem menschlichen Agieren verzahnt. Ohne Zweifel ist das, was eine Landschaft *schafft* oder hervorbringt mehr als eine geophysikalische Oberfläche, auf der sich die Ereignisse abspielen. Ohne Zweifel operiert eine bestimmte Konfiguration von Pflanzen, Gebäuden, Hügeln, Winden, Felsen und Stimmungen nicht einfach nur als Tableau für Handlungen, die Ihren Impetus von anderswoher beziehen.

Sie fragen mich nun, warum es mir falsch erscheint (nicht im moralischen Sinne, sondern ungenau bezüglich ihrer Wahrnehmung), von Materialität oder Landschaft so zu sprechen, als wären diese bloß eine stoffliche Angelegenheit. Es bleibt ungewiss, wie jemand dazu kommt, etwas zu glauben oder wahrzunehmen, wie er oder sie es nun einmal tut, doch ich unternehme den Versuch, zuerst von biografischen Einflüssen zu sprechen und benenne dann einige literarische und philosophische Einflüsse.

Der biografische Faktor ist Wahnsinn in meiner nächsten Verwandtschaft. Viele Jahre gescheiterter Versuche, meinen Bruder (der als „paranoid schizophren" diagnostiziert wurde) davon zu überzeugen, zu bedrängen, auszutricksen oder zu zwingen, akzeptablere Verhaltensweisen an den Tag zu legen, haben bei mir

1 Jane Bennett, *Vibrant Matter. A Political Ecology of Things*. Durham 2010.

"Assemblages are living, throbbing confederations that are able to function despite the persistent presence of energies that confound them from within. They have uneven topographies, because some of the points at which the various affects and bodies cross paths are more heavily trafficked than others ... Each member of the assemblage has a certain vital force, but there is also an effectivity proper to the grouping as such: an agency *of* the assemblage." Clearly, a landscape possesses an efficacy of its own, a liveliness intermeshed with human agency. Clearly, the scape of the land is more than a geophysical surface upon which events play out. Clearly, a particular configuration of plants, buildings, mounds, winds, rocks, moods does not operate simply as a tableau for actions whose impetus comes from elsewhere.

You ask how it came to pass that it now seems to me wrong (not morally wrong but perceptually imprecise) to speak as if materiality or landscape were mere matter. No one knows exactly how one comes to believe and perceive as one does, but I'll give it a try, speaking first of a biographical factor, and then naming some literary-philosophical influences.

The biographical factor is madness in my immediate family. Many years of failed attempts to convince, cajole, trick, or force my brother (diagnosed as "paranoid schizophrenic") to pursue more acceptable behaviors has taught me humility in the face of the agency of strange bodily assemblages. It revealed in an uncompromising fashion how dependent rational, communicable thought is upon a fortuitously congenial organization of various, *very powerful* materials of the body. Living alongside madness erased for me the figure of matter as essentially inanimate stuff; it was no longer possible, for instance, to think of the human body as a "landscape" for the exercise of "will." Body appears instead as a tangled composite of various active forces (one of which is called will and many of which are only moderately, if at all, susceptible to deliberate reformation).

Madness offers painfully strong evidence of the active powers of flesh, and this renders me more alert to, better sensitized toward, the vitality of materiality per se, including both natural and artificial complexes. It uncovers a world in which "things" vie alongside (as well as enter into) the workings of human will, intelligence, reason, desire. In other words, what holds true for the human body applies to the body of nature-culture as well: a geo-cultural landscape is no more passive, no more simply a context for action, than is the bodily terrain of my brother.

The first text that spurred (what could playfully be called) my neo-animist views was Hobbes' *Leviathan*, which presented Man as "matter in motion"

and human thought as one of the elements in a cascade of material effects. I was shaken by Hobbes' claim that thoughts share the volatile, mobile, vibratory character of bodies, but the starkness (and too mechanistic) materialism of Hobbes really jolted my anthropocentric prejudices about nature and self. Lucretius' *De Rerum Natura*, especially its brief remarks about the swerve (*clinamen*) in primordia. Epicurianism was also influential; it is nicely highlighting the material tendency to form and repeat patterns, even if its atomism understated the processual quality of configurations. I loved Henry Thoreau's account of his trek up the mountain Ktaadn, in The Maine Woods, where he speaks of the "Titanic" quality of flesh, and Kafka's stories (especially *Cares of a Family Man* and *The Castle*), which offered me an absurdist acknowledgment that material vitality is not confined to natural objects but resided as well in toys, artifacts, tools, furniture, buildings. Finally, there is Spinoza's *Ethics*, with its variegated holism of Substance, i.e., his "one-world" (immanent) metaphysics. I confess to being a certain kind of holist myself: not organic holism but the entangled character of complexes, the elements of which simultaneously impinge upon, interpenetrate, and exceed one another's powers. William Connolly describes this beautifully in *A World of Becoming*. And also Deleuze and Guattari's *A Thousand Plateaus*, with its peculiar brand of Spinozism, its eclectic natural-science-infused vocabulary, and its courage to say crazy, experimental things.

KKL: *Your work is most inclusive in that it accounts for its context of discourse in a conversational way. I understand* Vibrant Matter*'s conversational style as a technique or practice to actively do what you so convincingly promote: to assemble and to unfold agency between "things." As you present it, the intrinsic facets of active materiality seem to have developed and transformed in a lively manner.*

JB: There are relative strengths and weaknesses of using a conversational tone to address the "philosophical" themes of materialism, vitalism, the hegemony of the subject-object binary, etc. A strength may be that this tone reminds the writer and the reader alike that grand "ontological" questions (What is matter? What is life? What is it that we have called Nature?) are themselves questions of ordinary, daily life (What explains our collective tendency to "pave paradise and put up a parking lot"?) I also try to speak in a way that allows the material force of word-sounds, their ability to induce effects in the bodies of the readers and writers (a tingle of skin, a frown of face, a restlessness of the gaze, a vague or nameable mood), to come to the fore. It was also important to me to find ways to elide or work around the default grammar of description, which tends to present a world of agents and their objects rather than a world in which agency is distributed across an ontologically diverse range of bodies. Because I really do believe that the locus of agency is always an assemblage, it's important to me to write in a way that *invites readers into a collective project*—into, that is, an experiment of living with and as vibrant matter. Words are "actants," as are architectural objects: as Lilli Hollein noted with reference to your Observation Tower on the river Mur, "architecture is a wonderful means of representing, imposing, or arousing states of human nature."

A weakness of the conversational and sometimes eccentric/awkward voice of the book could be a certain slide toward a truistic rhetoric. Some readers have said that *Vibrant Matter* makes the rather obvious point that

Demut angesichts einer *agency* befremdlicher körperlicher Assemblagen erzeugt. Sie haben mich auf kompromisslose Weise erkennen lassen, wie sehr das vernünftige und kommunizierbare Denken von einer zufälligen Konstellation unterschiedlicher und *äußerst mächtiger* materieller Komponenten des Körpers abhängt. Mein Leben in unmittelbarer Nähe zu Wahnsinn hat für mich die Vorstellung getilgt, dass die Materie lediglich unbelebte Stofflichkeit sei. So war es zum Beispiel nicht länger denkbar, sich den menschlichen Körper als „Landschaft" vorzustellen, in der sich ein „Wille" zum Ausdruck bringt. Der Körper erscheint stattdessen als eine in mannigfaltig aktive Kräfte verwickelte Anordnung (und einer von diesen Kräften trägt den Namen „Wille" und viele andere sind, wenn überhaupt, nur in geringem Maße einer freiwilligen Umgestaltung zugänglich). Auf schmerzliche Weise liefert Wahnsinn den nachdrücklichen Beweis für die Aktivkräfte des Fleisches, und das lässt mich angesichts dessen aufmerksamer werden und sensibilisiert mich in dieser Hinsicht für die Lebendigkeit von Materie – welche natürliche wie künstliche Gefüge einschließt.

Dadurch enthüllt sich eine Welt, in der die „Dinge" mit dem Wirken des menschlichen Willens, der Klugheit, der Vernunft und des Begehrens wetteifern, um sich schließlich mit diesen zu vermischen. Mit anderen Worten – was für den menschlichen Körper gilt, kann genauso auch auf die stoffliche Substanz von Kultur – Natur übertragen werden: Eine geo-kulturelle Landschaft ist nicht passiv und auch nicht einfach der Kontext für eine Aktion, ebenso wenig wie es das körperliche Gelände meines Bruders ist.

Der erste Text, der mich hinsichtlich meiner neo-animistischen Ansichten (wie man das spielerisch nennen könnte) anspornte, war der *Leviathan* von Thomas Hobbes, der den Menschen als „Materie in Bewegung" vorstellt und das menschliche Denken als ein Element in einer Kaskade materieller Effekte. Mich hat Hobbes Behauptung erschüttert, dass Gedanken die wechselhaften, beweglichen und schwingenden Merkmale von Körpern tragen, doch die Schroffheit und der (allzu mechanistische) Materialismus erweckte gewisse anthropozentrische Vorurteile bezüglich Natur und Selbst. Da gab es Lukrez *De Rerum Natura* und diesbezüglich vor allem seine Bemerkungen zur entscheidenden Rolle des Schwankens (*clinamen*). Auch der Epikureismus war wichtig; er unterstreicht sehr schön die materielle Tendenz, Muster auszubilden und zu wiederholen, auch wenn gerade eine molekulare Betrachtung die prozessuale Qualität von Konfigurationen zu gering ansetzt. Ich liebe Henry Thoreaus Beschreibung seiner Besteigung des Ktaadn in den Wäldern Maines, wo er von den „titanischen" Qualitäten des Fleisches spricht, als auch Kafkas Erzählungen (vor allem *Die Sorge des Hausvaters* und *Das Schloss*), die mir eine absurde Bestätigung dafür zu sein scheinen, dass materielle Lebendigkeit nicht auf natürliche Objekte begrenzt bleibt, sondern sich auch auf Spielsachen, Artefakte, Werkzeuge, Einrichtungs-

gegenstände und Gebäude erstreckt. Und schließlich ist es die Ethik Spinozas mit ihrem vielfältigen Holismus der Substanz, das heißt mit ihrer „innerweltlichen" (immanenten) Metaphysik. Ich gestehe, dass ich auf eine gewisse Weise selbst Anhängerin des Holismus bin; nicht eines organischen Holismus, sondern einer verwobenen Beschaffenheit von Komplexen, von Elementen, welche sich gleichzeitig aneinander stoßen, sich durchdringen und Macht übereinander ausüben. William Connolly beschreibt das sehr schön in seinem Buch *A World of Becoming*. Selbstverständlich gab es auch Deleuze und Guattari mit ihren *Tausend Plateaus*, wo auf eigenwillige Art und Weise der Spinozismus zum Ausdruck kommt, mit all dem eklektischen naturwissenschaftlich durchdrungenen Vokabular und dem Mut, verrückte und experimentelle Dinge zu sagen.

KKL: *Ihre Arbeit ist besonders einbeziehend, indem sich der diskursive Kontext in Form des Gesprächs darbietet. Ich begreife diesen Konversationsstil in* Vibrant Matter *als eine Technik oder Praxis, genau das zu tun, was inhaltlich auch so überzeugend vertreten wird – die wechselseitige agency zwischen den „Dingen" zu versammeln und zu entfalten. Die Art, mit der Sie dies bewerkstelligen, scheint die immanenten Facetten der aktiven Materialität auf lebendige Weise zu entwickeln und umzusetzen.*

JB: Setzt man sich mit „philosophischen" Fragen von Materialismus, Vitalismus und Hegemonie der Subjekt-Objekt-Binarität etc. auseinander, dann zeigen sich Stärken und Schwächen bei der Anwendung eines solchen Gesprächstons. Eine Stärke mag darin liegen, dass dieser Ton den Schreiber und den Leser daran erinnert, dass die großen „ontologischen" Fragen (Was ist Materie? Was ist Leben? Was ist es, was wir Natur nennen?), an sich Fragen des gewöhnlichen Alltagslebens sind (Wie lässt sich unsere kollektive Neigung erklären, das „Paradies pflastern zu wollen, um dort einen Parkplatz zu errichten"?) Ich versuche auch auf eine Weise zu sprechen, die es den materiellen Kräften der Wortklänge selbst erlaubt, ihre Fähigkeit, Effekte auf die Körper der Leser und Schreiber auszuüben (ein Kribbeln auf der Haut, ein Runzeln der Stirn, die Rastlosigkeit des Blicks, eine vage oder deutliche Stimmung) in den Vordergrund treten zu lassen. Ebenso war es für mich wichtig Wege zu finden, um die vorgegebene Grammatik von Beschreibungen zu annullieren oder umzuarbeiten, die doch eher dazu neigt, eine Welt von Akteuren und deren Objekten darzulegen, anstelle einer Welt, in der sich Handlungsmacht über ein ontologisch vielgestaltiges Feld von Körpern verteilt. Denn ich bin fest davon überzeugt, dass der eigentliche Ort einer *agency* immer einer Assemblage entspringt und genau deshalb ist es für mich entscheidend so zu schreiben, dass *der Leser zu einem kollektiven Projekt eingeladen wird* – also etwa zu einem Experiment des Lebens mit und als dynamische Materie. Wörter sind Aktanten – wie es auch Architekturobjekte sind. Etwa in der Art, things exercise power over us. There is truth to the criticism, but I don't mind it. Sometimes the obvious gets lost or buried, in academic and (other) ethical-political forms of speech, and is worth repeating.

I'd be interested in hearing what you have to say about the question of the mode of presentation, a question of rhetoric or persuasion, especially since you come from a discipline that is more hospitable than political theory tends to be toward visuality and non-text-based forms of expression and modes of inquiry.

KKL: *Within a short genealogy of materialism, from Epicurus to the most recent accounts by Bruno Latour: "What kind of materialist are you ..."*

JB: I would have to be Michel Foucault to be able to offer even a short genealogy of materialism. Instead, I will name the two pragmatic problems that pushed me in the direction of affirming (and, to the extent that *Vibrant Matter* is a polemic, preaching) "vital materialism." The first was the intensification of an alarming trend in American public culture, wherein a rise in the invocations by politicians of otherworldly powers (the Judeo-Christian "Almighty" combatting "forces of Evil") was paired with the positioning of violence and torture as legitmate tools of state. (William Connolly speaks here of an "evangelical-capitalist resonance machine" and I think that Lucretius, Voltaire, Nietzsche, Foucault, and other iconoclasts of piety are right to remind us of the gruesome history of some variants of theism in the West.) This combination moved me to speak on behalf of an ethical outlook that was non-theistic and non-teleological (at least in the strongest sense of telos), to proclaim the possibility that an undesigned order of materiality could nevertheless possess the impressive, dynamic, incalculable, awesome and awful qualities elsewhere ascribed to God or *Geist* or "the human spirit" conceived as its highest expression. It is *materiality* that is wondrous.

A weakness of the conversational and sometimes eccentric/awkward voice of the book could be a certain slide toward a truistic rhetoric.

The second problem was ecological destruction, or the globalizing political economy devoted to extraction and exploitation, waste, commodification, human imperialism, and winner-take-all. I am a vital materialist who sees positive, pro-Green potential in raising the profile of the fact that any human "I" is itself made up of "its"—of a vast array of originally and to varying degress persistently nonhuman elements, such as bacteria, metals, ambient sounds, the "trains" of images of other bodies, etc. Here I have been inspired by the straightforwardness of Bruno Latour's rejection of the anthropocentric bias in the social sciences.

KKL: *For some time now in discourse, we have been arguing on modernity's seeming disenchantment with the world where the subject of modernity transcends its natural environment. A subsequent overcoming of the culture/nature divide leads towards a dissolution of modern binaries. But*

wie Lilli Hollein es hinsichtlich Ihres Murturms ausgedrückt hat: „Die Architektur ist ein wunderbares Mittel menschliche Zustände abzubilden, zu forcieren oder zu erwecken."

Eine Schwäche dieser Konversation betreibenden und zuweilen versponnen-verfänglichen Stimme des Buches könnte die Neigung zu einer axiomatischen Rhetorik sein. Manche Leser waren der Ansicht, *Vibrant Matter* vertrete den offensichtlichen Standpunkt, dass die Dinge Macht über uns ausüben. Diese Kritik hat etwas Wahres, doch das kümmert mich nicht besonders. Denn oftmals geht das Offensichtliche in den akademischen oder bei (anderen) ethisch-politischen Formen der Rede verloren oder unter, und ist doch der Wiederholung wert.

Es würde mich interessieren was Sie zur Frage der Modi von Präsentation zu sagen haben, eine Frage der Rhetorik und der Überzeugungskraft, gerade deshalb, weil Sie ja aus einer Disziplin kommen, die sich, im Unterschied zur politischen Theorie, in Bezug auf Visualisierung und nicht-textbasierten Formen des Ausdrucks und der Untersuchung etwas gastfreundlicher verhält.

KKL: *Innerhalb einer kurzen Geschichte des Materialismus, angefangen bei Epikur und bis hin zu den neuesten Ansätzen bei Bruno Latour – „Was für eine Art Materialistin sind Sie?"*

JB: Ich müsste Michel Foucault sein, wäre es mir auch nur möglich, eine kurze Genealogie des Materialismus aufzustellen. Anstelle dessen möchte ich die beiden pragmatischen Probleme anführen, die mich dazu leiteten, einen „lebendigen Materialismus" zu bejahen (und, insoweit *Vibrant Matter* eine Polemik ist, diesen auch zu predigen). Zuerst gab es da die Verstärkung eines besorgniserregenden Trends in der US-amerikanischen öffentlichen Kultur, wo im selben Zug mit der Anrufung außerweltlicher Mächte (der judeo-christliche „Allmächtige" kämpft gegen die „Mächte des Bösen"), nun auch Gewalt und Folter als legitime Mittel der Staatsraison betrachtet wurden. (In diesem Zusammenhang spricht William Connolly von einer „evangelikalen-kapitalistischen Resonanzmaschine" und ich bin der Ansicht, dass Lukrez, Voltaire, Nietzsche, Foucault und andere, die mit den Konventionen der Frömmigkeit brachen, uns auf sehr berechtigte Weise an die grausame Geschichte einiger Theismen des Okzidents erinnern.) Dieses Zusammenspiel bewegte mich dazu, über eine ethische Position nachzudenken, die weder theistisch noch teleologisch ist (zumindest nicht im strengen Sinn des *telos*), und damit auch die Möglichkeit bietet anzunehmen, dass auch ein ungestaltetes System von Materie die beeindruckenden, dynamischen, unberechenbaren, Ehrfurcht gebietenden und furchtbaren Qualitäten besitzen könnte, die man anderswo Gott oder Geist[2] oder „menschliche Seele" nennt, welche so als deren höchster Ausdruck erscheinen. Es ist Materialität, die bewunderungswürdig ist.

The second problem was ecological destruction, or the globalizing political economy devoted to extraction and exploitation, waste, commodification, human imperialism, and winner-take-all.

2 Im Original deutsch. A. d. Ü.

Das zweite Problem war die Umweltzerstörung oder die globalisierte politische Ökonomie, die sich völlig der Entnahme und Ausbeutung, der Vermüllung, menschlichem Imperialismus, der Vorstellung, dass der Gewinner alles einstreicht und die alles und jedes zur Ware macht, verschrieben hat. Ich bin eine vitale Materialistin, die positive und grüne Potenziale ausmachen kann, indem das Profil des Umstandes geschärft wird, dass jegliches menschliche „Ich" selbst aus verschiedenen „Es" zusammengesetzt ist – bestehend aus einem weitgreifenden Spektrum ursprünglicher und in unterschiedlichem Maße beeinflussbarer nicht-menschlicher Elemente, wie etwa Bakterien, Metalle, Umgebungsgeräusche, den wirkenden Bildketten anderer Körper und so weiter. In diesem Zusammenhang wurde ich von der geradlinigen Haltung Bruno Latours geprägt, der die anthropozentrische Ausrichtung der Gesellschaftswissenschaften zurückweist.

***KKL:** Seit geraumer Zeit führen wir nun den Diskurs um die scheinbare Verdrossenheit der Moderne mit dem Aspekt der Welt, welcher die Durchdringung mit der natürlichen Umwelt beschreibt. Eine weiterführende Überwindung der Trennung von Natur – Kultur führt zur Erosion dieser modernen Binaritäten. Aber wie können sich die Konsequenzen daraus entfalten? Für die weitere Entwicklung scheint Ihr Diskurs nun ganz besonders darauf abzuzielen, durch Einführung von Differenzierungen die Bühne für eine Anordnung zu errichten, wo beide Extreme herausgefordert werden – die der subjektiven Ideale ebenso, wie die eines natürlichen Materialismus.*

JB: Gut, dass Sie nach dem Verhältnis zwischen meinem Skeptizismus bezüglich der Verdrossenheit der Moderne einerseits und andererseits nach meiner Herausforderung sowohl der subjektiven Ideale und des natürlichen Materialismus fragen. Im Gegensatz zu Max Weber bin ich der Ansicht, dass sich in der Moderne überall Gebiete finden, die man als (säkular) reizvoll engagiert betrachten darf. Mit dieser reizvollen Verbindung meine ich eine Stimmung oder einen Affekt, der zwischen den menschlichen Körpern (worunter ich Komplexe verstehe, die aus menschlichen und nicht-menschlichen Komponenten zusammengesetzt sind) im Aufeinandertreffen mit anderen Tieren, Pflanzen und mineralischen Kräften, zirkuliert. Mit dieser reizvollen Bezüglichkeit verbinde ich das Gefühl, angesichts von Etwas, das wahrhaft wild und ungezügelt ist, zugleich fasziniert und verunsichert zu sein. Wichtig ist dabei, dass diese Art von Verzauberung nicht so sehr dem Glauben an einen energetischen Fluss folgt, der beim Zusammentreffen zwischen zwei Einheiten von aktiven Materialitäten entsteht, wobei die eine Einheit zum „Selbst" gerinnt und die andere zu etwas, das man gerne „Objekt der Beobachtung" zu nennen pflegt; die Lage kann jedoch besser beschrieben werden, wenn man Latour folgt und von Einheiten nicht-menschlicher Aktanten ausgeht. Diese dynamischen Tiere, Pflanzen, Viren, Wirbel-

how can the consequences unfold? For a subsequent development, your discourse appears as most lively—in making differences—in setting the stage with a set of protagonists that are challenging both ends—of subjective ideals as well as natural materialisms.

JB: I take you to be asking about the relationship between, on the one hand, my skepticism about the story of modernity as "disenchanted" and, on the other, my challenge to "both subjective ideals and natural materialisms." My view is that, contra Weber, modernity is full of sites of (secular) enchantment. By enchantment I mean a mood or affect circulating between human bodies (themselves conceived as complexes of human and nonhuman parts) and the other animal, vegetable, and mineral forces they encounter. I associate enchantment with the feeling of being simultaneously fascinated and unnerved in the presence of something truly wild and generative. The point is that enchantment is not so much a belief as it is an energetic current produced by the encounter between two sets of active materialities, one set congealed into a "self" and one into what is often called the "objects of experience" but is better described, following Latour, as a set of nonhuman "actants." These vibrant animals, plants, viruses, hurricanes, storms, pharmaceuticals, and other technological artifacts vie with, make demands upon, and impede and enable human agency. They make their presence known to us, or, one could say, make "calls" to which we are continually responding. The literary-visual-artistic ethical task at hand is, I think, to try to describe just what this "call" is without resorting to the framework of pregiven subjects and objects.

***KKL:** One path to dissipate ontotheological binaries, such as human/nature technological/organic, is favorizing ecology as the all-inclusive concept. While Slavoj Žižek warns of an unreflected application of this "opium for the masses," you may argue for another difference (in a purely horizontal juxtaposition of actants) within a cultural ecology—a politics of vital materialism.*

JB: Your question prompted me to go back to Žižek's problematic talk "Ecology: A New Opium for the Masses,"[2] the gist of which is his claim that there is no politically transformative power left in "ecology" as a rallying cry, and this for three reasons.

First, ecology has succumbed to the capitalist imperative of contemporary life, according to which "political action and consumption become fully merged." While I agree—who could deny?—that there is little "subversive edge" to Green marketing or to ecology reduced to a "problem of sustainable development," and that capitalism works ruthlessly and creatively to absorb its opponents, Žižek (deliberately) overstates his case. Can ecology (as a complex system of words, sounds, deeds, affects, narratives, propensities) really ever *fully merge* into the allegedly totalizing system of capitalism? Here I follow Deleuze and Guattari's claim that "from the viewpoint of micropolitics, society is defined by its lines of flight ... There is always something that flows or flees, that escapes ... the resonance apparatus, and the overcoding machine. Things that are attributed to a 'change in values,' to the youth, women, the mad, etc."[3]

2 Slavoj Žižek, "Ecology: A New Opium for the Masses," in the present GAM edition, pp. 32–51.

3 Gilles Deleuze, Félix Guattari, *A Thousand Plateaus: Capitalism and Schizophrenia* vol. II. London, New York 1987, pp. 238f.

Perhaps this is a question of a strategic choice between a rhetoric of purity (Žižek) and a rhetoric of encouragement. I know many non-duped people, from a mayor of a small Green town in Maryland, to community garden activists, to "Teach for America"[4] employees, to bird watchers and hunters, who find the idea that humans and nonhumans are profoundly interlinked to have the potential to alter the status quo. (See also, to cite just one recent book, Thomas Princen's *Treading Softly*.)

Žižek 's second objection to ecology concerns its allegedly necessary reliance on an image of nature as an intrinsically harmonious and moral order, which we can refer to for guidance in organizing a polity. He calls instead for an ecology without Nature. But this is precisely what *ecologists* have been pursuing for a while now, from Michel Serres' *notion* of noise in *Genesis* (1982) to Timothy Morton's more recent *Ecology without Nature* (2007). Here Žižek seems behind the times—he reduces any invocation of *natura naturans* to a secret longing for *natura naturata*. Thus it is that he can reject all ecological perspectives as valorizing stability and as *deeply conservative*, i.e., anti-revolutionary. That is his third objection to ecology: ecology is afraid of total, revolutionary change and aims instead to "to freeze the Earth's change, so that its ecology will remain basically the same, thus enabling humanity's survival ... This is why, although ecologists are all the time demanding that we change radically our way of life, underlying this demand is ... a deep distrust of change, of development, of progress: every radical change can have the unintended consequence of triggering a catastrophe. It is this distrust which makes ecology the ideal candidate for hegemonic ideology, since it echoes the ... post-political distrust of large collective acts."[5]

I think that Žižek is right that ecological thinking tends to harbor a distrust of grand and speedy collective acts. An ecological sensibility proceeds with the idea that all entities, forces, and activities are connected (in a not-fully-determinate way), and thus interventions always produce unanticipated effects that call for a certain degree of anticipatory caution. This caution is perhaps intensified once one acknowledges, as the vital materialist does, that "collective" action includes the actions of nonhuman members.

***KKL:** In distinction to other materialist thinkers, your objects unfold thing-power foremost in the state of assemblage, which unfolds through a contingency of their co-presence. In* Vibrant Matter*, you argue that "in this [state of] assemblage, objects appeared as things, that is, as vivid entities not entirely reducible to the contexts in which (human) subjects set them, never entirely exhausted by their semiotics."[6] At one point, when you argue for a culture of assemblages— "for a cognizant of our embeddedness in a natural-cultural-technological assemblage"[7]—I have to think of landscape (in its multi-dimensionality between matter and idea) as interface for this*

4 Teach for America is a nonprofit educational institution in the United States. For example, outstanding graduates work there at schools in low-income and underprivileged areas.

5 Slavoj Žižek 2011 (fn. 2).

6 Jane Bennett 2010 (fn. 1), p. 5.

7 See Jane Bennett, "The Force of Things: Steps Toward an Ecology of Matter," in: *Political Theory* 32/3 (2004), pp. 347–372, here p. 361.

stürme, Pharmazien und andere technologische Artefakte messen sich miteinander, stellen Ansprüche aneinander, behindern und ermöglichen die menschliche Vermittlung. Sie machen uns ihre Anwesenheit bewusst oder „rufen" uns, wie man sagen könnte; und wir antworten kontinuierlich auf diesen Impuls. Ich denke, wir haben die literarische und bild-künstlerische ethische Aufgabe, darzulegen, wie sich dieser „Impuls" formt, ohne dabei Zuflucht zu einem Rahmenwerk vorbestimmter Subjekte und Objekte zu nehmen.

***KKL:** Ein Weg, um die ontotheologischen Binaritäten wie Mensch/Natur, Technik/das Organische aufzulösen, favorisiert die Ökologie als allumfassendes Konzept. Dem gegenüber warnt uns Slavoj Žižek vor einer unreflektierten Anwendung eines solchen „Opium fürs Volk", wohingegen Sie für eine weitere Differenzierung (in Form einer rein horizontalen Aufreihung von Aktanten) innerhalb einer kulturellen Ökologie eintreten – für die Politik eines dynamischen Materialismus.*

JB: Ihre Frage bringt mich dazu, auf Žižeks problematischen Essay *Das Ökologische – Neues Opium fürs Volk*[3] einzugehen, dessen Kerninhalt darin besteht zu behaupten, dass bei der „Ökologie" keine Kraft der Veränderung mehr vorhanden ist, die als Parole in Anspruch genommen werden könnte. Das hat für ihn drei Gründe:

Erstens hat sich das Ökologische dem kapitalistischen Imperativ des gegenwärtigen Lebens unterworfen, indem „politische Tat und Konsum völlig ununterscheidbar" geworden sind. Während ich zustimme – Wer wollte dies auch abstreiten? – dass es kaum noch „subversive Brüche" im grünen Marketing gibt, das Ökologische auf ein „Problem einer nachhaltigen Entwicklung" reduziert und der Kapitalismus ungehemmt erfinderisch damit beschäftigt ist, seine Widersacher zu absorbieren, so übertreibt hier Žižek (wohlweislich) dennoch. Kann das Ökologische (als ein komplexes System von Wörtern, Geräuschen, Taten, Affekten, Erzählungen und Tendenzen) tatsächlich jemals *vollständig* mit dem angeblich totalisierenden System des Kapitalismus verschmelzen? Ich folge hier Deleuze und Guattaris Ansatz. „Aus der Sicht der Mikropolitik wird eine Gesellschaft durch eine Fluchtlinie definiert [...] Immer flieht und flüchtet etwas [...] dem Resonanzapparat, der Übercodierungsmaschine [...] – was man mit einem ‚Sittenwandel' erklärt, Jugendliche, Frauen, Verrückte etc."[4] Vielleicht ist das eine Frage der strategischen Wahl zwischen einer Rhetorik der Reinheit (Žižek) und der Rhetorik der Ermunterung. Ich kenne zahlreiche klarsichtige Menschen, angefangen von einem Bürgermeister einer kleinen grün-regierten Stadt in Maryland bis hin zu Aktivisten der Kleingartenbewegung,

3 Vgl. Slavoj Žižek, „Das Ökologische – Neues Opium fürs Volk", in diesem Heft, S. 32–51.

4 Gilles Deleuze, Félix Guattari, *Tausend Plateaus. Kapitalismus und Schizophrenie Bd. II*. Berlin 1992, S. 294f.

When humans act, they do not exercise exclusively human powers, but express and engage the agency of a variety of other actants—including food, micro-organisms, minerals, artifacts, sounds, bio- and other technologies, and so on. There is a difference between a human individual and a stone, but neither considered alone has real agency: the locus of agency is always a human–nonhuman collective. It seems to me here that what is called landscape is a paradigmatic example.

An assemblage has no sovereignty in the classical sense, for no one of its members can consistently determine its trajectory. The effects generated by an assemblage are emergent in that their ability to make something happen (a blackout, a hurricane, a war on terror, the border to Slovenia) is distinct from the sum of the force of each materiality considered alone.

von Mitarbeitern von „Teach for America"[5] bis hin zu Vogelbeobachtern und Jägern, welche die Vorstellung, dass Menschen und Nicht-Menschliches grundsätzlich miteinander verbunden sind, durchaus einsehen und auch davon ausgehen, dass hier das Potenzial liegt, den gegenwärtigen Stand der Dinge zu verändern. (Man kann hier auch, um nur eines der erst kürzlich erschienen Bücher zu erwähnen, auf Thomas Princens *Treading Softly* verweisen.)

Žižeks zweiter Einwand gegen das Ökologische richtet sich gegen die angeblich unumgängliche Anlehnung dieser an ein Bild der Natur, das an sich als harmonische oder moralische Ordnung erscheint und auf das wir uns als Leitbild beziehen, wenn wir eine dementsprechende Politik zu machen versuchen. Er verlangt stattdessen eine Ökologie ohne Natur. Doch gerade das ist es, was nun schon seit einiger Zeit *Ökologen* versuchen zu bewerkstelligen. Das fängt an bei Serres Idee vom Rauschen in seinem Buch *Genèse* (1982) an und reicht bis Timothy Mortons *Ecology without Nature* (2007). Es scheint so, als ob hier Žižek nicht ganz auf dem Stand der Zeit wäre – er reduziert jede Aufrufung der *natura naturans* auf die geheime Sehnsucht nach einer *natura naturata*. Aus diesem Grund kann er auch alle ökologischen Perspektiven verwerfen, indem er sie als *zutiefst konservativ* denunziert und sie beschuldigt, die bestehenden Verhältnisse aufrecht zu erhalten, kurz gesagt, anti-revolutionär zu sein.

Darin besteht sein dritter Einwand: Die Ökologie scheut sich vor dem völligen, revolutionären Wandel und zielt stattdessen darauf ab, „alle Veränderungen auf dem Erdball zu verhindern, damit dessen Ökosystem mehr oder weniger unverändert bliebe und dadurch auch das Überleben der Menschheit sichergestellt sein würde [...] Aus diesem Grunde fordern die Ökologen zwar die ganze Zeit, wir sollten unsere Lebensweise radikal ändern, doch dieser Forderung liegt etwas anderes zugrunde: [... das] post-politische Misstrauen gegenüber großen, kollektiven Taten".[6]

Ich bin der Ansicht, dass Žižek Recht damit hat, wenn er davon ausgeht, dass die Ökologie ein gewisses Misstrauen gegenüber großartigen und abrupt stattfindenden kollektiven Taten hegt. Ökologische Sensibilität verfährt gemäß der Vorstellung, dass alle Entitäten, Kräfte und Handlungen zusammenhängen (auf eine nicht vollständig zu bestimmende Weise), und dass demzufolge Eingriffe immer unerwartete Effekte zeitigen werden. Deshalb ist auch ein gewisses Maß an vorausschauender Vorsicht angebracht. Und diese Vorsicht wird unter Umständen noch dadurch verstärkt, dass jede „kollektive" Aktion auch die Aktion der nicht-menschlichen Teilnehmer

5 *Teach for America* ist eine gemeinnützige Bildungseinrichtung in den USA. Dort arbeiten zum Beispiel hervorragende Hochschulabsolventen an Schulen in einkommensschwachen und unterprivilegierten Gegenden. A. d. Ü.

6 Slavoj Žižek 2011 (Anm. 3).

mit betrifft, was nicht zuletzt die dynamischen Materialisten sehr genau wissen.

KKL: *Im Unterschied zu anderen materialistischen DenkerInnen entfalten die von Ihnen behandelten Objekte ihre thing-power vor allem dann, wenn sie zu einer Assemblage zusammengeschlossen sind, welche sich aus der Möglichkeit ihrer gemeinsamen Anwesenheit entfaltet. In* Vibrant Matter *argumentieren Sie, dass „in diesem Zustand der Assemblage Objekte als Dinge aufscheinen, das heißt als lebendige Einheiten, die nicht vollständig als Kontext reduziert werden können, als den sie das (menschliche) Subjekt positioniert und die sich auch niemals vollständig in ihrer Semiotik erschöpfen"*[7]*. An einer anderen Stelle, wenn Sie für eine Kultur der Assemblagen plädieren – „für das Bewusstsein, in ein Gefüge der Natur-Kultur-Technologie eingebettet zu sein"*[8] *– musste ich an eine Landschaft (in ihrer Multidimensionalität als Stoff und Idee) denken, die einer solchen vorgeschlagenen Praxis als Schnittstelle dient. Ein Beispiel für den lebendigen Materialismus unserer heutigen Landschaft ist Ihre Bezugnahme auf Infrastruktur.*

JB: Was ich in diesem Buch versucht habe war, die „Dinge" *sehr* ernst zu nehmen. Dies ist ein Projekt, das auch eine Gruppe objekt-orientierter Philosophen oder „spekulativer Realisten" (Graham Harman, Ray Brassier, Ian Hamilton Grant, Quentin Meillassoux, Timothy Morton und andere) unabhängig davon betreibt und deren Arbeiten ich zurzeit untersuche. Mit „Dingen" bezeichne ich die gewöhnlichen Sachen, die uns umgeben, die wir besitzen und gebrauchen und die von uns besessen und benutzt werden.

Unter menschlicher *agency* verstehe ich das Ergebnis oder den Effekt einer bestimmten Konfiguration von menschlichen und nicht-menschlichen Kräften. Wenn Menschen handeln, dann üben sie nicht bloß menschliche Macht aus, sondern sie reichern sich mit der *agency* einer ganzen Reihe anderer Aktanten an, oder drücken diese aus – das beinhaltet Nahrung, Mikroorganismen, Mineralien, Artefakte, Geräusche, biologische und andere Technologien und so weiter. Es gibt einen Unterschied zwischen einem menschlichen Individuum und einem Stein, doch keiner von diesen für sich allein kann eine Handlungsmacht beanspruchen. Der Ort der *agency* ist immer ein menschliches/nicht-menschliches Kollektiv. Mir scheint in dieser Hinsicht das, was man Landschaft nennt, ein paradigmatisches Beispiel zu sein. Was ich an Landschaftsarchitekten so bewundere, ist deren Geschick, gleichzeitig aufmerksam auf die sinnliche Qualität jedes diskreten Elements der Landschaft zu achten (so

7 Jane Bennett 2010 (Anm. 1), S. 5.

8 Vgl. Jane Bennett, „The Force of Things: Steps Toward an Ecology of Matter", in: *Political Theory* 32/3 (2004), S. 347–372, hier S. 361.

proposed practice. One example of a vital materialism of our contemporary landscape is your account on infrastructure.

JB: What I tried to do in the book is to take "things" *very* seriously. This is a project that a group of object-oriented philosophers or "speculative realists" (Graham Harman, Ray Brassier, Ian Hamilton Grant, Quentin Meillassoux, Timothy Morton, and others) were also pursuing independently, and whose work I am currently exploring. By "things" I mean the ordinary stuff around us that we possess and use, and are possessed and used by.

I experience human agency as the outcome or effect of a certain configuration of human and nonhuman forces. When humans act, they do not exercise exclusively human powers, but express and engage the agency of a variety of other actants—including food, micro-organisms, minerals, artifacts, sounds, bio- and other technologies, and so on. There is a difference between a human individual and a stone, but neither considered alone has real agency: the locus of agency is always a human–nonhuman collective. It seems to me here that what is called landscape is a paradigmatic example. One of the things I admire about landscape architects is their knack for being sensitive simultaneously to the sensuous specificity of each discrete element of a landscape (e.g., the "thing-power" of plant material) and to the overall mood-effect of the always-evolving *configuration*. An assemblage has no sovereignty in the classical sense, for no one of its members can consistently determine its trajectory. The effects generated by an assemblage are emergent in that their ability to make something happen (a blackout, a hurricane, a war on terror, the border to Slovenia) is distinct from the sum of the force of each materiality considered alone.

As you note, one example I work with in the book is the agency behind the widespread electricity blackout in 2003 in North America (and later in the year, in Europe). The government and industry response in the U.S. was to identify some human—some Enron executive or energy trader—who was the responsible agent, and then to punish him. Meanwhile, the relations between the infrastructure of the grid, the legislation deregulating energy trading, the structure of consumptive desire, and the natural tendencies of electricity itself were shuffled to the background. And so the likelihood of blackouts remains pretty much the same now as then. The tendency to define social problems as moral failures, exclusively the doing of individual or collective human agents (and the implicit assumption that we are in charge of nature) prevented us from discerning the real locus of agency—the assemblage of human and nonhuman actants—and attempting to alter the configuration of that human—nonhuman assemblage.

The guiding question of my book is this: How would our political analyses of events change were they to acknowledge an elemental, material agency distributed across bodies, human and nonhuman? Who or what would count as a "stakeholder"? How would a "public" be constituted? Would politics become less centered around finding and punishing individual human agents responsible for the public problems of, say, an electricity blackout or an epidemic of obesity, and more concerned with identifying how the complex human—nonhuman assemblage that's churning out the negative effect holds itself together? How it endures or feeds itself? Until we do that, political attempts to remedy the problem are likely to be ineffective. My point is really a pragmatic one: ethics and politics have more traction on material assemblages and the way they reproduce patterns

of effects than they can have on that elusive spiritual entity called the "moral agent."

KKL: *And there is more to account for—entire landscapes of trash, landfills, industrially driven agriculture, waterways, and a further category made up of, for example, geotectonic activities and flooding, or even of hyperobjects like global warming—all with negative attributes or "non-identity" in reference to Adorno and certainly hard to embrace … By way of contrast to his approach, you propose a surprising turn towards a positive or reflexive affirmation.*

JB: I have tended to emphasize the poetic, joyful, or bracing aspects of vibrant matter and I have argued that thing-power often first reveals itself as a negativity, a confounding or fouling up of an intention, desire, schema, or concept. But, as many thinkers have noted, such negativity is also the same stuff out of which positive things emerge. It is a negativity that is profoundly productive: the materiality that resists us is also the protean source of being, the essentially vague matrix of things. You are also asking me now to say something more about the repulsive, violent, or lethal aspects—the London Graduate School recently sponsored a conference on "Dark Materialism" (where I listened to the podcast) and I want to follow up on that lead, and to read Reza Negarestani's[8] work, which was an important reference point for the conference.

How would our political analyses of events change were they to acknowledge an elemental, material agency distributed across bodies, human and nonhuman? Who or wha would count as a "stakeholder"? How would a "public" be constituted?

I agree, of course, that there is a darker side yet to vibrant materialism. Several forces could recoil upon us in a way that eliminates the conditions for human life. There are no cosmic guarantees to be provided by vital materialism.

8 See http://backdoorbroadcasting.net/2011/01/dark-materialism/ and Reza Negerestani, *Cyclonopedia: Complicity with Anonymous Materials*. Melbourne 2008.

zum Beispiel auf die „Ding-Macht" des Pflanzenmaterials) und ebenso auf die übergreifenden Stimmungseffekte einer sich immer wieder ändernden *Konfiguration*. Eine Assemblage verfügt nicht im klassischen Sinn über Souveränität, da keine ihrer Bestandteile den Bahnungsverlauf konsequent zu bestimmen vermag. Die Effekte, die von einer Assemblage hervorgebracht werden, treten vielmehr durch deren Fähigkeit zu Tage, etwas geschehen zu lassen (ein Blackout, einen Wirbelsturm, Krieg gegen den Terror, die Grenze zu Slowenien), was sich von der Summe der einzelnen Mächte der Materialitäten für sich genommen unterscheidet.

Wie Sie angemerkt haben, ist eines der Beispiele, die ich in diesem Zusammenhang in meinem Buch behandle, die wirkende *agency* hinter dem Zusammenbruch der Stromversorgung im Jahr 2003 in Nordamerika (und später im selben Jahr dann in Europa). Die Regierung und die Industrie in den USA versuchte irgendeinen verantwortlichen Menschen namhaft zu machen – ein Vorstandsmitglied von Enron oder einen Stromhändler – der für die Sache verantwortlich sein sollte, um ihn dann zur Rechenschaft ziehen zu können. Doch dabei wurden die Bezüglichkeiten zwischen der Infrastruktur und dem Verteilernetz, der deregulierte Stromhandel, die Struktur des Konsumzwangs und die natürliche Weise, wie sich Elektrizität ausbreitet in den Hintergrund gedrängt. Aus diesem Grund bleibt die Wahrscheinlichkeit eines neuerlichen Zusammenbruchs wohl genauso hoch, wie sie es schon davor war. Der Hang, gesellschaftliche Probleme als moralisches Scheitern zu definieren, diese also ausschließlich individuellen oder kollektiv handelnden menschlichen Agenten zuzuschreiben (und die damit verbundene Vorstellung, wir hätten die Natur im Griff) hindert uns daran, den wahren Ort der Verschaltung auszumachen – nämlich die Assemblagen menschlicher und nicht-menschlicher Aktanten – wie es auch den Versuch behindert, die Konfigurationen dieser menschlichen und nicht-menschlichen Assemblagen zu verändern.

Die Leitfrage in meinem Buch ist die Folgende: In welcher Form würde sich die politische Analyse von Ereignissen verändern, würden wir eine elementare, materielle *agency* würdigen, die sich über die Körper, menschliche als auch nicht-menschliche, verteilt? Wer oder was vermöchte dann als „Interessenvertreter" aufzutreten? Wie würde sich eine „Öffentlichkeit" konstituieren? Würde sich die Politik weniger um die Frage kümmern, einen schuldigen menschlichen Verantwortlichen zu finden und zur Rechenschaft zu ziehen, der für öffentliche Probleme wie zum Beispiel einen großflächigen Stromausfall oder die epidemische Verbreitung von Fettleibigkeit einstehen muss, und sich stattdessen mehr der Aufgabe widmen, festzustellen, wie der Komplex menschlicher und nicht-menschlicher Assemblagen dazu beiträgt, negative Effekte zu produzieren, die sich hier zusammenschalten? Wie erhält sich derartiges aufrecht und befeuert sich immer weiter?

Solange wir zu einer solchen Sichtweise der Probleme nicht bereit sind, werden Versuche, diese Probleme zu kurieren, höchstwahrscheinlich wirkungslos bleiben. Tatsächlich vertrete ich eine pragmatische Anschauung: Politik und Ethik haben einen weit größeren Einfluss auf die materiellen Assemblagen und die Art und Weise, wie sich die Effekt-Muster wiederholen, als sie ihn auf die flüchtige geistige Einheit eines so genannten „moralisch Verantwortlichen" haben können.

KKL: *Und da ist ja noch mehr zu erfassen – ganze Müllberglandschaften, Deponien, eine industriell betriebene Landwirtschaft, Wasserstraßen, als auch eine weitere Kategorie, die sich beispielsweise aus geo-tektonischen Aktivitäten und Überflutungen oder gar aus Hyperobjekten wie der globalen Erderwärmung zusammensetzt; ihnen allen haften negative Attribute an oder sie sind „Nichtidentitäten" im Sinne Adornos und wohl schwer in Angriff zu nehmen ... Doch anders als bei seinem Ansatz schlagen Sie eine überraschende Wende vor, eine Wende hin zu einer positiven und reflexiven Affirmation.*

JB: Ich habe versucht die poetischen, fröhlichen und erfrischenden Aspekte der dynamischen Materie zu betonen und damit argumentiert, dass die *thing-power* sich oftmals zuerst als etwas Negatives zeigt, als eine Verdrehung oder Verschmutzung einer Absicht, eines Wunsches, eines Schemas oder eines Konzepts. Doch wie schon viele andere Denker festgestellt haben, ist eine solche Negativität aus demselben Stoff gemacht, aus dem auch die positiven Dinge entstehen. Es gibt eine Negativität, die grundsätzlich produktiv ist: Die Materialität, die uns widersteht ist auch die vielgestaltige Quelle des Seins, die prinzipiell unbestimmte Matrix der Dinge. Sie fragen mich jetzt auch, ob ich nicht mehr zu den widerwärtigen, gewalttätigen oder tödlichen Aspekten zu sagen habe – die *Graduate School* in London hat erst kürzlich eine Konferenz ausgerichtet, die sich mit dem Thema des „Dunklen Materialismus" beschäftigt hat. Ich habe das via Podcast verfolgt und möchte mich in dieser Hinsicht auch weiter mit dem Thema auseinandersetzen und Reza Negarestanis Arbeiten lesen,[9] die für diese Konferenz von äußerster Wichtigkeit waren.

Selbstverständlich stimme ich zu, dass es auch beim dynamischen Materialismus eine dunkle Seite gibt. Verschiedenste Kräfte können auf uns zurückwirken, und sie vermögen sogar die Grundlagen für unsere menschliche Lebensform zu vernichten. Auch der dynamische Materialismus kann keine kosmischen Garantien übernehmen.

Übersetzung Andreas L. Hofbauer und Klaus K. Loenhart

9 Vgl. http://backdoorbroadcasting.net/2011/01/dark-materialism/ und Reza Negerestani, *Cyclonopedia. Complicity with Anonymous Materials*. Melbourne 2008.

Contested Ecologies

1

1 *Birdfoot*: Wo sich Amerikas Fluss im Meer auflöst – Vogelschau Mississippi-Delta, CLUI (2008). *Birdfoot*: Where America's river dissolves into the sea—aerial view of the Mississippi Delta, CLUI (2008).

The Center for Land Use Interpretation

Birdfoot: Where America's River Dissolves into the Sea

The modes of address employed by the Center for Land Use Interpretation (CLUI)—research-based, documentary, archival—have obvious adjacencies with more traditional scientific and sociological ways of conceiving land and resource management, and assessments of the impact of the built environment on its surroundings.

Das Center for Land Use Interpretation. *Birdfoot: Wo sich Amerikas Fluss im Meer auflöst.* Die Adressierungsmethoden, die vom Center for Land Use Interpretation (CLUI) – forschungsorientiert, dokumentarisch, archivarisch – verwendet werden, zeigen eindeutige Bezüge zu traditionelleren wissenschaftlichen und soziologischen Auffassungen über Land- und Ressourcenmanagement sowie zur Bewertung der Auswirkungen der gebauten Umwelt auf ihre Umgebung. Da jedoch das Projekt des CLUI in einer Position außerhalb des herkömmlichen Rahmens einer solchen Untersuchung stattfindet, sind sie in der Lage, Aspekte eines offensichtlichen kulturellen und sozialen Mehrwerts zu mobilisieren, welche unweigerlich jene Orte begleiten, die sie untersuchen und katalogisieren.

JEFFREY KASTNER

Yet because CLUI's project proceeds from a position outside the conventional framework of such inquiry, they are able to mobilize some aspects of the obvious cultural and social surplus that inevitably attends the sites they investigate and catalog, producing portraits of locations that function not just as pedagogical accumulations of straight data, but also as markers for certain forms of poetic presences and absences.

This mixture of the analytical and the impressionistic is particularly vivid in CLUI's 2008 *Birdfoot* project, a research project-cum-travelogue that takes as its subject the southernmost terminus of the Mississippi, particularly the hundred or so miles of sparsely populated yet heavily industrialized wetlands between New Orleans and the Gulf of Mexico: a zone the project likens to an "anatomical orifice at the bottom of the country." This landscape has in recent years suffered two of the greatest environmental disasters in American history: Hurricane Katrina, which in August of 2005 killed more than 1,800 people and caused more than $ 81 billion in damage, and the April 2010 explosion of the Deepwater Horizon rig, whose extreme depth made the consequent leak almost impossible to stem, leading to the spillage of an estimated 180 million gallons of oil into marine habitats across some 180,000 km² of the Gulf. Although the BP spill occurred after *Birdfoot* was completed, the spectre of oil and gas extraction—along with associated industries like shipping and the large-scale earthworking necessary to create and maintain the physical environment—pervades the area on which the CLUI project focused.

This dynamic—a built intervention into a landscape that is paradoxically erasing the very landscape in which it is situated—is precisely the kind of problematic that the best of CLUI's work foregrounds. Projects like *Birdfoot* resist homogenous representations of the natural world, ones that acquiesce to the kinds of universalizing conventions which have come to dominate both discursive and visual models of "nature." In not simply accepting, but actually seeking out the stark, often disorienting contradictions that characterize the contemporary landscape (virtually the entirety of which must be understood as a hybrid of organic processes and industrial/technologic al techniques) CLUI's projects destabilize the generalizable, depoliticized rhetoric of much modern ecological activism. Their focus on minute particularities, and their commitment to producing and preserving a record of them, is an important piece in the larger movement to develop forward-looking political and pedagogical models.

Sie erzeugen dadurch Porträts von Schauplätzen, die nicht nur als pädagogische Sammlungen unverfälschter Daten wirken, sondern auch als Kennzeichnungen für bestimmte Formen von poetischen An- und Abwesenheiten.

Diese Mischung des Analytischen und Impressionistischen ist im *Birdfoot*-Projekt des CLUI aus dem Jahr 2008 besonders anschaulich – ein Forschungsprojekt mit Reisebericht, das den südlichsten Endpunkt des Mississippi, speziell die etwa hundertfünfzig Kilometer spärlich bewohnter und doch stark industrialisierter Auenlandschaft zwischen New Orleans und dem Golf von Mexiko, zu seinem Thema macht: eine Zone, die das Projekt mit einer „anatomischen Öffnung im Boden des Landes" vergleicht. Diese Landschaft hat in den letzten Jahren unter zwei der größten Umweltkatastrophen in der amerikanischen Geschichte gelitten: Durch den Hurrikan Katrina starben im August 2005 mehr als 1.800 Menschen und verursachte einen Schaden von mehr als 81 Milliarden Dollar, und im April 2010 folgte die Explosion der Ölbohrplattform Deepwater Horizon, deren extrem tiefliegende Bohrung die Schließung des Lecks fast unmöglich machte, und zum Austritt von geschätzten 670 Millionen Litern Öl in die Lebensräume des Meeres über etwa 180.000 km² des Golfes von Mexiko führte. Obwohl sich die BP-Ölkatastrophe nach der Fertigstellung von *Birdfoot* ereignete, überschattet die Öl- und Gasförderung – gemeinsam mit den zugehörigen Industrien, wie Schifffahrt und großmaßstäblichen Erdarbeiten, welche die entsprechende physische Umwelt erzeugen und erhalten – auch die Gegend, auf die sich das CLUI-Projekt konzentrierte.

Diese Dynamik einer Landschaft, die ausgerechnet dieselbe Landschaft auslöscht, in welcher sich ein Eingriff vollzieht – entspricht genau jener Art von Problematik, welche mit den besten Arbeiten des CLUI in den Vordergrund rücken. Projekte wie *Birdfoot* widerstehen homogenen Darstellungen der natürlichen Welt, die sich bestimmten verallgemeinernden Konventionen fügen und diskursive sowie visuelle Modelle einer „Natur" zunehmend dominieren. Indem sie die krassen und oftmals verwirrenden Widersprüche der Charakteristika unserer zeitgenössischen Landschaft (von der nahezu die Gesamtheit als ein Hybrid aus organischen Prozessen und industriellen/technologischen Techniken gesehen werden muss) nicht einfach akzeptiert, sondern vielmehr ausfindig gemacht haben, destabilisieren die Projekte des CLUI die generalisierende und entpolitisierte Rhetorik eines Großteils des modernen ökologischen Aktivismus. Ihr Fokus auf winzige Besonderheiten und ihre Bemühungen, Aufzeichnungen von diesen zu erzeugen und zu bewahren, sind wichtige Bestandteile in einer übergeordneten Bewegung, um fortschrittliche politische und pädagogische Modelle zu entwickeln.

Übersetzung Claudia Wrumnig

2 *Birdfoot*: Wo sich Amerikas Fluss im Meer auflöst – Vogelschau Mississippi-Delta, CLUI (2008). *Birdfoot*: Where America's river dissolves into the sea—aerial view of the Mississippi Delta, CLUI (2008).

1 *Untitled*, © Ilkka Halso.

Ecology – A New Opium for the Masses[1]

Marco Cicala, a Leftist Italian journalist, told me about his recent weird experience: when, in an article, he once used the word "capitalism," the editor asked him if the use of this term is really necessary—could he not replace it by a synonymous one, like "economy"? What better proof of the total triumph of capitalism than the virtual disappearance of the very term in the last two or three decades? No one, with the exception of a few allegedly archaic Marxists, refers to capitalism any longer.

Das Ökologische – Neues Opium fürs Volk[1]. Der linksgerichtete italienische Journalist Marco Cicala erzählte mir von einer seltsamen Begebenheit, die ihm neulich widerfahren war: Nachdem er in einem Artikel das Wort „Kapitalismus“ gebraucht hatte, fragte ihn der Herausgeber, ob es tatsächlich nötig sei, diesen Begriff zu benutzen – könnte man denn nicht einen anderen verwenden, zum Beispiel „Ökonomie“? Gibt es ein besseres Beispiel für den totalen Triumph des Kapitalismus, als das virtuelle Verschwinden genau dieses Begriffs in den letzten zwei oder drei Jahrzehnten? Nein – denn mit Ausnahme von ein paar vermeintlich vorsintflutlichen Marxisten bezieht sich heute niemand mehr auf den Kapitalismus.

SLAVOJ ŽIŽEK

The term was simply struck from the vocabulary of politicians, trade unionists, writers and journalists—even of social scientists … But what about the upsurge of the anti-globalization movement in the last years? Does it not clearly contradict this diagnostic? No: a close look quickly shows how this movement also succumbs to "the temptation to transform a critique of capitalism itself (centered on economic mechanisms, forms of work organization, and profit extraction) into a critique of 'imperialism.'" In this way, when one talks about "globalization and its agents," the enemy is externalized (usually in the form of vulgar anti-Americanism). From this perspective, where the main task today is to fight "the American empire," any ally is good if it is anti-American, and so the unbridled Chinese "Communist" capitalism, violent Islamic anti-modernists, as well as the obscene Lukashenko regime in Belarus may appear as progressive anti-globalist comrades-in-arms … What we have here is thus another version of the ill-famed notion of "alternate modernity": instead of the critique of capitalism as such, of confronting its basic mechanism, we get the critique of the imperialist "excess," with the (silent) notion of mobilizing capitalist mechanisms within another, more "progressive," frame.

So what is the problem here? It is easy to make fun of Fukuyama's notion of the End of History, but the majority today is "Fukuyamaian": liberal-democratic capitalism is accepted as the finally-found formula of the best possible society, all one can do is to render it more just, tolerant, etc. The only true question today is: do we endorse this "naturalization" of capitalism, or does today's global capitalism contain strong enough antagonisms which will prevent its indefinite reproduction? There are three (or, rather, four) such antagonisms:

The only true question today is: do we endorse this "naturalization" of capitalism, or does today's global capitalism contain strong enough antagonisms which will prevent its indefinite reproduction?

1. Ecology: In spite of the infinite adaptability of capitalism which, in the case of an acute ecological catastrophe or crisis, can easily turn ecology into a new field of capitalist investment and competition, the very nature of the risk involved fundamentally precludes a market solution—why? Capitalism only works in precise social conditions: it implies the trust into the objectivized/"reified" mechanism of the market's "invisible hand" which, as a kind of Cunning of Reason, guarantees that the competition of individual egotisms works for the common good. However, we are in the midst of a radical change. Till now, historical Substance played its role as the medium and foundation of all subjective interventions: whatever social and political subjects did, it was mediated and ultimately dominated, overdetermined, by the historical Substance. What looms on the horizon today is the unheard-of possibility that a subjective intervention will intervene directly into the historical Substance,

1 An expanded version of this paper has appeared at: http://www.lacan.com/zizecology1.htm.

Dieser Begriff wurde ganz einfach aus dem Repertoire der Politiker, Gewerkschafter, Autoren und Journalisten eliminiert – ja sogar bei den Sozialwissenschaftlern taucht er nicht mehr auf … Doch wie steht es um die heftigen Aufwallungen rund um die Antiglobalisierungsbewegung in den letzten Jahren? Ist nicht gerade das ein schlagender Gegenbeweis? Abermals nein: Sieht man näher hin, dann erkennt man rasch, dass diese Bewegung der Verführung erliegt, die Kritik des Kapitalismus an sich (basierend auf ökonomischen Mechanismen, Organisationsformen der Arbeit und Profitgewinnung) in eine Kritik des „Imperialismus" zu verwandeln. Spricht man also von der „Globalisierung und deren Vertreter", dann wird der Feind externalisiert (üblicherweise in Form eines vulgären Anti-Amerikanismus). So gesehen scheint dann die Hauptaufgabe darin zu bestehen, das „nordamerikanische Imperium" zu bekämpfen und jeder Verbündete ist willkommen, solange er sich nur gegen die USA stellt. Und deshalb werden der zügellose „kommunistische" Kapitalismus Chinas, ebenso wie die gewaltbereiten islamistischen Anti-Modernen und das obszöne Regime eines Lukaschenko in Weißrussland als fortschrittliche Waffenbrüder im Kampf gegen die Globalisierung akzeptiert. Wir haben es hier mit der übel beleumundeten Idee einer „Alternativ-Moderne" zu tun: Anstatt den Kapitalismus als solchen zu kritisieren und seinen grundlegenden Mechanismen die Stirn zu bieten, haben wir es mit einer Kritik des imperialistischen „Exzesses" zu tun, gekoppelt mit der (unter der Hand mitgeführten) Idee, kapitalistische Mechanismen in einem anderen, „fortschrittlicheren" Rahmen zu mobilisieren.

Worin liegt das Problem bei all dem? Fukuyamas Idee von einem *Ende der Geschichte* lächerlich zu machen, fällt leicht, doch letztendlich verhält sich die Mehrheit heutzutage ganz in seinem Sinne: Der liberal-demokratische Kapitalismus wird als die letztgültige Formel einer bestmöglichen Gesellschaft anerkannt und alles, was zu tun bleibt, ist, sie etwas gerechter, toleranter und so weiter zu gestalten. Die einzig wahre Frage, die sich heute noch stellt, lautet: Pflichten wir dieser „Naturalisierung" des Kapitalismus bei, oder beinhaltet der gegenwärtige globale Kapitalismus Antagonismen, die stark genug sind, um seine schrankenlose Reproduktion zu verhindern? Es gibt drei (oder vielmehr vier) derartiger Antagonismen:

1. Die Ökologie. Ungeachtet der unendlichen Anpassungsfähigkeit des Kapitalismus, der, im Falle einer akuten ökologischen Katastrophe oder Krise, die Ökologie sehr schnell in ein Feld verwandeln kann, das von der kapitalistischen Investition und vom Wettbewerb bestellt werden kann, so schließt doch das grundsätzlich damit verbundene Risiko eine Markt-

1 Eine erweiterte Fassung dieses Textes ist erschienen in: http://www.lacan.com/zizecology1.htm.

lösung aus. Warum? Der Kapitalismus funktioniert nur unter genau festgelegten gesellschaftlichen Bedingungen: Das impliziert das Vertrauen in den objektivierten/„vergegenständlichten" Mechanismus der „Unsichtbaren Hand" des Marktes, die, als eine Art „List der Vernunft", den Wettbewerb der jeweils egoistisch handelnden Individuen, die dadurch für das gemeinsame Wohl arbeiten, versichert. Bislang spielte die historische Substanz die Rolle des Mediums und war Grundlage für alle subjektiven Eingriffe: Was auch immer ein gesellschaftliches oder politisches Subjekt auch tat, es wurde von der historischen Substanz vermittelt und letztendlich bestimmt, ja sogar überdeterminiert. Was aber heute am Horizont heraufdämmert, ist die noch ungeahnte Möglichkeit eines subjektiven Eingriffs, der sich unmittelbar in die historische Substanz einmischen und auf katastrophale Weise deren Ablauf aus der Bahn werfen wird, wenn er eine ökologische Katastrophe auslöst, eine verhängnisvolle biogenetische Mutation hervorbringt, zu einem nuklearen oder einem ähnlichen militärischen Desaster führt und so weiter. Wir können uns nicht länger darauf verlassen, dass der Einflussbereich unserer Handlungen ein beschränkter ist: Nichts gewährleistet, dass die Geschichte, ungeachtet dessen, was auch immer wir tun, trotzdem weitergehen wird. Zum ersten Mal in der Geschichte der Menschheit kann die Tat eines einzelnen sozio-politischen Agenten den globalen historischen Prozess verändern oder gar abbrechen, so dass man demzufolge also ironischerweise gerade heute von der Geschichte behaupten kann, sie sei nicht länger nur als „*Substanz*, sondern ebenso sehr als *Subjekt*"[2] zu begreifen. Aus diesem Grunde können wir uns auch nicht länger auf die übliche Logik der „List der Vernunft" verlassen, die gerade der geschichtlichen Substanz die Vorrangstellung vor den handelnden Subjekten einräumt, wenn wir mit dementsprechend katastrophalen Perspektiven (zum Beispiel eine Gruppe, die ihre Gegner mit nuklearen oder biologischen Waffen angreifen will) konfrontiert werden. Man kann nicht länger den Standpunkt vertreten, man solle doch den „Feind, der uns bedroht, nur seine Potenziale ausschöpfen lassen, er werde sich dabei schon selbst zerstören" – der Preis, der zu zahlen ist, lässt man die geschichtliche Vernunft ihre Arbeit tun, ist mittlerweile zu hoch geworden, wenn wir dabei gemeinsam mit dem Feind zugrunde gehen. Man muss sich nur ein erschreckendes Detail aus den Zeiten der Kuba-Krise vor Augen führen: Erst im Nachhinein wurde ersichtlich, wie nahe wir einem Atomkrieg waren, als es am 27. Oktober 1962 zu einem Zwischenfall zwischen einem US-Zerstörer und einem sowjetischen B-59-U-Boot kam. Das Kriegsschiff setzte Unterwasserbomben unweit des U-Bootes ab, um dieses zum Auftauchen

2 Georg W. F. Hegel, *Phänomenologie des Geistes*. Vorrede. Frankfurt/M. 1970, S. 23; vgl. Slavoj Žižek, *The Sublime Object of Ideology*. London 1989, S. 201–231.

catastrophically disturbing its run by way of triggering an ecological catastrophe, a fateful biogenetic mutation, a nuclear or similar military-social catastrophe, etc. No longer can we rely on the safeguarding role of the limited scope of our acts: it no longer holds that, whatever we do, history will go on. For the first time in human history, the act of a single socio-political agent effectively can alter and even interrupt the global historical process, so that, ironically, it is only today that we can say that the historical process should effectively be conceived "not only as Substance, but also as Subject."[2] This is why, when confronted with singular catastrophic prospects (say, a political group which intends to attack its enemy with nuclear or biological weapons), we no longer can rely on the standard logic of the "Cunning of Reason" which, precisely, presupposes the primacy of the historical Substance over acting subjects: we no longer can adopt the stance of "let the enemy who threatens us deploy its potentials and thereby self-destruct himself"—the price for letting the historical Reason do its work is too high since, in the meantime, we may all perish together with the enemy. Recall a frightening detail from the Cuban missile crisis: only later did we learn how close to nuclear war we were during a naval skirmish between an American destroyer and a Soviet B-59 submarine off Cuba on October 27, 1962. The destroyer dropped depth charges near the submarine to try to force it to surface, not knowing it had a nuclear-tipped torpedo. Vadim Orlov, a member of the submarine crew, told the conference in Havana that the submarine was authorized to fire it if three officers agreed. The officers began a fierce, shouting debate over whether to sink the ship. Two of them said yes and the other said no. "A guy named Arkhipov saved the world," was a bitter comment of a historian on this accident.

2. Private Property: The inappropriateness of private property for the so-called "intellectual property." The key antagonism of the so-called new (digital) industries is thus: how to maintain the form of (private) property, within which only the logic of profit can be maintained (see also the Napster problem, the free circulation of music)? And do the legal complications in biogenetics not point in the same direction? Phenomena are emerging here which bring the notion of property to weird paradoxes: in India, local communities can suddenly discover that medical practices and materials they are using for centuries are now owned by American companies, so they should be bought from them; with the biogenetic companies patentizing genes, we are all discovering that parts of ourselves, our genetic components, are already copyrighted, owned by others …

The crucial date in the history of cyberspace is February 3, 1976, the day when Bill Gates published his (in)famous "Open Letter to Hobbyists," the assertion of private property in the software domain: "As the majority of hobbyists must be aware, most of you steal your software … Most directly, the thing you do is theft."[3] Bill Gates has built his entire empire and reputation on his extreme views about knowledge being treated as if it were tangible property. This was a decisive signal which triggered the battle for the "enclosure" of the common domain of software.

2 Georg W. F. Hegel, *Phänomenologie des Geistes*. Vorrede. Frankfurt/M. 1970, p. 23; see Slavoj Žižek, *The Sublime Object of Ideology*. London 1989, pp. 201–231.

3 Bill Gates, "Open Letter to Hobbyists," in: *Computer Notes* 1/9 (1976), p. 3.

zu zwingen, ohne zu wissen, dass dieses U-Boot über Torpedos mit Nuklearsprengköpfen verfügte. Vadim Orlov, ein Besatzungsmitglied des U-Bootes, teilte auf einer Konferenz in Havanna mit, dass das U-Boot dazu autorisiert gewesen sei, zurückzuschießen, wenn drei Offiziere diesem Befehl zustimmten. Es kam unter den Offizieren zu einer wilden Diskussion, wobei man sich anbrüllte, ob man nun das Schiff versenken solle oder nicht. Zwei von ihnen votierten dafür, einer war dagegen. „Ein Mann namens Arkhipov rettete die Welt", lautete der bittere Kommentar eines Historikers zu diesem Zwischenfall.

2. Das Privateigentum. Warum der Begriff des Privateigentums für das so genannte „geistige Eigentum" nicht angemessen ist. Der wesentliche Streitpunkt bezüglich der (Digital-)Industrie ist folgender: Wie kann man die Form des (privaten) Eigentums beibehalten, wenn durch diese ausschließlich die Logik des Profits gestützt wird (man denke dabei nur an *Napster* und das Problem, Musikdateien frei zirkulieren zu lassen)? Und geht es nicht bei den rechtlichen Problemen hinsichtlich der Biogenetik um etwas Ähnliches? Es tauchen hier Phänomene auf, welche die Idee, die man vom Eigentum hat, in verwegene Paradoxien treiben. So können zum Beispiel in Indien Dorfgemeinschaften herausfinden, dass die medizinischen Behandlungsverfahren und die dazu benötigten, selbst hergestellten Arzneimittel, die sie seit Jahrhunderten anwenden, plötzlich einem amerikanischen Pharmakonzern gehören, und dass die Menschen in Indien all das von nun an bei diesem Unternehmen käuflich erwerben sollen. Unternehmen auf dem Sektor der Biogenetik lassen Gene patentieren, und wir alle müssen nach und nach feststellen, dass Teile von uns selbst, unsere genetischen Bestandteile, bereits urheberrechtlich geschützt sind und jemand anderem gehören …

What looms on the horizon today is the unheard-of possibility that a subjective intervention will intervene directly into the historical Substance, catastrophically disturbing its run by way of triggering an ecological catastrophe, a fateful biogenetic mutation, a nuclear or similar military-social catastrophe, etc.

Das entscheidende Datum in der Geschichte des Cyberspace ist der 3. Februar 1976, der Tag also, an dem Bill Gates seinen berühmt-berüchtigten Brief „An Open Letter to Hobbyists" veröffentlichte, in dem er das Privateigentum von Software-Domains einmahnte. „Die Mehrheit der Hobby-Computeranwender muss sich klar darüber sein, dass ein Großteil der verwendeten Software gestohlen ist … Klipp und klar gesagt: Was Ihr hier macht ist Diebstahl."[3] Bill Gates hat sein ganzes Imperium und seine ganze Reputation auf der Grundlage seiner extremen Ansichten errichtet, man könne Wissen als konkret fassbares Eigentum behandeln. Das war ein entscheidendes Signal, das die Schlacht um die „Schließung" des allgemein zugänglichen Bereichs der Software eröffnete.

3. Die neuen technologischen und wissenschaftlichen Entwicklungen. Die gesellschaftlichen und ethischen Impli-

3 Bill Gates, „Open Letter to Hobbyists", in: *Computer Notes* 1/9 (1976), S. 3.

kationen der neuen techno-wissenschaftlichen Entwicklungen (vor allem in der Biogenetik). Selbst Fukuyama sah sich dazu genötigt zuzugeben, dass die biogenetischen Eingriffe in die menschliche Natur wohl die größte Bedrohung seiner Vision vom Ende der Geschichte seien.

Mit den neuesten biogenetischen Entwicklungen treten wir in eine Phase ein, in der es die Natur selbst ist, die zum Nichts verdampft: Die hauptsächliche Konsequenz des wissenschaftlichen Durchbruchs in der Biogenetik ist das Ende der Natur. Sobald wir ihren Bauplan durchschaut haben, transformieren die natürlichen Organismen zu Objekten, die der Manipulation zugänglich sind. Die menschliche und nichtmenschliche Natur wird demzufolge „entsubstanzialisiert" und von der undurchdringlichen Dichte abgelöst, die Heidegger noch „Erde" nannte. Und das zwingt uns auch, dem von Freud benutzten Titel vom *Unbehagen in der Kultur* eine neue Wendung zu verleihen. Mit den letzten Entwicklungen verschiebt sich das Unbehagen in der Kultur hinein in die Natur: Die Natur ist nicht länger „natürlich", nicht mehr der „solide" Hintergrund, vor dem wir unser Leben führen. Sie scheint zu einem fragilen Mechanismus geworden zu sein, der in jedem Augenblick explodieren und uns um die Ohren fliegen kann.

4. Die neuen Formen der Apartheid. *Last but not least* – neue Formen der Apartheid, neue Mauern und Slums. Am 11. September 2001 erfolgte der Anschlag auf die Twin Towers; zwölf Jahre vorher, am 9. November 1989 fiel die Berliner Mauer. Dieser 9. November kündigte die „fröhlichen 1990er-Jahre" an, den Traum vom Ende der Geschichte, wie es Francis Fukuyama vorschwebte. Das war der Glaube daran, dass die liberale Demokratie im Prinzip den Sieg davongetragen hätte und die Suche nun also vorbei sei. Der Advent einer globalen und liberalen Welt war nur noch einen Steinwurf weit entfernt und alle Hindernisse, die diesem übertriebenen Happy End à la Hollywood noch im Weg standen, waren bloß empirische und kontingente (ein paar Widerstandsnester, wo die jeweiligen Führer noch nicht verstanden hatten, dass ihre Zeit abgelaufen war). Dagegen wurde 9/11 zum Symbol einer anbrechenden Ära, wo überall wieder neue Mauern errichtet wurden – zwischen Israel und der West Bank, um die EU herum, an der Grenze zwischen Mexiko und den USA.

Was bedeutet es, wenn die neue proletarische Position nun die der Slumbewohner in den neuen Megalopolen ist? Das explosive Anwachsen der Slums in den letzten Jahrzehnten, vor allem in den Riesenstädten der Dritten Welt von Mexiko City und anderen lateinamerikanischen Hauptstädten bis hin nach Afrika (Lagos, Tschad) und Indien, China, den Philippinen und Indonesien, ist vielleicht *das* entscheidende geopolitische Ereignis unserer Tage. Dabei ist es erstaunlich, wie viele Merkmale auch auf die Bewohner dieser Slums zutreffen, folgt man der guten alten marxistischen Bestimmung,

3. New Techno-Scientific Developments: The socio-ethical implications of new techno-scientific developments (especially in bio-genetics)—Fukuyama himself was compelled to admit that the biogenetic interventions into human nature are the most serious threat to his vision of the End of History.

With the latest biogenetic developments, we are entering a new phase in which it is simply nature itself which melts into air: the main consequence of the scientific breakthroughs in biogenetics is the end of nature. Once we know the rules of its construction, natural organisms are transformed into objects amenable to manipulation. Nature, human and inhuman, is thus "desubstantialized," deprived of its impenetrable density, of what Heidegger called "earth." This compels us to give a new twist to Freud's title *Unbehagen in der Kultur*—discontent, uneasiness, in culture. With the latest developments, the discontent shifts from culture to nature itself: nature is no longer "natural," the reliable "dense" background of our lives; it now appears as a fragile mechanism which, at any point, can explode in a catastrophic direction.

4. New Forms of Apartheid: Last but not least, new forms of apartheid, new Walls and slums. On September 11th, 2001, the Twin Towers were hit; twelve years earlier, on November 9th, 1989, the Berlin Wall fell. November 9th announced the "happy '90s," the Francis Fukuyama dream of the "end of history," the belief that liberal democracy had, in principle, won, that the search is over, that the advent of a global, liberal world community lurks just around the corner, that the obstacles to this ultra-Hollywood happy ending are merely empirical and contingent (local pockets of resistance where the leaders did not yet grasp that their time is over). In contrast to it, 9/11 is the main symbol of the forthcoming era in which new walls are emerging everywhere, between Israel and the West Bank, around the European Union, on the U.S.-Mexico border.

So what if the new proletarian position is that of the inhabitants of slums in the new megalopolises? The explosive growth of slums in the last decades, especially in the Third World megalopolises from Mexico City and other Latin American capitals through Africa (Lagos, Chad) to India, China, Philippines and Indonesia, is perhaps the crucial geopolitical event of our times. It is effectively surprising how many features of slum dwellers fit the good old Marxist determination of the proletarian revolutionary subject: they are "free" in the double meaning of the word even more than the classic proletariat ("freed" from all substantial ties; dwelling in a free space, outside the police regulations of the state); they are a large collective, forcibly thrown together, "thrown" into a situation where they have to invent some mode of being-together, and simultaneously deprived of any support in traditional ways of life, in inherited religious or ethnic life-forms.

While today's society is often characterized as the society of total control, slums are the territories within a state boundaries from which the state (partially, at least) withdrew its control, territories which function as white spots, blanks, in the official map of a state territory. Although they are de facto included into a state by the links of black economy, organized crime, religious groups, etc., the state control is nonetheless suspended there, they are domains outside the rule of law. In the map of Berlin from the times of the now defunct GDR, the area of West Berlin was left blank, a weird hole in the detailed structure of the big city; when Christa Wolf, the well-known East German half-dissident writer, took her small daughter to the East Berlin's

high TV tower, from which one had a nice view over the prohibited West Berlin, the small girl shouted gladly: "Look, mother, it is not white over there, there are houses with people like here!"—as if discovering a prohibited slum Zone …

This is why the "de-structured" masses, poor and deprived of everything, situated in a non-proletarized urban environment, constitute one of the principal horizons of the politics to come. If the principal task of the emancipatory politics of the 19th century was to break the monopoly of the bourgeois liberals by way of politicizing the working class, and if the task of the 20th century was to politically awaken the immense rural population of Asia and Africa, the principal task of the 21st century is to politicize—organize and discipline—the "de-structured masses" of slum-dwellers. Hugo Chavez's biggest achievement is the politicization (inclusion into the political life, social mobilization) of slum dwellers; in other countries, they mostly persist in apolitical inertia. It was this political mobilization of the slum dwellers which saved him against the US-sponsored coup: to the surprise of everyone, Chavez included, slum dwellers massively descended to the affluent city center, tipping the balance of power to his advantage.

How do these four antagonisms relate to each other? There is a qualitative difference between the gap that separates the Excluded from the Included and the other three antagonisms, which designate three domains of what Hardt and Negri call "commons," the shared substance of our social being whose privatization is a violent act which should also be resisted with violent means, if necessary: the commons of culture, the immediately socialized forms of "cognitive" capital, primarily language, our means of communication and education (if Bill Gates were to be allowed monopoly, we would have reached the absurd situation in which a private individual would have literally owned the software texture our basic network of communication), but also the shared infrastructure of public transport, electricity, post, etc.; the commons of external nature threatened by pollution and exploitation (from oil to forests and natural habitat itself); the commons of internal nature (the biogenetic inheritance of humanity). What all these struggles share is the awareness of the destructive potentials, up to the self-annihilation of humanity itself, if the capitalist logic of enclosing these commons is allowed a free run. It is this reference to "commons" which justifies the resuscitation of the notion of Communism—or, to quote Alain Badiou:

"The communist hypothesis remains the good one, I do not see any other. If we have to abandon this hypothesis, then it is no longer worth doing anything at all in the field of collective action. Without the horizon of communism, without this Idea, there is nothing in the historical and political becoming of any interest to a philosopher. Let everyone bother about his own affairs, and let us stop talking about it. In this case, the rat-man is right, as is, by the way, the case with some ex-communists who are either avid of their rents or who lost courage. However, to hold on to the Idea, to the existence of this hypothesis, does not mean that we should retain its first form of presentation which was centered on property and State. In fact, what is imposed on us as a task, even as a philosophical obligation, is to help a new mode of existence of the hypothesis to deploy itself."[4]

4 See Alain Badiou, *Wofür steht der Name Sarkozy?* Berlin 2010; idem, *The Communist Hypothesis*. London 2010.

was ein proletarisches revolutionäres Subjekt sei: Sie sind im doppelten Wortsinne „frei", möglicherweise sogar in höherem Maße frei, als das für das klassische Proletariat galt (für sie gibt es keine substanziellen Bindungen mehr, sie leben im Freien, jenseits aller Regulative der staatlichen Verwaltung); sie bilden ein gewaltiges Kollektiv, das zu dieser Form des Lebens gezwungen wurde, sie sind in eine Situation „geworfen", in welcher sie die Arten und Weisen ihres Zusammenlebens selbst erfinden müssen, und sie sind gleichzeitig von jedweder herkömmlichen Unterstützung abgeschnitten, welche die überkommenen religiösen oder ethnischen Lebensmodelle anboten.

Oftmals werden die heutigen Gesellschaften als völlig der Kontrolle unterworfen beschrieben, doch Slums sind Territorien innerhalb der staatlichen Grenzen, aus denen sich der Staat (zumindest teilweise) zurückgezogen hat; sie sind Territorien, die als weiße Flecken, als Leerstellen, auf der Karte des staatlich kontrollierten Gebiets fungieren. Wenn sie auch *de facto* mit dem Staat durch diverse Gelenkstellen verbunden bleiben (etwa durch den Schwarzmarkt, das organisierte Verbrechen, religiöse Gruppierungen et cetera), so sind sie nichtsdestotrotz Gebiete, für welche die staatliche Kontrolle nicht mehr gilt, Gebiete außerhalb der Legalität. Nimmt man eine Landkarte aus den Zeiten der heute nicht mehr existierenden DDR zur Hand, dann ist Westberlin darauf als Leerstelle verzeichnet, ein seltsames Loch in der detailreichen Struktur der Großstadt. Als Christa Wolf, die bekannte ostdeutsche Schriftstellerin und Halbdissidentin ihre kleine Tochter auf den riesigen Fernsehturm Ostberlins mitnahm, von dem aus man eine gute Aussicht auf das unzugängliche Westberlin hatte, rief das kleine Mädchen begeistert: „Schau, Mama, da drüben ist ja gar nicht alles weiß, da gibt's Häuser und Menschen, genau wie hier!" – es war gerade so, als hätte man zum ersten Mal einen Blick auf die verbotene Slum-Zone geworfen …

Aus diesem Grunde sind es die „strukturlosen" Massen, arm und von allem abgeschnitten, die in einem nicht-proletarisierten urbanen Umfeld leben, die den prinzipiellen Vektor einer künftigen Politik angeben. War es die Hauptaufgabe einer emanzipatorischen Politik im 19. Jahrhundert, das Monopol der bürgerlichen Liberalen zu brechen, indem man die Arbeiterklasse politisierte, so war es die Hauptaufgabe des 20. Jahrhunderts, die riesige Landbevölkerung in Asien und Afrika zu wecken. Die Hauptaufgabe des 21. Jahrhunderts besteht in der Politisierung – Organisierung und Ausbildung – der „strukturlosen" Massen der Slumbewohner. Hugo Chavez' größte Leistung besteht in der Politisierung der Slumbewohner (da er sie in das politische Leben eingebunden und gesellschaftlich mobilisiert hat). In zahlreichen anderen Ländern verharren sie zumeist noch in unpolitischer Trägheit. Ihre politische Mobilisierung war es, die Chavez vor dem von den USA finanziell unterstützten Putsch retteten: Zur Überraschung aller, Chavez eingeschlossen, stiegen die Slumbewohner in

Massen zum reichen Stadtzentren ab und glichen damit die Machtverhältnisse zu seinem Vorteil wieder aus.

Wie hängen diese vier Antagonismen zusammen? Es gibt einen qualitativen Unterschied zwischen der Lücke, welche die Ausgeschlossenen von den Integrierten trennt und den anderen drei Antagonismen, welche die drei Bereiche bestimmen, die Hardt und Negri „Gemeingüter" nennen, eine geteilte Substanz unseres gesellschaftlichen Seins, deren Privatisierung einen Gewaltakt darstellt, gegen den man, wenn notwendig auch unter Anwendung von Gewalt, Widerstand leisten sollte: Es geht hier um das Gemeingut der Kultur, also die unmittelbar vergesellschafteten Formen des „kognitiven" Kapitals, wie sie vor allem in der Sprache, unseren Kommunikationsmitteln und bei der Bildung zum Tragen kommen (würde man Bill Gates ein Monopolrecht zugestehen, dann wären wir in die absurde Lage geraten, in der ein einzelnes Individuum buchstäblich den Quelltext der Software besäße, der dem basalen Netzwerk unserer Kommunikation zugrunde liegt), aber auch um die Infrastruktur, die wir alle gemeinsam teilen, sei es der öffentliche Nah- und Fernverkehr, die Stromversorgung, die Post et cetera. Das Gemeingut der äußeren Natur wird durch Umweltverschmutzung und Raubbau (von der Erdölgewinnung bis hin zur Rodung der Wälder und der Zerstörung unseres natürlichen Lebensraums im Allgemeinen) bedroht, und es geht um das Gemeingut der inneren Natur (das biogenetische Erbmaterial der Menschheit). All diesen Kämpfen ist das Bewusstsein gemeinsam, dass wir es hier mit einem zerstörerischen Potenzial zu tun haben, das sich bis zur Selbstauslöschung der Menschheit steigern kann, wenn man der kapitalistischen Logik erlaubt, in ihrem freien Walten diese Gemeingüter für sich zu vereinnahmen. Die Bezugnahme auf diese „Gemeingüter" ist es, welche die Wiederbelebung der Idee des Kommunismus rechtfertigt – oder, um Alain Badiou zu zitieren:

„Die Grundannahme des Kommunismus ist eine gerechtfertigte, und ich kann keine andere erkennen. Geben wir diese Vorstellung auf, dann hat es auch keinen Wert, hinsichtlich des gemeinsamen Handelns noch irgendetwas anderes zu tun. Ohne den Horizont des Kommunismus, ohne diese Idee, gibt es nichts, was im Werden des Historischen oder Politischen für einen Philosophen von Belang sein könnte. Dann möge sich jeder um seine eigenen Angelegenheiten kümmern, und wir können aufhören von all dem zu reden. In diesem Fall hätte der Ratten-Mann Recht, eben so, wie dies auch für viele Ex-Kommunisten gilt, die sich entweder um ihre Einkünfte sorgen oder ganz einfach den Mut verloren haben. Dennoch bedeutet es nicht, wenn man dieser Idee, der Existenz dieser Grundannahme, die Treue hält, dass wir deshalb auch ihre ursprüngliche Form wieder aufnehmen müssen, die sich um das Eigentum und den Staat herum entwickelte. In der Tat besteht unsere Aufgabe darin, ja das ist sogar eine philosophische Verpflich-

So where do we stand today with regard to communism? The first step is to admit that the solution is not to limit the market and private property by direct interventions of the State and state ownership. The domain of State itself is also in its own way "private": private in the precise Kantian sense of the "private use of Reason" in State administrative and ideological apparatuses:

"The public use of one's reason must always be free, and it alone can bring about enlightenment among men. The private use of one's reason, on the other hand, may often be very narrowly restricted without particularly hindering the progress of enlightenment. By public use of one's reason I understand the use which a person makes of it as a scholar before the reading public. Private use I call that which one may make of it in a particular civil post or office which is entrusted to him."[5]

What one should add here, moving beyond Kant, is that there is a privileged social group which, on account of its lacking a determinate place in the "private" order of social hierarchy, directly stands for universality: it is only the reference to those Excluded, to those who dwell in the blanks of the State space, that enables true universality. There is nothing more "private" than a State community which perceives the Excluded as a threat and worries how to keep the Excluded at a proper distance. In other words, in the series of the four antagonisms, the one between the Included and the Excluded is the crucial one, the point of reference for the others; without it, all others lose their subversive edge: ecology turns into a "problem of sustainable development," intellectual property into a "complex legal challenge," biogenetics into an "ethical" issue. One can sincerely fight for ecology, defend a broader notion of intellectual property, oppose the copyrighting of genes, while not questioning the antagonism between the Included and the Excluded—even more, one can even formulate some of these struggles in the terms of the Included threatened by the polluting Excluded. In this way, we get no true universality, only "private" concerns in the Kantian sense of the term. Corporations like Whole Foods and Starbucks continue to enjoy favor among liberals even though they both engage in anti-union activities; the trick is that they sell products that contain the claim of being politically progressive acts in and of themselves. One buys coffee made with beans bought at above fair-market value, one drives a hybrid vehicle, one buys from companies that provide good benefits for their customers (according to the corporation's own standards), etc. Political action and consumption become fully merged. In short, without the antagonism between the Included and the Excluded, we may well find ourselves in a world in which Bill Gates is the greatest humanitarian

There is nothing more "private" than a State community which perceives the Excluded as a threat and worries how to keep the Excluded at a proper distance.

5 Immanuel Kant, "Beantwortung der Frage: Was ist Aufklärung?," in: idem, *Was ist Aufklärung? Ausgewählte kleine Schriften*. Hamburg 1999, p. 22.

fighting against poverty and diseases, and Rupert Murdoch the greatest environmentalist mobilizing hundreds of millions through his media empire.

When politics is reduced to the "private" domain, it takes the form of the politics of FEAR—fear of losing one's particular identity, of being overwhelmed. Today's predominant mode of politics is post-political bio-politics—an awesome example of theoretical jargon which, however, can easily be unpacked: "post-political" is a politics which claims to leave behind old ideological struggles and, instead, focus on expert management and administration, while "bio-politics" designates the regulation of the security and welfare of human lives as its primal goal. It is clear how these two dimensions overlap: once one renounces big ideological causes, what remains is only the efficient administration of life ... almost only that. That is to say, with the depoliticized, socially objective, expert administration and coordination of interests as the zero-level of politics, the only way to introduce passion into this field, to actively mobilize people, is through fear, a basic constituent of today's subjectivity.

No wonder, then, that the by far predominant version of ecology is the ecology of fear, fear of a catastrophe—human-made or natural—that may deeply perturb, destroy even, the human civilization, fear that pushes us to plan measures that would protect our safety. This ecology of fear has all the chances of developing into the predominant form of ideology of global capitalism, a new opium for the masses replacing the declining religion: it takes over the old religion's fundamental function, that of putting on an unquestionable authority which can impose limits. The lesson this ecology is constantly hammering is our finitude: we are not Cartesian subjects extracted from reality, we are finite beings embedded in a bio-sphere which vastly transgresses our horizon. In our exploitation of natural resources, we are borrowing from the future, so one should treat our Earth with respect, as something ultimately Sacred, something that should not be unveiled totally, that should and will forever remain a Mystery, a power we should trust, not dominate. While we cannot gain full mastery over our bio-sphere, it is unfortunately in our power to derail it, to disturb its balance so that it will run amok, swiping us away in the process. This is why, although ecologists are all the time demanding that we change radically our way of life, underlying this demand is its opposite, a deep distrust of change, of development, of progress: every radical change can have the unintended consequence of triggering a catastrophe.

In short, without the antagonism between the Included and the Excluded, we may well find ourselves in a world in which Bill Gates is the greatest humanitarian fighting against poverty and diseases, and Rupert Murdoch the greatest environmentalist mobilizing hundreds of millions through his media empire.

tung, einen neuen Existenzmodus dieser Grundannahme auf den Weg zu bringen."[4]

Wo stehen wir heute also hinsichtlich des Kommunismus? In einem ersten Schritt müssen wir zugeben, dass die Lösung nicht darin bestehen kann, den Markt und das Privateigentum, durch direkte staatliche Interventionen zu beschränken und jene zu verstaatlichen. Die Sphäre des Staats ist selber auf ihre Weise eine „private": Privat genau im Sinne Immanuel Kants hinsichtlich des „Privatgebrauchs der Vernunft" im verwaltungstechnischen und ideologischen Staatsapparat.

„[D]er öffentliche Gebrauch seiner Vernunft muß jederzeit frei sein, und der allein kann Aufklärung unter Menschen zustande bringen; der Privatgebrauch derselben aber darf öfters sehr enge eingeschränkt sein, ohne doch darum den Fortschritt der Aufklärung sonderlich zu hindern. Ich verstehe aber unter dem öffentlichen Gebrauch seiner eigenen Vernunft denjenigen, den jemand als Gelehrter von ihr vor dem ganzen Publikum der Leserwelt macht. Den Privatgebrauch nenne ich denjenigen, den er in einem gewissen ihm anvertrauten bürgerlichen Posten oder Amte von seiner Vernunft machen darf."[5]

Man sollte hier ergänzen, und sich damit über Kant hinaus bewegen, dass es eine privilegierte gesellschaftliche Gruppe gibt, die aufgrund des Mangels eines bestimmten Platzes in der „privaten" Ordnung der gesellschaftlichen Hierarchie unmittelbar für die Universalität einsteht: Denn nur die Bezugnahme auf diese Ausgeschlossenen, auf diejenigen also, die in den Leerstellen des Staates hausen, ermöglicht die wahre Universalität. Nichts ist „privater" als ein Staat, der die Ausgeschlossenen als eine Bedrohung betrachtet und sich darum sorgt, wie er sie am Besten auf Distanz halten kann. Mit anderen Worten ist also in der Serie der vier Antagonismen derjenige der entscheidende, der zwischen den Integrierten und den Ausgeschlossenen besteht. Er ist der Bezugspunkt für die anderen drei. Ohne ihn büßen die anderen ihre subversiven Kanten ein: Die Ökologie wandelt sich zum „Problem einer nachhaltigen Entwicklung", geistiges Eigentum wird zu einer „komplexen rechtlichen Herausforderung", die Biogenetik wird zur „Frage der Ethik". Man kann aufrichtig für den Umweltschutz eintreten, eine breiter gefasste Idee des geistigen Eigentums verteidigen und sich dem Copyright auf Gene widersetzen, ohne sich die Frage nach dem Antagonismus zwischen den Integrierten und den Ausgeschlossenen überhaupt zu stellen – ja mehr noch: Man kann sogar einige dieser Kämpfe dergestalt formulieren, dass man den Eindruck gewinnt, die Integrierten stünden in Gefahr, vom Schadstoff der Ausgeschlossenen bedroht zu sein. Auf diese Weise erreichen wir keineswegs eine wahrhafte Universalität, sondern wir haben es nur mit „Privatangelegen-

4 Vgl. Alain Badiou, *Wofür steht der Name Sarkozy?* Berlin 2010; ders., *The Communist Hypothesis*. London 2010.

5 Immanuel Kant, „Beantwortung der Frage: Was ist Aufklärung?", in: ders., *Was ist Aufklärung? Ausgewählte kleine Schriften*. Hamburg 1999, S. 22.

heiten" im Sinne Kants zu tun. Unternehmen wie *Whole Foods* oder *Starbucks* werden immer noch von den Liberalen bevorzugt, wenngleich sie beide auch anti-gewerkschaftlich agieren; der Trick dabei ist, dass sie Produkte vertreiben, die an sich schon den Anschein erwecken, sie selbst – als Produkt – seien eine politisch fortschrittliche Tat. Man kauft Kaffee, der aus Bohnen gemacht wird, die nach fairen Marktpreisen gehandelt werden, man fährt ein Hybrid-Auto, man kauft bei Unternehmen ein, die ihre Umsatzgewinne an die Kunden weitergeben (selbstverständlich nach den Standards, die diese Unternehmen selber setzen) und so weiter. Die politische Tat und die Konsumation werden völlig ununterscheidbar. Kurz gesagt: Ohne den Antagonismus zwischen den Integrierten und den Ausgeschlossenen werden wir uns alsbald in einer Welt wiederfinden, in der Bill Gates der größte unter den Menschenfreunden ist, der gegen Armut und Seuchen kämpft; und Rupert Murdoch wird zum größten aller Umweltschützer, wenn er Abermillionen vermittels seines Medienimperiums mobilisiert.

Reduziert man also die Politik auf den Bereich des „Privaten", dann nimmt sie die Form einer Politik der Angst an – die Angst, seine eigene, besondere Individualität zu verlieren, überwältigt zu werden. Der heutzutage vorherrschende Modus der Politik ist die post-politische Biopolitik – ein staunenswertes Beispiel eines Theoriejargons, den man jedoch unschwer zerpflücken kann. Das „Post-Politische" ist eine Politik, die von sich behauptet, sich vom alten ideologischen Ballast befreit zu haben und sich stattdessen auf expertenbasiertes Management und Verwaltung konzentriert. „Biopolitik" bezeichnet die Tatsache, dass es das vorrangige Ziel ist, die Sicherheit und den Wohlstand des menschlichen Lebens zu regulieren. Es ist dabei ganz offensichtlich, dass diese beiden Sphären einander überschneiden: Wenn man sich erst einmal von den ideologischen Beweggründen distanziert hat, dann bleibt nur mehr die effiziente Verwaltung des Lebens übrig … beinahe nur mehr. Das heißt, dass mit der entpolitisierten, gesellschaftlich objektiven Expertenverwaltung und -administration und der Koordination der jeweiligen Interessen der Nullpunkt der Politik erreicht ist. Der einzige Weg, dieses Feld wieder mit Leidenschaft zu impfen, also die Menschen zu mobilisieren, besteht darin, Angst zu schüren, die konstitutive Grundlage der heutigen Subjektivität.

Wen wundert es also, dass die vorherrschende Ansicht hinsichtlich der Ökologie eine Ökologie der Angst ist. Angst vor der Katastrophe – sei diese nun vom Menschen verschuldet oder durch die Natur selbst –, welche die menschliche Zivilisation völlig verändern, ja sogar zerstören könnte. Eine Angst demnach, die uns dazu antreibt, nach Möglichkeiten, die unsere Sicherheit gewährleisten, zu suchen und diese bereitzustellen. Eine solche Ökologie der Angst hat gute Chancen, sich zu der alles bestimmenden Ideologie des globalen Kapitalismus zu mausern, ein Opium für die Massen zu werden und damit

It is this distrust which makes ecology the ideal candidate for hegemonic ideology, since it echoes the anti-totalitarian post-political distrust of large collective acts. This distrust unites religious leaders and environmentalists—for both, there is something of a transgression, of entering a prohibited domain, in this idea of creating a new form of life from scratch, from the zero-point. And this brings us back to the notion of ecology as the new opium for the masses; the underlying message is again a deeply conservative one—any change can only be the change for the worst—here is a nice quote from the *Newsweek* magazine on this topic:

"Behind much of the resistance to the notion of synthetic life is the intuition that nature (or God) created the best of possible worlds. Charles Darwin believed that the myriad designs of nature's creations are perfectly honed to do whatever they are meant to do—be it animals that see, hear, sing, swim or fly, or plants that feed on the sun's rays, exuding bright floral colors to attract pollinators."[6]

This reference to Darwin is deeply misleading: the ultimate lesson of Darwinism is the exact opposite, namely that nature tinkers and improvises, with great losses and catastrophes accompanying every limited success—is the fact that 90 percent of the human genome is "junk DNA" with no clear function not the ultimate proof of it? Consequently, the first lesson to be drawn is the one repeatedly made by Stephen Jay Gould: the utter contingency of our existence. There is no Evolution: catastrophes, broken equilibriums, are part of natural history; at numerous points in the past, life could have turned into an entirely different direction. The main source of our energy (oil) is the result of a past catastrophe of unimaginable dimensions. One should thus learn to accept the utter groundlessness of our existence: there is no firm foundation, a place of retreat, on which one can safely count. "Nature doesn't exist": "nature" qua the domain of balanced reproduction, of organic deployment into which humanity intervenes with its hubris, brutally throwing off the rails its circular motion, is man's fantasy; nature is already in itself "second nature," its balance is always secondary, an attempt to negotiate a "habit" that would restore some order after catastrophic interruptions.

With regard to this inherent instability of nature, the most consequent was the proposal of a German ecological scientist back in 1970s: since nature is changing constantly and the conditions on Earth will render the survival of humanity impossible in a couple of centuries, the collective goal of humanity should be not to adapt itself to nature, but to intervene into the Earth ecology even more forcefully with the aim to freeze the Earth's change, so that its ecology will remain basically the same, thus enabling humanity's survival. This extreme proposal renders visible the truth of ecology.

The lesson to be fully endorsed is thus that of another environmental scientist who came to the result that, while one cannot be sure what the ultimate result of humanity's interventions into geo-sphere will be, one thing is sure: if humanity were to stop abruptly its immense industrial activity and let nature on Earth take its balanced course, the result would have been a total breakdown, an imaginable catastrophe. "Nature" on

6 Lee Silver, "Scientists Push the Boundaries of Human Life," in: *Newsweek International*, June 4, 2007, http://www.newsweek.com/2007/06/03/life-2-0.html [accessed January 21, 2011].

Earth is already to such an extent "adapted" to human interventions, the human "pollutions" are already to such an extent included into the shaky and fragile balance of the "natural" reproduction on Earth, that its cessation would cause a catastrophic imbalance. This is what it means that humanity has nowhere to retreat: not only "there is no big Other" (self-contained symbolic order as the ultimate guarantee of Meaning); there is also no Nature qua balanced order of self-reproduction whose homeostasis is disturbed, thrown off the rails, by the imbalanced human interventions. Indeed, what we need is ecology without nature: the ultimate obstacle to protecting nature is the very notion of nature we rely on.

Alan Weisman's *The World Without Us* is a vision of what would have happened if humanity (and ONLY humanity) were suddenly to disappear from the earth—natural diversity blooming again, nature gradually regaining human artefacts. We, humans, are reduced to a pure disembodied gaze observing our own absence. (As Lacan pointed out, this is the fundamental subjective position of fantasy: to be reduced to *a*, the gaze which observes the world in the condition of the subject's non-existence—like the fantasy of witnessing the act of one's own conception, the parental copulation, or the act of witnessing one's own burial, like Tom Sawyer and Huck Finn. A jealous child likes to indulge in the fantasy of imagining how his parents would react to his own death, putting at stake his own absence.) "The world without us" is thus fantasy at its purest: witnessing the Earth itself retaining its pre-castrated state of innocence, before we humans spoiled it with our hubris. The irony is that the most prominent example comes from the catastrophe of Chernobyl: the exuberant nature taking over the disintegrating debris of the nearby city Pripyat which was abandoned, left the way it was.

Against this background, one should also render problematic Badiou's distinction between man qua mortal "human animal" and the "inhuman" subject as the agent of a Truth-procedure: man is pursuing happiness and pleasures, worrying about death, etc., it is an animal endowed with higher instruments to reach its goals, while only as a subject faithful to a Truth-Event does it truly raise above animality.[7] The problem with this dualism is that it ignores Freud's basic lesson: there is no "human animal," a human being is from its birth (and even before) torn out of the animal constraints, its instincts are "denaturalized," caught in the circularity of the (death-)drive, functioning "beyond the pleasure principle," marked by the stigma of what Eric Santner called "undeadness" or the excess of life.[8] This is why there is no place for "death drive" in Badiou's edifice, for the "distortion" of human animality which precedes fidelity to an Event. It is not only the "miracle" of a traumatic encounter with an Event which derails a human subject from its animality: its libido is already in itself derailed. One should thus turn around the usual criticism of Badiou: what is problematic is not the quasi-religious miracle of the Event, but the very "natural" order disturbed by the Event.

So, back to the prospect of ecological catastrophe, why do we not act? It is too short to attribute our disbelief in the catastrophe to the impregnation of our mind by scientific ideology, which leads us to dismiss the sane

7 See Alain Badiou, *L'être et l'événement*. Paris 1988.

8 See Eric L. Santner, *On the Psychotheology of Everyday Life*. Chicago 2001.

die absterbenden Religionen zu ersetzen: Sie übernimmt die Funktion, die früher die Religion innehatte, indem eine unhinterfragbare Autorität eingeführt wird, die in der Lage ist, Grenzen zu setzen. Die Lektion, die uns ununterbrochen vom Ökologischen eingehämmert wird, ist unsere Endlichkeit: Wir sind keine cartesianischen Subjekte, die aus der Realität herausgehoben sind, sondern wir sind endliche Wesen, die in eine Biosphäre eingebettet sind, die unseren Horizont bei weitem übersteigt. Wenn wir unsere natürlichen Ressourcen ausbeuten, dann borgen wir von der Zukunft. Aus diesem Grund sollten wir unsere Erde mit Respekt behandeln, als etwas, das im äußersten Maße heilig ist, etwas, das man nicht zur Gänze entschleiern soll, etwas, das für immer ein Mysterium bleiben wird, eine Kraft, auf die man vertrauen darf und die man nicht beherrschen soll. Obwohl wir unsere Biosphäre also nicht zur Gänze kontrollieren können, so liegt es dennoch unglücklicherweise in unserer Macht, sie aus der Bahn werfen zu können, ihre Balance so durcheinander zu bringen, dass sie völlig aus dem Ruder läuft und wir dabei gleich mit ihr untergehen. Aus diesem Grunde fordern die Ökologen zwar die ganze Zeit, wir sollten unsere Lebensweise radikal ändern, doch dieser Forderung liegt etwas anderes zugrunde: das nachgerade Gegenteil, der enorme Verdacht gegenüber jedwedem Wandel, jeder Entwicklung, gegenüber dem Fortschritt. Jeder radikale Wandel kann unbeabsichtigte Konsequenzen mit sich bringen und die Katastrophe auslösen.

Dieses Misstrauen ist es, welches die Ökologie zum perfekten Kandidaten für eine hegemoniale Ideologie macht, da wir es hier mit dem anti-totalitären post-politischen Misstrauen gegenüber großen, kollektiven Taten zu tun bekommen. Dieses Misstrauen bringt die religiösen Führer und die Umweltschützer ins selbe Boot – für beide liegt in der Idee, eine neue Form des Lebens von Grund auf zu befördern oder vom Nullpunkt her zu generieren, so etwas wie eine Überschreitung, ein Eindringen in eine verbotene Zone. Und das führt uns wieder zurück zur Vorstellung vom Ökologischen als einem neuen Opium fürs Volk. All dem liegt wieder eine zutiefst konservative Botschaft zugrunde. Jedweder Wandel kann nur ein Wandel zum Schlimmsten sein – und hier ist es angezeigt, *Newsweek* zu zitieren:

„Hinter dem Widerstand gegen die Idee vom Künstlichen Leben steht die Vermutung, dass die Natur (oder Gott) die beste aller denkbaren Welten bereitgestellt hätte. Charles Darwin war davon überzeugt, dass die Unzahl von Lebensformen, welche die Natur hervorgebracht hat, perfekt darauf abgestimmt seien, genau das zu vollbringen, wozu sie auch bestimmt wurden – mögen dies nun Tiere sein, die sehen, hören, singen, schwimmen oder fliegen können, oder Pflanzen, die durch das Sonnenlicht gedeihen, prächtige Farben entwickeln und damit Bestäuber anlocken."[6]

Diese Bezugnahme auf Darwin ist reichlich irreführend. Was Darwin tatsächlich sagt, ist das genaue Gegenteil davon.

Die Natur bastelt und improvisiert, und das ist mit großen Verlusten und Katastrophen verbunden, die jeden begrenzten Erfolg begleiten. Ist dafür die Tatsache, dass 90 Prozent des menschlichen Genoms „Junk-DNA" ist, Abfall also, der keine klare Funktion hat, nicht der beste Beweis? Konsequenterweise ist daher die erste Lektion, die wir lernen, die, welche Stephen Jay Gould wiederholt anbietet: Unsere Existenz ist völlig kontingent. Es gibt überhaupt keine Evolution: Katastrophen, gestörte Gleichgewichte, sind Teil der Geschichte der Natur; an zahlreichen Stellen in der Vergangenheit hätte die Entwicklung des Lebens einen völlig anderen Verlauf nehmen können. Unsere Hauptenergiequelle (das Erdöl) ist das Ergebnis einer Katastrophe unbegreiflichen Ausmaßes, die sich in der Vergangenheit ereignet hat. Man sollte daher anfangen, die Bodenlosigkeit unserer Existenz zu akzeptieren: Es gibt keinen unerschütterlichen Grund, keinen Platz, auf den man sich zurückziehen und den man als sicher bezeichnen kann. „Die Natur existiert nicht": Keine „Natur" im Sinne eines Bereichs der im Ausgleich befindlichen Reproduktion, einer organischen Entwicklung, in die sich die Menschheit mitsamt ihrer Hybris einmischen und die sie brutal aus dem Gleichgewicht zu bringen vermöchte. Das ist bloß ein Hirngespinst der Menschen. Die Natur ist in sich selbst bereits „zweite Natur"; jedes Gleichgewicht ist immer schon etwas Untergeordnetes, der Versuch, mit dem Etwas zu Rande zu kommen und nach katastrophalen Erschütterungen ein wenig Ordnung wiederherzustellen.

Hinsichtlich dieser der Natur innewohnenden Instabilität war der wissenschaftliche Vorschlag, den deutsche Ökologen in den 1970er-Jahren vorlegten, nur allzu konsequent: In ein paar Jahrhunderten wird sich zeigen, dass das Überleben der Menschheit unmöglich ist, und das gemeinsame Ziel sollte daher darin bestehen, sich mitnichten der Natur anzupassen, sondern sogar noch in verstärktem Maße daran zu arbeiten, alle Veränderungen auf dem Erdball zu verhindern, damit dessen Ökosystem mehr oder weniger unverändert bliebe und dadurch auch das Überleben der Menschheit sichergestellt sein würde. Dieser extreme Vorschlag macht nur allzu deutlich, worin die Wahrheit der Ökologie besteht. Denkt man diesen Vorschlag zu Ende, dann kommt man zu demselben Schluss, wie ein anderer Wissenschaftler des Umweltschutzes, der feststellte, dass wir zwar nicht sicher sein können, welche Auswirkungen unsere Eingriffe in die Geosphäre haben werden, eines jedoch sei in jedem Fall sicher: Wenn die Menschheit mit einem Schlag ihre immensen industriellen Aktivitäten einstellt und der Natur auf Erden ihren freien, ausgleichenden Lauf lässt, dann folgt daraus der totale Zusammenbruch, die

This is what it means that humanity has nowhere to retreat: not only "there is no big Other" (self-contained symbolic order as the ultimate guarantee of Meaning); there is also no Nature qua balanced order of self-reproduction whose homeostasis is disturbed, thrown off the rails, by the imbalanced human interventions. Indeed, what we need is ecology without nature: the ultimate obstacle to protecting nature is the very notion of nature we rely on.

6 Lee Silver, „Scientists Push the Boundaries of Human Life", in: *Newsweek International*, 4.6.2007, http://www.newsweek.com/2007/06/03/life-2-0.html [abgerufen am 21.1.2011].

And therein resides the horror of the Chernobyl accident: when one visits the site, with the exception of the sarcophagus, things look exactly the same as before, life seems to have deserted the site, leaving everything the way it is, and nonetheless we are aware that something is terribly wrong.

absehbare Katastrophe. Die „Natur" auf dieser Erde ist bereits so sehr an menschliche Interventionen angepasst, die durch den Menschen verursachten „Verunreinigungen" sind schon in einem derartigen Ausmaß in das wackelige und fragile Gleichgewicht der „natürlichen" Kreisläufe eingebaut, dass deren Aussetzung sofort ein katastrophales Ungleichgewicht zur Folge haben würde. Das heißt es also, wenn man sagt, es gäbe keinen Ort, an den sich die Menschheit zurückziehen kann: Nicht nur, dass der „große Andere nicht existiert" (die sich selbst beinhaltende symbolische Ordnung als ultimative Garantie der Bedeutung); es existiert auch keine Natur als ausgeglichene Ordnung der Selbstreproduktion, deren Homöostase durch die Eingriffe der Menschheit gestört oder aus der Bahn geworfen werden könnte. Was wir also in der Tat brauchen, ist eine Ökologie ohne Natur: Das entscheidende Hindernis, die Natur zu schützen, ist gerade die Vorstellung von Natur, auf die wir uns ständig beziehen.

Alan Weismans Buch *Die Welt ohne uns* ist eine Vision dessen, was geschehen würde, wenn alle Menschen (und zwar nur die Menschen) ganz plötzlich von der Erde verschwänden. Die natürliche Vielfalt würde wieder gedeihen, die Natur würde sich nach und nach wieder die Artefakte der Menschheit zurückerobern. Dabei werden wir, die Menschen, auf einen körperlosen Blick reduziert, der die eigene Abwesenheit betrachtet. (Lacan hat darauf hingewiesen, dass es sich bei derlei um die grundsätzliche Position des Subjekts in der Fantasie handelt: auf *a* reduziert zu sein, auf den Blick, der aus der Subjektposition der Nichtexistenz auf die Welt fällt. Das gleicht zum Beispiel der Fantasie, Zeuge seiner eigenen Zeugung zu sein, also die Eltern bei der Kopulation zu beobachten oder beim eigenen Begräbnis zugegen zu sein, wie es Tom Sawyer und Huck Finn geschieht. Ein eifersüchtiges Kind versenkt sich in den Tagtraum sich vorzustellen, wie wohl seine Eltern darauf reagieren würden, wenn diese erführen, dass es tot sei und damit bringt es seine eigene Abwesenheit ins Spiel). „Die Welt ohne uns" ist folglich eine Fantasie in Reinform: Wir werden Zeuge, wie die Welt ihren Zustand vor der Kastration wiedergewinnt, wieder zu dem Zustand zurückkehrt, noch bevor sie von den Menschen mit deren Hybris befleckt wurde. Die Ironie besteht dabei darin, dass das berühmteste Beispiel für eine solche Katastrophe die von Tschernobyl ist: Die üppige Natur überwuchert die verfallenden Trümmer der nahe gelegenen Stadt Prypjat, die von den Menschen Hals über Kopf verlassen wurde.

Vor diesem Hintergrund sollte man sich die Problematik vergegenwärtigen, die Badiou mittels seiner Unterscheidung zwischen dem Menschen als sterblichem „menschlichen Tier" und dem „unmenschlichen" Subjekt als Agenten im Prozess der Wahrheit einführt. Der Mensch strebt nach Glück und Genuss, sorgt sich ob seines Todes und so weiter; er ist ein Tier, das mit einem raffinierten Instrumentarium ausgestattet

ist, das ihm dabei hilft, seine Ziele zu erreichen. Doch nur ein Subjekt, das dem Wahrheitsereignis treu bleibt, vermag sich tatsächlich über seine Tierheit zu erheben.[7] Problematisch ist dieser Dualismus deshalb, weil er die grundlegende Basislektion von Freud ignoriert: Es gibt gar kein „menschliches Tier"; der Mensch ist von Geburt an (und schon vorher sogar) aus den tierischen Schranken herausgetreten, seine Instinkte sind „denaturalisiert", er ist gefangen in der Kreisläufigkeit des (Todes-)Triebs, der „jenseits des Lustprinzips" wirksam ist. Er ist mit dem Stigma behaftet, das Eric Santner das „Untote" oder „Exzess des Lebens" genannt hat.[8] In Badious Gedankengebäude gibt es keinen Platz für den Todestrieb, da die „Deformation" der menschlichen Tierheit der Treue zum Ereignis vorausgeht. Nicht allein das „Wunder" eines traumatischen Zusammenstoßes mit dem Ereignis ist es, welches das menschliche Subjekt aus seiner Tierheit herausbricht: Die Libido selbst ist bereits aus den Fugen. Man sollte daher die gängige Kritik an Badiou umkehren: Nicht das quasi-religiöse Wunder des Ereignisses ist das Problem, sondern gerade die „natürliche" Ordnung, die durch dieses Ereignis gestört wird.

Doch nun zurück zur Aussicht auf die ökologische Katastrophe; warum also handeln wir nicht? Es greift zu kurz, würde man einfach behaupten, dass unser Unglaube an die Katastrophe von der Imprägnierung unseres Geistes durch die wissenschaftliche Ideologie herrührt, die uns dazu verführt, uns zu weigern, vernünftige Schlüsse aus der allgemeinen Einsicht zu ziehen, das heißt: Unser Bauch sagt uns doch, dass an dieser ganzen wissenschaftlich-technischen Haltung etwas faul sein muss. Das Problem liegt viel tiefer. Es liegt in der Unzuverlässigkeit unseres gesunden Menschenverstandes selbst, der, angepasst an unsere Lebenswelt, wie er nun einmal ist, Mühe dabei hat, tatsächlich zu akzeptieren, dass der Lauf der Dinge in unserer alltäglichen Realität massiv gestört werden könnte. Unsere Haltung ist die der fetischistischen Spaltung: „Ich weiß sehr wohl (dass die globale Erderwärmung eine Bedrohung für die ganze Menschheit darstellt), trotzdem … (glaube ich es nicht). Es genügt doch, mich umzusehen und zu betrachten, wovon ich tagtäglich umgeben bin: das grüne Gras und die Bäume, das Säuseln des Windes, das Aufgehen der Sonne … kann man sich wirklich vorstellen, dass all das vergehen soll? Du sprichst vom Ozonloch – doch wie sehr ich auch in den Himmel starre, ich vermag keines zu erkennen. Alles was ich sehe, ist der Himmel, mal blau, mal grau."

Genau darin liegt der Horror des Tschernobyl-Unfalls: Wenn man den Ort besucht, dann sieht alles (mit Ausnahme des Betongrabes) genau so aus wie zuvor. Es scheint, als ob alles Lebendige diesen Ort verlassen hätte und alles so gelassen hätte, wie es war – trotzdem wissen wir, dass sich hier etwas

7 Vgl. Alain Badiou, *Das Sein und das Ereignis*. Berlin 2005.

8 Vgl. Eric L. Santner, *Zur Psychotheologie des Alltagslebens*. Zürich 2010.

concerns of our common reason, i.e., the gut sense which tells us that something is fundamentally wrong with the scientific-technological attitude. The problem is much deeper, it resides in the unreliability of our common sense itself which, habituated as it is to our ordinary life-world, finds it difficult really to accept that the flow of everyday reality can be perturbed. Our attitude here is that of the fetishist split: "I know very well (that the global warming is a threat to the entire humanity), but nonetheless … (I cannot really believe it). It is enough to look at my environs to which my mind is wired: the green grass and trees, the whistle of the wind, the rising of the sun … can one really imagine that all this will be disturbed? You talk about the ozone hole—but no matter how much I look into the sky, I don't see it—all I see is the same sky, blue or grey!"

And therein resides the horror of the Chernobyl accident: when one visits the site, with the exception of the sarcophagus, things look exactly the same as before, life seems to have deserted the site, leaving everything the way it is, and nonetheless we are aware that something is terribly wrong. The change is not at the level of the visible reality itself, it is a more fundamental one, it affects the very texture of reality. No wonder there are some lone farmers around the Chernobyl site who continued to lead their lives as before—they simply ignore all the incomprehensible talk about radiations. Do these farmers not behave like the madman in the old joke circulating among Lacanians to exemplify the key role of the Other's knowledge: a man who believes himself to be a grain of seed is taken to the mental institution where the doctors do their best to finally convince him that he is not a grain but a man; however, when he is cured (convinced that he is not a grain of seed but a man) and allowed to leave the hospital, he immediately comes back very trembling of scare—there is a chicken outside the door and that he is afraid that it would eat him. "Dear fellow," says his doctor, "you know very well that you are not a grain of seed but a man". "Of course I know that," replies the patient, "but does the chicken know it?" The chicken from the joke stands for the big Other which doesn't know. In the last years of Tito's life, he was effectively such a chicken: some archives and memoirs show that, already in the mid-1970s, the leading figures around Tito were aware that Yugoslavia's economic situation was catastrophic; however, since Tito was nearing his death, they made a collective decision to postpone the outbreak of a crisis till his death—the price was the fast accumulation of external debt in the last years of Tito's life. When, in 1980, Tito finally dies, the economic crisis did strike with revenge, leading to a 40 percent fall of standard of living, to ethnic tensions and, finally, civil and ethnic war that destroyed the country—the moment to confront the crisis adequately was missed. One can thus say that what put the last nail in the coffin of Yugoslavia was the very attempt by its leading circle to protect the ignorance of the Leader, to keep his gaze happy.

Is this not what, ultimately, culture is? One of the elementary rules of culture is to know when (and how) to pretend NOT to know (or notice), to go on and act as if something which happened did not happen. When a person near me accidentally produces an unpleasant vulgar noise, the proper thing to do is to ignore it, not to comfort him: "I know it was an accident, don't worry, it doesn't really matter!" We should thus understand in the right way the joke about the chicken: a madman's question is a quite pertinent question in many everyday situations. When parents with a young

child have affairs, fight and shout at each other, they as a rule (if they retain a minimum of decency) try to prevent the child to notice it, well aware that the child's knowledge would have had a devastating effect on him—so what they try to maintain is precisely a situation of "We know that we cheat and fight and shout, but the child/chicken doesn't know it." (Of course, in many cases, the child knows it very well, but merely feigns not to notice anything wrong, aware that in this way his parents' life is a little bit easier.) Or, at a less vulgar level, recall a parent in a difficult predicament (dying of cancer, in financial difficulties), but trying to keep this secret from his nearest and dearest …

And this is also our problem with ecology: we know it, but the chicken doesn't know it … The problem is thus that we can rely neither on scientific mind nor on our common sense—they both mutually reinforce each other's blindness. The scientific mind advocates a cold objective appraisal of dangers and risks involved where no such appraisal is effectively possible, while common sense finds it hard to accept that a catastrophe can really occur. The difficult ethical task is thus to "un-learn" the most basic coordinates of our immersion into our life-world: what usually served as the recourse to Wisdom (the basic trust in the background-coordinates of our world) is now THE source of danger.

One can learn even more from the Rumsfeldian theory of knowledge—the expression, of course, refers to the well-known accident in February 2002, when Donald Rumsfeld engaged in a little bit of amateur philosophizing about the relationship between the known and the unknown: "There are known knowns. These are things we know that we know. There are known unknowns. That is to say, there are things that we know we don't know. But there are also unknown unknowns. There are things we don't know we don't know." What he forgot to add was the crucial fourth term: the "unknown knowns," things we don't know that we know—which is precisely the Freudian unconscious, the "knowledge which doesn't know itself," as Lacan used to say. If Rumsfeld thinks that the main dangers in the confrontation with Iraq are the "unknown unknowns," the threats from Saddam about which we do not even suspect what they may be, what we should reply is that the main dangers are, on the contrary, the "unknown knowns," the disavowed beliefs and suppositions we are not even aware of adhering to ourselves. In the case of ecology, these disavowed beliefs and suppositions are the ones which prevent us from really believing in the possibility of the catastrophe, and they combine with the "unknown unknowns." The situation is like that of the blind spot in our visual field: we do not see the gap, the picture appears continuous.

The constellation is properly frustrating: although we (individual or collective agents) know that it all depends on us, we cannot ever predict the consequences of our acts – we are not impotent, but, quite on the contrary, omnipotent, without being able to determine the scope of our powers. The gap between causes and effects is irreducible, and there is no "big Other" to guarantee the harmony between the levels, to guarantee that the overall outcome of our interactions will be satisfactory. The problem is that, although our (sometimes even individual) acts can have catastrophic (ecological, etc.) consequences, the big Other prevents us from believing in it, from assuming this knowledge and responsibility: "Contrary to what the promoters of the principle of precaution think, the cause of our non-

Schreckliches ereignet hat. Der Wandel besteht nicht so sehr in dem, was sichtbar ist, sondern er ist viel fundamentaler und affiziert unmittelbar das Gewebe der Realität. Es verwundert deshalb auch nicht, dass es immer noch ein paar vereinzelte Bauern gibt, die um Tschernobyl herum ihr Leben gerade so wie zuvor führen – sie ignorieren schlicht und einfach das ganze unverständliche Gerede über die Strahlung. Verhalten sich diese Bauern dabei nicht wie die Verrückten in dem alten Witz, der unter Lacanianern kursierte und der die Schlüsselrolle des Wissens des Anderen beispielhaft wiedergibt? Ein Mann, der glaubt ein Saatkorn zu sein, wird in ein Irrenhaus gebracht, wo alle Ärzte sich verzweifelt darum bemühen ihm klarzumachen, dass er kein Korn sei, sondern ein Mensch. Als er schließlich geheilt ist (also eingesehen hat, dass er kein Korn, sondern ein Mensch ist) und es ihm gestattet wird, die Klinik zu verlassen, kommt er sofort wieder zurück, am ganzen Leib vor Angst schlotternd. Ein Huhn stünde da draußen und er fürchte, es würde ihn aufpicken. „Mein lieber Mann", sagt der Doktor zu ihm, „sie wissen sehr wohl, dass sie kein Korn sind, sondern ein Mensch!" „Na klar weiß ich das", antwortet der Patient, „aber weiß es auch das Huhn?" Das Huhn aus diesem Witz steht für den großen Anderen, der nicht weiß. In den letzten Jahren der Regierung Titos war dieser tatsächlich ein solches Huhn: Einige Archive und Erinnerungen belegen, dass schon Mitte der 1970er-Jahre die führenden Personen um Tito herum wussten, dass die wirtschaftliche Situation Jugoslawiens eine katastrophale war; dennoch beschlossen sie gemeinsam, da Titos Tod kurz bevorstand, den Ausbruch dieser Krise bis nach dessen Ableben aufzuschieben – und das ließ den Schuldenberg in den letzten Jahren Titos immens anwachsen. Als Tito 1980 schließlich starb, schlug die Wirtschaftskrise voll zurück und das hatte zur Folge, dass der Lebensstandard um 40 Prozent absackte; darauf folgten die ethnischen Konflikte und schließlich der Bürgerkrieg, der das ganze Land verwüstete – der Augenblick, in dem man der Krise hätte die Stirn bieten müssen, war versäumt worden. Man kann also sagen, dass der letzte Nagel im Sarg Jugoslawiens ausgerechnet der Versuch dieser Führungsgruppe war, die Ignoranz ihres Chefs schützend abzuschirmen – das heißt, ihm eine schöne Aussicht zu garantieren.

Ist das nicht die Kultur? Eine der Grundregeln der Kultur besteht doch darin zu wissen, wann (und wie) man behaupten muss, dass man nicht weiß (oder wie man sich weigert, etwas zur Kenntnis zu nehmen), also weiterzumachen, als ob etwas, das geschehen ist, einfach nicht geschehen sei. Wenn eine Person in meiner Nähe unabsichtlich ein unerfreuliches und unziemliches Geräusch verursacht, dann verhält man sich korrekt, wenn man darüber hinwegsieht und sie nicht mit Sprüchen, wie „Ich weiß schon, das war nicht absichtlich, keine Sorge, das kann jedem passieren!" beruhigt. Man sollte daher auch den Witz mit dem Huhn richtig verstehen: Die Frage des Verrückten ist eine ziemlich angemessene Frage für vielerlei Alltagssituatio-

nen. Wenn Eltern eines kleinen Kindes denken, der Partner hätte eine Affäre, dann streiten sie sich und brüllen einander an. Dabei achten sie in der Regel darauf (wenn sie ein Minimum an Anstand wahren), dass das Kind davon nichts mitbekommt, da sie genau wissen, dass das Wissen darob eine verheerende Wirkung auf das Kind haben würde – sie nehmen also eine Position ein, in der sie sich sagen können: „Wir wissen ganz genau, dass wir einander betrügen, miteinander streiten und uns gegenseitig anbrüllen, aber das Kind/Hühnchen weiß es nicht." (Natürlich weiß es das Kind in vielen Fällen sehr wohl, und es tut bloß so, als sei alles in Ordnung, weil es auch weiß, dass es damit das Leben seiner Eltern etwas leichter macht.) Oder, auf einem etwas weniger gewöhnlichen Niveau: Man denke an einen Elternteil, der sich in einer misslichen Lage befindet (er hat finanzielle Schwierigkeiten, Krebs wurde diagnostiziert), doch er versucht trotzdem, dies vor seinen Liebsten und Nächsten geheim zu halten …

Genau darin liegt unser Problem mit der Ökologie: Wir wissen Bescheid, aber das Huhn weiß es nicht … Folglich besteht auch die Schwierigkeit darin, dass wir uns weder auf unsere wissenschaftliche Denkweise verlassen können, noch auf den gesunden Menschenverstand – alle beide untermauern nur die Blindheit der jeweils anderen Position. Die wissenschaftliche Denkweise bevorzugt die kalte und objektive Beurteilung der Gefahren und Risiken, wohingegen es dem gesunden Menschenverstand schwer fällt zuzugeben, dass sich eine derartige Katastrophe überhaupt ereignen könnte. Eine schwierige ethische Aufgabe ist es deshalb, die grundlegendsten Vorstellungsmuster, dass und wie wir in unsere eigene Lebenswelt eingelassen sind, zu „verlernen": Was man üblicherweise unter der Zufluchtnahme bei der Weisheit versteht (also unser Urvertrauen auf den Hintergrund einer Welt, in der wir leben) ist jetzt zu der Gefahrenquelle schlechthin geworden.

Mehr noch kann man von der Theorie des Wissens lernen, die Rumsfeld vorgelegt hat – diese Aussagen beziehen sich auf das wohlbekannte Desaster, das im Februar 2002 seinen Anfang nahm und anlässlich dessen sich Donald Rumsfeld als Amateur präsentierte, der über die Beziehung des Gewussten und des Unbekannten philosophierte. „Es gibt Bekanntes, von dem wir wissen. Dinge also, von denen wir wissen, dass wir von ihnen wissen. Dann gibt es Dinge, von denen wir wissen, dass sie uns unbekannt sind. Das heißt Dinge, von denen wir wissen, dass wir nichts über sie wissen. Doch es gibt auch Unbekanntes, von dem wir nichts wissen. Und das wiederum sind die Dinge, von denen wir nicht wissen, dass wir sie nicht wissen." Doch was Rumsfeld vergaß, war die entscheidende vierte Position: Das „unbekannte Wissen" – das, von dem wir nicht wissen, dass wir es wissen. Das ist nichts anderes als das freudsche Unbewusste, „ein Wissen, das nicht von sich weiß", wie Lacan sagte. Denkt Rumsfeld also, dass die größte Gefahr im Krieg mit dem Irak vom Unbekannten ausgeht, von dem

The first to get it was Job—after Job is hit by calamities, his theological friends come, offering interpretations which render these calamities meaningful, and the greatness of Job is not so much to protest his innocence as to insist on the meaninglessness of his calamities (when God appears afterwards, he gives right to Job against the theological defenders of faith). The function of the three theological friends is to obfuscate the impact of the trauma with a symbolic semblance.

The legacy of Job prohibits us such a gesture of taking a refuge in the standard transcendent figure of God as a secret Master who knows the meaning of what appears to us as meaningless catastrophe, the God who sees the entire picture in which what we perceive as a stain contributes to global harmony.

man nichts weiß, von den Bedrohungen also, die Saddam bereithält und von denen wir nicht einmal wissen, worin sie bestehen könnten, dann müssen wir dem entgegenhalten, dass die Hauptgefahr im Gegenteil dort liegt, wo uns unbekannt ist, was wir selber wissen, also die verleugneten Glaubenssätze und Vermutungen, die wir nicht einmal uns selbst gegenüber zugeben wollen. Im Falle der Ökologie sind diese verleugneten Glaubenssätze und Vermutungen diejenigen, die uns davor schützen, tatsächlich an die Möglichkeit einer Katastrophe zu glauben und diese sind wiederum mit dem „Unbekannten, von dem wir nichts wissen" verschränkt. Die Lage entspricht also der des blinden Flecks in unserem Feld der Wahrnehmung: Wir sehen die Lücke nicht, das Bild scheint geschlossen.

Diese ganze Konstellation ist zutiefst frustrierend: Selbst wenn wir (als Einzelne oder als Agenten eines Kollektivs) auch wissen, dass alles von uns abhängt, so können wir dennoch niemals die Konsequenzen vorhersagen, die unsere Taten haben werden – wir sind nicht impotent, sondern ganz im Gegenteil omnipotent, ohne jedoch in der Lage zu sein, den Wirkungsbereich unserer Macht zu bestimmten. Die Lücke zwischen Ursache und Wirkung ist irreduzibel und es gibt keinen „großen Anderen", der den Ausgleich zwischen den verschiedenen Niveaus garantiert, der also versichert, dass das schlussendliche Ergebnis unserer Interaktionen ein befriedigendes sein wird. Das Problem dabei ist, dass der große Andere, wenngleich auch unsere (sogar individuellen Handlungen) katastrophale Konsequenzen (ökologische und so weiter) haben können, uns dennoch daran hindert, an derlei zu glauben. Er hindert uns daran, dieses Wissen in Rechnung zu stellen und die Verantwortung zu übernehmen. Ganz im Gegenteil zu dem, was die Vertreter des Prinzips eines vorsorglichen Denkens annehmen, liegt die Ursache für unser Nicht-Handeln gerade nicht in der Ungewissheit, die von der Wissenschaft vermittelt wird. Wir wissen es sehr wohl, aber wir können uns selbst nicht davon überzeugen, auch zu glauben, was wir wissen. Diese Situation bringt uns auch gleich in die radikale Auseinandersetzung mit der Sackgasse, wie sie sich als die gegenwärtige „Gesellschaft der freien Wahl" vorstellig macht. Der Normalzustand ist die erzwungene Wahl (eine Situation also, in der ich frei bin zu wählen, allerdings unter der Bedingung, auch die richtige Wahl zu treffen, was mir keine andere Wahl lässt, als mittels einer leeren Geste zu behaupten, ich träfe freiwillig eine Wahl, zu der ich nichtsdestotrotz gezwungen bin). Hier aber haben wir es im Gegenteil wahrhaftig mit einer freien Wahl zu tun, doch gerade aus diesem Grund ist das nur umso frustrierender: Wir müssen ununterbrochen Entscheidungen hinsichtlich von Angelegenheiten treffen, die unser Leben zwar grundsätzlich beeinflussen, ohne aber über das geeignete Wissen über die Sachlage zu verfügen. John Gray formuliert das so:

„Wir leben in Zeiten, in denen alles provisorisch ist. Neue Technologien verändern unser tägliches Leben. Die Traditio-

nen der Vergangenheit können nicht wieder hervorgeholt werden. Zur selben Zeit haben wir aber ziemlich wenig Ahnung davon, was die Zukunft bringen wird. Wir sind dazu gezwungen ein Leben zu führen, als wären wir frei.“[9]

Es reicht also nicht, das Standardmotiv der marxistischen Kritik zu modifizieren. „Obwohl wir angeblich in einer Gesellschaft der freien Wahl leben, so sind die Entscheidungen, die uns bleiben, trivial und ihre Vielzahl macht nur deutlich, dass wir es nicht mit wahren Entscheidungen zu tun haben, mit Entscheidungen, welche die Grundmuster unseres Lebens verändern würden …“ Das ist zwar richtig, schlimmer ist aber, dass wir gezwungen sind zu wählen, ohne das Wissen zur Verfügung zu haben, welches uns eine qualifizierte Wahl gestatten würde.

Die Lektion ist daher die alte von Lacan: Der große Andere existiert nicht. Der erste, der das begriffen hat, war Hiob. Nachdem er von allen möglichen Plagen heimgesucht worden war, besuchen ihn seine theologisierenden Freunde und versuchen, ihm Interpretationen vorzulegen, welche die Geschehnisse mit Bedeutung versehen sollen. Die Größe Hiobs ist nun nicht so sehr, dass er seine Unschuld beteuert, sondern dass er auf die generelle Sinnlosigkeit all dieser Plagen hinweist (und wenn schließlich Gott auftritt, dann gibt auch er Hiob recht und weist die theologischen Annahmen seiner Verteidiger zurück). Die Funktion der drei theologischen Freunde besteht darin, die Auswirkungen des Traumas mit dem Schein des Symbolischen zu verschleiern.

Dieses Bedürfnis, einen Sinn zu finden, ist im Zusammenhang potenzieller oder tatsächlicher Katastrophen – angefangen bei AIDS und der Umweltzerstörung bis hin zum Holocaust – wesentlich: Sie haben keine „tiefere Bedeutung“. Das Erbe Hiobs verbietet es uns, Zuflucht bei der Annahme zu suchen, die Figur eines transzendenten Gottes wäre eine Art geheimer Herr, der über die Bedeutung dessen Bescheid wüsste, was uns als sinnlose Katastrophe erscheint, Zuflucht also bei einem Gott zu suchen, der das ganze Bild sieht, in dem das, was uns Makel ist, nur zur allgemeinen Harmonie beiträgt. Sieht man sich etwa den Ereignissen des Holocaust gegenüber oder dem Tod von Millionen von Kongolesen in den letzten Jahren, dann scheint es vielmehr obszön zu behaupten, all diese Ereignisse hätten eine tiefere Bedeutung und würden dadurch zur Harmonie des Ganzen beitragen. Gibt es denn etwa ein Ganzes, das teleologisch ein Ereignis wie den Holocaust rechtfertigen kann? Christus Tod am Kreuz bedeutet folglich, dass wir rückhaltlos von der Vorstellung ablassen sollten, Gott wäre ein transzendenter Verwalter, der schon für den glücklichen Ausgang all unserer Taten sorgen werde, man muss die

9 John N. Gray, *Straw Dogs. Thoughts on Humans and Other Animals*. London 2002, S. 110.

action is not the scientific uncertainty. We know it, but we cannot make ourselves believe in what we know." This situation confronts us with the deadlock of the contemporary "society of choice" at its most radical. In the standard situation of the forced choice (a situation in which I am free to choose on condition that I make the right choice, so that the only thing left for me to do is the empty gesture of pretending to accomplish freely what is in any case imposed on me). Here, on the contrary, the choice really is free and is, for this very reason, experienced as even more frustrating: we find ourselves constantly in the position of having to decide about matters that will fundamentally affect our lives, but without a proper foundation in knowledge—as John Gray put it: "we have been thrown into a time in which everything is provisional. New technologies alter our lives daily. The traditions of the past cannot be retrieved. At the same time we have little idea of what the future will bring. We are forced to live as if we were free."[9]

It is thus not enough to vary the standard motif of the Marxist critique: "although we allegedly live in a society of choices, the choices effectively left to us are trivial, and their proliferation masks the absence of true choices, choices that would affect the basic features of our lives …" While this is true, the problem is rather that we are forced to choose without having at our disposal the knowledge that would enable a qualified choice.

The lesson is thus the old Lacanian one: there is no big Other. The first to get it was Job—after Job is hit by calamities, his theological friends come, offering interpretations which render these calamities meaningful, and the greatness of Job is not so much to protest his innocence as to insist on the meaninglessness of his calamities (when God appears afterwards, he gives right to Job against the theological defenders of faith). The function of the three theological friends is to obfuscate the impact of the trauma with a symbolic semblance.

This need to discover a meaning is crucial when we are confronting potential or actual catastrophes, from AIDS and ecological disasters to holocaust: they have no "deeper meaning." The legacy of Job prohibits us such a gesture of taking a refuge in the standard transcendent figure of God as a secret Master who knows the meaning of what appears to us as meaningless catastrophe, the God who sees the entire picture in which what we perceive as a stain contributes to global harmony. When confronted with an event like the holocaust or the death of millions in Congo in the last years, is it not obscene to claim that these stains have a deeper meaning in that they contribute to the harmony of the Whole? Is there a Whole which can teleologically justify an event like the holocaust? Christ's death on the cross thus means that one should drop without restraint the notion of God as a transcendent caretaker who guarantees the happy outcome of our acts, the guarantee of historical teleology—Christ's death on the cross is the death of this God, it repeats Job's stance, it refuses any "deeper meaning" that obfuscates the brutal real of historical catastrophes.

And the lesson of ecology is that we should go to the end here and accept the non-existence of the ultimate big Other, nature itself with its pattern of regular rhythms, the ultimate reference of order and stability.

9 John N. Gray, *Straw Dogs: Thoughts on Humans and Other Animals*. London 2002, p. 110.

However, this lack of the big Other does not entail that we are irrevocably caught in the misery of our finitude, deprived of any redemptive moments. In his *The Cattle Truck*, Jorge Semprun reports how he witnessed the arrival of a truckload of Polish Jews at Buchenwald; they were stacked into the freight train almost 200 to a car, traveling for days without food and water in the coldest winter of the war. On arrival all in the carriage had frozen to death except for 15 children, kept warm by the others in the centre of the bundle of bodies. When the children were emptied from the car the Nazis let their dogs loose on them. Soon only two fleeing children were left:

"The little one began to fall behind, the SS were howling behind them and then the dogs began to howl too, the smell of blood was driving them mad, and then the bigger of the two children slowed his pace to take the hand of the smaller … together they covered a few more yards … till the blows of the clubs felled them and, together they dropped, their faces to the ground, their hands clasped for all eternity."[10]

One can easily imagine how this scene should be filmed: while the soundtrack renders what goes on in reality (the two children are clubbed to death), the image of their hands clasped freezes, immobilized for eternity—while the sound renders temporary reality, the image renders the eternal Real. It is the pure surface of such fixed images of eternity, not any deeper Meaning, which allows for redemptive moments in the bleak story of the Shoah. One should read this imagined scene together with the final shot of Thelma and Louise: the frozen image of the car with the two women "flying" above the precipice: is this the positive utopia (triumph of the feminine subjectivity over death), or the masking of the miserable wreck the car IS in reality at that time? The weakness of the final shot from Thelma and Louise is that the frozen image is not accompanied by the soundtrack depicting what "really" went on (the car crash, terrible cries of the dying women)—strangely, this lack of reality undermines the very utopian dimension of the frozen image. In contrast to this scene, our imagined filmed scene from Semprun would fully assert the Platonic duality of temporal empirical reality and eternal Idea.

What this means is that, without shame, in conceiving art, we should return to Plato. Plato's reputation suffers because of his claim that poets should be thrown out of the city—a rather sensible advice, judging from my post-Yugoslav experience, where ethnic cleansing was prepared by poets' dangerous dreams (the Bosnian Serb leader Radovan Karadzic being only one among them). If the West has the industrial-military complex, we in the ex-Yugoslavia had a poetic-military complex: the post-Yugoslav war was triggered by the explosive mixture of the poetic and the military component. So, from a Platonic standpoint, what does a poem about the holocaust do? It provides its "description without place": it renders the Idea of holocaust.

Recall the old Catholic strategy to guard men against the temptation of the flesh: when you see in front of you a voluptuous feminine body, imagine how it will look in a couple of decades—the dried skin, sagging breasts … (Or, even better, imagine what lurks now already beneath the skin: raw flesh and bones, inner fluids, half-digested food and excrements …) Far from

10 Jorge Semprun, *The Cattle Truck*. London 1993, p. 39.

Idee, es gäbe eine Garantie durch die historische Teleologie fallen lassen – Christus Tod am Kreuz ist der Tod eines solchen Gottes und er wiederholt Hiobs Standpunkt. Er lehnt jede „tiefere Bedeutung" ab, welche die brutale Wirklichkeit historischer Katastrophen zu verschleiern trachtet.

Was das Ökologische angeht, sollten wir auch hier Schluss machen und akzeptieren, dass auch hier der ultimative große Andere nicht existiert; die Muster der Natur unterliegen keinen immer wiederkehrenden Rhythmen und sie selbst ist nicht der letzte Referenzpunkt für Ordnung und Stabilität.

Dieser Mangel am großen Anderen bedeutet aber nicht, dass wir unwiderruflich in der Misere unserer Endlichkeit gefangen sind und es keine Aussicht auf Erlösung gibt. In seinem Buch *Le grand voyage* (*Die große Reise*) berichtet Jorge Semprun davon, wie er Zeuge der Ankunft eines Transports polnischer Juden in Buchenwald wurde. Es waren etwa 200 Personen, die tagelang ohne Nahrung und Wasser, in einem Güterwagen zusammengepfercht, durch den kältesten Winter des Krieges gefahren waren. Bei der Ankunft waren alle erfroren, nur 15 Kinder hatten überlebt, die inmitten der Körper der anderen warm gehalten worden waren. Als man die Kinder aus dem Wagen herausgeholt hatte, ließen die Nazis ihre Hunde auf sie los. Schon bald gab es nur noch zwei Kinder, die zu flüchten versuchten:

„[D]er kleinere begann zurückzubleiben, die SS-Männer brüllten hinter ihnen, auch die Hunde begannen zu brüllen, der Blutgeruch brachte sie außer sich, aber da hielt der größere der Jungen im Laufen inne und nahm die Hand des kleineren, der schon stolperte, und sie legten zusammen noch ein paar Meter zurück, die linke Hand des jüngeren in der rechten des älteren, bis die Knüppel auch sie niederstreckten und sie nebeneinander mit dem Gesicht zu Boden fielen, ihre Hände auf immer vereint."[10]

Man kann sich unschwer vorstellen, wie man diese Szene verfilmen sollte: Während die Tonspur wiedergibt, was in Wirklichkeit geschieht (zwei Kinder werden erschlagen), friert das Bild ihrer Hände, die sich ineinander klammern, ein und bleibt so stehen – während auf diese Weise die Tonspur die Wirklichkeit des Zeitablaufs wiedergibt, zeigt das Bild das ewige Reale. Die reine Oberfläche solcher still gestellter Bilder der Ewigkeit ist es, und mitnichten eine tiefere Bedeutung, die uns einige erlösende Augenblicke in der trostlosen Geschichte der Shoah gewährt. Man mag diese Szene auch mit der letzten Einstellung aus dem Film *Thelma & Louise* zusammen betrachten: Das eingefrorene Bild eines Autos mit den beiden Frauen, die über den Abgrund hinaus „fliegen". Ist das die positive Utopie (Triumph weiblicher Subjektivität über den Tod), oder maskiert dieses Bild bloß das Wrack, welches das Auto in diesem

10 Jorge Semprun, *Die große Reise*. Berlin 1966, S. 207.

selben Augenblick tatsächlich geworden ist? Die Schwäche der letzten Einstellung aus *Thelma & Louise* liegt darin, dass das eingefrorene Bild nicht von einer Tonspur begleitet wird, die erkennbar werden lässt, was „wirklich“ geschieht (das Auto wird zertrümmert, schreckliche Schreie der sterbenden Frauen) – seltsamerweise unterläuft dieser Mangel an Realität die utopische Dimension des eingefrorenen Bildes. Im Gegensatz dazu würde die Filmsequenz, die wir uns für die Szene, die von Semprun beschrieben wird, ausgemalt haben, zur Gänze die Anforderungen einer platonischen Dualität von zeitlich-empirischer Wirklichkeit und der ewigen Idee zur Geltung bringen.

Das bedeutet, dass man sich keineswegs zu schämen braucht, wenn man sich in Sachen Kunst auf Platon bezieht. Seine Reputation ist zwar nicht die Beste, hatte er doch vorgeschlagen, man solle die Künstler aus der Stadt jagen – doch das ist ein beinahe sensibler Vorschlag, vergleiche ich ihn mit meinen post-jugoslawischen Erfahrungen, wo die ethnischen Säuberungen von den gefährlichen Träumen der Dichter herrührten (und Radovan Karadžic war nur einer von ihnen). Gab es im Westen den militärisch-industriellen Komplex, dann hatten wir im ehemaligen Jugoslawien den militärisch-poetischen Komplex. Der post-jugoslawische Krieg wurde durch die hochexplosive Mischung von dichterischen und militärischen Bestandteilen ausgelöst. Von einem platonischen Standpunkt aus betrachtet, stellt sich daher die Frage: Was kann ein Gedicht über den Holocaust bewirken? Es liefert eine „ortlose Beschreibung“, es trägt die Idee des Holocaust vor.

Man vergegenwärtige sich die katholische Strategie, Männer gegen die Versuchungen des Fleisches zu wappnen: Siehst du vor dir einen verlockenden Frauenkörper, dann stell’ dir vor, wie dieser in ein paar Jahrzehnten aussehen wird – die Haut wird runzelig sein, die Brüste herunter hängen … (Oder noch besser: Stell’ dir vor, was schon jetzt unter dieser Haut verborgen ist. Rohes Fleisch und Knochen, Körperflüssigkeiten, halb verdaute Nahrung und Exkremente …) Weit davon entfernt, eine Rückkehr zum Realen zu verordnen, gleicht ein solches Vorgehen der Flucht vor dem Realen, vor dem Realen nämlich, das sich selbst in der verführerischen Erscheinung des nackten Körpers ankündigt. In der Opposition zwischen der geisterhaften Erscheinung des sexualisierten Körpers und dem abstoßenden Körper des Verfalls, ist die geisterhafte Erscheinung das Reale und der verfallende Körper die Realität – wir nehmen Zuflucht beim verfallenden Körper, um der tödlichen Faszination des Realen auszuweichen, das droht, uns in den Strudel seines Genießens zu reißen.

Übersetzung Andreas L. Hofbauer

enacting a return to the Real destined to break the imaginary spell of the body, such a procedure equals the escape from the Real, the Real which announces itself in the seductive appearance of the naked body. That is to say, in the opposition between the spectral appearance of the sexualized body and the repulsive body in decay, it is the spectral appearance which is the Real, and the decaying body which is reality—we take recourse to the decaying body in order to avoid the deadly fascination of the Real which threatens to draw us into its vortex of jouissance.

1 Initiale Pflanzengemeinschaft auf fruchtbarem Ackerboden. Initial plant community on fertile agricultural soil.

Eco-Planning? Ecology as the New Opium for the People[1]

"Let's start by stating that after 'the rights of man,' the rise of 'the rights of Nature' is a contemporary form of the opium for the people. It is an only slightly camouflaged religion … It is a gigantic operation in the depoliticization of subjects."[2]

Öko-Planung? Ökologie – das neue Opium für das Volk.[1] „Beginnen wir mit der Behauptung, dass nach ‚den Menschenrechten' nun die ‚Rechte der Natur' eine Art modernes Opium für das Volk darstellen. Es ist eine nur schwach getarnte Religion … eine gigantische Operation zur Entpolitisierung bestimmter Themen."[2]

ERIK SWYNGEDOUW

1. Nature Does Not Exist! In the wake of the current environmental "crisis," "Nature" has gained considerable purchase in political debate, economic argument, and public intervention, and has become a leitmotiv in much of the urban planning and architecture literature. "Nature" poses indeed a considerable challenge in need of exploration for planning, urban and architectural theory. In his recent book, provocatively titled *Ecology without Nature*, Timothy Morton calls Nature "a transcendental term in a material mask [that] stands at the end of a potentially infinite series of other terms that collapse into it."[3] He distinguishes between at least three places or meanings of nature in our symbolic universe. First, as a floating signifier, the "content" of Nature is expressed through a range of diverse terms that all collapse in the Name of Nature: olive tree, parrot fish, SARS virus, love, reproduction, the Alps, mineral water, markets, desire, profits, CO_2, money, competition, ... "Nature" as metaphor is intrinsically empty; its meaning can only be gleaned from metonymic references to other, more ordinary signifiers. Second, Nature has "the force of law, a norm against which deviation is measured."[4] This is the sort of invocation of Nature that is mobilized, for example, to normalize heterosexuality and to think queerness as deviant and unnatural or that sees competition between humans as natural and altruism as a produce of "culture" (or vice versa). This is a view that sees Nature as something given, as a solid foundational (or ontological) basis that can be invoked to provide an anchor for ethical or normative judgments of ecological, social, cultural, political, or economic practices. Consider, for example, how many of recent sustainable planning efforts legitimize their activities by invoking some transcendental view of a Nature that is out of synch and requires re-balancing. And, third, Nature contains a plurality of fantasies and desires, like, for example, the dream of a sustainable nature, the desire for love-making on a warm beach under the setting sun, the fear for the revenge of Nature if we keep pumping CO_2 into the atmosphere. Nature is invoked here as the stand-in for other, often repressed or invisible, longings and passions—the Lacanian *object petit a* around which we shape our drives and that covers up for the lack of ground

In sum, the very uses of Nature imply simultaneously an attempt to fixate its unstable meaning while being presented as a fetishized "Other" that reflects or, at least, functions as a symptom through which our displaced deepest fears and longings are expressed.

1 Revised and abridged version of: "Trouble with Nature: Ecology as the New Opium for the People," in: Jean Hillier, Patsy Heale (eds.), *Conceptual Challenges for Planning Theory*. Farnham 2010, pp. 299–320.

2 Alain Badiou, "Live Badiou: Interview with Alain Badiou," Paris, December 2007, in: Oliver Feltham (ed.), *Alain Badiou: Live Theory*. London 2008, pp. 136–139, here p. 139.

3 Timothy Morton, *Ecology without Nature*. Cambridge, MA 2007, p. 14.

4 Ibid.

1. Es gibt keine Natur! Im Kielwasser der aktuellen „Umweltkrise" hat die Konjunktur des Themas „Natur" in politischen Debatten, Diskussionen zum Thema Ökologie und in öffentlichen Interventionen ungemein zugenommen. Auch wurde das Thema vielfach zum Leitmotiv stadtplanerischer Maßnahmen und architektonischer Abhandlungen. Der Begriff „Natur" stellt somit eine beachtliche Herausforderung für die Untersuchungen von Architekturtheorie, Planung und Stadtplanung dar. In seinem jüngsten Buch mit dem provokanten Titel *Ecology without Nature* [*Umwelt ohne Natur*] nennt Timothy Morton die Natur „einen metaphysischen Begriff in materieller Maske, [der] am Ende einer möglicherweise unendlichen Reihe von Begriffen steht, die auf ihn hinauslaufen".[3] Er unterscheidet zwischen mindestens drei Orten oder Bedeutungen der Natur in unserem symbolischen Universum. Erstens der „Inhalt der Natur" als freier Signifikant, ausgedrückt durch eine Reihe unterschiedlicher Begriffe, die alle unter den Begriff Natur fallen: Olivenbaum, Papageienfisch, SARS-Virus, Liebe, Reproduktion, die Alpen, Mineralwasser, Märkte, Begehren, Gewinne, CO_2, Geld, Wettbewerb usw. Die Bezeichnung „Natur" als Metapher ist per se leer; ihre Bedeutung erschließt sich erst durch metonymische Bezüge zu anderen, gebräuchlicheren Signifikanten. Zweitens die Natur, die „Gesetzeskraft [besitzt], eine Norm, an der die Abweichung gemessen wird".[4] Diese Art Natur wird zum Beispiel bemüht, wenn es darum geht, Heterosexualität als etwas Normales und Homosexualität als Abweichung und etwas Unnatürliches zu bezeichnen oder zu erklären, dass die Konkurrenz zwischen Menschen natürlich und Altruismus ein Produkt der „Kultur" – (oder umgekehrt) ist. Dies ist ein Standpunkt, von dem aus die Natur als etwas Gegebenes betrachtet wird, als eine solide grundlegende (oder ontologische) Basis, auf die man sich berufen kann, um über einen Fixpunkt für ethische oder normative Entscheidungen, für ökologische, soziale, kulturelle, politische oder wirtschaftliche Praktiken zu verfügen. Bedenken wir zum Beispiel, bei wie vielen der jüngsten nachhaltigen Planungsanstrengungen die Aktionen dadurch legitimiert werden, dass man sich auf eine transzendente Sicht der Natur beruft, die aus dem Gleichgewicht geraten ist und gleich gerückt werden muss. Und drittens die Natur, die eine Vielzahl von Fantasien und Wünschen beinhaltet, wie zum Beispiel den Traum von einer nachhaltigen Natur, den Wunsch sich bei Sonnenuntergang an einem Sandstrand zu lieben und die Angst vor der Rache der Natur, wenn

1 Überarbeitete und gekürzte Fassung von: „Trouble with Nature. Ecology as the New Opium for the People", in: Jean Hillier, Patsy Healey (Hg.), *Conceptual Challenges for Planning Theory*. Farnham 2010, S. 299–320.

2 Alain Badiou, „Badiou live. Interview mit Alain Badiou", Paris, Dezember 2007, in: Oliver Feltham (Hg.), *Alain Badiou. Live Theory*. London 2008, S. 136–139, hier S. 139.

3 Timothy Morton, *Ecology without Nature*. Cambridge, MA 2007, S. 14.

4 Ebd.

wir weiterhin CO_2 in die Atmosphäre pumpen. Die Natur wird hier in Vertretung anderer, häufig unterdrückter oder unsichtbarer Wünsche oder Leidenschaften heraufbeschworen – das Lacansche *objet petit a*, um das wir unsere Triebe bilden und das den Mangel an festem Boden, auf welchem unsere Subjektivität basiert, verdeckt.[5] Mit diesem Vorgehen investieren wir in die Natur, die auf die Ebene des „Anderen", auf unsere libidinösen Begehren und Ängste, verdrängt wird, eine Verdrängung des Abgrundes, der den verleugneten echten, „harten" Kern des Seins von der symbolischen Welt, in der wir uns aufhalten, trennt.

Zusammengefasst heißt das, dass die tatsächlichen Nutzungen der Natur zugleich den Versuch bedeuten, ihre instabile Bedeutung festzulegen, während sie als ein etwas fetischisiertes „Anderes" dargestellt wird, das ein Symptom reflektiert oder zumindest als ein Symptom fungiert, durch das unsere verdrängten tiefsten Ängste und Wünsche ausgedrückt werden. Als solches wird der Begriff „Natur" zur Ideologie *par excellence* und funktioniert ideologisch. Damit meine ich, dass er das Denken in Beschlag nimmt, die ihm innewohnende mangelnde Fassbarkeit seines Begriffs leugnet und somit dessen Vielfalt, Inkonsistenzen und Inkohärenzen ignoriert.[6] Jeder Versuch, die Bedeutung von Natur zu fassen, erschöpfend zu beschreiben und zu kolonisieren, ist Teil hegemonialer und im Grunde politischer Bestrebungen, die jedoch nicht als solche erkannt werden.[7] Eine Festlegung der Bedeutung von Natur wird selbstverständlich in allen öffentlichen Debatten, politischen Programmen, stadtplanerischen Analysen und Planungsdiskussionen, die sich auf Natur oder Umwelt berufen, systematisch betrieben. Das Leugnen des leeren Kerns von Natur durch Kolonialisierung ihrer Bedeutung, durch ein Füllen der Leere und durch eine Färbung mit ihr zugeschriebenen Bedeutungen, die in Folge verallgemeinert und homogenisiert werden, ist die Geste einer Entpolitisierung *par excellence*, einer Platzierung der Natur außerhalb des Politischen, also jenseits öffentlicher Debatten, Widersprüche und Uneinigkeiten. Morton schlägt in diesem Sinne vor, „Ökologie ohne Natur zu denken" und das Konzept „Natur" gänzlich aufzugeben. Das ist keine dumme oder törichte Geste, um „das Reale" aller mit der Natur verbundenen Dinge, Gefühle und Prozesse, die ich oben genannt habe, zu verleugnen. Im Gegenteil, es ist genau dieses Anerkennen der ihm innewohnenden Unsicherheit und Bedeutungsvielfalt, die von solch metonymischen Listen tatsächlich be-

5 Vgl. Slavoj Žižek, *The Ticklish Subject. The Absent Centre of Political Ontology*. London 1999.

6 Vgl. Morton 2007 (Anm. 3), S. 24.

7 Vgl. Ernesto Laclau, Chantal Mouffe, *Hegemony and Socialist Strategy*. London 2001; Yannis Stavrakakis, „On the Emergence of Green Ideology: The Dislocation Factor in Green Politics", in: David Howarth, Aletta J. Norval, Yannis Stavrakakis (Hg.), *Discourse Theory and Political Analysis. Identities, Hegemonies and Social Change*. Manchester 2000, S. 100–118.

on which to base our subjectivity.[5] This is a procedure by which we invest in Nature, displaced onto the plain of an "Other," our libidinal desires and fears, a displacement of the abyss that separates the disavowed Real "hard" kernel of being from the symbolic world in which we dwell.

In sum, the very uses of Nature imply simultaneously an attempt to fixate its unstable meaning while being presented as a fetishized "Other" that reflects or, at least, functions as a symptom through which our displaced deepest fears and longings are expressed. As such, the concept of Nature becomes ideology *par excellence* and functions ideologically, and by that I mean that it forecloses thought, disavows the inherent slippery of the concept, and ignores its multiplicities, inconsistencies, and incoherencies.[6] Every attempt to suture, to fill in exhaustively and to colonize the meaning of Nature is part of hegemonizing drives that are inherently political, but are not recognized as such.[7] Suturing Nature's meaning is of course systematically undertaken in almost all public debates, policy documents, urban analyses and planning discourses that invoke Nature or the environment. The disavowal of the empty core of Nature by colonizing its meaning, by filling out the void, staining it with inserted meanings that are subsequently generalized and homogenized, is the gesture *par excellence* of depoliticization, of placing Nature outside the political, that is outside the field of public dispute, contestation, and disagreement. It is in this sense that Morton proposes "to think ecology without nature," to abandon the concept of "Nature" altogether. This is not a stupid or silly gesture to disavow "the Real" of all the things, feelings, and processes associated with Nature that I listed above. On the contrary, it is exactly the recognition of the inherent slipperiness and multiplicities of meaning suggested by such metonymic lists of really existing things, emotions, and processes that urges us to consider that perhaps the very concept of Nature itself should be abandoned.

Bruno Latour, albeit from a completely different perspective, equally proposes to ditch the concept of Nature. For Latour, there is neither such thing as "Nature" in itself and for itself nor something like Society (or Culture).[8] For him, the collection of things (human and nonhuman) that fill in the world consists of continuously multiplying nature-culture hybrids. With Michel Serres and others, Latour argues that these socio-natural "messy" things are made up of proliferating sets of networked socio-natural assemblages that are defined as quasi-objects; they stand between the poles of nature on the one hand and culture on the other. Think of, for example, greenhouse gases, Dolly the cloned sheep, a dam, a bottle of milk, water networks, or electromagnetic waves. They are simultaneously social/cultural and natural/physical, and their coherence, i.e. their relative spatial and temporal sustainability, is predicated upon assembled networks of human and nonhuman relations.[9] This perspective, too, rejects retaining the concept of

5 See Slavoj Žižek, *The Ticklish Subject: The Absent Centre of Political Ontology*. London 1999.

6 See Morton 2007 (fn. 3), p. 24.

7 See Ernesto Laclau, Chantal Mouffe, *Hegemony and Socialist Strategy*. London 2001; Yannis Stavrakakis, "On the Emergence of Green Ideology: The Dislocation Factor in Green Politics," in: David Howarth, Aletta J. Norval, Yannis Stavrakakis (eds.), *Discourse Theory and Political Analysis: Identities, Hegemonies and Social Change*. Manchester 2000, pp. 100–118.

8 See Bruno Latour, *We Have Never Been Modern*. Cambridge, MA 1993.

9 See Erik Swyngedouw, "Circulations and Metabolisms: (Hybrid) Natures and (Cyborg) Cities," in: *Science as Culture* 15/2 (2006), pp. 105–121.

Nature and suggests in its stead to consider the infinite heterogeneity of the procedures of assembling—dissembling—reassembling the rhizomatic networks through which heterogeneous things, bodies, natures and cultures become enrolled and through which relatively stable quasi-objects come into purview.[10] This Latouran gesture also attempts to re-politicize Nature, to let quasi-objects enter the public assembly of political negotiations and considerations. For Latour too, there is nothing left to retain from the concept of Nature.[11]

For those attuned to the mess many of the world's environments are in, linguistic acrobatics as those introduced above might sound esoteric at best and nonsensical and counter-productive at worst, coming from the usual suspects of critical social theorists and sexy, but politically vacuous and pragmatically impotent, cultural musings. Interestingly, the work of Levins and Lewontin,[12] Harvard University biologists and ecologists, comes to strikingly similar conclusions. They hold to a relational and historically contingent view of biological differentiation and evolution. The world is in a process of continuous becoming through the contingent and heterogeneous recompositions of the almost infinite (socio-)ecological relations through which new natures come into being. They see the relations of parts to the whole and the mutual interaction of parts in the whole as the process through which both individuals and their environments are changed.[13] In other words, both individuals and their environments are co-produced and co-evolve in historically contingent, highly diversified, locally specific and often not fully accountable manners.

Both the critical cultural perspectives and anti-foundational evolutionary views explored above lead to a series of arguments and claims about Nature and how to think, conceptualize, and/or politicize it. This is the conceptual conundrum I wish to disentangle further in this contribution. Dissecting the conceptual challenges posed by the mobilization of Nature in a wide range of social sciences, political discourses and policy/managerial practices is absolutely vital in a world in which socio-ecological dynamics like resource depletion, climate change or environmental degradation pose challenges that, if unheeded, might possibly lead to the premature end of civilization as we know it, to the end of us before our sell-by date has expired.

2. The Empty Core of Nature—Multiple Natures. As suggested above, it is difficult, if not impossible, to define exactly what Nature is. Every attempt to nail down or to fix its meaning seems futile at best and politically problematic at worst; Nature is a *montage* of meaning, held together with quilting points (like the upholstery of a Chesterfield sofa). For example, in today's environmental parlance, "biodiversity," "eco-cities," "pollutants," "CO_2" can be thought of as quilting (or *points de capiton*) points through which certain meanings of Nature are knitted together. This emptying out of a fixed meaning of Nature has been a systematic feature of late modernity,

10 See Noel Castree, "Environmental issues: relational ontologies and hybrid politics," in: *Progress in Human Geography* 27/2 (2003), pp. 203–211; Bruce Braun, "Environmental issues: global natures in the space of assemblage," in: *Progress in Human Geography* 30/5 (2006), pp. 644–654.

11 See Bruno Latour, *Politics of Nature: How to Bring the Sciences into Democracy*. Cambridge, MA 2004.

12 See Richard Levins, Richard C. Lewontin, *The Dialectical Biologist*. Cambridge, MA. 1985; Lewontin, Levins, *Biology under the Influence. Dialectical Essays on Ecology, Agriculture, and Health*. New York 2007.

13 See also David Harvey, *Justice, Nature, and the Geography of Difference*. Oxford 1996.

stehender Dinge, Emotionen und Prozesse ausgeht, das uns zu der Überlegung zwingt, dass das Konzept „Natur" selbst aufzugeben sei.

Aus einer völlig anderen Richtung kommend schlägt Bruno Latour ebenfalls vor, den Begriff Natur fallen zu lassen. Für Latour gibt es weder so etwas wie „Natur" an und für sich, noch so etwas wie Gesellschaft (oder Kultur).[8] Für ihn besteht die Sammlung menschlicher und nicht-menschlicher Dinge, die diese Welt füllen, aus sich kontinuierlich vermehrenden Natur-Kultur-Hybriden. Latour argumentiert mit Michel Serres und anderen, dass diese sozionatürlichen „Dinge in Unordnung" aus wuchernden Sets vernetzter sozionatürlicher Verbindungen hervorgehen, die als Quasi-Objekte definiert werden. Diese Objekte stehen zwischen dem Pol der Natur auf der einen, und jenem der Kultur auf der anderen Seite. Denken wir zum Beispiel an Treibhausgase, Dolly, das Klonschaf, einen Damm, eine Milchflasche, Wassernetzwerke oder elektromagnetische Wellen. Sie sind zugleich sozial/kulturell und natürlich/physikalisch, und ihre Kohärenz, d. h. ihre relative räumliche und zeitliche Nachhaltigkeit wird mittels verbundener Netzwerke menschlicher und nicht-menschlicher Beziehungen bestimmt.[9] Auch diese Perspektive lehnt ein Festhalten am Konzept „Natur" ab und schlägt stattdessen vor, die unendliche Heterogenität der Verfahren des Zusammensetzens – Auseinanderbauens – Wiederzusammensetzens der rhizomatischen Netzwerke in Betracht zu ziehen, durch welche heterogene Dinge, Körper, Naturen und Kulturen registriert und relativ stabile Quasi-Objekte sichtbar werden.[10] Diese Geste Latours ist auch ein Versuch, die Natur zu re-politisieren und Quasi-Objekte in die öffentlichen politischen Verhandlungen und Betrachtungen einfließen zu lassen. Auch für Latour hat das Konzept Natur nichts, an dem weiter festzuhalten wäre.[11]

Für diejenigen, die sich auf das Ungleichgewicht eingestellt haben, das in manchen Gegenden der Welt herrscht, mag die zuvor betriebene linguistische Akrobatik bestenfalls esoterisch, im schlechtesten Fall sinnlos, kontraproduktiv und aus der Ecke der üblichen Verdächtigen stammend klingen: der Sozialtheoretiker und ihrer sexy, aber politisch leeren und praktisch einflusslosen, kulturellen Träumereien. Interessanterweise kommen Levins und Lewontin,[12] Biologen und Ökologen der Harvard

8 Vgl. Bruno Latour, *Wir sind nie modern gewesen. Versuch einer symmetrischen Anthropologie*. Berlin 1995.

9 Vgl. Erik Swyngedouw, „Circulations and Metabolisms: (Hybrid) Natures and (Cyborg) Cities", in: *Science as Culture* 15/2 (2006), S. 105–121.

10 Vgl. Noel Castree, „Environmental issues: relational ontologies and hybrid politics", in: *Progress in Human Geography* 27/2 (2003), S. 203–211; Bruce Braun, „Environmental issues: global natures in the space of assemblage", in: *Progress in Human Geography* 30/5 (2006), S. 644–654.

11 Vgl. Bruno Latour, *Das Parlament der Dinge: Für eine politische Ökologie*. Frankfurt/M. 2001.

12 Vgl. Richard Levins, Richard C. Lewontin, *The Dialectical Biologist*. Cambridge, MA. 1985; Lewontin, Levins, *Biology under the Influence. Dialectical Essays on Ecology, Agriculture, and Health*. New York 2007.

Universität, in ihrer Arbeit zu erstaunlich ähnlichen Schlussfolgerungen. Sie halten sich an eine relationale und historisch bedingte Sicht biologischer Differenzierung und Entwicklung. Die Welt befindet sich durch die zufälligen und heterogenen Neuanordnungen der nahezu unendlichen (sozio-)ökologischen Beziehungen, durch welche neue Naturen erzeugt werden, in einem kontinuierlichen Prozess des Werdens. Sie sehen die Beziehungen zwischen den Teilen und dem Ganzen und die Interaktion der Teile im Ganzen als einen Prozess, durch den sowohl Individuen als auch ihr Umfeld verändert werden.[13] Mit anderen Worten, sowohl Individuen als auch ihr Umfeld werden gemeinschaftlich produziert und entwickeln sich auf historisch zufälliger, höchst unterschiedlicher, örtlich spezifischer und oft nicht gänzlich erklärbarer Weise gemeinsam weiter.

Die zuvor untersuchten kritischen kulturellen Perspektiven und anti-positivistischen, evolutionären Sichtweisen führen zu einer Reihe von Argumenten und Aussagen über die Natur und wie sie zu denken, wie sie zu konzipieren und/oder zu politisieren ist. Dies ist das konzeptuelle Rätsel, das ich im Folgenden zu lösen versuche. Ein Sezieren der konzeptuellen Herausforderungen in Folge der Mobilisierung der Natur durch weite Bereiche der Sozialwissenschaften, politischer Diskurse und politisch-betriebswirtschaftlicher Praktiken ist absolut notwendig in einer Welt, in der sozioökologische Dynamiken wie die Erschöpfung der Ressourcen, der Klimawandel oder die Umweltzerstörung Herausforderungen darstellen, die, wenn sie nicht bewältigt werden, möglicherweise zu einem vorzeitigen Ende der Zivilisation führen, wie wir sie kennen – zu unserem Ende vor Ablauf unseres Verfallsdatums.

2. Der leere Kern der Natur – Multiple Naturen. Wie zuvor dargestellt, ist es schwierig oder nahezu unmöglich, zu definieren, was genau Natur ist. Jeder Versuch, ihre Bedeutung zu bestimmen oder zu fixieren, scheint im besten Falle vorläufig und im schlimmsten Falle politisch gesehen problematisch. Natur ist eine *Montage* von Bedeutungen, die durch Steppnähte (wie bei einem Chesterfield-Sofa) zusammengehalten wird. So kann man beispielsweise im heutigen Umweltschutzjargon Worte wie „Artenvielfalt", „Öko-Städte", „Schadstoffe", „CO_2" als Steppnähte (oder *points de capiton*) bezeichnen, die bestimmte Bedeutungen der Natur zusammenhalten. Das Lösen von einer bestimmten Bedeutung von Natur war ein systematisches Merkmal der späten Moderne, als sich die Bedeutungen dessen, was Natur „wirklich" ist, parallel zur Verbreitung sozialpolitischer, kultureller oder anderer Differenzierungen vervielfältigten. Ab dem 19. Jahrhundert, als die Natur-Wissenschaft-Vernunft-Vermischung sich durch die zunehmend rasantere Entwicklung der Naturwissenschaften und ihre faszinierenden Aus-

13 Vgl. auch David Harvey, *Justice, Nature, and the Geography of Difference*. Oxford 1996.

As suggested above, it is difficult, if not impossible, to define exactly what Nature is. Every attempt to nail down or to fix its meaning seems futile at best and politically problematic at worst; Nature is a *montage* of meaning, held together with quilting points (like the upholstery of a Chesterfield sofa).

particularly as signifying chains of what Nature "really" is multiplied in parallel to the proliferation of socio-political, cultural or other differentiations. From the 19th century onwards—while the Nature/Science/Rationality imbroglio consolidated itself, primarily through the increasingly successful development of the natural sciences and its mesmerizing applications in all domains of life—a plethora of other signifying chains began to quilt Nature's meaning. The contested process of modernization produced a cacophony of metonymic lists associated with Nature, none of which exhausted the vagaries, idiosyncrasies, and heterogeneous acting of the different and changing forms of nature that composed the world. Moreover, these forms proliferated as the number of socio-natural things, these hybrids of human and of nature—what Bruno Latour calls quasi-objects[14] or Donna Haraway Cyborgs[15]—multiplied with the intensifying assembling of human and non-human processes (like in, for example, nuclear energy, the making of trans-uranium elements, genetic manipulation, techno-natural constructs like water systems, energy lines, mega-cities, and the like). In recent years, and in particular as a result of the growing global awareness of "the environmental crisis," the inadequacy of our symbolic representations of Nature became more acute again as the Real of Nature, in the form of a wide variety of ecological threats (global warming, new diseases, biodiversity loss, resource depletion, pollution) invaded and unsettled our received understandings of Nature, forcing yet again a transformation of the signifying chains that attempt to provide "content" for Nature.[16]

In the call for a rebalanced environmental condition, many actors with very different and often antagonistic cultural, economic, political or social positions, interests and inspiration can find common cause in the name of a socially disembodied humanity.

The point of the above argument is that the natures we see and work with are necessarily radically imagined, scripted, and symbolically charged as Nature. These inscriptions are always inadequate, they leave a gap, a remainder and maintain a certain distance from the natures that are there, which are complex, chaotic, often unpredictable, radically contingent, historically and geographically variable, risky, patterned in endlessly complex ways, ordered along "strange" attractors.[17] In other words, there is no Nature out there that needs or requires salvation in name of either "Nature" itself or a generic "Humanity." There is nothing foundational in Nature that needs, demands, or requires sustaining. The debate and controversies over Nature and what to do with it, in

14 See Latour 1993 (fn. 8).

15 See Donna Haraway, *Simians, Cyborgs and Women: The Reinvention of Nature*. London 1991.

16 See Slavoj Žižek, *In Defense of Lost Causes*. London 2008.

17 See, for example, Ilya Prigogine, Isabelle Stengers, *Order out of Chaos: Man's New Dialogue with Nature*. London 1985.

wirkungen auf alle Lebensbereiche konsolidiert hatte, begann eine Fülle neuer Varianten die Bedeutung von Natur zu erweitern. Der umkämpfte Modernisierungsprozess verursachte eine Kakophonie metonymischer Bedeutungsvarianten von „Natur", von welchen aber keine die wunderlichen Einfälle, Idiosynkrasien oder heterogenen Aktionen der unterschiedlichen und sich verändernden Formen jener Natur wirklich ausschöpfte, die die Welt bildete. Überdies nahmen auch diese Formen zu, indem sich die Anzahl der sozionatürlichen Dinge, dieser Hybride aus Mensch und Natur, die Bruno Latour Quasi-Objekte[14] und Donna Haraway Cyborgs[15] nennt, durch die intensivierende Verbindung von menschlichen und nicht-menschlichen Prozessen vervielfältigte (wie zum Beispiel bei der Atomenergie, der Herstellung von angereichertem Uran, der Genmanipulation, bei technisch-natürlichen Bauten wie Kanalsystemen, Stromleitungen, Megastädten und ähnlichem). Während der letzten Jahre und vor allem als Ergebnis eines zunehmenden globalen Bewusstseins bezüglich der „Umweltkrise" wurde die Unzulänglichkeit unserer symbolischen Darstellungen von Natur wieder stärker sichtbar, als das Reale der Natur in Form zahlreicher Umweltbedrohungen (Klimaerwärmung, neue Krankheiten, Verlust der Artenvielfalt, Ressourcenabbau, Umweltverschmutzung) in unser überkommenes Verständnis von Natur eindrang, uns verunsicherte und damit eine erneute Transformation der Bedeutungsketten herbeiführte, die versuchen, die „Inhalte" von Natur zu vermitteln.[16]

Der Punkt dieser Argumentation ist, dass die Naturen, die wir sehen und mit denen wir arbeiten, notwendigerweise erdacht, konstruiert und symbolisch als Natur aufgeladen sind. Solche Zuschreibungen sind immer unzureichend, sie hinterlassen eine Lücke, einen Rest und halten eine gewisse Distanz zu den realen Naturen ein, die komplex, chaotisch und oft unvorhersehbar, vollkommen zufällig, historisch und geografisch variabel, riskant, voller unendlich komplexer Muster und anhand „seltsamer" Bezugspunkte angeordnet erscheinen.[17] Anders gesagt, gibt es dort draußen keine Natur, die eine Rettung im Namen der „Natur" selbst oder im Namen einer allgemeinen „Menschheit" verlangt oder benötigt. Es gibt nichts Grundlegendes in der Natur, das Erhaltung benötigt, begehrt oder erfordert. Die Debatten und Kontroversen zum Thema Natur und was damit zu tun ist, zeigen eher unsere Unfähigkeit, eine direkte politische oder soziale Argumentation und Strategien dafür zu entwerfen, dass Themen wie eine Neuordnung unserer sozio-ökologischen Koordinaten des Alltags, die Produktion neuer sozionatürlicher Konfigurationen und die Übereinkünfte der

14 Vgl. Latour 1995 (Anm. 8).

15 Vgl. Donna Haraway, *Simians, Cyborgs and Women: The Reinvention of Nature*. London 1991.

16 Vgl. Slavoj Žižek, *In Defense of Lost Causes*. London 2008.

17 Vgl. zum Beispiel Ilya Prigogine, Isabelle Stengers, *Order out of Chaos: Man's New Dialogue with Nature*. London 1985.

soziometabolischen Organisation, in der wir leben (allgemein „Kapitalismus" genannt), behandelt werden. In diesem Sinne hat sich einer der zentralen Signifikanten als „leerer" Schlüsselbegriff für die Beschreibung der wachsenden Besorgnis um eine Natur herausgestellt, die aus dem Gleichgewicht geraten zu sein schien: die „Nachhaltigkeit".

3. Nachhaltigkeit und nachhaltige Planung – ein Hirngespinst. Unabhängig von den verschiedenen Sichtweisen unterschiedlicher Personen und Gruppen auf Natur herrscht Einverständnis über den Ernst der Umweltsituation und darüber, dass das sozioökologische Gleichgewicht gefährdet ist. BP nennt sich nun „Beyond Petroleum", um seine umweltschützerischen Absichten zu beweisen, New Age Post-Materialisten stimmen in den Chor mit ein, der den irreversiblen Schwund ökologischer Annehmlichkeiten beklagt, bedeutende Wissenschaftler treten an die Öffentlichkeit, um vor der möglichen Umweltkatastrophe zu warnen, Politiker versuchen, sich im Hissen der ökologischen Flagge gegenseitig auszustechen und eine ganze Reihe politischer Initiativen und Praktiken, die dem Schlagwort der „Nachhaltigkeit" folgen, werden auf allen geografischen Maßstäben diskutiert, konzipiert und umgesetzt. Al Gore erhielt für *Eine unbequeme Wahrheit* den Friedensnobelpreis und das ist sicher eines der besten Beispiele dafür, wie Themen des Ökologischen nun auf die Ebene einer humanitären Angelegenheit gehoben werden. Es herrscht nahezu unangefochtene Einigkeit über die Notwendigkeit stärker „umweltschützerisch" tätig zu werden, wenn Katastrophen vermieden werden sollen.

In diesem Konsens werden Umweltprobleme im Allgemeinen als bedrohlich für das Überleben der Menschheit dargestellt, die ein vorzeitiges Ende der Zivilisation, wie wir sie kennen, ankündigen; das alles wird durch die „Ökologien der Angst", wie Mike Davis sie so passend nennt, untermauert.[18] Die diskursive Matrix, auf der sich die zeitgenössische Bedeutung der Umweltsituation entfaltet, wird durch die kontinuierliche Beschwörung von Angst und Gefahr und das Gespenst der ökologischen Auslöschung genährt. Dieses apokalyptische Imaginäre einer Welt ohne Wasser oder zumindest mit endemischem Wassermangel, verwüstet durch Hurrikans, deren Intensität durch den Klimawandel verstärkt wird, Bilder von ausgetrockneten Landschaften aufgrund der klimatischen Veränderung der Niederschlagsmenge und der Variabilität von Dürreperioden und Überschwemmungen durch die Klimaerwärmung, Eisberge, die um die Pole herum abbrechen und im Meer schmelzen, eine alarmierende Abnahme der Artenvielfalt durch bedrohte oder bereits verschwundene Arten, post-apokalyptische Bilder von öden Landschaften, Zerstörung durch Buschfeuer, Tsunamis, sich verbreitende Krankheiten wie SARS oder AIDS – mit all

18 Vgl. Mike Davis, *Ecology of Fear: Los Angeles and the Imagination of Disaster*. New York 1998.

contrast, signal rather our inability to engage in directly political and social argument and strategies about re-arranging the socio-ecological co-ordinates of everyday life, the production of new socio-natural configurations, and the arrangements of socio-metabolic organization (something usually called capitalism) that we inhabit. Indeed, one of the key signifiers that has emerged as the pivotal "empty" signifier to capture the growing concern for a Nature that seemed to veer off-balance is of course "sustainability."

3. The Fantasy of Sustainability and Sustainable Planning. Irrespective of the particular views of Nature held by different individuals and social groups, consensus has emerged over the seriousness of the environmental condition and the precariousness of our socio-ecological balance. BP has re-branded itself as "Beyond Petroleum" to certify its environmental credentials, New Age post-materialists join the chorus that laments the irreversible decline of ecological amenities, eminent scientists enter the public domain to warn of possible ecological catastrophe, politicians try to outmanoeuver each other in brandishing the ecological banner, and a wide range of policy initiatives and practices, performed under the motif of "sustainability," are discussed, conceived, and implemented at all geographical scales. Al Gore's *An Inconvenient Truth* landed him with the Nobel Peace price, surely one of the most telling illustrations of how ecological matters are elevated to the terrain of a global humanitarian cause. There is now a virtually unchallenged consensus over the need to be more "environmentally" sustainable if disaster is to be avoided.

In this consensual setting, environmental problems are generally staged as universally threatening the survival of humankind, announcing the premature termination of civilization as we know it and sustained by what Mike Davis aptly called "ecologies of fear."[18] The discursive matrix through which the contemporary meaning of the environmental condition is woven is one quilted systematically by the continuous invocation of fear and danger, the specter of ecological annihilation. This apocalyptic imaginary of a world without water or at least with endemic water shortages, ravaged by hurricanes whose intensity is amplified by climate change, pictures of scorched land as global warming shifts the geo-pluvial regime and the spatial variability of droughts and floods, icebergs that disintegrate around the poles as ice melts into the sea, alarming reductions in bio-diversity as species disappear or are threatened by extinction, post-apocalyptic images of derelict waste lands, the devastations raked by wildfires, tsunamis, spreading diseases like SARS or HIV, all these imaginaries of a Nature out of synch, destabilized, threatening, and out of control is paralleled by equally disturbing images of a society that continues piling up waste, pumping CO_2 into the atmosphere, deforesting the earth's lungs, etc. This is a process that Neil Smith appropriately refers to as "nature-washing," whereby the socio-ecological origins of the problems are recognized while this "socially changed nature becomes a new super determinant of our social fate."[19]

This scripting of Nature permits and sustains a post-political arrangement sutured by fear and driven by a concern to manage things so that we

18 See Mike Davis, *Ecology of Fear: Los Angeles and the Imagination of Disaster*. New York 1998.

19 Neil Smith, "Afterword to the Third Edition," in: Neil Smith (ed.), *Uneven Development*. London 2008, pp. 239–266, here p. 245.

can hold on to what we have.[20] This constellation leads Alain Badiou to insist that ecology has become the new opium for the masses, replacing religion as the axis around which our fear for social disintegration becomes articulated (but also from where redemption, if the warnings are heeded, can be retrieved). Such ecologies of fear ultimately conceal, yet nurture, a conservative or, at least, reactionary message. While clouded in rhetoric of the need for radical change in order to stave off immanent catastrophe, a range of technical, social, managerial, physical and other measures have to be taken to make sure that things remain the same; that nothing really changes, that life (or at least our lives) can go on as before. Is this not the underlying message of, for example, *An Inconvenient Truth* or of the report of the United Nation's Intergovernmental Panel on Climate Change (IPCC) on the human consequences of global climate change? Both these narratives, in their very different representational ways (popular/populist on the one hand, "scientific" on the other), urge radical changes in the techno-organizational management of the socio-natural environment in order to assure that the world as we know it stays fundamentally the same.[21] This sentiment is also shared by Frederic Jameson when he claims that "it is easier to imagine the end of the world than it is to imagine the end of capitalism."[22]

In the call for a rebalanced environmental condition, many actors with very different and often antagonistic cultural, economic, political or social positions, interests and inspiration can find common cause in the name of a socially disembodied humanity. It begs the rapid development of a whole battery of innovative environmental technologies, eco-friendly management principles and sustainable organizational forms so that the existing socio-ecological order really does not have to change radically. Consider, for example, how the real and uncontested accumulation of CO_2 in the atmosphere, the threat of peak-oil, the expanding demands for energy and other resources, are today among the greatest concerns facing large companies. Provided the correct techno-administrative apparatuses can be negotiated (like Agenda 21, the Kyoto protocol, recycling schemes, eco-friendly hard and soft technologies, eco-city planning, or biodiversity preservation management), the socio-ecological order as we know it can be salvaged, rescued from ecological Armageddon. It is ironic how in the context of climate change arguments, for example, technological fixes, searching for more energy effective and fossil fuel replacing technologies, combined with market-conform policy arrangements (like the Kyoto Protocol or the various schemes for carbon off-setting) stand to guarantee that the socio-ecological order we inhabit can be sustained for some time longer.

The container signifier that encapsulates these post-political attempts to deal with Nature is, of course, "sustainability." It refers to nothing and everything at the same time. Its prophylactic qualities can only be suggested by adding specifying metaphors. Hence, the proliferation of terms such as sustainable cities, sustainable planning, sustainable development, sustainable forestry, sustainable transport, sustainable regions, sustainable com-

20 See Erik Swyngedouw, "Impossible/Undesirable Sustainability and the Post-Political Condition," in: Rob Krueger, D. Gibbs (eds.), *The Sustainable Development Paradox*. New York 2007.

21 See Slavoj Žižek, "Ecology: A New Opium for the Masses," in the present GAM edition, pp. 32–51.

22 Frederick Jameson, "Future City," in: *New Left Review* 21 (2003), pp. 65–79, here p. 76.

diesen Vorstellungen einer aus dem Gleichgewicht geratenen, destabilisierten, bedrohlichen und nicht mehr kontrollierbaren Natur gehen ebenso verstörende Bilder einer Gesellschaft einher, die weiterhin Abfälle aufhäuft, CO_2 in die Atmosphäre pumpt, die Lunge der Erde abforstet etc. Dies ist ein Vorgang, den Neil Smith sehr passend als „nature-washing" bezeichnet, wodurch die sozioökologischen Ursachen der Probleme erkannt werden, während diese „sozial veränderte Natur zu einem neuen alles bestimmenden Faktor unseres sozialen Schicksals wird".[19]

Dieses Inszenieren der Natur erlaubt und unterstützt ein postpolitisches Arrangement, das durch Angst zusammengehalten und von der Sorge getrieben ist, die Dinge so zu handhaben, dass wir an dem, was wir haben, festhalten können.[20] Diese Konstellation veranlasst Alain Badiou zu seiner Behauptung, dass Ökologie zum neuen Opium für das Volk geworden sei und damit die Religion als Achse ersetzt, um die herum sich unsere Angst vor sozialem Zerfall artikuliert (von der aber auch Erlösung kommen kann, wenn wir auf die warnenden Stimmen hören). Solche Ökologien der Angst verbergen und nähren schließlich eine konservative oder sogar reaktionäre Botschaft. Vernebelt durch die Rhetorik der Notwendigkeit radikaler Veränderung mit dem Ziel, die drohende Katastrophe abzuwenden, werden eine Reihe technischer, sozialer, betriebswirtschaftlicher, physikalischer und anderer Maßnahmen ergriffen, damit alles beim Alten bleibt; damit sich nichts ändert und das Leben (oder zumindest unser Leben) so weitergehen kann wie bisher. Ist dies denn nicht die verborgene Botschaft von beispielsweise *Eine unbequeme Wahrheit* oder des IPCC–Berichtes (Zwischenstaatlicher Ausschuss für Klimaänderungen der Vereinten Nationen – Klimarat) zum Thema Auswirkungen des globalen Klimawandels auf die Menschen? Beide Narrative drängen in jeweils unterschiedlicher Darstellung (die eine populär/populistisch, die andere „wissenschaftlich") auf radikale Veränderungen im technisch-organisatorischen Management des sozionatürlichen Umfeldes, um sicherzustellen, dass die Welt, wie wir sie kennen, grundsätzlich die gleiche bleibt.[21] Auch Frederic Jameson teilt diese Einstellung, wenn er sagt, dass „es einfacher ist, sich das Ende der Welt als das Ende des Kapitalismus vorzustellen."[22]

In diesem Ruf nach Wiederherstellung des Gleichgewichtes der Umwelt finden sich viele Akteure mit sehr unterschiedlichen und oft antagonistischen kulturellen, wirtschaftlichen, politischen oder sozialen Positionen, Interessen und Inspirationen

19 Neil Smith, „Afterword to the Third Edition", in: Neil Smith (Hg.), *Uneven Development*. London 2008, S. 239–266, hier S. 245.

20 Vgl. Erik Swyngedouw, „Impossible/Undesirable Sustainability and the Post-Political Condition", in: Rob Krueger, D. Gibbs (Hg.), *The Sustainable Development Paradox*. New York 2007.

21 Vgl. Slavoj Žižek, „Das Ökologische – Neues Opium fürs Volk", in diesem Heft, S. 32–51.

22 Frederick Jameson, „Future City", in: *New Left Review* 21 (2003), S. 65–79, hier S. 76.

im Namen einer jenseits sozialer Schranken stehenden Humanität zusammen. Sie verlangt die rasche Entwicklung einer ganzen Reihe von innovativen Umwelttechniken, umweltfreundlichen Managementprinzipien und nachhaltigen Organisationsformen, damit die bestehende sozioökologische Ordnung tatsächlich nicht von Grund auf verändert werden muss. Nehmen wir zum Beispiel die Tatsche, dass die echte und unbestrittene Akkumulierung von CO_2 in der Atmosphäre, das Peak-Oil-Problem, der wachsende Bedarf an Energie und anderen Ressourcen heute zu den größten Sorgen großer Unternehmen gehören. Wenn es gelingt, die richtigen technisch-administrativen Systeme (wie z. B. die Agenda 21, das Kyoto-Protokoll, Recyclingverfahren, umweltfreundliche harte und weiche Technologien, umweltfreundliche Stadtplanung oder den Plan zur Erhaltung der Artenvielfalt) auszuhandeln, kann die sozioökologische Ordnung, wie wir sie kennen, bestehen bleiben und vor dem ökologischen Untergang gerettet werden. Es ist bezeichnend, dass technische Entwicklungen für energieeffizientere Technologien, die fossile Brennstoffe ersetzen sollen und mit marktkonformen politischen Abkommen (wie dem Kyoto-Protokoll oder den diversen Entwürfen für den Kohlendioxidemissionshandel) kombiniert werden, heute die Garanten dafür sind, dass die sozioökologische Ordnung, in der wir leben, noch länger erhalten bleibt.

Der Schlüsselbegriff, der solche post-politischen Versuche einschließt, mit der Natur zurechtzukommen, ist natürlich „Nachhaltigkeit". Sie bezieht sich auf alles und nichts zugleich. Ihre prophylaktischen Eigenschaften können nur durch das Hinzufügen erläuternder Metaphern angedeutet werden. Daher kommt die sprunghafte Vermehrung von Begriffen wie nachhaltige Stadt, nachhaltige Planung, nachhaltige Entwicklung, nachhaltiges Forstwesen, nachhaltiger Verkehr, nachhaltige Regionen, nachhaltige Gemeinden, nachhaltiger Ertrag, nachhaltiger Verlust, nachhaltige Ernte, nachhaltige Ressourcen-Nutzung von (fügen Sie ein, was immer Sie möchten), nachhaltiges Wohnen, nachhaltiges Wachstum, nachhaltige Architektur etc. Die Nennung von „Nachhaltigkeit" garantiert bereits, dass das Thema Natur und Umwelt ernst genommen wird, dass unsere Ängste von jenen, die an der Macht sind, gehört werden und dass der „Schutz der Heimat" in guten Händen ist.

Die Vorstellung von einer gutartigen und „nachhaltigen" Natur vermeidet die politisch sensible, aber wichtige Frage nach den sozioökologischen Übereinkünften und Strukturen, die wir schaffen möchten, wie dies erreicht werden kann und in welcher Art von Umgebung wir leben möchten, während wir gleichzeitig die radikale Zufälligkeit und Unvorhersehbarkeit von Natur anerkennen. Das ist der deutlichste Ausdruck der Struktur des Imaginären im Lacanschen Sinne. „Nachhaltigkeit" oder, genauer gesagt, die Steppnähte, um die ihre Bedeutung gewebt ist, sind das *Objekt klein a* der Aktivisten und Umweltplaner, die Sache, um die sich ihr Begehren dreht, und steht dennoch zugleich für das verleugnete Reale, den verdrängten

munities, sustainable yield, sustainable loss, sustainable harvest, sustainable resource (fill in whichever you fancy) use, sustainable housing, sustainable growth, sustainable architecture, etc. The gesture to "sustainability" already guarantees that the matter of Nature and the environment is taken seriously, that our fears are taken account of by those in charge, that "homeland security" is in good hands.

The fantasy of imagining a benign and "sustainable" Nature avoids asking the politically sensitive, but vital, question as to what kind of socio-environmental arrangements and assemblages we wish to produce, how this can be achieved, and what sort of environments we wish to inhabit, while at the same time acknowledging the radical contingency and undecidability of Nature. This is the clearest expression of the structure of fantasy in the Lacanian sense. "Sustainability," or more precisely the quilting points around which its meaning is woven, is the environmental planner and activist's *object petit a*, the thing around which desire revolves, yet simultaneously stands in for the disavowed Real, the repressed core, the state of the situation (i.e. the recognition that the world is really in a mess and really needs drastic and dramatic, that is revolutionary [a metaphor that of course can never be mobilized, that is banned, censured] action). It is in this phantasmagoric space that the proper political dimension (on which more below) disappears to be replaced by a consensually established frame that calls for techno-managerial action in the name of humanity, social integration, the earth and its human and nonhuman inhabitants.

The sequence of the de-politicization of Nature placed under the banner of "the environmental crisis," and re-assembled post-politically under the sign of "sustainability," corrals a series of interconnected processes.

The sequence of the de-politicization of Nature placed under the banner of "the environmental crisis," and re-assembled post-politically under the sign of "sustainability," corrals a series of interconnected processes. First, it is based on the expertise of an assumedly neutral natural scientific knowledge aristocracy. Yet, these experts partake directly in policy domains and become, as expert managers, integral to policy making forums and institutions. Here is a fundamentally duplicitous science and scientists at work, whereby "matters of fact" are seamlessly and without much political dispute translated into "matters of concern." This is a short-circuiting procedure, whereby "fact" and "value" are mixed, sometimes interchanged, and invariably translated without proper public political intermediation.[23] These normative values (like the idealized climate we ought to return to) become then universalized in the sustainability discourse. This discourse invokes THE people (as well as nonhumans) as a whole. Although socio-spatial differences and inequalities are acknowledged, the

23 See Latour 2004 (fn. 11).

Kern und den Status quo (d. h. die Erkenntnis, dass die Welt tatsächlich durcheinander ist, und drastische und dramatische Aktionen erfordert, d. h. revolutionäre (eine Metapher, die natürlich zensiert ist und nicht benutzt werden kann). In eben diesem phantasmagorischen Raum verschwindet die echte politische Dimension (im Weiteren mehr dazu), um durch einen einvernehmlich vereinbarten Rahmen ersetzt zu werden, der technisch-operative Maßnahmen im Namen von Humanität, sozialer Integration, der Erde und im Namen ihrer menschlichen und nicht-menschlichen Bewohner einfordert.

Der Ablauf der Entpolitisierung der Natur unter dem Banner der „Umweltkrise" und die post-politische Neuanordnung unter dem Zeichen der „Nachhaltigkeit" umfassen eine Reihe zusammenhängender Prozesse. Zunächst basieren sie auf der Expertise einer mutmaßlich neutralen Wissensordnung der Naturwissenschaftler. Allerdings sind diese Experten direkt auf politischem Gebiet aktiv und werden als Expertenmanager Teil politisch relevanter Foren und Diskussionen. Hier ist eine grundsätzlich heuchlerische Wissenschaft am Werk, durch welche „Tatsachen" nahtlos und ohne politische Diskussion zu „Sachverhalten" gemacht werden. Dies ist ein Kurzschlussverfahren, in dem „Tatsachen" und „Werte" vermischt, manchmal vertauscht und immer ohne ordentliche öffentliche politische Vermittlung übersetzt werden.[23] Diese normativen Werte (wie das idealisierte Klima, zu dem wir zurückkehren sollten) werden dann im Nachhaltigkeitsdiskurs verallgemeinert. Dieser Diskurs beruft sich auf die Bevölkerung (auch die nicht-menschliche) als Gesamtes: Trotz der Anerkennung sozialräumlicher Unterschiede und Ungleichheiten ist die Umweltbedrohung ein globales Symptom und betrifft alles und jeden.[24] Es gibt keine internen sozialen Spannungen oder produktive interne Konflikte; es ist eine populistische Geste, die die agonistische Heterogenität der „Bevölkerung" leugnet. Stattdessen wird der „Feind" externalisiert und objektiviert. Seine grundlegende Vorstellung ist die *eines Eindringlings*, der das System *korrumpiert* hat. Der „Feind" wird als vage und zweideutige, als sozial entleerte, homogenisierte und nichts sagende Figur externalisiert und letztlich fetischisiert. Bedenken wir zum Beispiel, dass die Kyoto-Verhandlungen (und anschließend jene in Kopenhagen und Cancún) CO_2 und die damit verbundenen Probleme als Versagen des Marktes darstellten, das durch Einführung eines Marktes, den es bisher noch nicht gegeben hatte, behoben werden könnte.[25] Die Forderung nach Nachhaltigkeit wendet sich an die Eliten mit Forderungen, die sich völlig im Rahmen

The fantasy of imagining a benign and "sustainable" Nature avoids asking the politically sensitive, but vital, question as to what kind of socio-environmental arrangements and assemblages we wish to produce, how this can be achieved, and what sort of environments we wish to inhabit, while at the same time acknowledging the radical contingency and undecidability of Nature.

23 Vgl. Latour 2001 (Anm. 11).

24 Vgl. Swyngedouw 2007 (Anm. 20).

25 Vgl. Diana Liverman, „Conventions of Climate Change: Constructions of Danger and the Dispossession of the Atmosphere", in: *Journal of Historical Geography* 35/2 (2009), S. 279–296; Adam G. Bumpus, Diana Liverman, „Accumulation by Decarbonization and the Governance of Carbon Offsets", in: *Economic Geography* 84/2 (2008), S. 127–155.

des Möglichen bewegen. Es handelt sich um eine Politik des Möglichen, die im Rahmen des Status quo operiert. Die Architektur eines solchen seinem Wesen nach populistischen Regierens äußert sich in Form einer Beteiligung von Entscheidungsträgern an der Regierungsgewalt, die über den Staat hinausgehend funktioniert und somit eine Art Selbstbestimmung, Selbstverwaltung und kontrollierter Selbstsanktionierung[26] unter der Schirmherrschaft einer unbestrittenen liberal-kapitalistischen Ordnung zulässt.

Zusammengefasst ruht die post-politische Nachhaltigkeit auf den folgenden Fundamenten: Erstens sind die sozialen und ökologischen Probleme, hervorgerufen durch die Moderne/den Kapitalismus externe Nebenwirkungen und nicht Bestandteil der Beziehungen zwischen liberaler Politik und kapitalistischer Wirtschaft. Zweitens kommt hier eine strikt populistische Politik zum Vorschein, eine, die die Interessen einer imaginären „Bevölkerung", einer imaginären „Natur" oder „Umwelt" auf die Ebene der Allgemeinheit hebt anstatt Räume zu öffnen, in denen die Ansprüche spezifischer Sozialnaturen, Umwelten oder spezifischer sozialer Gruppen oder Klassen verallgemeinert werden können. Drittens werden diese Nebenwirkungen als global, universell und bedrohlich dargestellt, sie sind eine totale Bedrohung. Viertens wird der „Feind" oder das Ziel der Sache dadurch natürlich kontinuierlich externalisiert und entmaterialisiert. Der „Feind" ist immer vage, zweideutig, namenlos und ungezählt, letztlich leer. Fünftens kann das Ziel der Sorge durch eine konsensorientierte dialogische Politik erreicht werden, wodurch Forderungen entpolitisiert und die Politik innerhalb einer vorgegebenen umweltpolitischen Ordnung, für die es anscheinend keine echte Alternative gibt, naturalisiert wird.[27]

4. Das Wesen der Stadtplanung. Für Slavoj Žižek, Chantal Mouffe[28] und andere[29] sind die einvernehmlich geäußerten Anliegen wie „Nachhaltigkeit", die um Ökologien der Angst angeordnet sind, welche eine reaktionäre Grundhaltung fördern und auf technisch-unternehmerische Interventionen drängen, ein Ausdruck des gegenwärtigen post-politischen und post-demokratischen Zustandes, der um spezifische biopolitische Gesten

26 Vgl. Mitchell Dean, *Governmentality. Power and Rule in Modern Society*. London 1999; Thomas Lemke, „'The Birth of Bio-Politics'. Michel Foucault's Lectures at the College de France on Neo-Liberal Governmentality", in: *Economy & Society* 30/2 (1999), S. 190–207; Swyngedouw, „Governance Innovation and the Citizen: The Janus Face of Governance-beyond-the-state", in: *Urban Studies* 42/11 2005), S. 1–16; ders., „Civil Society, Governmentality and the Contradictions of Governance-Beyond-the-State", in: Diana ' MacCallum et al. (Hg.), *Social Innovation and Territorial Development*. Aldershot 2009.

27 Vgl. Swyngedouw, „In Search of a Democratic Politics of Environmental Production", in: *International Journal of Urban and Regional Research* 33/3 (2009).

28 Vgl. Chantal Mouffe, *On The Political*. London 2005.

29 Vgl. Swyngedouw, „The Post-Political City", in: BRAVO (Hg.), *Urban Politics Now. Re-imagening Democracy in the Neo-liberal City*. Rotterdam 2007; ders., „The Antinomies of the Post-Political City", in: ebd.

environmental threat is global, and affects everyone and everything.[24] There are no internal social tensions or internal generative conflicts; it is a populist gesture that disavows the agonistic heterogeneity of "the people." Instead the "enemy" is externalized and objectified. Its fundamental fantasy is that of *an intruder* who has *corrupted* the system. The "enemy" is externalized, vague, and ambiguous, socially empty, homogenized, vacuous, and, ultimately, fetishized. Consider, for example, how the Kyoto (and subsequent Copenhagen and Cancun) negotiations elevated CO_2 and its problems to quintessentially an issue of market failure that can be rectified by instituting a market where hitherto there was none.[25] Demands for sustainability are addressed to the elites, demands that fully operate within contours of the possible; it is a politics of the possible operative within the framework of the given situation. The architecture of such inherently populist governing takes the form of stakeholder participatory governance that operates beyond-the-state and permits a form of self-management, self-organization, and controlled self-disciplining,[26] under the aegis of a non-disputed liberal-capitalist order.

In sum, post-political sustainability policies rest on the following foundations. First, the social and ecological problems caused by modernity/capitalism are external side-effects; they are not an inherent and integral part of the relations of liberal politics and capitalist economies. Second, a strictly populist politics emerges here; one that elevates the interest of an imaginary "the People," "Nature," or "the environment" to the level of the universal rather than opening spaces that permit to universalize the claims of particular socio-natures, environments, or social groups or classes. Third, these side-effects are constituted as global, universal, and threatening: they are a total threat. Fourth, the "enemy" or the target of concern is thereby of course continuously externalized and disembodied. The "enemy" is always vague, ambiguous, unnamed and uncounted, and ultimately empty. Fifth, the target of concern can be managed through a consensual dialogical politics whereby demands become depoliticized and politics naturalized within a given socio-ecological order for which there is ostensibly no real alternative.[27]

4. The Nature of Urban Planning. For Slavoj Žižek, Chantal Mouffe,[28] and others,[29] consensually established concerns, like "sustainability," struc-

24 See Swyngedouw 2007 (fn. 20).

25 See Diana Liverman, "Conventions of Climate Change: Constructions of Danger and the Dispossession of the Atmosphere," in: *Journal of Historical Geography* 35/2 (2009), pp. 279–296; Adam G. Bumpus, Diana Liverman, "Accumulation by Decarbonization and the Governance of Carbon Offsets," in: *Economic Geography* 84/2 (2008), pp. 127–155.

26 See Mitchell Dean, *Governmentality: Power and Rule in Modern Society*. London 1999; Thomas Lemke, "'The Birth of Bio-Politics': Michel Foucault's Lectures at the College de France on Neo-Liberal Governmentality," in: *Economy & Society* 30/2 (1999), pp. 190–207; Swyngedouw, "Governance Innovation and the Citizen: The Janus Face of Governance-beyond-the-state," in: *Urban Studies* 42/11 (2005), pp. 1–16; idem, "Civil Society, Governmentality and the Contradictions of Governance-Beyond-the-State," in: Diana MacCallum et al. (eds.), *Social Innovation and Territorial Development*. Aldershot 2009.

27 See Swyngedouw, "In Search of a Democratic Politics of Environmental Production," in: *International Journal of Urban and Regional Research* 33/3 (2009).

28 See Chantal Mouffe, *On The Political*. London 2005.

29 See Swyngedouw, "The Post-Political City," in: BAVO (ed.), *Urban Politics Now: Re-imagening Democracy in the Neo-liberal City*. Rotterdam 2007; idem, "The Antinomies of the Post-Political City," ibid.

tured around ecologies of fear that nurture a reactionary stance and urge techno-managerial forms of intervention, are an expression of the current post-political and post-democratic condition, one that is arranged around distinct bio-political gestures. Post-politics refers to a politics in which ideological or dissensual contestation and struggles are replaced by techno-managerial planning, expert management and administration, "whereby the regulation of the security and welfare of human lives is the primary goal."[30] Such post-political arrangement signals a de-politicized (in the sense of the disappearance of the democratic agonistic struggle over the content and direction of socio-ecological life) public space whereby expertise, interest intermediation, and administration through governance defines the zero-level of politics.[31] This depoliticized consensual arrangement is organized through post-democratic institutions of governance, like the Kyoto protocol, the European Union, or assorted other public-private governing arrangements that increasingly replace the political institutions of government.[32]

The challenges explored above are, I would argue, of vital importance for grappling with this post-political condition, for exploding the infernal process of de-politicization and for thinking planning again. The claim made above to abandon Nature in no way suggests ignoring, let alone forgetting, the Real of natures or, more precisely, the diverse, multiple, whimsical, contingent and often unpredictable socio-ecological relations of which we are part. On the contrary, it urges us to accept the extraordinary variability of natures, insists on the need to make "a wager" on natures, forces to choose politically between this rather than that nature, invites us to plunge in the relatively unknown, expect the unexpected, accept that not all there is can be known, and, most importantly, fully endorse the violent moment that is inscribed in any concrete or real socio-environmental intervention.

Indeed, the ultimate aim of urban planning and architecture is intervention, to change the given socio-environmental ordering in a certain manner. Like any intervention, this is a violent act, erases at least partly what is there in order to erect something new and different. Consider, for example, the extraordinary effect the eradication of the HI-Virus would have on sustaining livelihoods (or should we preserve/protect the virus in the name of biodiversity?). The recognition that planning acts are singular interventions, that any form of spatialization/environmentalization closes down, at least temporarily, the horizon of time, is of central importance. Such violent encounter, of course, always constitutes a political act, one that can be legitimized only in political terms, and not—as is customarily done—through an externalized legitimation that resides in a fantasy of "Nature" or "Sustainability." Any political act is one that re-orders socio-ecological co-ordinates and patterns, reconfigures uneven socio-ecological relations, often with unforeseen or unforeseeable, consequences.

The democratic planning process dwells, therefore, in two spheres simultaneously. Jacques Rancière defines these spheres respectively as "the

30 Žižek 1999 (fn. 5).

31 See David Marquand, *Decline of the Public: The Hollowing Out of Citizenship*. Cambridge 2004; Swyngedouw, "The Zero-Ground of Politics: Musings on the Post-Political City," in: *New Geographies* 2 (2009).

32 See Colin Crouch, *Post-Democracy*. Cambridge 2004.

angesiedelt ist. Post-Politik bezeichnet eine Politik, die ideologische oder auf Meinungsverschiedenheiten basierende Auseinandersetzungen und Anstrengungen durch technisch-unternehmerische Planung, Expertenmanagement und Administration ersetzt, „wobei die Steuerung der Sicherheit und des Wohlbefindens der Menschenleben das wichtigste Ziel ist".[30] Solch eine post-politische Vereinbarung lässt einen entpolitisierten (im Sinne des Verschwindens des demokratischen, widerstreitenden Ringens um Inhalt und Richtung sozioökologischen Lebens) öffentlichen Raum erkennen, in dem Fachkenntnis, Interessensvermittlung und Verwaltung durch politische Regierungsgewalt die Ebene Null von Politik festlegen.[31] Diese entpolitisierte, einvernehmliche Vereinbarung wird von post-demokratischen Regierungsinstitutionen wie beispielsweise dem Kyoto-Protokoll, der Europäischen Union oder verschiedenen anderen öffentlich-privaten Regierungsabkommen organisiert, die die politischen Regierungsinstitutionen zusehends ersetzen.[32]

Die oben untersuchten Herausforderungen sind, so würde ich behaupten, für die Auseinandersetzung mit diesem post-politischen Zustand, die Analyse des höllischen Prozesses der Entpolitisierung und das Nachdenken über Planung von entscheidender Bedeutung. Die oben genannte Forderung, die Natur aufzugeben, bedeutet keineswegs eine Nichtbeachtung oder gar ein Vergessen des Realen der Naturen oder, genauer gesagt, der unterschiedlichen, mannigfachen, skurrilen, zufälligen und meist unvorhersehbaren sozioökologischen Beziehungen, von denen wir ein Teil sind. Sie hält uns vielmehr dazu an, die außergewöhnliche Variabilität der Naturen anzuerkennen, beharrt auf der Notwendigkeit, auf die Naturen „zu wetten", zwingt uns, eine politische Entscheidung zwischen dieser oder jener Natur zu treffen, lädt uns ein, uns in das relativ Unbekannte zu stürzen, das Unerwartete zu erwarten, zu akzeptieren, dass nicht alles, was es gibt, verstanden werden kann, und was am allerwichtigsten ist, das gewaltsame Moment, das bei jedem konkreten oder realen sozioökologischen Eingriff mitspielt, vollkommen gutzuheißen.

Das letztendliche Ziel der Stadtplanung und Architektur ist die Intervention, um die bestehende sozioökologische Anordnung zu ändern. Wie jeder Eingriff ist das ein gewaltsamer Akt, der zumindest teilweise das Vorhandene auslöscht, um etwas Neues und Anderes zu schaffen. Bedenken wir beispielsweise die außerordentliche Auswirkung, die die Auslöschung des HI-Virus auf die Existenzsicherung hätte (oder sollten wir den Virus im Namen der Artenvielfalt erhalten/schützen?). Die

30 Žižek 1999 (Anm. 5).

31 Vgl. David Marquand, *Decline of the Public: The Hollowing Out of Citizenship*. Cambridge 2004; Swyngedouw, „The Zero-Ground of Politics: Musings on the Post-Political City", in: *New Geographies* 2 (2009).

32 Vgl. Colin Crouch, *Post-Democracy*. Cambridge 2004.

There are no internal social tensions or internal generative conflicts; it is a populist gesture that disavows the agonistic heterogeneity of "the people." Instead the "enemy" is externalized and objectified. Its fundamental fantasy is that of *an intruder* who has *corrupted* the system. The "enemy" is externalized, vague, and ambiguous, socially empty, homogenized, vacuous, and, ultimately, fetishized.

political" and "the police" (the policy order).[33] The (democratic) political is the space for the enunciation and affirmation of difference, for the cultivation of dissensus and disagreement, for asserting the presumption of equality of all and everyone. In contrast, the practice of planning interventions, when becoming concretely geographical or ecological, is of necessity a violent act of foreclosure of the democratic political (at least temporarily), of taking one option rather than another, of producing one sort of environment, of assembling certain socio-natural relations, of foregrounding some natures rather than others, of hegemonizing a particular metonymic chain rather than another. And the legitimation of such options cannot be based on corralling Nature or Sustainability into legitimizing service.

In conclusion, all socio-spatial processes are indeed invariably also predicated upon the circulation, the metabolism and the enrolling of social, cultural, physical, chemical, or biological processes, but their outcome is contingent, often unpredictable, immensely varied, risky. These metabolisms produce a series of both enabling and disabling socio-environmental conditions.[34] Indeed, these produced milieus often embody contradictory tendencies. Processes of metabolic (or socio-ecological) change are, therefore, never socially or ecologically neutral. For example, the unequal ecologies associated with uneven property relations, the commodification of all manner of natures, the impoverished socio-ecological life under the overarching sign of the commodity and of money in a neo-liberal order, and the perverse exclusions choreographed by the dynamics of uneven eco-geographical development at all scales suggest how the production of socio-ecological arrangements is always a deeply conflicting, and hence irrevocably political, process. All manner of social power geometries shape the particular social and political configurations as well as the environments in which we live. Therefore, the production of socio-environmental arrangements implies fundamentally political questions. The key issue is to tease out who gains from and who pays for, who benefits from and who suffers (and in what ways) from particular processes of socio-ecological change.

All manner of social power geometries shape the particular social and political configurations as well as the environments in which we live. Therefore, the production of socio-environmental arrangements implies fundamentally political questions.

Democratizing environments, then, become an issue of enhancing the democratic content of socio-environmental construction by means of identifying the strategies through which a more equitable distribution of social power and a more inclusive mode of producing natures can be achieved.

33 See Jacques Rancière, *Disagreement*. Minneapolis 1998.

34 See Swyngedouw 2006 (fn. 9).

Erkenntnis, dass Planungsakte einmalige Interventionen sind, dass jede Art von Verräumlichung oder „Verumweltlichung" den Zeitfaktor zumindest zweitweise außer Kraft setzt, ist von zentraler Bedeutung. Solch ein gewaltsames Aufeinandertreffen erzeugt selbstverständlich immer einen politischen Vorgang, der nur auf politischer Ebene legitimiert werden kann und nicht – wie üblich – durch eine externalisierte Legimitation, wie sie einer Einbildung von „Natur" und „Nachhaltigkeit" innewohnt. Jeder politische Akt ordnet sozioökologische Koordinaten und Muster neu und rekonfiguriert ungleiche sozioökologische Verhältnisse mit oft unvorhersehbaren Auswirkungen.

Der demokratische Planungsprozess wurzelt daher gleichzeitig auf zwei Ebenen. Jacques Rancière definiert diese beiden Bereiche als „das Politische" und „die Polizei" (die polizeiliche Ordnung).[33] Das (demokratisch) Politische ist der Raum für die Artikulation und Bejahung von Verschiedenheit, für Dissens und Meinungsverschiedenheiten, für die Durchsetzung der für alle geltenden Gleichheitsvermutung. Im Gegensatz dazu ist die Praxis der Planung von Eingriffen, sobald diese einen konkreten geografischen oder ökologischen Bezug aufweisen, notgedrungen ein gewaltsamer Akt, mit dem das demokratisch Politische (zumindest vorübergehend) aufgekündigt, eine Option gegenüber einer anderen bevorzugt, eine bestimmte Art von Umwelt und bestimmte soziale natürliche Beziehungen geschaffen, eine bestimmte Natur in den Vordergrund gerückt sowie bestimmten metonymischen Bedeutungsvarianten der Vorzug vor anderen gegeben wird. Doch die Legimitation solcher Optionen kann nicht darauf beruhen, die Natur oder Nachhaltigkeit darauf zu beschränken, dass sie zu Diensten sind.

Zusammenfassend basieren alle sozialräumlichen Prozesse also ausnahmslos auf Zirkulation, Formveränderung und der Einbeziehung sozialer, kultureller, physikalischer, chemischer oder biologischer Prozesse, aber ihr Resultat ist zufällig, oft unvorhersehbar, ungemein vielfältig und riskant. Diese Veränderungen erzeugen eine Reihe vorteilhafter und nachteiliger sozioökologischer Bedingungen.[34] Tatsächlich bestehen in diesen produzierten Milieus oft widersprüchliche Tendenzen. Prozesse metabolischen (oder sozioökonomischen) Wandels sind daher aus sozialer oder ökonomischer Sicht nie neutral. Die ungleichen Ökologien im Zusammenhang mit ungleichen Eigentumsverhältnissen, die Kommerzialisierung jeder Art von Natur, das verarmte sozioökologische Leben, das unter dem allumfassenden Zeichen der Konsumwaren und des Geldes in einer neoliberalen Ordnung steht, und die widersinnigen Ausgrenzungen, die von den Dynamiken unausgeglichener umweltgeografischer Entwicklungen auf allen Maßstabsebenen inszeniert

33 Vgl. Jacques Rancière, *Disagreement*. Minneapolis 1998.

34 Vgl. Swyngedouw 2006 (Anm. 9).

werden, zeigen somit, dass die Herstellung sozioökologischer Anordnungen stets ein zutiefst gegensätzlicher und daher unwiderruflich politischer Prozess ist. Soziale Machtgeometrien in allen möglichen Formen prägen die besonderen sozialen und politischen Strukturen, wie auch die Umgebungen, in denen wir leben. Daher schließt die Herstellung sozioökologischer Anordnungen grundsätzlich fundamentale politische Fragestellungen mit ein. Das Schlüsselproblem besteht darin, herauszufinden, wer aus bestimmten Prozessen sozioökologischen Wandels Gewinn schlägt und wer dafür bezahlt, wer davon profitiert und wer darunter leidet (und auf welche Weise).

Unsere Umwelten zu demokratisieren, handelt davon, den demokratischen Inhalt sozioökologischer Strukturen zu stärken, indem Strategien ermittelt werden, mit denen soziale Macht gerechter verteilt und Naturen in einer stärker integrierten Art und Weise produziert werden können. Das erfordert die Zurückeroberung einer vollwertigen Demokratie und vollwertiger demokratischer öffentlicher Räume (Räume für die Artikulation widerstreitender Auseinandersetzungen) als Grundlage und Bedingung für egalitärere sozioökologische Anordnungen, sowie für die Benennung eindeutig dargestellter, der Gleichheit verpflichteter, sozioökologischer Vorhaben, die unmittelbar umgesetzt werden können. Mit anderen Worten, in egalitären Ökologien geht es darum, das Unmögliche zu fordern und das Unwahrscheinliche zu verwirklichen.

This requires reclaiming proper democracy and proper democratic public spaces (as spaces for the enunciation of agonistic dispute) as a foundation for and condition of possibility for more egalitarian socio-ecological arrangements, the naming of positively embodied ega-libertarian socio-ecological futures that are immediately realizable. In other words, egalitarian ecologies are about demanding the impossible and realizing the improbable.

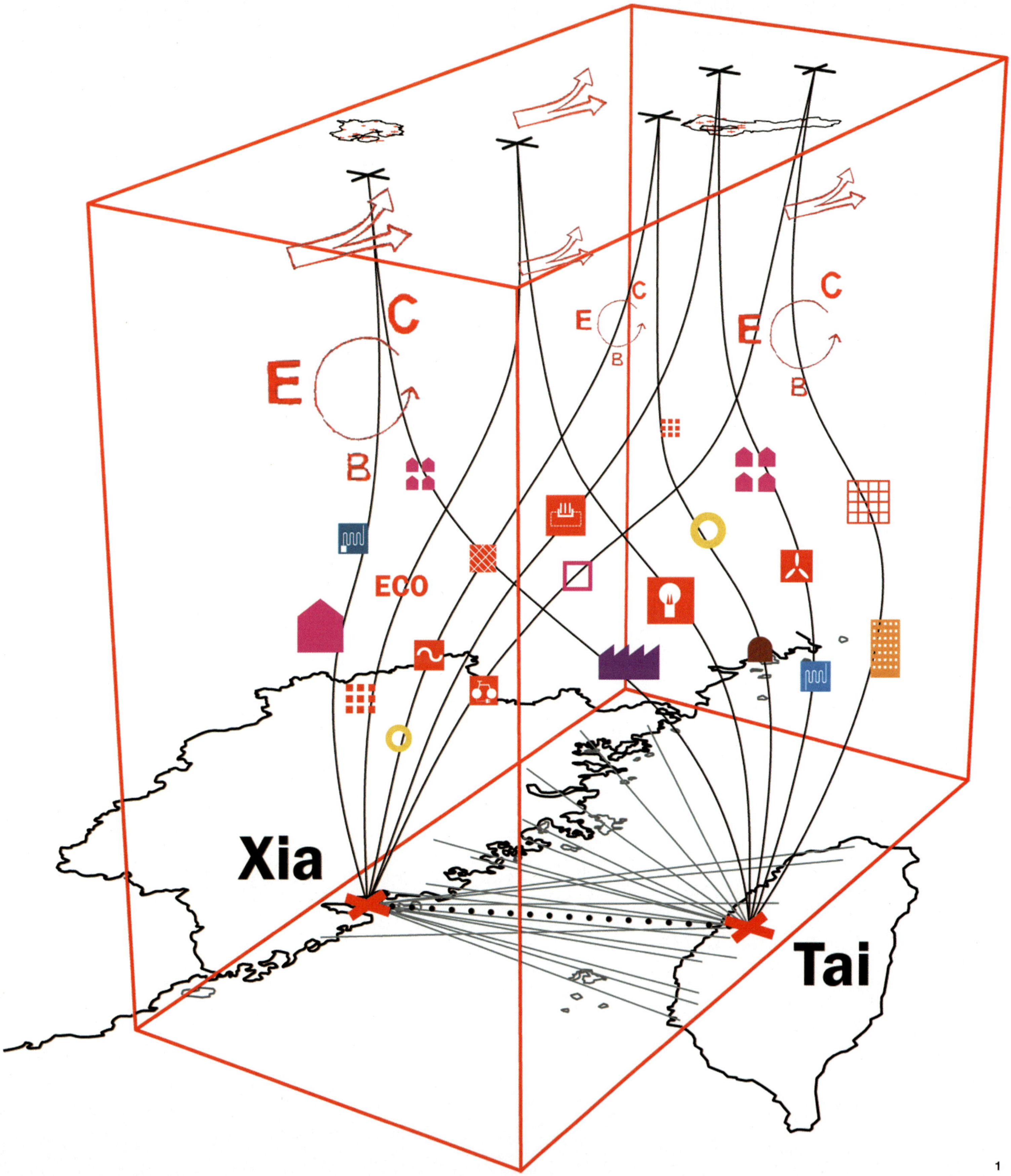

1 Taiwan Strait Incubator

A New Geography:

Climate Change and Post Oil Incubators

Imaging the low carbon city and low carbon society in the near future is a new pursuit. We have the technologies, we understand the urgency, and somehow the international community, through events such as Copenhagen, Tienjin, Cancun and Durban, are trying to create a continuation of the Kyoto Treaty, or to redesign it in some new form. But how does it look? How does it feel, and how does a society live in it?

Eine neue Geografie: Klimawandel und die Entstehungsbedingungen der Post-Oil-Ära. Die „Low-Carbon-City" und die „Low-Carbon-Society" der näheren Zukunft in Bildern vorzustellen, ist ein neuer Ansatz. Wir besitzen die Technologien, wir verstehen die Dringlichkeit und irgendwie versucht die internationale Gemeinschaft, mittels Veranstaltungen wie in Kopenhagen, Tianjin, Cancún und Durban das Kyoto-Protokoll fortzusetzen oder es in irgendeiner Art neu auszugestalten. Aber wie sieht das aus? Wie fühlt es sich an und wie lebt eine Gesellschaft damit?

RAOUL BUNSCHOTEN

A New Geography. Climate change is the cause of a new geography: the metaphor greenhouse has for a number of years been connected with the warming of the earth, so the "greenhouse effect" describes the capturing of the sun's heat in the atmosphere through the increase of CO_2 in the atmosphere. The diagram of sunlight bouncing back and forth between the skin of the earth and the outer edge of the atmosphere is a common image now and always referred to in the explanation of climate change and global warming. The thin layer of space wrapped around the earth has increasingly looked delicate, a mere wisp of air, and we are both safe in it, its oxygen giving us life, the sunlight passing through it giving energy, but we are also trapped in it, with no way to escape. This space, the thin periphery of the skin of the earth, is restless, dynamic, increasingly erratic, and possibly heating up irreversibly. Within this space and on this skin there are many regions and territories that will be affected in different, specific ways, where the changes will appear particularly strong, more tangible, faster, or in an invisible way. The movements of people, animals, the growth of plants, are affected by this restlessness, the skin of the earth itself is reacting to the changes, the shape of the world is different, this is the new geography of climate change. The new geography also describes the shifting of a society from total global and transnational dependency on fossil fuels to the new, post-oil-city world.

Maps. The maps describing this change are themselves new. Like the first maps of the geology of the skin of the earth, of the universe as far as we could see it, of the seas, horizons and new territories that were touched on by explorers, these maps describe new conditions where the effects are seen more clearly, or where causes of future effects can be read. The maps describe the peaks and troughs of the dynamics of weather, of impulsive and incremental climate change, of territorial windows on the specifics of a changing atmosphere.

Incubators. Incubators are places for the invention of thought or of new things, processes, institutions and symbolic forms. Incubating refers to the taking care of something, enabling it to grow, to become something new, autonomous, viable, a life form or new life. The incubator is a frame, a separation, the outline of a space, a territory, where these new things are nurtured. The incubator for a low carbon society is a condition of the new geography. It is a frame in the various maps belonging to climate change.

Choreography and Co-evolution. The incubator depends on planning and natural evolution. The planning refers to things in space, a composition of urban plans, projects, policies, technologies, infrastructures, buildings, organizations, etc., in time in the frame of the incubator. The incubator needs an imaginative plan of how all these things will exist with each other, follow each other up, support each other, form figures in space and sequences in time, clusters, rhythms, as well as juxtapositions, conflicts. But all these things sing and dance in a space which already contains other things that move, behave, change, and this is where co-evolution comes in: it is a concept that describes the intertwining of the different pathways of evolution of either existing life forms in the incubator, or the new ones, intertwining, interlinking, co-evolving with each other and older forms.

Eine neue Geografie. Der Klimawandel ist die Ursache für eine neue Geografie: Die Treibhaus-Metapher wird seit einigen Jahren für die Erderwärmung verwendet, wobei der „Treibhauseffekt" das Speichern der Sonnenhitze in der Atmosphäre durch den erhöhten CO_2-Gehalt der Atmosphäre beschreibt. Das Diagramm, das zeigt, wie das Sonnenlicht zwischen der Erdoberfläche und der äußeren Schicht der Atmosphäre hin und her springt, ist inzwischen allgemein bekannt und wird immer herangezogen, um Klimawandel und Erderwärmung zu erklären. Die dünne Raumschicht, die die Erde einhüllt, sieht immer empfindlicher aus, wie ein bloßer Lufthauch. Wir sind zwar sicher in ihr, ihr Sauerstoff gibt uns Leben und das hindurchstrahlende Sonnenlicht spendet Energie, aber wir sind auch gefangen in ihr und können nicht ausweichen. Dieser Raum, diese dünne Peripherie der Erdoberfläche ist in Bewegung, dynamisch, zunehmend ungleichmäßig und möglicherweise dabei, sich unumkehrbar zu erwärmen. Innerhalb dieses Raums und dieser Schicht gibt es viele Regionen und Gebiete, die auf verschiedene, spezifische Art und Weise betroffen sein werden und in denen der Wandel besonders stark, greifbarer, schneller oder auch unsichtbar auftreten wird. Die Bewegungen von Menschen und Tieren, das Pflanzenwachstum wird von diesem Wandel beeinflusst; die Erdoberfläche selbst reagiert auf die Veränderungen; die Gestalt der Welt ändert sich: Das ist die neue Geografie des Klimawandels. Diese neue Geografie beschreibt auch die Verlagerung einer Gesellschaft von einer totalen globalen und transnationalen Abhängigkeit von fossilen Brennstoffen zu der neuen, urbanen Welt im Post-Erdöl-Zeitalter.

Landkarten. Die Landkarten, die diesen Wandel beschreiben, sind selbst neu. Wie die ersten geologischen Karten der Erdoberfläche, also des Universums, so weit wir es damals erkennen konnten, der Ozeane, der Horizonte und neuen Gebiete, auf die die Entdecker stießen, beschreiben diese Landkarten die neuen Bedingungen, an denen die Auswirkungen klarer gesehen oder Ursachen zukünftiger Auswirkungen abgelesen werden können. Die Karten beschreiben die Höchst- und Tiefstpunkte der Wetterdynamiken, des impulsiven und zunehmenden Klimawandels und der territorialen Ausschnitte von den spezifischen Kennzeichen einer sich verändernden Atmosphäre.

Entstehungsherde. Entstehungsherde sind Orte der Erfindung von Gedanken oder neuen Dingen, Prozessen, Institutionen und symbolischen Formen. Etwas entstehen zu lassen, bedeutet, auf etwas Acht geben, ihm ermöglichen, zu wachsen, etwas Neues, Eigenständiges, Lebensfähiges zu werden, eine Lebensform oder neues Leben. Der Entstehungsherd als Inkubator ist ein Rahmen, eine Abtrennung, die Abgrenzung eines Raums, ein Territorium, in dem diese neuen Dinge gefördert

The maps describing this change are themselves new. Like the first maps of the geology of the skin of the earth, of the universe as far as we could see it, of the seas, horizons and new territories that were touched on by explorers, these maps describe new conditions where the effects are seen more clearly, or where causes of future effects can be read.

werden. Der Inkubator für eine „Low-Carbon-Society" ist eine Bedingung für die neue Geografie. Er ist ein Ausschnitt in den verschiedenen Karten, die zum Klimawandel gehören.

Choreografie und Koevolution. Der Inkubator hängt von Planung und natürlicher Evolution ab. Die Planung besteht aus Dingen im Raum, ist eine Zusammensetzung von Stadtplanungen, Projekten, Politiken, Technologien, Infrastrukturen, Gebäuden, Firmen etc. zu einer bestimmten Zeit im Rahmen des Inkubators. Der Inkubator braucht einen kreativen Plan, wie all diese Dinge gemeinsam existieren werden, einander nachfolgen und unterstützen, Figuren im Raum und Abfolgen in der Zeit, Gruppierungen, Rhythmen ebenso wie Gegenüberstellungen und Konflikte bilden. Aber all diese Dinge singen und tanzen in einem Raum, der schon andere Dinge enthält, die sich bewegen, sich verhalten, sich verändern, und dies ist der Punkt, an dem die Koevolution ins Spiel kommt: Sie ist ein Konzept, das die Verflechtung der verschiedenen Pfade der Evolution entweder schon existierender Lebensformen im Inkubator oder neue Formen beschreibt, die sich ineinander schlingen, verbinden und sich gemeinsam und mit älteren Formen entwickeln.

The incubator is a frame, a separation, the outline of a space, a territory, where these new things are nurtured. The incubator for a low carbon society is a condition of the new geography. It is a frame in the various maps belonging to climate change.

Die kuratorische Toolbox

Druck. Es besteht großer Druck, von fossilen Brennstoffen loszukommen, energieeffizientere Lebensweisen zu entwickeln und in diesem Kontext bei der Entwicklung urbaner und transnationaler Infrastrukturen, politischer Konzepte und Verträge zusammenzuarbeiten. So lastet auf der Region der Formosastraße, einem geopolitischen Hotspot, der Druck, die internationale Zusammenarbeit zu verstärken, überregionale Beziehungen zu entwickeln und die Spannung zu reduzieren. Die Sektoren T und E enthalten einige der am dichtesten besiedelten Gebiete in Europa und bilden eine Art Attraktor für verschiedene transnationale Strukturen, die in Europa entstehen: der „North-Sea-Ring" (Nordsee-Netzplan), Desertec, Nord-Süd-Energienetzwerke etc. Auf Europa lastet der Druck, sich im Post-Oil-Zeitalter und in einer Welt, in der Mexiko, Südafrika, Brasilien, Korea, Russland und vor allem Indien und China eine neue Rolle spielen und ein neues Gleichgewicht herstellen, zu positionieren.

Die Toolbox. Die Toolbox ist Teil dieser Neupositionierung, Teil des entstehenden Potenzials in Schwellenbereichen, in natürlichen Entstehungsherden und der Herstellung eines neuen Beziehungsgleichgewichts. Die Toolbox besteht auch daraus, was uns Menschen zur Verfügung steht, um uns an die Klimaveränderungen und an die Erderwärmung anzupassen und diese, sofern möglich, zu bremsen. Außerdem ist die

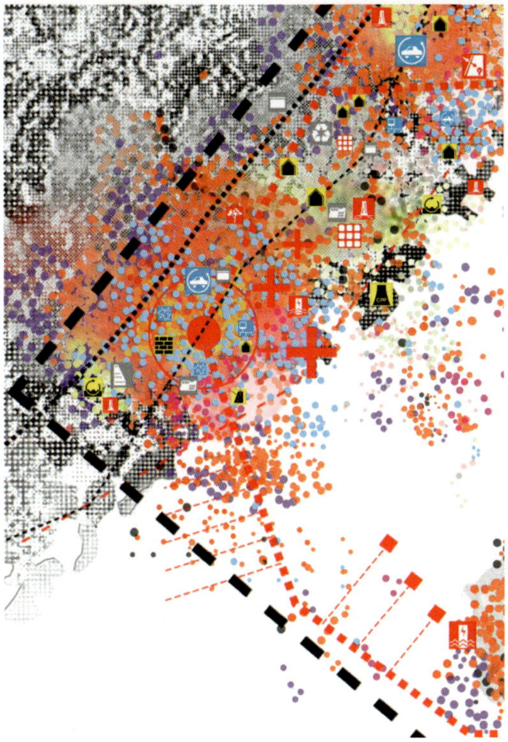

2

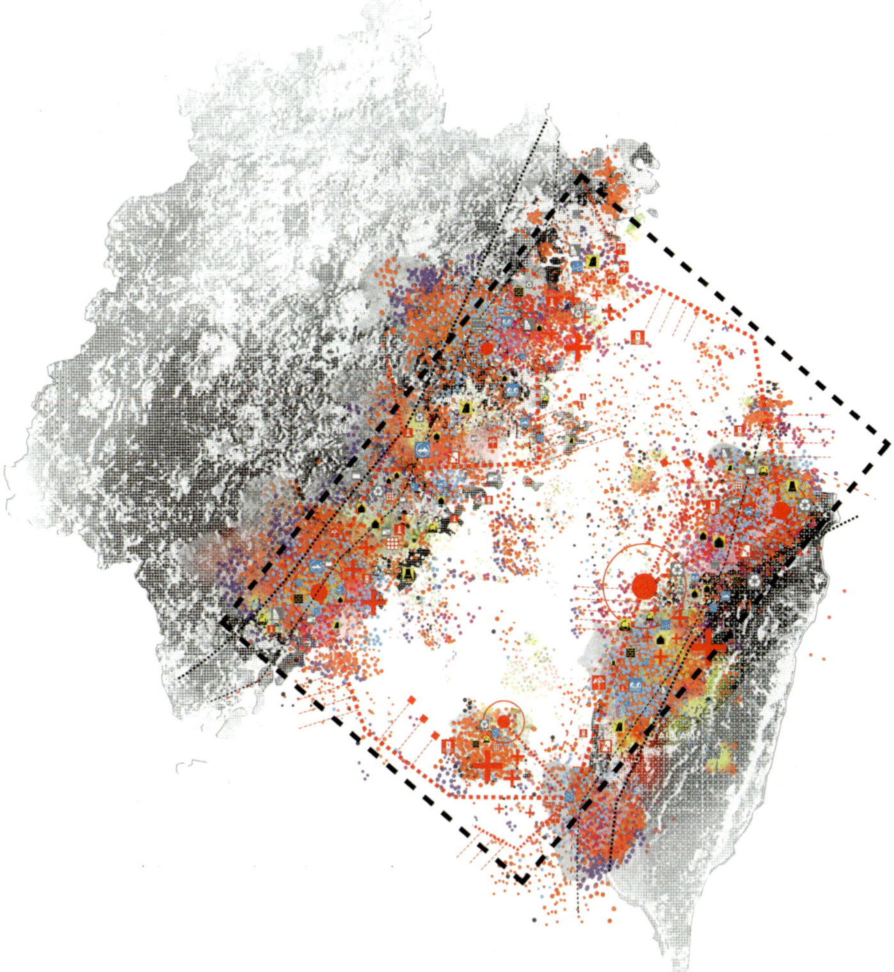

3

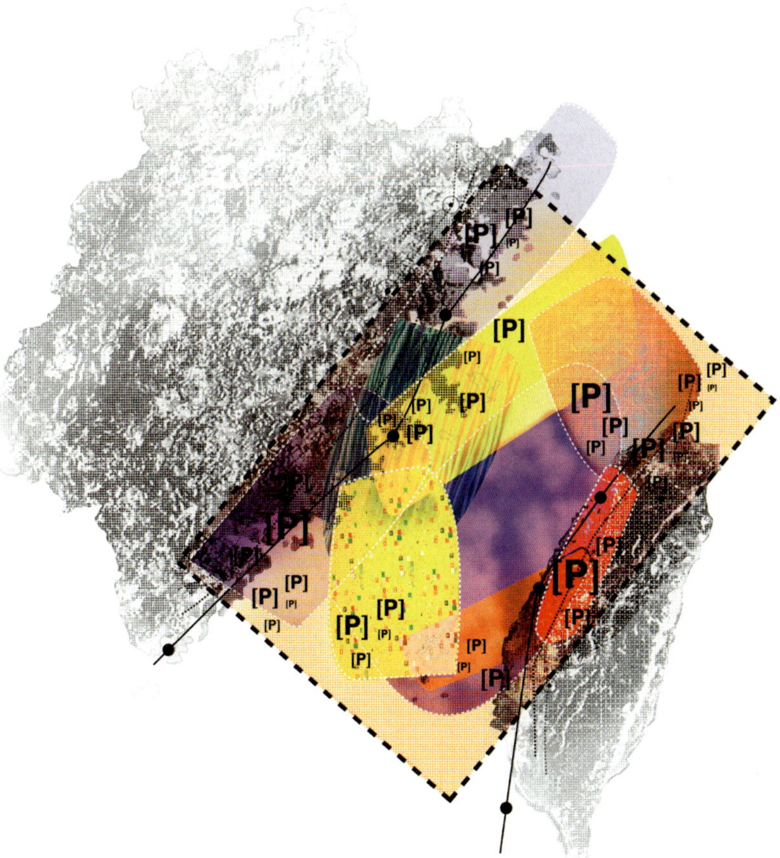

4

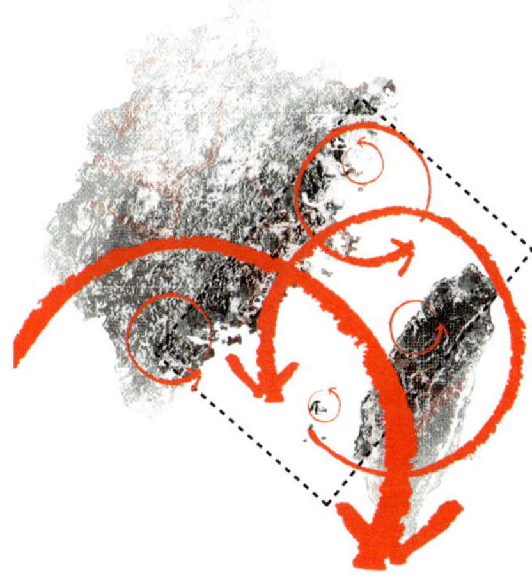

5

2–5 Taiwan Strait Incubator:
(2–3) Composite
(4) Branding
(5) Incorporation

6

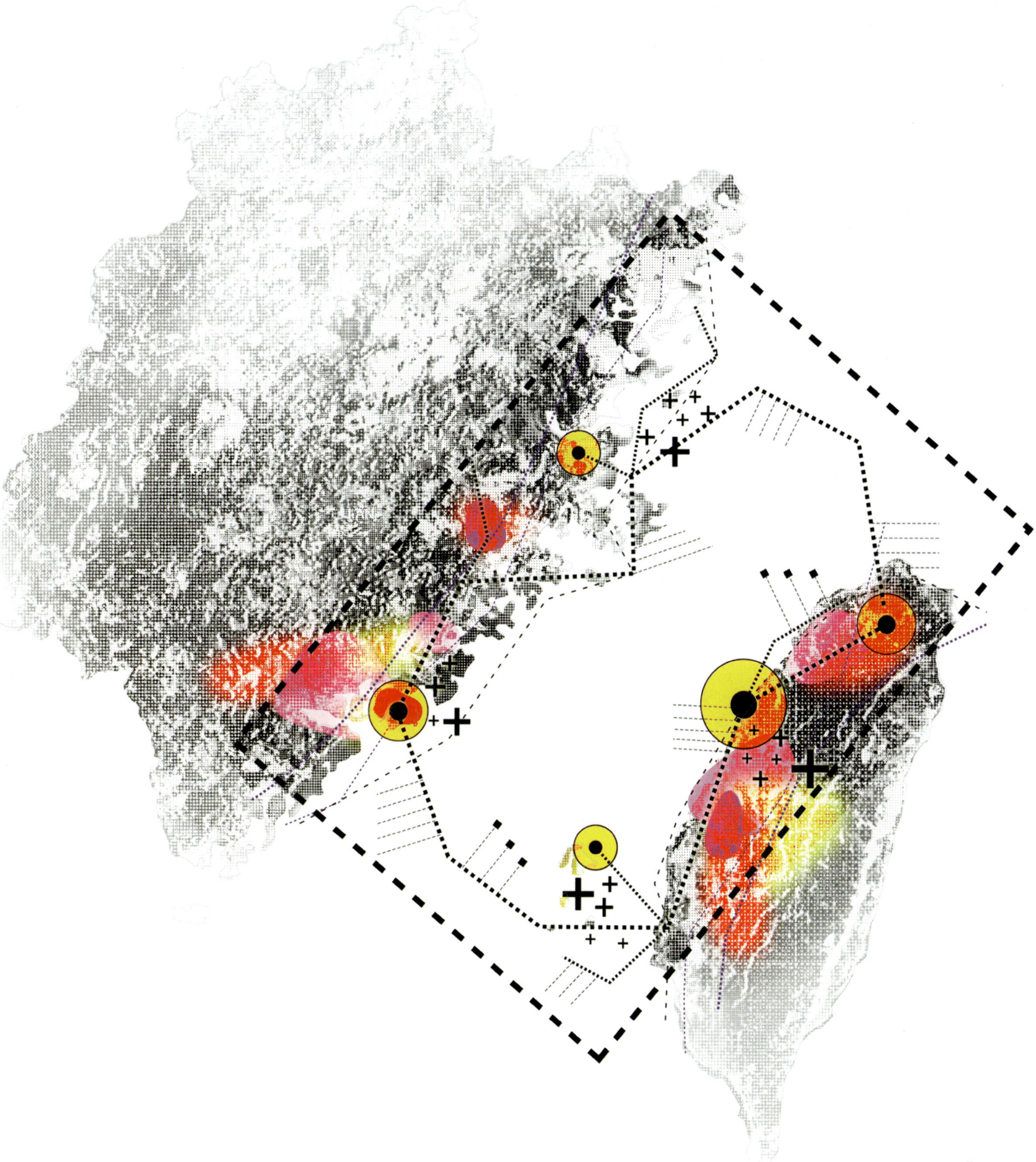

7 Taiwan Strait Incubator: Flow

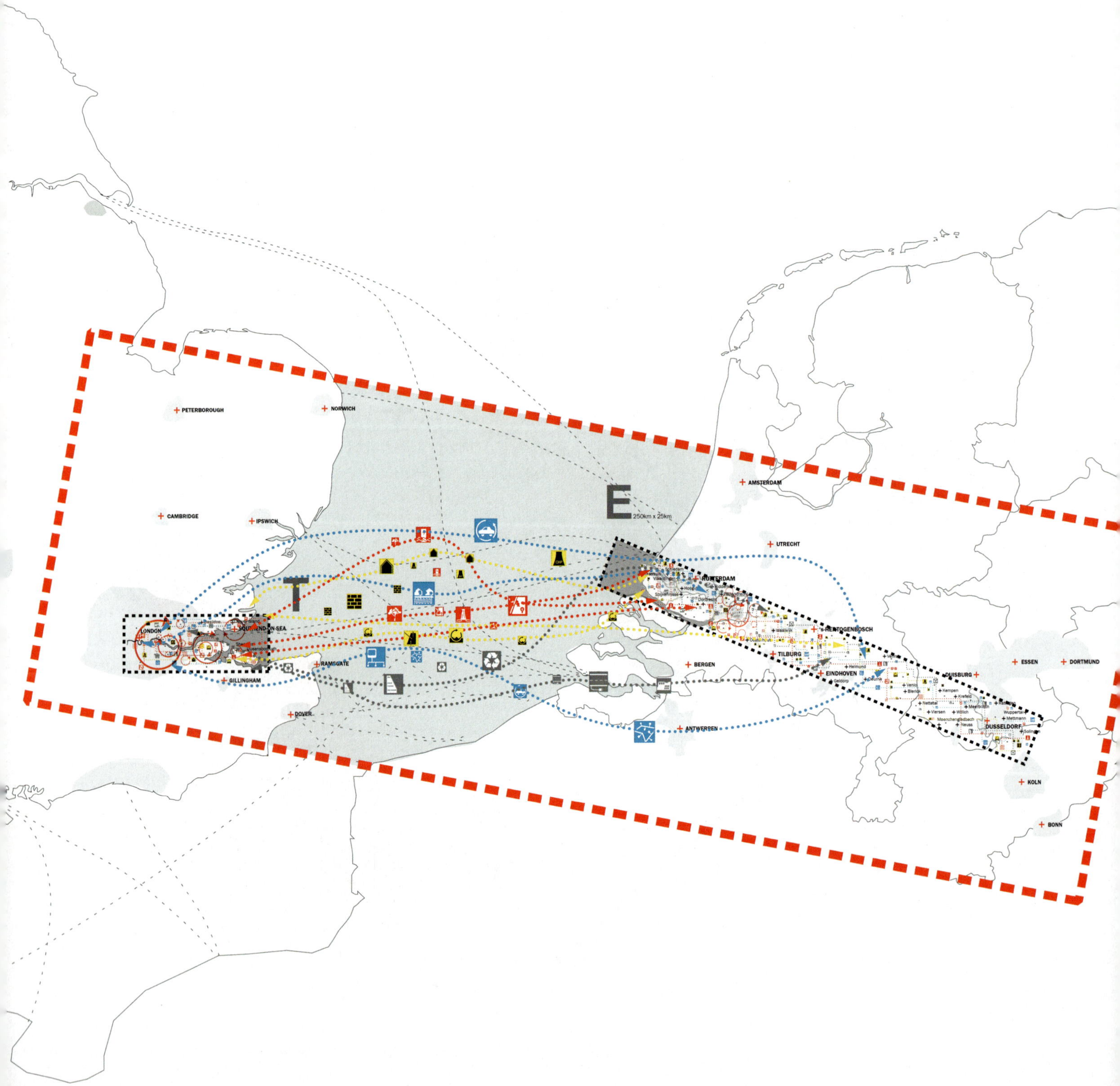

PETERBOROUGH
NORWICH
CAMBRIDGE
IPSWICH
AMSTERDAM
UTRECHT
E
250km x 25km
T
LONDON
SOUTHEND-ON-SEA
GILLINGHAM
RAMSGATE
DOVER
ROTTERDAM
BERGEN
ANTWERPEN
TILBURG
HERTOGENBOSCH
EINDHOVEN
DUISBURG
ESSEN
DORTMUND
DUSSELDORF
KOLN
BONN

8

Toolbox Stand der Technik und der Wissenschaft, das Erbe der Aufklärung und der industriellen Revolution oder gar sehr viel älterer Traditionen der Technik und Gestaltung wie zum Beispiel in China. Die Toolbox ist das, was wir in den Inkubator stellen und mit unserer Choreographie aktivieren und beleben. Die einzelnen Elemente der Toolbox werden zum Gefüge der Koevolutionsprozesse und zur Textur seiner Veränderungen.

Der Spin. Schließlich jedoch ist der Klimawandel ein kulturelles Projekt und braucht die Narrative und Kosmologien, die die Menschen immer schon im Umgang mit ihrer Umgebung, mit ihrer Welt und der Schaffung von Identitäten innerhalb dieser Welt anwandten. Der Inkubator hängt von Narrativen ab, um Komplizenschaft, Teilnahme, Organisation, Kooperation und Visionen vom Ende hervorzubringen, wenn er selbst nichts mehr hervorbringt, sondern wieder zurück mit den fluiden Schichten der Erdoberfläche verschmilzt. Der Spin ist natürlich in die Art und Weise eingebettet, wie diese Narrative Emotionen verursachen oder diese dirigieren und wie sie diese Emotionen verbreiten.

Die Bühne. Der Entstehungsherd ist eine Bühne, auf welcher diese Dinge, sowohl die Choreografie vieler „Low-Carbon" und ähnlicher Projekte, Entwürfe, Veranstaltungen als auch das natürliche Wachstum anderer Dinge, natürlicher Flüsse und der Fluss von Informationen, von Leben und Tod, für alle sichtbar gespielt werden, damit das Entstehen neuer Lebensformen, gemeinschaftlich aufgebauter, neu ausgedachter Räume und einer „Low-Carbon-Society", was auch immer das heißen mag, abgeschätzt werden kann. Dies ist sowohl eine Utopie als auch ein Mittel, um auszuprobieren, ob zumindest ein Teil dieser Utopie realisierbar ist, und um die Konsequenzen dieser Umsetzung als Modell, mit der Leitfigur einer Beatrice oder eines Mephisto, je nach Standpunkt zu erkennen.

The Curatorial Toolbox:

Pressure. Pressure is on to get rid of fossil fuels, to develop more energy-efficient ways of living and to cooperate on these in terms of urban and transnational infrastructures, policies and treaties. In the Taiwan Strait the pressure is on to increase cooperation, to develop cross-strait relations, to reduce the tension in this geopolitical hotspot. The Sectors T and E contain some of the most densely populated areas in Europe and form a kind of attractor for the various transnational structures emerging in Europe: the North Sea ring, Desertec, north south energy networks, etc. The pressure is on for Europe to define itself in a post-oil world and a world within which Mexico, South Africa, Brazil, Korea, Russia, and most of all India and China will play new roles and define new balances.

Toolbox. The toolbox is part of this redefinition, of the emergent potential in liminal zones, natural incubators and the rebalancing of relationships. The toolbox is what we as humans have to adapt to and mitigate where possible the changes in climate, including the warming up of the atmosphere. The toolbox is also the state of the art of technology and science, the legacy of the enlightenment and the industrial revolution, or of even much older traditions of technology and design as practices, for example in China. The toolbox is what we place in the incubator and activate, animate, with our choreography. The elements of the toolbox become the fabric of the processes of co-evolution, the texture of its changes.

Spin. In the end, climate change is a cultural project and needs the narratives and cosmologies that humans have always employed in dealing with their surroundings, their world and the creation of identities within that world. The incubator depends on narratives to create complicity, participation, organization and cooperation, and visions of the end, of when an incubator is not incubating anymore, but merging back into the fluid skin of the earth. The spin is of course embedded in the way these narratives engender or manage emotions, and in the way they proliferate those emotions.

The Stage. The incubator is a stage on which these things—both the choreography of many low carbon and related projects, designs, events, and the natural growth of other things, the flows of rivers and information, of love and death—are played out in full view in order to appreciate the emergence of new life forms, of cooperatively structured, of newly imagined spaces and of a low carbon society, whatever that means. It is both utopia, and the means to test the possibility of realizing at least part of this utopia, and to see the consequences of this realization as a model, a guide, a Beatrice or a Mephistopheles, depending on one's view.

1 Eisbergkalben an der Küste des Petermann Gletschers. Ice island calves at the coast of the Petermann Glacier. Advanced Land Imager (ALI) on NASA's Earth Observing-1 (EO-1) satellite. EO-1 ALI data provided courtesy of the NASA EO-1 team and the United States Geological Survey, öffentliche Domain public domain.

Zero Landscapes in the Time of Hyperobjects

"The vicissitudes of this life are like drowning in a glass pond."
Chögyam Trungpa

Zero Landscapes in den Zeiten der Hyperobjekte.
„Die Wechselfälle dieses Lebens sind wie Ertrinken in einem gläsernen Teich."
Chögyam Trungpa

TIMOTHY MORTON

Imagine you're eating an ice cream. You tell yourself that you will only have a lick after you have felt a moment of true happiness. The happiness never comes—and the ice cream also melts.

The ice cream is the world quite literally. It's melting. We have no time to think the right thoughts about it. We just have to save it. Objects are beginning to compel us, from outside the wall. The objects we ignored for centuries, the objects we created in the process of ignoring other ones: plutonium, global warming. I call them *hyperobjects*. Hyperobjects are real objects that are massively distributed in time and space. Good examples would be global warming and nuclear radiation. Hyperobjects are so vast, so long lasting, that they defy human time and spatial scales. They wouldn't fit in a landscape painting. They could never put you in the right mood.

If we're going to think beyond the modern period, beyond the era of philosophy, society and ecology in which we have been stuck for about two hundred years, then we will have to let go of the idea of landscape as a picture in a frame, even if the picture is liquid and motile, like a movie.[1] Why? The problem is the notion of the *frame*, and the distance the viewer has to assume for the landscape to appear as such. Because of this distance, the landscape embodies a subjective (whatever word works best for you here, "spiritual," "ideological," whatever) state. The picture is about the attitude you must assume to look at the picture. It's less about *land*, then, and more about *scape*. We talk about the mood of a landscape, the feeling it evokes in us. How ironic that this kind of aesthetic distancing, so woven into our social and cultural practices, not to mention actually existing structures and designs, was part of the modernity that summoned the hideous saviors, the hyperobjects, into our social, psychic and ecological space. After all, it's our supposed need for rolling hills and pastoral scenes that encourages us to fend off developers wanting to install wind farms to wean us off the oil that runs invisibly in pipes beneath the landscape.

The idea that landscape is about instilling an attitude presents us with a major problem. It's a profound form of idealism. Materialism, in all its varieties, just hasn't been powerful enough to break through the idealist tendencies of the last two centuries, perhaps because it's hell bent on reducing objects to their relations.[2] Idealism: it's all about the subject. It's all about me. What kind of an ecological view is that? To have a truly ecological view we must exit from this idea of landscape, based on a first- or third-person perspective, and instead look for a *zero-person perspective*, as absurd as this sounds from a traditional modernist point of view. We could at least allow other entities, sentient and non-sentient, to talk to us.

"If I can just get the attitude right, maybe I can change the world." By the time you find you can't get the right attitude, the world has changed already. We need to let in the rabbits, flowers, sea urchins, coral, granite and sand; the cities, villages, houses and churches—the entities that the technology and aesthetics of landscape organize into a picture for detached human consumption. But attempting to exit this Looking-Glass House of the aesthetic dimension proves fruitless. The clue is that hyperobjects, such

1 For an extensive discussion, see John Brinckerhoff Jackson, "Concluding with Landscapes," in: idem (ed.), *Discovering the Vernacular Landscape*. New Heaven 1984, pp. 145–158.

2 See Graham Harman, "Zero-Person and the Psyche," in: David Skrbina (ed.), *Mind that Abides: Panpsychism in the New Millennium*. Philadelphia 2009, pp. 253–282.

Stellen Sie sich vor, Sie essen eine Tüte Eis. Sie haben sich vorgenommen, dass Sie nur ein einziges Mal drüber schlecken, bis Sie diesen Moment vollkommenen Glücks empfinden. Das Glück stellt sich aber nicht ein – und das Eis schmilzt auch dahin.

Die Eistüte steht für unsere Erde. Sie schmilzt. Wir haben keine Zeit, um uns die richtigen Gedanken über sie zu machen. Wir müssen sie einfach retten. Dinge von außerhalb der Mauer ziehen uns plötzlich magisch an. Dinge, die wir jahrhundertelang ignoriert haben. Dinge, die wir selbst geschaffen haben, indem wir wiederum andere ignoriert haben: wie Plutonium oder die globale Erwärmung. Ich nenne diese Dinge *Hyperobjekte*. Hyperobjekte sind reale Dinge, die, in Zeit und Raum verteilt, massiv auftreten. Gute Beispiele für Hyperobjekte sind die bereits erwähnte globale Erwärmung und atomare Strahlung. Hyperobjekte sind riesig und so dauerhaft, dass sie die menschlichen Vorstellungen von Zeit und Raum sprengen. Hyperobjekte würden auch nicht in ein Landschaftsgemälde passen. Sie bringen einen nie in die richtige Stimmung.

Wenn wir versuchen, über unsere moderne Zeit hinaus zu denken, über diese Ära der Philosophie, Gesellschaft und Ökologie, in der wir über 200 Jahre befangen waren, dann müssen wir uns von dem Gedanken verabschieden, dass Landschaften als gerahmte Bilder an der Wand hängen, auch wenn diese Landschaften flüssig und beweglich sind, wie in einem Film.[1] Warum? Das Problem ergibt sich aus der Idee des *Rahmens*, und des Abstandes, den ein Betrachter einhalten muss, damit die Landschaft im Bild als solche erkennbar wird. Und erst durch diesen Abstand erhält die Landschaft einen subjektiven (spirituellen, ideologischen oder welches Wort Sie auch immer bevorzugen) Charakter. Denn im Bild geht es darum, welche Einstellung man braucht, um es betrachten zu können. Es geht dabei weniger um *Land* als um *Schaft*. Wir sprechen von der Stimmung einer Landschaft, von dem Gefühl, das sie in uns evoziert. Ironischerweise war es aber genau die ästhetische Distanzierung, die so sehr Teil unserer sozialen und kulturellen Praxis geworden ist, und da reden wir noch gar nicht von bestehenden Strukturen und Designs; diese Distanzierung also, die ein Teil jener Moderne war, die die abscheulichen Retter, die Hyperobjekte, in unseren sozialen psychischen und ökologischen Raum herein geholt hat. Schließlich ist es unser angebliches Bedürfnis nach sanften Hügeln und romantischen Schäferszenen, das uns dazu bringt, Entwickler abzuwimmeln, die Landschaft für Windparks erschließen wollen, die uns vom Öl unabhängig machen sollen, jenem Öl, das unter unseren Landschaften ungesehen in Rohren transportiert wird.

Die Idee, dass es die Aufgabe einer Landschaft sei, eine Stimmung in uns zu erwecken, stellt ein Problem dar, schließlich handelt es sich hierbei um eine tiefgreifende Form des

1 Für eine weiterführende Diskussion vgl. John Brinckerhoff Jackson, „Concluding with Landscapes", in: ders. (Hg.), *Discovering the Vernacular Landscape*. New Heaven 1984, S. 145–158.

Idealismus. Der Materialismus mit all seinen Abwandlungen war einfach nicht machtvoll genug, um die idealistischen Tendenzen der letzten zwei Jahrhunderte zu durchbrechen; vielleicht auch darum, weil er darauf versessen ist, die Objekte auf ihre Beziehungen zurückzuführen.[2] Idealismus, das bedeutet, es geht ausschließlich ums Subjekt, es geht ausschließlich um mich. Was für eine Ökologie soll das denn sein? Für eine ursächlich ökologische Weltanschauung müssen wir die Idee der Landschaft, die auf der Perspektive der 1. oder 3. Person basiert, hinter uns lassen, und uns stattdessen auf die Suche nach einer *Null-Person-Perspektive* machen, so absurd das auch aus einer traditionell modernistischen Sichtweise wirken mag. Wir könnten zumindest zulassen, dass andere Einheiten, seien sie nun fähig zu empfinden oder nicht, mit uns kommunizieren.

„Wenn ich nur die richtige Einstellung hinkriege, kann ich die Welt vielleicht verändern." Sobald man aber merkt, dass man die richtige Einstellung doch nicht hinkriegt, hat sich die Welt schon verändert. Wir müssen auch Raum schaffen für Kaninchen, Blumen, Seeigel, Korallen, Granit, Sand; die Städte, Dörfer, Häuser und Kirchen, jene Entitäten, welche die Technik und Ästhetik der Landschaften in ein Bild für abgelösten menschlichen Konsum verwandeln. Aber der Versuch, dieses Spiegel-Glashaus der ästhetischen Dimension zu verlassen, ist zum Scheitern verurteilt. Warum das so ist? Weil Hyperobjekte, wie globale Erwärmung und Plutonium, uns nie in Ruhe lassen. Ein Empfinden, das sich in einer Zeit der Hyperobjekte verändert haben wird, ist das Gefühl für den Abstand von Dingen und den Abstand der Dinge untereinander. Intimität wird das neue Schlüsselwort werden. Es wird kein „weg"-geben, wohin wir etwas werfen können. Eine *flache Ontologie*, in der es weder ideologische Verschränkungen noch Biegungen gibt, die unseren physischen und illusorischen Abfall in ein wie auch immer geartetes Jenseits entsorgen könnten.

Es wird keine „Welt" geben. In einer flachen Ontologie kann es keinen Hintergrund geben und daher auch keinen Vordergrund. Keine Entität und kein Ort werden hier gehätschelt werden, keinem wird besondere Bedeutung in Zusammenhang mit einer anderen Entität oder einem anderen Ort zugestanden werden. Umweltbewusstes Design wird also am Ende der Welt stehen. Entschuldigung, lieber Michael Jackson, aber: *We aren't the world*. All das bedeutet: *Etwas, das in einem neuen ökologischen Zeitalter vom Erdboden verschwinden wird, ist die Umweltschutzbewegung*. Das ist nicht leicht zu akzeptieren, aber es schaut ganz so aus, als ob jene Ideologie, die uns in die Richtung eines ökologischen Zeitalters getrieben hat, sich mit Beginn desselben auflösen wird.

Ich tausche nur zu gerne eine Welt, die aus Ganzem, Teilen und Abständen besteht, gegen eine, die Intimität erlaubt. Ich

Hyperobjects are real objects that are massively distributed in time and space. Good examples would be global warming and nuclear radiation. Hyperobjects are so vast, so long lasting, that they defy human time and spatial scales.

2 Vgl. Graham Harman, „Zero-Person and the Psyche", in: David Skrbina (Hg.), *Mind that Abides. Panpsychism in the New Millennium*. Philadelphia 2009, S. 253–282.

as global warming and plutonium, never leave us alone. One thing that will have changed in the time of hyperobjects will be our sense of proximity to other things. And to each other. Intimacy will be the new code word. There will be no "away" towards which we can throw anything. A *flat ontology* in which there are no ideological twists and bends to carry away our physical and philosophical waste into some illusory beyond.

There will be no "world." In a flat ontology, there can be no background; therefore there can be no foreground. No entity or place is pampered and special relative to any other entity or place. So ecological design will mark the end of the world. Sorry Michael Jackson: *We aren't the world*. All this means that *one thing that will disappear in a new ecological age will be environmentalism*. This really is hard to swallow, but it looks as if the ideology that started to propel us into the ecological age may dissolve as soon as we enter it.

I'm happy to swap a world of wholes and parts and distances for intimacy. I'm happy to swap knowing exactly what I'm doing and why for a more democratic argument among all beings as to what should be done. I'm happy for a time of zero landscape.

Objects, Objects, Everywhere. Imagine you have spent your whole life in a swimming pool. You have no idea that you are living in a swimming pool, but you see the rippling shadows and reflections. Then one day, the water in your pool starts to feel different. Something has changed, maybe the temperature or the composition of chemicals in the water. Slowly you begin to realize that the water you have been ignoring exists all around you. You are surrounded by a hyperobject. You exist in a hyperobject. You are inside an object! I can't stress how strange this is. Percy Shelley wrote "The awful shadow of some unseen Power / Floats through unseen among us" (*Hymn to Intellectual Beauty*, 1–2).[3] He thought he was writing about the life of the mind. Little did he know that he was writing a hymn to hyperobjects.

Yet we always imagined "world" and "reality" to be backgrounds to our foreground, neutral like stage sets—or like the distance in a landscape painting.

We are used to saying "We live in the world," "We live in reality." Yet we always imagined "world" and "reality" to be backgrounds to our foreground, neutral like stage sets—or like the distance in a landscape painting. Now we must get used to saying "We live inside an object." Sure, it's a massively distributed, changing object—but an object nonetheless. This is a supreme philosophical irony. Just when we thought we had gotten rid of stale, static, Aristotelian objects forever, and exchanged them for systems, processes, flows and ambience, back they come, bigger and stronger than ever. The result of systems thinking—thinking ecologically—has been the dis-

3 Donald H. Reiman, Neil Fraistat (eds.), *Shelley's Poetry and Prose*. New York 2002.

tausche gerne den Umstand, dass ich genau weiß, was ich gerade tue und warum ich es tue, für einen demokratischeren Diskurs aller Wesen darüber, was eigentlich getan werden müsste. Ich freue mich auf eine Zeit der *zero landscape*.

Objekte, Objekte überall. Stellen Sie sich einmal vor, Sie hätten Ihr Leben in einem Schwimmbecken verbracht. Sie wissen aber nichts davon; Sie sehen nur die verzerrten Schatten und Spiegelungen. Und eines Tages fühlt sich das Wasser in Ihrem Becken anders an. Irgendetwas hat sich verändert, vielleicht ist es die Temperatur, vielleicht die Konzentration der Chemikalien im Wasser. Und plötzlich werden Sie sich des Wassers, dessen Existenz Sie bisher ignoriert haben, bewusst. Sie merken, dass es Sie umgibt. Sie existieren in einem Hyperobjekt. Sie befinden sich innerhalb eines Objekts! Ich kann kaum ausdrücken, wie befremdend dieses Gefühl ist. Percy Shelley schrieb einst: „Der schreckliche Schatten einer unsichtbaren Macht / Gleitet ungesehen zwischen uns hindurch" (*Hymn to Intellectual Beauty*, 1–2).[3] Er dachte, er würde über das Leben des Geistes schreiben und hatte keine Ahnung, dass er eine Hymne an die Hyperobjekte schrieb.

Wir sagen immer „Wir leben in der Welt" oder „Wir leben in der Realität". Aber „Welt" und „Realität" bilden für uns den Hintergrund für unseren Vordergrund, und sie haben neutral zu sein, wie Bühnenbilder oder wie der Abstand zu einem Landschaftsbild. Und nun müssen wir uns daran gewöhnen, zu sagen: „Wir leben in einem Objekt." Natürlich handelt es sich dabei um ein weit verbreitetes, sich veränderndes Objekt, aber um ein Objekt. Das stellt die höchste philosophische Ironie dar. Gerade in jenem Moment, in dem wir glaubten, wir hätten uns von den abgestandenen, statischen, aristotelischen Objekten endlich befreit und sie durch Systeme, Prozesse, Abläufe und Milieus ersetzt, da kommen sie auch schon zurück, kräftiger und größer denn je. Das Ergebnis des Systemdenkens, eines ökologischen Denkens, führte zur Entdeckung der Hyperobjekte. Und als „Objekt" bezeichne ich nicht notwendigerweise etwas, das unbewegt und fest ist, aber doch etwas, das von uns verschieden ist und nicht nur darum existiert, weil wir es sehen können. Ich meine damit auch etwas, das finstere Tiefen aufweist und scheinbar endlose zeitliche Aussichten. Was heißt hier „endlos"? Sieben Prozent der Erderwärmung wird auch noch in *einhunderttausend Jahren* bestehen.[4] Was heißt hier groß? Die Erderwärmung ist das Ergebnis des Zusammenspiels von Photonen, also Lichtteilchen und Treibhausgasen. Sie ist so groß wie die Erde und der Abstand zwischen Erde und Sonne.

3 Donald H. Reiman, Neil Fraistat (Hg.), *Shelley's Poetry and Prose*. New York 2002.

4 David Archer, „How Long Will Global Warming Last?" in: realclimate.org/index.php/archives/2005/03/how-long-will-global-warming-last/; ders., *Global Warming. Understanding the Forecast*. Oxford 2007.

Wir werden uns nun Objekten wie der Erderwärmung bewusst, Hyperobjekten also, die unendlich viel größer sind und deutlich länger leben als wir. Keine Landschaft ist groß und langlebig genug, um ein Hyperobjekt in sich aufnehmen zu können. Hyperobjekte haben das erreicht, was jahrzehntelange Experimente der Avantgarde nicht erreicht haben: Sie haben den ästhetischen Rahmen, der den Betrachter und das Betrachtete voneinander trennte, der den ästhetischen Effekt des Abstands erzeugte, den Walter Benjamin als Aura bezeichnet hat, für immer aufgebrochen.

Und damit wären wir dann auch der Zeit der Romantik entkommen. Endlich haben wir das Zeitalter der schönen Seele hinter uns gelassen, die immer noch glaubt, dass man die Welt verändern kann, wenn man nur die perfekte Einstellung hat. Und das alles verdanken wir den Objekten mit ihrer glitzernden, dennoch zurückhaltenden Seltsamkeit.

Vier Axiome der Hyperobjekte: Zähflüssigkeit, Quetschung, Nonlokalität, Transdimensionalität. Dem Himmel sei Dank – den Objekten sei Dank. Aber jetzt kommen wir aus dem Regen der schönen Seele in die Traufe der Hyperobjekte. Die wir riefen, die Geister, werden wir nun nicht mehr los. Die Geister, die wir riefen, haben wir selbst erschaffen: die Erderwärmung zum Beispiel. Wir kommen von den Hyperobjekten nicht los. Und sie kommen von uns nicht los, denn unser Körper absorbiert radioaktive Strahlung und die Erderwärmung umgibt uns. Eine der Eigenschaften von Hyperobjekten ist ihre *Zähflüssigkeit*. Man wird sie nicht los. Daher müssen wir diese Zähflüssigkeit der Hyperobjekte in unsere Planungen miteinbeziehen. Man kann sie nicht ausschließen. Das ist wie bei der westafrikanischen Geschichte von Anansi und dem Teerbaby: Je mehr er versucht, wegzukommen, desto mehr ist er gefangen. Es handelt sich um eine Variation des „Alice-im-Garten-der-sprechenden-Blumen-Effektes".

Als Neo in *The Matrix* einen Spiegel berührt, bleibt dieser an seiner Hand haften und wird sofort von reflektierender Oberfläche zu viskoser Substanz. Das, was wir üblicherweise reflektieren, wird plötzlich zu einem eigenen Objekt, flüssig und dunkel wie Öl im schwachen Licht jenes Raumes, in dem Neo die rote Pille eingenommen hat.[5] Die übliche Interpretation dieser Szene ist, dass sich Neos Realität aufzulösen beginnt. Wenn wir auf der Ebene des klebrigen, öligen Spiegels bleiben, können aber wir eine genauso aufregende Interpretation durchführen. Denn dann löst sich nicht die Realität auf, sondern das Subjekt; die Fähigkeit, Dinge zu „spiegeln", sich von der Welt abzugrenzen so wie jemand, der eine Spiegelung in einem Spiegel betrachtet – von dem gespiegelten Objekt entrückt durch die ontologische Scheibe reflektierenden Glases. Der klebrige

5 *The Matrix*. Regie: Andy und Larry Wachowski. Warner Brothers, Village Roadshow Pictures 1999.

covery of hyperobjects. By "object" I don't mean something still and solid, necessarily, but I do mean something that is distinct from us, that doesn't only exist because we can see it. I also mean something that withdraws from access, something with shadowy depths and seemingly endless temporal vistas. How endless? Seven percent of global warming effects will still exist *one hundred thousand years from now*.[4] How big? Global warming is the result of interactions between photons and greenhouse gases. It's as big as Earth and the distance between Earth and the Sun.

We are now aware of objects such as global warming, hyperobjects that massively outsize us and outlast us. No landscape is big enough or long lasting enough to enclose hyperobjects in its frame. Hyperobejcts have finally done what decades of avant-garde experimentation have been unable to do: they have broken forever the aesthetic frame separating the viewer from the viewed and producing the aesthetic effect of distance, which Walter Benjamin called aura.

Finally we are out of the Romantic period, then. Finally we have exited the age of the beautiful soul, who imagines that having the perfect attitude will change the world. Thanks to objects, in all their glittering, withdrawn strangeness.

Four Axioms of Hyperobjects: Viscosity, Squishing, Nonlocality, Transdimensionality. Thank goodness—thank objects. But we are now out of the frying pan of the beautiful soul and into the fire of hyperobjects. It is as if we have summoned demons. Quite literally, we have: we created global warming. We are stuck with hyperobjects. They stick to us, literally: our bodies absorb nuclear radiation and we are totally surrounded by global warming. Hyperobjects have the property of being *viscous*. You can't shake them off. So we must build according to the viscosity of hyperobjects. There is no way to exclude them. It's like the story of Anansi and the Tar Baby: the harder he tries to pull away, the more he finds himself stuck. This is a modified version of the "Alice in the Garden of Talking Flowers" effect.

When Neo touches a mirror in *The Matrix* it adheres to his hand, instantly changing from reflective surface to viscous substance. The very thing that we use to reflect becomes an object in its own right, liquid and dark like oil in the dim light of the room in which Neo has taken the red pill.[5] The usual reading of this scene is that Neo's reality is dissolving. If we stay on the level of the sticky, oily mirror, however, we obtain an equally powerful reading. It's not reality that dissolves, but the subject, the very capacity to "mirror" things, to be separate from the world like someone looking at a reflection in a mirror—removed from it by an ontological sheet of reflective glass. The sticky mirror demonstrates the truth of what phenomenology calls *ingenuousness* or *sincerity*. Objects are what they are, in the sense that no matter what we are aware of, or how, there it is, impossible to shake off. In the midst of irony, there you are, being ironic. Even mirrors are what they are, no matter what they reflect. The mirror becomes a *substance*, an object. Hyperobjects push the reset button on sincerity, just as Neo discovers

4 David Archer, "How Long Will Global Warming Last?" in: realclimate.org/index.php/archives/2005/03/how-long-will-global-warming-last/; idem, *Global Warming: Understanding the Forecast*. Oxford 2007.

5 *The Matrix*. Directors: Andy and Larry Wachowski. Warner Brothers, Village Roadshow Pictures 1999.

that the mirror no longer distances his image from him in a nice, aesthetically manageable way, but sticks to him.

Hyperobjects are *squishy*. They are temporally foreshortened. Hyperobjects envelop us yet they are so massively distributed in time that they seem to taper off, like a long street stretched into the distance. Time bends them and flattens them, the same way that an electromagnetic wave front actually shortens at its leading edge. Because we can't see to the end of them, hyperobjects are necessarily uncanny. Like the empty streets and open doorways in the paintings of Giorgio de Chirico, hyperobjects seem to beckon us further into themselves, making us realize that we're already lost inside them. This recognition of being caught in and by hyperobjects is precisely a feeling of the Freudian "uncanny," a feeling of strange familiarity and familiar strangeness. We already know the weather like the back of our hand. But this is weird weather, this global warming weather. We already know light. But this is weird light, this radiation. Levi Bryant, exploring hyperobjects in a recent blog post, describes it thus:

"Hyperobjects are thus like our experience of a pool while swimming. Everywhere we are submersed within the pool, everywhere the cool water caresses our body as we move through it, yet we are nonetheless independent of the water. We produce effects in the water like diffraction patterns, causing it to ripple in particular ways, and it produces effects in us, causing our skin to get goosebumps."[6]

Space can thus no longer be construed as an absolute container, but as a spacetime manifold that is radically in the Universe, *of* it rather than ontologically outside it. Spacetime turns from a grid-like box into what Einstein fantastically calls a "reference-mollusk." Reference mollusks exist precisely *because* of hyperobjects that emanate gravitational fields. In these fields geometry is not Euclidean.[7] In an age without computer graphics that could morph a grid into rippling, swelling hollows and bumps, Einstein turns to the most squishy thing he can imagine. But I rather think we should bring back the mollusks. Hyperobjects are not infinitesimally small … thus they have Gaussian coordinates rather than Euclidean ones. *Hyperobjects are time-squished*. To this extent H. P. Lovecraft's monstrous god Cthulhu is a hyperobject, a giant squid-like being floating asleep in a non-Euclidean realm out there in the Universe. Our ecological devastation has summoned these Cthulhu-like hyperobjects to terrorize us.

Hyperobjects are *nonlocal*. You can only see parts of them in any one place at any one moment of time. I use the term "nonlocal" from quantum theory. To those great Victorian period discoveries—evolution, capital, the unconscious—we must now add three hyperobjects: spacetime, ecological interconnection (giving rise to global warming, for instance) and nonlocality. These discoveries all share something insofar as they humiliate the human, decisively decentering us from a place of pampered privilege in the scheme of things. Nonlocality is perhaps the most drastic of all of these, since it implies that the notion of being located at all is only an epiphenomenon to a deeper, atemporal implicate order. The hyperobjects concept is very handy

6 Levi Bryant, "Hyperobjects and OOO," in: larvalsubjects.wordpress.com/2010/11/11/hyperobjects-and-ooo/.

7 Albert Einstein, *The Meaning of Relativity*. New York 2003, p. 61.

Spiegel beweist, was die Phänomenologie *Offenheit oder Aufrichtigkeit* nennt. Objekte sind das, was sie sind. Ganz egal, ob und wie wir uns ihrer bewusst sind, wir können sie nicht loswerden. Mitten in der Ironie befinden wir uns und sind ironisch. Auch Spiegel sind das, was sie sind, gleichgültig, was sie widerspiegeln. Der Spiegel wird selbst zur Substanz, zu einem Objekt. Hyperobjekte drücken die Rückstelltaste für Aufrichtigkeit, so wie Neo merkt, dass der Spiegel sein Bild nicht mehr auf nette, ästhetisch handhabbare Weise auf Distanz bringt, sondern an ihm kleben bleibt.

Hyperobjekte sind *gequetscht*. Sie sind zeitweise verkürzt. Hyperobjekte hüllen uns ein, aber sind so massiv in der Zeit verstreut, dass sie sich zu entfernen scheinen, wie eine lange Straße, die sich in weite Ferne streckt. Die Zeit dreht und wendet sie, genauso wie eine elektromagnetische Welle an ihrem Anfang verkürzt ist. Da wir ihr Ende nicht erkennen können, sind Hyperobjekte per se unheimlich. Wie leere Straßen und offene Türen in den Bildern von Giorgio de Chirico, scheinen uns die Objekte in sich hineinbitten zu wollen, dadurch erkennen wir aber auch, dass wir uns schon in ihnen verloren haben. Das Gefühl, in und durch Hyperobjekte gefangen zu sein, entspricht genau dem Freud'schen „unheimlich", einem seltsamen Gefühl von Vertrautsein und Fremdsein. Wir kennen das Wetter schon wie unsere Westentasche. Aber dieses Wetter ist seltsam, dieses Wetter der Erderwärmung. Wir kennen auch schon das Licht. Aber es ist ein seltsames Licht, diese Strahlung. Levi Bryant beschreibt das in einem Posting über Hyperobjekte so:

„Hyperobjekte sind also so wie unsere Wahrnehmung von Schwimmbecken beim Schwimmen. Wir sind zwar zur Gänze in dem Becken untergetaucht, überall von Wasser umgeben, das unseren Körper liebkost, während wir hindurchschwimmen, und doch sind wir und das Wasser voneinander getrennt. Wir verursachen im Wasser Effekte wie Verzerrungen, wodurch spezielle Muster entstehen, aber auch in uns werden Effekte verursacht, wir bekommen Gänsehaut."[6]

Raum kann daher nicht mehr als absoluter Behälter konstruiert werden, sondern als raumzeitliche Mannigfaltigkeit, die zutiefst *im* und *vom* Universum existiert und sich nicht ontologisch außerhalb desselben befindet. Raumzeit verwandelt sich daher von einer gitterartigen Schachtel in das, was Einstein so fantastisch als „Referenz-Mollusken" bezeichnet hat. Referenz-Mollusken gibt es gerade, *weil* es Hyperobjekte gibt, die Gravitationsfelder erzeugen. In diesen Feldern ist die Geometrie nicht die euklidsche.[7] In einer Zeit ohne Computergrafiken, die ein Gitter in Schwingungen versetzen, Wellenberge und -täler erzeugen können, stürzt Einstein sich auf das

6 Levi Bryant, „Hyperobjects and OOO", in: larvalsubjects.wordpress.com/2010/11/11/hyperobjects-and-ooo/.

7 Albert Einstein, *The Meaning of Relativity*. New York 2003, S. 61.

Glitschigste, was er sich vorstellen kann. Ich glaube aber, dass wir die Mollusken wieder zurückbringen sollten. Denn Hyperobjekte sind nicht unendlich klein, daher sind ihre Koordinaten auch eher die von Gauß als von Euklid. *Hyperobjekte sind zeitgequetscht*. In diesem Sinne ist H. P. Lovecrafts monströser Gott Cthulhu ein Hyperobjekt, ein riesengroßes, tintenfischähnliches Wesen, das schlafend in einem nicht-euklidischen Reich irgendwo da draußen im Universum treibt. Unsere ökologische Verwüstung hat diese Cthulhu-artigen Hyperobjekte herbeigerufen, uns in Angst und Schrecken zu versetzen.

Hyperobjekte sind *nicht-lokal*. Man kann immer und überall nur Teile von ihnen sehen. Ich verwende den Terminus „nichtlokal" aus der Quantentheorie. Den herausragenden Entdeckungen des viktorianischen Zeitalters – die Evolution, das Kapital, das Unbewusste – müssen wir noch drei weitere Hyperobjekte hinzufügen: Raumzeit, ökologische Abhängigkeiten (wodurch zum Beispiel die Erderwärmung begünstigt wurde) und Nichtlokalität. Alle diese Entdeckungen haben eines gemeinsam: Sie demütigen den Menschen und verweisen ihn von einem privilegierten Platz an den Rand. Nonlokalität scheint das drastischste von allen zu sein, schließlich impliziert sie, dass die Idee der Ortsgebundenheit nur ein Epiphänomen einer tiefer gehenden, zeitlosen impliziten Ordnung ist. Das Konzept der Hyperobjekte ist für ein ökologisches Zeitalter sehr praktisch, denn es imaginiert augenscheinlich transzendente Dinge, wie Evolution oder Kapital, als diskrete *Objekte*, wie groß und seltsam sie auch sein mögen.

Halten Sie den Verlauf der Evolution an und Sie werden sie nicht sehen können. Stellen Sie sich unter eine Regenwolke und Sie werden nicht die Erderwärmung auf Ihren Kopf tropfen fühlen. Zerschneiden Sie Ihren Mantel in tausend Stücke und Sie werden kein Kapital darin finden. Und jetzt probieren Sie einmal, auf das Unbewusste zu zeigen. Haben Sie's? Das geht auch nicht, oder?

Wenn Sie spüren, wie Regentropfen auf Ihren Kopf fallen, fühlen Sie irgendwie immer auch das Klima. Genauer gesagt, fühlen Sie die Klimaveränderung, die als globale Erderwärmung bekannt ist. Aber die globale Erwärmung als solche spüren Sie nicht. Nirgends auf der langen Liste der Wetterkatastrophen werden Sie die globale Erwärmung aufgelistet finden. Aber die Erwärmung ist so real wie dieser Satz. Nicht nur das, sie ist auch zähflüssig. Sie klebt immer an einem, egal wo auf diesem Planeten man sich gerade befindet. Wie erklären wir uns das? Dadurch, dass die Erderwärmung, wie alle Hyperobjekte, nichtlokal ist: Man findet sie überall in Zeit und Raum.

Hyperobjekte sind *transdimensional*. Sie bestehen aus einem hochdimensionalen Phasenraum, jenem Raum, in dem sie mögliche Aktionen setzen. Darum kann man auch immer nur Teile davon gleichzeitig sehen. Für eine flache Welt, die aus zwei Dimensionen besteht, ist ein Apfel ein Hyperobjekt. Wenn der Apfel sich durch die flache Welt bewegt, sehen die

Nonlocality is perhaps the most drastic of all of these, since it implies that the notion of being located at all is only an epiphenomenon to a deeper, atemporal implicate order. The hyperobjects concept is very handy for an ecological age, because it imagines supposedly transcendental things such as evolution or capital as discrete *objects*, vast and strange though they are.

for an ecological age, because it imagines supposedly transcendental things such as evolution or capital as discrete *objects*, vast and strange though they are.

Stop the tape of evolution anywhere and you won't see it. Stand under a rain cloud and it's not global warming you'll feel falling on your head. Cut your coat into a thousand pieces—you won't find capital in there. Now try pointing to the unconscious. Did you catch it? Now try to point at a world tube. Same problem, right?

When you feel raindrops falling on your head, you are experiencing climate, in some sense. In particular you are experiencing the climate change known as global warming. But you are never directly experiencing global warming as such. Nowhere in the long list of catastrophic weather events will you find global warming. But global warming is as real as this sentence. Not only that, it's viscous. It never stops sticking to you, no matter where you move on planet Earth. How can we account for this? By arguing that global warming, like all hyperobjects, is nonlocal: it's massively distributed in time and space.

Hyperobjects are *transdimensional*. They exist in a high dimensional phase space, the space of possible actions they might take. This is why only pieces of them can be seen at a time. An apple is a hyperobject for a flat world of two dimensions. As the apple traverses the flat world, flat people see sections of the apple, growing larger and smaller over time and finally vanishing.

This way of seeing hyperobjects (using metaphors borrowed from relativity, quantum theory, engineering and phenomenology) affects the way we see all other objects. Think of a flower such as a daffodil. The crinkly, fractal edges of the yellow flower are the latest performances of algorithms buried in the genomic structure of the plant. The smooth bell-like curvature of the flower is a diagram of a slightly earlier execution of these algorithms. The harder, finger-like place where the flower joins the stem of the plant is a record of a still earlier algorithmic unfolding. The daffodil is a map of an algorithm in a three-dimensional phase space. Your face, with its lines and crevices, is a map of everything that happened to you. When you look at objects you are looking at time. Time is not a container of objects. It undulates inside them and ripples along their surfaces. Likewise, space is not a container of objects. Space is just a general word for large objects that contain us and daffodils and so on.

Design in the Time of Hyperobjects. The design we must do in an age of hyperobjects will inevitably take them into account, because we can't unthink our knowledge of them. This means that design must account for thousand, ten thousand, and hundred thousand year timescales. It must account for Plutonium 239, which remains dangerously radioactive for 24,100 years. Old landscape is predicated on hiding the artifice, appearances of naturalness and the erasure of traces. Design in the era of hyperobjects can't do this—however much it tries. This means that postmodern and deconstructive architecture, which revealed the production process, was strangely predictive of the new ecological age. However, while postmodern architecture still seems to make a point about human difference (from the nonhuman)—foregrounding artificiality as opposed to "nature" for instance—architecture and landscape design in the time of hyperobjects will precisely show that humans

Flachländer Teile des Apfels, die mit der Zeit größer und dann wieder kleiner werden, bis sie schließlich ganz verschwinden.

Die Art, wie wir Hyperobjekte betrachten (unter Verwendung von Metaphern, die wir der Relativitätstheorie, der Quantentheorie, der Technik und der Phänomenologie entlehnt haben), beeinflusst die Art, wie wir alle anderen Objekte sehen. Denken Sie zum Beispiel an eine Narzisse. Die zerknitterten fraktalen Ränder dieser gelben Blume sind der Ausdruck der letzten Ergebnisse von Algorithmen, die der genetischen Struktur der Pflanze zugrunde liegen. Die glatte glockenartige Rundung der Pflanze ist gleichsam ein Diagramm einer ein wenig früheren Ausprägung der Algorithmen; und der härtere, wie ein Finger geformte Ort, an dem die Blüte in den Stängel übergeht, ist der Ausdruck einer wiederum früheren Ausprägung der Algorithmen. Die Narzisse stellt sich als eine Karte von Algorithmen in einem dreidimensionalen Phasenraum dar. Genauso ist Ihr Gesicht mit all seinen Linien und Falten eine Landkarte all dessen, was Sie erlebt haben. Wenn Sie Objekte betrachten, betrachten Sie auch die Zeit. Zeit ist kein Behälter für Objekte. Sie bewegt sich vielmehr wellenförmig in ihnen und zieht Kreise auf ihrer Oberfläche. Und auch Raum ist kein Behälter für Objekte. Raum ist nur ein allgemeiner Begriff für größere Objekte, die uns und Narzissen und andere Dinge enthalten.

Design in den Zeiten der Hyperobjekte. Das Design in den Zeiten der Hyperobjekte wird diese selbstverständlich mit einbeziehen müssen, denn wir können unser Wissen um sie nicht ungewusst machen. Das bedeutet, dass Design sich in tausend, zehntausend, hunderttausend Jahren bewähren muss. Es muss Plutonium 239 miteinbeziehen, das 24.100 Jahre lang gefährlich radioaktiv bleibt. Alte Landschaften sind darauf ausgerichtet, das Künstliche zu verstecken, natürliches Aussehen zu bewahren und jedwede Spuren zu verwischen. Design kann das in den Zeiten der Hyperobjekte aber nicht leisten, ganz egal, wie oft es versucht wird. Die postmoderne, dekonstruktivistische Architektur, die den Produktionsprozess enthüllt hat, hat die neue ökologische Zeit vorhergesagt. Während die postmoderne Architektur noch immer die Unterscheidung des Menschlichen (vom Nicht-Menschlichen) feiert und dabei Künstlichkeit z. B. der „Natur" gegenüberstellt, werden Architektur und Landschaftsarchitektur in den Zeiten der Hyperobjekte klar aufzeigen, dass die Menschheit ganz klar „in" dem ist, was wir immer noch (fälschlich) die „Welt" nennen. Im Gegensatz zu postmodernen Versatzstücken wird sich hyperobjektives Design um das Thema Koexistenz drehen: fast dasselbe, nur ohne die zynische Distanz.

Von Malerei und Kino, den ästhetischen Formen der Landschaftsarchitektur, bewegen wir uns hin zu Landkarten von Algorithmen im Phasenraum. Das ist es, was Supercomputer heute tun können, wenn sie die Klimasituation darstellen. Das

Problem dabei ist natürlich, dass wir das selbst nicht mehr sehen, die Computer sehen für uns, wir sehen nur mehr Daten oder dünne Scheiben des Phasenraums, so dargestellt, dass es verwendbar ist. Panik und Leugnung sind daher beim Thema Klimaerwärmung durchaus verständlich. All das, vom Phänomen an sich bis zu der Art, wie wir es betrachten müssen, stellt für Eigennutz, Individualität, Nationalismus, Anthropozentrismus etc. eine fundamentale Bedrohung dar. Vielleicht sogar für den Kapitalismus selbst. Bald schon werden wir wissen, ob der Kapitalismus hierfür ein gangbares System ist. Nehmen wir nur das Beispiel von Plutonium 239. Keine Theorie des Eigennutzes, die bis dato entwickelt wurde, konnte bisher ein Endlager entwerfen, das das tödlich radioaktive Material für die 24.100 Jahre aufnehmen kann, die es zum Abbau braucht. Wir müssen also etwas entwerfen, das weder mit mir noch mit anderen Menschen auf der Welt heute etwas zu tun hat, schließlich wird niemand, der mit mir oder einem anderen Menschen der jetzt lebt, auch nur irgendwie verwandt ist, in 24.100 Jahren noch am Leben sein. Und doch wird jeder einzelne, der dann am Leben ist, von jenen Entscheidungen beeinflusst werden, die wir in Bezug auf Plutonium 239 treffen.[8] Sobald wir uns des Langzeiteffekts von Hyperobjekten bewusst werden, können wir dieses Bewusstsein nicht mehr ablegen, demzufolge korrodieren die Hyperobjekte unsere Fähigkeit, heute stimmige Entscheidungen zu treffen.[9] Hyperobjekte zwingen uns, in und mit diesem Paradoxon zu leben und damit zu entwerfen.

Wir können leicht überrascht sein über das, was passiert ist. Dies ist das Ende der Welt. Nicht im Sinne von Francis Fukuyama oder wie es sich in der Offenbarung des Johannes darstellt, aber das Ende der ästhetischen Idee der „Welt“ als einem umfangenden, Abstand haltenden und distanzierten Horizont. Wir leben jetzt nach dem Ende der Welt, in der Zeit der Hyperobjekte.

8 Vgl. Derek Parfit, *Reasons and Persons*. Oxford 1984, S. 355–357, hier S. 361.

9 Ebd., S. 371–377.

are radically "in" what we still (incorrectly) call "the world." Rather than postmodern pastiche, then, hyperobjective design will be about coexistence: almost the same thing, but without the cynical distance.

From painting and cinema, the aesthetic modes of landscape, we move to plots and maps of algorithms in phase space. This is what enormously powerful processors can now do when they map climate. The trouble is, of course, that we're not seeing it ourselves anymore. Computers see it for us, then we see data or slices of that phase space, rendered in some way to make it usable. The panic and denial about global warming is entirely justified. The whole thing, from the phenomenon itself to the ways we have to see it are profoundly threatening to self-interest, individualism, nationalism, anthropocentrism, you name it. Possibly even capitalism itself. We'll see fairly shortly whether capitalism is up for the job. Take Plutonium 239, for example. No self-interest theory yet devised can cope with building the right storage to house deadly radioactive materials for the 24,100 years they take to decay. Instead, we shall need to design without a view to look after Number 1, or Number 2, or even Number 1 million, because no one meaningfully related to me, not even by the craziest distance imaginable, will be alive 24,100 years from now. Yet *everyone* alive then will be affected by decisions we make regarding Plutonium 239.[8] Once we become aware of long-term effects of hyperobjects, we cannot abolish this awareness, and so they corrode our ability to make firm decisions in the present.[9] Hyperobjects force us to live this paradox, and design with it.

It's fine for us to be amazed at what has happened. This is the end of the world. Not as Francis Fukuyama or the Book of Revelations imagine it, but the end of the aesthetic idea of "world" as an environing, distancing and distanced horizon. We are now living after the end of the world, in the time of hyperobjects.

8 See Derek Parfit, *Reasons and Persons*. Oxford 1984, pp. 355–357, here p. 361.

9 Ibid., pp. 371–377.

1 *Molecular Invasion*, Installationsansicht installation view, The Corcoran, Washington, D.C.

Critical Art Ensemble

Molecular Invasion

The practice of "contestational biology" as practiced by Critical Art Ensemble (CAE)—a collective of artists and activists founded in the United States in the late 1980s—was developed as a response to the increasing ubiquity of bioengineering, and the effects of transgenics not only on the consumer food chain but also on conventional agricultural practice, the character of which has been forever changed by the scientific/economic impact of large-scale agribusiness industry.

Critical Art Ensemble. *Molekulare Invasion*. Das Verfahren einer „kontroversen Biologie", wie es von den Aktivisten und dem Künsterkolletiv des in den späten 1980er-Jahren gegündeten Critical Art Ensemble (CAE) praktiziert wird, wurde als Antwort auf die zunehmende Allgegenwart der Biotechnologie hin entwickelt. Entwickelt auch in Bezug auf Auswirkungen gentechnischer Eingriffe, welche nicht nur auf die Nahrungskette von Konsumenten wirken, sondern auch bezüglich wissenschaftlich/ökonomischer Einwirkungen der Agro-Business Industrie, mit denen der Charakter der konventionellen landwirtschaftlichen Praxis für immer verändert wurde.

JEFFREY KASTNER

CAE's program has involved various applications of tactical media—including publishing books and pamphlets, creating websites, and developing museological displays—both to examine and to formulate modes of social and political intervention within a range of contemporary biopolitical issues, from assisted reproductive technologies to electronic surveillance to military production. (The group gained visibility when one of its founders, Steve Kurtz, was arrested in 2004 on suspicion of terrorism after FBI agents discovered the art professor's home biology lab. After four years of hounding Kurtz, the government eventually dropped all charges against him in 2008.)

Molecular Invasion is representative of the group's ambitions and disciplinary breadth. Described as a "participatory science-theater work" made with the help of students from Washington D.C.'s Corcoran School of Art and Design and exhibited at the Corcoran Gallery in 2002, the project—spearheaded by CAE members Beatriz da Costa and Claire Pentacost—was built around a collective attempt to reverse-engineer various genetically-modified food crops (soy, canola, and corn). Operating along the margins of both science and cultural critique, *Molecular Invasion* was further accompanied by an elaborate Web presence, which included sites for fictitious firms like Bio Com, whose mission is described as seeking "to completely invade the flesh with vision and mapping technologies (initiating a program of total body control from its holistic, exterior configuration to its microscopic constellations), and to develop the political and economic frontiers of flesh products and services"; an expansive online mission statement ("With the combination of traditional, electronic, and biological means of resistance, hopefully enough inertia can be introduced into the biotech industries that there will be time to do long-term, replicated studies that will sort out the useful products from the pollutants for profits"); and a book of the same title, published by Autonomedia in New York.

Part dense jeremiad, part call to arms, part handbook for revolution, *The Molecular Invasion* proposes to expose the degree to which capital and a kind of imperialist politics have dictated the aspirations of biological science, not just in practical but, they argue, just as importantly in symbolic terms: "Representations of the transgenic face a deep contradiction," they write.

Part dense jeremiad, part call to arms, part handbook for revolution, *The Molecular Invasion* proposes to expose the degree to which capital and a kind of imperialist politics have dictated the aspirations of biological science, not just in practical but, they argue, just as importantly in symbolic terms: "Representations of the transgenic face a deep contradiction," they write. "The spectacle of transgenics, as usual, tends to consistently support profit initiatives, and promote the idea that the 'free' market always works

Das Programm des CAE umfasst diverse taktische Medienanwendungen wie die Herausgabe von Büchern und Broschüren, das Erstellen von Webseiten und die Entwicklung von Ausstellungen, um Methoden sozialer und politischer Intervention innerhalb der Bandbreite zeitgenössischer bio-politischer Themen – von Reproduktionstechnologien über elektronische Überwachung bis zu militärischer Entwicklung – zu untersuchen und zu formulieren. (Die Gruppe erreichte erste Publizität, als einer ihrer Gründer, Steve Kurtz, im Jahr 2004 aufgrund Terrorismusverdachts festgenommen wurde, nachdem FBI-Agenten das Biologielabor im Haus des Kunstprofessors entdeckt hatten. Nach einer vier Jahre andauernden Verdächtigung von Kurtz ließ die Regierung schließlich im Jahr 2008 alle Anschuldigungen gegen ihn fallen.)

Molekulare Invasion ist bezeichnend für die Ambitionen der Gruppe und ihre disziplinäre Bandbreite. Das als „partizipatorisches Wissenschaftstheater" beschriebe Projekt wurde mit Hilfe von Studenten der Corcoran School of Art and Design in Washington DC ausgeführt und 2002 in der Corcoran Galerie ausgestellt, behandelte den von CAE-Mitgliedern Beatriz da Costa und Claire Pentacost geleiteten kollektiven Versuch, einige genetisch veränderte Lebensmittel (Soja, Raps und Mais) technologisch zurückzuentwickeln. Das Projekt *Molekulare Invasion* agierte an den Rändern von Wissenschaft und Kulturkritik und wurde zusätzlich von einer ausgefeilten Webpräsenz begleitet, einschließlich Seiten fiktiver Firmen wie Bio Com, deren Mission als der Versuch beschrieben wurde, „die Fleischproduktion mit Bild- und Erfassungstechnologien vollkommen zu durchdringen (indem ein Programm zur totalen Kontrolle des Körpers von seiner ganzheitlichen, äußeren Konfiguration bis zu dessen mikroskopischen Konstellationen gestartet wird) und um die politischen und wirtschaftlichen Grenzen von Fleischprodukten und Dienstleistungen darzulegen." Begleitet war dies von einem umfangreichen Online *mission-statement* („Durch die Kombination von traditionellen, elektronischen und biologischen Mitteln kann hoffentlich eine gewisse Schwerfälligkeit in der Biotechnik-Industrie erzeugt werden, so dass genügend Zeit bleibt, um langfristige Versuchsreihen auszuführen, die nützliche Produkte von schädlichem Profittreiben trennt"), als auch von einem Buch gleichen Titels, das von Autonomedia in New York herausgegeben wurde.

Teils eine anspruchsvolle Hiobsbotschaft, teils ein Ruf zu den Waffen und teils ein revolutionäres Handbuch schlägt die *Molekulare Invasion* vor, jenen Grad freizulegen, bis zu welchem das Kapital und eine Form imperialistischer Politik die Anstrengungen der Biowissenschaft diktiert haben – nicht nur unter praktischen, sondern ebenso bedeutsam, wie sie feststellen – unter symbolischen Gesichtspunkten: „Darstellungen der Gentechnologie sehen sich mit einer tiefen Widersprüchlichkeit konfrontiert." „Das gentechnische Spektakel neigt

wie üblich zur konsequenten Unterstützung profitabler Initiativen und dazu, die Vorstellung zu verbreiten, dass der „freie" Markt immer zum Wohl öffentlicher Interessen arbeitet, indem er uns vor Umwelt-, Gesundheits- und Bevölkerungsproblemen bewahrt. Bedauernswert für diese Unternehmenskultur widersprechen die historischen Darstellungen der Ursachen von sozialer Armut und Umweltverschmutzung jedoch den utopischen Darstellungen gentechnisch veränderter Produkte." *Molekulare Invasion* und das Critical Art Ensemble arbeiten somit in einem Raum zwischen wissenschaftlichen Technologien und rhetorischen Strategien, um das etablierte Verständnis der Beziehung zwischen dem Natürlichen und dem Politischen zu erschüttern.

Übersetzung Claudia Wrumnig

in the public interest by saving us from environmental, health, and population problems. Unfortunately for corporate culture, the historical representation of the rules of social purity and pollution clash with the utopian representations of transgenic products." It's in a space between scientific technologies and rhetorical strategies that *Molecular Invasion*, and Critical Art Ensemble, work to unsettle received wisdom about the relationship between the natural and the political.

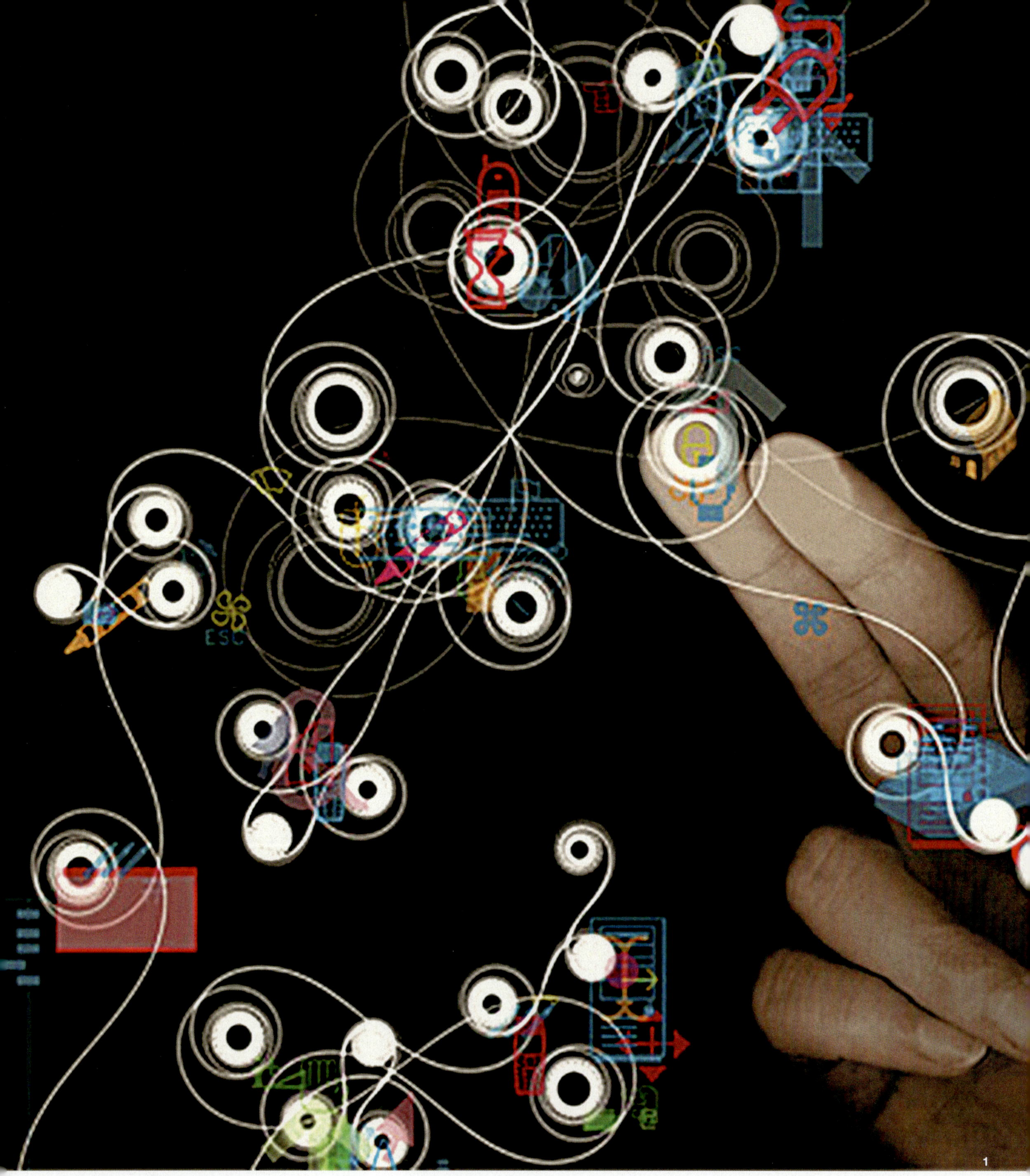

1

1 Filmstill, interaktives Interface, Design © Jonas Loh. Film-still, Interactive Interface, Design © Jonas Loh.

Auf dem Weg zu einem Landschaftsbegriff

für die urbane politische Ökologie

Landschaft, Macht und „Ökologie“. In den letzten Jahrzehnten wurde Landschaft in den Kulturwissenschaften zunehmend als eine „kulturelle Repräsentation“ bzw. „symbolische Form“ begriffen. Einige Analysen gingen dabei der Frage nach, wie die gegebenen historisch-geografischen Machtverhältnisse in der und durch die Landschaft naturalisiert und reproduziert werden.[1]

Towards a Landscape Idea for Urban Political Ecology. Landscape, Power and "Ecology." Over the past few decades, landscape has been increasingly understood as a "cultural representation" or a "symbolic form" in cultural sciences. In this context, some analyses have explored the question of how the historically-geographically given power relations are naturalized and reproduced in and via the landscape.[1]

ANA JEINIĆ

Der vorliegende Text gründet auf der These, dass die kulturellen Repräsentationen nicht nur passiv den Veränderungen der Machtverhältnisse „nachlaufen", sondern dass sie zu den Orten gehören, an denen sich gesellschaftlicher Wandel vollzieht.

Der Ausgangspunkt meiner Überlegungen ist ein bestimmter Prozess der Transformation des Landschaftsbegriffes, der sich in der gegenwärtigen landschaftsarchitektonischen Praxis vollzieht. Ursache dieser Transformation ist eine Reihe verschiedener Diskurse, die unter dem schwammigen Sammelbegriff „Ökologie" gefasst werden. Diese „Ökologisierung" des Landschaftsbegriffes hat zur Folge, dass auch die Frage nach der Beziehung zwischen *Landschaft* und *Macht*[2] sich im Zusammenhang mit der Frage nach der Beziehung zwischen *Umweltdiskursen* und *Macht* neu stellt. Es wäre also zu untersuchen, welche Umweltdiskurse (und die für sie charakteristischen Ökologiebegriffe) die landschaftsarchitektonische Praxis durchdringen, welche Änderungen des Landschaftsbegriffes dadurch ausgelöst werden, und ob die so geänderten Landschaftsbegriffe als Instrumente zur Transformation der Machtasymmetrien geeignet sind, oder ob sie selbst eher zu deren Maskierung und Reproduktion beitragen. Mit der Identifizierung eines Vektors, der die Landschaft in Richtung eines potenziell kritisch-transformativen Raumkonzeptes zu rücken vermag, geht somit die Identifizierung eines entsprechenden Ökologiebegriffes einher. Durch eine Diskussion des „Manifests für die urbane politische Ökologie"[3] werde ich untersuchen, ob dort ein solcher Ökologiebegriff enthalten ist, um einem ihm entsprechenden Landschaftsbegriff auf die Spur zu kommen. Vorangestellt sei die Interpretation von zwei anderen Umweltdiskursen (der „Systemökologie"[4] und der an das Konzept des „ökologischen Fußabdrucks" gebundenen Diskurse) sowie der ihnen entsprechenden Landschaftsbegriffe, da die urbane politische Ökologie als eine kritische Antwort auf andere Positionen in der Umweltdebatte entstanden ist.

Der vorliegende Text gründet auf der These, dass die kulturellen Repräsentationen nicht nur passiv den Veränderungen der Machtverhältnisse „nachlaufen", sondern dass sie zu den Orten gehören, an denen sich gesellschaftlicher Wandel vollzieht.

Untersuchung und Förderung der „ökologischen Gesundheit". Die *Produktion*, als ein Modell des Umweltbezuges, gehört zu den zentralen

1 Bezeichnend in dieser Hinsicht sind unter anderen die folgenden zwei Texte: Denis E. Cosgrove, *Social Formation and Symbolic Landscape*. Madison, Wisconsin 1984; und W. J. T. Mitchell (Hg.), *Landscape and Power*. Chicago und London 1994.

2 So der Titel eines berühmten Aufsatzes von W. J. T. Mitchell (Anm. 1).

3 Nik Heynen, Maria Kaika, Erik Swyngedouw, „Urban Political Ecology. Politicizing the Production of Urban Natures", in: dies. (Hg.), *In the Nature of Cities. Urban Political Ecology and the Politics of Urban Metabolism*. London und New York 2006.

4 Vgl. T. J. Demos, „The Politics of Sustainability: Art and Ecology", in: *Radical Nature. Art and Architecture for a Changing Planet 1969–2009*. Ausst.-Kat., London 2009.

The argument I pursue here is based on the assumption that cultural representations (including landscape) do not just passively follow the changes of power relations, but that they belong to the places in which social change takes place.

The starting point of my reflections is a certain process of change in the concept of landscape which is under way in current landscape design practice. This change was triggered by a series of different discourses gathered under the vague and ambiguous concept of "ecology." It results from this "ecologization" of the concept of landscape that the question of the relationship between *landscape* and *power*[2] needs now to be reformulated by relating it to the question of the relationship between *environmental discourses* and *power*. Thus it would be necessary to study which environmental discourses (and their specific concepts of ecology) penetrate landscape design practice and whether the new concepts of landscape emerging in this process can potentially contribute to change (or rather merely to a disguising and reproduction) of the existing power asymmetries. The identification of a vector that could shift the landscape in the direction of a potentially critical-transformative spatial tool (in regard to the aforementioned asymmetries) is thus accompanied by the identification of an adequate concept of ecology. I will try to ascertain, through a discussion of the "Manifesto for Urban Political Ecology,"[3] whether the latter contains such a concept, in order to track down an idea of landscape that could correspond to it. Since Urban Political Ecology has developed as a critical answer to other positions in the environmental debate, I shall begin with the interpretation of two other environmental discourses ("system ecology"[4] and the discourses bound to the "Ecological Footprint" concept) and of the corresponding concepts of landscape, in order to contextualize the emerging landscape idea for Urban Political Ecology in the existing dynamic field of mutually interrelated landscape architecture practice and environmental debate.

Examining and Promoting "Ecological Health." The *production* as a model of relation towards environment belongs to the core concepts of modernism – in modern discourses humans have primarily been considered as *productive subjects*. In Marxist discourses in particular, the aptitude to produce

1 The following two texts are particularly significant in this aspect: Denis E. Cosgrove, *Social Formation and Symbolic Landscape*. Madison, Wisconsin 1984; and W. J. T. Mitchell (ed.), *Landscape and Power*. Chicago and London 1994.

2 The title of a celebrated article by W. J. T. Mitchell (fn. 1).

3 Nik Heynen, Maria Kaika, Erik Swyngedouw, "Urban Political Ecology: Politicizing the Production of Urban Natures," in: idem (ed.), *In the Nature of Cities: Urban Political Ecology and the Politics of Urban Metabolism*. London and New York 2006.

4 See T. J. Demos, "The Politics of Sustainability: Art and Ecology," in: *Radical Nature: Art and Architecture for a Changing Planet 1969–2009*. Exhib. cat., London 2009.

(and to *work* in the sense of pursuing a productive activity) was considered the quality of the human species that enabled mankind to *dominate* nature and to *emancipate* itself from its constraints.

The early environmental movement evolved as a critical reaction to the modern *production-domination paradigm* insofar as it represented the ideological background of industrialization, which was considered responsible for the enormous environmental pollution and destruction.[5] Taking up these issues, a new current of the environmentalist movement—which I shall qualify as "system ecology," using the term deployed by T. J. Demos—developed in the early 1960s and 1970s.[6] This new environmental discourse shared with the ecological concepts formulated in the 19th century the assumption of the *unity of universal nature*[7] as well as the critical attitude towards the modernist idea of dominating nature. However, what was new was the rejection of the idea of *nurturing conservation* as the unique method for saving nature. The system-ecological theories confronted this idea with the concept of promoting nature's "fitness" (nature now being understood as the universal cybernetic system)—the optimum state of the environmental system (homeostasis)[8] being considered determinable by means of the rational methods developed in the ecological science. The system-ecological environmental discourse thus yielded a new paradigm of how to refer to the environment, a paradigm that was based neither on the idea of *conserving* nor on that of *dominating* nature, but rather on the concept of *"medical control"* of the environmental system. In other words, it was then neither about dominating nature, nor about returning to a presumed original state, but about "helping" it to maintain a "healthy" state, with that healthy state not necessarily being identical with the "original" one; because a healthy system can (and must) continuously change.

The modernist paradigm of the relation towards environment based on the conceptual pair *production/domination* allowed the revelation of the power asymmetry resulting from the unequal distribution of wealth (generated through production processes) amongst "producing subjects." Since within that conceptual frame only human actants could be acknowledged as producing subjects, whereas everything else was considered a passive object for productive interventions, another essential asymmetry remained largely invisible in modernist

5 For a detailed description of the early environmental movement, see: Ramachandra Guha, *Environmentalism: A Global History*. New York 2000.

6 See Demos 2009 (fn. 4).

7 Gregory Bateson, whose work is paradigmatic for the system-ecological discourse, stands for a certain variant of this idea. In his work nature is understood as the universal cybernetic system, to which the mind is immanent. See Gregory Bateson, *Steps to Ecology of Mind* [1972]. Chicago and London 2000.

8 Ibid.

Begriffen der Moderne – die Menschen wurden in den modernen Diskursen in erster Linie als *produktive Subjekte* betrachtet. Besonders in den marxistischen Diskursen wurde die Fähigkeit der Produktion (und die *Arbeit* als produktive Tätigkeit) als diejenige Eigenschaft der menschlichen Gattung gesehen, die es der Menschheit ermöglicht, die Natur zu *beherrschen* und sich dadurch von ihren Zwängen zu *emanzipieren*.

Die frühe Umweltbewegung entstand als eine kritische Reaktion auf das moderne *Produktion-Herrschaft*-Paradigma, insofern dieses den ideologischen Hintergrund der für die enorme Umweltverschmutzung und -zerstörung verantwortlichen Industrialisierung darstellte.[5] Daran anknüpfend entwickelte sich in den späten 1960er- und frühen 1970er-Jahren des 20. Jhs. eine neue Strömung der Umweltbewegung, die ich in Anlehnung an T. J. Demos als „Systemökologie" bezeichne.[6] Das system-ökologische Denken teilte mit den im 19. Jh. formulierten Umweltschutzideen die Annahme einer *Einheit der universalen Natur*[7] sowie die Kritik an der modernen Idee der Naturbeherrschung. Neu war hingegen der Abschied von der Idee der pflegenden Konservierung der Natur als der einzigen Methode zu ihrer Rettung. Dieser Idee wurde nun die Vorstellung von der Sorge um die „Fitness" der (im Sinne eines allumfassenden kybernetischen Systems konzeptualisierten) Natur entgegengestellt, wobei der optimale Zustand des Umweltsystems – die Homöostase[8] – durch rationale, in der ökologischen Wissenschaft entwickelte Methoden zu ermitteln war. Der system-ökologische Umweltdiskurs brachte somit ein neues Paradigma des Umweltbezuges hervor, das weder auf der Idee der Naturbeherrschung noch auf der Idee der Naturkonservierung, sondern eher auf der Idee einer *medizinischen Umweltsystemsteuerung* gründete. Anders gesagt, es ging jetzt weder darum, die Natur zu beherrschen, noch ihr die Rückkehr zu einem angenommenen ursprünglichen Zustand zu ermöglichen, sondern darum, ihr zu „helfen", einen „gesunden" Zustand zu erhalten, wobei der gesunde Zustand nicht immer ein ursprünglicher Zustand ist – ein gesundes System kann (und muss) sich stets verändern.

Das für die Moderne charakteristische, auf dem Begriffspaar Produktion/Naturbeherrschung gründende Paradigma des Umweltbezuges ermöglichte die Sichtbarmachung der Machtasymmetrie, die aus der ungleichen Verteilung der in den Produktionsprozessen erzeugten Werte unter den „produzierenden Subjekten" resultiert. Da innerhalb dieses begrifflichen Rahmens aber nur die menschlichen AkteurInnen als produzierende Subjekte anerkannt werden konnten, während alles andere als der passive Gegenstand für produktive Eingriffe betrachtet wurde, blieb eine andere grundlegende Asymmetrie für die modernen Diskurse weitgehend unsichtbar bzw. ihr kam der Status einer Selbstverständlichkeit oder sogar einer Norm zu. Es handelt sich um die Asymmetrie zwischen dem, was zum Bereich des Menschlichen (bzw. Sozialen), und dem, was zum Bereich des Nicht-Menschlichen (bzw. Biologischen) gezählt wurde. Obwohl sich der system-

5 Zur detaillierten Darstellung der frühen Umweltbewegung siehe: Ramachandra Guha, *Environmentalism. A Global History*. New York 2000.

6 Vgl. Demos 2009 (Anm. 4).

7 Eine bestimmte Variante dieser Idee vertritt Gregory Bateson mit seiner für den system-ökologischen Diskurs paradigmatischen Position, die Einheit der Natur im Sinne eines allumfassenden kybernetischen Systems zu verstehen, dem der Geist immanent sei. Vgl. Gregory Bateson, *Steps to Ecology of Mind* [1972]. Chicago und London 2000.

8 Ebd.

ökologische Diskurs kritisch zu dem für die Moderne charakteristischen Paradigma des Umweltbezugs verhielt, trug dieser Diskurs kaum zur Aufhebung der Herrschaft der Menschen über „Nicht-Menschen" bei. Vielmehr verschob die „medizinische Umweltsystemsteuerung" lediglich den Fokus von Fragen der Macht, Herrschaft und Ungleichheit hin zu Fragen der systemischen Funktionstüchtigkeit. Diese Blindheit für die historisch-geografisch kontextualisierten Machtasymmetrien charakterisiert auch den aus der Arbeit des Landschaftsarchitekten Ian McHarg hervorgegangenen Landschaftsbegriff, der mit der Idee der Umweltsystemsteuerung eng verknüpft ist.

Ian McHarg versuchte in seinem 1969 erschienen Buch *Design with Nature* eine Methode für eine „ökologisch informierte Gestaltung" zu entwickeln.[9] In Einklang mit dem Kern des system-ökologischen Denkens sah McHarg die Welt bzw. die „Natur" als ein komplexes kybernetisches System[10] an und teilte dem Menschen die Aufgabe zu, sein Wissen von der Funktionsweise dieses Systems permanent zu erweitern, um in der Zukunft für dessen Funktionieren sorgen bzw. *mitsteuern* zu können.[11] Um dies zu leisten, muss das sich ständig verändernde globale Umweltsystem erfassbar und darstellbar gemacht werden, was einen durch verschiedene technische und wissenschaftliche „Prothesen" vermittelten Blick von oben erfordert, der die Erdoberfläche in eine Plattform zur Steuerung von ökologischen Prozessen verwandelt. Der aus *Design with Nature* hervorgehende Landschaftsbegriff entspricht der Vorstellung von dieser Plattform. Dementsprechend zeigen die meisten Grafiken in diesem Buch die Draufsicht, die eine räumliche Konfiguration verschiedener ökologischer bzw. ökologisch relevanter Zusammenhänge darstellt.

Da die Werte im theoretisch-methodischen Konzept Ian McHargs (und innerhalb des system-ökologischen Diskurses generell) nicht als etwas von den AkteurInnen des Umweltsystems aktiv Produziertes begriffen werden, sondern der Fitness des Umweltsystems der Status eines universalen Wertes zukommt,[12] konnten auch seine Landschaftsdarstellungen keine Achsen der Herrschaft und Unterdrückung aufzeigen, die sich in den Prozessen der aktiven Werteerzeugung ausbilden. Anders gesagt, Ian McHargs Landschaften stellen die räumliche Konfiguration von „ökologischen" Prozessen und Werten dar, sagen aber nichts darüber aus, welche AkteurInnen in den genannten Prozessen privilegiert werden und welche nicht. Darüber hinaus erzeugt die für diesen Landschaftsbegriff charakteristische Vogelperspektive selbst eine weitere Asymmetrie – die Asymmetrie zwischen den UmweltexpertInnen, denen der steuernde Blick von oben vorbehalten ist, und denjenigen, die zu den Objekten der Steuerung werden.

Das Konzept des ökologischen Fußabdruckes. Während die system-ökologischen TheoretikerInnen die Methoden zur Erforschung des globalen Umweltsystems zu entwickeln versuchten, hatten sie Schwierigkeiten damit, den (positiven oder negativen) Einfluss konkreter Individuen oder Gemeinschaften auf die „Gesundheit" des Umweltsystems in Form von

9 Ian McHarg, *Design with Nature* [1969]. New York 1992.

10 Vgl. das Kapitel „World Is a Capsule", in: ebd., S. 95–101.

11 Ebd.

12 Vgl. die Kapitel „On Values", in: ebd., S. 67–79; „A Response of Values", S. 79–95 und „Processes as Values", S. 103–117.

discourses or was considered natural or even normative. This is the asymmetry between that which was counted as being part of the human (respectively the social) and that which was declared nonhuman (respectively biological). Although the system-ecological discourse was critical of the modernist paradigm of the relation to environment, the same discourse scarcely contributed to abolishing the domination of humans over "nonhumans." The new (system-ecological) paradigm rather merely shifted the focus from the sensitive questions of power, dominance and inequality to issues of systems' functional ability. This blindness for the historically and geographically contextualized power asymmetries also characterizes the concept of landscape derived from the work of landscape designer and environmentalist Ian McHarg, who tried to deploy the idea of eco-systems' steering in landscape design.

In his book *Design with Nature*, published in 1969, Ian McHarg attempted to develop a method for an "ecologically informed design."[9] In line with the core of the system-ecological approach, McHarg considered the world (or nature) as a complex cybernetic system[10] and attributed humanity the task of extending its knowledge of the structure and operating principles of this system, in order to ensure its proper functioning in the future.[11] In order to do this, the continuously changing global environmental system had to be made comprehensible and capable of representation, which required a view from above, supported by various technical and scientific prostheses; a view that would change Earth's skin into a platform for controlling ecological processes. The concept of landscape as developed in "Design with Nature" corresponds to the idea of this platform. Accordingly, most of the drawings in this book are top views representing spatial configuration of different ecological or ecologically relevant interrelations.

Since the values in Ian McHarg's theoretical and methodical concepts (and within the system-ecological discourse in general) were not understood as something actively produced by the actants of the environmental system, but the "fitness" of the system was considered a universal value,[12] his landscape representations were unable to reveal axes of domination and oppression, which are generated and perpetuated in the processes of active value production. In other words, Ian McHarg's landscapes show the spatial configuration of "ecological" processes and values, but do not reveal anything about which actants are privileged or disadvantaged in the said processes. Moreover, the bird's-eye view characteristic of this concept of landscape is another asymmetry in itself—the asymmetry

9 Ian McHarg, *Design with Nature* [1969]. New York 1992.

10 See the chapter "World is a Capsule," in: ibid., pp. 95–101.

11 Ibid.

12 See the chapters "On Values," in: ibid., pp. 67–79; "A Response of Values," pp. 79–95; and "Processes as Values," pp. 103–117.

between the environmental experts for whom the steering view from above is reserved, and those who function as mere objects of steering.

The Concept of the Ecological Footprint. While system-ecological theorists sought to develop methods for analyzing the global environmental system, they encountered difficulties in determining and representing the (positive or negative) influence of specific individuals or communities on system's "health" in precise numerical terms. The methods for determining such data were badly needed, because the development of the ecological crisis allowed the conclusion that people would only start to behave more "ecologically" if they were directly confronted with their own contribution to "environmental damage." Bearing this in mind, Mathis Wackernagel and William E. Rees formulated the concept of the "Ecological Footprint"[13] in the 1990s. This measure indicates "how much biologically productive land and water an individual, population or activity requires to produce all the resources it consumes and to absorb the waste it generates using prevailing technology and resource management practices."[14] Two other notions relating to the concept of the Ecological Footprint are "biocapacity" and the "ecological reserve" or the "ecological deficit." The first notion means "the capacity of ecosystems to produce useful biological materials and to absorb waste materials generated by humans, using current management schemes and extraction technologies."[15] "Ecological reserve" and the "Ecological deficit" mean the difference between "the biocapacity of a region or nation and its population's Footprint."[16]

As is clear from the definitions of these key terms, the concept of the Ecological Footprint inherited the notion of the "environmental system" from the system-ecological discourse. The perspective in which this system is seen, as well as the role man plays in it, however, is completely different. Whereas within the conceptual framework of the system-ecological discourse man was considered either an ignorant destroyer or a knowing manager of the environmental system, he now becomes its *"consumer"* and/or *indirect producer* (if, through his activities, he has a favorable impact on the biocapacity of his living environment). Whereas the system-ecological discourse ascribed an intrinsic value to the environmental system, the latter is now appreciated exclusively according to its ability to produce "biologically useful material" *for humans*. Simultaneously, human behavior is evaluated according to its

13 See Mathis Wackernagel, Bert Beyers, *Der Ecological Footprint: Die Welt neu vermessen*. Hamburg 2010.

14 Global Footprint Network, in: http://www.footprintnetwork.org/en/index.php/GFN/page/glossary/ [accessed on February 10, 2011].

15 Ibid.

16 Ibid.

exakten Zahlen darzustellen. Die Methoden, mit denen solche Zahlen ermittelt werden könnten, wurden dringend benötigt, weil der Verlauf der ökologischen Krise darauf schließen ließ, dass die Menschen nur dann anfangen würden, sich „umweltverträglicher" zu verhalten, wenn sie mit ihrem eigenen Beitrag zur „Umweltzerstörung" direkt konfrontiert würden. Mit dieser Absicht entwickelten Mathis Wackernagel und William E. Rees in den 1990er-Jahren das Konzept des „ökologischen Fußabdrucks".[13] Diese Größe gibt an, „wie viel biologisch produktive Land- und Wasserflächen ein Individuum, eine Bevölkerung oder eine Aktivität benötigt, um alle konsumierten Ressourcen zu produzieren und die anfallenden Abfälle zu absorbieren".[14] Zwei weitere Begriffe, die mit dem Konzept des ökologischen Fußabdrucks zusammenhängen, sind die „Biokapazität" und die „ökologische Reserve" bzw. „das ökologische Defizit". Der erste Begriff bezeichnet „die Fähigkeit von Ökosystemen, biologisch nutzbringendes Material zu produzieren und von Menschen produzierten Abfall unter heutigen Bedingungen aufzunehmen".[15] Die „ökologische Reserve" bzw. das „ökologische Defizit" bezeichnet „den Unterschied zwischen biologischer Kapazität und dem ökologischen Fußabdruck einer Region oder eines Landes".[16]

Zwei weitere Begriffe, die mit dem Konzept des ökologischen Fußabdrucks zusammenhängen, sind die „Biokapazität" und die „ökologische Reserve" bzw. „das ökologische Defizit".

Wie aus der Definition dieser Schlüsselbegriffe ersichtlich wird, übernimmt das Konzept des ökologischen Fußabdrucks den system-ökologischen Begriff des Umweltsystems. Die Perspektive auf dieses System bzw. die Rolle des Menschen darin ist aber eine völlig andere. Während die system-ökologische Denkweise den Menschen entweder als ignoranten Zerstörer oder als wissenden Verwalter auffasste, wird er nun zu seinem „Konsumenten" und zum indirekten Produzenten (wenn er durch seine Aktivität die biologische Kapazität seiner Lebensumwelt positiv beeinflusst). Während dem Umweltsystem innerhalb der system-ökologischen Diskurse ein intrinsischer Wert zugeschrieben wurde, wird es nun ausschließlich im Hinblick auf seine Fähigkeit bewertet, „biologisch nutzbringendes Material" für die Menschen zu produzieren. Gleichzeitig wird das menschliche Verhalten im Hinblick darauf bewertet, wie es die Produktion von biologisch nutzbringendem Material beeinflusst und durch welche (behutsame oder rücksichtslose) Formen der Konsumption dieses Materials gekennzeichnet ist. Das ermöglicht letztlich die Sichtbarmachung des asymmetrischen Verhältnisses zwischen der wenig

13 Vgl. Mathis Wackernagel, Bert Beyers, *Der Ecological Footprint. Die Welt neu vermessen*. Hamburg 2010.

14 Global Footprint Network, in: http://www.footprintnetwork.org/de/index.php/GFN/page/glossary/ [abgerufen am 10.2.2011].

15 Ebd.

16 Ebd.

produzierenden und übermäßig konsumierenden Stadt und ihrem viel produzierenden und mäßig konsumierenden Hinterland.

Dieses Konzept eröffnet den Raum für eine weitere Transformation des Landschaftsbegriffes. In Andre Viljoens Vision der „kontinuierlichen produktiven urbanen Landschaft“[17] fungiert diese als Instrument zur Aufhebung der zuvor erwähnten Asymmetrie, indem sie die produktive Funktion des Hinterlands in das städtische Territorium hinein zieht. Alle EinwohnerInnen einer urbanen Region werden nun durch ihre neuen landwirtschaftlichen Tätigkeiten zu (indirekten) ProduzentInnen des „biologisch nutzbaren Materials“, während sie gleichzeitig zu maßvollen KonsumentInnen werden, weil sie im Idealfall nur das konsumieren, was in ihrer lokalen Umwelt produziert wird. Alle anderen quälenden Ungleichheiten bleiben jedoch in dieser neuen Landschaft unsichtbar.

Darüber hinaus schränkt diese Idee von Landschaft selbst die Sichtbarkeit der mit den Mitteln des Konzepts des ökologischen Fußabdruckes begreifbaren Asymmetrie auf den städtisch-regionalen Maßstab ein, während Prozesse größeren Maßstabs ausgeblendet bleiben. Das hängt mit dem für das Konzept des „ökologischen Fußabdrucks“ charakteristischen Raumbegriff zusammen, der an die Vorstellung von frei addierbaren und dividierbaren Flächeneinheiten gebunden ist.[18] Demnach kann jeder beliebige lokale Maßstab zum Ausgangspunkt des gesellschaftlichen Wandels gewählt werden. Die Privilegierung des lokalen Maßstabs versperrt den Einblick in die Verflechtung von lokalen und globalen Prozessen und dadurch in die räumliche Komplexität der von diesen Prozessen reproduzierten Machtasymmetrien. Daraus können zahlreiche „unbeabsichtigte Konsequenzen“ hervorgehen – es passiert nämlich nicht selten, dass diverse alternative gesellschaftliche Modelle, die sich in ihrem engeren Umfeld von dominanten Beziehungen unterscheiden, in einem größeren Maßstab zur Reproduktion ebendieser dominanten Beziehungen beitragen.

Die Privilegierung des lokalen Maßstabs versperrt den Einblick in die Verflechtung von lokalen und globalen Prozessen und dadurch in die räumliche Komplexität der von diesen Prozessen reproduzierten Machtasymmetrien.

Die Position der urbanen politischen Ökologie. Sowohl der system-ökologische Diskurs als auch die ans Konzept des ökologischen Fußabdrucks gebundenen Diskurse lassen nicht viel Raum für die Sichtbarmachung und Transformation konkreter, historisch-geografischer Herrschaftsmechanismen – entweder bleiben sie unsichtbar oder sie werden ihrer Heterogenität beraubt, indem sie auf ein einziges asymmetrisches Verhältnis reduziert

17 Vgl. Andre Viljoen (Hg.), *Continuous Productive Urbane Landscapes: Designing Urban Agriculture for Sustainable Cities*. Oxford 2005.

18 Der ökologische Fußabdruck einer territorialen Einheit entspricht der Summe der ökologischen Fußabdrücke der kleineren territorialen Einheiten, aus denen die größere Einheit besteht.

impact on the production of "biologically useful material" and according to what (cautious or ruthless) forms of consumption this material is subject. This finally permits the revelation of a particular asymmetric relation, which in spatial terms is expressed as the asymmetry between the city (producing little and consuming excessively) and its hinterland (producing much and consuming little).

This perspective opens up the space for another transformation of the concept of landscape. In Andre Viljoen's vision of the "continuous productive urban landscape,"[17] the latter works as a tool for abolishing the above-mentioned asymmetry by making the hinterland's productive function overlap with urban territory. All (human) inhabitants of an urban region will now be equal in the sense that they will all become (indirect) producers of "biologically useful material" through their new agricultural activities, whereas they will simultaneously be moderate consumers consuming (in the ideal case) only the produce of their local environment. All other haunting inequalities, however, remain hidden in this new landscape.

Moreover, this concept of landscape reduces the visibility of the very asymmetry it strives to counteract to the scale of the urban region, disregarding larger-scale processes. The reason for this is the characteristic idea of space implicit in the concept of the "Ecological Footprint," which is bound to the idea of freely addable and dividable surface units.[18] According to this, any local scale can become the starting point of social change. Privileging local scales blocks the insight in the mutual interrelatedness of local and global processes and, accordingly, in the spatial complexity of the power asymmetries reproduced by these processes. This could yield many "unintended consequences" as it often happens that various alternative social models, which in their narrow environment generate socio-ecological relations different from the historically dominant ones, contribute, on a larger scale, to reproduction of these same dominant relations.

The Position of Urban Political Ecology. Both the system-ecological discourse and the discourses related to the concept of the Ecological Footprint provide only little room for the revelation and transformation of concrete historical-geographical mechanisms of domination—these mechanisms either remain hidden or are deprived of their heterogeneity by being reduced to a single asymmetric relation. The same is true for most all other environmental discourses (such as Deep Ecology, bioregionalism or eco-feminism); it is scarcely possible with the concepts developed in the framework of these dis-

17 See Andre Viljoen (ed.), *Continuous Productive Urban Landscapes: Designing Urban Agriculture for Sustainable Cities*. Oxford 2005.

18 The Ecological Footprint of a territorial unit corresponds to the sum of Ecological Footprints of the smaller territorial units of which the larger unit consists.

courses to grasp all the multifarious forms of domination and oppression.[19] This is why the disadvantaged inhabitants of the globalized world (such as most of the population of the so-called Third World) began to see the environmental discourses as an elitist affair unconcerned with their daily sufferings or even hostile to their subsistence strategies.

It is in this context that the discourse of Urban Political Ecology developed. The "Manifesto for Urban Political Ecology" written by Nik Heynen, Maria Kaika and Erik Swyngedouw declares at the beginning: "Environmental and social changes co-determine each other."[20] What is crucial for this linking of environmental questions with social ones is the concept of the metabolic environmental transformation characteristic of Urban Political Ecology as well as the specific interpretation of the idea of production connected to this concept. This particular idea of production, which will be explained further, enables comprehension of the field of the relations of humans to nonhumans (the subject of the conventional environmental discourses) and the field of the relations of humans to each other (the subject of the conventional social discourses) as one continuous field crisscrossed by manifold axes of domination and oppression.

Within the system-ecological discourse, humans and nonhumans were considered rather "functional components" of the environmental system than actants who actively transform their environment. The notion of productivity, as characteristic of the concept of the Ecological Footprint, was equally far from the idea of the conscious and active environmental transformation; productivity being understood above all as the ability of the environmental system to generate "biologically useful material." In opposition to this, the "Manifesto for Urban Political Ecology" relates the concept of production to the idea of active intervention of various actants in their respective environment: "environments are combined socio-physical constructions that are *actively* and historically *produced*."[21] Furthermore this active role is attributed not only to humans but also to various "nonhumans."[22] Whereas in modern social discourses, humans were considered the exclusive subjects and their nonhuman environment the mere object of production, this relationship has now been relativized by acknowledging the active role of nonhuman actants. This also implies the relativization of the concept of value insofar as through one and the same environmental transformation conditions can be produced that are positive for certain actants and negative for others.[23]

19 See David Harvey, *Justice, Nature & the Geography of Difference*. Cambridge, MA and Oxford 1996.

20 Heynen, Kaika, Swyngedouw 2006 (fn. 3), p. 11.

21 Ibid.

22 Ibid., p. 12.

23 Cf. Ibid.

werden. Das Gleiche gilt auch für die Mehrzahl anderer Umweltdiskurse (wie z. B. Tiefenökologie, Bioregionalismus oder Öko-Feminismus) – es ist kaum möglich, mit den dort entwickelten Begriffen die vielfältigen Herrschaft- und Unterdrückungsformen zu begreifen.[19] Daher sahen die mehrfach benachteiligten BewohnerInnen der inzwischen globalisierten Welt (wie z. B. der Großteil der Bevölkerung der sog. Dritten Welt) die Umweltdiskurse zunehmend als elitäre Angelegenheit, in denen ihr tägliches Leiden nicht vorkam und die oft auch ihre Überlebensstrategien zu unterbinden versuchten.

In diesem Kontext entwickelte sich der Diskurs der urbanen politischen Ökologie. Das von Nik Heynen, Maria Kaika und Erik Swyngedouw verfasste „Manifest für urbane politische Ökologie" stellt eingangs fest: „Environmental and social changes co-determine each other."[20] Zentral für diese Verbindung der ökologischen mit den gesellschaftlichen Fragestellungen ist der Begriff der *metabolischen Umwelttransformation*, mit dem auch eine für die urbane politische Ökologie charakteristische Deutung des Produktionsbegriffes zusammenhängt. Dieser spezifische Produktionsbegriff, der im Folgenden näher erläutert werden soll, eröffnet die Möglichkeit, das Feld der Beziehungen der Menschen zu ihrer nicht-menschlichen Umwelt (Schwerpunkt der herkömmlichen Umweltdebatte) und das Feld der Beziehungen zwischen den Menschen (Schwerpunkt der klassischen gesellschaftspolitischen Diskurse) als ein kontinuierliches, von vielfältigen Achsen der Herrschaft und Unterdrückung durchkreuztes Feld zu begreifen.

Innerhalb des system-ökologischen Diskurses wurden sowohl Menschen als auch Nicht-Menschen eher als „funktionelle Komponenten" des Umweltsystems betrachtet und weniger als AkteurInnen, die ihre Umwelt aktiv transformieren. Der für das Konzept des ökologischen Fußabdrucks charakteristische Begriff der Produktivität war auch weit von der Idee des bewussten und aktiven Umwelttransformierens entfernt – die Produktivität erschien in erster Linie als die Fähigkeit des Umweltsystems, das (für die Menschen) nutzbare biologische Material zu erzeugen. Demgegenüber ist im „Manifest für urbane politische Ökologie" der Begriff der Produktion an die Idee des aktiven Eingreifens diverser AkteurInnen in ihre jeweilige Umwelt gebunden: „Environments are combined socio-physical constructions that are *actively* and historically *produced*".[21] Dabei wird diese aktive Rolle nicht nur den Menschen, sondern auch verschiedenen „Nicht-Menschen" zugesprochen.[22] Während in den modernen sozialen Diskursen die Menschen als das exklusive Subjekt und ihre nicht-menschliche Umwelt als das bloße Objekt der Produktion begriffen wurden, wird dieses Verhältnis nun durch die Anerkennung der aktiven Rolle nicht-menschlicher AkteurInnen relativiert. Dies impliziert auch eine Relativierung des Wertbegriffes – durch eine und dieselbe Umwelttransformation können Bedingungen erzeugt werden, die für bestimmte AkteurInnen positiv, für andere hingegen negativ sein können.[23]

19 Vgl. David Harvey, *Justice, Nature & the Geography of Difference*. Cambridge, MA und Oxford 1996.

20 Heynen, Kaika, Swyngedouw 2006 (Anm. 3), S. 11.

21 Ebd.

22 Ebd., S. 12.

23 Vgl. ebd.

Dadurch erlaubt die politische Ökologie ein erweitertes Verständnis von den Asymmetrien, welche die Beziehungen zwischen den von den Umwelttransformationsprozessen betroffenen AkteurInnen charakterisieren. Während in den modernen gesellschaftspolitischen Diskursen vor allem die ungleiche Verteilung der produzierten Werte unter den an den Produktionsprozessen direkt oder indirekt beteiligten *Subjekten* (*ProduzentInnen*) im Mittelpunkt gestanden hat, erweitert der Diskurs der urbanen politischen Ökologie den Blick um mindestens zwei weitere asymmetrische Verhältnisse: jenem zwischen den AkteurInnen, die in den konkreten Umwelttransformationsprozessen den Status der exklusiven Subjekte für sich beanspruchen und denjenigen, denen ein reiner Objektstatus zugeschrieben wird; sowie jenem zwischen den AkteurInnen, für die der sie betreffende Teil des Gesamtoutputs konkreter Umwelttransformationsprozesse einen positiven und jenen, für die er einen negativen Wert darstellt.

Eine weitere Möglichkeit, welche der begriffliche Rahmen der urbanen politischen Ökologie eröffnet, ist die Berücksichtigung der *räumlichen* Dimension der sozio-ökologischen Beziehungen. Während die gesellschaftlichen Machtverhältnisse häufig als vertikale Schichtungen begriffen wurden,[24] für die der horizontale geografische Raum im wesentlichen irrelevant ist, rückt nun die Räumlichkeit dieser Verhältnisse ins Blickfeld. Räumlichkeit äußert sich dabei gleichzeitig in mehreren Maßstäben, wobei es keine direkte kausale Beziehung zwischen größeren und kleineren gibt.[25]

Durch den normativen Ansatz des system-ökologischen Diskurses, das „optimale Funktionieren" des globalen Umweltsystems zu gewährleisten, wurde der globale Maßstab privilegiert. Auf der anderen Seite erschienen innerhalb der ans Konzept des ökologischen Fußabdruckes gebundenen Diskurse die einzelnen lokalen Räume als unabhängig voneinander analysier- und planbar. Demgegenüber wird nun der Raum als dynamischer Kontext und Resultat der Umwelttransformationsprozesse verstanden, die gleichzeitig in mehreren Maßstäben operieren. Diese „Multimaßstäblichkeit" unterminiert die Vorstellung von der Isolierbarkeit einzelner physischer Räume bzw. die Privilegierung eines einzelnen Maßstabs – sei es der Maßstab der städtischen Nachbarschaft, der Stadt, des Ökosystems, der „Bioregion", des nationalen Staates oder der Erdkugel.

Mit der Idee von „Multimaßstäblichkeit" geht die für die urbane politische Ökologie charakteristische Deutung des *Urbanen* einher: „The urban world is a cyborg-world, part natural/part social, part technical/part cultural, but *with no clear boundaries, centers or margins*."[26] Das Urbane wird also weder durch den städtischen Maßstab, noch durch die Opposition gegen einen „natürlichen" oder landschaftlichen Raum definiert. Die Stadt begreift man als das veränderliche Resultat der metabolischen Umwelttransformationsprozesse, deren Maßstäbe nicht notwendigerweise mit jenen der physischen Stadt identisch sind. Die urbane politische Ökologie stellt dementsprechend kein Hindernis für die Entfaltung des Landschaftsbegriffs zwecks Transformation sozio-ökologischer Beziehungen in einer immer mehr urbanisierten Welt dar. Das Manifest lässt diese Möglichkeit nicht nur zu, sondern es impliziert sie sogar.

24 Vgl. Edward Soja, *Seeking Spatial Justice*. Minneapolis 2010.

25 Vgl. Heynen, Kaika, Swyngedouw 2006 (Anm. 3), S. 12.

26 Ebd.

Thus Urban Political Ecology enables an extended understanding of asymmetries characteristic of the relations between actants involved in (or affected by) processes of environmental transformation. Whereas the modern critical socio-political discourses focused mainly upon the unequal distribution of the produced values between directly or indirectly involved productive subjects, the discourse of Urban Political Ecology widens the potential field of critical analysis and transformative action by providing conceptual tools for revelation of at least two further asymmetric relations: the asymmetry between the actants who claim the exclusive subject status in the environmental transformation processes and those to whom a pure object status is ascribed; furthermore the asymmetry between the actants for whom the output of an environmental change process (insofar as they are affected by it) represents a positive value, and those for whom it represents a negative value.

Another possibility opened up by the specific conceptual frame of Urban Political Ecology is the consideration of the *spatial* dimension of socio-ecological relations. Whereas in common social discourses power relations used to be considered as vertical strata[24] for which the horizontal geographical space is irrelevant, the spatiality of these relations is now being put forward. This spatiality is simultaneously expressed on several scales, albeit there is no direct causal connection between the smaller and the larger scales.[25]

Through the objective of system-ecological discourses to ensure "optimum functioning" of the global environmental system, the *global* scale was privileged in the normative sense. On the other hand, within the discourses related the concept of the Ecological Footprint the individual *local* spaces appeared as analyzable and designable independently from each other. In opposition to this, the space is now considered as a dynamic context and a result of environmental transformation processes operating on more than one scale. This idea of multiplicity and interrelatedness of relevant spatial scales undermines the analytic and design concepts that assume separability of individual "spaces" and privilege thus a single spatial scale—be it the scale of urban neighborhood, of the city, of ecosystems, of the "bioregion," of a national state, or of the globe.

The idea of the interrelatedness of diverse spatial scales, as is pronounced in the "Manifesto for Urban Political Ecology," is accompanied by the particular interpretation of the *Urban*: "The urban world is a cyborg-world, part natural/part social, part technical/part cultural, but *with no clear boundaries, centres or margins*."[26] The Urban is thus defined neither by the urban scale nor by its opposition against landscape. The city is under-

24 See Edward Soja, *Seeking Spatial Justice*. Minneapolis 2010.

25 See Heynen, Kaika, Swyngedouw 2006 (fn. 3), p. 12.

26 Ibid.

stood as the changing result of metabolic processes of environmental transformation, the scales of which are not necessarily identical with those of the physical city. Thus Urban Political Ecology does not hinder the deployment of the concept of *landscape* as a spatial instrument for transformation of the existing socio-ecological relations in an ever more *urbanized* world. The Manifesto does not only admit this possibility, but even implies it in a sense.

Towards a Concept of Landscape for Urban Political Ecology. A clear-cut parallel between contemporary landscape design practice and Urban Political Ecology concerns the dissolution of the city-landscape dichotomy. This is particularly evident in "landscape urbanism"—the term already being significant. The main idea here is to have the landscape become a "lens," through which "the contemporary city is represented, and a medium in which it [the contemporary city] is constructed."[27] One of the most important reasons for this new role of landscape lies in the fact that the traditional concept of the city with its focus on the built urban structure (and not on processes producing it) proved to be inappropriate for dealing with (in both analytical and projective sense) all that which lies beneath, between and outside of this structure, although it is intrinsically related to it.[28] This "fault" of the traditional concept of the city became a major obstacle in the search for reasonable analytical and design strategies that could be deployed in the changing "rurban" territories. Because of its capacity to grasp and represent the processes and structures that depend on but are not reducible to the activity of human actants, the idea of landscape seemed to be an appropriate starting point in this context.

The emphasis on the processes in the contemporary landscape design practice also implies the relativization of spatial scale, since the concrete physical sites subject to design practices are intersected and determined by processes operating on scales different from the scale of these very sites. This leads to a new concept of place; the place appears now as a node in the net of socio-ecological processes, where different spatial scales collide.[29] Thereby the landscape becomes the materialization of this very network—a dynamic platform that relates the individual places to their environment (and makes them identifiable as places by means of this relational positionality). In precisely the same manner that a network is never perceived without nodes, the landscape understood as materialization of a net-

27 Charles Waldheim, "A Reference Manifesto," in: idem (ed.), *The Landscape Urbanism Reader*. New York 2006, p. 15.

28 See Linda Pollak, "Constructed Ground: Questions of Scale," in: ibid., pp. 125–140.

29 Anita Berrizbeitia analyzed this new concept of site using the example of James Corner/Field Operations' proposal for the Fresh Kills site, New York, and James Corner's and Stan Allen's proposal for Downsview Park, Toronto. See Anita Berrizbeitia, "Re-placing Processes," in: Julia Czerniak, George Hargreaves (eds.) *Large Parks*. New York 2007, pp. 195f.

Auf dem Weg zu einem Landschaftsbegriff für urbane politische Ökologie. Die deutlichste Parallele zwischen der zeitgenössischen Landschaftsarchitektur und der urbanen politischen Ökologie betrifft die fortschreitende Auflösung der Stadt-Land-Dichotomie. Besonders ausgeprägt ist dies bei der „Landschaftsurbanistik“ – bereits ihr Name ist bezeichnend. Ihre Hauptidee besteht darin, die Landschaft zu einer „Linse“ werden zu lassen, „durch die die gegenwärtige Stadt repräsentiert wird, und [zu einem] Medium, in dem sie [die gegenwärtige Stadt] konstruiert wird“.[27] Einer der wichtigsten Gründe für diese neue Rolle der Landschaft liegt darin, dass sich der herkömmliche Stadtbegriff wegen seiner Fixierung auf gebauten Strukturen als ungeeignet erwies, um all das, was sich unterhalb, zwischen und außerhalb dieser Strukturen befindet, aber unzertrennlich mit ihnen verbunden ist, darzustellen und für Eingriffe zu erschließen.[28] Dieser „Mangel“ des herkömmlichen Stadtbegriffes wurde wegen der zunehmende Zersiedlung zu einem schwer zu überwindenden Hindernis bei der Suche nach sinnvollen analytischen und entwerferischen Strategien für die sich wandelnden „rurbanen“ Territorien. Durch ihre Kapazität, Prozesse und physische Strukturen sicht- und handhabbar zu machen, die menschliche AkteurInnen einschließen, aber nicht ausschließlich auf deren Aktivitäten reduzieren, bot sich die Idee von Landschaft als Ausgangspunkt an.

Bei dem mit den systemökologischen Diskursen verbundenen Landschaftsbegriff konnten das Besondere und Lokale nur aus der Perspektive des imaginierten Ganzen (der globalen Einheit der Natur) wahrgenommen werden.

Mit der Hervorhebung der Prozesshaftigkeit in der zeitgenössischen landschaftsarchitektonischen Praxis geht eine Relativierung des Maßstabs einher, insofern die konkreten physischen Gestaltungsareale von Prozessen durchquert und bestimmt werden, deren Maßstab der räumlichen Ausdehnung des jeweiligen Gestaltungsareals nicht entspricht. Daraus ergibt sich ein neues Verständnis des Ortes, der als ein Knoten im Netzwerk sozioökologischer Prozesse erscheint, in dem unterschiedliche Maßstäbe aufeinandertreffen.[29] Landschaft wird in der Folge zur Materialisierung eben dieses Netzes – eine dynamische Plattform, welche die einzelnen Orte an ihre Umwelt bindet und sie durch eben diese Bindung überhaupt als Orte definiert. Ebenso wie kein Netzwerk ohne seine Knoten wahrgenommen werden kann, so kann auch die als Materialisierung eines Netzwerks begriffene Landschaft nicht ohne Bezug zum Partikulären (konkrete Körper, Orte, Milieus …) wahrgenommen und dargestellt werden.

27 Charles Waldheim, „A Reference Manifesto“, in: ders. (Hg.), *The Landscape Urbanism Reader*. New York 2006, S. 15.

28 Vgl. Linda Pollak, „Constructed Ground: Questions of Scale“, in: ebd., S. 125–140.

29 Anita Berrizbeitia untersuchte diesen neuen Ortsbegriff am Beispiel des Entwurfs für das *Fresh Kills Areal* in New York von James Corner/Field Operations und des Entwurfs für den *Downsview Park* in Toronto von James Corner und Stan Allen. Siehe Anita Berrizbeitia, „Re-placing Processes“, in: Julia Czerniak, George Hargreaves (Hg.), *Large Parks*. New York 2007, S. 195f.

Diese neue Idee von Landschaft unterscheidet sich also grundlegend von den zuvor dargestellten Landschaftsbegriffen. Bei dem mit den system-ökologischen Diskursen verbundenen Landschaftsbegriff konnten das Besondere und Lokale nur aus der Perspektive des imaginierten Ganzen (der globalen Einheit der Natur) wahrgenommen werden. Bei dem mit dem Konzept des ökologischen Fußabdrucks assoziierten Landschaftsbegriff erschienen die lokalen Räume als analysier- und verwaltbar ohne Rücksicht auf sozio-ökologische Konfigurationen, deren Maßstab sich von dem physischen Maßstab dieser lokalen Räume unterscheidet. Anders als bei diesen zwei Landschaftsbegriffen wird jetzt das Partikuläre durch die *Beziehungen* definiert, die es an andere verräumlichte sozio-ökologische Konfigurationen unterschiedlicher Maßstäbe binden. Damit werden die sozio-ökologischen Beziehungen und die durch diese Beziehungen konstituierten Differenzen (Partikularitäten) im Kontext des multimaßstäblichen geografischen Raumes begriffen und dargestellt.

Dieses Verständnis von Unterschieden sagt allein jedoch noch nichts über deren Charakter aus, denn „manche Unterschiede sind spielerisch, während die anderen die Pole der weltweiten Herrschaftssysteme darstellen".[30] Es ist die zweite Art von Differenzen, auf die sich das „Manifest für die urbane politische Ökologie" kritisch bezieht. Die Sichtbarmachung dieser „quälenden Asymmetrien" wird der urbanen politischen Ökologie erst durch eine spezifische Deutung des Produktionsbegriffes möglich.

> Landschaft erscheint zunehmend als dynamische Plattform, in der und durch die immer neue Formen sozio-ökologischer Interaktionen und Konfigurationen produziert werden.[32]

In der neueren landschaftsarchitektonischen Praxis wird auch häufig der produktive, aktive und innovative Aspekt der Landschaft in den Blick genommen.[31] Landschaft erscheint zunehmend als dynamische Plattform, in der und durch die immer neue Formen sozio-ökologischer Interaktionen und Konfigurationen produziert werden.[32] Dadurch nimmt der Begriff der Produktion eine neue Bedeutungsnuance an – Produktion erscheint in diesem Kontext zunehmend als *verräumlichtes sozio-ökologisches Experimentieren*.

Diese Idee deckt sich in einigen wichtigen Aspekten mit dem aus dem „Manifest für urbane politische Ökologie" hervorgehenden Produktionsbegriff – sie hebt die *Räumlichkeit* von Produktionsprozessen hervor und lässt auch die nicht-menschlichen AkteurInnen als mögliche Produktions-

30 „Some differences are playful, [while] some are poles of world historical systems of domination." Donna Haraway, „A Cyborg Manifesto: Science, Technology, and Socialist-Feminism in the Late Twentieth Century", in: dies., *Simians, Cyborgs and Women. The Reinvention of Nature*. New York 1991, S. 161.

31 Bezeichnend sind in dieser Hinsicht der Entwurf für das Fresh Kills Areal in New York von James Corner/Field Operations; der Landschaftspark Duisburg-Nord von Latz + Partner; der Parque del Rio Manzanares von West 8; der Los Angeles River Park von Hargreaves Associates; der Downsview Park in Toronto von James Corner/Stan Allen, um nur einige der bekanntesten Projekte in diesem Kontext zu nennen.

32 Vgl. James Corner, „Ecology and Landscape as Agents of Creativity", in: G. Thompson, F. Steiner (Hg.), *Ecological Design and Planning*. New York 1997.

work is never perceived or represented without relating to the particulars (concrete bodies, places, milieus, etc.).

This new idea of landscape is thus radically different from the two previously analyzed concepts. The concept of landscape associated with the system-ecological discourse allowed perceiving the particular and the local only from the perspective of the imagined whole (the universal environmental system). On the other hand the idea of landscape associated with the concept of the Ecological Footprint made local spaces appear as analyzable and manageable, regardless of socio-ecological processes operating on scales different from the physical scale of these local spaces. Unlike as it is true for those two concepts of landscape, the "particular" is now defined by relations that tie it to other spatialized socio-ecological configurations of various scales. Thus the socio-ecological relations and the differences (particularities) they constitute are now understood and represented in the context of the multi-scalar geographical space.

This spatial revelation of differences itself, however, says nothing about the nature of these differences, given that "some differences are playful, [while] some are poles of world historical systems of domination."[30] It is of course the second type of differences that the "Manifesto for Urban Political Ecology" critically refers to. In the discourse of Urban Political Ecology, it is the specific concept of production that enables revealing and representing such "haunting asymmetries."

In recent landscape architecture practice, the productive, active and innovative aspect of landscape is also often taken into consideration.[31] In this context landscape is increasingly interpreted as a dynamic platform, upon and through which ever novel forms of socio-ecological interactions and configurations are produced.[32] Thereby the concept of production adopts a new signifying nuance: the production is understood as a *spatialized socio-ecological experiment*.

In some important aspects, this idea is congruent with the concept of production as emerging from the "Manifesto for Urban Political Ecology; it underlines the spatiality of production processes and also lets the nonhuman actants appear as potential subjects (and not merely objects) of production. In

30 "Some differences are playful, [while] some are poles of world historical systems of domination." Donna Haraway, "A Cyborg Manifesto: Science, Technology, and Socialist-Feminism in the late Twentieth Century," in: idem, *Simians, Cyborgs and Women: The Reinvention of Nature*. New York 1991, p. 161.

31 In this context, the following design projects are significant: proposal for the Fresh Kills site in New York by James Corner/Field Operations; Landschaftspark Duisburg-Nord by Latz + Partner; Parque del Rio Manzanares by West 8; Los Angeles River Park by Hargreaves Associates; Downsview Park, Toronto, by James Corner/Stan Allen, just to mention a few of the most famous projects in this context.

32 See James Corner, "Ecology and Landscape as Agents of Creativity," in: G. Thompson, F. Steiner (eds.), *Ecological Design and Planning*. New York 1997.

this new context, however, production becomes a value in its own right by being bound to the idea of *creative invention*, whereas within the conceptual framework of Urban Political Ecology, the productive environmental transformation is understood as a process in the course of which the values (and the valueless) are yet to be defined, produced and distributed. The former interpretation of the concept of production suggests that production is positive for all actants involved. This interpretation causes the asymmetries generated in the production processes to drop out of view. Significant in this context is the promotion of the productive and active agency of landscape (which has almost become a commonplace in much of the contemporary landscape design), whereas the question of who exactly is privileged (and who is disadvantaged) in these innovative transformations is too often left aside. Thus landscape understood as a dynamic socio-ecological platform changes into a smooth surface from which any disagreeable roughness has been wiped away, as the differences it reveals are deprived of their darker aspect.

When searching for a concept of landscape that could become an emancipatory spatial tool in a time of environmental crises, we are called upon to dismiss the "narcissistic" interpretation of the idea of production, which is becoming prevalent in contemporary landscape design. Instead of understanding production as a value in itself—the interpretation which generates the naïve idea of landscape as a paradise of cultural and ecological inventive experimentation—it could be seen as the process of value creation, which is always interwoven with the threads of power and domination. Such an interpretation of the idea of production combined with the abolition of the landscape-city-polarity and with the idea of multiplicity of scales in landscape could in fact orientate the landscape towards an exquisite spatial instrument for achieving "a more equitable distribution of social power and a more inclusive form of production of nature."[33]

33 Heynen, Kaika, Swyngedouw 2006 (fn. 3), p. 13.

subjekte erscheinen. Durch ihre Bindung an die Idee der durchs Experimentieren erlangten *Invention* wird aber die Produktion in diesem Kontext zu einem Wert an sich, während innerhalb des begrifflichen Rahmens der politischen Ökologie die produktive Umwelttransformation als ein Prozess verstanden wird, im Zuge dessen die Werte (und das Wertlose) erst definiert, erzeugt und verteilt werden. Aus der ersten Deutung des Produktionsbegriffs geht hervor, dass die Produktion für alle involvierten AkteurInnen positiv ist, wodurch die in den Produktionsprozessen mitproduzierten Asymmetrien aus dem Blickfeld verdrängt werden. Bezeichnend dafür ist die in der zeitgenössischen Landschaftsarchitektur gängige Anpreisung der aktiven Wirkung der Landschaft in der Produktion der kulturell-ökologischen Innovation, wobei die Frage, wer genau in den konkreten Innovationsprozessen privilegiert bzw. benachteiligt ist, allzu oft ausgeblendet wird. Dadurch mutiert die als dynamische sozio-ökologische Plattform begriffene Landschaft zu einer glatten, von den unangenehmen Unebenheiten gereinigten Oberfläche, insofern die Unterschiede ihrer dunklen Seite beraubt werden.

Auf der Suche nach einem Landschaftsbegriff, der in den Zeiten der Umweltkrise(n) zu einem emanzipatorischen räumlichen Instrument werden könnte, gilt es, die in der zeitgenössischen Landschaftsarchitektur immer bedeutender werdende Idee der Produktion von ihrer „narzisstischen" Deutung zu befreien. Anstatt die mit der Landschaftsidee immer häufiger assoziierte Vorstellung von Produktion als einen Wert an sich zu begreifen (was eine naive Idee von Landschaft als einem unschuldigen *kulturell-ökologischen Inventionsparadies* impliziert), lässt sich die Produktion als ein mit den Fäden von Macht und Herrschaft verwobener Prozess der Werteerzeugung auffassen. Eine solche Deutung, kombiniert mit der Vorstellung von der Multimaßstäblichkeit der Landschaft und der Aufhebung der Stadt-Land-Polarität, könnte die Landschaft tatsächlich in Richtung eines vorzüglichen räumlichen Instruments für „eine gerechtere Verteilung der sozialen Macht und eine inklusivere Form der Produktion von Natur"[33] rücken.

33 Heynen, Kaika, Swyngedouw 2006 (Anm. 3), S. 13.

Of Agency and Matter

1

1 Buckmister Fuller, World Game, seminar 1972. "Energy Slaves," © The Estate of R. Buckminster Fuller.

The Productive Surface

From the legacy of high modernism, an emphasis on form, technique, function and technology has dominated the representation of surface in architecture and landscape architecture. This emphasis has perpetuated a binary interpretation of the role of the architectural surface—either form and technique driven or function and technology determined. Form privileges the expressive, a response to the question of what the surface could be; while function privileges the operational, a response to the question of what the surface should be.

Die produktive Oberfläche. Die Betonung von Form, Technik, Funktion und Technologie aus dem Erbe der Klassischen Moderne hat die Darstellung von Oberfläche in Architektur und Landschaftsarchitektur geprägt. Dieser Schwerpunkt hat eine binäre Interpretation der Rolle der architektonischen Oberfläche festgeschrieben – entweder durch Form und Technik motiviert, oder durch Funktion und Technologie bestimmt. Form begünstigt das Expressive, als Antwort auf die Frage, was die Oberfläche sein könnte; während Funktion eine Nutzungsorientierung begünstigt, als Antwort auf die Frage, was die Oberfläche sein sollte.

MASON WHITE

Certainly these hard-lined distinctions have not always been so clear, though they have organized camps of thought in 20th-century design histories and practices. Yet external to this pairing is an overlooked history of what could be called the "productive surface." The productive surface is a constructed terrain with the ability to—simply put—yield something. In other words, it has a tangible, positive byproduct—for example, energy, or biotic or abiotic components. The productive surface depends upon an intimate understanding of context, climate and natural processes. It may operate at the scale of a building or region, or at scales between—because of its networked and scalable logic. My goal here is to reveal a 20th-century history of the productive surface, establish its key progenitors, and interpret and assess its recent resurgence.

What Is the Productive? Earlier considerations of the productive within architecture and landscape were firmly embedded within the functionalist camp. This is understandable, given that the primary instigators have been agriculturists, technologists, botanists, material scientists and engineers. But contemporary design ambitions, and an increased interest in critical sustainability, ecology, and biological analogies, have posited new possibilities. Taken literally, the productive surface refers to the capacity for a designed surface to generate a usable component—agriculture, renewable energy systems, water harvesting systems, et al. Much as Reyner Banham exposed a previously suppressed lineage of environmental engineering in modern architecture, the field requires, once again, a sociological and methodological account of the impact of environmental technology on design.[1] Such an account is especially timely, given a contemporary design context increasingly littered with ecological metaphors, with sustainability as design justification, and with divergent understandings of the role of infrastructure.[2]

To begin this account of the productive surface, some questions: What does architecture and landscape already produce—intentionally or otherwise? And how is that component managed by design? Possible byproducts of any new construction include heat, light and waste; also shifts in air patterns, hydrology, species patterns and land value. The envelope, or outermost skin, is the principal plane of contact between a regulated interior and a fluctuating exterior. The main objective of this surface, in the case of architecture, has typically been preventive—to keep cool or warm air in or out. In landscape, the main objective has typically been to perform at the level of nature. But today the productive surface embraces a wider range of possibilities. Increasingly, design seeks to convert its very liability—an exposed surface—not only into a low-impact element but also into an economic and climatological asset. To return to a central question: How has the role of the horizontal surface—given its land uses, properties and resources—evolved toward the productive?

1 In the 1984 reissue of Reyner Banham's *The Architecture of the Well-tempered Environment*, the author chastises readers (and librarians) who "have put the first edition of this book among general introductions to technology—in which role it would leave much to be desired." Instead, Banham sought an integrated history of architecture and technology. Reyner Banham, *The Architecture of the Well-tempered Environment* [1969]. Chicago 1984, p. 9.

2 For a recent critique of sustainability, see especially Mark Jarzombek's "Sustainability: Fuzzy Systems and Wicked Problems," in which he argues that "sustainability as a field is dangerously afloat in ambiguity and indeterminacy." Mark Jarzombek, "Sustainability: Fuzzy Systems and Wicked Problems," in: *Log* 8 (Summer 2006), p. 11.

Mit Sicherheit waren diese strengen Unterscheidungen nicht immer so klar, doch haben sie verschiedene Denkrichtungen in der Entwurfsgeschichte und Praxis im 20. Jahrhundert nach sich gezogen. Doch über diese binären Paarungen hinaus gibt es eine Geschichte von dem, was man die „produktive Oberfläche" nennen könnte. Die produktive Oberfläche ist ein konstruiertes Terrain, das, einfach gesagt, fähig ist, etwas Nützliches hervorzubringen. Es hat, mit anderen Worten, ein konkretes, positives Nebenprodukt, etwa Energie, biotische oder abiotische Bestandteile. Die produktive Oberfläche hängt von einem genauen Verständnis des Kontexts, des Klimas und der natürlichen Prozesse ab. Sie kann aufgrund ihrer vernetzten und skalierbaren Logik im Maßstab eines Gebäudes oder einer Region – oder auf allen Stufen dazwischen – funktionieren. Mein Ziel ist es hier, eine Geschichte der produktiven Oberfläche im 20. Jahrhundert aufzuzeigen, ihre wichtigsten Protagonisten darzustellen und ihr Wiederaufleben in jüngster Zeit zu interpretieren und zu bewerten.

Was ist das Produktive? Frühere Erörterungen des Produktiven in Architektur und Landschaft waren fest im funktionalistischen Lager verankert. Dies ist verständlich, wenn man davon ausgeht, dass die ursprünglichen Verfechter Agraringenieure, Technologen, Botaniker, Materialwissenschaftler und Ingenieure waren. Doch heutige Bestrebungen im Design und ein vermehrtes Interesse an kritischer Nachhaltigkeit, Ökologie und biologischen Analogien haben neue Möglichkeiten geschaffen. Die produktive Oberfläche bezieht sich wörtlich genommen auf die Fähigkeit einer gestalteten Oberfläche, nutzbare Komponenten wie Landbau, erneuerbare Energiesysteme, Wassergewinnungssysteme und andere herzustellen. Ähnlich wie Reyner Banham die zuvor verdrängte Herleitung der umwelttechnischen Planung in der modernen Architektur offenlegte, erfordert das Gebiet abermals eine soziologische und methodologische Bestandsaufnahme des Einflusses der Umwelttechnologie auf den Entwurf.[1] Für eine solche Darstellung ist es höchste Zeit, da der gegenwärtige Entwurfskontext zunehmend von ökologischen Metaphern, Nachhaltigkeit als Rechtfertigung des Entwurfs und einer divergenten Auffassung der Rolle der Infrastruktur überschwemmt wird.[2]

Zu Beginn dieser Ausführung der produktiven Oberfläche einige Fragen: Was stellen Architektur und Landschaft – beab-

1 In der Neuauflage von 1984 von Reyner Banhams *The Architecture of the Well-tempered Environment* schilt der Autor Leser (und Buchhändler): „[they] have put the first edition of this book among general introductions to technology – in which role it would leave much to be desired." Stattdessen verfolgt Banham eine integrierte Geschichte von Architektur und Technologie. Reyner Banham, *The Architecture of the Well-tempered Environment* [1969]. Chicago 1984, S. 9.

2 Für eine neue Kritik zur Nachhaltigkeit, vgl. besonders Mark Jarzombek, „Sustainability: Fuzzy Systems and Wicked Problems," in dem er meint: „sustainability as a field is dangerously afloat in ambiguity and indeterminacy." Mark Jarzombek, „Sustainability: Fuzzy Systems and Wicked Problems," in: *Log* 8 (Sommer 2006), S. 11.

sichtigt oder nicht – bereits her? Und wie wird mit diesem Aspekt im Entwurf umgegangen? Mögliche Nebenprodukte jeder neuen Konstruktion schließen Wärme, Licht und Abfall mit ein; auch Verschiebungen bei Luftströmungen, Hydrologie, Artenverteilung und Grundstückswert zählen dazu. Die Hülle oder äußerste Schicht ist die hauptsächliche Kontaktfläche zwischen einem regulierten Innenraum und einem veränderlichen Außenraum. In der Architektur war die Hauptaufgabe diese Oberfläche betreffend typischerweise präventiv – um kalte oder warme Luft innen oder außen zu halten. Bei der Landschaft bestand die Hauptaufgabe typischerweise in der Ausübung natürlicher Prozesse. Doch heute umfasst die produktive Oberfläche einen erweiterten Bereich von Möglichkeiten. In zunehmendem Maße versucht das Design seine spezielle Leistungsfähigkeit – die freiliegende Oberfläche – umzuformen, nicht nur in Elemente mit möglichst geringen Auswirkungen, sondern auch mit einem ökonomischen und klimatologischen Gewinn. Zurück zur zentralen Frage: Wie hat sich die Rolle der horizontalen Oberfläche angesichts ihrer Landnutzung, Besitzverhältnisse und Ressourcen zum Produktiven hin entwickelt?

Produktion zonieren. Um den Aufstieg des Produktiven zu verstehen, müssen wir die unscharfe, aber dennoch zwingende Unterscheidung zwischen ökologischen und experimentellen Bestrebungen berücksichtigen. Meiner Meinung nach ist das Produktive eine Erweiterung und Entwicklung der Nachhaltigkeit – ohne jeden fragwürdigen empirischen oder technologischen Determinismus. Um die Geschichte der produktiven Oberfläche einzugrenzen, müssen wir weiters die Auswirkung der Zoneneinteilung und der Widmungsbestimmungen auf größere urbane Gefüge untersuchen. Die rasche Korporatisierung des Bodens während er 1970er- und 1980er-Jahre und die anschließende Deindustrialisierung der Städte sind gut dokumentierte Erscheinungen und haben innovative Vorschläge für neue Formen des Urbanismus nach sich gezogen.[3] Doch was sind die Ursprünge der industriellen Stadt?

Eines der dringlichen Ziele der Stadtplanung im frühen 20. Jahrhundert war, die zunehmende Komplexität und die unhygienischen Lebensbedingungen der sich ausbreitenden Stadt zu bewältigen, ebenso wie ihren Bezug zur rasanten Industrialisierung und den daraus folgenden Druck auf die Landwirtschaft zu steuern. Bis hin zur Jahrhundertwende entwickelten Planer und Entwerfer wie Ebenezer Howard, Patrick Geddes und Tony Garnier neue Modelle des Urbanismus, die versuchten, diesem schwierigen Übergang zu begegnen und dessen Herausforderungen aufeinander abzustimmen. Geddes zeigt

3 Vgl. vor allem Alan Berger, *Drosscape: Wasting Land in Urban America*. New York 2007; und Berger, *Reclaiming the American West*. New York 2002; ebenso Lars Lerup, *After the City*. Cambridge, MA 2001; im Speziellen zu Houston, Texas, eine Stadt ohne Bestimmungen zur Zoneneinteilung, und auch zur Begriffsklärung von „stim" und „dross".

Zoning Production. To understand the rise of the productive we need to acknowledge the blurred, yet empowering, distinction between ecological and experiential ambitions. My argument here is that the productive is an extension and evolution of sustainability—without any dubious empirical or technological determinism. In addition, to isolate a history of the productive surface, we need to understand the impact of zoning and land-use regulation upon larger urban assemblies. The rapid corporatization of land during the 1970s and '80s, and the subsequent deindustrialization of cities, are well-documented phenomena, and have provoked inventive propositions for new forms of urbanism.[3] But what are the origins of the industrial city?

One of the urgent goals of early 20th-century urban planning was to manage the increasing complexity and unhygienic conditions of the expanding city, and its relationship to both rapid industrialization and the resulting strains on agriculture. Leading up to the turn of the century, planners and designers including Ebenezer Howard, Patrick Geddes and Tony Garnier expounded new models of urbanism that sought to confront this difficult transition and coordinate these challenges. Geddes offered a biologist's view of urbanism, construing cities as forms of life.[4] Howard, trained as a stenographer, positioned the garden city as an ideal alternative to the current town form. Extending these provocations into a situated and detailed design proposition, Garnier developed the Cité Industrielle over a period of about 15 years, finally publishing his treatise in 1918. While each of these visionaries explored the form and format of the nascent industrial city, it is Garnier's proposition that most accurately reflects the early modern ambition to incorporate the productive amid the residential.

The productive surface depends upon an intimate understanding of context, climate and natural processes. It may operate at the scale of a building or region, or at scales between—because of its networked and scalable logic.

Influenced by the utopian socialism of Charles Fourier, the Cité Industrielle emerged within the context of early forays into regionalism.[5] Cité Industrielle, planned for a plateau in southeast France, incorporated residential, cultural, governmental, manufacturing and agricultural facilities into a gridded and zoned city; Garnier embraced the pre-condition of the site as both opportunity and obstruction. Unlike Ebenezer Howard's Garden City

3 See especially Alan Berger, *Drosscape: Wasting Land in Urban America*. New York 2007, and idem, *Reclaiming the American West*. New York 2002; also Lars Lerup, *After the City*. Cambridge 2001, for the particular case of Houston, Texas—a city without zoning ordinances—as well as clarification of the terms "stim" and "dross."

4 Patrick Geddes' *Cities in Evolution* (1915) was a seminal publication documenting his claim to a shift toward a "neotechnic" city. For more on Patrick Geddes, see the excellent Volker M. Welter, *Biopolis: Patrick Geddes and the City of Life*. Cambridge 2002.

5 For a more thorough account of regionalism and its relation to Garnier's Cité Industrielle, see Dora Wiebenson, *Tony Garnier: The Cité Industrielle*. New York 1969, pp. 16–20.

concept, Garnier's vision anticipated growth and evolution through an expandable linear framework. Various programs were located in dense homogenous clusters, which were strategically proximate to each other.

Divided into either residential or public zones, the plan used circulation, green belts and park areas to modulate separations as required. To address the industrial component, the plan specifically called for a metallurgic factory, a silk manufacturing factory, mining, a cattle farm, abattoirs, a vineyard, and a hydroelectric station and dam. Garnier's city was conceived and strategically programmed to absorb the productive capacities of industry for its own benefit—for the production of energy, food and a strong economy.

Garnier's preoccupation with hygiene determined many aspects of the city's configuration: its east-west alignment, the height of building masses, its intricate drainage systems and the separation of functions. The overall zoning strategy was intended to better facilitate future expansion, though it also espoused a separation of functions, which became increasingly common throughout the 20th-century. It might even be argued that this prompted the proliferation of segregated, enclaved urban environments—that it catalyzed the growing dominance of suburban, peri-urban, and exurban typologies. Frank Lloyd Wright would later extend and critique Garnier and others with the spatial order promoted in his suburban-utopian Broadacre City (1932–59).[6]

But today, the growing interest in urban agriculture, renewable energy technologies, and positive-energy developments invites are-reading of early modern planning with regard to the productive urban surface.

Howard, Geddes and Garnier struggled to realize their visions in their own time—which is not unusual for planners—and the subsequent course of modern planning would do little to rectify the neglect of most of the essential components of their plans. But today, the growing interest in urban agriculture, renewable energy technologies, and positive-energy developments invites a re-reading of early modern planning with regard to the productive urban surface.

Resource Terrains. More than four decades after Garnier and the early regionalists, another important provocateur propelled and expanded our understanding of the interrelationships among engineering, design and the productive surface. Operating at a significantly larger scale than his predecessors, and with a predisposition to comprehensive thinking, R. Buckminster Fuller was one of the most complex figures in 20th-century architecture. His transdisciplinary focus—which led some to dismiss him as a dilettante—spurred him to pursue a holistic understanding of energy, resources and urbanization. John McHale, a stalwart supporter, described Fuller as a

6 For more on Frank Lloyd Wright, Ludwig Hilberseimer, and Andrea Branzi and the positions of an "agrarian urbanism," see Charles Waldheim, "Notes Towards a History of Agrarian Urbanism," in: *Bracket 1: On Farming*. Barcelona 2010.

die Sicht eines Biologen auf den Urbanismus auf, der Städte als Lebensformen versteht.[4] Howard, ein ausgebildeter Stenograph, stellte die Garden City als ideale Alternative zur aktuellen Stadtgestaltung dar. Garnier erweiterte diese Denkanstöße zu einem ausgearbeiteten und detaillierten Entwurfsvorschlag, der Cité Industrielle, die er in einer Zeitspanne von 15 Jahren entwickelte und 1918 in seiner Abhandlung veröffentlichte. Während jeder dieser Visionäre die Form und das Ausmaß der entstehenden Industriestadt erforschte, war es Garniers Vorschlag, der am genauesten die frühe moderne Bestrebung widerspiegelt, das Produktive inmitten des Wohnens anzusiedeln.

Beeinflusst durch den utopischen Sozialismus von Charles Fourier entstand die Cité Industrielle im Zusammenhang mit frühen Ausflügen in den Regionalismus.[5] Die Cité Industrielle, die für eine Hochebene im Südosten Frankreichs geplant war, nahm die Einrichtungen für Wohnen, Kultur, Verwaltung, Produktion und Landwirtschaft in eine gerasterte und in Zonen eingeteilte Stadt auf; Garnier fasste die Vorgaben des Ortes zugleich als Gelegenheit und Schwierigkeit auf. Im Unterschied zu Ebenezer Howards Konzept der Garden City nahm Garniers Idealplan Wachstum und Entwicklung durch eine erweiterbare, lineare Struktur vorweg. Verschiedene Funktionen waren in dichten, homogenen Blöcken angesiedelt, die strategisch nahe beieinander lagen.

Der Plan, der öffentliche Bereiche und Wohngebiete trennte, nutzte die Zirkulation, die Grüngürtel und Parkgebiete, um Abgrenzungen je nach Bedarf zu schaffen. Um den industriellen Anteil einzubeziehen, berücksichtigte der Plan besonders eine Metallfabrik, eine seidenverarbeitende Fabrik, Bergbau, eine Rinderfarm, Schlachthöfe, einen Weingarten, ein Wasserkraftwerk und einen Staudamm. Garniers Stadt wurde geplant und strategisch programmiert, um die produktiven Kapazitäten der Industrie zu ihrem eigenen Nutzen zu integrieren – für die Produktion von Energie, Nahrungsmitteln und einer starken Wirtschaft.

Garniers Augenmerk auf Hygiene bestimmte viele Aspekte der Konfiguration der Stadt: ihre West-Ost-Ausrichtung, die Höhe der Verbauung, ihr durchdachtes Abwassersystem und die Trennung von Funktionen. Die übergeordnete Strategie der Zoneneinteilung zielte darauf ab, eine zukünftige Erweiterung besser zu ermöglichen, obwohl dies auch mit einer Trennung der Funktionen einherging, was im Laufe des 20. Jahrhunderts zunehmend üblich wurde. Man könnte sogar behaupten, dass

4 Patrick Geddes' *Cities in Evolution* war eine bahnbrechende Veröffentlichung, die seine Forderung nach einer Veränderung in Richtung einer „neutechnischen" Stadt dokumentierte. Vgl. Patrick Geddes, *Cities in Evolution*. London 1915. Mehr zu Geddes vgl. Volker M. Welter, *Biopolis: Patrick Geddes and the City of Life*. Cambridge, MA 2002.

5 Zu einer tiefgehenderen Darstellung des Regionalismus und seiner Beziehung zu Garniers Cité Industrielle vgl. Dora Wiebenson, *Tony Garnier: The Cité Industrielle*. New York 1969, S. 16–20.

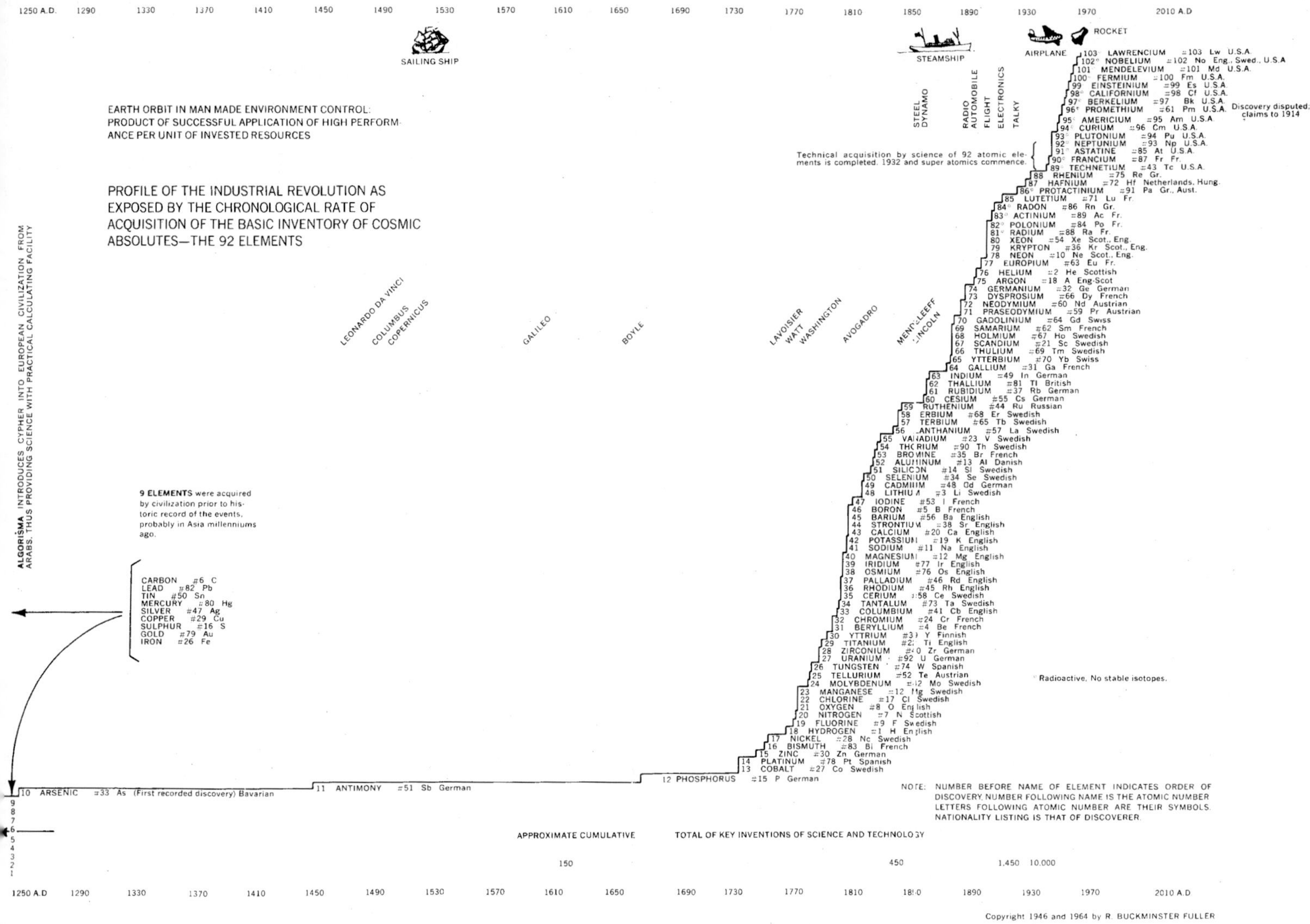

2

3

2 Buckmister Fuller, Struktur der Industriellen Revolution, 1946 (aktualisiert 1964), © The Estate of R. Buckminster Fuller.

3 Tony Garnier, *Une Cité Industrielle*, Luftbild aus der Ausstellung „Envois de Rome“, 1914.

2 Buckmister Fuller, profile of the industrial revolution, 1946 (updated 1964), © The Estate of R. Buckminster Fuller.

3 Tony Garnier, *Une Cité Industrielle*, aerial plan presented at the exhibit “Envois de Rome,” 1914.

dies die Verbreitung von abgegrenzten Enklaven städtischer Umgebung nach sich zog – und dass es den Anstoß zur wachsenden Vorherrschaft von suburbanen, periurbanen und exurbanen Typologien gab. Frank Lloyd Wright würde später mit dem räumlichen Ordnungssystem, das er in seiner suburbanutopischen Broadacre City (1932–1959) vorstellte, die Ideen von Garnier und anderen weiterentwickeln und kritisch hinterfragen.[6] Howard, Geddes und Garnier hatten Mühe, ihre Visionen zu ihrer Zeit zu realisieren – was für Planer nicht ungewöhnlich ist – und die nachfolgende Entwicklung der modernen Planung hat an der Mißachtung der wesentlichsten Bestandteile ihrer Entwürfe kaum etwas gutgemacht. Doch heute fordert das wachsende Interesse an städtischer Landwirtschaft, erneuerbaren Energietechnologien und Entwicklungen zur positiven Energiebilanz eine Relektüre der Entwürfe der frühen Moderne im Hinblick auf die produktive urbane Oberfläche.

McHale argued that both industry and agriculture needed to be reconceived and redesigned as "ecologically operating systems rather than piecemeal aggregates of unrelated processes."

Ressourcengebiete. Mehr als vier Jahrzehnte nach Garnier und den frühen Regionalisten hat ein anderer wichtiger Protagonist unser Verständnis der Wechselwirkungen zwischen Herstellung, Entwurf und produktiver Oberfläche angespornt und erweitert. R. Buckminster Fuller, der über eine besondere Fähigkeit zum ganzheitlichen Denken verfügte, bewegte sich in einer wesentlich weiteren Bandbreite als seine Vorgänger und war eine der komplexesten Persönlichkeiten der Architektur des 20. Jahrhunderts. Sein transdisziplinärer Schwerpunkt – der manche dazu verleitete, ihn als Dilettanten abzutun – trieb ihn dazu an, ein holistisches Verständnis von Energie, Ressourcen und Stadtentwicklung zu verfolgen. John McHale, ein unerschütterlicher Anhänger, beschrieb Fuller als ein Phänomen, das außerhalb des üblichen Kanons der Architekturbeurteilung liegt.[7]

Zwei Projekte seines umfangreichen Werkes ragen an dieser Stelle als besonders relevant heraus (bemerkenswerterweise erscheinen beide in den meisten Werksverzeichnissen etwas undeutlich). Das erste ist das „Profile of the Industrial Revolution", das zweite die Forschungsinitiative der World Design Science Decade 1965–1975, das zur Untersuchung und dem Entwurf des „World Game" führte.

In seinem „Profile of the Industrial Revolution" (1946 begonnen, 1964 aktualisiert) zeichnete Fuller die Entdeckung von 92 chemischen Elementen auf, beginnend 1250 als Albertus Magnus Arsen isolierte und bis zum Jahre 1961, als Wissenschaftler im Lawrence Berkeley Laboratorium Lawrencium

6 Mehr zu Frank Lloyd Wright, Ludwig Hilberseimer und Andrea Branzi und den Positionen des „agrarischen Urbanismus", bei Charles Waldheim, „Notes Towards a History of Agrarian Urbanism," in: *Bracket 1: On Farming*. Barcelona 2010.

7 „phenomenon [who] lies outside the customary canons of architectural judgment", John McHale, „Buckminster Fuller", in: *Architectural Review* 120/714 (Juli 1956), S. 12–20.

synthetisch herstellten. Fuller setzte die Grafik wirksam als Beweis für die Behauptung ein, die Menschheit habe „das komplette Inventar der Bauteile, aus denen das Universum aufgebaut sei, unter Kontrolle."[8] Die Elemente kommen in organischer und anorganischer Form vor, und werden durch Bergbau und andere den Boden verändernde Technologien extrahiert: kurz gesagt, werden sie aus dem Boden, dem Wasser oder der Luft gewonnen – durch eine Bewirtschaftung der Erdoberfläche oder Atmosphäre zum Zweck einer Neugestaltung und Umformung. In Fullers Schema werden biologische Ressourcen für pragmatische Zwecke entnommen (mit dem Ergebnis, Nahrung oder Energie zu gewinnen), während hingegen die elementaren Ressourcen als Ergebnis intellektuellen Wissensdrangs gefördert werden (mit dem Ergebnis, wissenschaftliche Erkenntnisse oder Materialien zu gewinnen).

Fuller griff seine Beschäftigung mit dieser Art von vollständiger Bestandsaufnahme in seiner Rede vor der International Union of Architects anlässlich des VII. Kongresses in London wieder auf. Die Architekturschulen müssten, behauptete er dort, „die nächsten zehn Jahre in das anhaltende Problem investieren, dass die gesamten Ressourcen der Erde, die derzeit nur 40 % dienen, durch kompetentes Design 100 % dienen."[9] Von da an produzierte Fuller in den Jahren 1965–1975 eine Reihe von Dokumenten, die alle unter dem Zeichen der World Design Science Decade standen. Fuller arbeitete eng mit dem Soziologen und Künstler John McHale zusammen, um beginnend mit „Inventory of World Resources, Human Trends, and Needs" diese ehrgeizigen Dokumente zu entwickeln. McHale engagierte sich zunehmend im WDSD Projekt und war der alleinige Autor des sechsten der Serie, die im Jahr 1967 unter dem Titel „The Ecological Context: Energy and Materials" erschien und später zu einem Buch erweitert wurde. Im Artikel und im Buch behauptete McHale, dass sowohl Industrie als auch Agrikultur neu erdacht und entworfen werden müssten als ökologisch operierende Systeme anstatt als bruchstückhafte Ansammlung unabhängiger Prozesse.[10] McHale schrieb weiter: „Unsere Absicht ist hier, die Rolle von anthropogenen Systemen umfänglicher zu bewerten, welche im gesamthaften Funktionieren des Systems auch natürliche Systeme sind."[11]

Das WDSD gipfelte 1965 im World Game, das auch im Hinblick auf die International and Universal Exposition, allgemein bekannt als Expo '67, die bald in Montreal eröffnet wer-

"phenomenon [who] lies outside the customary canons of architectural judgment."[7]

Two projects in his vast oeuvre stand out as particularly relevant here (notably, both have been somewhat obscured in most accounts of his work). The first is the "Profile of the Industrial Revolution"; the second is the research initiative World Design Science Decade 1965–75, which led to the study and proposition "World Game."

In his Profile of the Industrial Revolution (started 1946, updated 1964), Fuller charted the discovery of 92 chemical elements, beginning in 1250 when Albertus Magnus isolated arsenic and culminating in 1961 when scientists at Lawrence Berkeley Lab synthesized lawrencium. Fuller leverages the chart as evidence that humankind is in "command of the complete inventory of building components with which the universe is structured."[8] The elements occur organically and inorganically and are extracted through mining and other earth-altering techniques: in short, they are sourced from soil, water or air—farmed from the earth's surface or atmosphere for conversion and transformation. In Fuller's scheme, biological resources are extracted for pragmatic purposes (with food or energy as the results), while elemental resources are cultivated as a result of intellectual curiosity (with scientific knowledge or materials as the result).

Fuller's preoccupation with this kind of total inventory re-emerged in his 1961 speech to the International Union of Architects, at their VIIth Congress in London; there he argued that architecture schools must "invest the next ten years in a continuing problem of how to make the total world's resources, which now only serve 40 percent, serve 100 percent through competent design."[9] From this beginning Fuller then produced a series of documents, all under the banner of World Design Science Decade, 1965–75. Fuller worked closely with John McHale, a sociologist and artist, to develop these ambitious documents, starting in 1963 with "Inventory of World Resources, Human Trends, and Needs." McHale became increasingly involved in the WDSD project, and was sole author of the sixth in the series, the 1967 "The Ecological Context: Energy and Materials," later expanded into a book. In the article and book, McHale argued that both industry and agriculture needed to be reconceived and redesigned as "ecologically operating systems rather than piecemeal aggregates of unrelated processes."[10] McHale wrote that "[o]ur concern here is to more fully appraise the role of man-made systems which are also natural systems in the overall integral functioning of the system."[11]

The WDSD culminated in 1965 in World Game, which was also developed in anticipation of the International and Universal Exposition—known popularly as Expo '67—that would open soon in Montreal. The scale and ambition of Fuller's thinking is evident in his title—which to citizens of the 1960s would evoke not only the latest world's fair but also the World

8 Buckminster Fuller, „Earth, Inc.", in: James Meller (Hg.), *The Buckminster Fuller Reader*. London 1970, S. 223.

9 Buckminster Fuller, John McHale, *Phase I* (1963), vgl. Buckminster Fuller, John McHale, *Document 1: Inventory of World Resources Human Trends and Needs*. Carbondale 1963.

10 John McHale, *Phase II* (1967), vgl. John McHale, *Document 6: The Ecological Context: Energy and Materials*. Carbondale 1967, S. 7.

11 Ebd. S. 7.

7 John McHale, "Buckminster Fuller," in: *Architectural Review* 120/714 (July 1956), pp. 12–20.

8 Buckminster Fuller, "Earth, Inc.," in: James Meller (ed.), *The Buckminster Fuller Reader*. London 1970, p. 223.

9 Buckminster Fuller, John McHale, *Phase I* (1963), *Document 1: Inventory of World Resources Human Trends and Needs*. Carbondale 1963.

10 John McHale, *Phase II* (1967), *Document 6: The Ecological Context: Energy and Materials*. Carbondale 1967, p. 7.

11 Ibid.

Wars, the World Bank, the World Health Organization, etc. If Banham's *The Architecture of the Well-Tempered Environment* (1969) charted an overlooked environmental interior, then Fuller and McHale's WDSD Documents and World Game charted an overlooked environmental exterior. Each argued for a more efficient use of resources, land and materials—and did so years before the science of climate change emerged as a vital inquiry.

Specifically, the World Game located current and potential energy sources, resources, food trade, mobility patterns and education, all at the global scale. As Fuller explained: "[A] great world logistics game [could] be played by introducing into the computers all the known inventory and whereabouts of the various metaphysical and physical resources of the earth."[12] And in this way—though it would certainly be no easy undertaking—what Fuller called all "human trends, known needs and fundamental characteristics" could be calculated and mapped. According to Joachim Krausse and Claude Lichtenstein, editors of *Your Private Sky*, Fuller intended World Game to operate as a piece of software that could compute, "answers to the mounting social and ecological crisis, which he had been predicting since around 1950."[13]

It is significant that Fuller's argument for thinking comprehensively about planetary resources coincided with the famous images of Earth taken from space in the era's path-breaking space exploration program—enabling a view of the whole planet never before seen. Fuller's computational inventory and the astronauts' visual documentation: each encouraged thinking at ever larger scales. They also helped to launch the back-to-the-land movement of the 1970s counterculture, as chronicled in *The Whole Earth Catalog*, by Stewart Brand (an admirer of Fuller).[14]

The incorporation of resources, and the industries dependent on them, into design thinking is significant in the shift from mitigative sustainability to the productive surface. The inventories underlying the World Game, for example, were meant to offer not a single solution, but rather a resources framework for possible solutions.

Fuller wrote that to "accomplish the game's objective, the resources, pathways and dwelling points around the surface of our eight-thousand-mile-diameter, spherical Spaceship Earth must be employed by the players in such a way that the world's individual humans would each be able to exercise complete actional discretion."[15]

Much as aerial photography profoundly informed perceptions of the 20th-century landscape and thus influenced its uses, so today satellite imagery and Geographic Information Systems are changing 21st-century perceptions of land use and interpretation. These processes are bringing about new techniques for managing constructed surfaces, which geographer John May argues are not a type of infrastructure but instead "statistical-electrical

12 Joachim Krausse, Claude Lichtenstein (eds.), *Your Private Sky: R. Buckminster Fuller, The Art of Design Science*. Baden 1999, p. 473.

13 Ibid.

14 For more on *The Whole Earth Catalog* and cataloging, see Maya Przybylski, "The Catalog: From Ploughs to Clouds," in: *Bracket 1: On Farming*. Barcelona 2010. This was not the first effort at such cataloging. A century earlier, George P. Marsh published an impressively encompassing 644-page survey of current physical modifications to the environment and their quantifiable consequences. Marsh traces "the history of man's industry as exerted upon Animal and Vegetable Life, upon the Woods, upon the Waters, and upon Sands." See George P. Marsh, *The Earth as Modified by Human Action*. New York 1874, p. vii.

15 Krausse, Lichtenstein 1999 (fn. 12), pp. 473–479.

den sollte, entwickelt wurde. Der Maßstab und der Anspruch von Fullers Denken tritt in seinem Titel hervor – der bei Bürgern der 1960er-Jahre nicht nur die letzte Weltausstellung, sondern auch den Weltkrieg, die Weltbank und die Weltgesundheitsorganisation etc. ins Gedächtnis rief. Wenn Banhams *The Architecture of the Well-Tempered Environment* (1969) einen zu wenig beachteten, umweltbezogenen Innenraum aufzeigt, so stellen WDSD-Dokumente und World Game von Fuller und McHale einen zu wenig beachteten, umweltbezogenen Außenraum dar. Jeder setzt sich für eine effizientere Nutzung der Ressourcen, von Boden und Stoffen – und zwar Jahre bevor die wissenschaftliche Untersuchung des Klimawandels als wesentliches Forschungsgebiet auftauchte.

Vor allem das World Game setzte die aktuellen und potenziellen Energiequellen, Ressourcen, Lebensmittelgewerbe, Mobilitätsverhalten und Bildung mit einem globalen Maßstab in Verbindung. Fuller meint dazu: „Ein großartiges Weltlogistikspiel könnte gespielt werden, indem den Computern das gesamte bekannte Inventar und die Aufenthaltsorte der verschiedenen metaphysischen und physischen Ressourcen der Erde eingespeist würde."[12] Obwohl es sicherlich kein einfaches Unterfangen wäre, könnte auf diese Weise berechnet und ausgelegt werden, was Fuller zusammenfasst unter „human trends, known needs and fundamental characteristics" (menschliche Trends, bekannte Bedürfnisse und fundamentale Eigenschaften). Nach Joachim Krausse und Claude Lichtenstein, den Herausgebern von *Your Private Sky*, plante Fuller, dass das World Game wie ein Software Paket funktionieren sollte zur Berechnung der „Antworten zu der wachsenden sozialen und ökologischen Krise, welche er seit etwa 1950 vorhergesagt hatte."[13]

Bemerkenswert ist, dass Fullers Erörterung, ganzheitlich über die Ressourcen des Planeten zu denken, mit dem berühmten Bild der Erde zusammentraf, das vom Weltraum aus während des bahnbrechenden Programms zur Weltraumerforschung aufgenommen wurde – und das eine noch nie zuvor aufgenommene Ansicht des ganzen Planeten ermöglichte. Fullers rechnungsmäßige Bestandsaufnahme und die visuelle Dokumentation der Astronauten förderten beide eine Sichtweise in einem immer größeren Maßstab. Sie halfen auch bei der Gründung der back-to-the-land-Bewegung der 1970er-Gegenkultur, wie es in der Chronik *The Whole Earth Catalog* von Stewart Brand, einem Bewunderer Fullers, vermerkt ist.[14]

12 Joachim Krausse, Claude Lichtenstein (Hg.), *Your Private Sky: R. Buckminster Fuller, The Art of Design Science*. Baden 1999, S. 473.

13 Ebd., S. 473.

14 Über mehr zu *The Whole Earth Catalog* und zum Katalogisieren vgl. Maya Przybylski, „The Catalog: From Ploughs to Clouds", in: *Bracket 1: On Farming*. Barcelona 2010. Dieses Werk war nicht das erste Bestreben einer derartigen Katalogisierung. Ein Jahrhundert früher veröffentlichte George P. Marsh einen beeindruckend umfassenden 644-seitigen Überblick der aktuellen physischen Anpassungen an die Umgebung und ihre quantifizierbaren Folgen. Marsh skizziert „the history of man's industry as exerted upon Animal and Vegetable Life, upon the Woods, upon the Waters, and upon Sands." Vgl. George P. Marsh, *The Earth as Modified by Human Action*. New York 1874, S. vii.

Die Aufnahme der Ressourcen und der von ihnen abhängigen Industrie in das entwerferische Denken ist bedeutsam für den Übergang von einer mäßigen Nachhaltigkeit zur produktiven Oberfläche. Die Annahme, die beispielsweise dem World Game zugrunde liegt, sollte nicht eine einzelne Lösung aufzeigen, sondern vielmehr ein System an Hilfsmitteln für mögliche Lösungen.

Fuller schreibt: „Um das Ziel des Spiels zu erreichen, müssen die Ressourcen, die Wege und Aufenthaltsorte rund um die Oberfläche unseres achttausend Meilen Durchmesser großen kugelförmigen Raumschiffs Erde von den Spielern so eingesetzt werden, dass die menschlichen Individuen der Welt jedes für sich in der Lage wären, völlige Handlungsfreiheit auszuüben."[15]

Ebenso wie die Luftbildfotografie grundlegend die Wahrnehmung der Landschaft im 20. Jahrhundert beeinflusst hat und schließlich auch ihre Nutzung, verändern die Satellitenbilder und Geoinformationssysteme im 21. Jahrhundert die Wahrnehmung von der Bodennutzung und ihrer Interpretation. Diese Abläufe bringen auch neue Techniken mit sich, mit den gebauten Oberflächen umzugehen, die, wie der Geograf John May meint, nicht eine Form von Infrastruktur darstellen, sondern stattdessen „statistisch-elektrische Kontrollräume."[16] Und tatsächlich sind einige aktuelle Praktiken und Theoretiker als Protagonisten aus diesen Themen und Methoden hervorgegangen.[17]

Generative Flächen. Im letzten Jahrzehnt legte man den Schwerpunkt zunehmend auf die produktive Oberfläche. Massive Energieerzeugung, Wassergewinnung und Agrobusiness-Projekte verändern Gebäude und Landschaften – und zeigen Fullers Bestandsaufnahme als Bereiche der Intervention, Entwicklung und Gewinnung. Diese neuen Oberflächen bewirtschaften die Umwelt, ernten Erträge und erzeugen dabei Nebenprodukte, die selbst Bestandteil oder verteilt werden.

Ein Beispiel ist der bahnbrechende, 1100 Acre große River Rouge Complex von Ford Motors in Dearborn, Michigan, der von William McDonough + Partners 2003 neu gestaltet wurde, indem sie die Kapazität des großflächigen Daches in ein Wassergewinnungssystem umwandelten. Das begrünte Dach, das größte seiner Art in Nordamerika, reinigt nun ungefähr 10 Milliarden Gallonen Wasser jährlich durch ein System, das die Planer eine „industriegerechte" Landschaft nennen. Eine ähnliche Maßnahme wurde 2009 auf dem Dach des Atlantic City Convention Center in New Jersey durchgeführt. 13486 Photo-

15 Krausse, Lichtenstein 1999 (Anm. 12), S. 473–479.

16 John May, „The Logic of the Managerial Surface", Vortrag an der University of Toronto, 7.4.2010.

17 Das Center for Land Use Interpretation ist hier besonders hervorzuheben, ebenso Werk und Forschung von Keller Easterling, Albert Pope, Charles Waldheim, Alan Berger und P-REX, Pierre Belanger, Christopher Hight, Urban Lab, InfraNet Lab, und andere.

control spaces."[16] In fact, several contemporary practices and thinkers have emerged as proponents of these issues and methods.[17]

Generative Plots. In the last decade we find increasing focus on the productive surface. Massive energy generation, water harvesting, and agribusiness projects are transforming buildings and landscapes—turning Fuller's inventory into sites of intervention, development and generation. These new surfaces farm and harvest the environment, generating byproducts that are then integrated or distributed.

There is, for instance, the groundbreaking 2003 renovation of Ford Motors' 1,100-acre River Rouge Complex in Dearborn, Michigan, by William McDonough + Partners, which converted the liability of the massive roof into a water harvesting system. The living roof, the largest of its kind in North America, now cleans about 10 billion gallons of water annually in what the designers call an "industrial strength" landscape. A similar intervention was completed in 2009 on the roof of the Atlantic City Convention Center in New Jersey. 13,486 photovoltaic panels produce an average of 26 percent of the convention center's energy. Savings from the project are estimated at $4.4 million over the next 20 years. And in addition to water and solar, there is wind farming.[18] For example, the San Gorgonio Pass Wind Farm, installed during the 1990s and 2000s in southern California, comprises an array of 3,218 turbine units delivering 615 MW. Combined with the Altamont Pass and Tehachapi Pass wind farms, they account for 11 percent of the wind energy generated worldwide. Approval and development of these farms was initiated as early as 1981, in response to the 1970s energy crisis, meaning that some of the turbines are now significantly out of date. A renewal project that broke ground in 2008 at Tehachapi seeks to expand the field further, with ambitions to supply power to three million homes by 2013.

The shift in emphasis from the "function" of Modernism to the "production" of contemporary practice can be charted through relationship of architecture to the larger environment.

Then there are propositions and implementations of agriculture and the productive surface. Eurofresh Farms in Wilcox, Arizona—a place with no shortage of sunshine—houses some 318 acres of hydroponically grown tomatoes. In the United Kingdom, Thanet Earth, majority-owned by Fresca Group Ltd., has recently completed phase one of a massive greenhouse project in Kent. There tomatoes, peppers and cucumbers are grown in glass houses in which everything, according to its website, is "computer con-

16 John May, "The Logic of the Managerial Surface," lecture at the University of Toronto, April 7, 2010.

17 In particular, the Center for Land Use Interpretation is most notable here, but also the work and research of Keller Easterling, Albert Pope, Charles Waldheim, Alan Berger and P-REX, Pierre Belanger, Christopher Hight, Urban Lab, InfraNet Lab, among others.

18 For more on wind farms and agriculture, see Jason Sowell, "Cash Crops, Energy Landscapes," in: *Bracket 1: On Farming*. Barcelona 2010.

It is dynamic and responsive, yet occupiable and tangible. As the history of the productive surface emerges, its key provocateurs are likely to be corporations, venture capitalists, farmers and technologists. How might the productive surface generate new economies, programs, typologies and public realms? For the architect and landscape architect, the opportunity is ripe.

voltaik-Panele erzeugen durchschnittlich 26 Prozent des Energiebedarfs des Convention Center. Die Einsparungen durch dieses Projekt werden auf 4,4 Millionen Dollar für die nächsten 20 Jahre geschätzt. Zusätzlich zur Nutzung von Wasser- und Sonnenenergie findet auch die Energieerzeugung durch Wind statt.[18] Ein Beispiel dafür ist die San Gorgonio Pass Wind Farm, die während der 1990er- und 2000er-Jahre in Südkalifornien in Betrieb genommen wurde und aus einer Anzahl von 3218 Turbinenanlagen besteht, die 615 Megawatt liefern. Zusammen mit den Windfarmen von Altamont Pass und Tehachapi Pass beläuft sich ihre Leistung auf 11 Prozent der weltweit geförderten Windenergie. Zulassung und Entwicklung dieser Farmen wurden bereits 1981 als Antwort auf die Energiekrise der 1970er-Jahre in die Wege geleitet, so dass einige der Turbinen nun schon deutlich veraltet sind. Ein Erneuerungsprojekt, das 2008 in Tehachapi begonnen wurde, versucht dieses Gebiet zu erweitern und strebt an, drei Millionen Haushalte ab 2013 mit Energie zu versorgen.

Weitere Vorschläge und Anwendungen in Hinblick auf die Landwirtschaft und die produktive Oberfläche finden sich in den Eurofresh Farmen in Wilcox, Arizona – einem Ort mit mehr als genug Sonneneinstrahlung, an dem auf 318 Acre hydroponisch gezüchtete Tomaten gezogen werden. In Großbritannien hat Thanet Earth, das mehrheitlich der Fresca Group Ltd. angehört, vor kurzem die erste Phase einer großflächigen Treibhausanlage in Kent ausgeführt. Dort werden Tomaten, Paprika und Gurken in Glashäusern gepflanzt; auf ihrer Webseite ist der Ablauf folgendermaßen dargestellt: alles ist computergesteuert – von den Lamellen in der Decke zu den (zu öffnenden) Fenstern, der Zusammensetzung der Flüssigkeitszufuhr, der Heizung, dem Licht und der Kohlendioxidmenge. Die Planer wählten diesen Ort wegen seiner Lichtverhältnisse, der Nähe zur Energieversorgung, der regional hohen Arbeitslosigkeit und der guten Transportverbindungen. Besonders hervorzuheben, wenn auch von bescheidenerer Größenordnung, ist der vom Weißen Haus 2009 angelegte Gemüsegarten auf dem South Lawn, der Erste an diesem Ort seit Eleanor Roosevelts Victory Garden, welcher sich während des Zweiten Weltkrieges dort befand. In vielerlei Hinsicht sagt dies mehr aus als jede industrielle oder wissenschaftliche Entwicklung. Obwohl der Garten tatsächlich den Küchenchef des Weißen Hauses Sam Kass mit Produkten beliefert, verfolgt er freilich didaktische Ziele und seine Beete bringen Gemüse, Früchte, Kräuter und Honig hervor.[19] Um schädliche Käfer zu bekämpfen, verwendet das Team

18 Mehr zu Windfarmen und Landwirtschaft vgl. Jason Sowell, „Cash Crops, Energy Landscapes“, in: *Bracket 1: On Farming*. Barcelona 2010.

19 Um Obamas Gemüsegarten gab es einige Kontroversen, weil er auf dem „Volksrasen“ angelegt wurde. Viele meinten, dass der symbolische Wert des Rasens untergraben wurde. Die Ironie dieser Behauptung und Diskussion findet eine Parallele in der Forschung und den Projekten von Fritz Haeg und Heather Ring. Vgl. *Bracket 1: On Farming*. Barcelona 2010.

des Präsidenten nicht Pestizide, sondern Marienkäfer und Gottesanbeterinnen.

Entwürfe produzieren. Produktive Oberflächen formulieren einen neuen öffentlichen Raum und damit eine neue Öffentlichkeit – eine Öffentlichkeit ,die sich nicht dadurch kennzeichnet, dass sie urban, suburban oder ländlich ist, sondern dadurch, dass sie sich an der Erzeugung ihrer lebensnotwendigen Güter, ihrer Energie und Nahrung beteiligt. Die Verschiebung des Schwerpunkts von der „Funktion" des Modernismus zur „Produktion" der gegenwärtigen Praktiken kann mittels der Beziehung der Architektur zur Umgebung im weiteren Sinne aufgezeigt werden. Die produktive Oberfläche bringt Erzeugnisse hervor, und so reagiert sie nicht nur auf ihre Umwelt, sondern funktioniert in der Tat durch sie. Dies ist kein Mantra der Nachhaltigkeit, ebenso wie es keine biologische Politik verfolgt – das Ziel ist vielmehr eine Architektur der künstlichen Oberflächen, die in verschiedenen Maßstäben gebaute Gebiete versorgen, wozu auch das Dach, der Bauplatz ebenso wie das größere klimatologische und ökologische Gebiet gehören.

Die produktive Oberfläche schätzt und aktiviert das ihr innewohnende Potenzial zu saisonal bedingten oder regelmäßigen Erträgen. Sie ist dynamisch und interaktiv, doch auch benutzbar und konkret. Mit dem Hervortreten einer Geschichte der produktiven Oberfläche dürften ihre wichtigsten Protagonisten Unternehmen, Risikokapitalanleger, Landwirte und Technologen sein. Wie könnte die produktive Oberfläche neue Ökonomien, Programme, Typologien und eine neue Öffentlichkeit hervorbringen? Für Architekten und Landschaftsarchitekten ist die Gelegenheit günstig.

trolled—from the blinds in the ceilings to the [operable] windows, the liquid feed make-up, the heating, lighting and carbon dioxide levels." The project designers selected the site for its light levels, proximity to the national grid, high local unemployment and good transport links. Most notably, though more modest in scale, the White House installed a vegetable garden on the South Lawn in 2009, which is the first on that site since Eleanor Roosevelt's victory garden during World War II. In many ways, this is more telling than any industry or science development. Intended somewhat didactically—though it does provide produce for White House chef Sam Kass—the garden plots yield vegetables, fruits, herbs and honey.[19] And to control harmful bugs, the Presidential team deploys not pesticides but ladybugs and praying mantises.

Producing Design. Productive surfaces articulate a new public realm, and with that a new public—a public characterized not by whether it is urban, suburban, or rural, but by whether it participates in the cultivation of its necessities, of its energy and food. The shift in emphasis from the "function" of Modernism to the "production" of contemporary practice can be charted through relationship of architecture to the larger environment. The productive surface *yields*, making it not only responsive to its environment but indeed operational because of it. This is not a sustainability mantra so much as it is a biological one—the goal is an architecture of synthetic surfaces servicing variously scaled constructed environments, including the roof, the site, and the wider climatological and ecological territory.

The productive surface acknowledges and capitalizes on its innate potential for a seasonal or cyclical yield. It is dynamic and responsive, yet occupiable and tangible. As the history of the productive surface emerges, its key provocateurs are likely to be corporations, venture capitalists, farmers and technologists. How might the productive surface generate new economies, programs, typologies and public realms? For the architect and landscape architect, the opportunity is ripe.

"The Productive Surface" is excerpted from Bracket 1: On Farming, *edited by Mason White and Maya Przybylski.*

19 There was some controversy around the Obama's vegetable garden being constructed on the "people's lawn." Many felt that the symbolic value of the lawn had been compromised. The irony of this suggestion and controversy is paralleled in the research and projects of both Fritz Haeg and Heather Ring. See *Bracket 1: On Farming*. Barcelona 2010.

1 *Lunchbox Laboratory*; Materialien: Holz, recyceltes Plastik, Glas, Elektronische Bauteile, Algen; Futurefarmers (2008). *Lunchbox Laboratory*; materials: wood, recycled plastic, glass, electronics, algae; Futurefarmers (2008).

Futurefarmers

Lunchbox Laboratory

At once a practical tool for conducting environmental research and a symbolic gesture toward the democratization of such activity, *Lunchbox Laboratory*—a project created by the San Francisco-based collective Futurefarmers and Jonathan Meuser, a scientist with the Biological Sciences Team at the U.S. National Renewable Energy Lab—is a prototype for a portable lab designed to utilize distributed research methodologies to identify particularly productive strains of algae for use in renewable energy production.

Gleichzeitig ein praktikables Werkzeug zur Durchführung von Umweltforschung wie auch eine symbolische Geste in Richtung der Demokratisierung einer solchen Aktivität, ist *Lunchbox Laboratory* ein Projekt, das von der in San Francisco beheimateten Gemeinschaft Futurefarmers und Jonathan Meuser, Wissenschafter des Biological Sciences Teams am U.S. National Renewable Energy Lab, entwickelt wurde – ein Prototyp für ein tragbares Labor, um die wissenschaftliche Methode einer breit angelegten Identifizierung von produktiven Algenarten, welche in der Produktion von erneuerbarer Energie besondere Verwendung finden können, der Anwendung zuzuführen.

JEFFREY KASTNER

Founded in 1995 by artist Amy Franceschini, Futurefarmers is currently organized as a group of six individuals working at what is nominally a design studio, one whose projects typically involve political activism, interventions into social space, workshops, public actions, and what the team loosely defines as "sculpture." *Lunchbox Laboratory* is an example of the latter and took as its starting point the *DIY Algae/Hydrogen Kit*, a 2004 collaboration between Franceschini and Meuser at California's University of the Pacific that examined the potential for scalable, non-polluting hydrogen production using biophotolysis, or "water-splitting" carried out by modified strains of green algae. Yet as is often the case with Futurefarmers' work, the *DIY Algae* project was as much about making an argument for a particular mode of participatory activity as it was about reaching hard scientific results. *Lunchbox Laboratory* picks up this strategic thread and elaborates on it, identifying a particular physical form that allows for the research work to be conducted by a large group in a context that is both familiar and engaging.

Exhibited in the Museum of Modern Art's 2009 exhibition, *Design and the Elastic Mind*, the laboratory is a wooden case which instead of a school lunch contains a series of seven test tubes with which young scientists can gather algae samples for primary screening to determine their suitability for further research. The unit's functionality is belied by its extremely simple format and playful design—complete with easy-to-read step-by-step instructions and child-friendly logos. This egalitarian model operates in both political and instructional registers, producing a model of individual involvement with issues of ecological concern; marrying the practical and the symbolic with a kind of implicit critique in a way that only the best design can. It proposes a narrowing of the gap between the theoretical activities of a few and the pragmatic needs of the collective – bringing abstractions like "energy," "science," and indeed "nature," into a register both immediately understandable and eminently to hand.

Lunchbox Laboratory picks up this strategic thread and elaborates on it, identifying a particular physical form that allows for the research work to be conducted by a large group in a context that is both familiar and engaging.

Von Künstlerin Amy Francheschini 1995 gegründet umfasst Futurefarmers momentan eine Gruppe von sechs Personen, die in einem nominellen Designstudio arbeiten, dessen Projekte jedoch politischen Aktivismus, Interventionen im sozialen Raum, Workshops, öffentliche Aktionen, als auch das umfasst, was vom Team weitgehend als „Skulptur" definiert wird.

Lunchbox Labor ist ein Beispiel für Letzteres und nahm seinen Ausgangspunkt beim *DIY Algae/Hydrogen Kit* – Ergebnis der Zusammenarbeit zwischen Franceschini und Meuser an der University of the Pacific in Kalifornien im Jahr 2004, mit dem das Potenzial einer größenvariablen, ungiftigen Erzeugung von Wasserstoff unter Einsatz der Biophotolyse, oder „Wassertrennung" untersucht wurde, die mithilfe von modifizierten Arten grüner Algen umgesetzt werden kann. Wie bei der Arbeit von Futurefarmers oft der Fall handelte es sich bei dem *DIY Algae Projekt* gleichzeitig um eine Aussage bezüglich spezifischer Formen partizipatorischer Aktivitäten, wie es auch um die Erzeugung gesicherter wissenschaftlicher Resultate ging. *Lunchbox Laboratory* nimmt diesen strategischen Faden auf, um ihn weiter auszuführen, indem eine spezielle physische Form identifiziert wird, mit der die Forschungsarbeit in großer Gruppe und innerhalb eines Kontexts möglich wird, welcher gleichermaßen vertraut und anregend ist.

Die Laboreinheit, die 2009 im Museum of Modern Art im Rahmen der Ausstellung *Design and the Elastic Mind* gezeigt wurde, besteht aus einem hölzernen Gehäuse, das anstatt eines Pausenbrots sieben Reagenzgläser enthält, mit denen junge Wissenschaftler Algenproben für initiale Untersuchungen zusammentragen können, um deren Eignung zur weiteren Erforschung zu bestimmen. Die Funktionalität der Einheit straft ihr extrem einfaches Format und spielerisches Design Lügen, das mit leicht zu lesenden Schritt-für-Schritt-Anleitungen und kinderfreundlichen Logos ergänzt ist. Dieses egalitäre Modell operiert sowohl auf einer politischen wie erzieherischen Ebene und erzeugt ein Format von persönlicher Verbundenheit mit Themen von ökologischem Belang; so verbindet es das Praktische mit dem Symbolischen und einer Art impliziter Kritik, wie es nur das beste Design leisten vermag. Es schlägt die Verringerung der Lücke zwischen theoretischen Aktivitäten von Einigen wenigen und den praktischen Bedürfnissen einer Gemeinschaft vor, um abstrakte Begriffe wie „Energie", „Wissenschaft" und sogar „Natur" einem unmittelbaren Bezugssystem zuzuführen, welches gleichermaßen Verständlichkeit wie praktische Handhabbarkeit erzeugt.

Übersetzung Claudia Wrumnig

2 *Lunchbox Laboratory*; Materialien: Holz, recyceltes Plastik, Glas, Elektronische Bauteile, Algen; Futurefarmers (2008). *Lunchbox Laboratory*; materials: wood, recycled plastic, glass, electronics, algae; Futurefarmers (2008).

1 Ludwig Hilbersheimer, "The City in the Landscape," 1944, © Ryerson & Burnham Library Archives, The Art Institute of Chicago.

Notes Toward a History of Agrarian Urbanism

The categories of *agrarian* and *urban* are usually understood as distinct. Across many disciplines, and for centuries, the country and the city have been defined in opposition to one another. But today, in striking contrast, design culture and discourse abound with claims for the potential for urban agriculture.

Bemerkungen zu einer Geschichte des agrarischen Urbanismus. Die Kategorien *agrarisch* und *urban* werden für gewöhnlich als unterschiedlich angesehen. In vielen Disziplinen und über Jahrhunderte hinweg wurden das Land und die Stadt durch ihre Gegensätzlichkeit zueinander definiert. In bemerkenswertem Kontrast hierzu finden sich heute jedoch innerhalb der Design-Kultur und ihrem Diskurs reichlich Forderungen nach Möglichkeitsformen urbaner Agrikultur.

CHARLES WALDHEIM

As environmental literacy among designers and scholars has grown, so too has enthusiasm for agricultural production in and around cities; contributing to this trend is rising public interest in food and its production and distribution in a globalized world.

Contemporary interest in food is being shaped by various authors and interests, who argue for the more sustainable practices associated with local food production, reduced carbon footprint, better public health and the related benefits of pre-industrial farming techniques, including enhanced biodiversity and ecological health. Among the strongest advocates for these goals are the slow food and locavore movements.

While much has been written about the implications of urban farming for agricultural production, public policy, and food as an element of culture, little has been written about the potentially profound implications for the shape and structure of the city itself. To date the enthusiasm for slow and local food has been based, on the one hand, on the assumption that abandoned or underused brownfield sites could be remediated for their productive potential; and on the other it has been based on the trend toward conserving greenfield sites on city peripheries—on dedicating valuable ecological zones to food production and to limiting suburban sprawl. But these laudable goals are not much concerned with how urban farming might affect urban form. This suggests that we need to probe further into the possibilities of agricultural urbanism: so here I would like to outline a history of urban form perceived through the spatial, ecological and infrastructural import of agricultural production. In choosing the projects that comprise this tentative counter-history, I am conceiving of agricultural production as a *formative* element of city structure, rather than as an adjunct, something to be inserted into already existing structures. And I am seeking to construct a useful past from three projects organized explicitly around the role of agriculture in determining the economic, ecological and spatial order of the city.

> I am conceiving of agricultural production as a formative element of city structure, rather than as an adjunct, something to be inserted into already existing structures.

Many 20th century urban planning projects aspired to construct an agrarian urbanism—in some cases to reconcile the seemingly contradictory impulses of the industrial metropolis with the social and cultural conditions of agrarian settlement. In many of these projects, agrarianism offered a counterpoint to the increasingly dense metropolises that grew with the great migrations from farm villages to industrial cities in the 19th and early 20th centuries, especially in Western Europe and North America. Some early modernist proposals took their agrarian inspirations from the relatively decentralized industrial model favored by Henry Ford and others in the 1910s and 1920s—a preference that led to spatial decentralization and the abandonment of older, denser cities. A decade or so later, partly in response to the Great Depression, planners saw agrarianism as a kind of bridge between the rural practice of subsistence farming and the increasingly vulnerable urban workforce.

Mit den gestiegenen umweltpolitischen Kenntnissen von Designern und Wissenschaftlern ist auch der Enthusiasmus für agrikulturelle Produktion in und um die Städte gewachsen; das steigende öffentliche Interesse an Nahrungsmitteln, an deren Produktion und Verteilung in einer globalisierten Welt trägt zu diesem Trend bei.

Das gegenwärtige Interesse an Nahrungsmitteln wird von verschiedenen Autoren und Interessengruppen geteilt, die für nachhaltige Praktiken in Bezug auf lokale Nahrungsmittelproduktion, reduzierten Kohlenstoffausstoß, bessere Gesundheit der Bevölkerung und die damit verbundenen Vorteile der vorindustriellen landwirtschaftlichen Techniken eintreten, einschließlich höherer Artenvielfalt und ökologischer Gesundheit. Zu den wichtigsten Verfechtern dieser Ziele gehören die „slow food" und „locavore" Bewegungen.

Während viel über die Auswirkungen städtischer Landwirtschaft auf die agrikulturelle Produktion, öffentliche Planung und über Nahrungsmittel als kulturelle Werte geschrieben wurde, findet sich nur wenig über die möglicherweise tiefgreifenden Auswirkungen auf Form und Struktur der Stadt selbst. Bisher basierte der Enthusiasmus für „slow food" und regionale Lebensmittel einerseits auf der Annahme, dass aufgegebene oder zu wenig genutzte Brachfelder ihr produktives Potenzial wieder entfalten könnten, und andererseits gründete er auf dem Trend, Grünflächen an den Peripherien der Städte zu erhalten, indem man wertvolle ökologische Zonen der Lebensmittelproduktion widmet und die Ausbreitung der Vorstädte einschränkt. Diese lobenswerten Ziele befassen sich allerdings kaum mit der Frage, wie urbane Landwirtschaft die städtische Form beeinflussen könnte. Dies regt dazu an, die Möglichkeiten des agrikulturellen Urbanismus näher zu untersuchen: Ich möchte hier eine Geschichte der städtischen Form aufzeigen, die hinsichtlich einer räumlichen, ökologischen und infrastrukturellen Aneignung der Agrarproduktion in den Blick genommen wird. Indem ich Projekte wähle, die diese Art von Gegengeschichte in sich fassen, verstehe ich die Agrarproduktion als ein *formierendes* Element der Stadtstruktur, nicht als eine Ergänzung, die in bereits existierende Strukturen eingefügt werden müsste. So versuche ich einen überzeugenden Blick auf die Vergangenheit mit Hilfe von drei Projekten zu werfen, die explizit auf der Rolle der Landwirtschaft bei der Bestimmung der wirtschaftlichen, ökonomischen und räumlichen Struktur der Stadt aufbauen.

Viele Projekte zur Stadtplanung des 20. Jahrhunderts strebten nach der Entwicklung eines agrarischen Urbanismus – in manchen Fällen mit dem Ziel, die scheinbar widersprüchlichen Kräfte der industriellen Metropole mit den sozialen und kulturellen Bedingungen landwirtschaftlicher Erschließung in Einklang zu bringen. In vielen dieser Projekte bot Landwirtschaft ein Gegenstück zu den immer dichter besiedelten Metropolen, die durch die starke Migration von den bäuerlichen Dörfern in

die Industriestädte im 19. und im frühen 20. Jahrhundert besonders in Westeuropa und in Nordamerika wuchsen. Manche Vorschläge der frühen Moderne nahmen ihre landwirtschaftlichen Inspirationen von dem relativ dezentralisierten industriellen Modell, das Henry Ford und andere in den 1910er- und 1920er-Jahren bevorzugten – eine Tendenz, die zu räumlicher Dezentralisierung und zur Aufgabe älterer Städte mit höherer Bevölkerungsdichte führte. Etwa ein Jahrzehnt später sahen Planer die Förderung der Landwirtschaft als eine Art Verbindung zwischen der ländlichen Praxis der Subsistenzwirtschaft und der immer stärker in Anhängigkeit geratenen städtischen Arbeitskraft – auch als Antwort auf die „Große Depression". Durch die Koppelung von Industrie und Landwirtschaft entwarfen einige modernistische Stadtplaner ein rotierendes Beschäftigungssystem, in dem Arbeiter zwischen Fabrik und kollektiven Farmen wechselten; oft wurde diese neue räumliche Struktur als großflächige Landschaftsregionen geplant und ihre Darstellungen kombinierten Luftbilder und orthografische Karten.

Wir können diese neuen Tendenzen an drei ungebauten Projekten sehen, die für einen dezentralisierten agrarischen Urbanismus eintraten: Frank Lloyd Wrights „Broadacre City" (1934–1935), Ludwig Hilberseimers „New Regional Pattern" (1945–1949), und Andrea Branzis „Agronica" (1993–1994), sowie die Weiterentwicklung „Territory for the New Economy" (1999).[1] Obwohl Jahrzehnte zwischen diesen Projekten liegen und sie von drei sehr unterschiedlichen Autoren stammen, zeigen sie gemeinsam betrachtet viele der Auswirkungen von agrikultureller Produktion auf die urbane Form; sie besitzen auch eine zusammenhängende Ideengeschichte: Branzi verweist auf Hilberseimer, der sich wiederum an Wright orientierte. Jedes dieser Projekte schlug eine grundlegende Neuplanung der Stadt vor – eine radikale Dezentralisation und Auflösung der urbanen Gestalt in eine produktive Landschaft. Diese Auflösung der Gestalt im Feld machte die klassische Unterscheidung zwischen Stadt und Land irrelevant und ersetzte sie durch eine Kombination von Vorstadt und Region – ein suburbanisierter Regionalismus. Ausgehend vom gegenwärtigen Interesse an urbaner Landwirtschaft bieten diese Vorschläge anschauliche Alternativen zur klassischen Geschichte der städtischen Form.

Die Arbeiten dieser Urbanisten enthalten zwei große Annahmen: dass Städte weiter dezentralisiert und dass die *Landschaft* das primäre Medium der städtischen Form werden würden. Die suburbanen Landschaften in den Projekten von Wright, Hilberseimer und Branzi wurden mit agrikulturellen Landschaften – mit Farmen und Feldern – aufgefüllt; die Projekte

1 Frank Lloyd Wright, *The Living City*. New York 1958; Ludwig Hilberseimer, *The New Regional Pattern: Industries and Gardens, Workshops and Farms*. Chicago 1949; Andrea Branzi, D. Donegani, A. Petrillo und C. Raimondo, „Symbiotic Metropolis: Agronica", in: Ezio Manzini, Marco Susani (Hg.), *The Solid Side*. Netherlands 1995, S. 101–120; Andrea Branzi, „Preliminary Notes for a Master Plan", und „Master Plan Strijp Philips, Eindhoven 1999", in: *Lotus* 107 (2000), S. 110–123.

Through mixing industry with agriculture, some modernist urban planners imagined a rotational labor system in which workers alternated between factory jobs and collective farms; usually these new spatial orders were conceptualized as vast regional landscapes, and their representations conflated aerial views and orthographic maps.

We can read these emerging tendencies through three unbuilt projects that advocated for decentralized agrarian urbanism: Frank Lloyd Wright's "Broadacre City" (1934–35), Ludwig Hilberseimer's "New Regional Pattern" (1945–49), and Andrea Branzi's "Agronica" (1993–94), and its further development, "Territory for the New Economy" (1999).[1] Although produced decades apart by three very different authors, these projects, considered collectively, illustrate many of the implications of agricultural production for urban form; they also form a coherent intellectual genealogy, with Branzi referencing Hilberseimer, who earlier had been informed by Wright. Each of these projects proposed a profound reconceptualization of the city—a radical decentralization and dissolution of the urban figure into a productive landscape. The dissolution of figure into field rendered the classical distinction between city and countryside irrelevant, replacing it with a conflation of suburb and region—a suburbanized regionalism. Given contemporary interest in urban agriculture, these propositions offer compelling alternatives to what has become the canonical history of city form.

Implicit in the work of these urbanists were two large assumptions: that cities would continue to be decentralized, and that *landscape* would become the primary medium of urban form. The suburban landscapes in the projects of Wright, Hilberseimer and Branzi were fleshed out with agricultural landscapes—with farms and fields; the projects encompassed large territorial or regional networks of urban infrastructure that brought existing natural environments into new relationships with planned agricultural and industrial landscapes.

Broadacres/Usonia. In the depths of the Depression, lacking good projects and reasonable prospects for the recovery of his once towering reputation, Frank Lloyd Wright persuaded his lone remaining patron—Edgar J. Kauffman, who would later commission Fallingwater—to fund a traveling exhibition of Wright's grand proposal for an organic American urbanism. Broadacre City consisted of a large model—12 feet by 12 feet—and supporting materials produced by student apprentices at Taliesin in the winter of 1934–35. Although the intellectual premises of the project were evident in Wright's lectures as early as the 1920s, and fully articulated in his 1932 book *The Disappearing City*, the Broadacre model and drawings were not debuted until an exhibition in 1935 in New York City. Subsequently, the exhibition toured extensively, and the remarkably durable project was further disseminated in such publications as *When Democracy Builds* (1945) and *The Living City* (1958).[2]

1 Frank Lloyd Wright, *The Living City*. New York 1958; Ludwig Hilberseimer, *The New Regional Pattern: Industries and Gardens, Workshops and Farms*. Chicago 1949; Andrea Branzi, D. Donegani, A. Petrillo, and C. Raimondo, "Symbiotic Metropolis: Agronica," in: Ezio Manzini, Marco Susani (eds.), *The Solid Side*. Netherlands 1995, pp. 101–120; Andrea Branzi, "Preliminary Notes for a Master Plan," and "Master Plan Strijp Philips, Eindhoven 1999," in: *Lotus* 107 (2000), pp. 110–123.

2 The principles underpinning Wright's Broadacre project were published in 1932 in: Frank Lloyd Wright, *Disappearing City*. New York 1932; and subsequently reformulated as: idem, *When Democracy Builds*. Chicago 1945. For an historical overview of Broadacre's influences and contemporary reception, see Peter Hall, *Cities of Tomorrow*. Oxford 1996, pp. 285–90.

2 Andrea Branzi et al., „Masterplan Strijp Philips, Eindhofen", Modellansicht (1999–2000), © Andrea Branzi.
3 Andrea Branzi et al., „Masterplan Strijp Philips, Eindhofen", Modellansicht – Detail (1999–2000), © Andrea Branzi.
2 Andrea Branzi et al., "Masterplan Strijp Philips, Eindhofen," model view (1999–2000), © Andrea Branzi.
3 Andrea Branzi et al., "Masterplan Strijp Philips, Eindhofen," model view—detail (1999–2000), © Andrea Branzi.

umfassten weite gebietsbezogene oder regionale Netzwerke städtischer Infrastruktur, die die existierenden natürlichen Umgebungen in ein neues Verhältnis zu den geplanten agrikulturellen und industriellen Landschaften setzten.

Broadacres/Usonia. Als gute Projekte und vernünftige Aussichten auf eine Wiederherstellung seines einst überragenden Rufes am Tiefpunkt der wirtschaftlichen Depression nicht in Sicht waren, überzeugte Frank Lloyd Wright seinen einzigen verbleibenden Bauherrn – Edgar J. Kauffman, der später die Kommission Fallingwater leiten sollte, davon, eine Wanderausstellung von Wrights bedeutendem Entwurf für einen organischen Urbanismus für Amerika zu finanzieren. Broadacre City bestand aus einem 12 x 12 Fuß großen Modell und weiteren Unterlagen, die von studentischen Praktikanten in Taliesin im Winter 1934–1935 erstellt wurden. Obwohl die intellektuellen Thesen des Projekts bereits in Wrights Vorträgen in den 1920er-Jahren geäußert und in seinem Buch *The Disappearing City* von 1932 ausformuliert worden sind, wurden das Modell und die Zeichnungen von Broadacre erstmals 1935 bei einer Ausstellung in New York City vorgestellt. In der Folge wurde die Ausstellung vielerorts gezeigt und das Projekt fortwährend in Büchern wie *When Democracy Builds* (1945) und *The Living City* (1958) weiter publiziert.[2]

Broadacre City zeigte dem amerikanischen Publikum am deutlichsten die Kernthesen von Wrights vernichtender Kritik an der modernen Industriestadt; es schlug für die nordamerikanische Besiedelung ein einheimisches, organisch strukturiertes Modell auf einer prinzipiell grenzenlosen Ebene von kultivierter Landschaft vor. Broadacre vermied die traditionelle europäische Unterscheidung zwischen Stadt und Land und stellte eher ein Netzwerk von Transport- und Kommunikationsinfrastruktur auf Basis des Jeffersonschen Rasters als grundlegendem Ordnungssystem vor. Innerhalb dieses beinahe undifferenzierten Feldes sollte die Bezirksverwaltung (angeführt vom Bezirksarchitekten) weitere Regierungsebenen ersetzen und eine Bevölkerung von Landbesitzern als Bürger und Farmer verwalten. Wright war sicherlich mit Henry Fords Vorstellungen von dezentralisierter Besiedelung vertraut, denen er sehr aufgeschlossen gegenüberstand; das ähnlichste verwirklichte Vergleichsbeispiel zu Broadacre bilden Fords Bestrebungen, die zur Gründung der Tennessee Valley Authority führen sollten – der durch den New Deal initiierten Behörde, die die Konstruktion eines Netzwerkes von Wasserkraftwerken und Auto-

2 Die Prinzipien, die Wrights Broadacre Projekt zugrunde liegen, wurden 1932 publiziert in: Frank Lloyd Wright, *Disappearing City*. New York 1932; und anschließend formuliert in: ders., *When Democracy Builds*. Chicago 1945. Für einen historischen Überblick über den Einfluss von Broadacre und die aktuelle Rezeption vgl. Peter Hall, *Cities of Tomorrow*. Oxford 1996, S. 285–290.

Broadacre City offered American audiences the clearest crystallization of Wright's damning critique of the modern industrial city; it posited an indigenous organic model for North American settlement across an essentially boundless plain of cultivated landscape. Eschewing traditional European distinctions between city and countryside, Broadacre proposed a network of transportation and communication infrastructures, with the Jeffersonian grid as its principal ordering system. Within this nearly undifferentiated field, the county government (headed by the county architect) replaced other levels of government, administering a population of landowning citizen-farmers. Wright was clearly conversant with and sympathetic to Henry Ford's notion of decentralized settlement, and the closest built parallel for Broadacre can be found in Ford's instigation of what would become the Tennessee Valley Authority—the New Deal-authorized public agency that oversaw the construction of a network of hydroelectric dams and highways along the Tennessee River, enabling the electrification of the region and seeding its urbanization.[3]

With ownership of one acre of land per person as a birthright, residents of Broadacre (or Usonia, as Wright would later call it) would enjoy modern houses sited amid ample subsistence gardens and small-scale farms. This basic pattern of variously scaled housing and landscape types was interspersed with light industry, small commercial centers and markets, civic buildings and, of course, the ubiquitous highway. Despite Broadacre's extremely low density, most of the ground was cleared and cultivated. Occasionally this constructed and maintained landscape relented in favor of extant waterways, topographic features, or other existing ecologies. Presumably the extrapolation of Broadacre City from its chiefly middle-western origins to the margins of the continent would have been accomplished with varying degrees of accommodation to local climate, geography and geology, if not cultural or material history. The status of previously urbanized areas remained an open question; perhaps these would need to be abandoned in place, again following Ford's lead.

Within this nearly undifferentiated field, the county government (headed by the county architect) replaced other levels of government, administering a population of landowning citizen-farmers.

Wright's critique of private ownership, conspicuous consumption, and the accumulation of wealth associated with cities was no small part of the social critique embodied in Broadacre, which was conceived in the worst years of the Depression, when bankrupt family farmers were fleeing their mortgaged fields in the middle of the country and relocating to the East Coast or to California. Ironically, given his anxiety over the corrosive effects of wealth and speculative capital, Wright found in Ford's notion of regional infrastructure the basis for an American pattern of urban development:

3 For an overview of the Tennessee Valley Authority, see Walter Creese, *TVA's Public Planning*. Knoxville 1990; and Hall 1996 (fn. 2), pp. 161–163.

bahnen am Tennessee River überwachte und die Elektrifizierung und Urbanisierung der Region ermöglichte.[3]

Mit dem Besitz eines Acre Land als Geburtsrecht jeder Person könnten sich Bewohner von Broadacre (oder Usonia, wie Wright sie später nennen sollte) moderner Häuser erfreuen, die zwischen weitläufigen Hausgärten und kleinen Farmen lägen. Dieses Grundmuster verschieden großer Häuser und Landschaftstypen wurde von Kleinindustrie, kleinen Handelszentren und Märkten, öffentlichen Bauten und selbstverständlich der allgegenwärtigen Autobahn unterbrochen. Trotz Broadacres extrem geringer Dichte war der Großteil des Bodens gerodet und kultiviert. Gelegentlich wurde diese geplante und bewirtschaftete Landschaft von einem bestehenden Wasserlauf, topografischen Gegebenheiten oder anderer bereits vorhandener ökologischer Umwelt aufgelockert. Man kann annehmen, dass Broadacre City von ihren Ursprüngen hauptsächlich im mittleren Westen zu den Rändern des Kontinents mit unterschiedlichen Graden der Anpassung an das lokale Klima, die Geografie und Geologie, wenn nicht sogar an die kulturelle oder materielle Geschichte weitergeführt worden wäre. Der Status von bereits bestehenden städtischen Gebieten blieb eine offene Frage; vielleicht hätten diese, wenn man Fords Argumentation folgt, aufgegeben werden müssen.

Wrights Missbilligung von Privatbesitz, von zur Schau gestelltem Konsum und der Anhäufung von Wohlstand, den er mit Städten in Zusammenhang brachte, war ein beträchtlicher Teil der in Broadacre enthaltenen Sozialkritik; der Entwurf entstand in den schlimmsten Jahren der Depression, als bankrotte Farmerfamilien ihre mit Hypotheken belasteten Felder in der Mitte des Landes verließen, um an die Ostküste oder nach Kalifornien auszuwandern. Ironischerweise fand Wright, der über die negativen Effekte des Wohlstands und des spekulativen Kapitals besorgt war, gerade in Fords Begriff von regionaler Infrastruktur die Basis für ein amerikanisches Muster urbaner Entwicklung: Broadacre sollte einen Ausweg aus den unerbittlichen Anforderungen des Profitstrebens aufzeigen, das er mit Industriestädten in Zusammenhang brachte, obwohl sich die amerikanische Stadt, angetrieben durch die in hohem Maße kapitalistischen Strategien der fordistischen Produktionsweise, ebenfalls in Richtung Dezentralisierung bewegte.

Ironically, given his anxiety over the corrosive effects of wealth and speculative capital, Wright found in Ford's notion of regional infrastructure the basis for an American pattern of urban development: Broadacre was intended to provide a respite from the relentless demands of profit associated with the industrial city, even as the American city was well on a course toward decentralization, driven by the highly capitalist strategies of Fordist production.

Das neue regionale Muster/Die neue Stadt. Ein anderer modernistischer Architekt bzw. Urbanist, der sich mit den Einflüssen der Dezentralisierung auf die urbane Form auseinandersetzte, war Ludwig Hilberseimer. Er wurde in Karlsruhe, Deutschland, geboren und ausgebildet, und arbeitete gemeinsam mit Mies van der Rohe am Bauhaus, bis sie der Aufstieg

3 Für einen Überblick über die Tennessee Valley Authority vgl. Walter Creese, *TVA's Public Planning*. Knoxville 1990; und Hall 1996 (Anm. 2), S. 161–163.

des Faschismus im Jahre 1938 zur Emigration nach Chicago und an das Armour (später Illinois) Institute of Technology zwang. Während Hilberseimer vor allem durch seine Studien aus den 1920er-Jahren bekannt geworden ist, die im strikten, ja totalisierenden Rationalismus von Projekten wie etwa der *Hochhausstadt* gehalten sind, gab er deren Siedlungsformen rasch auf, um sich Aufgaben zuzuwenden, die eine Dezentralisierung als mögliches Mittel gegen die Übel der Industriestadt erforschten. Dies wurde bereits 1927 in einem Entwurf klar ersichtlich, der die „Großstadt als Gartenstadt“[4] darstellte; in den 1930er-Jahren wurde Hilberseimer immer stärker von europäischen Vorläufern der Gartenstadt beeinflusst. Seine Projekte aus dieser Zeit setzen Landschaft und Wohnbebauung mit unterschiedlichen Geschossen ein, um eine niedrige Bevölkerungsdichte zu schaffen; beginnend mit seiner *Mischbebauung* von 1930 sollte dieses Muster sein amerikanisches Werk über die nächsten Jahrzehnte hinweg bestimmen.

In den 1940er-Jahren nahm Hilberseimers Konzept der „Siedlungseinheit“ eine klare Form an, besonders in seiner Vorwegnahme eines Autobahnsystems über das ganze Land und in seiner präzisen Beschreibung der Beziehungen zwischen Transportnetzwerken, Siedlungseinheiten und der regionalen Landschaft. In den Nachkriegsjahren wurde sein Interesse am organischen Urbanismus durch die Anforderungen des Zivilschutzes weiter angeregt, der eine Dezentralisierung befürwortete.[5] In diesem Zusammenhang – und auch beeinflusst von Broadacre City, sowie der progressiven Tennessee Valley Authority und deren Befürwortern in der Regional Planning Association of America – entwickelte Hilberseimer sein neues regionales Muster als Strategie für eine Urbanisierung mit geringer Dichte, die auf regionalen Hauptverbindungsstraßen und natürlichen Umweltbedingungen basieren sollte; 1949 veröffentlichte Hilberseimer seine Ideen in *The New Regional Pattern: Industries and Gardens, Workshops and Farms*.[6]

Ebenso wie Broadacre war auch das „neue regionale Muster“ um Transport- und Kommunikationsnetzwerke angelegt, die eine im Wesentlichen horizontale, landschaftsdominierte, vorstädtische Siedlungsform vereinten. Häuser, Farmen, Kleinindustrie, Geschäftsgebäude und öffentlicher Raum: alles wurde über ein weitläufiges Gebiet hinweg errichtet. Doch das

4 Für einen Überblick über die Ursprünge von Hilberseimers Interpretation der Gartenstadt vgl. David Spaeth, „Ludwig Hilberseimer's Settlement Unit: Origins and Applications“, in: Richard Pommer, David Spaeth, Kevin Harrington (Hg.), *In the Shadow of Mies: Ludwig Hilberseimer, Architect, Educator, and Urban Planner*. New York/Chicago 1988, S. 54–68.

5 Hilberseimer und Caldwell befürworteten im Zuge von Hiroshima die Dezentralisierung als Strategie für den Zivilschutz. Vgl. Caldwell, „Atomic Bombs and City Planning“, in: *Journal of the American Institute of Architects* 4 (1945), S. 289–299; und auch Hilberseimer, „Cities and Defense“ [1945], Nachdruck in: Pommer, Spaeth, Harrington 1988 (Anm. 4), S. 89–93.

6 Vgl. auch Ludwig Hilberseimer, *The New City: Principles of Planning*. Chicago 1944; ders., *The Nature of Cities: Origin, Growth, and Decline, Pattern and Form, Planning Problems*. Chicago 1955.

Broadacre was intended to provide a respite from the relentless demands of profit associated with the industrial city, even as the American city was well on a course toward decentralization, driven by the highly capitalist strategies of Fordist production.

The New Regional Pattern/The New City. Another modernist architect/urbanist who grappled with the impacts of decentralization on urban form was Ludwig Hilberseimer. Born and educated in Karlsruhe, Germany, Hilberseimer worked with Mies van der Rohe at the Bauhaus until the rise of fascism precipitated their emigration to Chicago and the Armour (later Illinois) Institute of Technology in 1938. While Hilberseimer is most notoriously known for his 1920s studies for the strict, even totalizing rationalism of projects such as *Hochhausstadt* (Highrise City), Hilberseimer had in fact quickly abandoned those schemes in favor of projects that explored decentralization as a remedy for the ills of the industrial city. This was evident as early as 1927 in a sketch depicting "The Metropolis as a Garden-City";[4] and in the 1930s Hilberseimer was increasingly influenced by European precedents for the garden city. His projects from that time deploy landscape and mixed-height housing to create low-density settlement; starting with his 1930 *Mischbebauung* (Mixed Height Housing), this pattern would inform his U.S. work over the next decades.

By the 1940s, Hilberseimer's concept of the "settlement unit" was taking clear form, especially in its anticipation of an interstate highway system and its precise articulation of relationships among transportation networks, settlement units, and the regional landscape. In the postwar years Hilberseimer's interest in organic urbanism was further fueled by civil defense imperatives that encouraged decentralization.[5] In this context—and influenced too by Broadacre City as well as the progressive TVA and its proponents in the Regional Planning Association of America—Hilberseimer developed his New Regional Pattern as a strategy for low-density urbanization based on regional highways and natural environmental conditions, and he disseminated his ideas in the 1949 *The New Regional Pattern: Industries and Gardens, Workshops and Farms*.[6]

As was Broadacre, the New Regional Pattern was organized around transportation and communication networks that unified an essentially horizontal, landscape-dominated suburban settlement. Housing, farms, light industry, commercial buildings, and civic space: all were located across an extensive territory. But the New Regional Pattern did not defer to the abstraction of the grid; it was informed by the natural environment—by topography, hydrology, vegetation, wind patterns, et al. It conflated infrastructural systems with built landscapes and used environmental conditions to produce a radically reconceived type of North American settlement. Although

4 For an overview of the origins of Hilberseimer's interpretation of the garden city, see David Spaeth, "Ludwig Hilberseimer's Settlement Unit: Origins and Applications," in: Richard Pommer, David Spaeth, Kevin Harrington (eds.), *In the Shadow of Mies: Ludwig Hilberseimer, Architect, Educator, and Urban Planner*. New York, Chicago 1988, pp. 54–68.

5 Hilberseimer and Caldwell advocated for decentralization as a civil defense strategy in the wake of Hiroshima. See Caldwell, "Atomic Bombs and City Planning," in: *Journal of the American Institute of Architects* 4 (1945), pp. 289–299; and also Hilberseimer, "Cities and Defense" [1945], reprinted in: Pommer, Spaeth, Harrington 1988 (fn. 4), pp. 89–93.

6 See also Ludwig Hilberseimer, *The New City: Principles of Planning*. Chicago 1944; idem, *The Nature of Cities: Origin, Growth, and Decline, Pattern and Form, Planning Problems*. Chicago 1955.

Hilberseimer's exquisite drawings (many are the uncredited work of IIT colleague Alfred Caldwell) did not make an explicit case for the kind of ecological awareness apparent in contemporary landscape urbanism, they clearly inflected urban infrastructure to ambient environmental conditions.[7] In this regard the project offers a profound critique of traditional 19th-century urban form, as well as the associated architectural and urban practices that have persisted.

Agronica/Territory for the New Economy. The work of the Italian architect and urbanist Andrea Branzi is equally relevant to the emerging discourse on agrarian urbanism. Branzi's work reanimates the long tradition of using the urban project as a social and cultural critique—of seeing urban design as an opportunity not simply to illustrate a "vision" but also to demystify and critically describe ongoing social problems. In this sense Branzi's work is less concerned with utopian possibilities than with the critically engaged and politically literate delineation of the power structures, forces and flows shaping contemporary urbanism; and in the past four decades he has articulated a remarkably consistent critique of the failings—social, cultural, intellectual, also economic, environmental and aesthetic—of laissez-faire development and of the realpolitik assumptions of much design and planning.

Branzi's "weak work" maintains its critical and projective relevance for a new generation of urbanists.

Born and educated in Florence, Branzi studied architecture in the cultural milieu of the Operaists and the scholarly tradition of Marxist critique. He came to international visibility in the mid 1960s as a member of the collective Archizoom, which was based in Milan but associated with the Florentine Architettura Radicale movement. In projects such as "No-Stop City," Archizoom envisioned an urbanism of continuous mobility, fluidity and flux; indeed, though widely perceived as a satire of the British technophilia of Archigram, No-Stop City was really more an exploration of a kind of "degree zero" urbanization, an urbanism without qualities.[8] In their use, for instance, of typewriter keystrokes on A4 paper to represent the non-figural planning of No-Stop City, Archizoom anticipated contemporary studies in indexical and parametric formulations of the city. Their work also prefigured the current interest in mapping how financial and ecological flows shape the modern low-density metropolis; and it anticipates the focus on infrastructure and ecology as non-figurative drivers of urban form. A genera-

7 For a detailed account of Hilberseimer's professional relationship with Caldwell, see Caroline Constant, "Hilberseimer and Caldwell: Merging Ideologies in the Lafayette Park Landscape," in: Charles Waldheim (ed.), *CASE: Lafayette Park Detroit*. Cambridge and Munich 2004, pp. 95–111. On Caldwell's life and work, see Dennis Domer, Alfred Caldwell, *The Life and Work of a Prairie School Landscape Architect*. Baltimore 1997.

8 Archizoom Associates, "No-Stop City. Residential Parkings. Climatic Universal Sistem," in: *Domus* 496 (March 1971), pp. 49–55. For Branzi's reflections on the project, see Andrea Branzi, "Notes on No-Stop City: Archizoom Associates 1969–1972," in: Martin van Schaik, Otakar Macel (eds.), *Exit Utopia: Architectural Provocations 1956–1976*. Munich 2005, pp. 177–182. For more recent scholarship on the project and its relations to contemporary architectural culture and urban theory, see Kazys Varnelis, "Programming After Program: Archizoom's No-Stop City," in: *Praxis* 8 (May 2006), pp. 82–91.

neue regionale Muster fügte sich nicht in den Abstraktionsgrad des Rasters; es war vielmehr geprägt von der natürlichen Umgebung – von der Topografie, dem Wasserhaushalt, der Vegetation, den Windverhältnissen und vielem mehr. Es verband infrastrukturelle Systeme mit gestalteter Landschaft und nutzte die Umweltbedingungen, um eine radikal neuentworfene nordamerikanische Siedlungsform zu schaffen. Obwohl Hilberseimers ausgezeichnete Zeichnungen (viele sind das Werk des IIT-Kollegen Alfred Caldwell ohne dessen Namensangabe) zwar nicht explizit für jene Art ökologischen Bewusstseins sprechen, wie es im aktuellen Landschaftsurbanismus offensichtlich ist, so passten sie doch städtische Infrastruktur den sie umgebenden Bedingungen an.[7] In diesem Zusammenhang bietet das Projekt eine profunde Kritik an der traditionellen städtischen Form des 19. Jahrhunderts, sowie den damit verbundenen architektonischen und urbanen Praktiken, die weiter Bestand haben.

Agronica/Territorium für die neue Ökonomie. Die Arbeit des italienischen Architekten und Urbanisten Andrea Branzi ist ebenfalls bedeutsam für den zeitgenössischen Diskurs über agrarischen Urbanismus. Branzis Arbeit greift die lange Tradition auf, urbane Projekte als soziale und kulturelle Kritik zu formulieren – um den Städtebau nicht bloß als eine Möglichkeit zu sehen, um eine „Vision" darzustellen, sondern auch als Chance zur Entmystifizierung und kritischen Beschreibung von aktuellen sozialen Problemen. In diesem Sinne beschäftigt sich Branzis Arbeit weniger mit utopischen Möglichkeiten als mit dem kritischen, politisch gebildeten Aufzeigen von Machtstrukturen, Kräften und Einflüssen, die dem gegenwärtigen Urbanismus seine Formen verleihen; und so formulierte er in den letzten vier Jahrzehnten eine auffallend konsistente Kritik der Fehler – sozialer, kultureller, intellektueller, wie auch ökonomischer, umweltbezogener und ästhetischer – der laissez-faire-Entwicklung und der realpolitischen Annahmen der meisten Gestaltungen und Planungen.

Geboren und aufgewachsen in Florenz studierte Branzi Architektur im kulturellen Milieu des Operaismus und in der Tradition der marxistischen Kritik. Mitte der 1960er-Jahre wurde er als Mitglied der Gruppe Archizoom international bekannt, die zwar in Mailand gegründet wurde, doch zu der Architettura Radicale Bewegung in Florenz gehörte. In Projekten wie „No-Stop City" entwarf Archizoom einen Urbanismus, der von kontinuierlicher Mobilität, fließendem Übergang und ständigem Wechsel gekennzeichnet ist; obwohl No-Stop

7 Für eine detaillierte Darstellung der professionellen Beziehung von Hilberseimer mit Caldwell vgl. Caroline Constant, „Hilberseimer and Caldwell: Merging Ideologies in the Lafayette Park Landscape", in: Charles Waldheim (Hg.), *CASE: Lafayette Park Detroit*. Cambridge und München 2004, S. 95–111. Über Caldwells Leben und Arbeit, vgl. Dennis Domer, Alfred Caldwell, *The Life and Work of a Prairie School Landscape Architect*. Baltimore 1997.

4 Ludwig Hilbersheimer, „Vogelperspektive der Gewerbegebiete und Wohneinheiten“, 1944, © Ryerson & Burnham Library Archives, The Art Institute of Chicago. Ludwig Hilbersheimer, “Bird’s-eye view of commercial area and settlement unit,” 1944, © Ryerson & Burnham Library Archives, The Art Institute of Chicago.

tion of contemporary urbanists—ranging from Stan Allen and James Corner to Alex Wall to Alejandro Zaero-Polo—has thus drawn from Branzi's intellectual commitments.[9] Still more recently, Pier Vittorio Aureli and Martino Tattara's "Stop-City" project directly references Branzi's use of non-figurative urban projection as a kind of social and political critique.[10] Branzi's projects have also informed contemporary attention to such diverse topics as animalia, indeterminacy and genericity.

Just as he has influenced younger designers, Branzi himself was influenced by the leading postwar thinkers; in his focus on urban design as social critique, No-Stop City drew upon the projects and theories of Hilberseimer, especially the New Regional Pattern.[11] Not coincidentally, both Branzi and Hilberseimer chose to illustrate the city as a continuous *system* of relational forces and flows, as opposed to a collection of objects—which makes them particularly relevant to contemporary discussions of ecological urbanism. What is more, Branzi occupies a singular historical position as a hinge figure between the social and environmental aspirations of mid-century planning and the politics of 1968.

Branzi's Agronica, of 1993–94, illustrates the relentlessly horizontal spread of capital across thinly settled territory, and the resulting "weak urbanization" that neo-liberal economics has enabled. Commissioned by Philips Electronics, and created in association with the Domus Academy—a research institute Branzi cofounded in the '80s—Agronica explores the potential relationships among agricultural and energy production, new versions of post-Fordist industrialism, and the cultures of consumption that follow.[12] More recently, in 1999, Branzi extended this work in a project in Eindhoven; here too he shows, with typical wit, a "territory for the new economy," in which agricultural production shapes urban form.[13]

Branzi's "weak work" maintains its critical and projective relevance for a new generation of urbanists. His longstanding call for the development of what he defines as weak urban forms and non-figural fields—forms and fields that are flexible, mobile, open to change—influenced the formulation of landscape urbanism over a decade ago and promises to animate the emerging discussions of ecological urbanism.[14] Just as much, his projective and polemic propositions illuminate the possibilities for agrarian urbanism.

My brief pre-history of agricultural urbanism raises more questions than it answers, and it might not convince contemporary readers of the efficacy

9 On field conditions and contemporary urbanism, see James Corner "The Agency of Mapping: Speculation, Critique and Invention," in: Denis Cosgrove (ed.), *Mappings*. London 1999, pp. 213–300; and Stan Allen, "Mat Urbanism: The Thick 2-D," in: Hashim Sarkis (ed.), *CASE: Le Corbusier's Venice Hospital and the Mat Building Revival*. Munich 2001, pp. 118–126. On logistics and contemporary urbanism, see Susan Nigra Snyder, Alex Wall, "Emerging Landscape of Movement and Logistics," in: *Architectural Design Profile* 134 (1998), pp. 16–21; and Alejandro Zaera Polo, "Order out of Chaos: The Material Organization of Advanced Capitalism," in: *Architectural Design Profile* 108 (1994), pp. 24–29.

10 See Pier Vittorio Aureli, Martino Tattara, "Architecture as Framework: The Project of the City and the Crisis of Neoliberalism," in: *New Geographies* 1 (September 2008), pp. 38–51.

11 Ludwig Hilberseimer, *The New Regional Pattern: Industries and Gardens, Workshops and Farms*. Chicago 1949.

12 Andrea Branzi, D. Donegani, A. Petrillo, C. Raimondo, "Symbiotic Metropolis: Agronica," in: Ezio Manzini, Marco Susani (eds.), *The Solid Side*. Netherlands 1995, pp. 101–120.

13 Andrea Branzi, "Preliminary Notes for a Master Plan," and "Master Plan Strijp Philips, Eindhoven 1999," in: *Lotus* 107 (2000), pp. 110–123.

14 Andrea Branzi, "The Weak Metropolis," in: *Ecological Urbanism Conference*. Harvard Graduate School of Design, April 2010.

City weithin als eine Satire über die britische Technophilie von Archigram wahrgenommen wurde, war der Entwurf eigentlich eher die Erforschung einer Art „Nullpunkt"-Urbanismus, eines Urbanismus ohne Eigenschaften.[8] Indem Archizoom etwa die Tastenanschläge von Schreibmaschinen auf einem A4-Papier benutzte, um die nicht-figurale Planung von No-Stop City darzustellen, nahm Archizoom aktuelle Arbeiten in ihren indexikalischen und parametrischen Konzepten der Stadt vorweg. In ihrer Arbeit ist auch bereits das heutige Interesse an Diagrammen lesbar, die zeigen, wie Finanzströme und ökologische Verläufe die moderne Metropole mit geringer Bevölkerungsdichte beeinflussen; auch setzten sie zukunftsweisend den Schwerpunkt auf Infrastruktur und Ökologie als nicht-figurative Triebkräfte der urbanen Form. Eine heutige Generation von Urbanisten – von Stan Allen und James Corner zu Alex Wall und Alejandro Zaero-Polo – hat Branzis intellektuelle Überzeugungen übernommen.[9] In jüngster Zeit bezog sich Pier Vittorio Aureli und Martino Tattaras „Stop-City"-Projekt direkt auf Branzis Verwendung der nicht-figurativen urbanen Projektierung als soziale und politische Kritik.[10] Branzis Arbeiten haben gegenwärtig auf so verschiedene Themen wie „animalia", „indeterminacy" und „genericity" aufmerksam gemacht.

Ebenso wie Branzi jüngere Designer bis heute beeinflusst, wurde auch er selbst von den führenden Theoretikern der Nachkriegszeit beeinflusst; mit seinem Schwerpunkt auf urbanen Entwürfen als Sozialkritik bezog er sich in No-Stop City auf Projekte und Ansätze von Hilberseimer, besonders auf die neuen regionalen Muster.[11] Nicht von ungefähr stellten Branzi und Hilberseimer beide die Stadt als ein kontinuierliches System miteinander in Beziehung stehender Kräfte und Einflüsse – und eben nicht als eine Ansammlung von Objekten – dar, was sie für gegenwärtige Diskussionen des ökologischen Urbanismus besonders relevant macht. Darüber hinaus hat Branzi eine be-

8 Archizoom Associates, „No-Stop City. Residential Parkings. Climatic Universal Sistem", in: *Domus* 496 (März 1971), S. 49–55. Zu Branzis Gedanken zu diesem Projekt vgl. Andrea Branzi, „Notes on No-Stop City: Archizoom Associates 1969–1972", in: Martin van Schaik, Otakar Macel (Hg.), *Exit Utopia: Architectural Provocations 1956–1976*. München 2005, S. 177–182. Für die aktuelle Forschung über das Projekt und seine Beziehungen zur zeitgenössischen architektonischen Kultur und urbanen Theorie vgl. Kazys Varnelis, „Programming After Program: Archizoom's No-Stop City," in: *Praxis* 8 (Mai 2006), S. 82–91.

9 Zu Feldforschung und zeitgenössischen Urbanismus vgl. James Corner, „The Agency of Mapping: Speculation, Critique and Invention", in: Denis Cosgrove (Hg.), *Mappings*. London 1999, S. 213–300; und Stan Allen, „Mat Urbanism: The Thick 2-D", in: Hashim Sarkis (Hg.), *CASE: Le Corbusier's Venice Hospital and the Mat Building Revival*. München 2001, S. 118–126. Über Logistik und zeitgenössischen Urbanismus vgl. Susan Nigra Snyder, Alex Wall, „Emerging Landscape of Movement and Logistics", in: *Architectural Design Profile* 134 (1998), S. 16–21; und Alejandro Zaera Polo, „Order out of Chaos: The Material Organization of Advanced Capitalism", in: *Architectural Design Profile* 108 (1994), S. 24–29.

10 Vgl. Pier Vittorio Aureli, Martino Tattara, „Architecture as Framework: The Project of the City and the Crisis of Neoliberalism", in: *New Geographies* 1 (September 2008), S. 38–51.

11 Ludwig Hilberseimer, *The New Regional Pattern: Industries and Gardens, Workshops and Farms*. Chicago 1949.

sondere historische Position als Verbindungsglied zwischen den sozialen und ökologischen Planungsbestrebungen in der Mitte des 20. Jahrhunderts und der Politik von 1968 inne.

Branzis Agronica von 1993–1994 zeigt die unaufhaltsame, horizontale Ausbreitung von Kapital über ein dünn besiedeltes Territorium und die daraus resultierende „schwache Urbanisierung", die durch die neoliberale Wirtschaft ermöglicht wurde. Beauftragt von Philips Electronics und in Zusammenarbeit mit der Domus Academy – ein in den 1980er-Jahren von Branzi mitbegründetes Forschungsinstitut – erforscht Agronica die möglichen Beziehungen zwischen landwirtschaftlicher Produktion und Energiegewinnung, neue Versionen einer postfordistischen Industrialisierung und die sich daraus ergebenden Konsumkulturen.[12] In jüngerer Zeit (1999) weitete Branzi dieses Konzept auf ein Projekt in Eindhoven aus; auch hier zeigt er mit typischem Humor ein „Territorium für die New Economy", in dem landwirtschaftliche Produktion die städtische Form prägt.[13]

Branzis „weiche Theorie" hat ihre kritische und projektive Relevanz für eine neue Generation von Urbanisten behalten. Sein anhaltender Aufruf zur Entwicklung dessen, was er als „weiche" urbane Formen und nicht-figurative Felder bezeichnet – Formen und Felder, die flexibel, beweglich und offen gegenüber Veränderungen sind – beeinflusste die Definition des Landschaftsurbanismus vor über einem Jahrzehnt und verspricht, auch die aktuellen Diskussionen über ökologischen Urbanismus zu beleben.[14] Ebenso beleuchten seine projektiven und polemischen Vorschläge die Möglichkeiten eines landwirtschaftlichen Urbanismus.

Meine knappe Vorgeschichte des agrarischen Urbanismus wirft mehr Fragen auf, als sie beantwortet und es könnte sein, dass sie zeitgenössische Leser nicht von der Wirksamkeit der Maßnahmen überzeugt, eine Stadt auf diese Art zu organisieren; aber es scheint ein nützlicher Schritt zum Verständnis der größeren Konsequenzen des aktuellen Umgangs mit Nahrungsmitteln für die Entwurfsdisziplinen zu sein. Wright, Hilberseimer und Branzi betrieben landwirtschaftlichen Urbanismus als Teil einer kritischen Auseinandersetzung mit wirtschaftlicher Ungleichheit, sozialer Gerechtigkeit und ökologischer Gesundheit. Jeder von ihnen hat heutigen Agrar-Urbanisten wichtige Lehren hinterlassen.

of organizing the city in this way—but it seems a useful step in understanding the larger implications of contemporary food culture for the design disciplines. Wright, Hilberseimer and Branzi each pursued agricultural urbanism as part of critical positions that engaged economic inequality, social justice, and environmental health. Each has contributed an important legacy for today's agrarian urbanists.

"Notes Towards a History of Agrarian Urbanism" is excerpted from Bracket 1: On Farming, *edited by Mason White and Maya Przybylski.*

12 Andrea Branzi, D. Donegani, A. Petrillo, C. Raimondo, „Symbiotic Metropolis: Agronica", in: Ezio Manzini, Marco Susani (Hg.), *The Solid Side*. Netherlands 1995, S. 101–120.

13 Andrea Branzi, „Preliminary Notes for a Master Plan", und „Master Plan Strijp Philips, Eindhoven 1999", in: *Lotus* 107 (2000), S. 110–123.

14 Andrea Branzi, „The Weak Metropolis", in: *Ecological Urbanism Conference*. Harvard Graduate School of Design, April 2010.

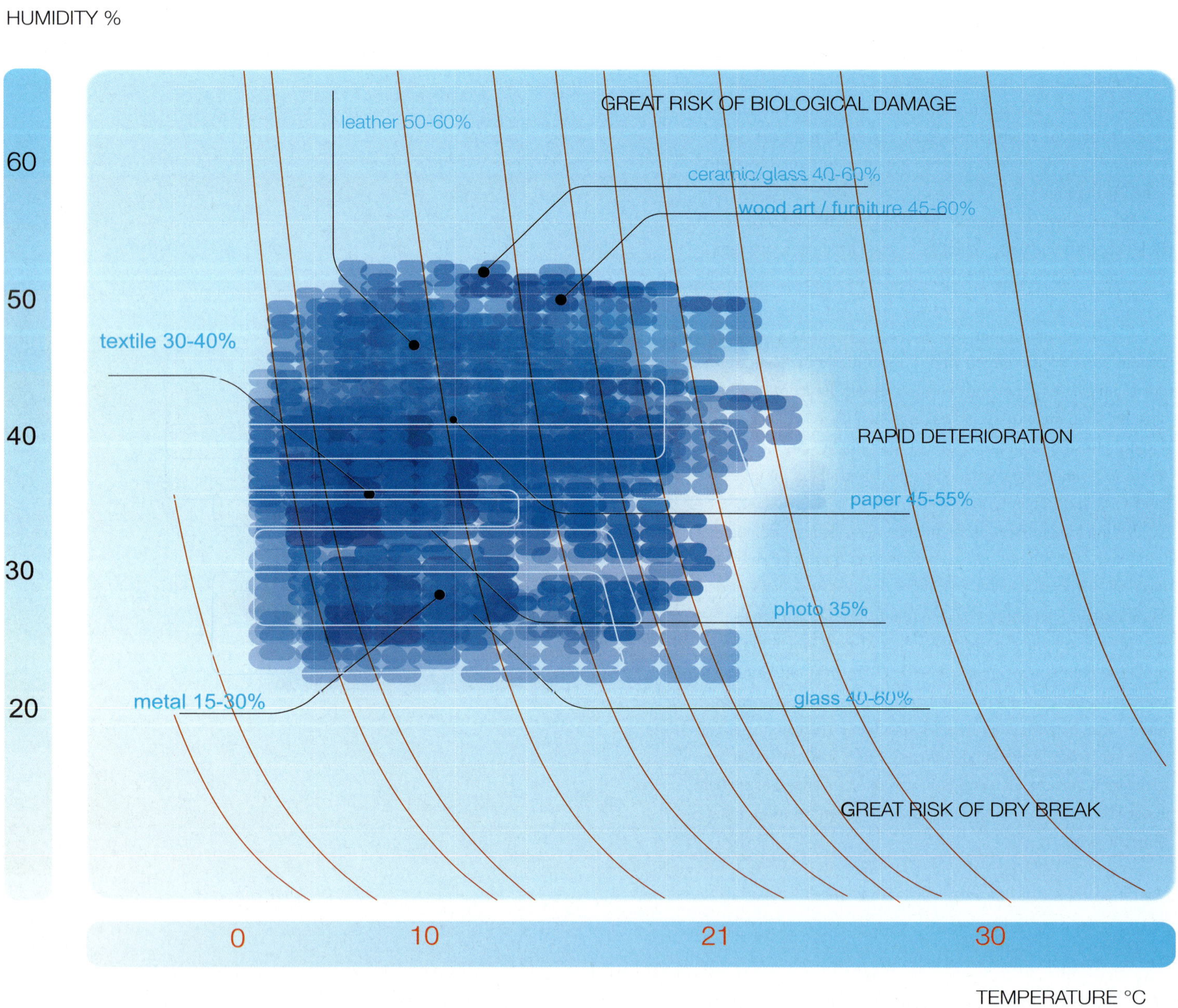

1

1 Evaporation, meteorological typologies, meteorologische Typologien, Philippe Rahm architectes

Architecture of Meteorology and Atmosphere

The "climate" has taken on a role of major importance as a subject in architecture ever since the challenges of sustainable development arose as an answer to the problem of global warming. In architecture, climate means the management of heating and cooling in a building, in order to achieve a comfortable temperate average.

Architektur aus Meteorologie und Atmosphäre. Der Begriff „Klima" ist angesichts der Herausforderungen der nachhaltigen Entwicklung als Antwort auf die Klimaerwärmung in der Architektur zu einem Hauptthema geworden. Unter Klima versteht man in der Architektur das Management von Erwärmung und Kühlung im Inneren von Gebäuden, um eine angenehme mittlere Temperierung zu erzielen.

PHILIPPE RAHM

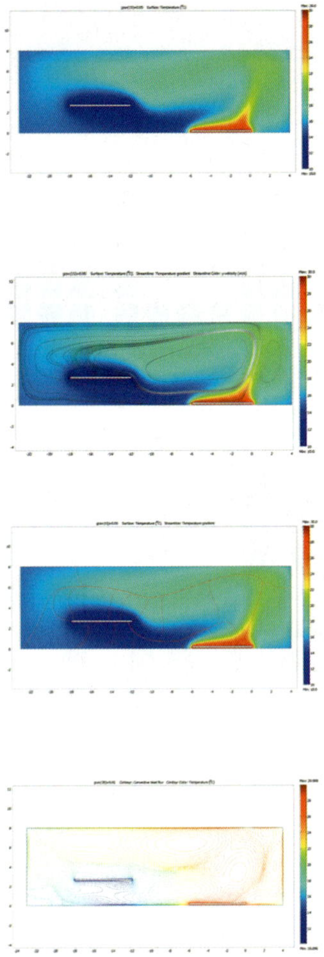

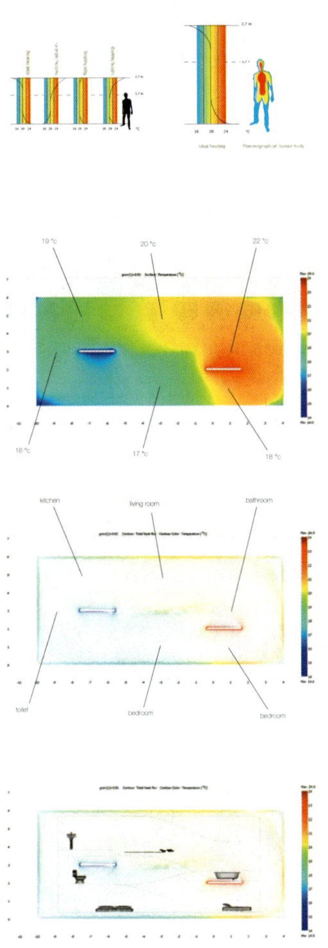

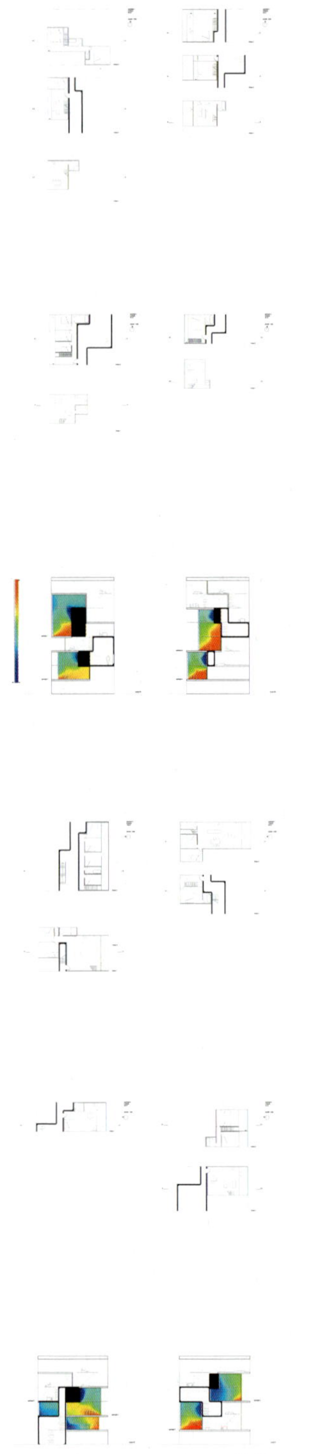

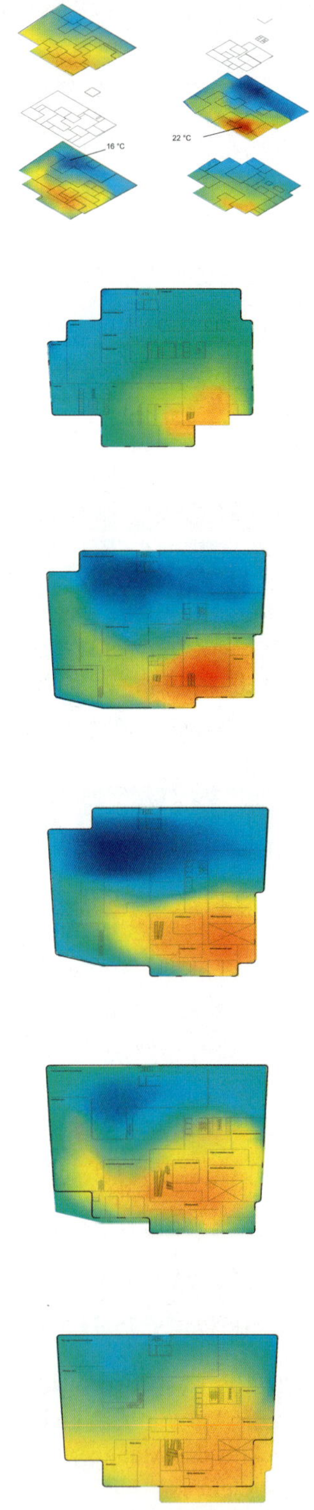

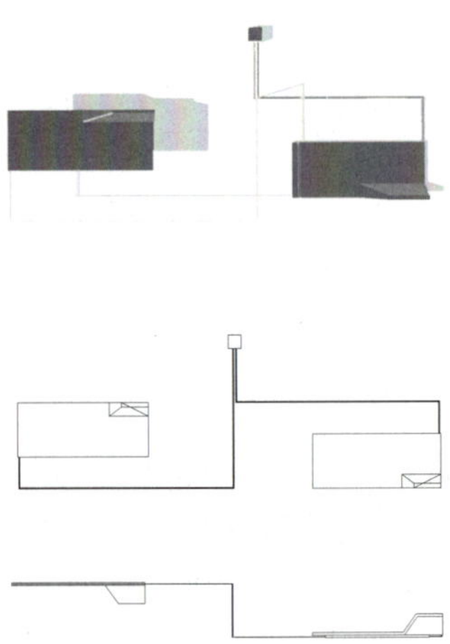

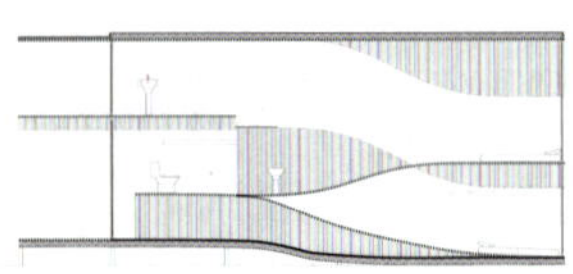

INTERIOR GULF STREAM

Modernity led to uniform, consistent spaces in which the temperature is regulated around 21 degrees. The aim here is to restore diversity to the relation that the body maintains with space, with its temperature, to allow seasonal movement within the house, migrations from downstairs to upstairs, from cold to warm, winter and summer, dressed and undressed. For people to feel comfortable in a heated room there must be equilibrium in the exchange of heat occurring via convection between their bodies and the surrounding air. This equilibrium is of course relative to clothing, from nudity in the bathroom, to the thermal protection of blankets, to light clothing worn in the living room. Today, confronted with the will to economize energy resources, the demand is to set up in each building, and even each room, a precisely calculated thermal capacity in order to expend only the energy that is strictly necessary. The Swiss construction norm SIA 3842 thus gives the following indicative values for ambient temperature: Bathroom: 22°C, Living room: 20°C, Kitchen: 18°C, Bedroom: 16°C. Instead of warming all the space at the good temperature around 20°C, we propose to create in the house two sources of heat, like two different thermal poles creating a thermodynamic tension inside the all house: one pole is cold at 15 °C and situated in the upper layers of air of the house. The opposite pole is warm, at 22°C situated in the lower layers of the space. A movement of air will be generated by this difference of temperatures and positions in the space. With the help of thermal model software, we analyze the variation of temperature and his distribution in all the space and find then places for activities, according to specific temperatures. The project process is thus reversed: a indoor climate is first produced and after, functions are freely chosen anywhere in the space related to the thermal quality required depending of activities, clothes, personal desires. The floors and the open spaces are therefore designed to follow the form taken by the air in the entire height of the building, in accordance with vertical air movements in relation to temperature, and the functions that are suggested as a result. Next, various functions take their places in an obvious manner on this stratification from the coldest to the warmest.

DIGESTIBLE GULF STREAM

The problem of global warming has placed as the relationship between climate and architecture at the center of current preoccupations. A 'Digestible Gulf Stream' is the prototype for architecture that works between the neurologic and the atmospheric, developing like a landscape that is simultaneously gastronomic and thermal.

Architecture should no longer builds spaces, but rather create temperatures and atmospheres. Here, two horizontal metal planes are extended at different heights. The lower plane is heated to 28°C, the upper one is cooled to 12°C. Like a miniature Gulf Stream, their position creates a movement of air using the natural phenomenon of convection, in which rising hot air cools on contact with the upper cool sheet and, falling, is then reheated on contact with the hot sheet, thus creating a constant thermal flow, akin to an invisible landscape. What interests us here is not the creation of homogeneous, established spaces, but of a plastic, climatic dynamic, the activation of forces and polarities that generate a landscape of heat. In this case the architecture is literally structured on a current of air, opening up a fluid, airy, atmospheric space. This architecture is based on the construction of meteorology. The inhabitant may move around in this invisible landscape between 12°C and 28°C, temperatures at the two extremities of the concept of comfort, and freely choose a climate according to his or her activity, clothing, dietary, sporting or social wishes.

Our architecture extends between the microscopic and the macroscopic, the gastronomic and the atmospheric, the visible and the invisible. Architecture becomes a 'Gulf Stream' that polarises the contrasts on different scales (hot/cold, low/high, clothed/unclothed, internal/external, rest/activity) to give rise to architecture as a convective movement of air, creating a place like geography, designing space like climate, atmosphere and gastronomy.

CLIMATIC TYPOLOGIES

Each apartment has a unique spatial quality achieved with different heights, different depths. The layout of the apartments is made according to calculations of temperature change depending on the input of fresh air in the apartment at the sheath. In a thermographic physical study, we manage the various functions in relationship with the movement of interior temperatures linked to the recommendations of the standard SIA 384 / 2 by placing the functions that require the cooler temperatures near the sheath (rooms, wc, kitchen) and those that require higher temperatures higher, under the law of Archimedes, following the upward movement of heat.

CONVECTIVE MUSEUM

This project for the contemporary art museum in Wroclaw in Poland is defined by the introduction in the space of two poles of heat (like two radiators), one more cold at 16° Celsius, the other more warm at 22° Celsius. We choose these 2 temperatures because they set the low and high temperatures limits required in the program of a museum: 16° C corresponding to storage or minor used local or quickly. 22 ° C correspond to the maximum temperatures in the offices, while 19°C serves for the exhibition's rooms for walking people dressed normally . We first draw out a volume covering the whole former block of the 19th century. We introduce then in the diagonal, the two poles, hot and cold, which, by their difference of temperatures generate a thermodynamic imbalance that move air masses and draw a atmospheric landscape. Using a climatic software, we model the climate which defines areas of air more or less hot, layers of different temperature, atmospheric zones, spaces and volumes that have each have thermal qualities, like different landscapes, temperate here, cold there, tropical further.

After modeling the climate with the software, we put the program seeking places in plans and sections where the temperatures are good, following the thermal recommendations for museum. The shape of the building, the indoor composition of the program drift from this climatic method and thermodynamic tension. Nothing is truly closed in this volume, so the air can circulate everywhere and the glaze often too. To leave move freely air, floors and ceilings are most of the time specially designed slatted with a percentage of full-blank range depending on the needs of the program. The walls are also slatted to allow air circulation and sometimes the eyes, except for exhibition's room where the slats are closed for becoming cimaises. More than a building, it is an atmosphere that we propose as the new place of a museum.

2

Eine der Hauptaufgaben der Architektur besteht natürlich darin, dafür zu sorgen, dass es während der Winterkälte in den Häusern wärmer ist als draußen und dass wir umgekehrt im Sommer in kühlen Innenräumen vor Hitze und Hundstagen geschützt sind. Paradoxerweise tragen die zum Heizen und zur Kühlung von Innenräumen verbrannten fossilen Brennstoffe zum Treibhauseffekt und zur Klimaerwärmung bei.

Wir müssen heute diese Klimaaufgabe der Architektur hinterfragen und sie nicht mehr allein als Ziel, sondern auch als Mittel akzeptieren. Das Klima muss von Anfang eines Entwurfs an, das heißt bereits in der Sprache, mitbedacht werden. Es muss in die Bestandteile, das Tragwerk, die Gliederung und schließlich die ästhetischen Kriterien einfließen. Die Architektur als Klima erweitert ihren Bewegungsradius um weiche, thermische, plastische, materielle Dimensionen. Sie öffnet sich neuen Wahrnehmungen durch Nase, Haut und hormonelle Reize. Das Feld der Architektur muss sich heute vom Physiologischen hin zum Atmosphärischen neu bestimmen und ihre Formen und Typologien neu definieren, indem den neuen ökologischen Herausforderungen, wie sie mit dem Klima verbunden sind, verantwortungsvoll begegnet wird.

Während sich herkömmlicherweise die Form eines Gebäudes und die Qualität eines Raums aus Fläche und Kubatur ergeben, möchten wir hier eine Architektur aus Meteorologie und Atmosphäre vorschlagen. Der Grund für diesen Paradigmenwechsel von der Fläche zur Meteorologie, von der Kubatur zum Atmosphärischen liegt in unserer Überzeugung, dass die gegenwärtigen Herausforderungen im Zusammenhang mit Klima, Schutz vor der Erderwärmung und Erschöpfung der Ressourcen nicht mehr nur als besorgniserregendes Problem gesehen werden dürfen, sondern dass man dafür völlig neuartige Tools und Lösungen erfinden muss. Die Architekten sollten sich der neuen klimatischen Daten mit Lust und Neugierde annehmen, anstatt sie als zusätzliche technische Einschränkungen bloß hinzunehmen. Nicht um die Akzeptanz geht es hier, sondern vielmehr darum, dafür zu sorgen, dass die physikalischen Aspekte des Klimas – Druck, Tiefdruck, Temperatur, relative Feuchtigkeit – als Material für die Architektur, als neue Werkzeuge für den Architekturentwurfsprozess herangezogen werden. Architektur unter dem Aspekt „Klima“ zu denken, bedeutet, sich in eine andere Ordnung des Raums zu projizieren, ein sinnlicheres Verhältnis zum Raum aufzubauen und einen Innenraum wie eine Atmosphäre zu bewohnen, samt deren unterschiedlichen Klimazonen, Wetterwechseln und Verläufen.

Nach Jahrzehnten unter dem Primat des Sichtbaren, in denen das Subjektive und die Narration die fortschrittlichen, anspruchsvollen Pläne der Moderne dreist ersetzt haben, befinden wir uns jetzt auf dem Weg in ein neues Zeitalter, das von einer allgemeinen Verlagerung vom Sichtbaren zum Unsichtbaren hin gekennzeichnet ist, wodurch sich das Feld der Architektur zum Mikroskopischen und Atmosphärischen, vom Bio-

It is of course one of the chief tasks of architecture to ensure that it is warmer inside than outside in winter, and when it is hot outside that a building provides shelter from the summer sun and scorching heat in cool rooms. Paradoxically, it is by heating and cooling the interior climate that fossil fuels are burnt, emitting gasses that contribute to the greenhouse effect and to global warming.

We must question ourselves about this climatic task of architecture today, and instead of accepting it merely as a goal, we must see it as a means. The climate must be integrated upstream of an architectural project, and this even in the architectural language. It must modify the elements, structure, modes of composition and finally the aesthetic criteria of the building. Architecture as a climate increases its sphere of action by adding sensitive, thermal, plastic, material dimensions. It opens towards other—olfactory, cutaneous, hormonal—perceptions. It is time to reevaluate the field of architecture, to pass from the physiological to the atmospheric, to redefine its forms and typologies by taking responsibility for the new ecological concerns relating to the climate.

Whereas the form of buildings and the quality of space have traditionally been expressed in terms of surface and volume, we would like to propose here architecture as meteorology and atmosphere. The reason for this shifting of paradigms from surface to meteorology, from volume to the atmospheric lies in our conviction that today's challenges linked with the climate, its protection against warming and with the exhaustion of resources, must no longer be considered as a problem or a worry, but must provoke completely new tools and solutions. Architects should seize the new climatic data with sensual pleasure and enthusiasm, instead of simply accepting them as further technical constraints. This is not simply a matter of accepting them, but rather about transforming the physical elements of the climate—pressure, low pressure, temperature, relative humidity—into architecture's raw materials, into new architectural design tools. To think of architecture in terms of climate means to project oneself into another spatiality, a more sensual relationship with space, means to inhabit the inner space as an atmosphere with its diversity of climates, its meteorological variations and its gradients.

After decades of attachment to the visible, where the subjective and the narrative had insolently replaced the progressive and moral ideas of modernism, we are now setting out into a new period in which a general shift from the visible to the invisible is taking place, displacing the field of architecture towards the microscopic and atmospheric, from the biological to the meteorological. The wonderful achievements of the sciences now resound with the climate and our worries about its warming. Between these two extremes, the field of the visible, which until now has been saturated with symbols, morality, narrations and singular interests, is in decline, emptying, diffracting, becoming clearer, lighter, deforming and deprogramming itself. Spread out between the physiological and the climatic, between determinism and freedom, the now open, floating, indecisive in-between is about to become the space for a new humanist landscape.

We want to re-establish the language of architecture following this shift towards the invisible; stretching architecture between the infinitesimal and the infinite, between the physiological and the meteorological. We want to safeguard the essence of the elements of architecture in the light of the

Architects should seize the new climatic data with sensual pleasure and enthusiasm, instead of simply accepting them as further technical constraints. This is not simply a matter of accepting them, but rather about transforming the physical elements of the climate—pressure, low pressure, temperature, relative humidity—into architecture's raw materials, into new architectural design tools.

logischen zum Meteorologischen verschiebt. Die wunderbaren wissenschaftlichen Errungenschaften hallen im Klima und unserer Sorge um die Klimaerwärmung wider. Zwischen diesen beiden Extremen schrumpft nun das Feld des Sichtbaren, das bis jetzt von Symbolen, Moral, Erzählungen und speziellen Interessen gesättigt war; es leert sich, zersplittert, hellt sich auf, wird leichter, verformt und deprogrammiert sich. Aufgespannt zwischen dem Physiologischen und dem Klimatischen, zwischen Determinismus und Freiheit ist dieses nunmehr offene, schwebende, unbestimmte Zwischending der Raum für eine neue humanistische Landschaft.

Wir möchten die Architektursprache als Reaktion auf diese Verschiebung hin zum Unsichtbaren neu fassen; die Architektur zwischen dem unendlich Kleinen und dem unendlich Großen, zwischen der Physiologie und der Meteorologie neu aufspannen. Wir möchten angesichts des Niedergangs des Sichtbaren das Wesen der Architekturelemente neu aufstellen. Die Mittel der Architektur müssen unsichtbar und leicht werden, müssen Orte als offene, freie Landschaften, neue Geografien und andere Meteorologien hervorbringen. Das Konzept der Form und der Nutzung zwischen Gefühl und Erscheinungsform, zwischen dem Neurologischen und dem Meteorologischen, zwischen dem Physiologischen und dem Atmosphärischen erneuern. Wir suchen Räume ohne Bedeutung, ohne Narration, interpretierbare Räume, in denen sich die Grenzen verflüchtigen und die Strukturen auflösen. Es geht nicht mehr um die Konstruktion von Bildern und Funktionen, sondern darum, Klimata und Interpretationen zu öffnen, mit Leere, der Luft und ihren Bewegungen, mit den Phänomenen der Leitung, Transpiration und Konvektion als meteorologischen Übergangsbedingungen und gleichzeitig neuen Paradigmen der Gegenwartsarchitektur zu arbeiten. Es geht darum, von dem metrischen zum thermischen Entwurf, vom Tragwerksdenken zum Klimadenken, vom narrativen Denken zum meteorologischen überzugehen. Es geht um die Verknüpfung stündlicher Lufterneuerung mit einem Grundriss nach der relativen Luftfeuchtigkeit, der Wohnwärmeströmung, der Temperaturoptimierung, dem Verlauf der Luftströme, dem Druck und Tiefdruck, um die Schichtung der Temperaturen als neue Vorgaben für den Architekturentwurf und hernach um das Aufzeigen programmatischer, plastischer und sensorischer Potenziale. Der Raum, der bis jetzt als leer und abstrakt aufgefasst wurde, materialisiert sich als elektromagnetische, chemische, sinnliche Atmosphäre, in die wir getaucht sind und die wir neu hervorbringen, indem wir in ihr wohnen, d. h. atmen, schwitzen, und in der wir mit unserem Körper, unserer physischen und hormonalen Aktivität, unseren Bewegungen und unserer Kleidung Wärme abstrahlen. Zwischen dem unendlich Kleinen des Biologischen und dem unendlich Großen des Meteorologischen muss die Architektur einen sinnlichen Austausch zwischen Körper und Raum, den Sinnen, der Haut, der Atmung und

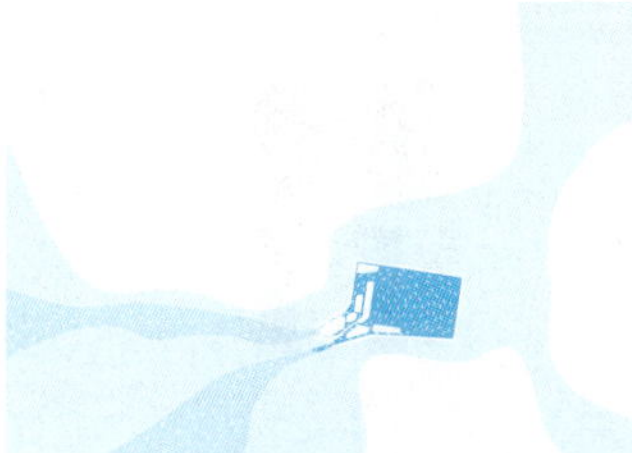

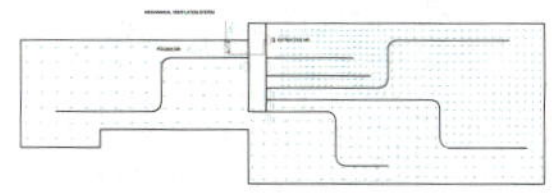

AIRFLOW

In this project, the architectural design is the articulation of the movement of air as an inhabitable airflow: an architecture as a drawing of wind, where its qualities express themselves in terms of velocity, volume, movement,propulsion, and extraction are transformed, both poetically and spatially, into an issue of ventilation. From the start, the plan is composed according to the requirements of the management of air flow, all the while prioritizing the matter (issue) of the hourly rate of air renewal. The project is developed according to the requirements of airflow management (automatic ventilation of fresh air with heat recovery / Minergie, Switzerland) so as to reduce, by a factor of 8, the building's energy consumption. Thus it embodies the subject of the hourly rate of air renewal / recirculation (calculated in m3 of air per hour). The recirculation of interior air is then determined by a particular rate that is a function of its usage, of the number of occupants, the duration of their stay within the space, and of their level of physical activity: a sparse or physically inactive occupation will require a lower rate of air renewal than a more densely occupied space or one where more vigorous physical activity will demand a higher hourly rate. Air renewal is essential to the metabolic process because it brings in fresh oxygen, which is consumed 500 times faster than its usual rate during periods of strenuous physical exercise; it functions to flush out metabolic wastes such as hydrogen, carbon dioxide, and lactates. From 7.5 liters during times or rest, the output of the ventilation process is raised to over 120 liters per minute during physical activity. This increase is made possible by a parallel increase in breathing rate, which necessitates a more rapid exchange between fresh and stale air. There exists therefore a very precise relationship between the geometry of the space and the quantity of air that needs to be recycled and renewed, reinitiating the issue of a building's ventilation as being a decisive factor in its architectural form. Architecture here is designed as the continuous movement of air, whose streams join together to shape the mass of air moving through space. The architecture is formed in the manner of a gust of wind, sculpting itself not unlike a stream of air whose flow gradually increases as a result of the respiration of its occupants, the rate of respiration itself being a function of their activity level and the quantity of water vapor they produce.

PUBLIC AIR

Reintroducing physiological needs in city planning principles is a responsible and attractive attitude today, as the management of the earth's resources and safeguarding of ecosystems has become paramount. Public space becomes the place where the quality of the air is defined. Its temperature is heated in the winter or cooled in summer in relation to the climate, albedo and vegetation, creating a depollution process in public. Air organizes the form, shape and materials of public space. It updates the meaning of public space as certain physiological need not fulfilled by interior space, where a social life and exchange between the inhabitants could be born.

The urban agenda of our project is to build two spaces, one cold, one warm, at the ends of the site and stretching the buildings between them. The buildings are woven between these two public spaces. The circulation corridors of the buildings become inhabitable ventilation ducts, increased to human scale. The ends of these ventilation ducts are connected to the two public spaces, drawing on their ambient airs. The air of the mineral space to the northwest will have a high thermal quality and the air near the forest to the southeast will have a low thermal quality.

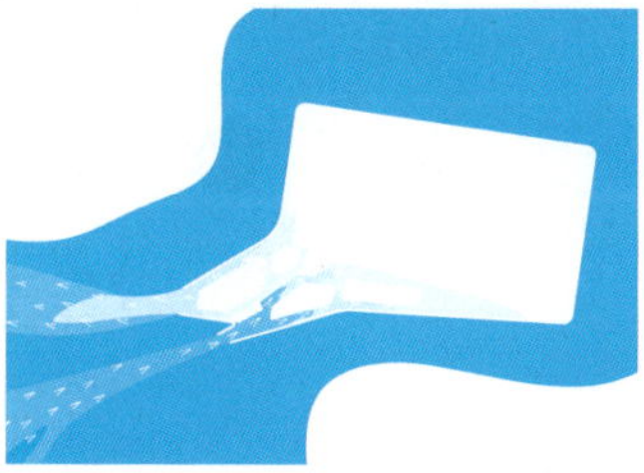

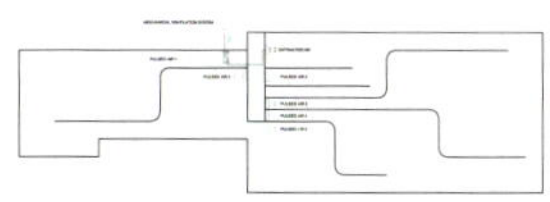

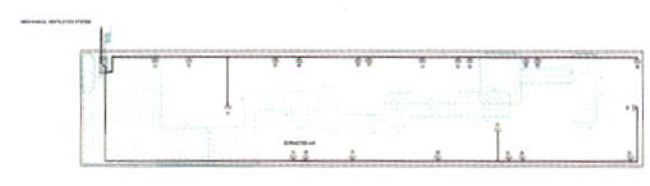

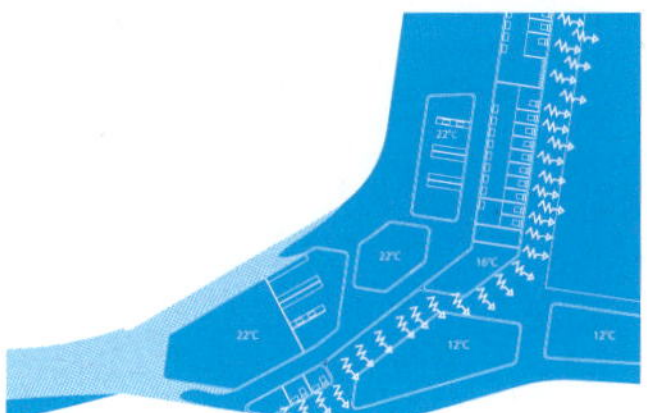

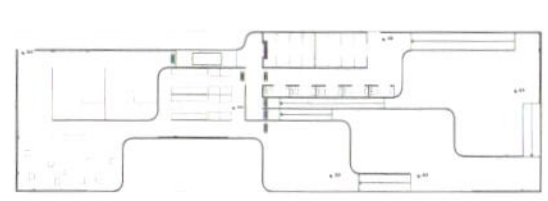

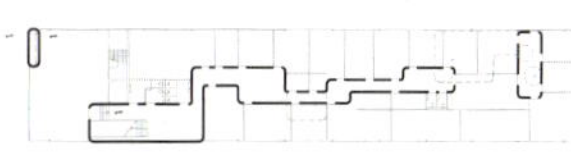

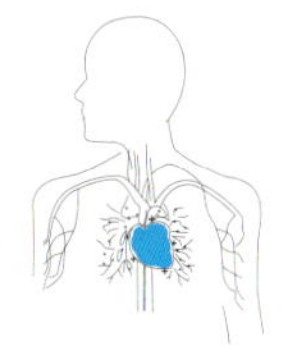

Augmentation of the heart beat rate depending on the sport activity

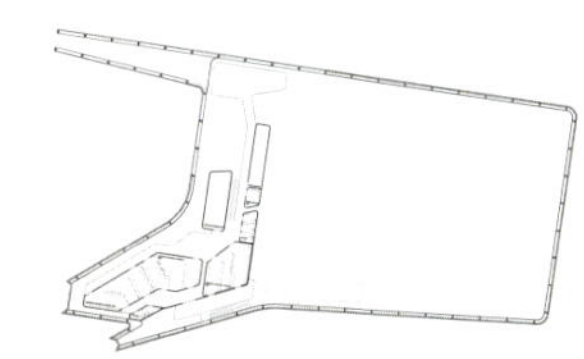

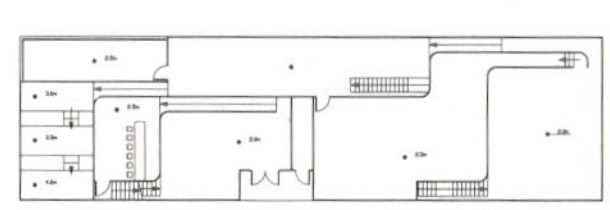

FILTERED REALITIES

The project is organized according to the requirements of managing its airflow (automatic ventilation system with heat recovery / Minergie, Switzerland), so as to cut back by a factor of four the energy consumed by the building. The design prioritizes the building's air supply, thus transforming the technical issue of the ventilation duct and its distribution of air into one that is in principle architectonic, spatial, and poetic. The diameter of the duct is essentially widened until it becomes itself an inhabitable space which slides, bends, contracts and expands along the entire length of the building. Instead of a system of galvanized steel paneling, this ventilation shaft is made of solid load-bearing limestone, reproducing along its length, in miniature from West to East, the geological stratification of soil eroded by the wind, from the Atlantic Ocean to the Parisian basin, from Le Havre to Paris. The architectural quality we are proposing is essentially an atmosphere—a scent, a particular perfume—of the air of Paris having come all the way from the sea to its west and which will be infused, at the heart of the building, with the nuanced mineral scents of the different types of stone. A few oak trees are planted along its path, and their presence adds a certain vegetal element to the complex perfume of the air.The realized form of these issues generates the architectural form of the building and its functional organization as well as its spatial poetry. It is made up of certain elements, whose potentials we have amplified to the point that they create new architectural typologies. It is thus the movement of air through the building which determines its form and poetic implications, imparting to it a more sensual presence. It is an architecture formed by a breeze. The project reconstructs a terrain within its interior space, taking into consideration its technical requirements of ventilation and heat recovery. The terrains we design are natural, yet contained within the interior. Characterized by the nature of a particular land and its geological underside, these interior terrains release their perfumes and their tastes into the surrounding air. The limestone blocks, extracted from soils scented with the sea breezes that traverse the terrain between Paris and the ocean, diffuse their perfumes into the surrounding air; meanwhile, the all the other materials used in the construction—glass, polyurethane, and stainless steel—remain chemically neutral within this olfactory architectural composition.

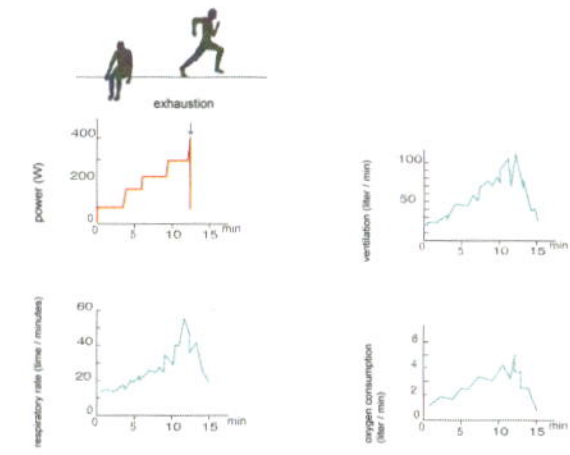

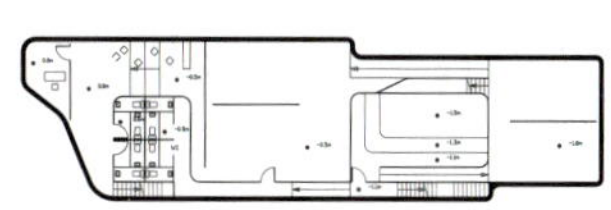

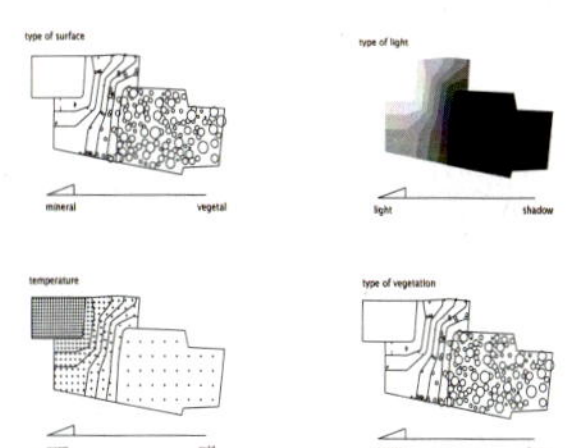

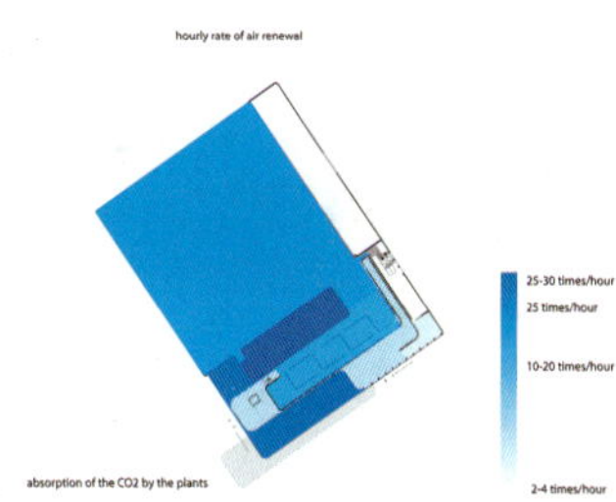

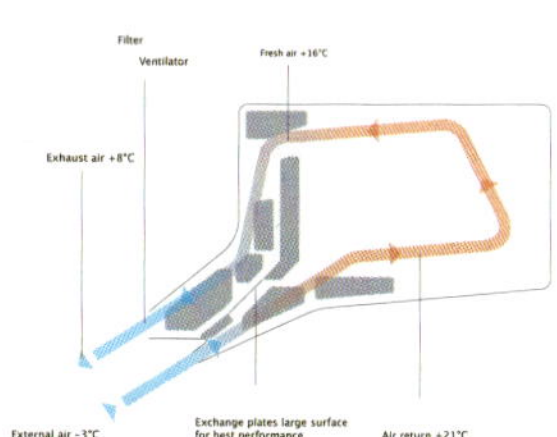

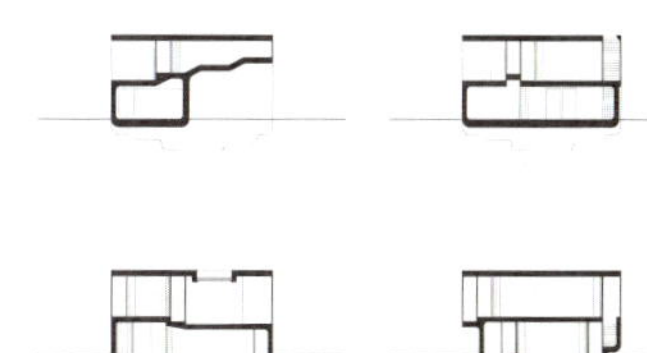

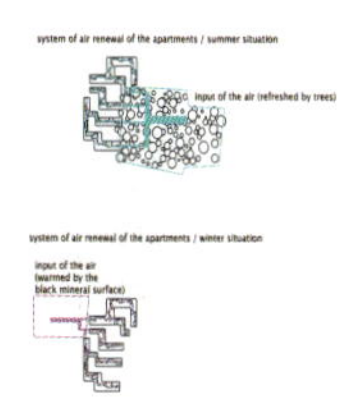

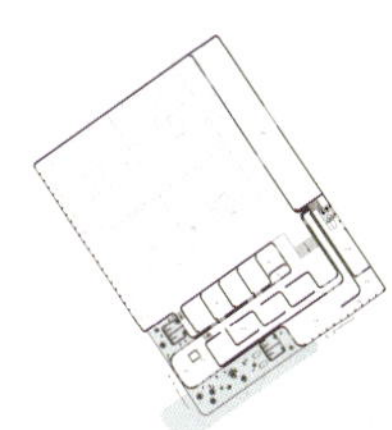

WINTRAP

Our project for a new sports hall in Slovenia is an architecture as weather, placed in the site as a wooden object slipped in the course of the wind. It captures the warm scent from the south and rejects the stale air to the north, after removing its heat. The sports hall emerges as a slight inflection in the natural movement of wind. Technically, this building, perfectly isolated, uses a system of double flow ventilation, which warms the incoming air with the warmth of the exhaust air, by an exchange between large conductive metal surfaces. In the winter, this allows the exhaust air to give its heat to the cold incoming air.

The project spatially expands the double flow heat exchange air renewal system, which is normally the size of a machine, to the size of the entire building. So, all the rooms of the building participate in the exchange of heat, depending on recommended temperatures related to the functions: from the hottest at 22 ° C for the showers and changing rooms, to the coldest at 12 ° C for storage room. The toilets and corridors form the chemically-sealed boundary between the incoming fresh air and the returning hot air, and are where the heat exchange to the metal walls happens, warmer at the north of the building and colder at the south of the building.

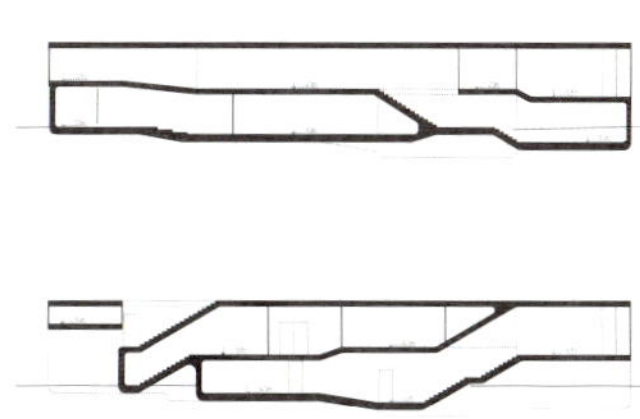

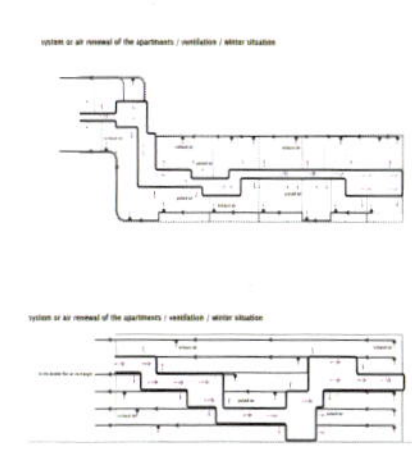

AIRFLUX

The architecture design as a movement of air. Reducing the question of the architecture of a sports hall to that of ventilation and aeration, that is to say re-establish the architectural project literally for the need to bring oxygen into the building and to air out the waste produced during respiration. What is the deep relationship between space and sporting activity? It is undoubtedly one of oxygen to your muscles, the athlete whose consumption is multiplied 500 times during important muscular work compared to rest activities. Our project consists ordered, then formed specifically from management of air into the building through its course, speed, volume, and rate of renewal. The architecture becomes a system of ventilation and the spaces are literally shaped ducts in which air flows at low pressure. The building is proposed as a continuous movement of air, with its tributaries increasing the amount of air brought into space. The architecture consists of a gradually increasing rate of ventilation. First therefore, the spaces where we spend the least time where our body is little muscular activity, which occurs under water vapor, and then gradually increases while

Our project consists therefore gradually, like a stream of air which, joined by other streams, progressively becomes a river, a sea and architecture that we propose is an air flow space, a wind that is emerging and is growing by the average hourly rate of renewal of fresh air in the type of space. So the sports hall is defined as an air path following the rate of air change per hour: Storage: 3 to 10 times per hour, Hall: 2 to 4 times per hour, Toilet: 10 to 15 times per hour, Closets Sports: 10 to 20 times per hour, Sports Hall : 10 to 25 times per hour, Shower: 20 to 30 times per hour.

Thus our project is organized, where the architecture itself as a wind, as a movement of air that grows gradually by increasing its frequency of renewal based on the respiration of the people, their activities and amount of steam they generate.

3

3 Low-pressure, meteorological typologies **Unterdruck, meteorologische Typologien,** Philippe Rahm architectes

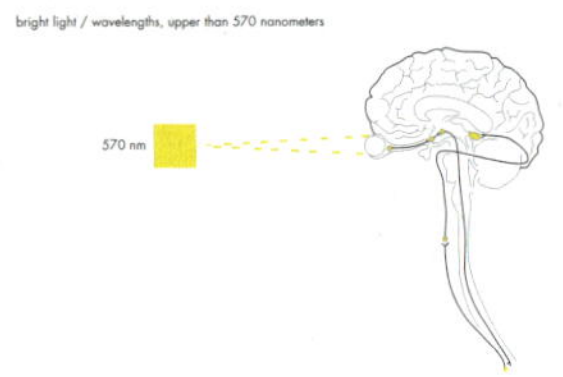

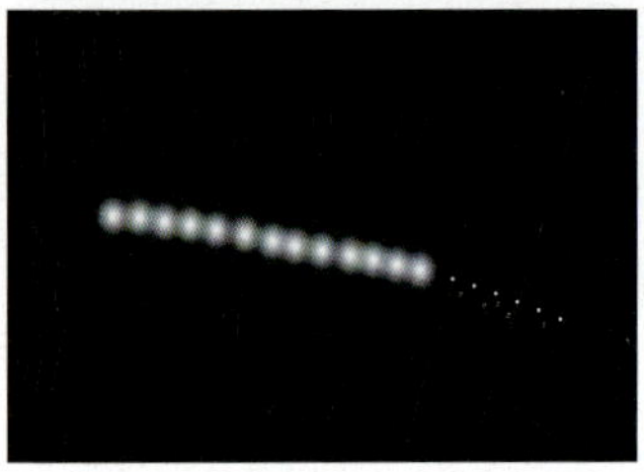

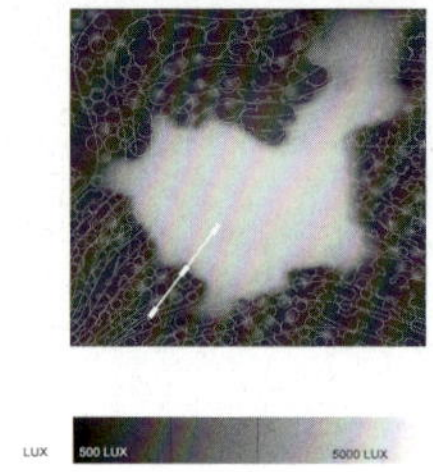

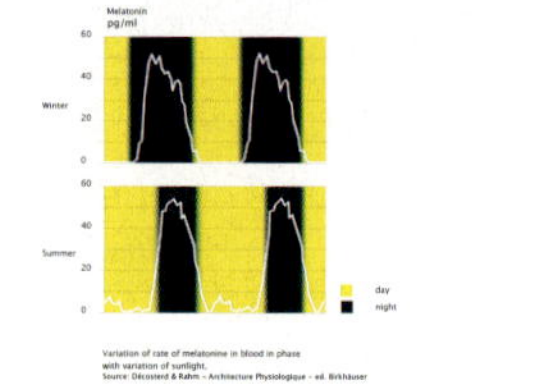

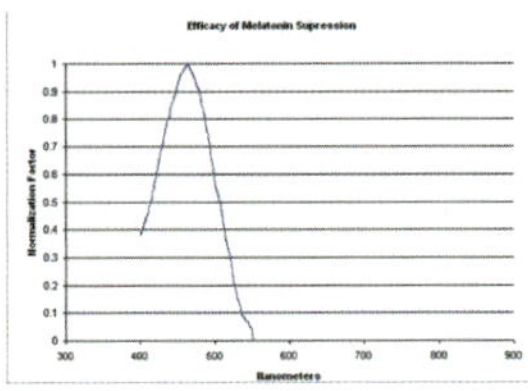

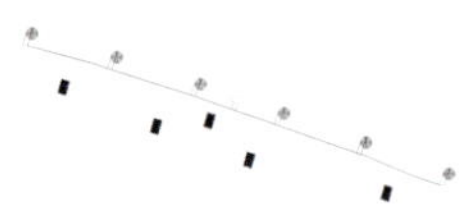

HOUSE DILATION

The proposal is to dilate a house on the site, to disperse its rooms and its layout over the whole of the site, selecting particular places for their particular climates. The house then, is no longer a compact and closed object; it bursts, disseminating its layout and its spaces in different locations over the site, multiplying the views, the situations, the sites, the atmospheres and the climates.

The idea is that a house can be disseminated throughout the landscape, finding the rooms in various places, according to hours of the day, to the environment, to the desires of the moment and the season. The thresholds between two rooms, normally a doorway of a few centimeters thick, dilates then over hundreds of meters. The apartment does not measure any more 50 square meters, but one square kilometers. And the inhabitant lives in this dilated space on a landscape scale.

Our project for Grizedale works on the whole of the site. It dilates the functions through various places, various climates and various qualities of light, temperature and moisture, chosen according to the moments of the day or the seasons. In this situation, architecture removes its outer skin or jacket and it is the environment which then takes on this role, becoming this last skin, filtering the light, containing or repelling moisture, heating or cooling, according to the place and the moment of the day. Three sites are selected: in the meadow, at the boundary of field and forest and in the forest itself. Each site is determined by its specific climatic qualities: the light, temperature and humidity created by the trees. According to the hour of the day and the time of season, the interior quality of the rooms will vary. Activity in each dilation, will relate to the particular and required climate: the heat of the night forest, the warmth of the field in the winter during the day, the freshness of the forest edge in the spring.

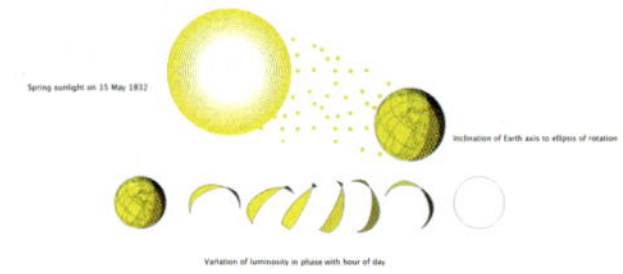

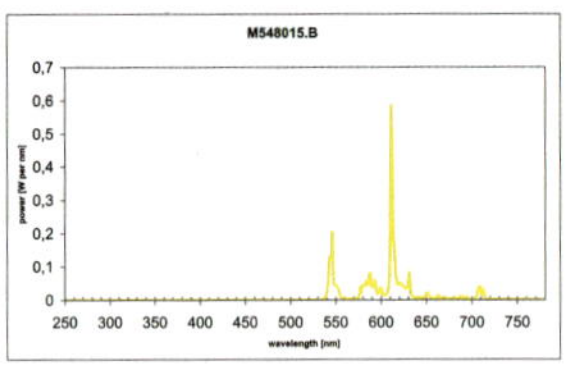

JOUR NOIR

The introduction of the street lighting in the city during the 19-century was at the origin of one the most important social and political revolution of the urban practice and of the form of the city. The ambition was demiurgic: to make the day during the night. The street lighting caused new urban typologies (the boulevard for example) but was also the cause of new behaviors, those of the noctambulism, sauntering the evening on the boulevards, dancing in the balls. It is an ambition of the same order that we want to produce today but more contemporary, more ambiguous: that to create the night during the day.

Our project is that to invent a negative urban standard lamp, producing the night during the day, physically. It's a perverted answer to the perpetual day created by the modernity, Internet and the contemporary globalization. After the "Nuit blanche" ("white night" in French means All-nighter) we would like to invent the "Jour noir", the Black day (All-Dayer). After the noctambulism we would like to propose the diambulism. To create, in the streets, the night during the day, we work on the emitted electromagnetic radiation, as the traditional outdoor lamp. If the traditional outdoor lighting, like a mini-sun, emits a visible radiation of light (artificial electromagnetic radiations of the sunlight), our outdoor lamp emits an invisible and cold electromagnetic radiation, like that emitted by the night sky.

Our lighting consists of a diffuser like a mini night celestial vault, cooled by the flow of glycolic water at the temperature close to 0°C. Its surface is black, absorbing the whole of the luminous spectrum. As it is the case the night with the icy night vault of heaven, our body, with 37°C, will lose energy by infrared radiation in direction of this cold vault. It will cool by thermal phenomenon of balance. A hot body always loses heat to the profit of a cold body. Our outdoor lamps will produce the night thus a black and cold light like the electromagnetic spectrum of the night sky vault.

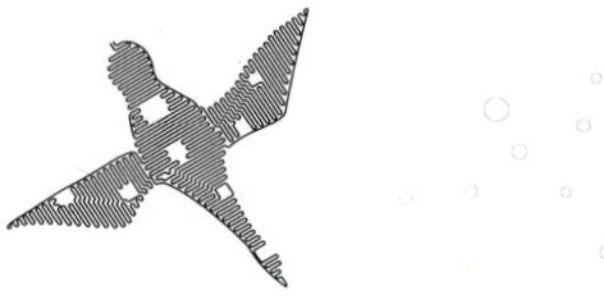

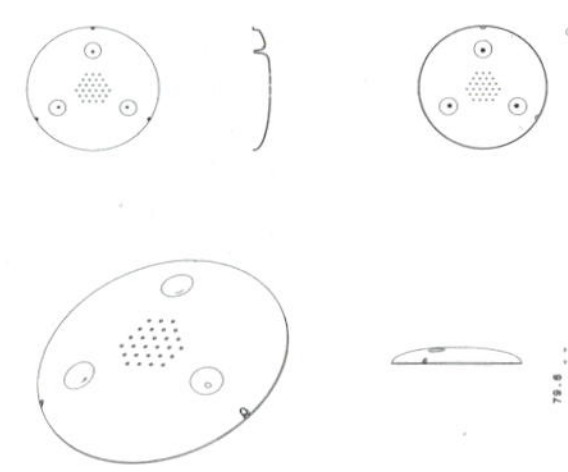

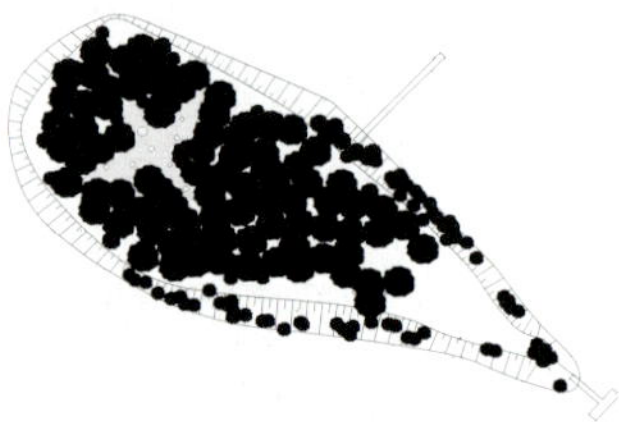

DE-TERRITORIALISED MILIEUS

If modernity has de-territorialised and de-phased light by making it available anywhere at any time, thanks to the research of Alfred Lewy in the early 80s, we now know that certain circadian hormonal cycles are in phase with the luminosity of natural light, between day and night. Studies focusing on the modern-day rupture of this natural physiological relationship between the human body and the astronomical rhythm of the sun's movement tend to show that it is a cause of disorders that are both organic and psychological. In view of this, I propose reinstating the time dimension of electrical light by re-synchronising it with the solar cycle. This translates into a lamp that can be used in two modes. The first is automatic mode, which pilots a daily light cycle corresponding to a spring day, 15 May in Paris. This mode automatically induces variations in the intensity of light emission over 24 hours, with artificial sunset at 9.26pm and artificial sunrise at 6.07am. This default mode is satisfying from the physiological viewpoint, since it enables synchronization of the body-clock to the cycle of natural luminescense. Mode n°2 is manual, with 24 positions available via a switch, thus enabling the user to choose the desired intensity of light at any given time of the reference day, 15 May, the lamp responding as programmed. Adjustable to needs, here the bodyclock is asked to correspond to luminous intensity.

By using archived meteorological data and digital models of climate conditions, I have captured the solar cycle of the day 15 May, 1831, morning to midnight, from 0 hour to 24 hours. The choice of the year 1831 corresponds to the year before the coming into service of the first coal-powered factory in France, which marks the beginning of the disruption of the ecologicalcycle by vaporisation into the atmosphere of fossil carbon, the phenomenon responsible for the hot-house effect and climate change. What I propose is a "day before" to be experienced in an interior, comparable to a fine spring day in Paris in 1832.

DIURNISME

The introduction of the street lighting in the city during the 19-century was at the origin of one the most important social and political revolution of the urban practice and of the form of the city. The ambition was demiurgic: to make the day during the night. And we live henceforth in this endless artificial day in the city. The street lighting caused new urban typologies (the boulevard for example) but was also the cause of new behaviors, those of the noctambulisme, sauntering the evening on the boulevards, dancing in the balls. It is an ambition of the same order that I want to produce today but more contemporary, more ambiguous: to create the night during the day. My project is to reinvent a new form of night in the continuous artificial day of the modernity. It is to produce the night during the day, physically. It's a reversed answer to the perpetual day created by the modernity, Internet and the contemporary globalization, a second perversion. After the "Noctambulisme" I would like to invent the "Diurnisme", using an orange-yellow bright light which wavelengths, upper than 570 nanometers, are perceived by the body through the melatonin rhythm as a true night. The room becomes a paradox between the visible and the invisible, the visual and the physiological: a night which looks like a bright day. Reversed "nocturnes for the piano" by the early 19 century Irish musician John Field, the inventor of this "form" of music, are diffused in the space.

SPLIT TIME CAFE

Architecture becomes not only the design of the space but of the time too. To construct a night, to construct a day: it becomes challenging possibilities for the architectural design. "Split times café" is an architectural project splitting the time in three parallel spaces and customers could shift instantly from one moment of the day to an other. Architecture becomes a time –machine, permitting to cross the time, to pass instantly from the day to the night, to shift from the naturalness to the artificial in a fragment of second. Architecture is here literally the art of the construction of time. The first temporality, taken in an envelope of clear glass, is, in real time, the time of the natural solar course. Classic furniture of a café is there, tables and chairs. An envelope of blue glass defines the second temporality. The wavelengths of this blue light block the secretion of the melatonin in the body. It is therefore a kind of endless day, which becomes a bar, with high tables only, where customers stay upright for short stays. The third temporality is built with a yellow colored glass envelope, blocking the wavelengths of the light responsible for the fall of the melatonin in the body. It reproduces a true physiological night while being luminous like a day. Furniture is here closer to a lounge and approaches the sofa to the bed. The furniture choice is consequently in association with these temporalities.

"Split times café" is an architectural project for a café for the FOC Eybesfeld. It is given like a cellular division, from a time unique and single at the beginning, to a split in two parallel times, the night and the day, but both present at the same time. Actually, "Split times Café" gives the possibility of live in three temporalities: The first one is natural; the other two are artificial, physiologically produced. Furniture is drawn consequently, offering a variety of use and atmosphere, to choose freely. The project is thus a machine to cross the time, to pass instantly from the day to the night, to shift from the naturalness to the artificial in a fragment of second. Architecture is here literally the art of the construction of time.

THE SECOND SUMMER

The island is marshy. An acre or so in a river's ox-bow. Forever casting their shadows, mighty black-barked elms almost totally cover it. What we want to create here is another time, outside astronomical rhythms. A time that is adrift, a seasonal shift, lost on an island, hidden somewhere in a forest. Here, summer will go on indefinitely. It will stretch away into the year, pass through autumn, and make its way through winter into next spring. It is a sort of second summer, a seasonal alteration, an Indian summer, but even more vigorous, astray in the Austrian winter, a climate in suspension. At the heart of the island, behind a dark mass formed by tall deciduous trees, we can make out a clearing, like some improbable, supernatural space. Our project tries to prolong the island's darkness and its mystery, first making it denser, then, disguised in the heart of the island, opening up a space to the sky and the light.

There is a perimeter of about 200 m2 defined by a light, the light of the summer solstice, on 21 June, with its brightness and its variations, which is here perpetuated throughout the year. In the clearing, daybreak comes at 5.03 a.m., and the sun goes down at 11.51 p.m, each day the same, all year round. In the clearing the days will invariably last for 15 hours and 53 minutes. Even on 21 December, whereas beyond the clearing the day will be only 8 hours and 30 minutes long, and the sun will set at 4.10 p.m. The vegetation in the clearing will last throughout this summer. It will be out of season, it will not really change colour, photosynthesis will not cease, the joints of the branches will not snap, the leaves will not completely fall, because the se seasonal phenomena are brought on by the shorter day's length, and because, here, the day's length will forever be that of the first day of summer. An artificial light, whose electromagnetic spectrum reproduces that of sunlight, will each day make up for the shorter day, prolonging photosynthesis beyond autumn, beyond winter. In the clearing, on the ground, the electric light is installed beneath great circles of opaline glass whose arrangement and number borrow those of the stars in the Cygnus constellation. Alpha, gamma, delta, epsilon, beta and three other stars create summer days in the heart of an island in winter.

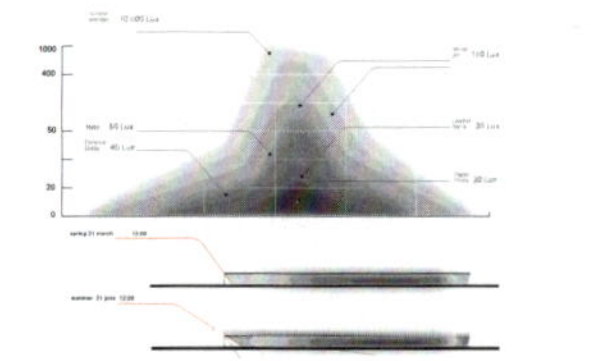

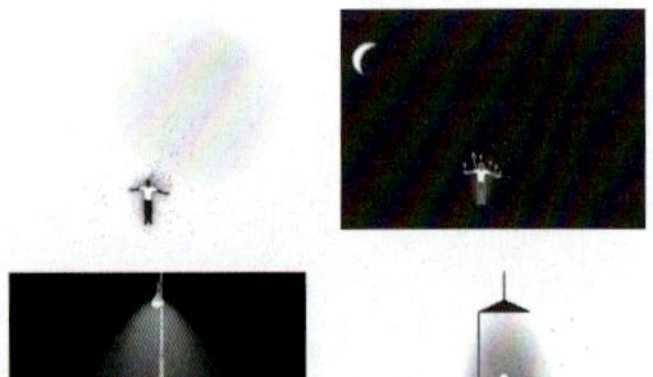

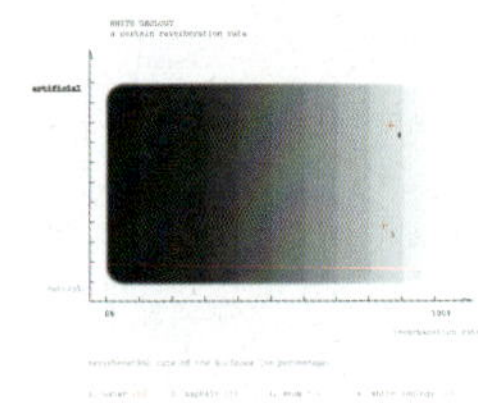

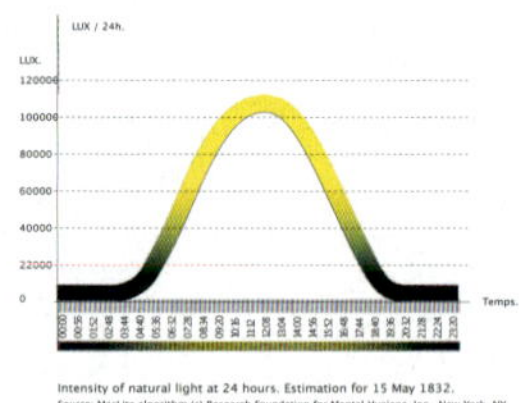

Intensity of natural light at 24 hours. Estimation for 15 May 1832.
Source: MacLite algorithm (c) Research Foundation for Mental Hygiene, Inc., New York, NY.

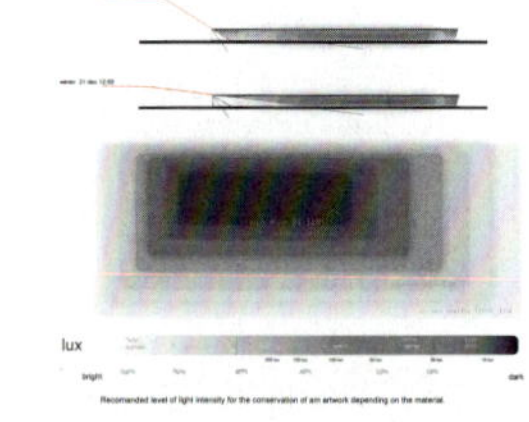

Recomanded level of light intensity for the conservation of an artwork depending on the material

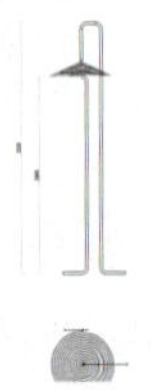

WHITE GEOLOGY

White Geology planned for La Force de l'Art 02, the second triennial contemporary art exhibition at the Grand Palais, is an exploration of the reflection of a background and the power of a white surface to emit light and create optical reflection. The material used for the background serves simply to ensure a high degree of reflection, 80%, and diffract and diffuse the light. It is a white landscape, a white museum cube unfolded to provide a stand for the art works which are set like natural objects on and in front of it. Their shapes and colours stand out sharply against this neutral white background, which blurs the distinction between vertical and horizontal. It is a simplified, white geological form.

Our proposal is more than an architectural project. It is an impoverished geological process that is triggered by the forces in the art works themselves. It is therefore the opposite of exhibition design in the sense that it is not the work of art that fits into the architecture, but the architecture which yields to the demands of the work of art. The exhibits will work together to shape the landscape through the simultaneous play of pressure and checks and balances. A landscape that evolves, sinking and swelling, making shady spaces underneath away from the light of the Grand Palais and bright areas above exposed to the changing daylight that floods through the roof. Shallow, objective and devoid of mystery, White Geology has a reflection level that is similar to snow – 80% –, where all shadows and architectural ornament are obliterated.

Architecture does not construct images and functions. Instead it creates environments and interpretations. It works in emptiness, on air and light, on the phenomena of reflection, effusion and reverberation, like so many mild and fluctuating meteorological conditions, which are becoming the new paradigms for contemporary architecture. It is shifting from metric design to thermal design, from structural thinking to climate-oriented

Variation de la position du soleil dans le ciel et de son intensité en fonction des heures de la journée

LOWERING CLIMATES

Relative humidity and variations of temperature, light intensity and colour range are the key elements that we typically explore in the development of our architectural projects. It is not the use of space that determines the shape of these buildings but their form which produces various practical interpretations. The climate is modulated according to the specific organic or mineral characteristics of each of the artworks. For example, an acceptable quantity of light is assigned to each piece. Light brings about a molecular change in the materials, both by photochemical deterioration (for the shortest wavelengths, such as ultraviolet), as well as by heating (for longer wavelengths approaching infrared radiation). For this reason, paper must be preserved at an approximate maximum intensity of 20 lumens (lx) while wood or metal withstand stronger luminosities. Our project was therefore developed around the reduction of the natural climate, progressing rigorously and rhythmically from the exterior toward the interior, from the most humid spaces to the driest, from the brightest to the darkest, from the strongest in ultraviolet light to the weakest. The natural light intensity decreases as the visitor penetrates the museum, descending progressively from 5,000lx to 10lx in the innermost part.

The character of the architecture attempts to offer some kind of material reification of this invisible sequence. A museum visit is arranged as a gradual immersion into the chemical and physical parameters of the artworks' preservation. Accordingly, the exhibition rooms form a continuum, unfurling between storage spaces through which one may freely circulate, to more controlled climatic migrations. The visitor is offered a cultural experience but also a sensory one. The works are no longer grasped by sight alone but also through the physiology of space and the body, through a descent into obscurity, through the perception of increasingly dry air. In the very physical phenomenon of preservation, in the physiological perception of a 4

dem Klima, der Temperatur, den Schwankungen von Feuchtigkeit und Licht konstruieren.

Bis jetzt haben die Prozesse der Herstellung von Stadt oder Gebäuden versteinerte Erzählungen, vereiste Formen sozialer, politischer und moralischer Konventionen hervorgebracht. Sie haben unflexible Kulturlandschaften gebildet, die früher im Widerspruch zu der fluktuierenden, unvernünftigen Natur von Land und Klima standen. Inzwischen wurde diese Dichotomie vom Fortschritt und den jüngsten Fehlschlägen der biologischen Entwicklung und der Luftverschmutzung eingeholt. Es ist an der Zeit, uns die Werkzeuge der physischen Geografie anzueignen, um Städte und Bauten zu erzeugen, aus denen Narration, Funktionalismus und Determinismus entfernt wurden; Bauten und Städte also, die sich als reine Präsenz offenbaren. Fluktuierende Atmosphären, offene Landschaften, Ziele „ohne schmückendes Beiwerk", die man bewohnt, indem man sie interpretiert. Die Architektur als neue Atmosphäre und zweite Meteorologie ist nicht mehr der geschlossene und „subjektive" Ort der Repräsentation sozialer Verhältnisse und der Politik, sondern wird vielmehr zum „objektiven", offenen Ort, an dem neue soziale und politische Beziehungen entstehen können.

demise of the visible. The means of architecture must become invisible and light, producing places as open and free landscapes, as new geographies and other meteorologies. Renewing the idea of form and function between sensation and the phenomenon, between the neurological and the meteorological, between the physiological and the atmospheric. We are looking for spaces without significance, narration, interpretable spaces in which boundaries evaporate and structures dissipate. No longer is it about constructing images and functions, but about opening up climates and interpretations. About working the void, the air and its movements, the phenomena of conduction, perspiration, convection as if it were transitory meteorological conditions and the new paradigms of contemporary architecture. It is about passing from the metric outline into a thermic outline, from the structural idea to a climate one, from the narrative to the meteorological. About hourly air exchange, relative humidity-of-air plans, habitable convection, thermic design, air movement layouts, pressure and depression, the stratification of temperature as new modes of architectural composition and then revealing the programmatic, plastic and sensitive potentials. The space which has been understood until now as empty and abstract materializes itself as an electromagnetic, chemical, sensorial atmosphere in which we are immersed and which we re-create by inhabiting it, breathing, perspiring in it and in which our body radiates heat, in which we act physically, hormonally by moving and wearing clothes. Between the infinitesimal of the biological and the infinitely grand of the meteorological, architecture must build the sensual exchanges between body and space, the senses, the skin, respiration and the climate, temperature, the variations of humidity and light.

Until now, the processes of producing the city or buildings have yielded petrified narrations, frozen forms of social, political and moral conventions. They formerly shaped frozen cultural landscapes contrasting with the fluctuating and unreasonable disposition of the countryside and the climate. Overcome by progress and the recent failures of biology and air pollution, this dichotomy no longer exists. We can now say that it is our turn to appropriate the tools of physical geography, in order to generate cities and buildings void of their narration, their functionality and their determinism; buildings and cities that would thus be revealed as mere presences. As fluctuating atmospheres, open objective landscapes without adjectivity which can be inhabited by interpreting them. Architecture as a new atmosphere and secondary meteorology is no longer the "subjective," closed place of representation of social interaction and politics, but is becoming an "objective" and open place in which new social and political interaction may take place.

1

1 Pazifische Qualle Pacific jellyfish, Foto photo: © Lindsey Hoshaw.

SUPERFAST JELLYFISH

Matter, Agency, and Emergent Properties of Landscape

"No man is an island, entire of itself;
every man is a piece of the continent,
a part of the main …"
John Donne (1572–1631)

ISLAND ONE: A Matter of POP, Plastic, and Sedimentation. Es sind die seltenen Momente pop-kultureller Innovation, „wenn eine neue Formel gefunden wird“, die Pop-Theoretiker Diedrich Diederichsen mit der Betrachtung bestimmter Praktiken der zeitgenössischen Popmusik zu entdecken vermag, und die zu Modellen einer kommenden Kulturpraxis avancieren oder mit denen bestehende Praktiken aufgelöst werden können.

ISLAND ONE: A Matter of POP, Plastic, and Sedimentation. The rare moments of pop-culture innovation "when a new formula is found" are those discovered by pop theorist Diedrich Diederichsen in considering certain approaches in contemporary pop music—moments which advance to become models of an up-and-coming cultural practice or which facilitate an untangling of existing practices.

KLAUS K. LOENHART

Ein solches im Entstehen begriffenes Modell identifiziert er in der Tendenz, nicht die eigene subjektive Verfassung, sondern den Blick auf die Welt in Texten, Bildern und Bedeutungen zu vernähen. Heute, so stellt er fest, ist es nicht mehr die vordringliche Aufgabe, „die Zerlegbarkeit der Einheiten von Form, Grammatik und Ideologie zu demonstrieren", sondern vielmehr die „Erkennbarkeit von Zusammenhängen zu betonen", also die Bezüglichkeiten jenseits unterschiedlicher ideologischer und kultureller Sphären zusammenzuschreiben.[1] Für Diederichsen entstehen auf diese Weise nicht nur ganz unerwartet diskursive Orte, sondern, wie er betont, auch eine „Interkreativität" bei der „Begegnung der Künste mit gesellschaftlichen Praktiken".[2]

So besingt auf dem aktuellen Album der britischen Konzept-Band Gorillaz der Gast-Artist Lou Reed „Some Kind of Nature". Diese wird auf dem Album *Plastic Beach*[3] der Band mit einer tropischen Insel lokalisiert, deren übergroßes Modell im Studio mit akribischen Details aufgebaut ist. Während das Modell in der Totale das überzeichnete Bild einer schwimmenden Insel erzeugt, offenbaren sich im Zoom deren Eigenschaften. In der „making-of documentary" gleitet die Kamera über den Modellkörper und macht dessen Agglomeration aus Trümmern, aus unzähligen Fragmenten unserer Konsumgesellschaft sichtbar – eine *Plastic Island*.[4]

„Some kind of nature ... Some kind of soul ... Some kind of mixture ... Some kind of gold ... Some kind of majesty ... Some chemical load". Songs wie *Some Kind of Nature* oder *Superfast Jellyfish* des hoch eklektischen Albums erzählen uns im Refrain – in der Manier eines *site-seeings* – von einer fragmentierten Welt in naher Zukunft, in der die Artefakte unserer überschäumenden Konsumproduktion eine neue, fremdartige Körperlichkeit entwickeln und sich mit der natürlichen Umwelt vermengt haben.

Eine oberflächliche Bilderreferenz zu den Konsumpraktiken unserer Zeit oder eine grelle Ästhetisierung von Müll mit dem Ziel *to sell records*? Vielleicht ein Ergebnis des sozialen Engagements mit Charity Oxfam? Gorillaz-Sänger Damon Albarn und Cartoonist Jamie Hewlett verstehen es, ihren spektralen Blick auf die Welt in Texten, Bildern und Bedeutungen zu vernähen – verdichtet zu *Environments* ihrer musikalischen Avatars.

Tatsächlich erinnert die Körperlichkeit von *Plastic Island* an ein geologisches Konglomerat, an ein Sedimentgestein aus miteinander verkitteten Komponenten. Die Sprache des Modells stiftet Verwirrung, denn sein Zusammengebackensein erzeugt eine „fremdartige Natürlichkeit" – *„Some kind of nature ...*" Mit *Plastik Island* sedimentieren sich, der Analogie selektiver geologischer Akkumulation folgend, die grobkörnigen mit den feinkörnigen Fragmenten unserer Konsumkultur zu einem geologisch anmutenden Stratum.

Ein Rückblick auf Robert Smithsons Beobachtung der Fragmentierung unserer modernen sprachlichen und geologischen Umwelt deutet auf eine künstlerische Parallele: „Words and rocks contain a language that follows a syntax of splits and ruptures. Look at any word long enough and you will

1 Diedrich Diederichsen, „Karg, scharf, grau und genau", in: *Süddeutsche Zeitung*, 30.1.2011.

2 Diedrich Diederichsen, „Das Bürgertum besteht nur aus Subkulturen", in: *Welt am Sonntag*, 25.5.2008.

3 Damon Albarn, *Plastic Beach*, Gorillaz Partnership, EMI Records, 2010.

4 Damon Albarn, „Making-of Plastic Beach Documentary", ebd.

Today, he observes, the primary task is no longer "to demonstrate how units of form, grammar, and ideology may be taken apart," but rather "to emphasize how causal relationships may be recognized," that is, to associate the referentialities beyond different ideological and cultural spheres.[1] Developing in this way, for Diederichsen, are not only quite unexpectedly discursive places, but, as he emphasizes, also an "intercreativity" in the "encounter of the arts with social practices."[2]

It is along these lines that Lou Reed, guest artist on the current album by British conceptual band Gorillaz, besings "Some Kind of Nature." The song is localized on the band's album *Plastic Beach*[3] by a tropical island, which is depicted by an ultra-large model constructed in the studio of meticulous details. While the model in its entirety produces the exaggerated image of a swimming island, its features are revealed upon zooming in. In the "making-of documentary," the camera glides over the model body, making visible its agglomeration of rubble, countless fragments from our consumer society—a *Plastic Island*.[4]

"*Some kind of nature ... Some kind of soul ... Some kind of mixture ... Some kind of gold ... Some kind of majesty ... Some chemical load*." On this highly eclectic album, songs such as "Some Kind of Nature" or "Superfast Jellyfish" in their refrains give an account—in a "site-seeing-like" manner—of a fragmented world in the near future where artifacts of our excessive consumer production have developed a new, unfamiliar physicality, intermingling with the natural environment.

Does this all merely represent a superficial pictorial reference to the consumer practices of our age, or a glaring aestheticization of trash with the aim of selling records? Perhaps it is the result of social involvement with the charity Oxfam? Gorillaz singer Damon Albarn and cartoonist Jamie Hewlett expertly weave their spectral view of the world into texts, images, and meanings—condensed into the environments of their musical avatars.

The physicality of *Plastic Island* is in fact reminiscent of a geological conglomerate, a sedimentary rock consisting of conflated components. The model's language causes confusion, for its state of agglomeration produces an "unfamiliar naturalness"—"*Some kind of nature ...*" In *Plastic Island* sedimentation occurs in line with an analogy of selective geological accumulation, where coarse- and fine-grained fragments of our

1 Diedrich Diederichsen, "Karg, scharf, grau und genau," in: *Süddeutsche Zeitung*, January 30, 2011.

2 Diedrich Diederichsen, "Das Bürgertum besteht nur aus Subkulturen," in: *Welt am Sonntag*, May 25, 2008.

3 Damon Albarn, *Plastic Beach*, Gorillaz Partnership, EMI Records, 2010.

4 Damon Albarn, "Making-of Plastic Beach Documentary," ibid.

2

3

2–3 Filmstills, Making-of-Dokumentation des Albums *Plastic Beach*, Gorillaz Partnership 2010.

2–3 Film stills, making-of *Plastic Beach* documentary, Gorillaz Partnership 2010.

see it open up into a series of faults, into a terrain of particles each containing its own void. This discomforting language of fragmentation offers no easy gestalt solution."[5]

In seinem künstlerischen Tun, das er als *sedimentation of the mind* bezeichnet, sind umweltliche Dinge Anlass, um in Folge scheinbar zusammenhanglose Bilder, Beobachtungen, Worte, Objekte und Materialien zueinander zu fügen – als Assemblage und zeitgebundene Konstellation. Folgt das Bandprojekt Gorillaz um Damon Albarn einem ähnlichen Prozess des Zusammenschreibens assoziativ sinnstiftender Konstellationen, dann ließe sich *Plastic Island* jenseits eines ökologischen Diskurses auch als die popkulturelle Artikulation einer gesellschaftlichen Kontroverse und Problemstellung deuten.

Das Modell selbst gleicht einer Versuchsanordnung. Mit dem dargestellten Prozess der Akkumulation und Sedimentierung werden Bruchstücke zusammengeführt, die sich aus ihren Kontexten gelöst haben und im Konsumkreislauf überflüssig geworden sind: Materialien – „Matter" der Konsumkultur im Stadium des Trash. Der ursprünglichen Funktion im Warenkreislauf folgt nun eine neue Einbindung der funktionslos gewordenen Objekte. In Analogie zu Smithsons künstlerischer Praxis, formiert sich eine neu gestaltete Landschaft zwischen musikalischen Texten und Trash-Island zur *Assemblage* – zum „terrain of particles each containing its own void".[6] *Plastic Island* wandelt die moderne Dingwelt von einer „Tatsache" in einen „Sachverhalt"[7] der Materie, welche nach dem Konsum nicht hinter uns liegt, sondern sich vor uns am Horizont ansammelt. Dabei entsteht in der gewonnenen Körperlichkeit dann sogleich auch eine „Schnittstellen-Topografie" separater Realitäten der Moderne – eine Projektionsfläche nicht nur für kulturelle Zustände, sondern auch für verschiedene Auffassungen von Materialität, Landschaft, Humanismus, Subjektivität,[8] die darauf zielt, deren verworrenes Gefüge gesellschaftlich offenzulegen. „Populär sind Künstler nicht zuletzt", stellt Diederichsen fest, „weil sie immer unübersichtlichere und gebrochenere Ereignis- und Objektverkettungen"[9] unserer Gesellschaft zu einem Narrativ zusammenschreiben.

Plastic Island wandelt die moderne Dingwelt von einer „Tatsache" in einen „Sachverhalt"[7] der Materie, welche nach dem Konsum nicht hinter uns liegt, sondern sich vor uns am Horizont ansammelt.

ISLAND TWO: Modernist Controversies, Vibrant Materiality and Matter of Concern. Eine solche Objektverkettung inszeniert die Pop-Rea-

5 Robert Smithson, „A Sedimentation of the Mind", in: Jack D. Flam (Hg.), *Robert Smithson. The Collected Writings*. New York 1996, S. 107.

6 Ebd.

7 Bruno Latour, „Spinoza Lecture I", in: *What Is the Style of Matters of Concern?* Amsterdam 2008, S. 38ff.

8 Tom Holert, „Strudel und Wüsten des Politischen: Michelangelo Antonioni, Robert Smithson und Michael Snow", in: *Medien Kunst Netz*, http://www.mediaartnet.org/themen/kunst_und_kinematografie/wuesten_des_politischen/, 2004 [abgerufen am 20.1.2011].

9 Diederichsen 2008 (Anm. 2).

consumer culture combine to become what seems to be a geological stratum.

A review of Robert Smithson's consideration of the fragmentation of our modern linguistic and geological environment indicates an artistic parallel: "Words and rocks contain a language that follows a syntax of splits and ruptures. Look at any word long enough and you will see it open up into a series of faults, into a terrain of particles each containing its own void. This discomforting language of fragmentation offers no easy gestalt solution."[5]

In his artistic activity, which he calls "sedimentation of the mind," environmental things are the grounds for consequently joining together apparently unconnected images, observations, words, objects, and materials—as an assemblage and time-bound constellation. If Damon Albarn's Gorillaz band project pursues a similar process of coalescing associatively meaningful constellations, then *Plastic Island* could also be interpreted beyond an ecological discourse, as the pop-cultural articulation of a social controversy and its definition of a challenge.

The model itself resembles an experimental exploration. Through the depicted process of accumulation and sedimentation, fragments are reassembled that have broken away from their contexts and become superfluous in the cycle of consumption: material—consumer-culture "matter" in the stage of trash. Its original function in the product life cycle is followed by a new integration of these now functionless objects. By analogy to Smithson's artistic practice, a reconfigured landscape takes shape between musical lyrics and trash island to become an assemblage—a "terrain of particles each containing its own void."[6] *Plastic Island* transforms a modern world of things from a *matter of fact* into a *matter of concern*[7] which, after being consumed, lies not behind us but rather assembles itself before us—at the horizon. Within this newly achieved corporeality, an "interface-topography" of separate realities of modernity then instantly develops—a projection surface not only for cultural conditions, but also for different conceptions of materiality, landscape, humanism, and subjectivity[8] aspiring to bare to society its abstruse fabric. "Artists are popular," Diederichsen notes, "not lastly because they [write up] the increasingly confusing and broken chains of events and objects"[9] of our society into a new narrative.

5 Robert Smithson, "A Sedimentation of the Mind," in: Jack D. Flam (ed.), *Robert Smithson: The Collected Writings*. New York 1996, p. 107.

6 Ibid.

7 Bruno Latour, "Spinoza Lecture II," in: *What Is the Style of Matters of Concern?* Amsterdam 2008, pp. 38ff.

8 Tom Holert, "Strudel und Wüsten des Politischen: Michelangelo Antonioni, Robert Smithson und Michael Snow," in: *Medien Kunst Netz*, http://www.mediaartnet.org/themen/kunst_und_kinematografie/wuesten_des_politischen/, 2004 [accessed January 20, 2011].

9 Diederichsen 2008 (fn. 2).

ISLAND TWO: Modernist Controversies, Vibrant Materiality, and Matter of Concern. The pop-reality of the composite entity *Plastic Island* stages such a threading of objects in that Damon Albarn combines discursive filaments to a concrete discovery and its momentarily unfolding controversy:

On his way home from the Transpac sailing regatta—spanning a distance of 2,225 nautical miles between Los Angeles and Japan—Captain Charles Moore took a shortcut through the horse latitudes, which sailors like to avoid because of the calm seas generally prevailing in this Pacific convergence zone. Midway he unexpectedly sailed through an area teeming with plastic waste. For days, bottles, styrofoam, canisters, wrappers, plastic buoys, and bits of something or other floated past his boat. Charles Moore had discovered a new continent, the "Great Pacific Garbage Patch" (GPGP).[10]

This confirmed what oceanographer Curtis Ebbesmeyer had long suspected, for ocean currents in the North Pacific—driven by winds and the Earth's rotation—form a gigantic "gyre" that causes flotsam refuse to accumulate between Japan, China, and North America.[11] Beyond all territorial waters, fragments converge to create a massive soup consisting of artificial materials. Suspended forever in an area of 1.5 million square kilometers (about four times as large as Germany or twice the size of Texas) is any semblance of a clear boundary between cultural agency and natural ecosystem. While an average of 18,000 pieces of plastic are found in each square kilometer of ocean on our planet, in the GPGP a significantly higher number of plastic parts of any imaginable size and origin accumulate. Besides the large, visible fragments, it is primarily the smaller particles that make a separation from the surrounding ecosystem impossible. Since plastic will not degrade biologically but only photochemically, years or decades must pass before the particles sink to the ocean floor to ultimately be deposited as sediment.

The sediment on Kamilo Beach in Hawaii contains more plastic particles than grains of sand—all the way down to a depth of thirty centimeters. And in 2010, there were already forty-seven times more plastic particles than zooplankton in GPGP waters.[12] Moore has already documented plastic particles in a large number of zoological species, even in the bodies of transparent jellyfish. Because many sea dwellers mistake them for zooplankton, the synthetic materials thus start their journey through the food chain, ultimately ending up in the human organism. Within this cessation of water flow in the Pacific Ocean, as caused by winds and the Earth's rotation,

10 Peter Haffner, "Eine Ahnung von Apokalypse," in: *Neue Zürcher Zeitung*, NZZ Folio, September 2007.

11 Dietmar Bartz, "Bade-Entchens letztes Ufer," in: *Neue Zürcher Zeitung*, NZZ Folio, February 2004.

12 Richard Grant, "Drowning in Plastic," in: *The Telegraph*, April 24, 2009.

lität des Mischwesens *Plastic Island*, indem Damon Albarn diskursive Fäden zu einer konkreten Entdeckung und ihrer sich erst im Entfalten befindenden Kontroverse knüpft:

Auf der Heimfahrt von der sich über 2.225 Seemeilen erstreckenden Transpac-Segelregatta zwischen Los Angeles und Hawaii nahm Kapitän Charles Moore eine Abkürzung durch die Rossbreiten, die von Seglern gerne vermieden werden, da in dieser pazifischen Konvergenzzone üblicherweise Windstille herrscht. Auf halber Strecke durchquerte er unerwartet eine Zone von Plastikmüll. Tagelang zogen an seinem Boot Flaschen, Styropor, Kanister, Hüllen, Plastikbojen, Schnipsel von irgendetwas vorüber. Charles Moore hatte einen neuen Kontinent entdeckt, den *Great Pacific Garbage Patch* (GPGP).[10]

Bestätigt war damit, was Ozeanograf Curtis Ebbesmeyer lange vermutet hatte, denn angetrieben von Winden und der Erdrotation bilden Meeresströmungen im Nord-Pazifik einen gigantischen Wirbel, mit dem sich Treibgut zwischen Japan, China und Nordamerika ansammelt.[11] Außerhalb aller Hoheitsgewässer verdichten sich dort die Fragmente zu einer Suppe künstlicher Stoffe mit gewaltiger Ausdehnung. Auf rund 1,5 Millionen Quadratkilometern (einer Fläche viermal so groß wie Deutschland oder der doppelten Größe des Bundesstaats Texas) sind Vorstellungen der klaren Abgrenzung zwischen kulturellem Handlungsraum und natürlichem Ökosystem für immer außer Kraft gesetzt. 18.000 Plastikteile finden sich im Durchschnitt in jedem Quadratkilometer Ozean auf unserem Planeten, im GPGP jedoch akkumuliert sich ein Vielfaches dieser Menge an Plastikteilen jeder erdenklichen Größe und Herkunft. Neben den großen sichtbaren Fragmenten sind es vor allem die kleineren Partikel, die keine Trennung zum umgebenden Ökosystem mehr möglich machen. Da Plastik nicht biologisch, sondern lediglich fotochemisch abbaubar ist, dauert es Jahre oder Jahrzehnte, bis die Partikel zu Boden sinken, um sich schließlich als Sediment abzulagern.

Am Kamilo Beach in Hawaii finden sich in seinen Sedimenten bis zu einer Tiefe von 30 Zentimetern mehr Plastikpartikel als Sandkörner. Im Jahr 2010 wiederum befanden sich in den Gewässern des GPGP bereits 47 Mal mehr Plastikpartikel als Zooplankton.[12] Moore hat Plastikpartikel bereits in vielen zoologischen Spezies dokumentiert, selbst in den Körpern durchsichtiger Quallen. Da viele Meeresbewohner sie mit Zooplankton verwechseln, treten die synthetischen Stoffe so ihren Weg durch die Nahrungskette an, um schließlich in den menschlichen Organismus zu gelangen. An der durch Winde und Erdrotation in Gang gesetzten strömungstechnischen Leerstelle im Pazifischen Ozean bilden sich hybride Konstellationen zwischen der entwerteten Konsumwelt und einer natürlichen Meeresökologie, die als organisch/anorganische Müllhybride nunmehr aus dem Hintergrund komfortabler Unsichtbarkeit treten. Andreas Nebelung beschreibt dieses Phänomen als „abgedrängte umweltliche Kategorie" im Grenzbereich zwischen System und Umwelt.[13]

10 Peter Haffner, „Eine Ahnung von Apokalypse", in: *Neue Zürcher Zeitung*, NZZ Folio, 2007/09.

11 Dietmar Bartz, „Bade-Entchens letztes Ufer", in: *Neue Zürcher Zeitung*, NZZ Folio, 2004/02.

12 Richard Grant, „Drowning in Plastic", in: *The Telegraph*, London, 24.4.2009.

13 Andreas Nebelung, *Ökologische Soziologie. Zwischenräume*. Gießen 2003.

4

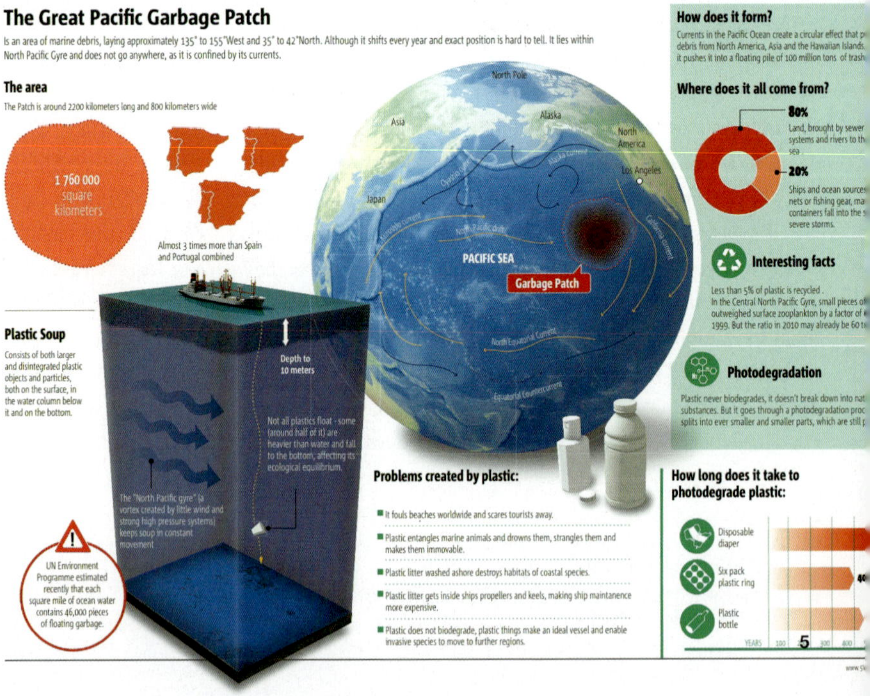

5

4 Müllansammlung im *Great Pacific Garbage Patch*, Foto: © Lindsey Hoshaw.

5 Systemgrafik des GPGP, Illustration: © 5Wgraphics.com

4 Trash agglomeration *Great Pacific Garbage Patch*, photo: © Lindsey Hoshaw.

5 GPGP system graphic, illustration: © 5Wgraphics.com

hybrid constellations develop between a devaluated world of consumption and a natural marine ecology, where organic/inorganic waste hybrids are now emerging from the background of comfortable invisibility. Andreas Nebelung describes this phenomenon as a "relegated environmental category" on the borderline between system and environment.[13]

Generally speaking, the presence of garbage rarely manifests in our Western sphere of culture, yet the continental dimensions of the GPGP to date have exceeded the stage of invisibility. Though communicated following Moore's discovery in research and media reports, the GPGP continues to elude personal categorization—since none of the observations made are part of our collective memory.

With "modern separations," fundamental fallacies develop between cultural artifacts and environment,[14] initially turning this *Plastic Island*, actually floating in the Pacific, into error or anomaly. Yet far away, a network of fundamental relationships between our day-to-day habit of excessive disposal and the consequences of its suppression connect up to this island of trash. Leading us above all to the margins of separability in terms of cultural and natural spheres, besides the realization of its sheer dimensions, is an imagining of the systemic consistency of this marine landscape: "How can the dictum 'In ecosystems, everything is used' be made to work with plastic?"[15] The GPGP establishes plastic waste in a landscape of continental dimensions and, in so doing, attests to the end of dialectics between nature and culture—a reversal that may have asserted itself in design theories but that has yet to yield any sweeping consequences. Perhaps it is necessary to take a step toward more closely relating the theory with the *matter* of the issue itself.

In their sheer materiality, the objects floating in the Pacific gyre, fragmented and devoid of their previous function and recognizability, develop a phenomenon which political scientist Jane Bennett refers to as *thing-power*: "Thing-power materialism figures materiality as a protean flow of matter-energy and figures the thing as a relatively composed form of that flow. It hazards an account of materiality even though materiality is both too alien and too close for humans to see clearly. It seeks to promote acknowledgment, respect, and sometimes fear of the materiality of the thing and to articulate ways in which human being and thinghood overlap."[16] The materiality of the

13 Andreas Nebelung, *Ökologische Soziologie: Zwischenräume*. Gießen 2003.

14 Bruno Latour, *We Have Never Been Modern*, trans. Catherine Porter. Cambridge, MA 1993.

15 Charles Moore, "Trashed: Across the Pacific Ocean, Plastics, Plastics, Everywhere," in: *Natural History* 112, no. 9 (November 2003), http://www.mindfully.org/Plastic/Ocean/Moore-Trashed-PacificNov03.htm [accessed January 20, 2011].

16 Jane Bennett, "The Force of Things: Steps toward an Ecology of Matter," in: *Political Theory* 32/3 (June 2004), p. 349.

Üblicherweise tritt die Präsenz von Müll in unserem westlichen Kulturraum selten in Erscheinung, doch die mittlerweile kontinentalen Ausmaße des GPGP haben den Grad der Unsichtbarkeit überschritten. Obwohl nach Moores Entdeckung durch Forschungs- und Medienberichte kommuniziert, entzieht sich der GPGP weiterhin einer persönlichen Kategorisierung – denn keine der dort gemachten Beobachtungen sind Teil unseres kollektiven Bilderarchivs.

Mit „modernen Trennungen" zwischen kulturellen Artefakten und Umwelt entstehen grundlegende Täuschungen,[14] welche die im Pazifik tatsächlich treibende *Plastic Island* zunächst als Irrtum oder Störung erscheinen lässt. Doch knüpft sich an diese Trash-Insel in weiter Ferne ein Netz grundlegender Bezüge zwischen unserer alltäglichen Wegwerfhandlung und den Konsequenzen ihrer Verdrängung. Neben der Realisierung der schieren Größe, führt uns vor allem die systemische Konsequenz, diese Meereslandschaft zu denken, an die Grenze der Trennbarkeit von Kultur- und Naturraum: „How can the dictum ‚In ecosystems, everything is used' be made to work with plastic?"[15] Der GPGP etabliert den Plastikmüll in landschaftlichem, kontinentalem Maßstab und bestätigt damit erneut das Ende der Dialektik von Natur und Kultur – eine Aufhebung, die sich in den Gestaltungstheorien zwar weitgehend durchgesetzt, aber bislang kaum durchschlagende Konsequenzen gezeitigt hat. Vielleicht bedarf es dazu des Schritts, die Theorie mit der *Materie* der Sache selbst enger in Beziehung zu setzen.

Da Plastik nicht biologisch, sondern lediglich fotochemisch abbaubar ist, dauert es Jahre oder Jahrzehnte, bis die Partikel zu Boden sinken, um sich schließlich als Sediment abzulagern.

Die im pazifischen Wirbel treibenden Objekte, zerstückelt und ihrer früheren Funktion und Erkennbarkeit entzogen, entfalten in ihrer bloßen Materialität ein Phänomen, das die Politikwissenschaftlerin Jane Bennett als Ausdruck einer *thing-power* fasst: „Thing-power materialism figures materiality as a protean flow of matter-energy and figures the thing as a relatively composed form of that flow. It hazards an account of materiality even though materiality is both too alien and too close for humans to see clearly. It seeks to promote acknowledgment, respect, and sometimes fear of the materiality of the thing and to articulate ways in which human being and thinghood overlap."[16] Der Materialität der Dingwelt wird so eine Lebendigkeit und Performativität zugesprochen, die nicht zuletzt auch die antimaterielle Neigung[17] unserer Konsumgesellschaft erkennbar macht. In immer schnel-

14 Bruno Latour, *Wir sind nie modern gewesen. Versuch einer symmetrischen Anthropologie*. Frankfurt/M. 2008.

15 Charles Moore, „Trashed: Across the Pacific Ocean, Plastics, Plastics, Everywhere", in: *Natural History* 112, Nr. 9, November 2003, http://www.mindfully.org/Plastic/Ocean/Moore-Trashed-PacificNov03.htm [abgerufen am 20.1.2011].

16 Jane Bennett, „The Force of Things. Steps toward an Ecology of Matter", in: *Political Theory* 32, Nr. 3, 2004, S. 349.

17 Ebd., S. 350.

leren Zyklen bewegen wir uns durch die Prozesse von Erwerb, Gebrauch, Entwertung und Entsorgung mit der Tendenz, die jeweilige Materialität der Dinge durch den Vorbehalt ihres Austauschs durch neue Artefakte unwiderruflich zu diskreditieren.

Der Schlüsselmoment des „Wiedereintritts" des Trashs in unsere gelebte Realität spiegelt dann nicht nur die Systeme des Austritts, des Wegwerfens und der Prozesse der Entwertung wider, sondern ermöglicht es, die Agglomeration von Kunststoffpartikeln im Pazifischen Ozean quasi als „Co-Aktanten" unserer gesellschaftlich-ökologischen Realität zu erkennen. Mit dem Wiedereintritt ändert sich augenblicklich die Wirklichkeit in ihren Assoziationen der vielen Beziehungen und Verantwortlichkeiten. Mit diesem Moment wird deutlich, dass die Aufgabe vielmehr darin besteht, die Wirkkraft und Bedeutung der nun hervortretenden „nichtmenschlichen Akteure" für unsere gesellschaftlichen Handlungen erkennbar zu machen. Konzipiert als lebendiges, „vibrierendes" Bezugssystem menschlicher- und nichtmenschlicher Akteure, entfaltet sich in Folge ein ökologisch-politisches Netzwerk, das einer genaueren Analyse bedarf. Wie aber lässt sich ein solches Netzwerk von Akteuren darlegen?

Diese Frage erläutert Bruno Latour anhand des Unglücks der US-amerikanischen Raumfähre Columbia: Nach dem tragischen Bersten der Raumfähre beim atmosphärischen Wiedereintritt, wurde eine akribische Rekonstruktion eingeleitet, welche das Verhalten von Politik, Menschen, Naturgesetzen (etwa Thermodynamik, Gravitation), die technische Konzeption, Materialität und Stofflichkeit (Atmosphäre, Staub) in Beziehung setzte. Jedem Element wurde im Zuge der Rekonstruktion eine spezifische Rolle im Ablauf und in den Wirkzusammenhängen der einzelnen Handlungen, Entscheidungen und Materialien zugeordnet. In einem Hangar der NASA wurden alle gefundenen Teile des Shuttle auf einem Rasterplan in Beziehung gesetzt, eine Art stoffliches Performanzdiagramm herstellend, das die Beziehung zwischen den Teilen erkennbar machte: „Look at any object [das Shuttle], at first it looks as self-containing to itself, with well-delinated edges and limits, then something happens: A strike, an accident, a catastrophy [...] and suddenly you discover a swarm of entities [von Bezüglichkeiten und Performanz], that seem to have been there all along, but were not visible before, and that appear in retrospect necessary for its sustainance."[18]

Nach dem anfänglichen Erkennen eines „Schwarms von Einheiten" entwickelt sich in der Folge eine dynamische Assemblage aus Material, menschlichen Handlungen, politischer Entscheidungsfindung, wissenschaftlicher Analyse, subjektivem und naturgesetzlichem Verhalten. „You thought for instance, the Columbia shuttle was an object, ready to fly in the sky, and then suddenly, after a dramatic 2003 explosion, you realize that it needed the NASA, and it's complex organizational body, to fly safely in the sky. [...] The action of flying a technical object, has been redistributed through-

18 Bruno Latour, „Networks, Societies, Spheres: Reflections of an Actor-Network Theorist", The International Network Theory Conference, University of Southern California, 19.2.2010, in: http://www.youtube.com/watch?v=Bj7EDMRJrbU, 6'42" [abgerufen am 20.1.2011].

world of things is thus awarded a vibrancy and performativity that not lastly renders visible an antimaterial propensity[17] of our consumer society. As we move through the processes of acquisition, usage, devaluation, and disposal in ever more rapid cycles, a tendency emerges to irrevocably discredit the respective materiality of things, subject to the condition that they can be substituted by new artifacts.

The pivotal moment of the "reentry" of trash into our lived reality then reflects not only the systems of discharge, throwing away, and the processes of devaluation but makes it possible to recognize the agglomeration of plastic particles in the Pacific Ocean as conceivable "co-agents" in our socioecological reality. With this reentry, reality is instantly transformed in its associations of numerous relationships and responsibilities. It is this moment that foremost demonstrates how the task lies in making recognizable the efficacy and meaning of those now emerging "nonhuman agents" for our social activities. Conceived as a lively, "vibrant" reference system of human and nonhuman agents, an ecopolitical network thus unfolds, one requiring more precise analysis. Yet how might such a network of agents be depicted?

Bruno Latour illustrates this question in reference to the U.S. space shuttle Columbia disaster: after it tragically burst upon reentry into the Earth's atmosphere, a meticulous reconstruction was initiated that associated politics, human behavior, laws of nature (such as thermodynamics, gravitation), its technical conception, and materiality (atmosphere, dust). Over the course of this reconstruction, each element was assigned a specific role in the order of events and cause-effect relationships of the individual activities, decisions, and materials. Spread out in a large NASA hangar, all parts of the shuttle that had been found were placed into relation with one another on a grid, producing a kind of material performance diagram that rendered discernable the relationship between individual pieces:

"Look at any object [the shuttle]—at first it looks self-containing to itself, with well-delineated edges and limits, then something happens: a strike, an accident, a catastrophe ... and suddenly you discover a swarm of entities [of referentialities and performance] that seem to have been there all along but were not visible before, and that appear in retrospect necessary for its sustainance."[18]

After the initial recognition of a "swarm of entities," a dynamic assemblage was subsequently developed, consisting

17 Ibid., p. 350.

18 Bruno Latour, "Networks, Societies, Spheres: Reflections of an Actor-Network Theorist," The International Network Theory Conference, University of Southern California, February 19, 2010, in: http://www.youtube.com/watch?v=Bj7EDMRJrbU, 6'42" [accessed on January 20, 2011].

6 Plastikteile vermischt mit Zooplankton beim GPGP, Foto: © Lindsey Hoshaw. Plastic particles to be confused with zooplankton in the GPGP, photo: © Lindsey Hoshaw.

7 Untersuchung des Columbia-Shuttle-Absturzes im Kennedy Space Center in Cape Canaveral, Florida, März 2003, Foto: © NASA. Columbia Shuttle Crash Investigation at Kennedy Space Center in Cape Canaveral, Florida, March, 2003, photo: © NASA.

of material, human actions, political decision-making, scientific analysis, and behavior related to subjectivity and laws of nature: "You thought for instance, the Columbia shuttle was an object, ready to fly in the sky, and then suddenly, after a dramatic 2003 explosion, you realize that it needed the NASA and its complex organizational body to fly safely in the sky. … The action of flying a technical object has been redistributed throughout a highly composite network, where bureaucratic routine is just as important as equations and material resistances."[19]

Just as the evocative processes of the Columbia crash in its relational dynamics were first understood in retrospect, the lines of action related to the GPGP can also be reconstructed retrospectively through the visible contradictions presented by the modern commodity system: here, *matter* has taken on an enormous mediating role in most direct relation to the social and political decisions which are now equivalent parts of this assemblage. It is the materiality of things, in particular, that has already removed itself from an original contextuality, opening up new perspectives—through its ruptures and gaps, so to speak—on the network of relationships associated with its own existence. For Jane Bennett, this gives rise to a necessity of a practice of reading and detecting these relationships. She speaks of a practice of agency in which one primarily recognizes the "discipline of looking always at what is to be seen."[20]

Continuing along this train of thought, the incorporation of (artificial) material in the organic tissue of Pacific jellyfish, for example, hence displays a double hybridity—material (organic/nonorganic) and political (nature/culture). It is the transformation from *matters of fact* into *matters of concern* that allows the newly identified and abstruse contextuality to become visible—"objects become things, that is, when matters of fact give way to their complicated entanglements and become matters of concern."[21] Consequently, things in their contested environmental relatedness emerge out of a neutral world of objects, thus fostering discourse on associated social controversies.

ISLAND THREE: The Ecological Turn, Its Design-Practice, and Protocols of Controversy. And there are signs of an emerging awareness for making these respective "matters of concern" visible and for protocolling them as social controversy: this occurs at precisely that moment when "the dimen-

19 Ibid., 6'55".

20 Bennett 2004 (fn. 16), p. 350, in reference to Henry Thoreau.

21 Bruno Latour, "From Realpolitik to Dingpolitik or How to Make Things Public," in: idem, Peter Weibel (eds.), *Making Things Public: Atmospheres of Democracy*. Karlsruhe, Cambridge, MA, and London 2005, p. 31.

out a highly composite network, where bureaucratic routine is just as important as equations and material resistances."[19]

Ebenso wie die Vorgänge des Columbia-Absturzes erst retrospektiv in ihrer beziehungsreichen Dynamik verstanden wurden, lassen sich auch beim GPGP die Handlungsstränge aus den sichtbaren Widersprüchen des modernen Warensystems nachträglich rekonstruieren: „*Matter*" hat hier eine gewaltige Vermittlungsrolle eingenommen im direkten Bezug zu den sozialen und politischen Entscheidungen, welche nun gleichwertige Teile dieser Assemblage sind. Besonders die Materialität der Dinge selbst, welche sich einer ursprünglichen Kontextualität bereits entzogen hat, eröffnet neue Blicke – sozusagen durch die Risse und Sprünge hindurch – auf das Beziehungsgeflecht ihrer Existenz. Für Jane Bennett erwächst daraus die Notwendigkeit einer Praxis des Lesens und Erkennens dieser Beziehungen. Sie spricht von einer Handlungspraxis als Disziplin, in der man vordringlich das erkennt, „was sich in seiner Bezüglichkeit offenbart" („the discipline of looking always at what is to be seen").[20]

Dieser Betrachtung folgend, bildet sich beispielsweise mit den (kunst-)stofflichen Einlagerungen in das organische Gewebe pazifischer Quallen (Jellyfish) sogar eine doppelte Hybridität ab – eine stoffliche (organisch-nichtorganisch) und eine politische (Natur-Kultur): Es ist der Wandel von einer Tatsache zu einem Sachverhalt, der die neu erkannte und verworrene Kontextualität sichtbar werden lässt – „Objects become things, that is, when matters of fact give way to their complicated entanglements and become matters of concern".[21] Aus der neutralen Objektwelt treten in Folge die Dinge in ihrer umkämpften umweltlichen Bezüglichkeit hervor und ermöglichen einen Diskurs um die damit verbundenen gesellschaftlichen Kontroversen.

Aus der neutralen Objektwelt treten in Folge die Dinge in ihrer umkämpften umweltlichen Bezüglichkeit hervor und ermöglichen einen Diskurs um die damit verbundenen gesellschaftlichen Kontroversen.

ISLAND THREE: The Ecological Turn, Its Design-Practice and Protocols of Controversy. Und es finden sich Anzeichen für eine entstehende Aufmerksamkeit, jene bezüglichen „Sachverhalte" (*matters of concern*) sichtbar zu machen und als gesellschaftliche Kontroverse zu protokollieren: Dies geschieht just in dem Moment, in dem „die Dimensionen der anstehenden Aufgaben durch die verschiedenen ökologischen Krisen fantastisch vergrößert worden sind" und ein öffentliches Bewusstsein notwendig gemacht haben dafür, „was es bedeutet zu handeln".[22] Sollte sich etwa diese

19 Ebd., 6'55".

20 Bennett 2004 (Anm. 16), S. 350, mit Bezugnahme auf Henry Thoreau.

21 Bruno Latour, „From Realpolitik to Dingpolitik or How to Make Things Public", in: ders., Peter Weibel (Hg.), *Making Things Public. Atmospheres of Democracy*. Karlsruhe, Cambridge, MA und London 2005, S. 31.

22 Bruno Latour, „Ein vorsichtiger Prometheus", in: Mark Jongen, Sjoerd van Tuinen, Koenraad Hemelsoet (Hg.), *Die Vermessung des Ungeheuren*. München 2009, S. 360.

Versammlung aktueller ökologischer, gesellschaftlicher und politischer Ereignisse – in ihren durchdringenden Verbindungen – als „evolutionäres" Produkt und kontinuierliche Landschaft unserer zivilisatorischen Handlungen zu erkennen geben?

Um durchdringende Assemblagen sichtbar zu machen, bedarf es in Annäherung an Bennett's Argument der Entwicklung einer Praxis des Lesens und Protokollierens – nun im gesellschaftlichen Maßstab – um zu erkennen, „was sich als ‚*agency of assemblage*' in seiner Bezüglichkeit offenbart".[23] Notwendig ist hierfür ein Moment der Wendung, Neujustierung, ein „*turn*" unserer Praktiken. Trotz vielfältiger Auslegung der räumlichen Metapher des *turn* transportiert der Begriff in geeigneter Weise die Bemühungen der letzten Jahre, konzeptionelle Wendungen von der Kategorie der Zeit zu der des Raumes zu beschreiben. Im Zusammenspiel mit dem Begriff der Ökologie bezeichnet dies keineswegs einen Weg zurück zur Natur, sondern eher den Bedarf, auf ein Netzwerk dynamischer, materieller und performativer Beziehungen hinzuweisen und dessen Charakteristik als performatives „Arbeitssystem" in den Vordergrund zu rücken.[24] Die Praktik eines „*Ecological Turn*" ist dann auch eine Raumpraktik, die sich der stofflichen Grundlage der Landschaft und deren Performanz von Ökologien menschlicher und nicht-menschlicher Akteure zuwendet.

An diesem Punkt lässt sich „Landschaft" selbst als verbindendes Medium, als bündelnde Linse beziehungsweise als Handlungsraum eines solchen *Ecological Turn* entwickeln.

An diesem Punkt lässt sich „Landschaft" selbst als verbindendes Medium, als bündelnde Linse beziehungsweise als Handlungsraum eines solchen *Ecological Turn* entwickeln. Denn sie bietet die Möglichkeit zur kritischen Auseinandersetzung mit gesellschaftlichen Kontroversen und Anliegen, indem sie als aktive Handlungsträgerin (*active agent*) und landschaftliche Wirklichkeit eine Relektüre der klassischen Dichotomie zwischen „Natur" und „Kultur" erlaubt.

Wenn, wie wir eingangs festgestellt haben – unsere derzeitige gesellschaftliche Situation tatsächlich geprägt ist von den Möglichkeiten, „eine neue Formel" zu finden, um die „Erkennbarkeit von Bezüglichkeiten" jenseits von ideologischen und kulturellen Sphären und Realitäten zu protokollieren – dann wäre nun weiterführend zu prüfen, inwieweit eine gestaltende Praxis diese lesbar machen könnte. Hier wird ein weiterer „Wiedereintritt" von Materialität in ihrer Performanz interessant. Denn wo sich die typisch moderne Trennung von „Materialität auf der einen Seite und Design auf der anderen Seite" im Zuge unserer gesellschaftlichen Verabschiedung der modernen Trennungen langsam auflöst,[25] erscheinen gestaltende räumliche Praktiken – im Folgenden dargelegt als Landschaftspraxis, als Arbeits-

23 Jane Bennett, „Agency of Assemblage", in: *Vibrant Matter. A Political Ecology of Things*. Durham und London 2010, S. 20.

24 Bennett 2004 (Anm. 16), S. 365.

25 Latour 2009 (Anm. 22), S. 358.

sions of the tasks at hand have been fantastically amplified by the various ecological crises," and a collective awareness becomes necessary for "what it means to act."[22] Should this accumulation of current ecological, social, and political occurrences—in their pervasive connections—reveal itself as an "evolutionary" product and continuous landscape emerging of our civilization-induced actions?

In order to make these pervasive assemblages visible, it is necessary to approach Bennett's argument regarding the development of a practice of *discerning* and *protocolling*—now in a social dimension—with an aim of recognizing "what reveals itself as an 'agency of assemblage' in its relatedness."[23] For this to unfold, a moment of conversion, a readjustment, a "turn" in our practices becomes compelling. Despite the varied interpretation of the spatial metaphor of the turn, this concept aptly transports recent efforts to describe conceptional adaptations from a category of time to that of space. In conjunction with the concept of ecology, this in no way connotes a path back to nature, but more the need to allude to a network of dynamic, material, and performative relationships and to foreground its characteristic as performative "working-system."[24] The practice of an "ecological turn" is then also a *practice of space* that turns to the material basis of landscape and its performance by ecologies of human and nonhuman agents.

At this point, "landscape" itself can evolve as a connecting medium, as a focusing lens, or as a space of action for such an ecological turn. Indeed, it provides the opportunity for a critical examination of social controversies and concerns in that it allows—as active agent and landscape reality—a rereading of the classic dichotomy between "nature" and "culture."

When reviewing the original assessment—that our current social situation is in fact characterized by possibilities of finding "a new formula" for protocolling the "visibility of referentialities" beyond ideological and cultural spheres and realities—one finds an indication for furthermore exploring the extent at which a formative practice could render this percipient. Here, a further "reentry" of materiality in terms of its performance becomes of interest. For where the typically modern division of "materiality on the one hand and design on the other is slowly being dissolved away" over the course of our social dismissal of modern separations,[25] practices of designing space—demonstrated in the following as landscape practice, as a working-

22 Bruno Latour, "A Cautious Prometheus: A Few Steps Toward a Philosophy of Design (with Special Attention to Peter Sloterdijk)," in: http://www.bruno- latour.fr/articles/2008.html, p. 3 [accessed on January 20, 2011].

23 Jane Bennett, "Agency of Assemblages," in: *Vibrant Matter: A Political Ecology of Things*. Durham and London 2010, p. 20.

24 Bennett 2004 (fn. 16), p. 365.

25 Latour 2008 (fn. 22), p. 2.

system between medium and materiality—manifest as a fitting space of action for addressing this division. Landscape then can be explored in the spectrum of its agency—in its simultaneity as a platform (idea/culture) and matter (space/ecology) for future cultural practices.

This is to suggest a simultaneous focus on materiality *and* topological connecting and networking. "Landscape becomes connected through networks of thoughts where every atom can be traced to its original place on this planet as societal action and can be put in active relationship to a place on the planet and made visible."[26] Extended by topological space, "landscape" as a practice of the ecological turn is no longer exclusively bound to an Euclidean grid, with fixed contiguities or measurable distances; rather, different standards—or better: beyond standards—may now be assigned their respective positions and roles within the scope of a spatio-social complex of agency. However, easily severable threads, which connect the one with the other,[27] demand a slower, more cautious practice oriented toward a tangible world.

Designing our lived world according to this ecological turn would then imply developing those methods that facilitate a pursuit of a network of things, material, persons, whose relations of subordination are uncertain. Required in order to meet this aspiration is the development of original methods capable of articulating networks as spaces of agency in terms of matter and ecological processuality. Consequently, what is called for is an experimental design practice that is no longer claiming absoluteness—thus a practice of curating a significantly extended group of agents.[28] Reviewing the De Biesbosch project by the office of Michele Desvigne may illustrate how such a practice can be discursively apprehended as landscape practice.

The term "Biesbosch" denotes a landscape expanse that is part of the Rotterdam-Dordrecht agglomeration, which, like many areas near the coast, is characterized by excessive cultural impact as well as natural, ecological dynamics. The name De Biesbosch ("forest of rushwoods") refers to the original vegetation, the saline marshland of the local tidal zone. As one of the last freshwater tidal landscapes in Europe, sections of Biesbosch are maintained as a national park.

For decades, the landscape expanse was modernized so as to protect from flooding, and as a result landscape "simplifications" were introduced in order to make the hybrid tidal landscape productive. Since the great flood of the 15th century at the latest, this landscape can no longer be correlated with a

26 Latour 2010 (fn. 18).

27 Bruno Latour, *Pandora's Hope: Essays on the Reality of Science Studies*. Cambridge, MA 1999.

28 Latour 2008 (fn. 22).

system zwischen Medium und Stofflichkeit – als ein geeigneter Handlungsraum, um diese Trennung zu thematisieren. Landschaft kann dann im Spektrum ihrer *agency* – in ihrer Gleichzeitigkeit als Plattform (Idee/Kultur) und Materie (Raum/Ökologie) – für künftige kulturelle Praktiken erkundet werden.

Vorgeschlagen wird so ein gleichzeitiges Augenmerk auf Stofflichkeit *und* topologisches Verbinden und Vernetzen: „Landscape becomes connected through networks of thoughts where every atom can be traced to its original place on this planet as societal action and can be put in active relationship to a place on the planet and made visible."[26] Um den topologischen Raum erweitert, ist „Landschaft" als Praktik des *Ecological Turn* dann nicht länger ausschließlich in ein euklidisches Raster eingebunden – mit festgelegten Nachbarschaften oder messbaren Entfernungen und Distanzen – vielmehr lassen sich in einem räumlich-sozialen Handlungsgefüge nun unterschiedliche Maßstäbe, oder besser: maßstabsunabhängig ihre jeweiligen Plätze und Rollen zuordnen. Leicht zerreißbare Bänder, die das Eine mit dem Anderen verbinden,[27] verlangen jedoch nach einer langsamen, bedächtigen, sich an der erfahrbaren Welt orientierenden Praxis.

Eine Gestaltung unserer gelebten Welt nach jenem *Ecological Turn* hieße dann, jene Verfahren zu entwickeln, die es möglich machen, einem Netzwerk von Dingen, Materialien, Personen zu folgen, deren Unterordnungsverhältnisse ungewiss sind. Um diesem Anspruch gerecht werden zu können, bedarf es auch der Entwicklung originärer Techniken, die Netzwerke als Handlungsräume im Bezug auf Materie und ökologische Prozessualität artikulieren können. Zu entwickeln ist daher eine experimentelle gestalterische Praxis, die keinen Absolutheitsanspruch mehr erhebt – eine Praktik des Kuratierens einer deutlich erweiterten Gruppe von Aktanten.[28] Ein Beispiel, wie eine solche Praktik als Landschaftspraxis diskursiv erfasst werden kann, zeigt die Betrachtung des Projekts *De Biesbosch* des Büros Michele Desvigne.

„Biesbosch" bezeichnet einen Landschaftsraum und Teil der Agglomeration Rotterdam-Dordrecht, der wie viele küstennahe Gebiete geprägt ist von kultureller Überformung sowie naturräumlicher, ökologischer Dynamiken. Der Name De Biesbosch („Wald aus Riedgräsern") verweist auf die ursprüngliche Vegetation, das saline Marschland der örtlichen Gezeitenzone. Als eine der letzten Süßwasser-Gezeitenlandschaften Europas werden Teile von Biesbosch als Nationalpark verwaltet.

Über Jahrhunderte hinweg wurde der Landschaftsraum modernisiert, um ihn vor Überflutung zu schützen, und es wurden in der Folge landschaftliche „Vereinfachungen" eingeführt, um die hybride Tiedenlandschaft einem produktiven Zweck zuzuführen. Spätestens seit der großen Flut im 15. Jahrhundert lässt sich diese Landschaft keinesfalls mehr einem „natürlichen" Kosmos zuordnen – ist sie doch hoffnungslos verstrickt in ein Beziehungsgeflecht aus menschlichen und nicht-menschlichen Faktoren. Diese Ver-

26 Latour 2010 (Anm. 18).

27 Bruno Latour, *Die Hoffnung der Pandora. Untersuchungen zur Wirklichkeit der Wissenschaft*. Frankfurt/M. 2002, S. 59.

28 Latour 2009 (Anm. 22), S. 359.

strickungen gingen aus dem Glauben an eine technische Verwaltbarkeit der natürlichen Dynamiken hervor. Die funktionsbezogene Verwaltung der Landschaft als Infrastruktur führt heute jedoch zum Kollaps des Systems.

Die modernen Ingenieurstechniken, mit denen die Landschaft von Biesbosch geformt wurden, haben ein faszinierendes Phänomen von „Inversion" erzeugt: Nachdem das kultivierte Land hinter den Poldern aufgrund von anhaltender Drainage kontinuierlich abgesunken war, änderte sich das relative Niveau zum Netzwerk der Wasserläufe, deren Höhenlage jedoch fast unverändert blieb. Ein Paradox – liegt doch das kultivierte Land nun tiefer als die umgebende Wasserlandschaft. Das Ergebnis ist, wie Desvigne feststellt, eine Deltalandschaft in Umkehrung, bei der die ursprünglichen topografischen Vertiefungen und Furchen des Wassernetzes als Höhenrücken in der Landschaft angehoben erscheinen.

Aus Anlass einer zunehmenden Überflutungsgefahr soll nun ein großräumiges Netz aus Wasserläufen zu einem Binnen-Flussdelta umgestaltet werden. Für das Netzwerk aus durch Gezeiten beeinflusste Flussarme, Deiche, Inseln und Farmland hat das Büro Michele Desvigne, Paris, ein künftiges Handlungsszenario vorgelegt, das sich als Beispiel besonders eignet, eine reflexive Landschaftspraxis im Sinne des *Ecological Turn* zu skizzieren.[29]

Wie beim *Great Pacific Garbage Patch* verursacht die gesellschaftliche Auseinandersetzung mit dessen Materialität und ungewünschter *agency* einen „Wiedereintritt" derselben in die nun als Kontroverse wahrgenommene Realität einer künftigen Kulturlandschaft.

Desvigne versucht nun antizipativ, diese naturräumlich-ingenieurtechnische Kontroverse mit einer Referenz sowohl zu vergangenen wie künftigen „Proto-Aktanten" abzubilden. „Alle Aktanten mischen sich ein" – im wörtlichen Sinne: Beispielsweise schlägt er vor, Sedimente aus Teilbereichen des historischen Netzwerks auszuheben, um die alten Gerinne und Wasserläufe dem hydrologischen Flussnetz anzubinden. Die ausgehobenen Sedimente sind jedoch vorrangig dem modernen Industriezeitalter zuzuschreiben und teils mit Schwermetallen belastet.

Wie beim *Great Pacific Garbage Patch* verursacht die gesellschaftliche Auseinandersetzung mit dessen Materialität und ungewünschter *agency* einen „Wiedereintritt" derselben in die nun als Kontroverse wahrgenommene Realität einer künftigen Kulturlandschaft. Desvigne praktiziert eine Art „feeding off controversies", d. h. er will von vorgefundenen Widersprüchen und den entstandenen Kontroversen inhaltlich profitieren,[30] indem er beispielsweise die gestalterische Einbindung „belasteter Materie" (Schwermetalle in Sedimenten) untersucht und auch deren Umdeutung und Fort-

29 Michele Desvigne, Paris, „Biesbosch Stad", Studie für die 2. Internationale Architektur Biennale Rotterdam, 2005.

30 Bruno Latour, *Reassembling the Social. An introduction to actor-network-theory*, Oxford 2005, S. 25.

"natural" cosmos—for it is hopelessly intertwined in a network of relationships made up of human and nonhuman factors. These entanglements materialized from a belief in the technical administrability of natural dynamics. Today, however, the function-related administration of the landscape as an infrastructure leads to a collapse of the system.

Modern engineering technologies, with which the Biesbosch landscape has been shaped, have produced a fascinating phenomenon of "inversion": since the cultivated land behind the polders was continually sinking due to sustained drainage, the relative level in relation to the network of watercourses, whose height above sea level remained virtually unchanged, shifted. A paradox—as the cultivated land is now of lower level than the surrounding waterscape. The result, as Desvigne has established, is a delta landscape in reverse where the original topographic depressions and trenches of the water network are elevated and appear to formate ridges in the landscape.

Due to the increasing danger of flooding, an extensive reorganization of the watercourse network is in planning, in view of forming an inland river delta. The office of Michele Desvigne in Paris has submitted a projected future scenario for the network comprised of river branches, dikes, islands, and farmland influenced by tides. It is a particularly fitting example of sketching a reflexive landscape practice in the sense of an ecological turn.[29]

Desvigne is now anticipatively attempting to depict this controversy of geophysical engineering with reference to both past and future "proto-agents." "All agents are involved"—in a literal sense: he suggests, for example, excavating sediments out of sections of the historical network in order to tie the old conduits and watercourses to the hydrological river network. However, the excavated sediments can primarily be attributed to the modern industrial age and are in part polluted with heavy metals.

As is the case with the Great Pacific Garbage Patch, social involvement with its materiality and undesired agency causes a "reentry" of the same into the reality of a future cultural landscape, which is now perceived as controversy. Desvigne practices a kind of "feeding off controversies," that is, he aims to profit in terms of content from the encountered contradictions and the resulting controversies[30]—for instance by examining the structural inclusion of "polluted matter" (heavy metals in sediments) and also by initiating their reinterpretation and perpetuation. According to his suggestion, it is precisely the polluted material that can be removed from the hydrological cycle and, by way of a phytoremediation, concentrated into islands

29 Michele Desvigne, Paris, "Biesbosch Stad," study for the 2nd International Architecture Biennale Rotterdam, 2005.

30 Bruno Latour, *Reassembling the Social: An introduction to actor-network-theory*, Oxford 2005, p. 25.

6 De Biesbosch, Modellansicht, Foto: © Michele Desvigne, Paris. De Biesbosch, model view, photo: © Michele Desvigne, Paris.

schreibung initiiert. Gerade das belastete Material nämlich könnte, so der Vorschlag, dem Wasserkreislauf entzogen und nach einer Phytoremediation zu Inseln innerhalb der hydrologischen Gerinneräume vormaliger Wasserläufe verdichtet werden, um in Folge die tieferliegenden Weiden einer erneuten Überflutung und dem Tiedenhub auszusetzen.

In der Praxis dieses Zusammenschreibens handelt es sich dann nicht um eine rein ästhetische Umkehrung, sondern um einen reflexiven Akt, der die Künstlichkeit der Intervention innerhalb der hydrologisch geprägten Landschaftsmorphologie verortet, sie dort quasi „implantiert“. Aus dem identifizierten „Schwarm von Akteuren“ würde sich in Folge eine dynamische Assemblage aus angesammelten Material und menschlicher Handlung, aus politischer Entscheidungsfindung, wissenschaftlicher Analyse, subjektivem und naturgesetzlichem Verhalten entwickeln. So entsteht – ähnlich wie bei *Plastic Island* doch nun in gestaltender Anwendung – eine Art „Schnittstellen-Topografie“ zwischen separaten Teilen moderner Praktiken, nicht nur eine „Projektionsfläche“ für den faktischen Umgang mit historischem Erbe, sondern auch eine experimentell hergestellte hybride Kultur- und Naturform.

Bemerkenswert ist hierbei der Verzicht auf eine gestalterische Überformung, welche erneut Proportion und Maßstab nach euklidischen Prinzipien bemisst, denn die Formkräfte der materiellen Eigenschaften – deren stoffliche *agencies* – werden zum Formenanlass des Designs. Diese auf den ersten Blick anmutende „natürliche Einbindung“ in die Morphologie der hydrologischen Tektonik, folgt der Überlegung, sowohl den künftigen dynamischen *agencies* des Mündungsdeltas als auch der modernen Historie Rechnung zu tragen. Mit diesem wie auch vielen weiteren Details versammelt Desvigne eine Landschaft aus „Proto-Aktanten“, deren künftige Beziehungen noch vollkommen offen sind und nicht in ein vorab festgelegtes und in sich geschlossenes Beziehungsnetz münden. Doch genau an dieser Stelle tut sich auch eine Schwachstelle auf, welche auf den Entwicklungsbedarf der kuratierenden Praxis verweist. Denn zur Entfaltung jenes radikalen Kontextualismus fehlt ein kommunizierendes Handlungsmuster, ein Notationsmodell, um eine dynamische Topologie aller Aktanten gemeinschaftlich zu praktizieren.

Denn zur Entfaltung jenes radikalen Kontextualismus fehlt ein kommunizierendes Handlungsmuster, ein Notationsmodell, um eine dynamische Topologie aller Aktanten gemeinschaftlich zu praktizieren.

Doch hiervon abgesehen ist eine kuratierende Handlungspraxis denkbar, die vordringlich erkennt, was sich „in seiner Bezüglichkeit offenbart“: Sie erlaubt, die *agency* der materiellen und „natürlichen“ Ökologie in Biesbosch mit den Akteuren einer politischen Ökologie zu involvieren. Beide so unterschiedlichen und zu unterscheidenden Formen von Ökologie – die landschaftlich stoffliche, wie auch die politische, könnten in dieser Landschaftspraxis gleichzeitig, wenn auch nicht als Einheit, praktiziert werden. Für die Neuausrichtung der gestaltenden Praktiken eines *Ecological Turn* liegt hierin ein wichtiges Detail: Anstelle eines rein landschaftlich „ökologisch

within the hydrological conduit regions of former watercourses, thus subjecting the lower-lying pastures to renewed flooding and tidal amplitude.

So this practice of coalescing involves not a purely aesthetic reversal but a reflexive act that situates the artificialness of the intervention within the hydrologically influenced landscape morphology—as “implant,” so to speak. As a result, a dynamic assemblage of accumulated material and human action, of political decision-making, scientific analysis, subjective and natural behavior, would develop out of the “swarm of agents” that has been identified. What thus emerges—similar to the *Plastic Island* but now in formative adaptation—is a kind of “interface-topography” between separate parts of modern practices; not only a “target of projection” for the actual handling of a historical legacy, but also an experimentally produced hybridity of cultural and natural aspects.

Notable here is a waiving of the excessive structural impact reassessing proportion and scale according to Euclidean principles, for the material features’ force of form—their material agencies—becomes the motive for the design configuration. This at first glance seemingly “natural incorporation” into the morphology of hydrological tectonics acts on the consideration of allowing for both future dynamic agencies of the estuary delta as well as modern history. With this and many other details, Desvigne assembled a landscape out of “proto-agents” whose future relationships are still completely open and do not lead to a predetermined and self-contained relationship network. Yet it is precisely at this juncture that a weak point opens up to reference the developmental need for curatorial practice. Because, in order for this radical contextualism to unfold, a communicating pattern of action is necessary, a notation model, so that a dynamic topology of all of the agents may be collectively practiced.

But apart from this, a curating practice of action is conceivable that recognizes in advance what is a “discipline of looking always at what is to be seen.” It allows the agency of the material and the “natural” ecology in Biesbosch to become intervolved with the agents of a political ecology. Both of these inherently different and distinct forms of ecology—the landscape-related material as well as the political—could be followed simultaneously in this landscape practice, although not as a unit. Herein lies an important detail for the reorientation of the designing practices of an ecological turn: instead of pursuing a purely landscape-related, “ecologically correct” design, Desvigne inscribes reflexive elements of the contradictory and controversial nature of modern action into his design. The vibrant frame of reference of human, nonhuman, and material agents thus displays the potential for a “negotiative” political ecology: “*Some kind of nature … Some kind of soul … Some kind of mixture … Some kind of gold …*”—a space of design for protocolling social controversies.

The future therefore lies not in an obvious "greening" of an ecological landscape practice and a longed-for surmounting of modern practices of separation—for that would be an illusion. "Floating assemblages"—islands of architectures or landscapes of an idealized and purely ecological multiplicity—will not be capable of enduring. For operating at their conceptual and material edges, at its topographical interface—despite ruptures and cracks and meanwhile in green guise—is the modernization of our world. "... *Some kind of majesty ... Some chemical load*."

Translation Rebecca van Dyck

korrekten" Designs schreibt Desvigne reflexive Momente der widersprüchlichen und kontroversen Natur des modernen Handelns in sein Design ein. Im vibrierenden Bezugssystem menschlicher, nicht-menschlicher und materieller Akteure, zeigen sich so die Potenziale einer „verhandelnden" politischen Ökologie: „*Some kind of nature ... Some kind of soul ... Some kind of mixture ... Some kind of gold ...*" ein Gestaltungsraum für Protokolle gesellschaftlicher Kontroversen.

Die Zukunft liegt somit nicht in der so naheliegenden Grünfärbung einer ökologischen Landschaftspraxis und einem ersehnten Überwinden trennender moderner Praktiken – denn das wäre eine Illusion. „Freischwebende Assemblagen", Inseln von Architekturen oder Landschaften einer idealisierten und rein ökologischen Vielheit werden nicht bestehen können, denn wie an ihren gedanklichen und stofflichen Rändern – der topografischen Schnittstelle – sichtbar wird, agiert weiterhin – trotz Rissen und Sprüngen und nun im grünen Gewand – die Modernisierung unserer Welt. „... *Some kind of majesty ... Some chemical load*".

1 Raster aus Pfählen Grid of poles

Interaction Between the Elements. Terschelling

The symbiosis between human activity and impressive natural processes makes Terschelling into an enormous attraction to inhabitants and outsiders alike. According to Rietveld Landscape, this fact should guide all attempts at dealing with the rising of the sea level.

Zusammenspiel der Elemente. Terschelling. Durch die Symbiose von menschlicher Aktivität und eindrucksvollen Naturprozessen entwickelt Terschelling eine enorme Anziehungskraft sowohl für seine Bewohner als auch für Menschen von außerhalb. An dieser Tatsache sollten sich nach den Vorstellungen des Büros Rietveld Landscape alle Versuche messen, mit dem Ansteigen des Meeresspiegels umzugehen.

RIETVELD LANDSCAPE

2

3

4

5

6

2–5 Formende Agencies der Dünenlandschaft
6 Temporärer Zustand der Tidenlandschaft
2–5 Shaping *agencies* of the dune landscape
6 Temporay state of the tidal landscape

Da es unmöglich ist, mit ausreichender Sicherheit vorherzusagen, wann der Meeresspiegel welches Niveau erreicht, müssen für Ost- und West-Terschelling flexible Strategien entwickelt werden – Maßnahmen, die sich nach den Bewegungen des Wassers richten und die über die Zeit hinweg angepasst werden können.

Zwar wurden die vorgeschlagenen Interventionen speziell für Terschelling konzipiert, doch die zugrunde liegende Strategie kann angesichts ähnlicher Bedrohungen und Gefahren durch das Meer auch auf andere Inseln in der Nordsee übertragen werden.

Ost-Terschelling. Mit dem Ansteigen des Meeresspiegels werden das Wattenmeer und die Südseite der Boschplaat durch zusätzliche Sandanlagerungen vor der Küste weiter wachsen. Der Norden der Boschplaat hingegen wird keine derartige Entwicklung nehmen. Der in diesem Teil der Insel bestehende Flugsanddeich soll aktiviert werden, indem der derzeitige Bewuchs entfernt wird. In der Folge wird sich eine riesige Flugsanddüne bilden. Ein Raster aus alten Hafenpfählen macht die Bewegungen des Flugsandes und die Prozesse der Dünenbildung über die Zeit hinweg sichtbar. Nach Jahren des beständigen Anwachsens soll der Flugsanddeich nun, so der Vorschlag, mit einer Reihe von Perforationen versehen werden. Diese sorgfältig geplanten Perforationen werden für neue Überspülungen durch das Meer sorgen. Auf diese Weise entsteht ein faszinierendes Zusammenspiel zwischen der Gewalt des Meeres, dem System der Pfähle und dem Prozess der Dünenbildung. Durch das Ansteigen des Meeresspiegels wird die Boschplaat wachsen, auch ihr ökologischer Wert wird sich dank der Überspülungen erhöhen. Der Entwurf von Rietveld Landscape hebt sowohl die Rolle menschlicher Interventionen als auch die dynamische Interaktion zwischen den Elementen hervor.

Because it is impossible to predict with sufficient certainty when the sea will have what level, flexible strategies for East and West Terschelling are needed; interventions that follow the movement of the water and can be adjusted through time. Although the proposed interventions have been designed specifically for Terschelling, the strategy informing it can be exported to other islands in the North Sea. These are after all threatened by the sea in a similar manner.

East Terschelling. The Wadden See and the south side of the Boschplaat will grow with the rising of the sea level because of sand replenishments in front of the coast. The northern part of the Boschplaat is unable to grow in this way. There, the existing drift dike will be activated by removing the current vegetation. A huge drifting sand dune will consequently develop. A grid of old mooring bollards ensures that the processes of sand drift and dune formation are readable through time. After years of heightening, a series of perforations in the drift dike is now proposed. These carefully selected perforations will bring about new wash-overs. In this way, an exciting interaction between the power of the seawater, the bollard grid and the dune formation process is created. The Boschplaat will grow with the rising of the sea level and will become ecologically more valuable because of the wash-overs. Both the role of human intervention and the dynamics of the interaction between the elements are made visible by Rietveld Landscape's design.

7

8

9

10

7 Temporärer Zustand der Tidenlandschaft
8 Scenario einer Springflut
9 Initiale Überspülung
10 Gänzliche Überspülung
11 Initiale Ausgangslage
12 Einführung des Systems aus Pfählen
13 Aktivierung der Dünenbildung
14 Erste Deichüberspülung
7 Temporay state of the tidal landscape
8 Scenario of extreme flooding
9 Initial wash-over
10 Total wash-over
11 Initial state of the landscape
12 Introduction of the system of poles
13 Activation of drifting dunes
14 First wash-over of dike

11

12

13

14

1–6 Agrikulturelle Zeittafel der landwirtschaftlichen Entwicklungen während der vergangenen 8000 Jahre. Timeline of agricultural and agrarian developments during the past 8,000 years.

The Agronomic Landscape

A Brief 8,000-Year Timeline of Soil & Plants, Techniques & Technologies, Crops & Cultures, Industries & Ecologies, Empires & Urbanization

Between 2007 and 2008, the price of food and fiber commodities skyrocketed across the world.[1] From milk to meat, soybean to sugarcane, rice to wheat, the price for cereals and grains almost doubled or tripled internationally.

Die agronomische Landschaft. Ein chronologisches Mapping von Boden & Pflanzen, Verfahren & Technologien, Saaten & Züchtungen, Industrien & Ökologien, Imperien & Urbanisierung entlang einer Zeitachse von 8000 Jahren. Weltweit schoss der Preis für Lebensmittel und Naturfaserrohstoffe zwischen den Jahren 2007 und 2008 plötzlich in die Höhe[1] – von Milch zu Fleisch, Soja zu Zucker, Reis zu Weizen – der Preis für Getreide und Korn hatte sich international annähernd verdoppelte bzw. verdreifacht.

PIERRE BÉLANGER • CURTIS ROTH

Attributed to depleting food stocks and crop shortfalls, the international spike in food prices was actually the result of several compounding conditions: the rise of raw material prices such as petroleum for transportation and potash for fertilizers, increased urban demand from rapidly developing countries across Asia, and diversion of crops from foodstuffs to feedstocks for biofuels in Europe.[2] Dealing a hard blow to countries worldwide both rich and poor, the food price spike ricocheted in a series of geo-economic effects across the world that include riots in underdeveloped countries such as Bolivia and Bangladesh where food staples consume more than half of household income, or the spontaneous installment of protectionist policies and export bans by net food exporters such as Brazil and Russia, creating food deficits in net importing and conflict countries such as Somalia, Congo, Haiti and Bosnia.[3]

While the world price crisis exposed both the volatility of the global commodities exchange and the perishability of transnational price agreements, it also put into question the fragile foundation upon which rests the centralization of commodities exchange that has dominated the industrialized world since the 20th century. Economically, it triggered a chain reaction across the foodshed[4] of global manufacturing and crop specialization, a natural and perhaps inevitable effect of trade liberalization. However, in a total upset of the Malthusian principle[5] that populations outpace food production, it also shed light on the inseparability of the cultivation of food and how cities, with their increasing populations, are fed. While contemporary discourse has focused on the lopsidedness of liberalization and the drawbacks of foreign farmland investment as well as on the environmental repercussion of food and fiber production (consider that world agriculture consumes over 60 percent of the world's total freshwater resources and produces 50 percent of greenhouse gas emissions), the intrinsic reciprocity and complex ecology of soil—the basic medium of plant growth and crop cultivation—and patterns of urbanization

… this research proposes a longer, more nuanced view of the agricultural, political and technological transformations which have lent contemporary global change the appearance of inevitability and irreversibility.

1 UN Department of Public Information, News and Media Division, "Press Conference by World Food Programme Executive Director on Food Price Crisis," New York, April 24, 2008.

2 For a greater discussion on the paradox of the world food price crisis amidst record harvest, see Eric Holt-Giménez, Loren Peabody, "From Food Rebellions to Food Sovereignty: Urgent call to fix a broken food system," in: *Institute for Food and Development Policy* 14/1 (Spring 2008).

3 See Francis Ng, M. Ataman Aksoy, "Who Are the Net Food Importing Countries?" in: *Policy Research Working Paper 4457*. The World Bank Development Research Group, 2008; and M. Ataman Aksoy, "The Evolution of Agricultural Trade Flows," in: idem, John C. Beghin (eds.), *Global Agricultural Trade and Developing Countries*. Washington, D.C. 2005.

4 The concept of the foodshed refers to the network of food and distribution for an urban region. See Pierre Bélanger, Angela Iarocci, "Foodshed: The Global Infrastructure of the Ontario Food Terminal," in: John Knechtel (ed.), *Food*. Cambridge, MA 2008, pp. 208–239.

5 Thomas R. Malthus, *An Essay on the Principle of Population: Influences on Malthus, Selections from Malthus' Work, Nineteenth-Century Comment, Malthus in the Twenty-First Century*. New York 2004.

Die weltweite Steigerung der Lebensmittelpreise wurde der Erschöpfung von Nahrungsmittelvorräten und Ernteausfällen zugeschrieben, war in Wirklichkeit aber das Resultat von mehreren sich überlagernden Umständen: dem Preisanstieg von Rohstoffen wie Erdöl für den Transport und Kaliumkarbonat für Dünger, der gestiegenen urbanen Nachfrage aus sich rasch entwickelnden Ländern in Asien und der Umwandlung von bisher als Nahrungsrohstoffe genutzten Pflanzen in Rohmaterialien für Biosprit in Europa.[2] Der Anstieg der Lebensmittelpreise versetzte weltweit armen und reichen Ländern gleichermaßen einen harten Schlag, der zu einer Reihe von geo-ökonomischen Folgeerscheinungen auf der ganzen Welt führte, von Aufständen in unterentwickelten Ländern wie Bolivien und Bangladesh, in denen Grundnahrungsmittel mehr als die Hälfte des Haushaltseinkommens aufbrauchen, zu der spontanen Einsetzung von protektionistischen Bestimmungen und Exportverboten durch Nahrungsmittel-Nettoexporteure wie Brasilien und Russland, die dadurch Nahrungsdefizite in Nettoimport- und Krisenländern wie Somalia, Kongo, Haiti und Bosnien verursachten.[3]

Die weltweite Preiskrise entlarvte die Schwankungsanfälligkeit der globalen Rohstoffbörse und die Vergänglichkeit von länderübergreifenden Preisabkommen gleichermaßen, sie stellte aber ebenso das fragile Fundament infrage, auf dem die Zentralisierung des Warenaustausches ruht, welche die industrialisierte Welt seit dem 20. Jahrhundert dominiert. In wirtschaftlicher Hinsicht löste sie eine Kettenreaktion im gesamten *Foodshed*[4] von globaler Produktion und Anbau-Spezialisierung aus, eine natürliche und vielleicht unvermeidbare Folge der Handelsliberalisierung. Als totale Umkehrung des Malthusianischen Prinzips,[5] nach welchem das Wachstum der Bevölkerung immer jenes der landwirtschaftlichen Produktion überholt, gab sie auch Aufschluss über die Untrennbarkeit von Nahrungsanbau und der Weise, wie Städte mit ihren steigenden Einwohnerzahlen ernährt werden. Während sich der zeitgenössische Diskurs auf die Einseitigkeit der Liberalisierung

1 UN Department of Public Information, News and Media Division, „Press Conference by World Food Programme Executive Director on Food Price Crisis", New York, 24.4.2008.

2 Für eine ausführlichere Diskussion des Paradoxons der weltweiten Nahrungspreiskrise inmitten einer Rekordernte vgl. Eric Holt-Giménez, Loren Peabody, „From Food Rebellions to Food Sovereignty: Urgent call to fix a broken food system", in: *Institute for Food and Development Policy* 14/1 (Frühling 2008).

3 Vgl. Francis Ng, M. Ataman Aksoy, „Who Are the Net Food Importing Countries?", in: *Policy Research Working Paper* 4457. The World Bank Development Research Group, 2008; und M. Ataman Aksoy, „The Evolution of Agricultural Trade Flows", in M. Ataman Aksoy, John C. Beghin (Hg.), *Global Agricultural Trade and Developing Countries*. Washington, D.C. 2005.

4 Das Konzept des Foodshed bezieht sich auf das Netzwerk von Nahrungsmitteln und deren Verteilung für eine urbane Region. Siehe Pierre Bélanger, Angela Iarocci, „Foodshed: The Global Infrastructure of the Ontario Food Terminal", in: John Knechtel (Hg.), *Food*. Cambridge 2008, S. 208–239.

5 Thomas R. Malthus, *An Essay on the Principle of Population: Influences on Malthus, Selections from Malthus' Work, Nineteenth-Century Comment, Malthus in the Twenty-First Century*. New York 2004.

und die Nachteile von Investitionen in ausländisches Ackerland, sowie auf die Auswirkungen der Lebensmittel- und Naturfaserproduktion auf die Umwelt konzentriert (man bedenke, dass die weltweite Landwirtschaft über 60 % der gesamten Süßwasservorkommen verbraucht und 50 % der Treibhausgasemissionen produziert), ist die immanente Wechselseitigkeit und komplexe Ökologie des Bodens – des grundlegenden Mediums für Pflanzenwachstum und Nahrungsmittelanbau – und der Muster der Urbanisierung, großteils übersehen worden. Städtische Infrastruktur zum Beispiel wird selten mit Ernährungssicherung assoziiert, noch werden die Planung des städtischen Wachstums oder gesundheitliche Probleme wie Fettleibigkeit jemals mit der Flächennutzungsordnung in Verbindung gebracht. Als Antwort auf die Polarisierung gegenwärtiger Debatten über die weltweite Nahrungspolitik und lokale landwirtschaftliche Tendenzen schlägt diese Untersuchung einen weitsichtigeren, differenzierteren Blickwinkel auf die landwirtschaftlichen, politischen und technologischen Transformationen vor, die der gegenwärtigen globalen Veränderung den Anschein von Unvermeidbarkeit und Unumkehrbarkeit verleihen. Mit der Präsentation einer Zeitachse der landwirtschaftlichen Entwicklungen während der vergangenen 8000 Jahre hebt die folgende Forschungsarbeit die Untrennbarkeit der Diskurse über Nahrungsproduktion, Boden- und Energievorkommen, technologische Innovationen, logistische Netzwerke, Konsumregimes und Muster der Urbanisierung hervor.

Peak Soil & globale Landnahme. In den letzten zehn Jahren hat die globale Agrarwirtschaft einen noch nie da gewesenen Anstieg an hochwertigen Käufen großer Teile von fruchtbarem Ackerland im globalen Süden (es beschränkt sich jedoch keineswegs auf ein Nord-Süd-Muster) durch reichere, bodenarme oder klimatisch benachteiligte Regionen (Naher Osten, Japan, Nordeuropa) und mächtige Agrarkonzerne (Archer Daniels Midland, Cargill, British Petroleum, die Carlyle Group) erlebt. Das *International Food Policy Research Institute* (IFPRI) schätzt den Gesamtwert dieser landwirtschaftlichen Transaktionen seit 2006 auf 20 bis 30 Milliarden USD jährlich ein.[6] Die Welternährungsorganisation der Vereinten Nationen und andere Experten schätzten letztes Jahr, dass fast 20 Millionen Hektar (50 Millionen Morgen) Ackerland – ein Gebiet etwa halb so groß wie der gesamte landwirtschaftlich nutzbare Boden in Europa – innerhalb von nur sechs Monaten verkauft wurden oder sich in Verkaufs- bzw. Pachtverhandlungen befanden.[7] Das überrascht nicht, wenn man bedenkt, dass in einigen Fällen ein Hektar fruchtbaren afrikanischen Bodens mit einer Pacht auf 99 Jahre für einen US-Dollar pro Jahr hergegeben wird.

6 Joachim von Braun, Ruth Meinzen-Dick, „‚Land Grabbing' by Foreign Investors in Developing Countries: Risks and Opportunities", in: *IFPRI Policy Brief* 13 (April 2009).

7 Ebd.

have largely been overlooked. Urban infrastructure for example, is seldom associated with food security, nor is the planning of urban growth or health-related problems like obesity ever linked to land use zoning. In response to the polarized current debates on global food politics and local agricultural tendencies, this research proposes a longer, more nuanced view of the agricultural, political and technological transformations which have lent contemporary global change the appearance of inevitability and irreversibility. Presenting a timeline of agricultural and agrarian developments during the past 8,000 years, the following research proposes the inseparability between the discourses on food production, soil and energy resources, technological innovation, logistical networks, consumption regimes, climate zones and patterns of urbanization.

Peak Soil & Global Land Grabbing. In the last ten years, the global agricultural economy has seen an unprecedented rise in high-value purchases of large swaths of arable farmland in the Global South (yet it is by no means limited to a North-South pattern) by wealthier, soil-starved or climate-handicapped regions (Middle East, Japan, Northern Europe) and major agricultural corporations (Archer Daniels Midland, Cargill, British Petroleum, the Carlyle Group). Since 2006 the International Food Policy Research Institute (IFPRI) estimates the total value of these agricultural transactions to be between 20 and 30 billions USD annually.[6] The United Nation's food and agricultural organization and other analysts estimated last year that nearly 20 million hectares (50 million acres) of farmland—an area roughly half the size of all arable land in Europe—was sold or had been negotiated for sale or lease in the space of just six months.[7] This is not surprising considering that, in some cases, a hectare of fertile African land, a 99-year lease and all goes for 1 US dollar a year. Food-importing nations with land and water constants, but rich in capital, such as the Gulf States, are pioneering a new relationship between food production and urbanization in the global economy.

Population & Proteins. Arable land, or foreign soil, is literally being transacted—in the form of private negotiations, federal land leases and concessions in exchange for the development of agricultural infrastructure, irrigation systems, roads—between countries at a breakneck pace. Characterized as a relatively new phenomenon, the process is known today as the the global soil economy or, in some cases, as the global land grab.[8] Contracting and stretching the contours of cultivation, new boundaries between countries and corporations are being drafted by soil trade agreements and large land purchases as we witness a structural change in the postwar era of importing foodstuffs from foreign producers. However, as a result of the creation of specialized crops, agricultural economies are susceptible to rapid spikes in the prices of land, crops, fertilizers and water; and capable of collapsing entire economies by inflating food prices to unsustainable levels. The food strikes and political collapse of Madagascar in 2009[9] are

6 Joachim von Braun, Ruth Meinzen-Dick, "'Land Grabbing' by Foreign Investors in Developing Countries: Risks and Opportunities," in: *IFPRI Policy Brief* 13 (April 2009).

7 Ibid.

8 Ibid., p. 1.

9 Lauren Ploch, "Madagascar's 2009 Political Crisis," in: *Congressional Research Service*, 7-5700 R40448, May 18, 2009.

the most explicit example of this threat. In 2006–2007, the agro-economic bubble created by extensive foreign land sales—totaling nearly half of the nation's superficies—led first to widespread hunger and later, in 2009, led to complete political collapse and fall of the Ravalomanana presidency by Andry Rajoelina. Demonstrating the fragility of this global land trading system, regional alternatives are currently emerging in the wake of the over-exertion of the liberalization of transnational trade. Concepts such as slow food, farm-to-fork, food miles and foodsheds are fin-de-siècle strategies that, for the most part, have formed in the Western World in the wake of new corporate power relationships, predatory industrial practices, trade policies and prohibitive zoning practices that have historically increased the gap between urban markets, food production and land cultivation. Soil, as opposed to simply crops, is now being recognized as a national resource in countries worldwide, an underlying agent in food security and the infrastructure of urban economies. According to *The Financial Times*, "food now rivals oil as a basis for power and economic security."[10]

Dirt Research: From Crop to Commodity to Capital to Culture. Using the format of a visual timeline, the research is based on the guiding notion that the history of agriculture, that of food production, energy resources, soil and water systems, cannot and should not be read as distinct from the history of urbanization. On the smallest scale, the timeline documents the slow, cumulative evolution of agricultural practices and soil sciences, while on the largest scale, the project posits the notion that these processes are often overlooked in humankind's interactions with soil while having played an immeasurable role in the historic events we think of as our most exceptional (consider for example, the role of the depletion of soil in the Fall of the Rome,[11] or in the legacy of wars and famines in drought-stricken Ethiopia, or in the rise of Brazil as a global food-and-feed superpower). In this way, the research advocates for a re-reading of the geo-economic and proto-ecological significance of agriculture and its continual role in shaping global politics and urban economies.

Using the format of a visual timeline, the research is based on the guiding notion that the history of agriculture, that of food production, energy resources, soil and water systems, cannot and should not be read as distinct from the history of urbanization.

As a brief 8,000 year history of these revolutionary processes, the timeline advances the idea of an uneven yet cyclical pattern of urbanization's

10 "Fix the land deals" (Editorial), in: *The Financial Times*, May 26, 2009.

11 In his classic 1874 account *The Earth, as Modified by Human Action*, George Perkins Marsh explains the physical decay of the territory of the Roman Empire in section titles "Causes of the Decay" (pp. 3–8), from North Africa to the greater Arabian Peninsula, as a result of massive deforestation and strip farming, resulting in the large-scale depletion of soil fertility, erosion and drought that now characterizes the Mediterranean Region and the Middle East. See also David R. Montgomery, *Dirt: Erosion of Civilizations*. Berkeley 2008.

Nahrungsmittelimportierende Nationen wie die Golfstaaten, mit begrenzten Boden- und Wasserressourcen, jedoch reich an Kapital, bereiten in der Weltwirtschaft den Weg für eine neue Beziehung zwischen der Produktion von Nahrungsmitteln und der Urbanisierung.

Population & Proteine. Ackerland, oder fremder Boden, wird im wörtlichen Sinn in einem halsbrecherischen Tempo zwischen Ländern übergeben, in Form von privaten Verhandlungen und bundesstaatlichen Verpachtungen und Konzessionen im Austausch für die Entwicklung landwirtschaftlicher Infrastruktur von Bewässerungssystemen und Straßen. Gekennzeichnet als ein relativ neues Phänomen, ist der Vorgang heute als globale Bodenwirtschaft oder, in einigen Fällen, als globale Landnahme bekannt.[8] Durch Handelsabkommen für Boden und große Landkäufe werden neue Grenzen zwischen Ländern und Konzernen definiert, welche die Ausmaße des Ackerbaus vertraglich festlegen und ausweiten, während wir Zeugen eines strukturellen Wandels in der Nachkriegsära des Importierens von Lebensmitteln ausländischer Erzeuger werden. Als Konsequenz der Schaffung von spezialisiertem Saatgut sind Agrarwirtschaften jedoch anfällig für rapide Steigerungen der Preise für Land, Lebensmittel, Dünger und Wasser; und in der Lage durch die Erhöhung der Lebensmittelpreise auf untragbare Niveaus ganze Volkswirtschaften zu zerstören. Die Nahrungsstreiks und der politische Zusammenbruch von Madagaskar im Jahr 2009[9] sind das ausdrücklichste Beispiel dieser Bedrohung. In den Jahren 2006–2007 führte die agro-ökonomische Blase – erzeugt durch umfangreiche Landverkäufe an das Ausland, die insgesamt fast die Hälfte der Gesamtfläche des Landes ausmachten – erst zu weit verbreitetem Hunger und später, im Jahr 2009, zum völligen politischen Zusammenbruch und dem Sturz des Präsidenten Ravalomanana durch Andry Rajoelina. Dass dieses System des globalen Landhandels zerbrechlich ist, zeigen die regionalen Alternativen, die momentan als Folge der überzogenen Liberalisierung des länderübergreifenden Handels auftauchen. Konzepte wie *Slow Food*, *Farm-to-Fork*, *Food Miles* und *Foodsheds* sind Strategien der Jahrhundertwende, die zum größten Teil in der westlichen Welt als Folge der Machtbeziehungen von Großunternehmen, rücksichtslosen industriellen Praktiken, Handelspolitiken und prohibitiven Zonierungsmaßnahmen, welche die Lücke zwischen urbanen Märkten, der Nahrungserzeugung und der Bodenbewirtschaftung historisch ausgedehnt haben, entstanden sind. Weltweit wird in Ländern nun Boden, anstatt einfach nur Ernte als nationale Ressource und als ein grundlegender Repräsentant in der Nahrungssicherung und der Infrastruktur von urbanen Ökonomien ent-

8 Ebd., S. 1

9 Lauren Ploch, „Madagascar's 2009 Political Crisis“, in: *Congressional Research Service*, 7-5700 R40448, 18.5.2009.

spice globalizes the world's agricultural economy
Depleted Roman Soil Kills 90% of Rome's Population
The Great Famine Kills 50Million Europeans Giving Rise to the Black Death
in medival europe, agricultural policies of communal land promoted animal husbandry and responsible soil management
as the european population expanded, roman deforestation strategies were adopted to feed growing populations
decreasing soil productivity due to eroded soils, in combination with larger urban cores, resulted in emerging food crises throughout
wet weather for two straight years, combined with underperforming land resulted in the great famine of 1315-1317, which toppled urban settlements and lead to pervasive malnutrition, and the black plaugue, ultimately killing one quarter of the european population.
massive population growth around 1000AD resulted in widespread urbanization of europe, the development of a middle class, and global agricultural trade with asia.
surplus in the 10th and 11th centuries leads to the first medieval urban conditions
the aftermath of the punic wars spreads a practice of feudal farming throughout the near east
by the renaissance europe's population had once again risen, forcing major spikes in food prices
"persistant famine between 1690 and 1710 stalked a population larger than could be reliably fed"
"real hunger, as much as the hunger for empire or freedom, helped launch Europe toward the new wo
feudal farming practices re-establish agricultura
the collapse of rome diminishes global agricultural export economies
ibn al-baitar develops the botany that leads to the arab agricultural revolution
alexandria, might with a amine." -caesar augustus
sweet potato: used as an important source of starch and sugar in asia, europe and the western hemisphere
anise: imported to western europe for its licorice-like flavor
camphor: cultivated in the middle east, transported to western europe
mandrake: first cultivated in the middle east, one of the first medicinal uses of agriculture
cinnamon: the primary imported spice of the spice trade, used as currency in europe
the banana: an important plan
maize: the counterpoint to wheat in the new world, the primary source of cultivated food

e and congestion force
e west for greener pastures
Export Farming Strategies Erode Southern Soil Productivity by 75
the new world's agricultural economy was based almost entirely on the exportation of tobacco
"tobacco strips more than ten times the nitrogen, and more than thirty times the phosphorus from the soil than do traditional crops"
columbus discovers the new world in response to overpopulation in europe
slave trading suppor
agricultural economy a
"once individual family farms coalesced into slave-worked tobacco plantations, the region became trapped in an instable socioeconomic system that fed on fresh land."
continued malnourishment in europe leads to peasant revolts in france and britain
with westward expansion an economic necessity for new world farms, British restrictions on westward expansion, along with high tobacco taxes helped feul the american revolution
large native american communities are of the south to allow plantations to expa
an abundance of land and high export prices require an abundance of cheap, plentiful labor
charles townsend taxes agricultural exports in the new world
charles
the agric
the slave trade establishes the first global agricultural economy
dried tobacco becomes the number one agricultural export of the new world
jethro tull brings about the british agricultural revolution
s in europe
BROMLEY'S
best Virginia,
Friday Street
COLUMBUS
bombyx mori (silkworm): bred in china to produce textiles, augmenting the space trade in europe
ed in eastern europe, the main source of sugar in middle ages europe
agricultural revolution
beat: an important source of sugar following the collapse of the spice trade
clover: part of the emerging science of botany, used to re-deposit nitrogen into depleted soils
the tomato: part of the early science of companion plants
the carrot: a companion to the tomato, harbors predatory wasps
rum: the most popular product of sugar canes in the american colonies
sugarcane: an important sweetener in the new world, part of the triangular trade o
tobacco: the primary
the lemon: an important source of vita

deckt. Laut der *Financial Times*, „konkurriert Nahrung jetzt mit Öl als Basis von Macht und wirtschaftlicher Stabilität."[10]

Dirt Research: Von Anbau zu Rohstoff zu Kapital zu Kultur. Unter Verwendung des Formats einer visuellen Zeitachse basiert die Forschung auf dem Leitgedanken, dass die Geschichte der Landwirtschaft – jene der Nahrungsproduktion, Energievorkommen, Boden- und Bewässerungssysteme – nicht unabhängig von der Geschichte der Urbanisierung gelesen werden kann und sollte. Im kleinsten Maßstab dokumentiert die Zeitachse die langsame, kumulative Entwicklungsgeschichte der landwirtschaftlichen Praktiken und der Bodenwissenschaften, während das Projekt im größten Maßstab die Ansicht postuliert, dass diese Prozesse in der Interaktion der Menschheit mit dem Boden oft übersehen werden, obwohl sie eigentlich eine unschätzbare Rolle in historischen Ereignissen spielen, die wir für unsere außergewöhnlichsten halten (siehe, zum Beispiel, die Rolle der Bodendegradation im Niedergang des Römischen Reiches[11] oder die Kriege und Hungersnöte des von der Dürre geplagten Äthiopien oder den Aufstieg von Brasilien zu einer globalen *Food-and-Feed* Supermacht). Auf diese Weise tritt die Forschung für eine Neubewertung der geo-ökonomischen und proto-ökologischen Bedeutung der Landwirtschaft und deren anhaltender Rolle in der Weltpolitik und in der Formung urbaner Volkswirtschaften ein.

Als eine kurze 8000-jährige Geschichte dieser revolutionären Prozesse unterstützt die Zeitachse die Idee eines unausgeglichenen und doch periodischen Musters der Beziehung zwischen Urbanisierung und Boden und postuliert die Auffassung, dass jeder große Fortschritt in der landwirtschaftlichen Technologie zwangsläufig dazu genutzt wurde, immer größere und größere Gebiete von Boden zu bewirtschaften, was zum Phänomen der stellvertretenden Bewirtschaftung führte, vom Nil-Delta als Kornkammer während des Römischen Reiches zu dem entfernten Anbau von Früchten, Hülsenfrüchten und anderen Keimlingen im subsaharischen Afrika für Entwicklungsländer heute. Die Verwendung von Ersatzboden oder fremdem Land hat historisch gesehen immer mehr in Richtung spezifischer Muster der Landnutzung geführt, in denen kurzfristiger Ertrag der langfristigen Bodenerhaltung vorgezogen wird. Es muss erkannt werden, dass die wachsende internationale Kommerzialisierung des Bodens, das Abfallprodukt der

10 „food now rivals oil as a basis for power and economic security." „Fix the land deals" (Editorial), in: *The Financial Times*, 26.5.2009.

11 In seinem Klassiker von 1874 *The Earth, as Modified by Human Action* erklärt George Perkins Marsh den physischen Zerfall des Territoriums des Römischen Reiches im Abschnitt unter dem Titel „Causes of the Decay" (S. 3–8), von Nordafrika bis zur größeren Arabischen Halbinsel, als Resultat massiver Waldrodungen und Streifenanbaus welche zu einer großmaßstäblichen Erschöpfung der Fruchtbarkeit des Bodens, zu Erosion und Dürren geführt hat, die nun die Mittelmeerregion und den mittleren Osten charakterisieren. Vgl. auch David R. Montgomery, *Dirt: Erosion of Civilizations*. Berkeley 2008.

relationship with soil, positing the notion that every major advancement in agricultural technology has inevitably been harnessed towards the cultivation of larger and larger territories of soil, leading to a condition of surrogate farming, from the Nile Delta-as-breadbasket during the Roman Empire to the remote cultivation of fruits, legumes and other crops in Sub-Saharan Africa for developing countries today. The use of surrogate soil or foreign land, historically, has tended more and more towards specific land-use patterns whereby industrial agriculture promoting short-term crop yield is prioritized over long-term soil replenishment. What needs to be recognized is that the growing international commodification of soil, the dirt of urban civilization, often prioritizes cash-crops produced through the practices of monocultures, overgrazing, use of chemical fertilizers and pesticides, and a lack of cover crops. In the long run, cut-and-run farming tactics which deplete organic nutrients in soil and promote topsoil erosion threaten the longevity of vast sections of the world's arable land.[12] Together, these soil-mining and industrial farming practices have historically laid the groundwork for some of the largest social collapses in history.[13] Dubbed as 21st century agro-imperialism, the significance of the global land grab in the 8,000-year history of urbanization is undeniable and, to some extent, inevitable. While historically not new, this phenomenon could accurately be interpreted as the most wide-scale operation of long-distance farming in human history, and one which needs to be studied through its influence in the transformation of global agricultural practices.

The graphic format of the timeline enables multiple readings of these lineages, both synchronically (changes during a single period) and diachronically (changes throughout time).

Soil Empires & Plant Societies. The timeline is organized horizontally into a series of lineages and interconnected histories that are continually converging, overlapping and splintering. The graphic format of the timeline enables multiple readings of these lineages, both synchronically (changes during a single period) and diachronically (changes throughout time). As a result, readings of these dynamics operate across a range of different interpretations: they can be reciprocal and synergistic, or they can be contradictory and paradoxical. Consequently, innovations have naturally blossomed from technology and engineering, as well as from disaster or widespread dispersal. Plant species have been discovered by chance, by transnational exchange or by centuries of cultivation.[14] Crop failures have

12 Amy Westervelt, "Peak Soil Has a Simple Fix, But Will We Manage It?" November 19, 2009, in: http://solveclimatenews.com/news/20091119/peek-soil-has-simple-fix-will-we-manage-it [accessed on February 20, 2011].

13 One of the most important and early texts illustrating essential links between farming practices, soil cultivation and urban land uses is a study for the U.S. Soil Conservation Service by W.C. Lowdermilk, "Conquest of the Land through Seven Thousand Years," in: *USDA Bulletin* 9. U.S. Department of Agriculture Natural Resources Conservation Service, 1939.

14 Herbert G. Baker, *Plants and Civilization: Fundamentals of Botany Series*. Belmont, CA 1965.

agro-chemicals and synthetic fertilizers substitute slaves
Plantations Exhaust 5Million Acres of
new world
s the atlantic
john bennet lawes first develops agro-chemistry
acco depletes southern soils 30x faster than standard cereal grains forcing new agricultural land to constantly be procured
the widescale abolition of slavery occured at the same time as major scientific discoveries regarding chemical application to soils
the slave trade from the third to the first world was substituted with the trade of agro-chemicals, mined in the third world and applied to first world soils
franklin pierce signs the foreign lands act
the african slave trade is replaced by early agro-chemical mines in western africa
the civil war erupts over the question of slavery's expansion west
john froelich invents the first gasoline powered tractor
eugene hilgard, the father of modern soil science
wilhelm II pursues foreign occupation of africa
soil loss in southern plantations forced tobacco farms to cultivate western states, the necessity for these states to be pro-slavery states, sparked the american abolitionist movement and later the civil war.
benjamin disreali encourages agro-chemical mining in africa
guano mines in western peru become important sources for phospherous
animal husbandry is widely praised but largely ignored in the american south
george washington carver proposes agricultural alternatives for the american south
fritz huber developes synthetic ammonia
the first to propose
peter kropotkin founds the first agricultural coopérative
poor sharecroppers in the US turn to nutrient application over nutrient
shortages in fertile land in europe forces european colonization of africa and asia
a combination of mechanized farming and agro-chemical application soon stripped the midwest farmlands bare
omas malthus publishes 'an essay the principles of population'
john deere develops the first steel plow
by the 1930s, much of the midwestern soi been robbed of significant nutrient value, the stage for the great american dustbowl would eventually displace seven hundred thousand midwestern farmers
justus von liebig discovers the value of nitrogen in plant growth
eli whitney invents the cotton gin
locomotive technology allows perishable foods to become valuable exports
native american communities are confined to reservations to free up the midwest for agriculture
STARVED
LACK OF
NT FOOD
NOURISHED
ON
PHOSPHATE
AND LIME
MILLIONS OF ACRES
IOWA NEBRASKA
LANDS
population
cost of oil
BUNGE
CARGILL
Dow AgroSciences
DUPONT
nd rum
safflower: cultivated in the new world as an important source of medicine and cooking oils
coffee bean: transplanted to the new world to replace the coffee trade from the middle east
important non-perishable export of the colonies
ort of the new world
from the east
lime: an important source of vitamin c
palm: used as an important source of oil and exported to europe
the melon: first cultivated in the middle east, prized as an export commodity for its

urbanen Zivilisation, häufig kurzfristige, zum Verkauf bestimmte Ernten bevorzugt, die durch die Praktiken der Monokulturen, Übergrasen, Verwenden von chemischen Düngemitteln und Pestiziden und ohne Gründüngung produziert werden. Auf lange Sicht brauchen diese *cut-and-run*-Anbauweisen die organischen Nährstoffe im Boden auf und fördern die Erosion des Oberbodens, wodurch sie die Langlebigkeit großer Bereiche des fruchtbaren Bodens der Welt bedrohen.[12] Zusammen genommen haben diese den Boden ausbeutenden und industriellen Anbauverfahren in der Geschichte die Grundlage für einige der größten sozialen Zusammenbrüche geliefert.[13] Betitelt als *Agro-Imperialismus des 21. Jahrhunderts*, ist die Bedeutung der globalen Landnahme in der 8000-jährigen Geschichte der Urbanisierung unleugbar und gewissermaßen auch unausweichlich. Obwohl es historisch betrachtet nicht neu ist, kann dieses Phänomen zu Recht als die großmaßstäblichste Umsetzung des Fern-Ackerbaus in der menschlichen Geschichte bezeichnet werden und es muss in seiner Auswirkung auf die Transformation globaler landwirtschaftlicher Praktiken untersucht werden.

Boden-Imperien & Pflanzen-Gesellschaften. Die Zeitachse ist horizontal in eine Serie von Abfolgen und abhängigen Geschichten organisiert, die sich ständig annähern, überlappen und absplittern. Das grafische Format der Zeitachse ermöglicht verschiedene Lesearten dieser Abfolgen – gleichermaßen synchron (Veränderungen während einer einzelnen Zeitperiode) und diachron (Veränderungen über die Zeit). Daraus ergibt sich, dass die Lesearten dieses Kräftespiels über eine Bandbreite verschiedener Interpretationsmöglichkeiten operieren: Sie können wechselwirkend und synergetisch sein oder auch unvereinbar und widersprüchlich. Folglich sind Neuerungen auf natürliche Weise aus der Technologie und Technik erblüht, sowie aus Katastrophen und weit verbreiteter Verteilung. Pflanzenarten wurden durch Zufall entdeckt – durch überregionalen Handel oder durch Jahrhunderte der Bodenbewirtschaftung.[14] Ernteausfälle haben zu Hungersnöten geführt, Kriege ausgelöst, aber oft folgten ihnen auch einschneidende Veränderungen in politischen Regimen.

Von Nahrungssuche zu Nahrungsanbau. Der markante Wechsel auf der Zeitachse kann als der Übergang von einer präurbanen Kultur der Nahrungssuche zu sesshaften Formen der Landbesiedelung verstanden werden. Ermöglicht durch die

12 Amy Westervelt, *Peak Soil Has a Simple Fix, But Will We Manage It?* 19.11.2009, in: http://solveclimatenews.com/news/20091119/peek-soil-has-simple-fix-will-we-manage-it [abgerufen am 20.2.2011].

13 Einer der wichtigsten und frühesten Texte, der diese wesentliche Verbindung zwischen landwirtschaftlichen Praktiken, Bodenbearbeitung und urbaner Landnutzung aufzeigt, ist eine Studie für den U.S. Soil Conservation Service von W.C. Lowdermilk, „Conquest of the Land through Seven Thousand Years," in: *USDA Bulletin* 9. U.S. Department of Agriculture Natural Resources Conservation Service, 1939.

14 Herbert G. Baker, *Plants and Civilization. Fundamentals of Botany Series*. Belmont, CA 1965.

generated famines, triggered wars, but very often, they are also followed by watershed changes in political regimes.

Foraging to Farming. The distinctive shift in the timeline can be understood as the transition from a pre-urban culture of foraging to sedentary formats of land settlement. Facilitated by plant selection, domestication or cultivation, this momentous turning point provides the initiating stage for the research. Geospatially, the timeline works backward from the recent occurrence of the global land grab between 2006 and 2008 (India holds soybean projects in Brazil, China has farms in Zambia, Norway has biofuel projects in Ghana)[15] and the prominence of industrial monocultures and vast glass regions (consider Almeria in Spain, one of the largest greenhouse complexes in the world),[16] towards the early origins of urban civilization transformed by agricultural dispersals and species transplants during the Age of Discovery or, by the intentional cultivation of wild grains, producing the first stationary human settlements in Prehistoric Mesopotamia.[17] Geobotanically, a lineage of plant species in the foreground of these changes—as well as fruits and flowers, roots and grafts, oils and sugars, weeds and seeds, clones and cultivars, chromosones and cultigens—reveals the development of urban civilization in close proximity with plant life, by necessity or luxury, and the cross-dependencies on the solar energy stored by photosynthesis in plants and on the nitrogen-fixing attributes of their root systems.

Phytogeography & Geobotany. From the recent advances in plant genomics and pollen biotechnology in the 20th century (algae and cyanobacteria for biofuels) to the first domesticated plants for cultivation (papyrus for vellum, hexaploid wheat for bread, taro as staple root, grapes for wine, baobabs for water storage) or animals (sheep for livestock, dromedaries for transport) to the first recorded cultivated plants for medicinal and nutritional purposes to the plant trade (ginger, lemon, mandrake, camphor)[18] through the early of use of foraged plants (hemp, agave, milkweed), the foreground simultaenously illustrates how the knowledge of soils and plants has profoundly shaped economic, cultural and political histories. Consider penicillin harvested from artificially cultivated fungi, curare used for its anesthetic properties during WWII, the research on peanuts and sweet potatoes by George Washington Carver that contributed to modern chemistry through alcohol fermentation,[19] the coffee bean transplanted to South America that supplanted Middle East trade, the cotton plant as a central export to the European colonies and major source of slave labor, corn as the major counterpoint to wheat in the New World as the primary source of cultivated food, or the banana as a crucial plant in the Arab agricultural revolution.

15 Braun, Meinzen-Dick 2009 (fn. 6).

16 The most recent and authoritative assessment of the rise of the Almeria greenhouse region was completed by a group of 8 scientists from Wageningen University on a study tour of the vast greenhouse complex. See J.M. Costa, E. Heuvelink (eds.), *Greenhouse horticulture in Almeria (Spain)*. Wageningen, January 2000.

17 See Section "Evolution, Agriculture, History," in: Marcel Mazoyer, Laurence Roudart, *A History of World Agriculture: From the Neolithic Age to the Current Crisis*. New York 2006, p. 65.

18 See Herbert G. Baker's discussion of "Plants as Stimuli of Exploration and Exploitation," in: idem, *Plants and Civilization: Fundamentals of Botany Series*, Belmont, CA 1965, pp. 29–42; and Judith M. Taylor, "Early Botanists and the Introduction of Drug Specifics," in: *Bulletin of the New York Academy of Medicine* 60 (1979), p. 685.

19 Ibid., see Baker's explanation of "The Utilization of Drug Plants," pp. 145–159; and George Carver, "How to Grow the Peanut and 105 Ways of Preparing it for Human Consumption," in: idem; and the section on Organic Synthesis Chemicals in: Aaron John Ihde, *The Development of Modern Chemistry*. Toronto 1964, pp. 687–688.

Culture & Cultivation. In addition to the bioeconomic outcomes of soil and plant cultivation in the botanical foreground, the evolution and transplanting of the knowledge and use of flora also registers the first traces of modern botanical chemistry. The early use of companion plants in China more than 1,000 years ago (mosquito ferns with rice crops to increase nitrogen fixation), the four-field rotational crop system in Europe during the Middle Ages (wheat, turnips, barley, clover), and the development of botanic gardens for phytotherapy during the Renaissance (medicinal herbs used to treat the Medici Family) are precursors to contemporary research in vitaminology, permaculture and modern genetic science, on which major pharmaceutical and biotechnological research corporations have staked billions of dollars of funding.[20] Across the timeline, these small developments can be seen historically as revolutions. From gene shuffling to protein engineering to molecular breeding, these developments work in parallel with a series of statistical progressions that connect the dots and fill in the gaps between seemingly disparate data. World population growth and decline, the price of oil and other world commodities, can then establish the interconnectedness between fluctuations in plant industries, land investments, agricultural economies, regional economies, climate change and global urbanism. For example, the tight relationship between the 2006–2007 Atlantic hurricane season which dramatically affected oil production in the Gulf of Mexico and the simultaneous spike in world food prices in 2006–2007 can be compared, albeit to a lesser degree, to the Great Famine between 1849–1851 caused by potato blight that killed 1 million Irish and forced the migration of 2.5 million more to England, America and Australia.

World population growth and decline, the price of oil and other world commodities, can then establish the interconnectedness between fluctuations in plant industries, land investments, agricultural economies, regional economies, climate change and global urbanism.

Power & Capital. Moving beyond the statistical and economic world view, a series of maps in the furthest layer of the background reveal changing world views based on urban empires, food trading systems and power relationships. Period representations of the world track the rise and fall of civilizations—from monarchies to dictatorships to democracies—while simultaneously tracing the mobility of plants and flow of foodstuffs across continents drawing new borders. Each worldly representation characterizes the geography of urban empires and shifts in centers of power drawn by large-scale geo-politics, resource wars, technological innovation, capital mobility, mineral wealth, climate change and disease onslaught. Examples of this ecological imperialism abound: After the col-

20 Michael Howell, Melanie Trull and Mark D Dibner, "The rise of European venture capital for biotechnology," in: *Nature Biotechnology* 21 (2003), pp. 1287–1291.

Selektion, Domestizierung oder Kultivierung von Pflanzen, stellt dieser bedeutsame Wendepunkt die einleitende Phase für die Forschung zur Verfügung. Aus geografisch-räumlicher Sicht arbeitet die Zeitachse rückwärts, von der kürzlich auftretenden globalen Landnahme zwischen 2006 und 2008 (Indien unterhält Sojabohnen-Projekte in Brasilien, China hat Farmen in Sambia, Norwegen hat Biosprit-Projekte in Ghana)[15] und der Bedeutung von industriellen Monokulturen und riesigen Treibhaus-Regionen (siehe Almeria in Spanien, einer der größten Treibhaus-Komplexe der Welt[16]) in Richtung der frühen Ursprünge urbaner Zivilisation, die durch landwirtschaftliche Verteilungen und Artenumpflanzungen während des Zeitalters der Entdeckungen oder durch den bewussten Anbau von Wildgetreide, der im prähistorischen Mesopotamien zu den ersten ortsgebundenen Ansiedelungen führte, umgeformt wurde.[17] Aus geografisch-botanischer Sicht enthüllt eine Abfolge von Pflanzenarten im Vordergrund dieser Veränderungen – wie auch von Früchten und Blumen, Wurzeln und Setzlingen, Gräsern und Samen, Klonen und Kultursorten, Chromosomen und Kulturpflanzen, Ölen und Zucker – die Entwicklung der urbanen Zivilisation in unmittelbarer Nähe der Pflanzenwelt, aus Notwendigkeit oder Luxus, und die Abhängigkeit von der Sonnenenergie, die durch Photosynthese in Pflanzen gespeichert wird, und von den stickstoff-fixierenden Eigenschaften ihrer Wurzelsysteme.

Pflanzengeografie & Geobotanik. Von den letzten Fortschritten in der Pflanzengenetik und der Pollen-Biotechnologie im 20. Jahrhundert (Algen und Cyanobakterien für Biosprit) zu den ersten domestizierten Pflanzen zum Anbau (Papyrus für Pergament, hexaploider Weizen für Brot, Taro als Grundnahrungswurzel, Weintrauben für Wein, Affenbrotbaum zur Wasserspeicherung) oder Tieren (Schafe als Nutztiere, Dromedare für den Transport), bis zu den ersten aufgezeichneten Kulturpflanzen für medizinische und ernährungsbedingte Zwecke und zum Handel mit Pflanzen (Ingwer, Zitronen, Alraune, Kampfer)[18] durch die frühe Verwendung von gesammelten Pflanzen (Hanf, Agave, Seidenpflanze), demonstriert der Vordergrund gleichzeitig, wie das Wissen über Böden und Pflanzen die wirtschaftlichen, kulturellen und politischen Geschichten grundlegend geformt hat. Man denke an Penicillin, das von künstlich

15 Braun, Meinzen-Dick 2009 (Anm. 6).

16 Die jüngste und gründlichste Bewertung des Aufstiegs der Almeria Glashaus-Region wurde von einer Gruppe von acht Wissenschaftern der Wageningen Universität auf einer Studienreise durch den gigantischen Glashauskomplex erstellt. Vgl. J.M. Costa, E. Heuvelink (Hg.), *Greenhouse horticulture in Almeria (Spain)*. Wageningen, Januar 2000.

17 Vgl. die Sektion „Evolution, Agriculture, History", in: Marcel Mazoyer, Laurence Roudart, *A History of World Agriculture: From the Neolithic Age to the Current Crisis*. New York 2006, S. 65.

18 Vgl. Herbert G. Bakers Diskussion der „Plants as Stimuli of Exploration and Exploitation", in: ders., *Plants and Civilization. Fundamentals of Botany Series*, Belmont, CA 1965, S. 29–42; und Judith M. Taylor, „Early Botanists and the Introduction of Drug Specifics", in: *Bulletin of the New York Academy of Medicine*, 60 (1979), S. 685.

western farming strategies spread
from the first world to the third world
agro-imperialism tr
Famine in Africa kills 30Million People in One Yea
gaafar nimeiry overthrown after massive famine in the sudan
leonid brezhnev overthrows kruse
of the virgin lands campaign and
haile selassie overthrown after massive f
food prices soar with
artificial nitrogen production becomes widespread
during WWI due to port blockades
mechanized farming depletes poor midwestern
soils resulting in the great american dust bowl
the proliferation of oil furthers export economies
and the development of petro-chemistry
norman borlaug fathers the green agricultural revolution
henry ford's assembly line allows mechanical farming to become the worldwide standard
previously unfarmable land could finally be cultivated
through the use of agro-chemicals and mechanization
nikita kruschev founds the virgin lands campaign
post WWI nitrogen plants are converted to agro-chemical factories
with much of US farmland exhausted, and a free africa post
WWII, the attention of global agricultural trade shifts to africa
dustbowls in africa, asia and the south pacific lead to
wordwide famine, killing millions
WWI trench warfare requires ten times
the gunpowder of any previous conflict
post war food shortages result
in global agricultural trade
adolph hitler uses agricultural trade as a
weapon to starve poland into submission
TIME
FOOD PRICES:
The Big Beef
FOOD IS A WEAPON
the fordson becomes the first
mass-produced tractor
POOL
POOL
15 McDONALD'S 15
FAMOUS
HAMBURGERS
BUY'EM BY THE BAG
OR EUROPEAN REC
SUPPLIED BY THE
STATES OF AM
ConAgra Foods
Tyson
the soy bean: a multiuse plant, perfected through early genetic manipulations
strophanthus: isolated for the production of cortisone, used medicinally
mushrooms: a valuable foraged agricultural commodity
the rubber plant: facilitated modern industrial farming through vulcanized rubber
t: one of the plants that gave birth to modern chemical botany
pene
poppies: imported to south an
curare: used for its anaesthetic properties during WWI and WWII
early gene modification attempted to protect corn from common diseases
5

angebauten Pilzen geerntet wurde, Kurare, das während des Zweiten Weltkriegs aufgrund seiner betäubenden Eigenschaften verwendet wurde, an die Forschung über die Erdnusspflanze und die Süßkartoffel von George Washington Carver, welche erheblich zur Entstehung der modernen Chemie durch Alkoholfermentation beigetragen hat,[19] die Kaffeebohne, verpflanzt nach Südamerika, die den Handel mit dem Nahen Osten verdrängte, die Baumwollpflanze als zentrale Exportware in die europäischen Kolonien und als Hauptquelle für Sklavenarbeit, Mais als der wichtigste Kontrapunkt zu Weizen in der neuen Welt und als die primäre Quelle von kultivierter Nahrung oder die Banane als eine entscheidende Pflanze in der arabischen Landwirtschaftsrevolution.

In addition to the linear layout of technological agriculture history, a cyclic pattern of rise and fall emerges from the accumulation of layers of information when seen over time.

Zucht & Anbau. Zusätzlich zu den bio-ökonomischen Resultaten der Bodenbewirtschaftung und des Pflanzenanbaus im botanischen Vordergrund, registriert die Entwicklung und Übertragung des Wissens und der Verwendung der Pflanzenwelt auch die ersten Spuren der modernen botanischen Chemie. Die frühe Verwendung von Mischkulturen in China vor mehr als 1000 Jahren (Algenfarn mit Reis zur Erhöhung der Stickstofffixierung), die Vierfelderwirtschaft in Europa während des Mittelalters (Weizen, Weißrübe, Gerste, Klee) und die Entstehung von botanischen Gärten für die Phytotherapie während der Renaissance (medizinische Kräuter für die Behandlung der Medici-Familie) sind Vorgänger der zeitgenössischen Forschung in der Vitaminbiologie, der Permakultur und der modernen Genforschung, in deren Finanzierung große pharmazeutische und biotechnologische Forschungskonzerne Milliarden von Dollars gesteckt haben.[20] Diese kleinen Entwicklungen können auf der Zeitachse historisch als Revolutionen gesehen werden. Von der Mischung der Gene über das Arrangement von Proteinen bis zu der molekularen Zucht arbeiten diese Entwicklungen parallel zu einer Serie von statistischen Entwicklungen, die einen Zusammenhang zwischen scheinbar verschiedenen Daten herstellen und Lücken füllen. Das Wachstum und der Rückgang der Weltbevölkerung, sowie der Preis für Öl und andere Weltgüter können somit einen Zusammenhang zwischen Schwankungen in Pflanzenindustrien, Landinvestitionen, Agrarwirtschaften, regionalen Wirtschaften, dem Klimawandel und globalem Urbanismus herstellen. Die enge Verbindung zwischen der atlantischen Hurrikan-Saison 2006–2007, welche auf dramatische Weise die Ölproduktion im Golf von Mexiko beeinflusste, und der gleichzeitigen Steigerung der weltweiten Nahrungsmittelpreise 2006–2007 kann, wenn auch in geringerem

19 Ebd., vgl. Bakers Erklärung „The Utilization of Drug Plants", S. 145–159; und George Carver, „How to Grow the Peanut and 105 Ways of Preparing it for Human Consumption", in: ebd. und der Abschnitt über „Organic Synthesis Chemicals", in: ders., *The Development of Modern Chemistry*. Toronto 1964, S. 687–688.

20 Michael Howell, Melanie Trull und Mark D. Dibner, „The rise of European venture capital for biotechnology", in: *Nature Biotechnology* 21 (2003), S. 1287–1291.

Grad, mit der großen Hungersnot zwischen 1849–1851 verglichen werden, die von Kartoffelfäule verursacht wurde und eine Million Iren tötete, sowie die Migration weiterer 2,5 Millionen nach Europa, Amerika und Australien erzwang.

Macht & Kapital. Bewegt man sich über die statistische und ökonomische Weltansicht hinaus, enthüllt eine Serie von Karten auf der entferntesten Ebene des Hintergrunds wechselnde Weltansichten, basierend auf urbanen Weltreichen, Systemen des Nahrungshandels und Machtbeziehungen. Darstellungen verschiedener Weltepochen zeichnen den Aufstieg und Fall von Zivilisationen nach – von Monarchien über Diktaturen zu Demokratien – während sie gleichzeitig die Wanderung von Pflanzen und den Fluss von Lebensmitteln auf Kontinenten kennzeichnen und neue Grenzen ziehen. Jede materielle Darstellung charakterisiert die Geografie von urbanen Weltreichen und den Wechsel von Machtzentren, gezogen von großformatigen Geo-Politiken, Ressourcen-Kriegen, technologischen Innovationen, Bewegungen des Kapitals, Reichtum an Bodenschätzen, Klimawandel und den Angriff von Krankheiten. Beispiele dieses ökologischen Imperialismus sind zahlreich: Nach dem Zusammenbruch seines landwirtschaftlichen Systems im 5. Jahrhundert trug der Fall des Römischen Reiches zur Dezentralisierung des regionalen Handels, zur Öffnung von neuen Routen, zur Verteilung der urbanen Bevölkerung und zur Bildung einer neu aufkommenden globalen Agrarwirtschaft bei. Oder der Wettlauf um Afrika, in Zuge dessen 90 % des gesamten Kontinents (sechsmal größer als die EU) durch die Herrschaft von nur sieben europäischen Nationen (Belgien, Deutschland, Frankreich, Großbritannien, Niederlande, Portugal und Spanien) auf der Berlin-Konferenz von 1884–1885 zur Ressourcengewinnung aufgeteilt wurde und dessen Grenzen heute noch vorhanden sind.

Spieler & Strategien. Zwischen dem geobotanischen Vordergrund aus Pflanzenarten, Saatgutauswahl und Nahrungsanbau und dem kartografischen Hintergrund aus imperialistischer Entwicklung liegt ein anderer, breiterer Bereich aus Meilensteinen, Schlüsselfiguren, transformierenden Techniken und einflussreichen Publikationen. Die Einwohner dieses Bereichs sind einflussreiche Wissenschaftler in der Entwicklung der modernen Agrarchemie und -technologie, wie Jethro Tull,[21] dessen Erfindung von frühen mechanischen, von Pferden gezogenen Drillmaschinen und Hacken nicht nur zur Britischen Agrarrevolution im 18. Jahrhundert führte, sondern auch den Grundstein für die moderne mechanische Landwirtschaft und die im industriellen Maßstab gemessenen landwirtschaftlichen Abläufe legte, welche die Anbaumethoden über die folgenden Jahrhunderte dominieren sollten. Oder, man bedenke, wie der Haber-Bosch Prozess der Synthetisierung von Ammoniak die

21 Charles Albert Browne, *A Source Book of Agricultural Chemistry*. New York 1944, S. 92–96.

lapse of its agricultural systems in the 5th century, the fall of Roman Empire contributed to the decentralization of regional trading, the opening of new routes, the distribution of urban population, and the formation of a nascent global agricultural economy. Or, consider the Scramble for Africa, where 90 percent of the entire continent (six times larger than the EU) was partitioned by the dominion of just seven European nations (Belgium, France, Germany, Great Britain, Netherlands, Portugal, and Spain) during the 1884–1885 Berlin Conference, for purposes of resource extraction and whose borders are still in place today.

Players & Policies. In between the geobotanical foreground of plant species, seed selection and crop cultivation and the cartographic background of imperial evolution is a another, thicker field of milestone events, key figures, transformative techniques and influential publications. Populating this field are influential scientists in the development of modern agricultural chemistry and technology such as Jethro Tull[21] whose development of early mechanical horse-drawn seed drills and hoes led not only to the British Agricultural Revolution in the 18th century, but also laid the foundation for modern mechanical farming and the industrial-scaled agricultural operations which would dominate farming practices for centuries to come. Or, consider how the Haber-Bosch process of synthesizing ammonia divorced the production of fertilizer from natural deposits and lead to unprecedented levels of nitrogen bioaccumulation.[22] Along with these pioneers of agricultural science and technology, the timeline also documents how urbanists and policy makers have reconfigured or rethought civilization's relationship to soil cultivation and land development, as well as the major world events which transformed global agricultural paradigms. Consider the General Enclosure Act of 1845 which amalgamated more than 7 million acres of farmland (21 percent of England) for increased productivity and modern machinery,[23] or Nikita Khrushchev's Virgin Lands Campaign which, in the 1950s, transformed over 300,000 square kilometers of Kazakhstan's stepped landscape into the breadbasket of the Soviet Union through the labor of hundreds of thousands of relocated Russian civilians, only to collapse due to soil erosion less than five years after the campaign began, hastening Khrushchev's political demise and the early fracturing of the iron curtain as the USSR was forced to import 20 million tons of Canadian grain.[24] Below Khrushchev and above Haile Selassie I (the Ethiopian who fell under the Wollo famines in the early 1970s) emerges Frank Lloyd Wright's Broadacre City, a midwestern agricultural urbanism and precursor to suburban expansion in the mid 20th century and as critique of the separation between industry, agriculture and cities.[25] These characterizations are often preceded by technological innovations a few decades earlier, such as the advent of the Fordson (first mass-produced mechanized tractor), American fast-food (part of a changing food culture in the U.S.), and the quintessential U.S. highway system.

21 Charles Albert Browne. *A Source Book of Agricultural Chemistry*. New York 1944, pp. 92–96.

22 Scott C. Doney, "Growing Human Footprint on Coastal and Open-Ocean Biogeochemistry," in: *Science* 328 (2010), p. 1513.

23 Gilbert Slater, "Historical outline of land ownership in England," in: *The land: the report of the Land Enquiry Committee*. London 1913.

24 From a complete discussion of the demise of Soviet agricultural policies, see Medvedev Zhores, *Soviet Agriculture*. New York 1980.

25 Frank Lloyd Wright, *The Living City*. New York 1958.

Soil: Dirt of Urban Civilization, Medium of the Future. In addition to the linear layout of technological agriculture history, a cyclic pattern of rise and fall emerges from the accumulation of layers of information when seen over time. This long view charts major shifts in population growth as outcomes of a spectrum of specific agronomic practices, and their attendant urban patterns. At one extreme of this spectrum are courtyard gardens of the Middle East, serving as bio-climactic conditioners and water reservoirs in the desert during the Golden Age, or agrarian cities like Montreuil, a suburb of Paris built of south-facing walls and espaliers for the growth of pears and peaches for Louis XVII, or more recently, the "organopónicos" (organic urbanism) of Havana the former communist Antillean colony that developed into a self-fed metropolis following the fall of the Soviet Union in the late 1980s,[26] or agricultural regions like Guandong, home to the oldest aquaculture areas in the heavily urbanized estuary of the Pearl River Delta, the medieval manors of single-family open field strip farming across Europe from the Middle Ages, or the megacity of Bangkok amidst the Chao Phraya Delta of rice paddies and shrimp farms since the middle of the 15th century.

Slaves & Substitutes, Syntheses & Systems. At another extreme of the spectrum are the failed agricultural experiments where industrial monocultures secularized and volatilized urban development. The case of the mono-cultural tobacco economy in early colonial America is one its most profound examples. Tobacco, one of the only agricultural products to survive the journey from New World fields back to European coffers, is also a crop, which strips 10–30 times the soil nutrients of standard cereal grains. In the 18th century alone, vast territories of the colonies' soil and labor forces were depleted, forcing a general population movement westward. The expansion of slavery practices to the much-needed Western lands, required by the South's exhaustion due to monocultural tobacco crops, ultimately triggered the American Civil War in 1865.[27] When considered synchronically, the timeline sheds light on the failure of policy and planning to restructure agricultural practices in the post-Civil War era. Instead, labor forces were merely substituted by the application of higher-yield agro-chemical fertilizers recently discovered by the founding fathers of modern chemistry, such as British scientist John Bennet Lawes. Reconsidered, the era which is typically thought of as the end of slavery practices in the U.S. was merely the exportation of slavery, as massive labor forces were re-deployed by the tens of thousands to the western coasts of Africa and South America

Reconsidered from a distance, this specific instance of monocultural urbanism is, however not an isolated incident.

26 Hugh Warwick, "Cuba's Organic Revolution," in: *The Ecologist* 29/8 (December 1999).

27 For an account of the antebellum period, see Avery Craven, *The Coming of the Civil War*. Chicago 1942. One of the earliest and most vocal abolitionists, William Lloyd Garrison, was also staunch opponent of tobacco farmers, who disproportionally committed slavery. See Walter M. Merrill, *Against Wind and Tide: A Biography of Wm. Lloyd Garrison*. Cambridge, MA 1963. For a capsule history of the tobacco plant, see Gene Borio, "The Tobacco Timeline," in: http://www.tobacco.org/History/Tobacco_History.html.

Erzeugung von Düngemittel von natürlichen Ablagerungen getrennt hat.[22] Zusammen mit diesen Pionieren der Agrarwissenschaft und -technologie dokumentiert die Zeitachse auch, wie Stadtplaner und politische Entscheidungsträger die Beziehung der Menschheit zur Flächennutzung und Landentwicklung neu gestaltet oder gedacht haben, sowie die großen Weltereignisse, welche globale landwirtschaftliche Paradigmen umwandelten. Das *Allgemeine Flurbereinigungsgesetz* von 1845 beispielsweise vereinigte mehr als 7 Millionen Morgen Ackerland (21 % von England), um die Produktivität zu erhöhen und die Maschinerie zu modernisieren.[23] Nikita Chruschtschow's *Virgin Lands*-Kampagne verwandelte in den 1950er-Jahren über 300.000 Quadratkilometer von Kasachstans Steppenlandschaft durch die Arbeitskraft von hunderttausenden umgesiedelten russischen Zivilisten in die Kornkammer der Sowjetunion, nur um weniger als fünf Jahre nach dem Start der Kampagne aufgrund von Bodenerosion zusammenzubrechen, was Chruschtschow's politischen Untergang beschleunigte und einen frühen Riss im Eisernen Vorhang erzeugte, da die UdSSR gezwungen war, über 20 Millionen Tonnen kanadischen Getreides zu importieren.[24] Unter Chruschtschow und über Haile Selassie I (der Äthiopier, der in den Wollo-Hungersnöten in den frühen 1970er-Jahren fiel), tritt Frank Lloyd Wright's *Broadacre City* in Erscheinung – eine mittelwestliche Agrarstadt, Vorläufer der suburbanen Erweiterung in der Mitte des 20. Jahrhunderts und eine Kritik an der Trennung zwischen Industrie, Landwirtschaft und Städten.[25] Diesen Darstellungen gehen oft, ein paar Jahrzehnte früher, technologische Innovationen voraus, wie die Produktion des *Fordson* (des ersten als Massenprodukt hergestellten motorisierten Traktors), amerikanisches *Fast-Food* (Teil einer sich wandelnden Esskultur in den USA) und das essenzielle Highway-System der USA.

Boden: Abfallprodukt der urbanen Zivilisation, Medium der Zukunft. Zusätzlich zum linearen Aufbau der Geschichte der technologischen Landwirtschaft entsteht ein periodisches Muster von Aufstieg und Fall, das durch die Ansammlung von Informationsebenen in Erscheinung tritt, wenn diese über die Zeit betrachtet werden. Dieser breite Blickwinkel erfasst bedeutende Veränderungen im Bevölkerungswachstum, die als Resultate eines Spektrums von spezifischen landwirtschaftlichen Praktiken und deren zugehörigen urbanen Mustern aufgezeich-

22 Scott C. Doney, „Growing Human Footprint on Coastal and Open-Ocean Biogeochemistry", in: *Science* 328 (2010), S. 1513.

23 Gilbert Slater, „Historical outline of land ownership in England", in: *The land; the report of the Land Enquiry Committee*. London 1913.

24 Für eine vollständige Diskussion des Niedergangs der Sowjetischen Landwirtschaftsplanung, vgl. Medvedev Zhores, *Soviet Agriculture*. New York 1980.

25 Frank Lloyd Wright. *The Living City*. New York 1958.

net werden. Am einen Extrem dieses Spektrums stehen Hofgärten im Nahen Osten, welche während der Blütezeit des Islams als bio-klimatische Luftkühlanlagen und Wasserbehälter dienten, oder Agrarstädte wie Montreuil, ein Vorort von Paris geformt aus südseitigen Wänden und Spalieren für den Anbau von Birnen und Pfirsichen für Louis XVII, oder in jüngerer Zeit die „Organopónicos" (organischer Urbanismus) von Havanna, der ehemaligen kommunistischen Kolonie auf den Antillen, die sich nach dem Fall der Sowjetunion in den späten 1980er-Jahren zu einer selbsternährenden Metropole entwickelt hat[26] oder landwirtschaftliche Regionen wie Guandong, Heimat der ältesten Anbaugebiete mit Aquakulturen, welche die Mündung des Perlfluss-Delta stark urbanisierten, die mittelalterlichen Landgute mit Streifenanbau einzelner Familien im offenen Feld in Europa während des Mittelalters oder die Metropole Bangkok inmitten des Chao Phraya-Deltas mit Reisfeldern und Krabbenfarmen seit der Mitte des 15. Jahrhunderts.

Sklaven & Surrogate, Synthesen & Systeme. An einem anderen Extrem des Spektrums stehen gescheiterte landwirtschaftliche Experimente, in denen industrielle Monokulturen die urbane Entwicklung säkularisierten und flüchtiger machten. Der Fall der monokulturellen Tabakwirtschaft im frühen kolonialen Amerika ist eines der umfassendsten Beispiele dafür. Tabak, eines der wenigen landwirtschaftlichen Produkte, das die Reise von den Feldern der neuen Welt zurück in die europäischen Schatzkammern überlebte, ist auch eine Pflanze, die dem Boden 10–30 Mal so viele Nährstoffe entzieht als übliche Getreidearten. Schon im 18. Jahrhundert waren enorme Teile des kolonialen Bodens und der Arbeitskräfte erschöpft und erzwangen eine generelle Wanderung der Bevölkerung in westliche Richtung. Die Ausweitung der Sklaverei auf die, aufgrund der Erschöpfung des Südens durch den monokulturellen Tabakanbau, dringend benötigten westlichen Ländereien, löste am Ende den amerikanischen Bürgerkrieg im Jahr 1865 aus.[27] In synchronischer Abfolge betrachtet, beleuchtet die Zeitachse das Versagen von Politik und Planung, die landwirtschaftlichen Praktiken in der Nachkriegs-Ära zu restrukturieren. Stattdessen wurden Arbeitskräfte einfach durch die Anwendung ertragsreicherer agro-chemischer Dünger ersetzt, welche kurz zuvor von den Gründungsvätern der modernen Chemie, wie dem britischen Wissenschaftler John Bennet Lawes, erfunden worden waren. Im Rückblick war die Ära, welcher man typischer-

26 Hugh Warwick, „Cuba's Organic Revolution", in: *The Ecologist* 29/8 (Dezember 1999).

27 Für eine Darstellung der sog. antebellum Periode in den USA vgl. Avery Craven, *The Coming of the Civil War*. Chicago 1942. Einer der ersten und lautstärksten Sklavereigegner, William Lloyd Garrison, war auch ein überzeugter Gegner der Tabakfarmer, welche überproportional viel Sklaverei betrieben. Vgl. Walter M. Merrill, *Against Wind and Tide: A Biography of Wm. Lloyd Garrison*. Cambridge, MA 1963. Für eine Kurzgeschichte der Tabakfabrik vgl. Gene Borio, „The Tobacco Timeline", in: http://www.tobacco.org/History/Tobacco_History.html.

to phosphorous mines. Back in North America, these practices ultimately increased the rates of soil degradation by exponential proportions until the complete collapse of the central and western agricultural region, now known as the Dust Bowl. Reconsidered from a distance, this specific instance of monocultural urbanism is, however not an isolated incident. It is indicative of a longer trend which has re-occurred continually from the collapse of the Egyptian Old Kingdom to the great famines of Africa during the 1970s, in which urban land use privileged soil mining and industrial farming over replenishable soil practices, rotational farming techniques and distributed land use patterns.

From the early methods of rotational farming and permaculture in the Nile Delta to the contemporary practice of precision farming in Brazil and India, or the future of carbon farming in the urban world, the groundwork research presented here thus proposes that the landscape of agriculture and the current discourse of food production cannot be separated from the geospatial distribution of population and the culture of urban markets. Nor can it be separated from the design of urban territories, the botanic sciences, farming practices and techniques, or shifts in geo-political power throughout history. Whether the current discourse is focused on global commodity exchanges, regional agricultural economies, or low density urban spread, contemporary advances—including the advent of global land grabbing, soilless greenhouses, bioengineering, biosolids recycling, and agrarian urbanism—all represent the contemporary manifestation of the nascent potential pattern lying in between urbanization and the cultivation of food.

Acknowledgments: This project is made possible in part with funding from the Canada Council for the Arts. Seed funding was originally provided by the Professional Prix de Rome Award for research on the interrelationship between watersheds, foodsheds and urban patterns. The authors would also like to thank Daniel Rabin, Michelle Dobbie and David Christensen for their graphic research in the early stages of the timeline project.

Anmerkungen References

Der grafische Inhalt der Zeitachse wurde erstellt unter Verwendung von Information, Daten und Bildern aus den folgenden Publikationen: The graphic content of the timeline was developed using information, data and illustrations from the following titles:

Thomas Anderson, *Elements of Agricultural Chemistry*. Charleston 2010.
Liberty Hyde Bailey, *The Horticulturist's Rule-Book: A Compendium of Useful Information for Fruit Growers, Truck Gardeners, Florists, and Others*. New York 1895.
Herbert G. Baker, *Plants and Civilization: Fundamentals of Botany Series*, Belmont, CA 1965.
Miguel Barcelo, Francois Sigaut, *The Making of Feudal Agricultures?* Boston 2004.
Graeme Barker, *The Agricultural Revolution in Prehistory: Why did Foragers become Farmers?* Oxford 2009.
Peter Bellwood, *First Farmers: The Origins of Agricultural Societies*. New York 2004.
Wendell Berry, *The Unsettling of America: Culture and Agriculture*. San Francisco 1996.
Charles Corn, *The Scents of Eden: A History of the Spice Trade*. New York 1999.
Alfred W. Crosby, *Ecological Imperialism: The Biological Expansion of Europe, 900–1900. Studies in environment and history*. Cambridge and New York, 1986.
Cyril D. Darlington, E. K. Janaki Ammal, *Chromosome Atlas of Cultivated Plants*. London 1945.
Gabriel De Herrera, *Ancient Agriculture: Roots and Application of Sustainable Farming*. Layton 2006.
Kenneth Deffeyes, *Beyond Oil: The View from Hubbert's Peak*. New York 2006.
Arthur Demarest, *Ancient Maya: The Rise and Fall of a Rainforest Civilization*. Cambridge 2005.
Georges Duby, Cynthia Postan, *Rural Economy and Country Life in the Medieval West*. Philadelphia 1998.
Giovanni Federico, *Feeding the World: An Economic History of Agriculture, 1800–2000*. Princeton 2008.
Evan D. G. Fraser, *Empires Of Food: Feast, Famine, and the Rise and Fall of Civilizations*. New York 2010.
Walter Page Hedden, *How Great Cities are Fed*. Boston, New York et al. 1929.
Sir Albert Howard, *An Agricultural Testament*. Oxford 2010.
Edward Hyams, *Soil and Civilization*. New York 1976.
Icon Group International, *Agrochemicals, Webster's Timeline History, 1987–2007*. Washington, D.C. 2009.
Calestous Juma, *The New Harvest: Agricultural Innovation in Africa*. Oxford 2010.
Franklin H. King, *Farmers of Forty Centuries: Or Permanent Agriculture in China, Korea and Japan*. Kent 2010.
Petr Kropotkin, *Fields, Factories and Workshops: Or, Industry Combined with Agriculture and Brain Work with Manual Work*. London 1913.
John Bennet Lawes, *Reply to Baron Liebig's Principles of Agricultural Chemistry*. London 1855, reprint 2010.
Estele Levetn, Karen McMahon, *Plants and Society*. New York 2003.
Carl von Linné, Johann Christian Daniel Schreber, *Materia Medica*. Editio quinta auctior curante D. Io. Christ. Dan. Schrebero … ed. Lipsiae, Erlangae, 1739–1810.
William Bryant Logan, *Dirt: The Ecstatic Skin of the Earth*. New York 2007.
Thomas R. Malthus, *An Essay on the Principle of Population: Influences on Malthus, Selections from Malthus' Work, Nineteenth-Century Comment, Malthus in the Twenty-First Century*. New York 2004.
Coyne S. Mark, James A. Thompson, *Fundamental Soil Science*. Delmar 2005.
Marcel Mazoyer, Laurence Roudart, *A History of World Agriculture: From the Neolithic Age to the Current Crisis*. New York 2006.
Peter McClelland, *Sowing Modernity: America's First Agricultural Revolution*. Ithaca 1997.
David R. Montgomery, *Dirt: Erosion of Civilizations*. Berkeley 2008.
Clement Moore, *Images of Development: Egyptian Engineers in Search of Industry*. Cairo 2006.
Marion Nestle, *Food Politics: How the Food Industry Influences Nutrition and Health*. Berkeley 2007.
Mark Overton, *Agricultural Revolution in England: The Transformation of the Agrarian Economy 1500–1850*. Cambridge 1996.
Pliny, the Elder, *Natural History*. Cambridge, MA 1962.
Michael Pollan, *The Omnivore's Dilemma: A Natural History of Four Meals*. New York 2007.
Paul Roberts, *The End of Food*. Boston 2009.
Marie-Monique Robin, *The World According to Monsanto*. New York 2010.
Robert Sallares, *Malaria and Rome: A History of Malaria in Ancient Italy*. Oxford 2002.
Carl Ortwin Sauer, *Seeds, Spades, Hearths, And Herds: The Domestication Of Animals And Foodstuffs*. 2nd ed. Cambridge 1969.
Carl Ortwin Sauer, *Agricultural Origins and Dispersals. Bowman Memorial Lectures*; Vol. 2, Ser. 2. New York 1952.
Londa L. Schiebinger, *Plants And Empire: Colonial Bioprospecting in the Atlantic World*. Cambridge, MA 2004.
Vandana Shiva, *Stolen Harvest: The Hijacking of the Global Food Supply*. Brooklyn 2000.
Jimmy Skaggs, *The Great Guano Rush: Entrepreneurs and American Overseas Expansion*. New York 1995.
Jack Turner, *Spice: The History of a Temptation*. New York 2005.
Nikolai I. Vavilov, "The Problem of the Origin of the World's Agriculture in the Light of the Latest Investigations," in: *Science at the Crossroads*, Papers Presented to the International Congress of the History of Science and Technology Held in London from June 29–July 3, 1931 by the Delegates of the U.S.S.R. London, 1931.
Tony Weis, *The Global Food Economy: The Battle for the Future of Farming*. London 2007.
Michael Woods, Mary B. Woods, *Ancient Agriculture, From Foraging to Farming*. Minneapolis 2000.
Aaron Woolf, *King Corn*. New York 2008.
Medvedev Zhores, *Soviet Agriculture*. New York 1980.

weise das Ende der Sklaverei in den USA zuschreibt, lediglich ein Export der Sklaverei, da die Arbeitskräfte zu Zehntausenden an die westlichen Küsten von Afrika und Südamerika in Phosphorminen umgeschichtet wurden. In Nordamerika ließen diese Praktiken schließlich den Grad der Bodendegradation in exponentiellen Größenverhältnissen ansteigen, bis zum vollständigen Zusammenbruch der zentralen und westlichen Landwirtschaftsregionen – heute bekannt als der *Dust Bowl*. Aus Distanz betrachtet, ist dieses spezifische Beispiel eines monokulturellen Urbanismus jedoch kein Einzelfall. Es deutet auf eine längerfristige Tendenz hin, welche sich kontinuierlich wiederholt – vom Zusammenbruch des alten Königreichs in Ägypten zu den großen Hungersnöten in Afrika während der 1970er-Jahre, in denen die urbane Flächennutzung der Bodenausbeutung und dem industriellen Anbau den Vorzug gab vor nachhaltiger Bodennutzung, Methoden des Fruchtwechsels auf Feldern und verteilten Flächennutzungsmustern.

Von den frühen Methoden des Fruchtwechsels und der Permakultur im Nildelta zu der gegenwärtigen Praktik des Präzisionsackerbaus in Brasilien und Indien, oder der Zukunft des *Carbon Farming* in der urbanen Welt – die hier präsentierte Grundlagenforschung schlägt vor, dass die Landschaft des Ackerbaus und der derzeitige Diskurs über die Lebensmittelproduktion nicht von der geografisch-räumlichen Verteilung der Bevölkerung und der Kultur der urbanen Märkte getrennt werden können. Dies kann auch nicht getrennt betrachtet werden vom Entwurf urbaner Territorien, den botanischen Wissenschaften, Anbaumethoden und -techniken oder den Veränderungen in der geo-politischen Macht im Lauf der Geschichte. Egal ob sich der derzeitige Diskurs auf globale Rohstoffbörsen, regionale Landwirtschaften oder urbane Ausbreitung mit niedriger Dichte konzentriert, die zeitgenössischen Fortschritte – einschließlich dem Aufkommen der globalen Landnahme, Gewächshäusern mit Hydrokulturen, Biotechnik, Abwasser-Wiederaufbereitung und des agrarischen Urbanismus – präsentieren alle den zeitgenössischen Ausdruck eines neu aufkommenden möglichen Musters, zwischen Urbanisierung und dem Anbau von Lebensmitteln.

Übersetzung Claudia Wrumnig

Danksagung: Dieses Projekt wurde durch das Canada Council for the Arts gefördert. Anschubfinanzierung wurde ursprünglich durch den Professional Prix de Rome Award für Forschung über den Zusammenhang zwischen Wassereinzugsgebieten, Foodsheds und urbanen Besiedlungsmustern zur Verfügung gestellt. Der Autor dankt Daniel Rabin, Michelle Dobbie und David Christensen für ihre grafische Forschung in den Anfangsstadien des Zeitachsen-Projekts.

agro-imperialism triggers a new global land grab
Famine in Africa kills 30Million People in One Yea
south korean land grab of mozambique results in widespread food shortages and political upheaval
open oil crisis cripples global agricultural trade
gaafar nimeiry overthrown after massive famine in the sudan
leonid brezhnev overthrows kruschev after the failure of the virgin lands campaign and the russian dustbowl
genetically modified crops seen as the solution to world hunger
haile selassie overthrown after massive famine in etheopia
soil-less agricultural landscapes of almeria spain respond to the need for year-round produce
food prices soar with the increasing cost of oil
TIME
FOOD PRICES:
The Big Beef
nikita kruschev founds the virgin lands campaign
SORRY NO GAS
FLITE-FUEL
POLICE
BIOFUELS = "CRIME AGAINST HUMANITY"
IS A WEAPON
R EUROPEAN RECOVERY
SUPPLIED BY THE
STATES OF AMERICA
WHEAT
atlantic hurricane season causes $50 billion in damages
genetically modified soybeans
genetically modified cotton
genetically modified corn
opec embargo quadruples oil prices
BAYER
BASF
Chemical
early genetic manipulations
penecillin: harvested from artificially cultivated fungi
poppies: imported to south america for narcotics production, funded afghani war with ussr
curare: used for its anaesthetic properties during WWI and WWII
early gene modification attempted to protect corn from common diseases
genetically engineered seed-crop sought to make crops larger, brighter and more sweet

1 Die Ermöglichung morphodynamischer Prozesse an der Isar schafft eine Vielzahl unterschiedlicher Lebensräume sowohl für die Menschen als auch Flora und Fauna.
Enabling morphodynamic processes at the Isar creates a variety of habitats for humans as well as flora and fauna.

Die *Agencies* der Landschaft orchestrieren

Landschaft ist das Ergebnis der Wirkung und Wechselwirkung von natürlichen und menschlichen Faktoren, so die Europäische Landschaftskonvention aus dem Jahre 2000. Diese knappe, kluge und auf breitem Konsens aufbauende Definition weist auf die zwei entscheidenden Elemente von Landschaft hin: ihre Dynamik durch die wechselwirkenden Prozesse und ihre Hybridität durch die Vermischung natürlicher und menschlicher Faktoren.

Orchestrating Agencies of Landscape. Landscape is the result of the action and interaction of natural and human factors, according to the European Landscape Convention of 2000. This concise and clever definition builds upon a broad consensus and emphasizes the two key elements of landscape: its dynamics through the interacting processes and their hybridity by the mixing of natural and human factors.

MARTIN PROMINSKI

Im Folgenden möchte ich zeigen, dass die Betonung dieser zwei Elemente nicht selbstverständlich ist, sondern eine erst in jüngster Zeit möglich gewordene, grundlegend neue Orientierung. Die Anerkennung des hybriden und dynamischen Charakters von Landschaft bedeutet einen neuen Ausgangspunkt für die Frage, wie deren *Agencies* in einem zukunftsorientierten Entwerfen von Landschaft orchestriert werden sollen.

Hybridität. Falls wir heute den Common Sense zur Landschaft befragten, würde die Mehrheit der Menschen sie wahrscheinlich als etwas Grünes, Natürliches bezeichnen. Bestätigt wird diese These durch zahlreiche Untersuchungen von Gerhard Hard zum alltagssprachlichen Verständnis von Landschaft.[1] Aber diese einseitige Zuordnung von Landschaft zur Sphäre des Natürlichen wird immer fragwürdiger, da heute die Existenz von Natur als Gegensatz zur Kultur zunehmend infrage gestellt wird. Im Jahre 1988 bemerkte beispielsweise der französische Philosoph Gilles Deleuze in einem Interview, er möchte als nächstes Projekt „eine Art Naturphilosophie machen – im Augenblick, in dem sich jeder Unterschied zwischen Natur und Artefakt verwischt",[2] und entwickelte zusammen mit Felix Guattari eine hybride „Geophilosophie".[3] Diese durch die Vermischung von Natürlichem und Künstlichem motivierte Geophilosophie ist im Grunde eine Landschaftsphilosophie, denn die Autoren betonen, dass Philosophie nichts mit abstrakten Ideen zu tun hat, sondern immer in konkreten Kontexten der Geografie stattfindet und sich aus ihnen entwickelt. Diese konkreten Kontexte sind physisch, human und mental, wie die Landschaft.[4] Für sie ist die Geo- oder Landschaftsphilosophie angesichts der totalen Verwischung von Natur und Kultur die neue Naturphilosophie.

Aber diese einseitige Zuordnung von Landschaft zur Sphäre des Natürlichen wird immer fragwürdiger, da heute die Existenz von Natur als Gegensatz zur Kultur zunehmend infrage gestellt wird.

Auch der Frankfurter Philosoph Martin Seel betont diese hybride Qualität von Landschaft: „Ohnehin ist daran zu erinnern, dass beinahe alle heutigen Landschaften, auch diejenigen weit am Rand der Zivilisation, nie nur Natur sind, sondern immer auch, wenn auch in ganz unterschiedlichem Maß, Legierungen von Natur und Kultur darstellen".[5]

Diese hybriden Thesen von Philosophen zur Landschaft laufen parallel zu Erkenntnissen in der Theorie der Ökologie. Das traditionelle Ökologieverständnis externalisiert den Menschen und trennt zwischen „natürlichen"

1 Vgl. Gerhard Hard, „Landschaft als professionelles Idol", in: *Garten + Landschaft* 3 (1991), S. 13–18.

2 Gilles Deleuze, *Unterhandlungen*. Frankfurt/M. 1992, S. 226.

3 Gilles Deleuze, Felix Guattari, *Was ist Philosophie?* Frankfurt/M. 1996, S. 97–131.

4 Vgl. ebd., S. 109.

5 Martin Seel, „Das Unsichtbare sichtbar machen. Zur aktuellen Lage des Austauschs von Kunst und Natur", in: Volker Adolphs (Hg.), *Ferne Nähe. „Natur" in der Kunst der Gegenwart*. Köln 2009, S. 175.

Below I will argue that the emphasis of these two elements is not self-evident, but it rather represents a fundamental new orientation that has only recently become possible. The recognition of the hybrid and dynamic nature of the landscape represents a new starting point for the question of how their agencies are to be orchestrated in a future-oriented design of landscape.

Hybridity. If we would determine the common sense about landscape with a survey, the majority of people would probably describe it as something green and natural. This hypothesis is confirmed in numerous studies by Gerhard Hard concerning the colloquial meaning of "landscape."[1] But this univocal assignment of landscape to the natural sphere is becoming questionable, as the existence of nature as opposed to culture is put increasingly in question today. In 1988, for example, the French philosopher Gilles Deleuze remarked in an interview that as his next project he wanted to "produce a sort of philosophy of Nature, now that any distinction between nature and artifice is becoming blurred,"[2] and so together with Felix Guattari he developed a hybrid "geophilosophy."[3] In its mixing of the natural and the artificial, geophilosophy is basically a philosophy of landscape, as the authors argue that philosophy has nothing to do with abstract ideas but always takes place in and grows from specific geographical contexts. These concrete contexts are physical, human and mental, like the landscape.[4] Because of the total blurring of nature and culture, the geo- or landscape philosophy is for them the new natural philosophy.

Also the Frankfurt philosopher Martin Seel emphasizes the hybrid quality of landscape: "one should remember that almost all of today's landscapes, even those at the far edge of civilization, are never just nature, but always represent alloys of nature and culture, albeit to very different degrees."[5]

Such philosophical theses about the hybridity of landscapes run parallel to findings in ecological theory. The traditional understanding of ecology externalizes the human being and separates between "natural" and "artificial" systems.[6] The former are characterized by a high degree of stability and harmony and are thus regarded as something positive. The human being stands for the artificial. Although in some way part of the system, the human being is not integrated in it, because basically the development processes do not require a human presence.

1 See Gerhard Hard, "Landschaft als professionelles Idol," in: *Garten + Landschaft* 3 (1991), pp. 13–18.

2 Gilles Deleuze, *Negotiations*. New York 1995, p. 155.

3 Gilles Deleuze, Felix Guattari, *What is Philosophy?* London 1994, pp. 85–114.

4 See ibid., p. 96.

5 Martin Seel, "Ushering the Invisible into View: On the Current Exchange between Art and Nature," in: Volker Adolphs (ed.), *Ferne Nähe: "Natur" in der Kunst der Gegenwart*. Cologne 2009, p. 175.

6 See Peter Eisenhardt et al., "Traditionelle und kritische Ökologie," in: idem (eds.), *Wie Neues entsteht*. Reinbek 1995, pp. 218ff.

Such a view is rejected by the "new ecology" or "critical ecology."[7] It recognizes the human being as a major factor in most ecosystems and makes no idealized distinction between "natural" and "artificial" systems. Furthermore, these theories criticize the orientation towards an "ecological balance" that would represent an ideal state. Instead of a gradual, orderly and predictable series of developmental stages leading to a climax, these new theories emphasize the importance of disturbances. They are not seen as exceptions in an otherwise orderly sequence, but conditions for high biodiversity. The frequency, intensity or spatial extension of the disturbances can be affected by humans who no longer occupy only the position of a detached spectator and instead are seen as active players within the interdependent elements of ecosystems. In this way, ecology relinquishes its traditional univocal and exclusive orientation to nature and focuses instead on layerings of nature and culture, just like landscape. In this sense, the French sociologist Bruno Latour claims that ecology dissolves boundaries and reconfigures the players; radically, he speaks only of a "political ecology" which does not try and has never tried "to protect nature. On the contrary, it wants to assume in an even more complete, more complex manner an even wider variety of entities and destinies."[8] Thus it is clear that similar theoretical developments have taken place both as regards landscape and ecology: if landscape was for a long time understood simply as the green counterpart of the cultural sphere and ecology was the synonym for the natural, both are now seen as the interweaving of the natural and the artificial, a view which allows for more complex perspectives.

If such a perspective is adopted, exciting spatial developments are possible. An example is the project by the Amsterdam office of Rietveld Landscape for the Boschplaat nature reserve on the Dutch island of Terschelling. An attractive nature reserve was formed in the lee of a drift dike but it is now endangered by the sea level rise caused by climate change. The dike is the relic of a past experiment to connect all the Dutch Wadden Sea islands. This cultural relic, which originally led to the emergence of the nature reserve, could also be the reason for its downfall, because it prevents the flushing of the surface with sediment that would increase its height. In order to preserve the Boschplaat, the landscape architects of Rietveld suggest two measures:

First, the stabilizing grass skin of the dike is removed in order to make it into a sand dune. Second, a strict grid of bollards are to be placed on the surface of the Boschplaat. These measures will rearrange the agencies of water, wind and sand movement. The wind blows the sand from the dune in the direction of Boschplaat where the bollards will halt it, causing

7 Ibid., pp. 226ff.

8 Bruno Latour, "Modernisierung oder Ökologisierung?" in: *ARCH+* 196/197 (2010), pp. 12–21.

und „künstlichen" Systemen.[6] Erstere zeichnen sich durch ein hohes Maß an Stabilität und Harmonie aus und gelten daher als Positivum. Als das Künstliche wird der Mensch betrachtet. Er ist zwar irgendwie Teil des Systems, aber nicht integriert, denn im Grunde wird er für die Entwicklungsprozesse nicht benötigt.

Im Gegensatz dazu steht die „Neue Ökologie" oder „Kritische Ökologie".[7] Sie erkennt den Menschen als einen der wichtigsten Faktoren der meisten Ökosysteme an und trifft keine idealisierende Unterscheidung in „natürliche" und „künstliche" Systeme. Weiters kritisieren diese Theorien eine Orientierung am „ökologischen Gleichgewicht", das einen idealen Zustand darstellt. Statt einer gradualen, geordneten und vorhersagbaren Folge von Entwicklungsstadien hin zum Klimaxstadium betonen diese neuen Theorien die Bedeutung von Störungen. Sie sind nicht als Ausnahme eines ansonsten geordneten Ablaufes zu betrachten, sondern wichtig für hohe Biodiversität. Diese Störungen können in ihrer Frequenz, Intensität oder räumlichen Ausdehnung vom Menschen gestaltet werden. Er verlässt damit die Zuschauerposition und wird aktiver Mitspieler innerhalb der wechselwirkenden Elemente der Ökosysteme. Ökologie löst sich damit aus einer einseitigen, exklusiven Zuordnung zur Natur und thematisiert stattdessen, ebenso wie Landschaft, Legierungen von Natur und Kultur. In diesem Sinne behauptet der französische Soziologe Bruno Latour, dass Ökologie Grenzziehungen auflöst und die Akteure neu verteilt, und spricht daher radikal nur noch von „Politischer Ökologie". Diese „versucht nicht und hat nie versucht die Natur zu schützen. Sie will sich im Gegenteil auf eine noch vollständigere, noch komplexere Art einer noch größeren Vielfalt von Entitäten und Schicksalen annehmen".[8] Es wird also deutlich, dass sowohl für die Landschaft als auch für die Ökologie ähnliche theoretische Entwicklungen stattgefunden haben: War Landschaft lange nur das grüne Gegenüber der kulturellen Sphäre und Ökologie das Synonym für das Natürliche, werden beide heute als Verwebungen von Natürlichem und Künstlichem gesehen, was komplexere Perspektiven erlaubt.

Wenn eine derartige Perspektive eingenommen wird, sind spannungsreiche Raumentwicklungen möglich, wie beispielsweise das Projekt „Boschplaat Naturschutzgebiet" auf der niederländischen Insel Terschelling vom Büro Rietveld Landscape aus Amsterdam zeigt. Hier hat sich im Windschatten eines Flugsanddeiches ein attraktives Naturschutzgebiet entwickelt, das nun durch den klimawandelbedingten Anstieg des Meeresspiegels gefährdet ist. Der Deich ist das Relikt eines länger zurückliegenden Versuches, alle holländischen Wattenmeer-Inseln zu verbinden. Dieses kulturelle Überbleibsel, das möglicherweise erst zum Entstehen des Naturschutzgebietes geführt hat, wird zukünftig der Grund seines Untergangs, denn er verhindert das Überspülen der Fläche mit Sedimenten, so dass es sich aufhöhen kann. Um nun die kulturell bedingte Zielsetzung des Erhalts der Boschplaat zu gewährleisten, schlagen die Landschaftsarchitekten von Rietveld zwei Maßnahmen vor: Erstens soll dem Deich seine stabilisierende Rasenhaut genommen werden, um ihn zur sandigen Düne zu machen. Zweitens sollen auf der Fläche des Boschplaat in strengem Raster Pfähle gesetzt werden. Auf diese Weise

6 Vgl. Peter Eisenhardt et al., „Traditionelle und kritische Ökologie", in: dies. (Hg.), *Wie Neues entsteht*. Reinbek 1995, S. 218ff.

7 Ebd., S. 226ff.

8 Bruno Latour, „Modernisierung oder Ökologisierung?" in: *ARCH+* 196/197 (2010), S. 12–21.

setzen sie ein völlig neues Zusammenwirken der *Agencies* von Wasser, Wind und Sand in Bewegung. Der Wind weht den Sand von der Düne in Richtung Boschplaat, wo die Pfähle als Anlandungspunkte dienen und sich so das Niveau rund um die Pfähle durch den angewehten Sand langsam anhebt. Wenn sich das Niveau genügend gehoben und stabilisiert hat, soll die Düne des ehemaligen Deiches durchbrochen werden, so dass das Wasser eindringen kann und durch weitere Sedimentierung das Niveau erhöhen kann (Abb. 2). Insgesamt ist dieses Projekt ein komplexes Zusammenspiel von gewollten (Erhalt der Boschplaat) und ungewollten (Klimawandel) kulturellen Setzungen sowie den nahezu unvorhersehbaren natürlichen Prozessen.

Dynamik. Lange Zeit war der Umgang mit Landschaft von sehr statischen Bildern geprägt. Die vorindustrielle Kulturlandschaft mit ihrer kleinteiligen Gliederung von Wiesen, Hecken und Baumgruppen galt als ideale Zielvorstellung. Die Landschaftsplanerin Beate Jessel spricht hier selbstkritisch von der „Schwierigkeit, daß wir Landschaft nur allzu gerne als Idealbild auffassen [...]. Gerade in der Landschaftspflege meinen wir oft, quasi bildhaft konstruierte landschaftliche Idealzustände schaffen bzw. unter hohem, bis ins Detail geregeltem Pflegeaufwand aufrechterhalten zu müssen“.[9] Die *Agency* der Landschaft wurde unter Kontrolle gebracht, um ein sehr eingeschränktes und einschränkendes Ideal zu realisieren. Von vielen Seiten regte sich spätestens seit den 1980er-Jahren Widerstand gegen diese Limitierung: Auf Seiten der Theorie entwickelte beispielsweise John Brinckerhoff Jackson seine dynamische „Landschaft Drei“,[10] und der Landschaftsarchitekt George Hargreaves stellte für Landschaftsprojekte fest: „Why are static landscapes – frozen in space and time – the norm? Maybe it's time to change that and the concept of beauty.“[11]

Seitdem hat sich eine Menge getan bezüglich einer dynamischen Landschaftsvorstellung. Einer der radikalsten Prozessdenker der Landschaft ist der Niederländer Louis Le Roy. Sein Projekt „Öko-Kathedrale“ agiert an der Schnittstelle von Landschaftsarchitektur, Architektur und Kunst und kann als eine der konsequentesten Übertragungen einer dynamischen, evolutionären Haltung in räumliche Gestalt interpretiert werden. Nach Meinung des Architekturkritikers Piet Vollaard ist die Öko-Kathedrale das einzige Beispiel einer prozessorientierten, zeitlich offenen Architektur in den Niederlanden.[12]

Seit über dreißig Jahren lässt sich der Kunsterzieher Le Roy sämtliche Straßenbauabfälle, die in der niederländischen Gemeinde Heerenveen anfallen, auf ein ihm von der Gemeinde überlassenes Grundstück am Rande des Dorfes Mildam bringen. Inzwischen sind 15.000 Tonnen abgekippt worden, die Le Roy auf dem vier Hektar großen Gelände zwischen Restbeständen von Wald verteilt hat. Dieses Schuttmaterial schichtet er ohne irgendeine maschinelle Hilfe in Trockenbauweise zu aztekisch anmutenden Bauwerken auf (Abb. 3). Die Strukturen, an denen er gerade nicht baut, werden so lange

9 Beate Jessel, „Dimensionen des Landschaftsbegriffs“, in: *Laufener Seminarbeiträge* 04 (1995), S. 8.

10 John Brinckerhoff Jackson, „Concluding with Landscapes“, in: ders. (Hg.), *Discovering the vernacular landscape*. New Haven 1984, S. 145–157; vgl. Martin Prominski, „Designing Landscapes as Evolutionary Systems“, in: *Design Studies* 8/3 (2005), S. 25–34.

11 George Hargreaves, „Most Influential Landscapes“, in: *Landscape Journal* 12/2 (1993), S. 177.

12 Vgl. Piet Vollard, „Time-based Architecture in Mildam“, in: Louis Le Roy (Hg.), *Nature Culture Fusion*. Rotterdam 2002, S. 22.

the level of sand to slowly rise around them. Once the sand level is high and stable enough, the former levee will be breached, so that water can penetrate and raise the Boschplaat further by sedimentation (fig. 2). Overall, this project represents the complex interplay of intentional goals (maintaining the Boschplaat), unwanted cultural effects (climate change) and the almost unpredictable natural processes.

Dynamics. For a long time, the conceptions of the landscape were influenced by very static images. The pre-industrial cultural landscape with its small-scale structure of lawns, hedges and trees was held as the ideal. Self-critically, the landscape architect Beate Jessel speaks of the "difficulty that we are only too eager to think of landscape as a pictorial ideal ... Especially in site preservation, we often think of creating ideal landscapes that are conceived as images or preserving such conditions even if it required detailed maintenance."[9] The agency of the landscape was brought under control in order to realize a very narrow and restrictive ideal. Since the 1980s, opposition to such a limitation has arisen from many areas: from the side of theory, for example, John Brinckerhoff Jackson proposed the dynamic concept of "the third landscape"[10] and the landscape architect George Hargreaves asked: "Why are static landscapes—frozen in space and time—the norm? Maybe it's time to change that and the concept of beauty."[11]

Since then a lot has been done to develop a dynamic conception of landscape. One of the most radical processual thinkers of landscape is the Dutchman, Louis Le Roy. His project Eco-Cathedral operates at the interface of landscape architecture, architecture and art and can be interpreted as one of the most consistent negotiations of a dynamic, evolutionary thought into spatial form. According to the architecture critic Piet Vollaard, the Eco-Cathedral is the only example of a process-oriented, open-ended architecture in the Netherlands.[12]

For over thirty years, the art teacher Le Roy has had all road construction waste generated in the Dutch municipality of Heerenveen transported to his lot, donated by the municipality, at the outskirts of the village of Mildam. To date, 15,000 tons of debris have been dumped on the lot and Le Roy has distributed it on the four-acre site between the remnants of a forest. Without any mechanical assistance, he erects out of the debris vaguely Aztec-looking buildings in dry construction (fig. 3).

9 Beate Jessel, "Dimensionen des Landschaftsbegriffs," in: *Laufener Seminarbeiträge* 04 (1995), p. 8.

10 John Brinckerhoff Jackson, "Concluding with Landscapes," in: idem (ed.), *Discovering the vernacular landscape*. New Haven 1984, pp. 145–157; see Martin Prominski, "Designing Landscapes as Evolutionary Systems," in: *Design Studies* 8/3 (2005), pp. 25–34.

11 George Hargreaves, "Most Influential Landscapes," in: *Landscape Journal* 12/2 (1993), p. 177.

12 See Piet Vollard, "Time-based Architecture in Mildam," in: Louis Le Roy (ed.), *Nature Culture Fusion*. Rotterdam 2002, p. 22.

The structures which Le Roy is not presently working on are taken over by vegetation, until he devotes his attention to them again and builds them up. Inspired by Ilya Prigogine's question, "What can one man achieve in space and time?"[13] Le Roy does not let anyone else work on the Eco-Cathedral as long has he is alive, but a foundation has already been established in order to continue the work after his death. The time horizon that Le Roy envisages for his project reaches up to the year 3000; physically he anticipates reaching a height of up to 200 meters.[14] In which direction exactly the Eco-Cathedral is supposed to develop is not important to Le Roy because he is primarily concerned with the creative openness of evolutionary processes. In terms of open-endedness, he compares his project to medieval cathedrals such as Chartres, where at the beginning of the construction, no one could tell what the building would eventually look like.

For this reason, Le Roy criticizes the static approach of most designers who begin with a set plan. Buildings, plantations and open areas are defined, and constant care is needed to maintain this state. Instead, Le Roy takes the view that every garden is a process which can not be frozen in time: "In my projects, nothing is fixed, everything works as a process and changes every day."[15] In his opinion, evolutionary processes are endless. They are based on a partnership of people, plants and animals, which is driven by "free energy." With this energy, nature constructs itself, and the goal of this evolution is to achieve the greatest possible complexity.[16] Le Roy's project is certainly one of the most radical examples of a dynamic conception of landscape. However, Le Roy's principle of "strong self-organization" (allowing dynamic processes with a minimum degree of design or structural requirements)[17] works best for private experimental spaces. In the design of other landscapes, the method can run into implementation difficulties, as illustrated by his projects in public spaces (e.g. Kennedylaan, Heerenveen or Lewenborg). In my view, "low self-organization" (limiting dynamic processes with predetermined design rules or frames)[18] provides more promising opportunities.

Landscape, Agency, and Design. For our future landscapes, it is crucial how we orchestrate the hybrid processes. How can we design with the agencies of the landscape? In the following I wish to describe transdisciplinarity and process orientation as the two aspects that I think are important starting points for this kind of landscape design.

13 Le Roy 2002 (fn. 12), p. 12.

14 Ibid.

15 Ibid., p. 34.

16 Ibid.

17 Martin Prominski, "Die Unordnung planen," in: *Garten + Landschaft* 10 (1996), pp. 12–14.

18 See ibid.

von Pflanzen überwuchert, bis er sich ihnen wieder widmet und höher aufbaut. Mit Ilya Prigogine fragt er: „Was kann ein einzelner Mensch in Raum und Zeit erreichen?“[13] weshalb zu seinen Lebzeiten ausschließlich er selbst an der Öko-Kathedrale arbeitet. Eine Stiftung ist schon gegründet, um nach seinem Tode die Arbeit weiterzuführen. Der zeitliche Horizont, den Le Roy für sein Projekt angibt, liegt beim Jahr 3000, räumlich kann er sich Höhen von 200 Metern vorstellen.[14] Wohin sich aber die Öko-Kathedrale genau entwickelt, ist Le Roy nicht wichtig, denn es geht ihm gerade darum, mit der prinzipiellen Offenheit evolutionärer Prozesse kreativ zu arbeiten. Er vergleicht sein Projekt bezüglich dieses zeitlich offenen Charakters gerne mit mittelalterlichen Kathedralen wie beispielsweise Chartres, bei denen am Anfang der Bauzeit auch niemand wusste, wie das Bauwerk am Ende aussehen würde. Le Roy kritisiert deshalb den statischen Ansatz der meisten Entwerfer, die mit einem alles festlegenden Plan beginnen. Bauwerke, Pflanzungen und freie Flächen werden definiert, und ständige Pflege ist notwendig, um diesen Zustand aufrecht zu erhalten. Le Roy dagegen meint, dass jeder Garten ein Prozess ist, den man zeitlich nicht festhalten kann: „In meinen Projekten ist nichts fixiert, alles funktioniert als Prozess und verändert sich jeden Tag“.[15] Evolutionäre Prozesse sind seiner Meinung nach ewig andauernd. Sie basieren auf einer Partnerschaft von Menschen, Pflanzen und Tieren, die von „freier Energie“ angetrieben wird. Mit dieser Energie konstruiert sich die Natur selbst, und das Ziel dieser Evolution ist das Erreichen einer größtmöglichen Komplexität.[16] Le Roys Projekt ist sicherlich eines der radikalsten Beispiele einer dynamischen Landschaftsauffassung. Für das Entwerfen von Landschaften jenseits privater Experimentierräume hat Le Roys Ansatz von „starker Selbstorganisation“ (Zulassen dynamischer Prozesse mit einem Minimum gestalterisch-struktureller Vorgaben)[17] allerdings Grenzen, was die Umsetzungsprobleme seiner Arbeiten im öffentlichen Raum (z. B. Kennedylaan, Heerenveen oder Lewenborg) zeigen. „Schwache Selbstorganisation“ (Zulassen dynamischer Prozesse innerhalb gestalterisch vorgegebener Regeln oder Rahmen)[18] bietet aus meiner Sicht vielversprechendere Möglichkeiten.

Angesichts ihres hybriden Charakters ist Landschaft ein Feld, das von vielen Disziplinen gemeinsam beackert werden sollte, um es fruchtbar zu machen.

Landschaft, *Agency* und Entwerfen. Für unsere zukünftigen Landschaften ist es nun entscheidend, wie wir die hybriden Prozesse orchestrieren. Wie können wir mit *Agencies* der Landschaft entwerfen? Im Folgenden möchte ich mit Transdisziplinarität und Prozessorientierung zwei Aspekte

13 Le Roy 2002 (Anm. 12), S. 12.

14 Ebd.

15 Ebd., S. 34.

16 Ebd.

17 Martin Prominski, „Die Unordnung planen“, in: *Garten + Landschaft* 10 (1996), S. 12–14.

18 Vgl. ebd.

darstellen, die ich für wichtige Ausgangspunkte für diese Art des Landschaftsentwerfens halte.

Transdisziplinarität. Angesichts ihres hybriden Charakters ist Landschaft ein Feld, das von vielen Disziplinen gemeinsam beackert werden sollte, um es fruchtbar zu machen. Bislang wird die Gestaltung der räumlichen Umwelt allerdings von relativ autonomen Fraktionen geleistet, die Zuständigkeiten sind klar verteilt: für Gebäude die Architekten, für Infrastruktur die verschiedenen Ingenieure für Wasser, Verkehr etc., für Tiere und Pflanzen die Ökologen, für Landschaft und Freiräume die Landschaftsarchitekten und Umweltplaner, usw. Diese Trennung manifestiert sich bis heute in jedem Organigramm der Bauverwaltungen oder auch Universitäten. Disziplinäres Wissen ist zwar für die Gestaltung der „neuen" Landschaft unerlässlich, sollte aber dringend durch Transdisziplinarität ergänzt werden.[19]

Diese Notwendigkeit für zukünftiges räumliches Gestalten ist Teil eines breiten kulturellen Diskurses. Beispielsweise wird in der aktuellen Wissenschaftstheorie eine neue Form der Wissensproduktion gefordert, die den komplexen Fragestellungen heutiger Forschung besser gerecht wird als klassische Ansätze. Letztere werden von einer Gruppe um Helga Nowotny, Michael Gibbons und Peter Scott als „Modus 1" der Wissensproduktion bezeichnet, in denen disziplinär organisiert nach universalem, allgemeingültigem Wissen geforscht wird.[20] Da dieser Ansatz für Probleme der Gen-, Klima- oder Gehirnforschung alleine nicht angemessen ist, plädieren die Autoren für zeitgenössische Formen der Wissensproduktion, die sie als „Modus 2" der Wissensproduktion bezeichnen. Dieser ist durch Anerkennung spezifischer Kontexte, Anwendungsorientierung und Transdisziplinarität charakterisiert. Zahlreiche Beispiele für transdisziplinäre Wissensproduktion finden sich im Umweltbereich. So arbeiten bei der Erforschung des „Treibhauseffektes" nicht nur eine Vielzahl verschiedenster Disziplinen zusammen, sondern dieses „Modus 2-Objekt" integriert auch verschiedenste Institutionen – universitäre, privatwirtschaftliche und Forscher aus Umweltorganisationen sitzen in einem Boot.

Die Integration des Wissens ist entscheidend für Transdisziplinarität – durch die Hybridisierung der verschiedenen disziplinären Beiträge entsteht neues Wissen, das nicht einer bestehenden Disziplin zuzuordnen ist. Im Gegensatz dazu bleiben die disziplinären Grenzen bei der Multi- beziehungsweise Pluridisziplinarität bestehen – ein Forschungsthema wird ohne Integration aus den verschiedenen Perspektiven bearbeitet.[21]

Die Autoren betonen einerseits, dass sie Transdisziplinarität nicht als positiven Wert an sich verstehen und warnen davor, sie vorsätzlich, d. h. ohne Kenntnis des spezifischen Problemgegenstandes, zu „konstruieren". Diese auch gerne im universitären Bereich gemachten Versuche sind alle gescheitert – Transdisziplinarität entsteht immer erst als Folge einer spezifischen Problemorientierung. Andererseits bedarf Transdisziplinarität immer disziplinären Wissens, so dass „Modus 1" und „Modus 2" in komplementärem Verhältnis stehen.

19 Vgl. Hille von Seggern et al., *Creating Knowledge. Innovationsstrategien im Entwerfen urbaner Landschaften*. Berlin 2008.

20 Vgl. Helga Nowotny et al., *Re-Thinking Science*. Cambridge 2001; Michael Gibbons et al., *The New Production of Knowledge*. London 1994.

21 Vgl. Helga Nowotny, *Es ist so. Es könnte auch anders sein*. Frankfurt/M. 1999, S. 106.

Transdisciplinarity. Given its hybrid nature, landscape is a field that needs to be plowed with instruments from many disciplines in order to make it fruitful. Nonetheless, the design of the physical environment has so far been effected by relatively autonomous groups whose responsibilities are clearly separated: buildings are made by architects; the infrastructure by specialized engineers for water, transport, etc.; animals and plants are taken care of by the ecologists; while landscape architects and environmental planners design the landscape and open spaces. This separation manifests itself today in every organization chart of the planning departments or universities. Disciplinary knowledge is indeed essential to design the "new" landscape, but should be strongly complemented by interdisciplinarity.[19]

This need for future spatial design is part of a broader cultural discourse. For example, current philosophy of science demands a new form of knowledge production that is better suited for the complex issues of today's research than traditional approaches. A group led by Helga Nowotny, Michael Gibbons and Peter Scott describes the traditional approach as "Mode 1 knowledge production" in which research follows along disciplinary lines towards universal, general knowledge.[20] Since this approach alone is not adequate to meet the demands of genetic, environmental or brain research, the authors argue for contemporary forms of knowledge production, which they call "Mode 2 knowledge production." This is characterized by recognition of specific contexts, orientation to particular applications, and transdisciplinarity. Numerous examples of transdisciplinary knowledge production can be found in environmental research. A case in point, the study of the greenhouse effect brings not only a variety of different disciplines together, but this "Mode 2 object" also integrates a variety of organizations—universities, private research institutions and environmental groups are all sitting in one boat.

The integration of knowledge is crucial for transdisciplinarity—the hybridization of the various disciplinary contributions produces new knowledge that cannot be assigned to any traditional discipline. By contrast, in multidisciplinary research, disciplinary boundaries are not transgressed, for the different perspectives are not integrated.[21]

On the one hand, the authors emphasize that they do not see transdisciplinarity as a positive value in itself and they caution against constructing it without the understanding of the specific research object. All attempts by universities to intentionally produce transdisciplinarity have failed: it only arises as a result of a specific problem orientation. On the other hand, transdis-

19 See Hille von Seggern et al., *Creating Knowledge: Innovation Strategies for Designing Urban Landscapes*. Berlin 2008.

20 See Helga Nowotny et al., *Re-Thinking Science*. Cambridge 2001; Michael Gibbons et al., *The New Production of Knowledge*. London 1994.

21 See Helga Nowotny, *Es ist so: Es könnte auch anders sein*. Frankfurt/M. 1999, p. 106.

2

3

4

2 Das von Rietveld Landscape vorgeschlagene Pfostenraster für die Boschplat in Terschelling sorgt für Anlagerung von Sand und damit zur Erhöhung des Inselniveaus angesichts des durch den Klimawandel steigenden Meeresspiegels.

3 Louis Le Roys Ökokathedrale in Mildam mit ihren aztekisch anmutenden Bauwerken, die er alleine aus Bauschutt aufgerichtet hat.

4 An der Isar in München sichern Treppen kritische Engstellen und machen die Ufer bis an das Wasser nutzbar.

2 The pattern for the post proposed by Rietveld Landscape for the Boschplat in Terschelling causes the accretion of sand and thus increases the levels of the island according to the increasing sea levels caused by climate change.

3 Louis Le Roy's Eco-cathedral in Mildam with Aztec-style buildings, which he has raised only from rubble.

4 At the Isar in Munich stairs safeguard the critical bottlenecks and make the banks up to the water usable.

Bei den ambitionierten Wettbewerben zur Gestaltung der Landschaft ist die Forderung nach transdisziplinärer Zusammensetzung der Entwurfsteams daher inzwischen zur Selbstverständlichkeit geworden. Bei den Wettbewerben zu den Lower Don Lands in Toronto (2007) oder der Müllkippe Fresh Kills in New York (2001) bestanden die Gewinnerteams jeweils aus zehn verschiedenen Disziplinen.

Prozessorientierung. Neben der Transdisziplinarität ist die Prozessorientierung eine wesentliche Voraussetzung für das Orchestrieren der verschiedenen *Agencies* von Landschaft. Hier möchte ich einen Aspekt aufgreifen, der schon bei der Beschreibung der zwei Projekte von Rietveld und Le Roy angedeutet wurde. Entscheidend für die Offenheit gegenüber Prozessen ist die Setzung von gestalterischen Rahmengerüsten, innerhalb derer Raum ist für das Zusammenwirken unvorhersehbarer Prozesse (schwache Selbstorganisation, siehe oben). Das Gegenmodell wäre die Festsetzung aller Entwurfskomponenten zu einem Bild, das so und nicht anders sein kann. Alle einwirkenden, verändernden Prozesse wären dann unerwünscht, denn sie zerstören das vom Entwerfer angedachte Bild. Solche Landschaften sind häufig eindimensional und wenig resilient, denn jede Veränderung muss behoben werden, um den festgesetzten Zustand wiederherzustellen.

Ich möchte dieses Entwerfen von Rahmengerüsten, innerhalb derer Raum ist für unvorhersehbare, dynamische Entwicklungen, an einem Projekt erläutern, das auf den ersten Blick gar nicht entworfen aussieht – die Isar in München. Hier werden dem Fluss durch das Projekt Isar-Plan (2000 bis heute) teils sichtbare, teils unsichtbare Grenzen gesetzt, innerhalb derer morphodynamische Veränderungen möglich sind.[22]

> Das Gegenmodell wäre die Festsetzung aller Entwurfskomponenten zu einem Bild, das so und nicht anders sein kann.

Die Isar ist ein kiesgeprägter, voralpiner Gebirgsfluss mit heftigen, zum Teil plötzlichen Hochwasserereignissen. Das Projektgebiet des so genannten Isar-Plans beginnt vor der eigentlichen Kernstadt und zieht sich bis in dicht bebaute Strukturen. Der Isar-Plan ist ein Gemeinschaftsprojekt der Landeshauptstadt München und des Freistaates Bayern, vertreten durch das Wasserwirtschaftsamt München. Auf einer Strecke von acht Kilometern wurde bzw. wird die Isar zwischen der Wehranlage Großhesselohe und dem Deutschen Museum umgestaltet.

Der Isar-Plan verfolgt in seiner Umsetzung seit 2000 neben ökologischen Aufwertungen auch eine Verbesserung des Hochwasserschutzes und die Qualitätssteigerung für Erholungssuchende. Für den Hochwasserschutz wurde das Mittelwasserbett aufgeweitet und die bestehenden Deiche stabilisiert, indem im Deichkern eine Dichtwand eingezogen wurde. Durch die Aufweitung konnte auf eine Erhöhung der Deiche verzichtet und damit der alte Baumbestand auf den Deichen erhalten werden.

Um der Isar einen Teil ihrer Eigendynamik zurückzugeben, war es zunächst nötig, sie aus ihrem kanalartigen Korsett zu befreien. Das Aufbrechen

22 Vgl. Martin Prominski, Antje Stokman, Daniel Stimberg, Hinnerk Voermanek, Susanne Zeller, *Fluss Raum Entwerfen*. Basel 2011.

ciplinarity requires disciplinary knowledge, so that "Mode 1" and "Mode 2" stand in a complementary relationship.

In ambitious competitions of landscape design, the demand for transdisciplinary teams has therefore become a matter of course. In the competitions of the Lower Don Lands in Toronto (2007) or the Fresh Kills landfill in New York (2001), the winning teams each represented ten different disciplines.

Process orientation. In addition to transdisciplinarity, process orientation is essential for the orchestration of the various agencies of the landscape. Here I would like to pick one issue which was already indicated in the description of the projects by Rietveld and Le Roy. It is decisive to define a framework within which there is room for the interaction of unpredictable processes (weak self-organization, see above). The opposing model is to fix all design components in an image that can only be one way and not otherwise. For the latter model, all processes of change are undesirable because they destroy the image conceived by the designer. Such landscapes are often one-dimensional and not very resilient, because each change must be rectified in order to restore the predetermined condition.

To illustrate the design of frameworks for unpredictable and dynamic developments, I want to discuss a project that at first glance appears not to have been designed at all—the river Isar in Munich. In this case, the Isar-Plan (from 2000 to present) sets visible and invisible boundaries that allow morphodynamic changes to take place.[22]

Dominated by gravel soil, the Isar is a pre-Alpine mountain river with violent, sometimes sudden floods. The project area of the Isar-Plan begins before the actual urban area and reaches up to the densely built fabric. The Isar-Plan is a joint project of the capital city of Munich and the Free State of Bavaria, represented by the water board of Munich. Along the stretch of eight kilometers, between the Großhesselohe weir and the German Museum, the river has been or will be transformed.

Besides purely ecological goals, the implementation of the Isar-Plan is intended to improve flood protection and enhance the quality of the environment for recreational use. For better flood protection, the main channel bed was widened and the existing dikes stabilized by collecting the dike core in a diaphragm wall. Because the main channel bed was broadened, it was not necessary to increase the height of the dikes, and so the old tree population could be preserved.

To give the Isar some of its own momentum back, it was first necessary to free it from its channel-like corset. The breaking and flattening of the trapezoidal profile, fortified with masonry and concrete, allows the river to form its bed through erosion and sedimentation processes. However, the design sets a limit to these processes in the form of a "dormant" embankment. The

22 See Martin Prominski, Antje Stokman, Daniel Stimberg, Hinnerk Voermanek, Susanne Zeller, *River. Space. Design*. Basel 2011.

shape of the river can change until it reaches an embedded wall positioned just under the ground surface, behind which the meadow can continue to be used for recreational purposes.

Thus, long sections of the Isar can change their longitudinal and transverse profiles. Overall, the Isar today has several different types of banks: close to buildings, the concrete embankments are retained or transformed into useable sitting areas (fig. 4). In places where the flood meadows function as playgrounds, the banks are flattened and secured with gravel. The points with embedded structures are described by the Water Authority as developing banks. Here are, depending on the situation in the river, very shallow gravel banks or bluffs. The floodplain has been zoned for different uses (fig. 1). Besides recreation, environmental concerns are also taken into account: for example a special seed mixture featuring wild plants typical of the river is used as bank vegetation. In addition to a fixed "deadwood island" and several gravel islands, a special willow island will also be constructed. After citizen protestations, it was decided that a part of the old bank with its willows should be retained and built as a new island in the widened river bed. The willow island will be a refuge for animals and plants while people can enjoy it from amphitheater-like seating on the opposite bank.

As can be seen in the areas that have already been given a more natural appearance, the expansion of the river bed with flat sloping banks supports the formation of gravel islands and banks. As a result, these sections gain both aesthetic and environmental value. In particular, the gravel banks provide different biotopes for a variety of animal and plant species. Numerous small animals and rare fish species have found new habitats as the gravel banks are rearranged during higher flow conditions. Each flood also brings large amounts of deadwood which is washed up on the banks. The maintenance concept leaves as much of the debris as possible there at the spot: as a disturbance to the water flow and important structural element for the development of rare insect species.

The example of the Isar shows what can be achieved by activating and orchestrating the agencies of landscape. By operating with the natural processes of water erosion and sedimentation, the design team of water engineers, ecologists and landscape architects were able to achieve significant quality improvements as regards ecology, flood protection and recreational use of the river. Such a processual involvement of the agencies is only possible if the designers accept a degree of uncertainty. Since one cannot exactly predict in which direction the dynamic interaction of the hybrid processes will lead, many things are inevitably beyond the control of the designer. This requires humility to which not all designers are accustomed …

Translation Grace Quiroga

und Abflachen des mit Steinen und Beton befestigten trapezförmigen Profils ermöglicht es dem Fluss, sein Bett durch Erosions- und Sedimentationsprozesse wieder selbst zu entwickeln. Diesen Prozessen wird allerdings im Entwurf eine Grenze in Form einer „schlafenden" Sicherung gesetzt. Bis zu diesem knapp unterhalb der Erdoberfläche liegenden und damit unsichtbaren Bauelement kann sich der Flussraum verändern, dahinter können die Wiesen wie bisher zur Erholungszwecken genutzt werden.

Die Isar kann so über weite Abschnitte ihre Lage und die Ausbildung des Längs- und Querprofils selbst entwickeln. Insgesamt hat die Isar heute mehrere Ufertypen: In Bereichen von Bauwerken werden die Sicherungen erhalten oder zu nutzbaren Sitzstufen umgestaltet (Abb. 4). An Stellen, wo die Flutwiesen als Spielwiesen erhalten wurden, sind die Ufer abgeflacht und die neue Sicherung mit Kies überdeckt. An den Stellen mit zurückgelegten „schlafenden" Sicherungen spricht das Wasserwirtschaftsamt von Entwicklungsufern. Hier bilden sich je nach Lage im Flusslauf sehr flache Kiesbänke oder Steilufer. Über Zonierungen wurde die Aue für verschiedene Nutzungen erschlossen (Abb. 1). Neben der Erholung finden auch die ökologischen Ansprüche verstärkt einen Raum, unter anderem wird eine besondere Saatmischung isartypischer Wildkräuter als Uferbewuchs verwendet. Eine Besonderheit neben einer fest gebauten „Totholzinsel" und angelegten Kiesinseln stellt die Weideninsel dar. Die alten Weiden am ehemals befestigten Ufer der Isar wurden trotz der Aufweitung des Flussbettes erhalten, insbesondere nach Willensbekundungen der Bürgerschaft. Sie stehen jetzt auf einer Insel, die ein neuer Nebenarm vom Ufer trennt. Von Treppenstufen gegenüber lässt sich die Insel genießen. Für den Menschen unzugänglich soll sich die Insel zu einem Refugium für Tiere und Pflanzen entwickeln. Wie in den bereits naturnäher gestalteten Bereichen zu beobachten ist, fördert die Aufweitung des Flussbetts mit abgeflachten Uferpartien die Bildung vielfältiger Gewässerstrukturen wie Kiesinseln und Kiesbänke. Dadurch gewinnt dieser Abschnitt nicht nur ästhetisch an Reiz, sondern auch ökologisch an Wert. Insbesondere Kiesbänke bieten unterschiedliche Lebensräume für eine Vielzahl von Tier- und Pflanzenarten. Zahlreiche Kleinlebewesen und rar gewordene Fischarten finden durch Kiesumlagerungen bei höheren Wasserführungen neue Lebensräume. Jedes Hochwasser führt darüber hinaus große Mengen an Totholz mit sich, welches am Isarstrand angeschwemmt wird. Das Pflegekonzept sieht vor, dieses so weit wie möglich an Ort und Stelle zu belassen: als Störelement für den Gewässerlauf und wichtiges Strukturelement für die Entwicklung seltener Insektenarten.

Das Beispiel der Isar macht deutlich, was durch das Aktivieren und Orchestrieren der *Agencies* von Landschaft möglich ist. Das Entwurfsteam aus Wasserbauingenieuren, Ökologen und Landschaftsarchitekten hat die durch das Wasser angetriebenen Prozesse der Erosion und Sedimentation bewusst einbezogen und damit für Ökologie, Hochwasserschutz und Freiraumnutzung deutliche Qualitätssteigerungen erreicht. Ein derartiges prozessorientiertes Einbeziehen der *Agency* erfordert von den Entwerfern die Hinnahme von Ungewissheit. Da nicht exakt vorherzusagen ist, in welche Richtung sich das dynamische Zusammenspiel der hybriden Prozesse entwickelt, laufen viele Dinge jenseits der Kontrolle der Entwerfer. Dieses erfordert eine Bescheidenheit, die für einige Entwerfer noch ungewohnt ist …

1 Landwirtschaftlich genutzte Fläche Agricultural landscape, © National Wildlife Federation International Team

Activating the Global and Regional Landscape

"Margaret: What if you get stuck in the middle of nowhere?
Travis: Ma, I don't think there's a 'nowhere' anymore."[1]

Aktivierung der Globalen und Regionalen Landschaft.

„Margaret: Was ist, wenn du mitten im Nirgendwo stecken bleibst?
Travis: Mama, ich denke nicht, dass es irgendwo noch ein ‚Nirgendwo' gibt."[1]

KATRINA STOLL

Urbanization, with the aid of infrastructure, has redefined our concept of the extents, limits, and territories of space. Historically confined to city commercial centers, urban forms have cut across dimensions, expanding to territories, creating new configurations on global scales. With increasing access to information, centrality is no longer geographically defined, but rather functions through a diverse network of trans-territorial centers. As a result, the scale of urbanism will continue to be reframed as new connections are formed. As Marc Angélil and Cary Siress point out: "The classical model of the city as a unified organism is eclipsed by an entirely different creature, one with organs, but this time without the support of a cohesive body."[2] The support of ecological systems intertwined with human systems can produce this cohesive structure.

The connectivity of the globe has been achieved, both physically and intangibly, through new linkages that strengthen communication and exchange. Saskia Sassen terms these connections "inter-city geographies," which are accountable for "contributing a critical infrastructure for a new global political economy, new cultural spaces and new types of politics."[3] I would add that these new infrastructures contributed also to a new ecology. The forces of globalization cannot be reversed. The human and natural systems have evolved together to form higher degrees of complexity and organization from the hunter-gatherer phase, to agricultural, industrial, and finally post-industrial societies.[4] Unlike any other species, there are no longer any regions of the globe unaffected by human existence, especially when the effects of acid rain on soil biology and carbon dioxide enrichment of the atmosphere on climate systems are taken into account.[5]

The global network of urban space continues to mutate as a result of social and economic shifts that have transformed the built and natural environments. Statistics showing that more than 50 percent of the human population is now living in urban conditions suggest a dichotomy between the urban and rural that is misleading. The urban condition is almost omnipresent. Edward Soja and Miguel Kanai write: "Not only is urbanization increasingly reaching everywhere, everywhere is increasingly reaching into the city, contributing to a major reconfiguration of the social and spatial structures of urbanism and creating the most economically and culturally heterogeneous cities the world has ever known."[6] The transformation of urban space has moved towards the arrangement of indeterminate assemblages in constant flux.

In the United States, the expansion of urban space has been acknowledged by expanding the parameters of cities and labeling them as metropolitan areas that include both rural and urban habitats. The 100 largest metropoli-

1 Tommy Nohilly, *Blood From a Stone*, 2010, Act 3.

2 Marc Angélil, Cary Siress, "City of 'and … and … and'," in: Ilka Ruby, Andreas Ruby (eds.), *Urban Transformations*. Berlin 2008, p. 18.

3 Saskia Sassen, "Why Cities Matter," in: Richard Burdett, Sarah Ichioka (eds.), *Cities: People, Society, Architecture*. Exhib. cat. 10th Venice Architecture Biennale, New York 2006, p. 27.

4 See Zev Naveh, Yohay Carmel, "Landscape Complexity versus Ecosystem Complexity—Implication for Landscape Planning and Management," in: *XII Congresso Nazionale della Società Italiana di Ecologia, Atti 00*. Urbino, September 16–18, 2002, p. 39.

5 See Peter Del Tredici, "Brave New Ecology," in: *Landscape Architecture Magazine* 96 (February 2006), p. 48.

6 Edward Soja, Miguel Kanai, "The Urbanization of the World," in: Ricky Burdett, Deyan Sudjic (eds.), *The Endless City*. London 2007, p. 54.

Die Urbanisierung hat mithilfe der Infrastruktur unser Konzept von räumlichen Ausmaßen und territorialen Gebieten neu definiert. Die urbanen Formen, welche historisch an Handelszentren der Stadt gebunden waren, haben Dimensionen durchschnitten und sich zu Territorien ausgedehnt und somit auf globaler Ebene neue Konfigurationen erzeugt. Durch den zunehmend einfacheren Zugriff auf Information ist Zentralität nicht länger geografisch definiert, sondern funktioniert vielmehr als ein vielfältiges Netzwerk aus gebietsübergreifenden Zentren. Der urbane Maßstab wird folglich durch die Entstehung neuer Verbindungen weiterhin umformuliert werden. Marc Angélil und Cary Siress meinen dazu: „Das klassische Modell der Stadt als ein einheitlicher Organismus wird von einem völlig anderen Wesen in den Hintergrund gedrängt. Dieses hat ebenfalls Organe, wird aber nicht von einem zusammenhängenden Körper gestützt."[2] Durch die Unterstützung von ökologischen Systemen, die mit menschlichen Systemen verflochten sind, kann diese zusammenhängende Struktur erzeugt werden.

Die Vernetzung der Welt wurde, materiell und ideell gleichermaßen, durch neue Verbindungen erreicht, die Kommunikation und Austausch fördern. Saskia Sassen bezeichnet diese Verbindungen als „Intercity-Geografien", welche „zu einer wichtigen Infrastruktur für eine neue globale politische Ökonomie, neue Kulturräume und eine neue Art von Politik beigetragen haben."[3] Ergänzend trugen diese neuen Infrastrukturen auch zu einer neuen Ökologie bei. Die Kräfte der Globalisierung können nicht umgekehrt werden. Menschliche und natürliche Systeme haben sich gemeinsam zu höheren Komplexitäts- und Organisationsgraden entwickelt – vom Zeitalter der Jäger- und-Sammler zu landwirtschaftlichen, industriellen und schließlich postindustriellen Gesellschaften.[4] Es gibt auf der Welt keine Regionen mehr, die von der menschlichen Existenz unbeeinflusst bleiben, vor allem wenn man die Auswirkungen des sauren Regens auf die Bodenbiologie und der Anreicherung von Kohlendioxid in der Atmosphäre auf Klimasysteme in Betracht zieht.[5]

In Folge von sozialen und wirtschaftlichen Veränderungen, welche die gebaute und natürliche Umgebung transformiert haben, mutiert das globale Netzwerk des urbanen Raumes weiterhin. Statistiken, die belegen, dass mehr als 50 Prozent der menschlichen Bevölkerung heute in urbanen Verhältnissen lebt,

1 Tommy Nohilly, *Blood From a Stone*, 2010, 3. Akt.

2 Marc Angélil und Cary Siress, „City of ‚and … and … and'", in: Ilka Ruby, Andreas Ruby, *Urban Transformations*. Berlin 2008, S. 18.

3 Saskia Sassen, „Why Cities Matter", in: Richard Burdett, Sarah Ichioka (Hg.), *Cities: Architecture and Society. Ausst.-Kat. 10th Venice Architecture Biennale*. New York 2006, S. 27.

4 Vgl. Yohay Carmel, Zev Naveh, „Landscape Complexity versus Ecosystem Complexity – Implication for Landscape Planning and Management", in: *XII Congresso Nazionale della Società Italiana di Ecologia, Atti 00*. Urbino, 16.–18. September 2002, S. 39.

5 Vgl. Peter Del Tredici, „Brave New Ecology", in: *Landscape Architecture Magazine* 96 (Februar 2006), S. 48.

deuten eine irreführende Gegensätzlichkeit von urban und ländlich an. Urbane Lebensverhältnisse sind nahezu allgegenwärtig. Edward Soja und Miguel Kanai schreiben: „Die Urbanisierung breitet sich nicht nur zunehmend überall aus, die Ubiquität erreicht auch zunehmend die Stadt, was zu einer bedeutenden Umgestaltung der sozialen und räumlichen Strukturen des Urbanismus führt und die wirtschaftlich und kulturell verschiedenartigsten Städte erzeugt, welche die Welt je gesehen hat."[6] Die Transformation des urbanen Raumes hat sich einer Anordnung von unbestimmten Zusammenfügungen in ständigem Fluss angenähert.

In den Vereinigten Staaten reagierte man auf die Expansion des urbanen Raumes mit einer Ausweitung der Parameter von Städten und bezeichnete diese als Metropolregionen, die ländliche und urbane Lebensräume gleichermaßen einschließen. Die 100 größten Metropolregionen machen zwei Drittel der Bevölkerung der Vereinigten Staaten aus und generieren 74 % des Bruttoinlandsprodukts.[7] In 50 Prozent der Metropolregionen der USA existieren ländliche Gebiete[8], die aus wirtschaftlichen, politischen, kulturellen und ökologischen Gründen zusammengefasst werden. Der Zusammenschluss dieser Gebiete ist menschlichen und ökologischen Systemen zu verdanken, die in der Versorgung der gebauten Umwelt als hilfreiche Kräfte auftreten. Für die Zwecke dieser Arbeit werden größere Metropolregionen und die darüber hinausgehenden Territorien als Regionen bezeichnet, da dies Bereiche von höherer und niedrigerer Bevölkerungsdichte miteinbezieht. Sie machen die Gestaltung der globalen Landschaft aus, welche das zugrunde liegende Medium für die Verbindung dieser Regionen ist.

Die gebaute Umwelt wird von Territorien versorgt, die wesentlich größer sind als eine Region und sie hat die Ausmaße des ländlichen „Hinterlandes" neu definiert. Der Zugang zu Wasserversorgung, Energie, Nahrung und Abfall geht üblicherweise über die traditionellen Grenzen einer Stadt hinaus. Die Stadt Los Angeles, zum Beispiel, bezieht den Großteil ihres Wassers vom 970 Kilometer entfernten Colorado River, während Mexiko City, auf 2.240 Metern gelegen, vom kostspieligen Pumpen von Wasser tausend Meter aufwärts und aus 150 Kilometer Entfernung abhängig ist. Den Rekord stellt Peking mit seinen Plänen auf, Wasser aus dem Flussbecken des Yangtze aus über 1.200 Kilometer Entfernung zu beziehen.[9] Die Kommunikation wird von unter Wasser verlegten Glasfaserkabelsträngen unterstützt, die sich über den Meeresboden ausbreiten, während Energie in Öl- oder Erdgaspipelines politische und

6 Edward Soja, Miguel Kanai, „The Urbanization of the World", in: Ricky Burdett, Deyan Sudjic (Hg.), *The Endless City*. London 2007, S. 54.

7 Vgl. Bruce Katz, „City Centered", in: *Time*, 21.10.2010.

8 Vgl. Derek Douglas, „White House Advisor to Urban Affairs and Urban and Metropolitan Policy Issues", in: *Global Metro Summit*, 8.12.2010.

9 Vgl. Lester R. Brown, *Plan B 3.0: Mobilizing to Save Civilization*. New York 2008, S. 194.

tan areas constitute two-thirds of the population of the United States and generate 74 percent of the gross domestic product.[7] Rural areas exist in 50 percent of the metropolitan areas of the United States and are grouped together for economic, political, cultural, and ecological reasons.[8] Binding these areas together is the performance of human and ecological systems that are instrumental agents in servicing the built environment. For the purposes of this paper I will refer to the larger metropolitan areas and the territories beyond as regions, since this incorporates areas consisting of both higher and lower human population densities. They constitute the composition of the global landscape, which is the underlying medium that connects these regions.

The built environment is serviced by territories far larger than the scale of a region and has redefined the extents of the rural "hinterland." Access to a water supply, energy, food, and waste usually extends beyond the traditional limits of the city. Los Angeles, for example, draws much of its water from the Colorado River 970 kilometers away, while Mexico City, at an altitude of 2,240 meters, depends on the costly pumping of water 1,000 meters up in elevation from 150 kilometers away. Beijing will set the record with plans to draw water from the Yangtze River basin 1,200 kilometers away.[9] Communication is aided by fiber-optic submarine cable strands that stretch across the ocean floor, while energy pipelines of oil and natural gas cross political and geographical boundaries around the globe. New Energy Algeria is currently constructing an undersea cable to export solar energy from the Sahara Desert to Europe. Known as the Desertec Initiative, it aims to supply 15 percent of Europe's electricity by 2050.

The transformation of urban space has moved towards the arrangement of indeterminate assemblages in constant flux.

The global distribution of food has created highly specialized agro-industrial landscapes that have dramatically changed and isolated themselves from surrounding ecological conditions. These fields still depend on photosynthetic conversion, but are greatly subsidized by fossil energy. Heavy chemical inputs have supplanted much of their natural control mechanisms, creating serious environmental impacts on the surrounding and connected landscapes. This includes wildlife and biodiversity, the quality of natural resources, such as soil and water, and human health.[10] The United States exports approximately 80 million tons of grain each year, containing basic plant nutrients of nitrogen, phosphorus, and potassium. The ongoing export of these nutrients will eventually decrease the fertility of the United States' cropland if the nutrients are not replaced.[11] Japan, with limited farmland to

7 See Bruce Katz, "City Centered," in: *Time*, October 21, 2010.

8 See Derek Douglas, "White House Advisor to Urban Affairs and Urban and Metropolitan Policy Issues," in: *Global Metro Summit*, December 8, 2010.

9 See Lester R. Brown, *Plan B 3.0: Mobilizing to Save Civilization*. New York 2008, p. 194.

10 See Zev Naveh, "Ten Major Premises for a Holistic Conception of Multifunctional Landscapes," in: *Landscape and Urban Planning* 57 (2001), p. 281.

11 See Brown 2008 (fn. 9), p. 34.

The global landscape is made up of a field of regions that work together and are influenced by each other through connections humans have established, affecting the political, economic, cultural, and ecological networks. Cities will become "spatial peaks within stretching regional fields."[13] No longer restricted by boundaries such as mountain ranges and oceans, these infrastructural linkages have strengthened the influence of cities and regions, and diminished the significance of nation-states.

geografische Grenzen auf der ganzen Welt überquert. New Energy Algeria verlegt gegenwärtig ein Unterwasserkabel zum Export von Solarenergie aus der Sahara nach Europa. Bekannt als Desertec Initiative, ist das Ziel dieses Unternehmens, bis zum Jahr 2050 15 % der europäischen Stromversorgung zu übernehmen.

Die globale Nahrungsverteilung hat hochspezialisierte industrielle Agrarlandschaften erzeugt, die sich erheblich verändert und von ihren umgebenden ökologischen Bedingungen abgegrenzt haben. Diese Pflanzenfelder sind noch stets von der Fotosynthese abhängig, werden aber von fossiler Energie stark unterstützt. Reichlich chemische Eingaben haben viele ihrer natürlichen Kontrollmechanismen verdrängt, was zu ernsten Konsequenzen für die Umwelt der umgebenden Landschaften führt. Dazu zählen die Tier- und Pflanzenwelt und die Biodiversität, die Qualität der natürlichen Ressourcen wie Boden und Wasser und die menschliche Gesundheit.[10] Die Vereinigten Staaten exportieren jährlich etwa 80 Millionen Tonnen Getreide, die grundlegende pflanzliche Nährstoffe, wie Stickstoff, Phosphor und Kalium, enthalten. Der laufende Export dieser Nährstoffe wird irgendwann die Ergiebigkeit der amerikanischen Ackerflächen verringern, sollten die Nährstoffe nicht ersetzt werden.[11] Japan, das selbst über beschränkte Anbauflächen zur Nahrungsversorgung seiner Bevölkerung verfügt, empfängt Weizen, Korn und Sojabohnen-Importe aus den USA, Australien und Brasilien.[12] Die Ausmaße der Netzwerke, die die gebaute Umwelt versorgen, bewegen sich jenseits der Region zu einem globalen Maßstab.

Jenseits von politischen Grenzen. Regionen sind von Natur aus mit einer bestimmten Kultur und Ökologie verbunden, was durch die Verbindung neuer Infrastrukturen mit anderen Regionen nah und fern fortwährend befruchtet wird. Es wird nicht nur MTV im ländlichen China übertragen, sondern man findet auch Sushi und Essstäbchen in fast jeder Stadt der Vereinigten Staaten, Europas und Australiens. Während die Wirtschaft, Kultur und Politik zunehmend globaler wurden, haben auch unsere regionalen Ökosysteme diesen Prozess mit derselben Komplexität abgebildet. Die berühmte Kopoubohne, welche fünf Zentimeter pro Stunde wachsen kann, wurde im Jahr 1876 zur Dekoration des japanischen Pavillons auf der Ausstellung zur Hundertjahrfeier Philadelphias in die Vereinigten Staaten gebracht. Die Pflanze gedieh und verteilte sich rasch über eine breite Vielfalt von Lebensräumen, was heute oft mit dem Kommentar: „Die Pflanze, die den Süden aß“ versehen wird. Diese Beispiele formellen und informellen Aus-

10 Vgl. Zev Naveh, „Ten Major Premises for a Holistic Conception of Multifunctional Landscapes“, in: *Landscape and Urban Planning* 57 (2001), S. 281.

11 Vgl. Brown 2008 (Anm. 9), S. 34.

12 Vgl. ebd., S. 195.

tausches erzeugen neue und verändern existierende Räume, Ökologien, Wirtschaften, Kulturen und Politiken. Die beschränkte Kapazität des Nationalstaates, diesen globalen Austausch zu beeinflussen, verändert den urbanen Zustand ständig.

Die globale Landschaft setzt sich aus einem Feld von Regionen zusammen, die gemeinsam arbeiten und sich gegenseitig durch menschlich erzeugte Verbindungen beeinflussen, was sich auf politische, wirtschaftliche, kulturelle und ökologische Netzwerke auswirkt. In Städten „türmen sich die [...] räumlichen Aspekte gesellschaftlichen Zusammenlebens [...] auf, um dann – mit zunehmender Entfernung zum Zentrum – wieder abzuflachen."[13] Diese infrastrukturellen Verbindungen, die nicht länger von Begrenzungen wie Gebirgsketten oder Ozeanen eingeschränkt werden, haben den Einfluss der Städte und Regionen gestärkt und die Bedeutung der Nationalstaaten herabgesetzt. Während der Nationalstaat von einer politischen Einheit überlagert und definiert wird, existieren Regionen schon seit einer sehr langen Zeit. Sie bilden eine im Fließen begriffene räumliche Struktur und „es sind nicht nur deren Grenzen, die nicht feststehen, auch die Aktivitäten sind ungebunden."[14]

Wassereinzugsgebiete werden oft als entscheidende ökologische regionale Indikatoren bezeichnet, da alle Lebewesen untrennbar durch deren gemeinsamen Wasserlauf verbunden sind. Obwohl Wassereinzugsgebiete, aufgrund wechselnder Grenzen, ebenso veränderlich sind, gibt es eine generelle Tendenz oder eine Einflusszone, die einem Bereich zugeordnet werden kann. Dort, wo Regionen politische Grenzen überschreiten, existieren vielfältige Vertretungen, um die internationalen Bemühungen zu koordinieren. Der Bodensee, zum Beispiel, liegt auf dem Grenzgebiet zwischen Deutschland, Österreich und der Schweiz und fließt über den Rhein in den Atlantik, nachdem er die Niederlande passiert hat. Der See ist ein bedeutender Trinkwasserlieferant für den Südwesten von Deutschland und ein beliebtes Naherholungsgebiet. Zum Zweck der Regulierung wurde im Jahr 1959 die Internationale Gewässerschutzkommission für den Bodensee (IGKB) von Deutschland, Österreich und der Schweiz gegründet, als ein Beratungsorgan zum Schutz des Ökosystems des Bodensees vor einer weiteren Verschlechterung. Die Hauptverantwortlichkeiten der Kommission liegen in der Beobachtung und Diskussion der Benützung des Sees, der Bestätigung von Verschmutzungsursachen und der Aufstellung von Vorschlägen für koordinierte Schutzmaßnahmen. Die IGKB kann keine Regeln festlegen oder Handlungen zum Schutz des Sees vollziehen, die regionale Regierung ist jedoch durch eine Abmachung dazu verpflich-

13 Ronald Wall, „Global/Local", in: MVRDV (Hg.), *The Regionmaker: RheinRuhrCity*. Ostfildern-Ruit 2002, S. 28.

14 Winy Maas, Penelope Dean, „Interview with Bert van de Knaap", in: ebd., S. 66.

supply food for its population, receives its wheat, corn, and soybean imports from the United States, Australia, and Brazil.[12] The extents of networks that support the built environment move beyond the region to a global scale.

Beyond Political Boundaries. Regions are inherently connected with a particular culture and ecology, which continues to be cross-fertilized as new infrastructures connect with other regions near and far. Not only is MTV broadcast in rural China, but also sushi and mastery of chopsticks can be found in almost any city in the United States, Europe, and Australia. As the economy, culture, and politics have become globalized, so too have our regional ecosystems mirrored this process with every bit of complexity. The famous kudzu vine, which is able to grow at two inches an hour, was brought to the United States to decorate the Japanese Pavilion at the Philadelphia Centennial exposition in 1876. The plant prospered and spread swiftly through a wide variety of habitats, often now being referred to as "the plant that ate the South." These examples of formal and informal exchange produce new, and alter existing, spaces, ecologies, economics, cultures, and politics. The limited capacity of the nation-state to influence these global exchanges continually modifies the urban condition.

The global landscape is made up of a field of regions that work together and are influenced by each other through connections humans have established, affecting the political, economic, cultural, and ecological networks. Cities will become "spatial peaks within stretching regional fields."[13] No longer restricted by boundaries such as mountain ranges and oceans, these infrastructural linkages have strengthened the influence of cities and regions, and diminished the significance of nation-states. Whereas the nation-state is superimposed and defined by a political unit, regions have existed for a very long time. They are fluid spatial structures and "not only fluid in the sense that the boundary is not fixed but also because the activities are not fixed."[14] Watersheds are often attributed as defining ecological regional indicators, as all living things are intrinsically connected by their common watercourse. Though watersheds are also fluid with shifting boundaries, there is a general tendency or zone of influence that can be attributed to an area. Multiple agencies exist to coordinate international efforts where regions cross political boundaries. For example, Lake Constance is situated between the borders of Germany, Austria, and Switzerland and drains into the Atlantic, via the Rhine, after passing through the Netherlands. The lake is a major supplier of drinking water to southwestern Germany and a popular recreation area. In need of regulation, the Internationale Gewässerschutzkommision für den Bodensee (IGKB) was founded in 1959 by Germany, Austria, and Switzerland as an advisory agency to preserve the Lake Constance ecosystem from further degradation. The main responsibilities of the agency are to observe and discuss uses of the lake, confirm any causes of pollution, and produce recommendations for coordinated preventive measures. The IGKB cannot make rules or take action in pro-

12 Ibid., p. 195.

13 Ronald Wall, "Global/Local," in: MVRDV (ed.), *The Regionmaker: RheinRuhrCity*. Ostfildern-Ruit 2002, p. 29.

14 Winy Maas, Penelope Dean, "Interview with Bert van de Knaap," in: ibid., p. 67.

tecting the lake, but by agreement the regional governments are obliged to convert the recommendations of the IGKB into national law.[15]

Regions are connected not only by watersheds, but also by weather patterns that transmit effects of ecological and human activity beyond political boundaries.[16] In 2010 the Eyjafjallajokull volcano in Iceland notably created the longest closure of European airspace since the Second World War. Affecting millions of travelers, more than 100,000 flights were cancelled and it is estimated to have cost the airline industry US $ 1.7 billion.[17] The eruption crossed multiple international boundaries, highlighting the interconnectedness of these regional fields, or the so-called butterfly effect.[18] Giulio A. De Leo and Simon Levin write that "ecosystems are not uniquely identified entities, nor are they defined by sharp boundaries. Instead, they are loosely defined assemblages that exhibit characteristic patterns on a range of scales of time, space, and organization complexity."[19] As systems become more complex, they become less predictable.[20] Thus, we can say that an ecosystem, as defined by Marina Alberti, consists of "hybrid, multi-equilibria, hierarchical systems, in which patterns at higher levels emerge from the local interactions among multiple agents interacting among themselves and with their environments … [They are] prototypical complex adaptive systems, which are open, nonlinear, and highly unpredictable."[21] They cannot be cordoned off by political boundaries, city limits, or a Cartesian grid.

Activating an Underlying Global Landscape. Similar to questioning the dichotomy of the rural and urban, I would like to question the dichotomy between "natural" and "human" systems. Cities and the built environment are often directly influenced and related to the underlying landscapes, such as the geology, topography, rivers and harbors, climate, and of course development over time.[22] Formerly cities were strategically located along rivers for ease of transport and trade or on higher ground for safety and preservation of agricultural land. New infrastructures that have enabled alternative flow patterns have allowed the city to develop independently. Automobiles, truck and train freight, the Internet, and other connective

15 See Marion Hammerl, Udo Gattenlöhner, "Lake Constance/Bodensee," paper presentation from the Lake Basin Management Initiative Regional Workshop for Europe, Central Asia and the Americas, June 18–21, 2003, p. 14. Another example in the United States is the Appalachian Trail. Benton MacKaye devised this ecological corridor as a "transportation project" to connect the eastern part of the country.

16 There are many examples of natural systems crossing political boundaries, caused by both humans and "natural" occurrences. Pollution from forest fires in Indonesia frequently crosses into neighboring countries, notably Singapore and Malaysia. Most recently in October 2010 forest fires in Indonesia's second largest island of Sumatra caused both Singapore and Malaysia to offer help to put out more than 200 fires deliberately set to clear land. The Pollutant Standards Index (PSI) reached up to 108, the worst reading in four years. Schools were closed and respiratory illnesses were noted to be on the rise. See En-Lai Yeoh, "Indonesia Seeks to Stem Haze," in: *Wall Street Journal*, October 22, 2010.

17 See Susan Stellin, "Lessons From the Icelandic Volcano Eruption," in: *The New York Times*, May 2, 2010.

18 The meteorologist Edward Lorenz famously asked: "Does the flap of a butterfly's wings in Brazil set off a tornado in Texas?" The butterfly effect is a metaphor for how one small change can potentially have far-reaching and seemingly unrelated effects.

19 Giulio A. De Leo, Simon Levin, "The Multifaceted Aspects of Ecosystem Integrity," in: http://www.consecol.org/vol1/iss1/art3/ (2007).

20 See Naveh, Carmel 2002 (fn. 4), p. 36.

21 Marina Alberti, *Advances in Urban Ecology: Integrating Humans and Ecological Processes*. New York 2008, p. 258.

22 See Elizabeth Mossop, "Landscapes of Infrastructure," in: Charles Waldheim (ed.), *The Landscape Urbanism Reader*. New York 2006, p. 172.

tet, die Vorschläge der IGKB in ein nationales Gesetz umzuwandeln.[15]

Regionen werden nicht nur durch Wassereinzugsgebiete, sondern auch durch das Wettergeschehen verbunden, das Konsequenzen von ökologischer und menschlicher Aktivität über politische Grenzen hinausträgt.[16] Im Jahr 2010 löste der isländische Vulkan Eyjafjallajokull die längste Schließung des europäischen Luftraums seit dem Zweiten Weltkrieg aus. Mehr als 100.000 Flüge wurden gestrichen, wovon Millionen von Reisenden betroffen waren und was die Flugzeugindustrie schätzungsweise 1,7 Milliarden USD gekostet hat.[17] Der Ausbruch überquerte verschiedenste internationale Grenzen und wies auf die Vernetzung dieser regionalen Felder oder auf den so genannten Schmetterlingseffekt hin.[18] Giulio A. De Leo und Simon Levin schreiben, dass „Ökosysteme keine besonders gekennzeichneten Einheiten sind, noch sind sie durch klare Grenzen definiert. Stattdessen sind sie lose definierte Ansammlungen, die charakteristische Muster auf einer Reihe von Maßstäben der Zeit, des Raumes und der organisatorischen Komplexität ausstellen."[19] Je komplexer ein System wird, desto schwerer lässt es sich vorhersagen.[20] Wir können also sagen, ein Ökosystem, wie es von Marina Alberti definiert wird, besteht aus „hybriden, mehrfach-gleichgewichtigen, hierarchischen Systemen, in denen Muster auf höheren Ebenen aus den lokalen Interaktionen zwischen mehreren Agenten hervorgehen, die untereinander und mit ihren Umgebungen interagieren [… Sie sind] prototypische, komplexe, adaptive Systeme, die offen, nicht-linear und im höchsten Grad unvorhersehbar sind."[21] Sie können nicht mit politischen Grenzen, Stadtgrenzen oder dem kartesianischen Raster abgeriegelt werden.

15 Vgl. Marion Hammerl, Udo Gattenlöhner, „Lake Constance/Bodensee", Vortrag zum Lake Basin Management Initiative Regional Workshop for Europe, Central Asia and the Americas, 18.–21.6.2003, S. 14. Ein anderes Beispiel in den USA ist der Appalachian Trail. Benton MacKaye entwickelte diesen ökologischen Korridor als ein „Transportprojekt" zur Verbindung des östlichen Teils des Landes.

16 Es gibt viele Beispiele von natürlichen Systemen, die politische Grenzen überschreiten, sei es aufgrund von menschlichen oder „natürlichen" Vorfällen. Verschmutzungen aufgrund von Waldbränden in Indonesien wandern regelmäßig in dessen Nachbarländer, insbesondere nach Singapur und Malaysia. Erst kürzlich, im Oktober 2010, führten Waldbrände auf der zweitgrößten indonesischen Insel Sumatra zu Hilfeleistungen aus Singapur und Malaysia. Mehr als 200 Brände, die absichtlich gelegt wurden um Land zu roden, mussten gelöscht werden. Der *Pollutant Standards Index* (PSI) erreichte den Wert von 108, der höchste Stand in vier Jahren. Schulen wurden geschlossen und Erkrankungen der Atemwege zeigten sich im Steigen begriffen. Vgl. En-Lai Yeoh, „Indonesia Seeks to Stem Haze", in: *Wall Street Journal*, 22.10.2010.

17 Vgl. Susan Stellin, „Lessons From the Icelandic Volcano Eruption", in: *The New York Times*, 2.5.2010.

18 Der Meteorologe Edward Lorenz stellte bekanntlich die Frage: „Kann der Flügelschlag eines Schmetterlings in Brasilien einen Wirbelsturm in Texas auslösen?" Der Schmetterlingseffekt ist eine Metapher für die Annahme, dass eine kleine Veränderung weit reichende und scheinbar zusammenhangslose Effekte auslösen kann.

19 Giulio A. De Leo, Simon Levin, „The Multifaceted Aspects of Ecosystem Integrity", in: http://www.consecol.org/vol1/iss1/art3/ (2007).

20 Vgl. Naveh, Carmel 2002 (Anm. 4), S. 36.

Aktivierung einer zugrundeliegenden globalen Landschaft. Auf ähnliche Weise wie die Gegensätzlichkeit von ländlich und urban infrage zu stellen ist, kann man jene von „natürlichen" und „menschlichen" Systemen anzweifeln. Städte und die gebaute Umwelt werden oft direkt von den zugrunde liegenden Landschaften, wie der Geologie, Topografie, Flüssen und Häfen, Klima und natürlich Entwicklung über die Zeit, beeinflusst und auf diese bezogen.[22] Früher wurden Städte strategisch an Flüssen platziert, um Transport und Handel zu erleichtern oder auf Anhöhen aus Gründen der Sicherheit und der Bewahrung von Ackerflächen. Neue Infrastrukturen, die alternative Verteilungsmuster ermöglicht haben, haben die unabhängige Entwicklung der Stadt erlaubt. Autos, Lastwagen und Güterzüge, das Internet und andere Verbindungsnetzwerke haben zur Neudefinierung des gebauten Gefüges beigetragen. Der Versuch, die Natur zu dominieren, ist jedoch zum Scheitern verurteilt, da „natürliche" und „menschliche" Systeme so eng verflochten sind, dass sie nicht länger als unabhängige oder getrennte Kräfte betrachtet werden können. Die Regulierung von Flussläufen ohne Rücksicht auf die Konsequenzen hat ehemalige Trockengebiete in Hochwassergebiete verwandelt; Abholzung und Überweidung haben die Ausdehnung von Wüsten, wie der Sahara und der Wüste Gobi in China, begünstigt. Ökosysteme unterstützen die menschliche Existenz durch die Versorgung mit Diensten, die den Material-, Energie- und Informationsfluss aus der Biosphäre einbeziehen.[23]

Der amerikanische Landschaftsplaner Benton MacKaye war ein Befürworter der regionalen Planung und verstand seinen Ansatz als „liquid planning", der die vielen aktiven Kräfte innerhalb unserer Landschaft umfasste. Dies schloss verschiedenste Bestandteile ein, vom Fruchtwechsel auf Feldern bis zu Autobahnen, Schienen und Häfen, welche als Netzwerke zur Versorgung des Warenflusses operieren. MacKaye verstand diese flüssige Dynamik, „das ‚eiserne Netz' der Zivilisation als einen Kreislauf, dessen Stränge ‚hohl' seien und das ‚vitale, flüssige Element' wie ‚Adern' trügen."[24] Dieser Ansatz ist dabei behilflich, menschliche und ökologische Systeme als zusammenhängende, flüssige Netzwerke zu begreifen, die das Leben unterstützen. Jedoch sind sogar diese Flüsse unsicher und benötigen eine gewisse Offenheit, um Flexibilität und Anpassung zu ermöglichen. Marina Alberti schreibt, diese Funktionen seien „bewegliche Ziele mit verschiedenartigen und unvorhersehbaren Zukunftsaussichten; folglich verursachen Politiken, die feste Ziele erreichen wollen, einen Verlust an Elastizität und

Similar to questioning the dichotomy of the rural and urban, I would like to question the dichotomy between "natural" and "human" systems. Cities and the built environment are often directly influenced and related to the underlying landscapes, such as the geology, topography, rivers and harbors, climate, and of course development over time.[22]

21 Marina Alberti, *Advances in Urban Ecology: Integrating Humans and Ecological Processes*. New York 2008, S. 258.

22 Vgl. Elizabeth Mossop, „Landscapes of Infrastructure", in: Charles Waldheim (Hg.), *The Landscape Urbanism Reader*. New York 2006, S. 172.

23 Vgl. Edward O. Wilson, *The Future of Life*. New York 2002, S. 106.

24 Keller Easterling, *Organization Space: Landscapes, Highways, and Houses in America*. Cambridge, MA 1999, S. 54.

networks have aided in the redefinition of the built fabric. However, the attempt to dominate nature is not feasible as "natural" and "human" systems are so well intertwined that it is no longer possible to perceive these as independent and separate forces. Re-routing rivers without considering consequences has turned previously dry territories into flood land, and deforestation and overgrazing has spread the stretch of deserts such as the Sahara and the Gobi in China. Ecosystems support human existence by providing services that include the flow of materials, energy, and information from the biosphere.[23]

The American planner Benton MacKaye was an advocate for regional planning and conceived of his approach as "liquid planning" that was comprised of the many active forces within our landscape. This included diverse components from rotating crop fields to highways, railroads, and ports, which operate as networks that service the flow of goods. MacKaye described these fluid dynamics by conceiving "the 'iron web' of civilization as a circulatory system, the strands of which were 'hollow' and, like 'veins,' carried the 'vital liquid element.'"[24] It is instrumental to conceiving of human and ecological systems as interrelated fluid networks that support life. Yet, even these flows are uncertain and require a level of openness to allow for flexibility and adaptation. Marina Alberti writes that these functions are "moving targets with multiple and unpredictable futures; thus, policies that aim to achieve fixed goals cause a loss of resilience and are destined to fail."[25] A strategy to enforce support for the fluidity of both human and ecological functions in tandem is needed.

Ecosystems support human existence by providing services that include the flow of materials, energy, and information from the biosphere.[23]

Compounded on these systems are the impacts of human development, which have led to urban sprawl, automobile congestion, pollution, over harvesting of materials, and species endangerment and extinction. These impacts extend beyond the immediate fields of human influence, presenting challenges for the ecosystem. Appropriate systems are needed to adapt to these changes that are occurring at an exponential rate, leading to predictions of shortages in food, water, and energy. Ecologists Zev Naveh and Arthur S. Lieberman have suggested, as a result of the human domination on Earth, the supersystem Total Human Ecosystem (THE) as the highest level of the global ecological hierarchy, or the "co-evolutionary geo-bio-anthropological entity" that is formed between humans and their total environment.[26] This system rises beyond to include not only the physical and geographical space and ecological processes but also the cognitive space.[27] This "Gestalt" system

23 See Edward O. Wilson, *The Future of Life*. New York 2002, p. 106.

24 Keller Easterling, *Organization Space: Landscapes, Highways, and Houses in America*. Cambridge, MA 1999, p. 54.

25 Alberti 2008 (fn. 21), p. 261.

26 See Naveh, Carmel 2002 (fn. 4), p. 42.

sind zum Scheitern verurteilt."[25] Was benötigt wird, ist eine Strategie, um die Flüssigkeit von menschlichen und ökologischen Funktionen gleichermaßen und im Zusammenhang zu verstärken.

Vermischt mit diesen Systemen sind die Auswirkungen der menschlichen Entwicklung, die zu Zersiedelung, Stau, Verschmutzung, Überproduktion von Materialien und der Gefährdung und Auslöschung von Arten geführt haben. Diese Auswirkungen entziehen sich dem unmittelbaren Einflussbereich des Menschen und stellen somit eine Herausforderung für Ökosysteme dar. Um sich an diese Veränderungen anzupassen, die im exponentiellen Maß auftreten und zu einem Mangel an Nahrung, Wasser und Energie führen können, sind geeignete Systeme nötig.

Die Ökologen Zev Naveh und Arthur S. Lieberman haben als Folge der Vorherrschaft des Menschen auf der Erde das Supersystem Total Human Ecosystem (THE) als die höchste Ebene auf der globalen ökologischen Hierarchie – die „koevolutionäre geo-bio-anthropologische Einheit",[26] die sich zwischen den Menschen und ihrer gesamten Umwelt bildet – vorgeschlagen. Dieses System entsteht abseits, um nicht nur den physischen und geografischen Raum und ökologische Prozesse einzuschließen, sondern auch den kognitiven Raum.[27] Landschaften sind in diesem „Gestalt"-System mehr als die Summe ihrer Teile, da „alle ihre Teile durch den allgemeinen Zustand des Ganzen miteinander in Beziehung stehen".[28] Die „Wälder, Weide- und Buschlandschaften, ihre Sumpfgebiete und Flüsse, ihre landwirtschaftlichen Felder, ihre Wohn- und Industriegebiete, ihre Straßen, Verkehrslinien und Stromleitungen, und deren Geschichte tragen zu diesem wahrhaft ganzheitlichen Gestaltcharakter der Landschaft bei. Diese Elemente umfassen ihre verschiedenen bio- und humanökologischen, sozialen, wirtschaftlichen, psychologischen, spirituellen, ästhetischen und funktionalen Aspekte. In den Landschaften erfahren und benutzen wir diese als konkrete Ganzheit."[29]

Durch die Verknüpfung dieser zwei komplexen Systeme als nicht-statische Einheiten, konzipiert man diese als ständigen Transformationsprozess, der Materialien, Energie, Information und Abfall in den Regionen verarbeitet und verteilt.[30] Der Einsatz von Rohstoffen und Recyclingmaterialien in Nahrung, Waren oder Energie muss auch dem Abfall und dessen Verbreitung, Umwandlung oder Lagerung Beachtung schenken. Pierre

25 Alberti 2008 (Anm. 21), S. 261.

26 Vgl. Naveh, Carmel 2002 (Anm. 4), S. 42.

27 Ebd.

28 Naveh 2001 (Anm. 10), S. 273.

29 Ebd.

30 Vgl. Brad Allenby, „The Autonomic City", in: http://www.greenbiz.com/blog/2005/12/31/autonomic-city (31.12.2005). Vgl. auch das Earth Systems Management (ESM), ein Ansatz zur Überwachung und Organisation von Ökosystemen und deren innewohnender Unsicherheit.

Bélanger schreibt treffend: „Die urbane regionale Landschaft sollte, einfach gesagt, als Infrastruktur verstanden werden."[31] Wassereinzugsgebiete sind grundlegende Systeme, die in die Planung von „Straßennetzen, Kanalisation und Wohnsiedlungen" miteinbezogen werden müssen; das Gleiche gilt für Abfalleinzugsgebiete und „Mülldeponien, Bodenflächen mit biologischem Abbau von Schadstoffen, Abstell- und Lagerplätze und Sortiereinrichtungen".[32] Eine globale Aktivierung des THE muss auf der Ebene der Region überwacht und angeleitet werden.

Aktivierung regionaler Felder. Im Jahr 1968 schrieb Garrett Hardin einen Aufsatz mit dem Titel „The Tragedy of the Commons", in dem er Probleme ansprach, die nicht durch die Technik, sondern durch verantwortungsbewusste Regierungsführung gelöst werden können. Er machte darauf aufmerksam, dass die rationale Verfolgung eigener Interessen zum kollektiven Ruin führe.[33] Viele der heutigen Herausforderungen – die ökologische Unausgeglichenheit aufgrund des sich ausdehnenden bebauten Raumes, Überforstung, Überfischung und die Knappheit an Wasser, Öl und Materialien, wie Blei, Zinn und Kupfer – müssen durch verantwortungsbewusste Regierungsführung gelöst werden. Als Antwort auf die globalen infrastrukturellen Netzwerke und den weltweiten Austausch ist eine vernetzte Regierungsführung nötig, die länderübergreifende und vielseitige regionale Räume erzeugt. Da Information, Transport, Energie, Materialien und Finanzen zunehmend alle urbanisierten Systeme vernetzen, weiten sich noch nie da gewesene Räume über traditionelle politische und geografische Grenzen aus. Eine vernetzte Regierungsführung folgt den Verbindungen, die Wirtschaft, Kultur und Ökologie erzeugt haben und beruht auf der Verteilung von Information durch mehrere Akteure. Das führt zu einer raschen Durchführung von Handlung und der Verwendung von existierenden Institutionen zur Nutzbarmachung von Fachkenntnis, Wissen und gesetzgebender Gewalt. Zur Unterstützung der menschlichen Existenz könnten diese vereinten Kräfte die Bildung, Anwendung und Verteilung von Infrastruktur-Management-Systemen beeinflussen.

Als Gestalter muss der Architekt eine integrierte Rolle spielen und neue langfristige Methoden von anhaltender Verbindlichkeit konstruieren. Architekten müssen ständig auf sich wandelnde und anpassende Systeme reagieren und diese neu bewerten und Projekte nicht länger mit einem Anfangs- und Enddatum versehen. Die unglaubliche Komplexität dieser Systeme muss anerkannt und innerhalb ihres Kontexts behan-

31 Pierre Bélanger, „Landscape as Infrastructure", in: *Landscape Journal* 28 (2009), S. 91.

32 Ebd.

33 Vgl. Garrett Hardin, „The Tragedy of the Commons", in: *Science* V, 162 (13.12.1968), S. 1243–1248.

identifies landscape as more than the sum of its parts because "all their parts are related to each other by the general state of the whole."[28] A regional landscape's "forests, grass- and shrublands, its wetlands and rivers, its agricultural fields, its residential and industrial areas, its roads, traffic- and power-lines, and their history contribute to this truly holistic Gestalt character of the landscape. These elements comprise its various biological- and human-ecological, social, economic, psychological, spiritual, aesthetic and functional aspects. We experience these and use these in the landscapes as concrete wholes."[29]

Coupling these two complex systems as non-static entities, they are conceived in constant transformation, processing and distributing materials, energy, information, and waste across regions.[30] The input of raw and recycled materials into food, goods, or energy must equally consider the waste and its distribution, transformation, or storage. Pierre Bélanger aptly writes: "Put simply, the urban-regional landscape should be conceived as infrastructure."[31] Watersheds are essential systems to be taken into consideration for the planning of "highway networks, sewage systems, and subdivisions" and similarly waste sheds for "landfills, landfarms, laydown and storage areas, and sorting facilities."[32] A global activation of the THE needs to be monitored and guided at the scale of the region.

Activating Regional Fields. In 1968, Garrett Hardin wrote an essay titled "The Tragedy of the Commons," addressing problems that cannot be solved by engineering, but by good governance. He proposed that a rational pursuit of individual self-interest leads to collective ruin.[33] Many of the challenges faced today, including ecological imbalance from expanding built space, overforesting, overfishing, and shortages of water, oil, and materials such as lead, tin, and copper need to be solved with good governance. In response to these global infrastructure networks and exchanges, networked governance is needed to produce trans-national and multilateral regional spaces. Unprecedented spaces extend beyond traditional political borders and geographical boundaries as information, transportation, energy, materials, and finance increasingly interconnect each urbanized system. Following the linkages that economics, culture, and ecology have established, networked governance relies on distributed intelligence with multiple actors leading to a rapid delivery of action and utilizing existing institutions to harness expertise, knowledge, and legislative power. This combined effort could influence the formation, implementation, and distribution of infrastructural management systems to support human existence.

As designer, the architect must play an integrated role, constructing new long-term methods of sustained engagement. No longer assigning

27 Ibid.

28 Naveh 2001 (fn. 10), p. 273.

29 Ibid.

30 See Brad Allenby, "The Autonomic City," in: http://www.greenbiz.com/blog/2005/12/31/autonomic-city (December 31, 2005). Also see Earth Systems Management (ESM), a monitoring and management approach to ecosystems and their inherent uncertainty.

31 Pierre Bélanger, "Landscape as Infrastructure," in: *Landscape Journal* 28 (2009), p. 91.

32 Ibid.

33 See Garrett Hardin, "The Tragedy of the Commons," in: *Science V* 162 (December 13, 1968), pp. 1243–1248.

projects with a start and end date, architects must continually respond to, and reevaluate, transforming and adaptive systems. The incredible complexity of these systems needs to be acknowledged and treated within its context in order to produce appropriate interventions. This may require the re-zoning of land in response to the stresses of ecological and, for example, economic or social networks. It also demands attention beyond the typical political boundaries established, but to examine the larger networks that feed into and leave the given region. This leads to a design based on anticipation and scenario-planning for long-term transformation rather than fixed results.

Sustainability is often packaged in independent products, such as singular buildings, technological improvements, or energy conservation or generation methods that can be fed back into the urban grid. Though these improvements are important and necessary, governance needs also to be applied towards the larger scale of a region. A multi-scaled space with distributed intelligence and networked by varying actors is needed to develop these regional fields that can coordinate with the global landscape. It will form new spaces in the built environment through carrying the flows of exchange, allocating stocks, transforming processes, and providing living, industrial, and commercial spaces. An exchange of population, information, material, and capital flows, while the distribution of food, energy, and water become valuable stocks to sustain population settlements.

At this multiregional scale, a looped system of composite infrastructures, combined with the THE, produces an extensive network. A scalable system should be designed to reactivate regional fields by providing for social demand flows, managing circulation of resources, improving energy and water efficiency, transforming waste, managing spatial reserves, and increasing the resilience of the urban metabolism. Great opportunities exist to benefit from built density, where economies of scale reduce net resource demands and improve the efficiency of buildings and transport systems; this is accomplished through decreasing the travel distance of resources, such as energy, water, and waste flows, and managing distribution regionally.

Located along this macro space of exchange, a series of nodes and switches process stocks and flows of the network. These nodes and switches are transit stations and distribution points that are connected to fields that filter waste, clean water, and produce agriculture. The nodes would appropriately form living, industrial, and commercial space, linking living units with public space, retail, and regions further away. At any given point, a cross section will reveal multiple intersecting regions, each forming their own locale. Thus, simultaneously occupying both macro and micro spaces. The regional fields have the potential to spatialize these newly formed geographies of built space that extend across the global landscape.

The networked effects of globalized space have made previous definitions of city, rural, and hinterland spaces obsolete. Rather, fields should be reconfigured as regions with equal attention to human and ecological systems. These regions overlap and interact with each other and the underlying global landscape that interconnects the larger network of global space.

delt werden, um geeignete Interventionen hervorzubringen. Dies bedarf möglicherweise einer Neuaufteilung der Landzonen als Maßnahme gegen die Belastung der ökologischen und, zum Beispiel, ökonomischen und sozialen Netzwerke. Es verlangt auch Aufmerksamkeit über die typischen politischen Grenzen hinaus, also die Untersuchung von größeren Netzwerken, die in die gegebene Region einleiten und diese verlassen. Daraus entsteht ein Entwurfsansatz, der auf der Vorwegnahme und Planung von Szenarien beruht und langfristige Transformationen über vorgefasste Ergebnisse stellt.

Die Nachhaltigkeit wird oft in unabhängige Produkte verpackt, beispielsweise einzelne Gebäude, technologische Fortschritte oder Energieeinsparungs- oder Erzeugungsmethoden, die ins urbane Netz rückgespeist werden können. Diese Fortschritte sind wichtig und notwendig, die Regierung muss jedoch auch im größeren Maßstab einer Region Anwendung finden. Um diese regionalen Felder, die mit der globalen Landschaft gut zusammenarbeiten können, zu entwickeln, ist ein mehrfach gestaffelter Raum mit verteilter Information nötig, der von verschiedenen Akteuren vernetzt wird. Innerhalb der gebauten Umwelt werden sich neue Räume bilden, die auf dem Fluss von Austausch, der Verteilung von Vorräten, Umwandlungsprozessen und der Bereitstellung von lebendigen, industriellen und kommerziellen Räumen beruhen. Bevölkerung, Information, Materialien und Kapitalflüsse werden ausgetauscht, während die Verteilung von Nahrung, Energie und Wasser zu einem wertvollen Vorrat für die Aufrechterhaltung von Ansiedelungen wird.

Auf dieser multiregionalen Ebene erzeugt eine Schleife zusammengesetzter Infrastrukturen – kombiniert mit dem THE – ein ausgedehntes Netzwerk. Um regionale Felder zu reaktivieren, muss ein anpassbares System entworfen werden, das den Fluss sozialer Nachfrage zur Verfügung stellt, die Zirkulation von Ressourcen leitet, die Energie- und Wassereffizienz verbessert, Abfall umwandelt, räumliche Ressourcen verwaltet und die Belastbarkeit des urbanen Stoffwechsels erhöht. Dort wo Größenvorteile die Netto-Nachfrage nach Ressourcen reduzieren und die Effizienz von Gebäuden und Transportsystemen verbessern, finden sich große Chancen von der gebauten Dichte zu profitieren; durch die Reduzierung des Transportweges von Ressourcen, wie Energie, Wasser und Müll, und deren regionaler Verteilung wird das erreicht.

In diesem Makro-Raum des Austausches verarbeitet eine Abfolge von Knoten und Schaltern die Vorräte und Flüsse des Netzwerks. Diese Knoten und Schalter sind Durchfahrtsstationen und Verteilungspunkte, die mit Feldern verbunden sind, welche Abfälle filtern, Wasser reinigen und Landwirtschaft betreiben. Die Knoten bilden idealerweise lebendige, industrielle und kommerzielle Räume, die lebhafte Einheiten mit dem öffentlichen Raum, Einzelhandel und weiter entfernten Regionen verbinden. An jedem gegebenen Punkt wird ein

Querschnitt mehrere sich überschneidende Regionen zum Vorschein bringen, von denen jede ihre eigene Örtlichkeit bildet und somit gleichzeitig Makro- und Mikro-Räume gleichermaßen einnimmt. Die regionalen Felder verfügen über das Potenzial, diese neu geformten Geografien gebauten Raumes, die sich über die globale Landschaft ausbreiten, zu verräumlichen.

Die vernetzten Auswirkungen des globalisierten Raumes haben frühere Definitionen von Stadt, ländlich und Hinterland überholt. Vielmehr sollten Felder zu Regionen umgestaltet werden, die auf menschliche und ökologische Systeme gleichermaßen Rücksicht nehmen. Diese Regionen greifen aufeinander über und interagieren miteinander und mit der zugrunde liegenden globalen Landschaft, die das größere Netzwerk des globalen Raumes in Verbindung setzt.

Übersetzung Claudia Wrumnig

Uneven Topographies

1 http://chevronthinkswerestupid.org

The Yes Men

Rainforest Action Network/Amazon Watch/ "We Agree"/Chevron Intervention

The unstable matrix of relationships that expresses itself as "nature" is in large part held together by agreed-upon linguistic structures and visual forms, many of which are constructed explicitly to abet commercial interests.

The Yes Men. Aktionsnetzwerk Regenwald/Amazonas-Wache/„Wir stimmen zu"/Chevron Intervention. Die instabile Beziehungsmatrix, welche sich selbst als „Natur" ausdrückt, wird in großen Teilen von vereinbarten linguistischen Strukturen und visuellen Ausprägungen zusammen gehalten, von denen jedoch viele ausdrücklich zur Begünstigung geschäftlicher Interessen geschaffen wurden.

JEFFREY KASTNER

It's in this terrain of language and image that the Yes Men deploy their culture jamming scenarios, creating elaborate media hoaxes whose targets typically consist of international businesses, politicians, and entities like the World Trade Organization. (The latter provided the basis of one of their first notable interventions, a fake website for the institution—gatt.org—with links to policy documents featuring titles like "Is petroleum useful, essential, or somewhere in-between? Ask the American Petroleum Institute" and "WTO Announces Formalized Slavery Market For Africa.")

The performance-cum-activist group, led by Jacques Sevrin and Igor Vamos (under the aliases Andy Bichlbaum and Mike Bonanno) and including hundreds of other actors and performers, has in a number of cases focused on the ecological effects of global industry on local populations. One of their most famous interventions was the hoax perpetrated in 2004, on the 20th anniversary of the Bhopal disaster, when Bichelbaum, impersonating a Dow Chemical spokesman, managed to get himself interviewed on the BBC and announced that the company—which had long fought the lawsuits brought against it for what is widely considered the most lethal industrial accident in history, when a gas leak from the then-Union Carbide Plant in the Indian state of Madhya Pradesh killed nearly 4,000 people—had changed its position and agreed to compensate the local population. And their most recent project, carried out in the autumn of 2010, similarly took on a corporate giant with a troubled ecological history, in this case Chevron and its operations between 1964 and 1990 in the Amazonian rainforest of Ecuador (a situation that is also the subject of the current film *Crude*, whose director Joe Berlinger has been sued by Chevron in an effort to suppress the 600+ hours of footage he shot in South America).

Having learned of the oil company's plans for a $50 million advertising campaign designed to "greenwash" their questionable reputation, the Yes Men worked with other environmental groups to produce a shadow campaign that aped exactly the form of the real campaign. However, instead of the empty, anodyne sentiments to which the firms leaders announced their "agreement" ("Oil Companies Should Get Real") the group substituted alternative images and "improved" slogans such as "Oil Companies Should Clean Up Their Messes" and "Oil Companies Should End the Wars They Started." The highly sophisticated propaganda, inserted into the media stream ahead of the actual Chevron campaign, effectively blunted the expensive message of the oil giant's public relations machine, putting it on the defen-

The performance-cum-activist group, led by Jacques Sevrin and Igor Vamos (under the aliases Andy Bichlbaum and Mike Bonanno) and including hundreds of other actors and performers, has in a number of cases focused on the ecological effects of global industry on local populations.

Auf diesem Terrain der Sprache und des Bildes positionieren die Yes Men ihre Szenarien des *Culture Jammings* und erzeugen so ausgeklügelte mediale Falschmeldungen, mit denen sie üblicherweise auf internationale Firmen, Politiker und Verbände wie die Welthandelsorganisation zielen. (Letztere schuf die Basis für eine ihrer ersten bemerkenswerten Interventionen, eine gefälschte Webseite für diese Institution [gatt.org] mit Links zu Richtlinienpapieren, die Titel, wie „Ist Erdöl nützlich, essenziell oder irgendwas dazwischen? Fragen Sie das American Petroleum Institute" und „WHO gibt die formalen Regeln des Sklavenmarktes für Afrika bekannt" trugen.)

Die Performance- und Aktivistengruppe, die von Jacques Sevrin und Igor Vamos (unter den Pseudonymen Andy Bichlbaum und Mike Bonanno) geführt wird und hunderte andere Akteure und Künstler umfasst, hat sich in mehreren Fällen auf ökologische Beeinträchtigungen lokaler Bevölkerungsgruppen konzentriert, welche durch die globalisierte Industrie ausgelöst wurden. Einer ihrer bekanntesten Interventionen war die Falschmeldung aus dem Jahr 2004 bezüglich des zwanzigsten Jahrestages der Katastrophe von Bhopal. Bichlbaum, der sich als Sprecher von Dow Chemicals ausgab, gelang es in einem BBC-Interview zu verkünden, dass die Firma – welche lange gegen die Klagen aufgrund des wohl schlimmsten Industrieunfalls in der Geschichte angekämpft hatten, der durch ein Gasleck in der damaligen Union Carbide Fabrikanlage im indischen Bundesstaat Madhya Pradesh verursacht wurde und fast 4.000 Menschen tötete – ihre Meinung geändert habe und Entschädigungszahlungen an die lokale Bevölkerung befürworten würde.

Ihr jüngstes im Herbst 2010 ausgeführtes Projekt nahm es auf ähnliche Weise mit einem Riesenkonzern mit einer konfliktreichen ökologischen Geschichte auf, der in diesem Fall Chevron hieß. Das Projekt bezog sich auf die Tätigkeiten des Konzerns zwischen 1964 und 1990 im amazonischen Regenwald von Ecuador (dies wurde auch im aktuellen Film *Crude* thematisiert, dessen Regisseur Joe Berlinger von Chevron verklagt wurde, um die mehr als 600 Stunden Filmmaterial, die er in Südamerika aufgenommen hatte, geheim zu halten.)

Da sie von den Plänen des Ölkonzerns gehört hatten, mit einer 50 Millionen Dollar schweren Werbekampagne dessen fragwürdigen Ruf durch *greenwashing* zu verbessern, arbeiteten die Yes Men mit anderen Umweltorganisationen zusammen, um eine Scheinkampagne zu produzieren, welche exakt die Form der echten Kampagne nachahmte. Statt der leeren, neutralen Gefühle, mit denen die Firmenchefs ihr „Übereinkommen" verkündeten („Ölkonzerne müssen auf dem Boden bleiben"), setzte die Gruppe jedoch alternative Bilder ein und „verbesserte" die Slogans zu „Ölkonzerne sollten ihre Verschmutzungen selbst aufräumen" und „Ölkonzerne sollten die Kriege beenden, die sie begonnen haben." Diese raffinierte Meinungsmache, die vor der Chevron-eigenen Kampagne in

die Medienwelt geschleust wurde, dämpfte erfolgreich die kostspielige Botschaft der PR-Maschine des Ölgiganten, was diesen in die Defensive drängte und damit genau das Gegenteil der ursprünglichen Intention erzeugte. Wie die besten ihrer Arbeiten hat auch die Chevron Parodie von Yes Men das Potenzial von Agitprop vorgeführt, sich innerhalb der konventionellen Medienlandschaft einzubinden anstatt in Opposition zu agieren.

Übersetzung Claudia Wrumnig

sive and producing precisely the opposite effect that was intended. Like the best of their work, the Yes Men's Chevron spoof demonstrated the potential of agitprop inserted into, rather than opposed against, the conventional media landscape.

1 American Museum of Natural History (AMNH), Hall of Biodiversity, © Dom Dada

The Economics of Ecosystems and Biodiversity

When the iconic architect Frank Lloyd Wright said "study nature, love nature, stay close to nature. It will never fail you,"[1] he had no idea that in the first decade of the new millennium a major study would take place to bring the natural sphere and economics closer together in order to show not just the value of what our natural environment provides us, but also the cost for our societies, if we continue to fail it.

Die Ökonomie von Ökosystemen und Biodiversität. „Studiere die Natur, liebe die Natur, suche die Nähe der Natur. Sie wird dich nie im Stich lassen."[1] Als der berühmte amerikanische Architekt Frank Lloyd Wright diesen Ausspruch tat, hätte er sich wohl nicht träumen lassen, dass in der ersten Dekade des neuen Jahrtausends eine umfassende Studie durchgeführt werden würde mit dem Ziel, die Kluft zwischen natürlicher Sphäre und Ökonomie zu verringern, und dass es in dieser Studie nicht nur darum gehen würde, den Wert unserer natürlichen Umwelt aufzuzeigen, sondern auch die auf uns zukommenden Kosten, wenn wir unsere Hilfe versagen.

PAVAN SUKHDEV

This global study *The Economics of Ecosystems and Biodiversity* (TEEB) was initiated by the European Commission and Germany; moreover, this first phase of the TEEB initiative highlighted important issues that had not hitherto occupied "center-stage" in global political discourse, such as the correlation between biodiversity/ecosystem losses and impacts of climate change, links with poverty, as well as the importance of openly recognizing the role of ethics in our treatment of risks and uncertainty. The interim report of TEEB I also highlighted examples of efforts to achieve "win-win" solutions for biodiversity conservation and economic growth.

However, at the *9th Conference of the Parties to the Convention on Biological Diversity* (CBD COP9) in Bonn, Germany, delegates pointed out that scientific challenges still remain to be addressed. They stressed the need for further input from the scientific community to elaborate the valuation framework and methodologies used in TEEB I and to focus on engaging end-users of this work: namely, policymakers, business executives, consumers and local communities.

The second phase of TEEB, which commenced in 2009, responds to these concerns with a focus on improving understanding of the economic costs of biodiversity loss and ecosystem degradation and on communicating this understanding to key stakeholders. Our ongoing study Economics of Ecosystems and Biodiversity (TEEB) involves hundreds of experts from around the world: policymakers, scientists, economists, business people, all united in illustrating why it is not only good sense, but good economics to recognize the flows from nature, to demonstrate their economic value and to share the benefits of conservation with local communities. The study is comprised of a suit of reports aimed at decision makers from different stakeholder audiences: national policy, business and local and regional contexts. In addition a website and video tools to help convey the value of nature to citizens and consumers were also created.

An ecosystem is a dynamic, complex of plant, animal and micro-organism communities and their non-living environment interacting as a functional unit. Examples of ecosystems include deserts, coral reefs, wetlands, rainforests, boreal forests, grasslands, urban parks and cultivated farmlands.

An ecosystem is a dynamic, complex of plant, animal and micro-organism communities and their non-living environment interacting as a functional unit. Examples of ecosystems include deserts, coral reefs, wetlands, rainforests, boreal forests, grasslands, urban parks and cultivated farmlands. Ecosystems can be relatively undisturbed by people, such as virgin rainforests, or can be modified by human activity. Ecosystem services are the

Initiiert wurde diese globale Studie mit dem Titel *Die Ökonomie von Ökosystemen und Biodiversität* [*The Economics of Ecosystems and Biodiversity* – TEEB] von der Europäischen Kommission sowie von der Bundesrepublik Deutschland. In der ersten Phase der Initiative wurden wichtige Fragen und Probleme behandelt, die bis dato im globalen politischen Diskurs keine zentrale Rolle gespielt hatten. Dazu zählten u. a. die Wechselbeziehungen zwischen dem Verlust von Ökosystemen/Biodiversität und den Auswirkungen des Klimawandels, Verkettungen mit dem Problem der Armut sowie die Notwendigkeit, die Rolle der Ethik im Umgang mit Risiken und Unsicherheiten klar anzuerkennen. Der TEEB I-Zwischenbericht zeigte auch Beispiele für Versuche auf, Win-Win-Lösungen für den Schutz der Biodiversität einerseits und das wirtschaftliche Wachstum andererseits zu erzielen.

Dennoch wiesen auf der *9. Vertragsstaatenkonferenz des Übereinkommens über die biologische Vielfalt* in Bonn [*9th Conference of the Parties to the Convention on Biological Diversity* – CBD COP9] einige deutsche Delegierte darauf hin, dass eine Reihe von wissenschaftlichen Fragen bislang noch nicht berücksichtigt worden war. Sie hoben die Notwendigkeit hervor, die in TEEB I verwendeten Bewertungssysteme und Methoden mithilfe der Wissenschaft noch weiter auszuarbeiten und die Endnutzer des Projekts stärker einzubinden: politische Entscheidungsträger, Führungskräfte aus der Wirtschaft, Konsumenten und lokale Gemeinschaften.

Die zweite TEEB-Phase, die im Jahr 2009 begann, trägt diesen Bedenken Rechnung und legt den Schwerpunkt auf ein verbessertes Verständnis der ökonomischen Kosten, die entstehen, wenn Biodiversität verlorengeht und Ökosysteme zerstört werden. Gleichzeitig gibt es Bemühungen, diese Erkenntnisse an wichtige Interessengruppen zu vermitteln. In die TEEB-Studie sind zurzeit hunderte Experten aus der ganzen Welt eingebunden: politische Entscheidungsträger, Wissenschaftler, Nationalökonomen, Vertreter der Wirtschaft – sie alle verbindet das Bestreben aufzuzeigen, warum es nicht nur vernünftig, sondern auch wirtschaftlich sinnvoll ist, die Leistungen der Natur anzuerkennen, ihren ökonomischen Wert darzulegen und die Vorteile des Naturschutzes mit lokalen Gemeinschaften zu teilen. Die Studie besteht aus einer Reihe von Berichten, die sich an die Entscheidungsträger unterschiedlicher Interessengruppen in der nationalen Politik, im Bereich der Wirtschaft sowie in lokalen und regionalen Zusammenhängen wenden. Auch eine Website und diverse Videotools wurden geschaffen, um den Bürgern und Konsumenten den Wert der Natur näher zu bringen.

Ein Ökosystem ist ein komplexes dynamisches Gefüge, in dem Pflanzen-, Tier- und Mikroorganismengemeinschaften sowie die unbelebte Umwelt interagieren und eine funktionale

1 As quoted in Carla Lind, *The Wright Style*. New York 1992, p. 4.

1 Zitiert nach Carla Lind, *The Wright Style*. New York 1992, S. 4.

Einheit bilden. Beispiele für verschiedene Ökosysteme sind: Wüsten, Korallenriffe, Feuchtgebiete, Regenwälder, boreale Nadelwälder, Grasland, städtische Parks und landwirtschaftlich genutzte Ackerflächen. Es gibt Ökosysteme, die relativ ungestört von menschlichen Einflüssen bestehen (z. B. unberührte Regenwälder), und solche, die durch humane Aktivitäten verändert werden. Ökosystemleistungen sind der Nutzen, den Menschen aus Ökosystemen ziehen. Dazu zählen: Nahrung, Süßwasser, Holz, Regulierung des Klimas, Schutz vor natürlichen Gefahren, Erosionsschutz, pharmazeutische Substanzen und Erholung. Unter Biodiversität versteht man die Quantität und Variabilität lebender Organismen innerhalb der Arten (genetische Diversität) und zwischen den Arten sowie die Vielfalt der Ökosysteme. Biodiversität an sich ist keine Ökosystemleistung, sondern liegt diesen Leistungen bzw. „öffentlichen Gütern" zugrunde. Die Annahme, dass uns „öffentliche Güter" dieser Art im Überfluss und ohne Einschränkungen zur Verfügung stehen, geht jedoch weit an der Realität vorbei. Wir sind mit einem ständigen signifikanten Verlust an natürlichen Lebensräumen konfrontiert, dessen Folgen für das menschliche Wohlergehen offenkundig sind. Aus diesem Grund ist die ökonomische Unsichtbarkeit des Naturkapitals ein zentrales Anliegen von TEEB, d. h. die Unfähigkeit des derzeit vorherrschenden Wirtschaftssystems, den ökonomischen und gesellschaftlichen Wert unserer natürlichen Umwelt anzuerkennen. Im Mittelpunkt der Arbeit von TEEB steht das Problem, dass wir üblicherweise davon ausgehen, die von Biodiversität und Ökosystemen erbrachten Leistungen stünden jedem in ausreichender Menge zur Verfügung. Das fehlende Verständnis für die begrenzte Verfügbarkeit von natürlichen „öffentlichen Gütern", für ihren Beitrag zur Wirtschaftsleistung und für ihre umfassende Bedeutung für das menschliche Wohlergehen ist nicht auf bestimmte gesellschaftliche Schichten beschränkt. Von einzelnen Menschen bis hin zu nationalen Regierungen – überall muss ein Bewusstsein für die facettenreichen Beziehungen zwischen Mensch und Natur geschaffen werden. TEEB zeigt, dass die Probleme im Zusammenhang mit den gesellschaftlichen Auswirkungen auf die natürliche Umwelt und ihrer Nutzung häufig im freien Zugang zu natürlichen Ressourcen liegen, verstärkt durch unklare Eigentumsrechte und einen Mangel an einschlägigen nationalen Gesetzen bzw. effektiven internationalen Verträgen. In einer Abwärtsspirale führen all diese Faktoren zu einer Erschöpfung der verfügbaren Biodiversitäts- und Ökosystemleistungen, ein Prozess, der auch als „Tragödie der Allmende" bezeichnet wird. In diesem ausbeuterischen und auf Dauer unhaltbaren System sind es die Armen, die am stärksten leiden, denn ihr Lebensunterhalt hängt in hohem Maße von Umweltressourcen ab. Selbstverständlich wird die Wirtschaft auch weiterhin wachsen und auch die Umwandlung von natürlichen Ökosystemen in landwirtschaftlich genutzte Flächen wird weitergehen. Wir können – und dürfen – dem legitimen Streben von Staaten und

benefits that people obtain from ecosystems. Examples include food, freshwater, timber, climate regulation, protection from natural hazards, erosion control, pharmaceutical ingredients and recreation. Biodiversity is the quantity and variability among living organisms within species (genetic diversity), between species and between ecosystems. Biodiversity is not itself an ecosystem service but underpins the supply of services or "public goods." The cornucopian assumption of abundant and unfettered availability of these "public goods" simply does not reflect harsh reality. Ongoing losses of natural areas are significant, and their impact on human welfare benefits is palpable. As a consequence, a central concern of TEEB is the economic invisibility of natural capital—the inability of our dominant economic model to recognize economic and societal value delivered by the natural environment. Central to TEEB's work is addressing the problem that biodiversity and ecosystem services have conventionally been seen as enough for everyone and available to everyone. The lack of understanding of the finite nature of natural "public goods," of their contribution to the economy, and of their larger significance in maintaining human well-being is not bound to any specific social strata. From individuals to national governments, awareness has to be built to understand the multiple facets of the relationship between humankind and the natural world. TEEB explains that the problems related to societal impact on and use of the natural environment often lie with open access to natural resources, coupled with unclear property rights, and the lack applicable national laws or effective international treaties. Together, these factors lead to depletion of biodiversity and ecosystem services, in a race to the bottom called "the tragedy of the commons." Within this exploitative and unsustainable framework, it is the poor that are the worst sufferers as their livelihoods depend heavily on environmental resources. Economic growth and the conversion of natural ecosystems to agricultural production will of course continue. We cannot—and should not—put a brake on the legitimate aspirations of countries and individuals for economic development. However it is essential to ensure such development takes proper account of the real value of natural ecosystems. This is central to both economic and environmental management. As illustrated in the TEEB reports there are some common messages for developing the economics of ecosystems and biodiversity: rethink today's subsidies to reflect tomorrow's priorities; reward currently unrecognized ecosystem services and make sure the costs of ecosystem damage are accounted for, by creating new markets and promoting appropriate policy instruments; share the benefits of conservation; measure the costs and benefits of ecosystem services.

The long-term purpose of TEEB is to compile and communicate the best available scientific and economic analysis on the economics of ecosystems and biodiversity. Through this exercise, our goal is to help policymakers, administrators, businesses and citizens formulate responses to address the losses we see all around us. These actions collectively have the power to halt and reverse the losses of natural capital and to improve well-being for humanity, especially the poor. Considering the rapid loss of biodiversity and ecosystems and the ensuing effects on the welfare of the poor in particular, the question of whether we have any choice in the characterization of global public goods becomes important. Do public goods always have to remain public? This is largely dependent on policy choices that we make, which determine whether a good is private or public. In the *TEEB*

The long-term purpose of TEEB is to compile and communicate the best available scientific and economic analysis on the economics of ecosystems and biodiversity. Through this exercise, our goal is to help policymakers, administrators, businesses and citizens formulate responses to address the losses we see all around us. These actions collectively have the power to halt and reverse the losses of natural capital and to improve well-being for humanity, especially the poor.

Individuen nach wirtschaftlicher Entwicklung keinen Riegel vorschieben. Es muss jedoch unbedingt sichergestellt werden, dass diese Entwicklung den wahren Wert natürlicher Ökosysteme entsprechend berücksichtigt. Das ist für den Umgang mit wirtschaftlichen wie umweltpolitischen Fragen gleichermaßen von zentraler Bedeutung. Wie aus den TEEB-Berichten hervorgeht, gibt es einige allgemein gültige Aspekte für die Entwicklung eines ökonomischen Umgangs mit Ökosystemen und Biodiversität: Überdenken derzeitiger Subventionen und Förderungen mit Blick auf zukünftige Prioritäten, Belohnung bislang nicht anerkannter Ökosystemleistungen und zwingende Einberechnung der Kosten von Umweltschäden durch Schaffung neuer Märkte und Förderung adäquater Instrumente, Teilen des aus Naturschutzmaßnahmen erwachsenden Nutzens sowie Messung der Kosten und Vorteile von Ökosystemleistungen.

Das langfristige Ziel von TEEB besteht darin, die besten wissenschaftlichen und wirtschaftlichen Analysen zur Ökonomie von Ökosystemen und Biodiversität zusammenzustellen und zu kommunizieren. Dies soll als Hilfestellung für Entscheidungsträger, Verwaltungsexperten, Unternehmen und Bürger dienen, um Lösungen für den Umgang mit den Verlusten in unserer Umwelt zu formulieren. Zusammengenommen sind diese Aktionen in der Lage, den Verlust an Naturkapital zu stoppen bzw. rückgängig zu machen und das Wohlbefinden der Menschheit, insbesondere der Armen, zu verbessern. Angesichts des rasanten Verlustes an Ökosystemen und Biodiversität und der daraus resultierenden Folgen für das Wohl speziell der armen Bevölkerung gewinnt die Frage an Bedeutung, inwieweit wir bei der Kennzeichnung von globalen öffentlichen Gütern eine Wahl haben. Müssen öffentliche Güter immer öffentlich bleiben? Dies hängt weitgehend von den von uns gewählten Vorgehensweisen ab, denn sie bestimmen, ob ein Gut privater oder öffentlicher Natur ist. In dem im November 2009 veröffentlichten Bericht *TEEB for Policy Makers* haben wir gezeigt, dass es *die* Lösung nicht gibt, da jedes Land verschieden ist, jede Ökonomie in unterschiedlicher Weise von der Natur abhängt und der Ausgangspunkt in jedem Land aufgrund bestehender Instrumente und Strategien anders ist. Dennoch haben die folgenden beiden Empfehlungen in nahezu allen Fällen Gültigkeit, unabhängig von den jeweiligen Rahmenbedingungen: Die Maßnahmen und Aktivitäten sollten nicht auf Prozesse der Umweltpolitik beschränkt sein, sondern auch andere Sektoren wie Fischereiwesen, Land- und Forstwirtschaft, Energie, Nahrungsmittel- und Getränkeversorgung, Grundstoffindustrie, Verkehr, Tourismus und Gesundheit einbeziehen – um nur einige wenige zu nennen. Der Wert unseres Naturkapitals kann in Entscheidungsprozessen weitaus besser berücksichtigt werden, wenn er möglichst umfassend dargelegt wird – von der volkswirtschaftlichen Gesamtrechnung und Gesetzgebung über die Fiskalpolitik und das öffentliche und private Beschaffungswesen bis hin zu den Staatsausgaben. Der Einsatz eines einzigen

for Policy Makers report released in November 2009 we showed that there is no single "solution" as each country is different, each economy relies on nature in a different way and each country starts with a different set of policies already in place. However, the following two recommendations may apply in almost all cases, irrespective of the specific setting: the policy response should not be limited to "environmental" policy-making processes, but also needs to come from other sectoral policies like fisheries, agriculture, forestry, energy, food and beverages, extractive industries, transport, tourism and health—to name but a few. The value of our natural capital can be much better reflected in decision-making if broadly considered—from national accounting, regulation and fiscal policy, to public and private procurement and government spending. The application of single-policy instruments may sometimes work, but more often the appropriate policy response will involve a flexible and "smart" policy mix. Such a mix can be delivered through a step-wise approach that starts with the most easily available opportunities, i.e. the "low-hanging fruit."

TEEB studies and analyses highlight various options for robust policy responses and describe what instruments and measures are already available. However, as noted above, different instruments will suit different situations and there is no single policy solution for all countries. It is therefore very helpful that each country first review the situation on the ground. This assessment can be done in the following steps:

Step I: Consider what ecosystem and biodiversity means for your economy: countries are urged to carry out their own reviews of how ecosystem services relate to their economic growth, employment, and prosperity and what risks are associated with their loss. Several countries are already working on national assessments, such as France,[2] the United Kingdom (UK National Ecosystem Assessment), Japan and India.

Step II: Evaluate current policies and identify potential improvements: building on the insights of national reviews, the existing policy framework can be evaluated to reveal inconsistencies and identify the potential for better managing natural capital.

There are numerous examples where policy initiatives of national governments and investments by the private sector are changing this dynamic by rewarding unrecognized benefits. In Costa Rica for example, payments for environmental services are virtually a country-wide strategy for forest and biodiversity conservation as well as sustainable development.[3] Private corporations are increasingly seeing value in biodiversity preservation and recognizing the interconnectivity with long-term business durability. Insurance firms and shipping companies are financing the reforestation of the Panama Canal to restore freshwater flow and prevent the mounting of

2 See Bernard Chevassus-au-Louis et al., "Approche économique de la biodiversité et des services lies aux ecosystems," Centre d'analyse stratégique, April 2009, in: http://www.strategie.gouv.fr/IMG/pdf/rapport_bio_v2.pdf [accessed on February 21, 2011].

3 See *TEEB – The Economics of Ecosystems and Biodiversity for National and International Policy Makers* (2009), chapter 5; S. Pagiola, "Payments for Environmental Services in Costa Rica," in: *Ecological Economics* 65/4 (2008), pp. 712–725; R. Portela, M. C. Rodriguez, "Environmental Services Payment in Costa Rica," 2008, unpublished manuscript, Conservation International; S. Wunder, S. Wertz-Kanounnikoff, "Payments for Ecosystem Services: A New Way of Conserving Biodiversity in Forests," in: *Journal for Sustainable Forestry* 28 (2009), pp. 576–596.

shipping premiums caused by Canal closures.[4] In Guyana, a private equity firm has bought the rights to 20 percent of the value of environmental services from a 370,000 hectare rainforest reserve anticipating that its carbon storage, water storage, biodiversity maintenance, and rainfall regulation services will only become more valuable and be recognized.[5] At a national level, strong opportunities exist for governments to capture the worth of biodiversity, generate revenue streams internally and through international agreements, and create appropriate domestic institutional arrangements to protect it. National governments have the responsibility to effectively integrate conservation of resources into environmental and forestry policies and beyond, into finance and planning agendas of the country. Governments should further provide fiscal or other incentives for people to encourage participation from a diverse set of stakeholders that can change the common property exploitative design of public goods and inspire innovation in the environmental sector.

Architects are no strangers to the idea of incorporating the natural environment into their design proposals, but TEEB is also pushing for city and regional planners to do more to integrate natural systems and biodiversity and its value into public planning schemes and policies. For the first time in human history over half of the world's population lives in cities. China already has 100 cities with a population of over one million; India has 35. By 2050, the UN predicts that up to 80 percent of the global population could be urban.[6] The environmental challenges of this trend are significant: for example, of China's 669 cities, 60 percent suffer water shortages, and in 2005 nearly half lacked wastewater treatment facilities.[7] If living standards and environmental conditions in cities fail to improve, the social and political implications are also clear. At present about 30 percent of the population of the world's city-regions lives in extreme poverty. By 2030 this proportion will increase to about 40 percent under "business as usual" assumptions.[8] Integrating ecosystem services into urban planning is essential for our urban futures.

For this vision to unfold, innovations in city planning and architecture, and an unprecedented step change in infrastructure investment, will be required to transform the world's rapid urbanization over the next two decades into a suite of new models for sustainable urban living. Initial examples are on their way, for a number of cities worldwide are approaching new strategies and policies and are blazing trails for others. Singapore has for decades prided itself in being a "garden city," with a model National Parks service, and it continues its experiment in "greening" the city even further with rooftop gardens and a very well maintained set of wilderness areas for the

4 See *TEEB – The Economics of Ecosystems and Biodiversity: An Interim Report* (2008); Bradford S. Gentry et al., *Emerging Markets for Ecosystem Services: A Case Study of the Panama Canal Watershed*. Binghamton, NY 2007; "The New Eco-Warriors: Can Markets Succeed Where Tree-Huggers Failed?" in: *The Banker* 1 (2007), pp. 32–37.

5 See *TEEB* 2008 (fn. 4); iNSnet Foundation, http://www.insnet.org/printable.rxml?id=9199&photo [accessed on January 31, 2011].

6 See *TEEB – The Economics of Ecosystems and Biodiversity Report: Mainstreaming the Economics of Nature: A Synthesis of the Approach, Conclusions and Recommendations of TEEB* (2010); UNDESA – United Nations Department of Economic and Social Affairs, "World Urbanization Prospects: The 2009 Revision," in: http://esa.un.org/unpd/wup/ [accessed on February 20, 2011].

7 See *UNDP Human Development Report* 2006.

8 Ibid.

Instruments mag in manchen Fällen zielführend sein, doch in der Regel wird die adäquate Vorgehensweise in einer Kombination aus verschiedenen flexiblen und klug gewählten Mitteln bestehen. Dies wird erreicht durch einen stufenweisen Zugang, der mit den am leichtesten verfügbaren Möglichkeiten beginnt („Strategie der niedrigen Schwelle").

Die Studien und Analysen von TEEB untersuchen verschiedene Optionen für nachhaltige und effektive Strategien und beschreiben, welche Instrumente und Maßnahmen bereits verfügbar sind. Wie jedoch zuvor bereits erläutert, erfordern unterschiedliche Situationen unterschiedliche Instrumente – es gibt keine Lösung, die auf alle Länder anwendbar ist. Aus diesem Grund ist es sinnvoll, wenn jeder Staat erst einmal die eigene Ausgangsposition analysiert. Dies kann in folgenden Schritten geschehen:

1. Festlegung der Bedeutung von Ökosystemen und Biodiversität für die eigene Wirtschaft. Die Staaten sind dazu angehalten, selbst zu überprüfen, wie Ökosystemleistungen mit ihrem Wirtschaftswachstum, ihrer Beschäftigungssituation und ihrem Wohlstand zusammenhängen und welche Risiken ein Verlust bedeuten würde. Einige Länder arbeiten bereits an nationalen Bewertungssystemen, darunter Frankreich,[2] Großbritannien (UK National Ecosystem Assessment), Japan und Indien.

2. Evaluierung der derzeitigen Strategien und Identifizierung möglicher Verbesserungen. Ausgehend von den Ergebnissen der oben dargestellten Bewertung kann der aktuelle Strategierahmen evaluiert werden, um Widersprüche und Inkonsistenzen aufzudecken und das Potenzial für einen besseren Umgang mit dem Naturkapital zu ermitteln.

Es gibt unzählige Beispiele dafür, dass Initiativen nationaler Regierungen und Investitionen durch den privaten Sektor zu einer Veränderung dieser Dynamik führen, indem bislang nicht anerkannte Leistungen belohnt werden. In Costa Rica beispielsweise sind Zahlungen für Ökosystemleistungen eine nahezu landesweite Strategie zum Schutz von Wäldern und Biodiversität sowie für die nachhaltige Entwicklung.[3] Private Unternehmen erkennen zunehmend den Wert, der in der Erhaltung von Biodiversität liegt, sowie die Auswirkungen auf den langfristigen Bestand von Unternehmen. So finanzieren Versicherungen und Reedereien die Wiederaufforstung der

2 Vgl. Bernard Chevassus-au-Louis et al., „Approche économique de la biodiversité et des services lies aux ecosystems", Centre d'analyse stratégique, April 2009, in: http://www.strategie.gouv.fr/IMG/pdf/rapport_bio_v2.pdf [abgerufen am 21.2.2011].

3 Vgl. *TEEB – The Economics of Ecosystems and Biodiversity for National and International Policy Makers* (2009), Kap. 5; S. Pagiola, „Payments for Environmental Services in Costa Rica", in: *Ecological Economics* 65, 4 (2008), S. 712–725; R. Portela und M. C. Rodriguez, „Environmental Services Payment in Costa Rica", 2008, unveröffentlichtes Manuskript, Conservation International; S. Wunder und S. Wertz-Kanounnikoff, „Payments for Ecosystem Services: A New Way of Conserving Biodiversity in Forests", in: *Journal for Sustainable Forestry* 28 (2009), S. 576–596.

Region rund um den Panamakanal, um die Versorgung mit Süßwasser wiederherzustellen und das Steigen der Schifffahrtskosten zu verhindern, die durch das Schließen des Kanals verursacht werden.[4] In Guyana hat eine Private-Equity-Firma die Rechte an 20 Prozent der Umweltleistungen erworben, die durch ein 370.000 Hektar großes Regenwaldschutzgebiet erbracht werden. Das Unternehmen geht davon aus, dass die Vorteile in Form von Kohlenstoff- und Wasserspeicherung, Erhalt der Biodiversität und Niederschlagsregulierung in Zukunft weiter an Wert gewinnen und Anerkennung finden werden.[5] Auf nationaler Ebene haben die Regierungen umfassende Möglichkeiten, den Wert der Biodiversität zu erfassen, innerstaatlich und durch internationale Übereinkommen Einkommensströme zu generieren und adäquate nationale Institutionen zu ihrem Schutz ins Leben zu rufen. Es liegt in der Verantwortung der nationalen Regierungen, den Schutz von Ressourcen effektiv in ihre Umwelt- und Forstwirtschaftspolitik sowie, darüber hinausgehend, in ihre staatlichen Finanzierungs- und Planungsaktivitäten zu integrieren. Darüber hinaus sollten die Regierungen fiskalische und andere Anreize entwickeln und so eine Einbindung unterschiedlichster Interessengruppen fördern, die den ausbeuterischen Umgang mit freien bzw. öffentlichen Gütern verändern und Innovationen auf dem Umweltsektor anstoßen kann.

Architekten sind mit der Idee vertraut, die natürliche Umgebung in ihren Entwürfen zu berücksichtigen, doch TEEB fordert auch von Stadt- und Raumplanern, natürliche Systeme, Biodiversität und deren Wert stärker in öffentliche Planungsprogramme und -strategien zu integrieren. Zum ersten Mal in der Geschichte der Menschheit lebt mehr als die Hälfte der Weltbevölkerung in Städten. In China gibt es bereits 100 Städte mit mehr als 1 Million Einwohnern, in Indien 35. Nach Schätzungen der UNO werden bis zum Jahr 2050 bis zu 80 Prozent aller Menschen weltweit in urbanen Zentren leben.[6] Die mit diesem Trend einhergehenden Umweltprobleme sind beträchtlich. So leiden 60 Prozent der 669 chinesischen Städte unter Wassermangel und 2005 gab es in nahezu der Hälfte keine Anlagen zur Abwasseraufbereitung.[7] Wenn sich der Lebensstandard und die Umweltbedingungen in den Städten nicht bessern,

TEEB looks to take this one step further and encourages the calculation of the *economic value* of city biodiversity and ecosystems. These aspects of quality of life are important, are valued by citizens, but because they come free as "public goods and services" from our natural environments, they tend to be forgotten.

4 Vgl. *TEEB – The Economics of Ecosystems and Biodiversity: An Interim Report* (2008); Bradford S. Gentry et al., *Emerging Markets for Ecosystem Services: A Case Study of the Panama Canal Watershed*, Binghamton/New York 2007; „The New Eco-Warriors: Can Markets Succeed Where Tree-Huggers Failed?" in: *The Banker* 1 (2007), S. 32–37.

5 Vgl. *TEEB* 2008 (Anm. 4); iNSnet, http://www.insnet.org/printable.rxml?id=9199&photo [abgerufen am 31.1.2011].

6 Vgl. *TEEB – The Economics of Ecosystems and Biodiversity Report: Mainstreaming the Economics of Nature: A Synthesis of the Approach, Conclusions and Recommendations of TEEB* (2010); UNDESA – United Nations Department of Economic and Social Affairs, „World Urbanization Prospects: The 2009 Revision", in: http://esa.un.org/unpd/wup/ [abgerufen am 20.2.2011].

7 Vgl. *UNDP Human Development Report 2006*.

public—Sungei Buloh (a mangrove park restored from disused shrimp farms), Bukit Timah Nature Reserve (a hilly area of primary and secondary tropical rainforest), and McRitchie Reservoir (another natural area which serves as the catchment for the island city's main freshwater reservoir).[9] Singapore has also taken the lead in setting up a "City Biodiversity Index" which is worth emulating. This "Index" is a grading system to measure how cities worldwide are conserving their plant and animal species. *The Singapore Index on Cities' Biodiversity* (CBI)[10] measures performance and assigns scores based on three categories: biodiversity—the number of plant, animal and other species in a city; the services that these plants and animals provide, such as pollination and as carbon sinks; and how well a city manages its biodiversity—for instance, by setting up a conservation agency or a museum to document species and habitats. This index and its proposed international propagation will help cities benchmark the success of their efforts to reduce biodiversity loss and hopefully enhance urban biodiversity in the longer term, adding to the quality of life, including the health and recreation benefits of city biodiversity.

> Critics of this economic approach to the natural environment regularly question the concept of adding a price tag onto the natural sphere, assuming this is an approach to trade biodiversity along with other goods.

TEEB looks to take this one step further and encourages the calculation of the *economic value* of city biodiversity and ecosystems. These aspects of quality of life are important, are valued by citizens, but because they come free as "public goods and services" from our natural environments, they tend to be forgotten. This economic invisibility of the natural sphere is in fact one of the main reasons for its relentless and ongoing loss, and we as citizens of cities need to be aware of the problem, its causes, its impacts on our well-being, and of course, of solutions that require better management. City biodiversity and its inherent value can take many forms. About 400,000 trees planted in Canberra are estimated to have a combined energy reduction, pollution mitigation and carbon sequestration value of \$20–67 million during the period 2008–2012 in Canberra.[11] The forest ecosystems of Beijing intercept approximately 1.43 billion m^3 of annual rainfall and 277.82 million m^3 of soil water under ideal conditions, while supplying 286.67 million m^3 of fresh water. The

9 See *TEEB* 2010a (fn. 6).

10 See *TEEB – The Economics of Ecosystems and Biodiversity Report for Local and Regional Policy Makers* (2010), chapter 4. TEEBcase by S. Rodricks (2010), "The Singapore Index on Cities' Biodiversity," in: http://www.TEEBweb.org.

11 See *TEEB* 2010b (fn. 10), chapter 1; C. L. Brack, "Pollution Mitigation and Carbon Sequestration by an Urban Forest," in: *Environmental Pollution* 116 (2002), pp. 195–200.

sind auch die sozialen und politischen Folgen absehbar. Zum gegenwärtigen Zeitpunkt leben ca. 30 Prozent der Bevölkerung in den urbanen Regionen dieser Welt in extremer Armut. Wenn wir weitermachen wie bisher, wird sich dieser Anteil bis zum Jahr 2030 auf etwa 40 Prozent erhöhen.[8] Unsere urbane Zukunft hängt wesentlich davon ab, dass Ökosystemleistungen in der Stadtplanung Berücksichtigung finden.

Damit diese Vision Gestalt annehmen kann, sind Innovationen in Stadtplanung und Architektur ebenso erforderlich wie eine beispiellose und radikale Umgestaltung im Bereich der Infrastrukturinvestitionen. Ziel dabei ist es, die rasante weltweite Urbanisierung im Laufe der nächsten beiden Jahrzehnte in neue, nachhaltige Modelle für das Leben in Städten zu transformieren. Erste Beispiele dafür zeichnen sich bereits ab – Städte auf der ganzen Welt entwickeln neue Strategien und Richtlinien und leisten dabei Pionierarbeit für die anderen. Singapur mit seinem vorbildhaften Nationalparkservice beispielsweise, das seit Jahrzehnten auf seinen Ruf als „Gartenstadt" stolz ist, treibt sein Stadtbegrünungsexperiment mit der Einrichtung von Dachgärten und verschiedenen gut geführten und für die Öffentlichkeit zugänglichen Wildnisgebieten weiter voran: Sungei Buloh (ehemalige Shrimpsfarmen, die in einen Mangrovenpark umgewandelt wurden), Bukit Timah Nature Reserve (ein hügeliges Gebiet mit primärem und sekundärem tropischem Regenwald) und McRitchie Reservoir Park (ein Naturareal, das als Einzugsgebiet für das wichtigste Süßwasserreservoir der Stadt dient).[9] Singapur ist auch führend in der Entwicklung eines nachahmenswerten Biodiversitätsindex für Städte. Dieser besteht aus einem Bewertungssystem, das misst, welche Maßnahmen Städte auf der ganzen Welt zum Schutz ihrer Pflanzen- und Tierarten ergreifen. Der *Singapore Index on Cities' Biodiversity* (CBI)[10] erfasst die jeweiligen Leistungen anhand dreier Kategorien und weist ihnen eine bestimmte Punkteanzahl zu. Zu diesen Kategorien zählen: Biodiversität (Anzahl der Pflanzen-, Tier- und sonstigen Arten in einer Stadt); Leistungen, die von diesen Pflanzen und Tieren erbracht werden (z. B. Bestäubung und Kohlenstoffspeicherung); Qualität des städtischen Biodiversitätsmanagements (z. B. Einrichtung eines Naturschutzbüros oder Museums zur Dokumentation von Arten und Habitaten). Der Index, der auch international Anwendung finden soll, wird den Städten dabei helfen, den Erfolg ihrer Bemühungen zur Reduzierung von Biodiversitätsverlusten einzuschätzen. Es steht zu hoffen, dass dieses Instrument die urbane Biodiversität sowie die daraus resultierenden

8 Ebd.

9 Vgl. *TEEB* 2010a (Anm. 6).

10 Vgl. *TEEB – The Economics of Ecosystems and Biodiversity Report for Local and Regional Policy Makers* (2010), Kap. 4. TEEBcase (Fallbeispiel) von S. Rodricks (2010), „The Singapore Index on Cities' Biodiversity", in: http://www.TEEBweb.org.

Vorteile für Gesundheit und Erholung auf längere Sicht verbessern und somit zu einer Erhöhung der Lebensqualität beitragen wird.

TEEB möchte noch einen Schritt weiter gehen und schlägt vor, den *ökonomischen Wert* von urbanen Ökosystemen und Biodiversität zu berechnen. Diese Aspekte der Lebensqualität sind wichtig und werden von den Bürgern geschätzt, da sie jedoch als „öffentliche Güter und Leistungen" von der Natur kostenlos zur Verfügung gestellt werden, erhalten sie häufig nicht die Aufmerksamkeit, die sie verdienen. Tatsächlich ist die ökonomische Unsichtbarkeit der Natur einer der Hauptgründe für ihren fortwährenden, erbarmungslosen Verlust. Wir als urbane Bürger müssen dieses Problem, seine Ursachen und seine Auswirkungen auf unser Wohlbefinden zur Kenntnis nehmen. Gleichzeitig müssen wir Lösungen entwickeln, die einen besseren Umgang mit unseren natürlichen Ressourcen implizieren. Die urbane Biodiversität und der ihr innewohnende Wert können viele verschiedene Formen annehmen. So wurden in Canberra 400.000 Bäume gepflanzt, deren Gesamtwert für den Zeitraum 2008–2012 – basierend auf Beiträgen zur Energiereduktion, Minderung der Schadstoffbelastung und Kohlenstoffspeicherung – auf 20–67 Millionen Dollar geschätzt wird.[11] Die Waldökosysteme in Peking fangen unter idealen Bedingungen jährlich ca. 1,43 Milliarden Kubikmeter Niederschlag sowie 277,82 Millionen Kubikmeter Bodenwasser auf und liefern 286,67 Millionen Kubikmeter Süßwasser. Im Bereich des Gewässerschutzes betrug der von den Pekinger Wäldern bereitgestellte ökonomische Wert insgesamt 0,63 Milliarden Dollar, der ökonomische Nutzen pro Hektar belief sich auf 688 Dollar.[12] Eine in Hongkong durchgeführte Studie über die Auswirkungen von Nachbarschaftsparks auf den Verkaufspreis von Privatwohnungen in Hochhäusern hat ergeben, dass solche Grünanlagen die Preise um bis zu 17 Prozent erhöhen können (Verfügbarkeit: 15 Prozent, Aussicht: 2 Prozent).[13]

Im Jahr 2005 verabschiedete die Stadt Toronto ein Gesetz zur Schaffung eines Grüngürtels.[14] In der Folge initiierte die David Suzuki Foundation eine Studie, um die Bedeutung des Naturkapitals sowie die Ökosystemleistungen und Vorteile des Grüngürtels aufzuzeigen. Der Bericht analysierte den Wert von Naturkapital innerhalb der Zone drei Jahre nach ihrer offiziel-

11 Vgl. *TEEB* 2010b (Anm. 10), Kap. 1; C. L. Brack, „Pollution Mitigation and Carbon Sequestration by an Urban Forest", in: *Environmental Pollution* 116 (2002), S. 195–200.

12 Vgl. Zhang Biao et al., „Water Conservation of Forest Ecosystem in Beijing and Its Value", in: *Ecological Economics* 69/7 (Mai 2010), S. 1416–1426.

13 Vgl. C. Y. Jim, W. Y. Chen, „Value of Scenic Views: Hedonic Assessment of Private Housing in Hong Kong", in: *Landscape and Urban Planning* 91/4 (Juli 2009), S. 226–234.

14 Vgl. *TEEB* 2010b (Anm. 10), Kap. 4; TEEBcase (Fallbeispiel) von K. Almack, S. Wilson, „Economic Value of Toronto's Greenbelt". Canada 2010, in: http://www.TEEBweb.org.

total economic value of water conservation provided by Beijing's forests was $0.63 billion, and the economic benefit per hectare was equal to $688.[12] Hong Kong did a study on the effects of neighborhood parks on the transaction price of high-rise private residential units in Hong Kong, which indicated that neighborhood parks could lift prices by 17 percent, including 15 percent for availability and 2 percent for view.[13]

The City of Toronto established a legislated "greenbelt" in 2005.[14] The David Suzuki Foundation then initiated a study to show the importance of natural capital and the ecosystem services or benefits provided by the greenbelt. The report examined the value of natural capital within the greenbelt region three years after it had been legally designated, in order to provide legitimacy to the existing regulation, and to consolidate and enlarge the greenbelt surrounding the Greater Toronto Area. They used a variety of methods to value the ecosystem's services—replacement cost for: wetland habitat (annualized cost of local restoration of wetlands); avoided cost for: forest/wetland water filtration services (avoided water treatment cost), biodiversity value, carbon sequestration services of forests, loss of seed dispersal services, sewage treatment, habitat damage, drinking water treatment, loss of forest for carbon values; contingent valuation or "willingness to pay" studies for: cultural values, recreation values; benefit transfer approach can be used for: watershed services, erosion control, soil retention, agricultural services, and pollination services, but it should be cautioned that this approach has limitations, and can only ever be a temporary measure, to be replaced by site- and location-specific valuation studies later on. The report quantified the value of the ecosystem services provided by the greenbelt's natural capital, revealing the annual value of the region's measurable non-market ecosystem services at an estimated $2.6 billion annually; an average value of $3,487 per hectare of Greenbelt.

Critics of this economic approach to the natural environment regularly question the concept of adding a price tag onto the natural sphere, assuming this is an approach to trade biodiversity along with other goods. The TEEB approach does not advocate this but also recognizes the principle of our market economic model that there are just some things one cannot put a price on. This is why the word "value" has a central role in the recommendations put forward by the study. The value of the natural environment also must include and recognize the intrinsic value, the spiritual and cultural values of nature—these are hard to economically quote, but this sense of value is nevertheless just as valid and important as straight economic gains or losses. As such, TEEB urges a conservative approach to the economics of the natural sphere, but argues that with economics a dialogue can be opened up between the often polarized camps of conservation and finance. Being able to illustrate the impacts on our natural world in monetary terms can go a long way towards arguing for investment in natural ecological values as opposed to disregarding it.

12 See Zhang Biao et al., "Water Conservation of Forest Ecosystem in Beijing and Its Value," in: *Ecological Economics* 69/7 (May 2010), pp. 1416–1426.

13 See C.Y. Jim, W.Y. Chen, "Value of Scenic Views: Hedonic Assessment of Private Housing in Hong Kong," in: *Landscape and Urban Planning* 91/4 (July 2009), pp. 226–234.

14 See *TEEB* 2010b (fn. 10), chapter 4; TEEBcase by K. Almack and S. Wilson, *Economic Value of Toronto's Greenbelt*, Canada, 2010, in: http://www.TEEBweb.org.

len Einrichtung, um die Legitimität der bestehenden Regelung unter Beweis zu stellen und den Bestand des Grüngürtels rund um die Greater Toronto Area zu sichern bzw. zu erweitern. Zur Bewertung der Ökosystemleistungen wurden verschiedenste Methoden eingesetzt: Wiederherstellungskosten für Feuchtgebiet-Habitate (auf das Jahr umgerechnete Kosten für die lokale Wiederherstellung von Feuchtgebieten); Vermeidungskosten für Wasserfiltrationsleistungen durch Wälder/Feuchtgebiete (vermiedene Kosten für Wasseraufbereitung), Biodiversitätswert, Kohlenstoffsequestrierung durch Wälder, reduzierte Samenverbreitung, Abwasserreinigung, Beeinträchtigung von Lebensräumen, Trinkwasseraufbereitung, Verlust an Wald/Kohlenstoffwerte; kontingente Bewertungsstudien („Bereitschaft zu zahlen") für kulturelle Werte, Erholungswerte. Der Einsatz eines Benefit-Transfer-Ansatzes ist möglich für Wasserschutzleistungen, Erosionsschutz, Schutz vor Erdrutschen, Leistungen für die Landwirtschaft und Bestäubung. Es muss jedoch warnend hinzugefügt werden, dass dieser Ansatz Grenzen hat und nur einen provisorischen Maßstab darstellen kann, an dessen Stelle in Zukunft orts- und standortspezifische Bewertungsstudien treten müssen. Der Bericht der David Suzuki Foundation quantifizierte den Wert der vom Naturkapital des Grüngürtels erbrachten Vorteile und schätzte den Wert der messbaren, nicht-marktbasierten Ökosystemleistungen in der Region auf 2,6 Milliarden Dollar pro Jahr. Dies entspricht einem Durchschnittswert von 3.487 Dollar pro Hektar Grüngürtel.

Critics of this economic approach to the natural environment regularly question the concept of adding a price tag onto the natural sphere, assuming this is an approach to trade biodiversity along with other goods.

Kritiker dieser ökonomischen Herangehensweise an unsere natürliche Umwelt bemängeln zumeist die Idee, der natürlichen Sphäre ein Preisschild umzuhängen, und sehen sie als Versuch, mit Biodiversität wie mit anderen Gütern auch Handel zu treiben. Der Ansatz von TEEB unterstützt diese Sichtweise nicht, erkennt aber das Prinzip unseres marktwirtschaftlichen Modells an, demzufolge es nur wenige Dinge gibt, deren Bedeutung nicht in Form von Preisen gemessen werden kann. Daher spielt der Begriff des „Wertes" auch eine zentrale Rolle für die in der vorliegenden Studie gemachten Empfehlungen. Die Bewertung unserer natürlichen Umwelt muss auch ihren intrinsischen Wert, ihre spirituellen und kulturellen Werte, inkludieren und berücksichtigen – diese lassen sich nur schwer ökonomisieren, sind jedoch ebenso gültig und wichtig wie unmittelbare Vermögensgewinne oder -verluste. Aus diesem Grund mahnt TEEB eine vorsichtige Herangehensweise an die Ökonomie der Natursphäre ein, vertritt aber auch die Ansicht, dass der Ansatz einen Dialog zwischen den oft völlig entgegengesetzten Bereichen Naturschutz und Finanzwelt erlaubt. Die Möglichkeit, Auswirkungen auf unsere natürliche Umwelt in monetärer Form darzustellen, kann viel dazu beitragen, Investitionen in natürliche, ökologische Werte zu fördern, statt sie wie bisher zu ignorieren.

Seit ihrem Beginn im Jahr 2008 hat die TEEB-Studie weltweit Aufsehen erregt. Mittlerweile geht es jedoch nicht mehr so sehr darum, die Dimension der Probleme und mögliche Lö-

sungen aufzuzeigen, im Vordergrund steht nun die Implementierung von Programmen, um TEEB in verschiedenste Kontexte einzubinden. Indien hat angekündigt, zur Bewertung seines Naturkapitals eine eigene TEEB-Studie durchzuführen mit dem Ziel, die volkswirtschaftliche Gesamtrechnung des Landes bis 2015 durch ökologische Werte zu ergänzen. Brasilien arbeitet an einem ähnlichen Plan und auch die Wirtschaft des Landes initiiert eine Studie, um die ökonomische Dimension der Beziehungen zwischen Wirtschaft und Natur in Brasilien zu untersuchen. TEEB hat viele Anfragen von Ländern, regionalen Behörden und Wirtschaftssektoren erhalten, die um Hilfestellungen für die Entwicklung eines TEEB-Ansatzes bitten. All diese Initiativen sind lobenswert, denn sie bringen uns einer Zukunft näher, in der wir erkennen, wie sehr wir von unserer natürlichen Umwelt abhängen und was wir tun können, um unsere Beziehung zu ihr aufrechtzuerhalten oder zu verbessern.

Der *TEEB Report for Business* zeigt, dass im Jahr 2009 27 Prozent der von PricewaterhouseCoopers befragten CEOs weltweit befürchteten, der Verlust an Biodiversität könnte Auswirkungen auf das Wachstum ihres Unternehmens haben. Noch aufschlussreicher war jedoch, in welchen Ländern diese Sorge am größten war. Mehr als 50 Prozent der lateinamerikanischen und 45 Prozent der afrikanischen CEOs sahen den Rückgang der Artenvielfalt als eine Herausforderung für die Entwicklung ihres Betriebes. Im Gegensatz dazu teilten weniger als 20 Prozent ihrer Kollegen in Westeuropa diese Bedenken.[15] Die Ergebnisse lassen erkennen, dass Firmenlenker, die den nachhaltigen Umgang mit Biodiversität nicht in ihre Pläne integrieren, langsam den Anschluss an die Märkte verlieren könnten. Eine andere aktuelle Erhebung, die ebenfalls im *TEEB Report for Business* angeführt wird, belegt das zunehmende Interesse der Konsumenten an dem Thema: 60 Prozent der befragten Verbraucher in Amerika und Europa und mehr als 90 Prozent in Brasilien sind sich über den Verlust der Artenvielfalt im Klaren. Mehr als 80 Prozent der Befragten gaben an, sie würden keine Produkte mehr von Firmen kaufen, die bei der Beschaffung keine ethischen Standards beachten.[16] Die in Großbritannien ansässige Beratungsfirma TruCost schätzte in einer von UNPRI in Auftrag gegebenen Studie, dass die von den 3.000 größten börsennotierten Unternehmen weltweit verursachten Schäden bzw. „Umweltexternalitäten" jährlich rund 2,2 Billionen Dollar betragen.[17]

15 Vgl. *TEEB – The Economics of Ecosystems and Biodiversity Report for Business* (2010), Kap. 1; PricewaterhouseCoopers, „Analysis for TEEB", 2009.

16 Vgl. *TEEB* 2010c (Anm. 15), Kap. 1; Union for Ethical BioTrade, „Biodiversity Barometer 2010", in: http://www.countdown2010.net/2010/wpcontent/uploads/UEBT_BIODIVERSITY_BAROMETER_web-1.pdf [abgerufen am 21.1.2011].

17 Vgl. *TEEB* 2010c (Anm. 15), Kap. 2; UNPRI, UNEPFI und Trucost, *Universal Ownership and Environmental Externalities* (erscheint in Kürze).

Since its initiation in 2008, the TEEB study has attracted worldwide attention, and by now attention has turned from illustrating the dimension of the problems and how we might solve them, to implementing programs to bring TEEB into a range of contexts. The Indian government has announced that it is establishing its own TEEB study to assess the value of its Natural Capital, with the intention to incorporating ecological values into its national accounts by the year 2015. Similarly, Brazil is also looking at a similar plan, and its business community is likewise initiating a study on the economic dimension of the relationship between Brazilian business and nature. TEEB has received many expressions of interest from countries, regional authorities and business sectors for advice on how they might start to take a TEEB approach. Each of these initiatives should be commended and all contribute to moving us all towards a future where we recognize just how much we depend upon our natural environment and identify what we can do to maintain or improve our relationship with it.

The *TEEB Report for Business* highlighted that in 2009 27 percent of global Chief Executive Officers (CEOs) surveyed by PricewaterhouseCoopers expressed concern about the impacts of biodiversity loss on their business growth prospects. What was even more interesting was where this concern was mostly centered. Over 50 percent of CEOs surveyed in Latin America and 45 percent in Africa see declines in biodiversity as a challenge to business growth. In contrast, less than 20 percent of their counterparts in Western Europe share such concerns.[15] The findings indicate that corporate bosses who fail to make sustainable management of biodiversity part of their business plans may find themselves increasingly out of step with the marketplace. Another recent survey, also spotlighted in the *TEEB Report for Business*, shows rising interest among consumers with 60 percent of those surveyed in America and Europe and over 90 percent in Brazil aware of biodiversity loss. Over 80 percent of those consumers surveyed said they would stop buying products from companies that disregard ethical considerations in their sourcing practices.[16] The UK-based consultancy TruCost, on behalf of the UN's Principles for Responsible Investment, estimated in a study on the activities of the world's top 3,000 listed companies that their negative impacts or "environmental externalities" total around $2.2 trillion annually.[17]

However, public acceptance of biodiversity loss is declining, leading to calls for low-impact production and compensation for impacts on biodiversity and ecosystems. Many companies are exploring how to manage the adverse impacts of their activities on biodiversity and ecosystem services (BES). A few companies have made public commitments to "No Net Loss," "Ecological Neutrality," or even "Net Positive Impact" on biodiversity, or on specific ecosystem services such as water resources. In some

15 See *TEEB – The Economics of Ecosystems and Biodiversity Report for Business* (2010), chapter 1; PricewaterhouseCoopers, "Analysis for TEEB," 2009.

16 See *TEEB* 2010c (fn. 15), chapter 1; Union for Ethical BioTrade, "Biodiversity Barometer 2010," in: http://www.countdown2010.net/2010/wpcontent/uploads/UEBT_BIODIVERSITY_BAROMETER_web-1.pdf [accessed on January 21, 2011].

17 See *TEEB* 2010c (fn. 15), chapter 2; UNPRI, UNEPFI and Trucost, *Universal Ownership and Environmental Externalities* (forthcoming).

cases, even relatively straightforward ecological restoration can deliver biodiversity benefits that may exceed those of the original land use. One such example is where, in support of a request to extend an existing quarry in North Yorkshire, Aggregate Industries UK (a subsidiary of Holcim) proposed to create a mix of wetlands for wildlife habitat as well as a lake for recreational use, following extraction of sand and gravel from land currently used for agriculture. Stakeholders were consulted to determine their preferences. Ecosystem valuation was undertaken in 2009–2010 to estimate the benefits associated with wetland restoration. Using a 50-year time horizon and a 3 percent discount rate, the study concluded that the value of biodiversity benefits generated by the proposed wetlands ($2.6 million in 2008), the recreational benefits of the lake ($663,000) and increased flood storage capacity ($417,000) would, after deducting restoration and opportunity costs, deliver net benefits to the local community of about $2 million, in present value terms. Moreover, the marginal benefits of wetland restoration far exceeded the current benefits derived from agricultural production. The study further shows that the costs of ecosystem restoration and aftercare are low compared to both the economic benefits of wetland restoration and the financial returns from sand and gravel extraction.[18]

The TEEB study shows us that we cannot take natural ecological values for granted. The examples of my argumentation shall help to illustrate that all sectors of society can contribute to addressing the loss of biodiversity and to mainstreaming the sense of value and the economics of nature into everyday decision-making. For architects and landscape designers, the TEEB approach can help catalyze an even greater shift towards not only linking humanity with the built environment but also linking us inextricably with the natural sphere. We must start to recognize its value, account for it in our decision-making, reward those who manage it better, and act now. Considering the environment must become a central part of our decision-making, and the idea of a green economy must be realized if we really are to enjoy a sustainable future.

18 See *TEEB* 2010c (fn. 15), chapter 2; N. Olsen and D. Shannon, "Valuing the Net Benefits of Ecosystem Restoration: The Ripon City Quarry in Yorkshire, Ecosystem Valuation Initiative," Case Study No. 1, WBCSD and IUCN, Geneva and Gland 2010.

Doch die Öffentlichkeit ist immer weniger bereit, den Verlust an Biodiversität hinzunehmen, was zur Forderung nach umweltfreundlicheren Produktionsweisen und Kompensationen für Schäden an Ökosystemen und Biodiversität führt. Viele Unternehmen suchen derzeit nach dem richtigen Umgang mit den negativen Auswirkungen ihrer Operationen auf Ökosystem- und Biodiversitätsleistungen. Einige wenige haben sich im Hinblick auf die biologische Vielfalt oder spezielle Ökosystemleistungen wie z. B. Wasserressourcen öffentlich zu Strategien wie „No Net Loss" (keine Nettoverluste), „Ecological Neutrality" (ökologische Neutralität) oder sogar „Net Positive Impact" (positiver Nettoeffekt) bekannt. Manchmal können sich auch relativ einfache Maßnahmen zur Behebung von Umweltschäden positiver auf die Biodiversität auswirken, als dies die ursprüngliche Form der Landnutzung vermochte. Beispielsweise schlug Aggregate Industries UK, ein Tochterunternehmen von Holcim, im Rahmen eines Ansuchens um die Ausweitung eines bestehenden Steinbruchs in North Yorkshire vor, nach erfolgter Entnahme von Sand und Kies in einem zurzeit landwirtschaftlich genutzten Gebiet eine Reihe von Feuchtgebiet-Habitaten für Pflanzen und Tiere sowie einen See für Erholungszwecke zu schaffen. Die betroffenen Interessengruppen wurden konsultiert und zu ihren Präferenzen befragt. In den Jahren 2009/2010 wurde eine Bewertung des Ökosystems vorgenommen, um die Vorteile der Wiederherstellung des Areals in Form von Feuchtgebieten zu beurteilen. Unter Annahme eines Zeitrahmens von 50 Jahren und eines Diskontsatzes von drei Prozent kam die Studie zu dem Schluss, dass der Wert der durch die geplanten Feuchtgebiete generierten Biodiversitätsleistungen (2,6 Millionen Dollar im Jahr 2008), der Nutzen des Sees für Freizeit- und Erholungszwecke (663.000 Dollar) und die erhöhte Speicherkapazität bei Überschwemmungen (417.000 Dollar) nach Abzug der Wiederherstellungs- und Opportunitätskosten den Menschen vor Ort einen Nettonutzen von etwa zwei Millionen Dollar (heutiger Wert) bringen würden. Darüber hinaus würde der Grenznutzen im Falle der Schaffung von Feuchtgebieten die derzeitigen Leistungen durch die landwirtschaftliche Produktion bei weitem übertreffen. Die Studie zeigte weiters, dass die Kosten für die Behebung der verursachten Umweltschäden und die Nachbetreuung niedrig sind im Vergleich zu den wirtschaftlichen Vorteilen durch die Schaffung von Feuchtgebieten und den finanziellen Erträgen durch die Sand- und Kiesgewinnung.[18]

Aus der TEEB-Studie geht hervor, dass wir natürliche, ökologische Werte nicht als selbstverständlich hinnehmen können. Die oben angeführten Beispiele sollen demonstrieren,

18 Vgl. *TEEB* 2010c (Anm. 15), Kap. 2; N. Olsen, D. Shannon, „Valuing The Net Benefits of Ecosystem Restoration: The Ripon City Quarry in Yorkshire, Ecosystem Valuation Initiative", Case Study No. 1, WBCSD und IUCN, Genf und Gland 2010.

dass alle Bereiche der Gesellschaft dazu beitragen können, dem Verlust an Biodiversität entgegenzuwirken. Ziel ist es, den Wert und die Ökonomie der Natur als fixen Bestandteil der alltäglichen Entscheidungsfindung zu etablieren. Für Architekten und Landschaftsdesigner kann der TEEB-Ansatz einen noch umfassenderen Wandel anstoßen hin zu einer Haltung, die die Menschen nicht nur mit ihrer gebauten Umgebung, sondern auch untrennbar mit der Natur verbindet. Wir müssen den Wert natürlicher Ressourcen anerkennen und in unseren Entscheidungen berücksichtigen sowie jene belohnen, die bessere Lösungen gefunden haben. Der Zeitpunkt zum Handeln ist gekommen. Denn wir werden nur dann eine nachhaltige Zukunft haben, wenn wir die Umwelt zu einem Schlüsselelement in Entscheidungsprozessen machen und das Konzept einer „ökologischen Ökonomie" Wirklichkeit werden lassen.

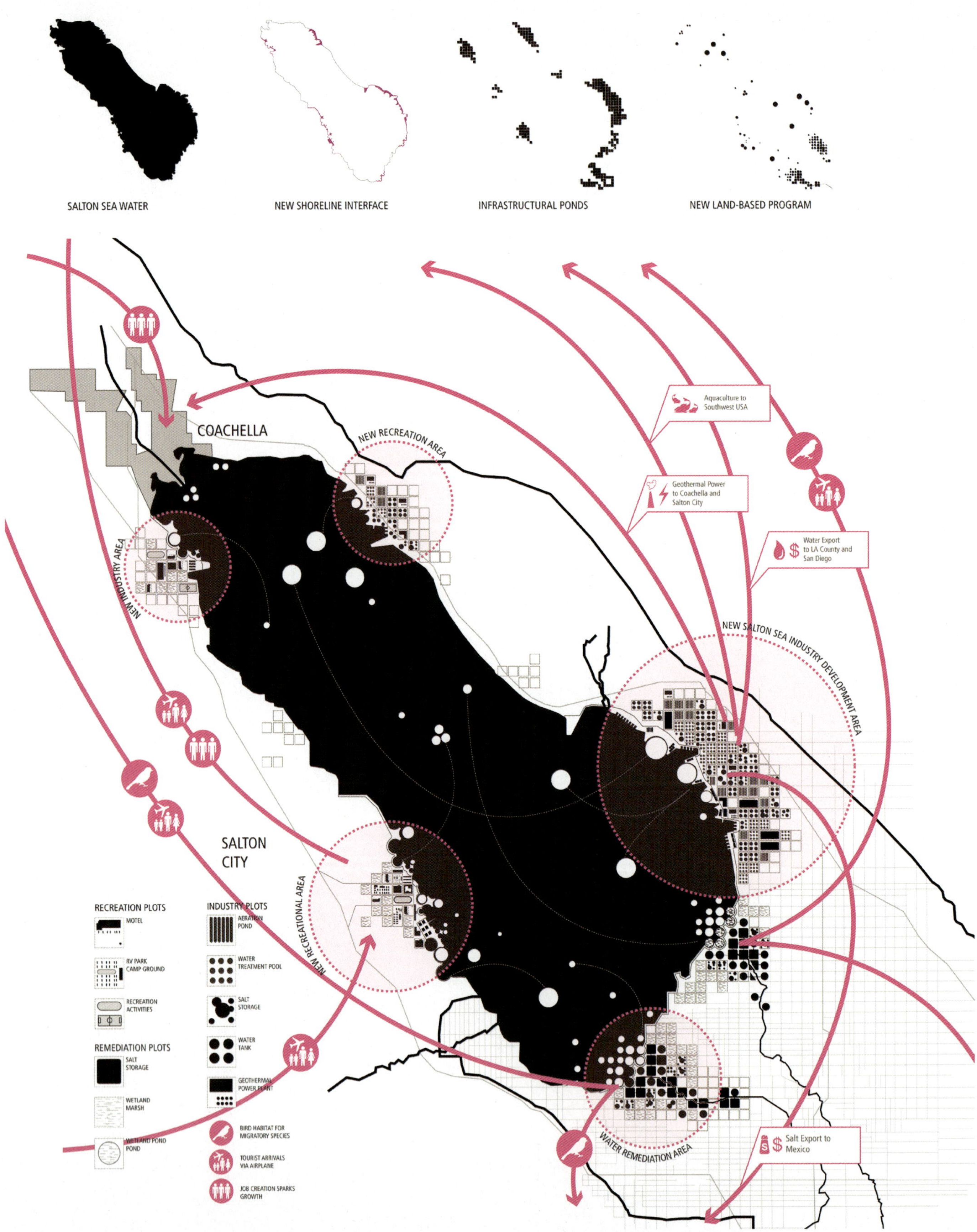

1

1 Neue Ökonomie-, Ökologie- und Freizeitströme reaktivieren den Saltonsee. New flows of economies, ecologies, and recreation re-activate the Salton Sea.

On Water Economies & Ecologies

This text on water economies and ecologies is discussing not a landscape project *per se*, but rather a project engaged in questions of how landscape, infrastructure and urbanism might operate at a territorial scale. The project embraces a notion of "extrinsic architecture"—an architecture that embraces the expanded effects and potentials of architecture. Such an approach shifts or extends the discussion beyond architecture into economics, ecology, energy, and technology.

Über Ökonomien und Ökologien des Wassers. Dieser Text über Ökonomien und Ökologien des Wassers diskutiert kein Landschaftsprojekt *per se*, sondern vielmehr ein Projekt, das sich mit Fragen beschäftigt, wie Landschaft, Infrastruktur und Urbanismus auf einer territorialen Ebene funktionieren könnten. Das Projekt vertritt die Vorstellung einer „extrinsischen Architektur" – einer Architektur, welche die erweiterten Auswirkungen und Potenziale der Architektur umfasst. Solch ein Ansatz verschiebt oder erweitert die Diskussion über Architektur hinaus in die Ökonomie, Ökologie, Energie und Technologie.

LOLA SHEPPARD • MASON WHITE

The project *Farming the Salton* charts the impacts of excessive hydrological manipulation in the driest regions of America, and proposes new models of water infrastructure. The project seeks to raise the question: How might one organize territorial, or in this case aqueous, networks? And how might one imagine an intensified agency for landscapes and infrastructures?

Within the design disciplines, the term "infrastructure" presents increasingly divergent and often conveniently contradictory conditions. In fact, between landscape, architecture, and urbanism a nascent tug-of-war has emerged with the term, its uses, and applications. It seems essential to first establish the various guises of infrastructure within the expanded field of architecture.

In Rosalind Krauss' 1979 essay "Sculpture in the Expanded Field" Krauss observed that the practice of sculpture had been obscured and could only qualify itself in opposition to architecture and landscape.[1] Using a Klein group structure, she identifies three additional practices of sculpture that sculpture had previously been burdened with, and names them "site-construction," "marked sites," and "axiomatic structures." These three uncovered practices become disciplinary parallels that are equal yet tangential to sculptural practices.

Landscape theorist Elizabeth Meyer took on Krauss' project in her 1997 essay "The Expanded Field of Landscape," in order to define a set of practices within the discipline of landscape.[2] Meyer's new terms largely address the visual and formal configurations of landscape: "minimal garden," "articulated space," "figured ground," "landscape for architecture." Projects such as *Farming the Salton*, however, seek to extend positions of landscape, infrastructure and architecture into a more performative realm—to include economic, ecologic, or social performance.

Within the design disciplines, the term "infrastructure" presents increasingly divergent and often conveniently contradictory conditions. In fact, between landscape, architecture, and urbanism a nascent tug-of-war has emerged with the term, its uses, and applications.

One might argue that architecture—previously absorbed within Krauss' group—is similarly in need of a range of situational qualifiers to establish its position amongst the rapidly expanding disciplinary terrain of landscape architecture and urbanism. So architecture is removed from the original group and replaced with urbanism. Sculpture is replaced with a term that, like sculpture, has been so obscured of late: *infrastructure*.

Marking the expanded field of architecture reveals new formats and functions for architecture as a conduit, container, and surface found within

1 Rosalind E. Krauss, "Sculpture in the Expanded Field," in: *October* 8 (Spring 1979), pp. 30–44.

2 Elizabeth Meyer, "The Expanded Field of Landscape Architecture," in: George Thompson, Frederick Steiner (eds.), *Ecological Design and Planning*. New York 1997, pp. 45–80.

Unser Projekt, *Farming the Salton*, erfasst die Auswirkungen übermäßiger hydrologischer Manipulation in den trockensten Gebieten von Amerika und schlägt neue Modelle für Wasserinfrastrukturen vor. Das Projekt möchte die Frage aufwerfen: wie kann man territoriale, oder in diesem Fall wassergestützte Netzwerke organisieren? Und wie kann man sich eine verstärkte *Agency* für Landschaft und Infrastrukturen vorstellen?

In der Entwurfsdisziplin stellt der Begriff „Infrastruktur" zunehmend unterschiedliche und oftmals praktisch gegensätzliche Bedingungen dar. Tatsächlich hat sich zwischen Landschaft, Architektur und Urbanismus ein Tauziehen um den Begriff, sowie um seinen Gebrauch und seine Anwendungen entwickelt. Es scheint daher von grundlegender Bedeutung zu sein, zuerst die verschiedenen Erscheinungsformen der Infrastruktur innerhalb des erweiterten Feldes der Architektur herauszustellen.

In ihrem Aufsatz „Skulptur im erweiterten Feld" aus dem Jahr 1979 beobachtete Rosalind Krauss, dass die Praxis der Skulptur undeutlich geworden sei und sich nur in Opposition zu Architektur und Landschaft selbst bestimmen könne.[1] Mithilfe einer Kleinschen Gruppenstruktur identifiziert sie drei zusätzliche Praktiken der Skulptur, mit denen diese kürzlich belastet worden sei, die sie „Orts-Konstruktion", „markierte Orte" und „axiomatische Strukturen" nennt. Diese drei freigelegten Praktiken entwickeln sich zu disziplinären Entsprechungen, die den skulpturalen Praktiken gleichwertig und doch andersartig sind.

Die Landschaftstheoretikerin Elizabeth Meyer nahm in ihrem Aufsatz „The Expanded Field of Landscape Architecture" im Jahr 1997 Bezug auf Krauss' Projekt, um eine Reihe von Praktiken innerhalb der Landschaftsdisziplin zu definieren.[2] Die neuen Begriffe von Meyer beziehen sich großteils auf die visuellen und formalen Gestaltungen von Landschaft: „minimal garden", „articulated space", „figured ground", „Landschaft für Architektur". Projekte wie *Farming the Salton* bemühen sich darum, die Positionen von Landschaft, Infrastruktur und Architektur in einen performativeren Bereich auszuweiten – um auch Ökonomie, Ökologie oder soziale Leistungen zu berücksichtigen.

Man könnte anmerken, dass die Architektur – zuvor innerhalb der Gruppe von Krauss absorbiert – ebenso eine Reihe von situativen Bedingungen benötigt, um ihre Position innerhalb des sich schnell ausdehnenden Bereichs der Landschaftsarchitektur und des Urbanismus zu begründen. Die Architektur

1 Vgl. Rosalind E. Krauss, „Skulptur im erweiterten Feld", in: dies., *Die Originalität der Avantgarde und andere Mythen der Moderne*. Amsterdam und Dresden 2000, S. 331–346.

2 Vgl. Elizabeth Meyer, „The Expanded Field of Landscape Architecture", in: Frederick Steiner, George Thompson (Hg.), *Ecological Design and Planning*. New York 1997, S. 45–80.

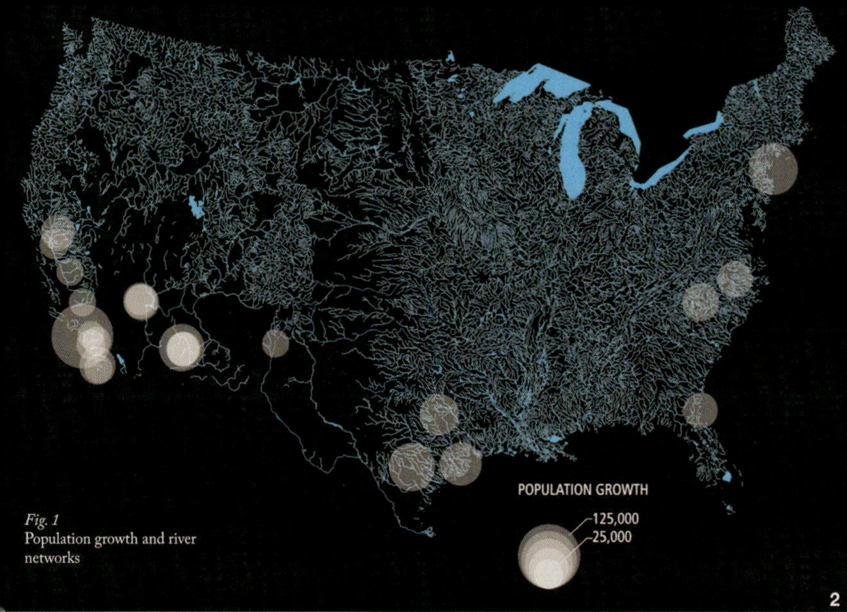

2

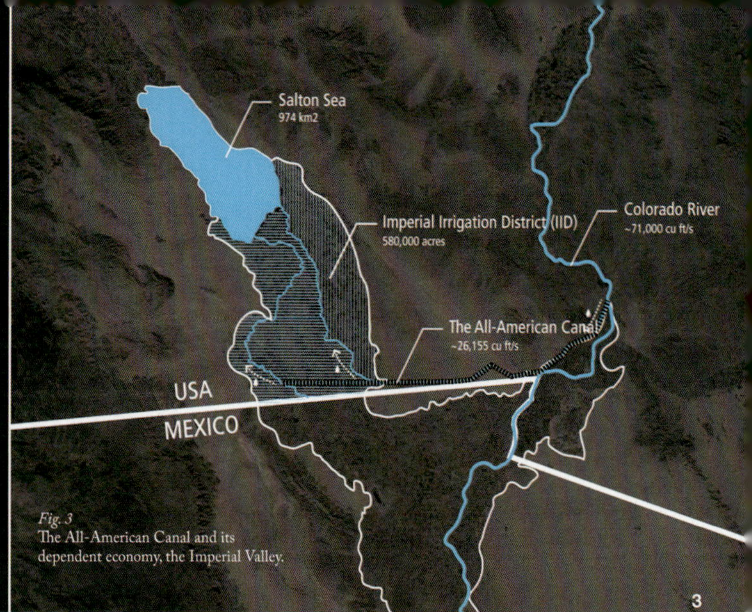

3

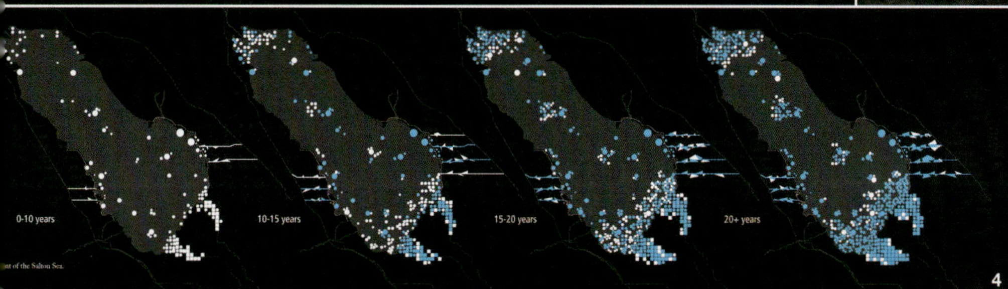

4

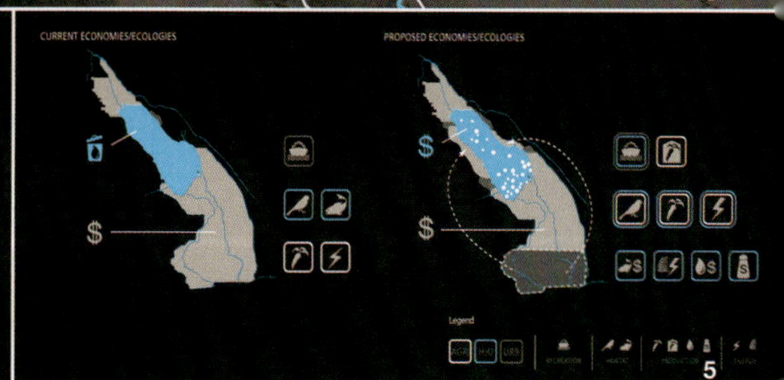

5

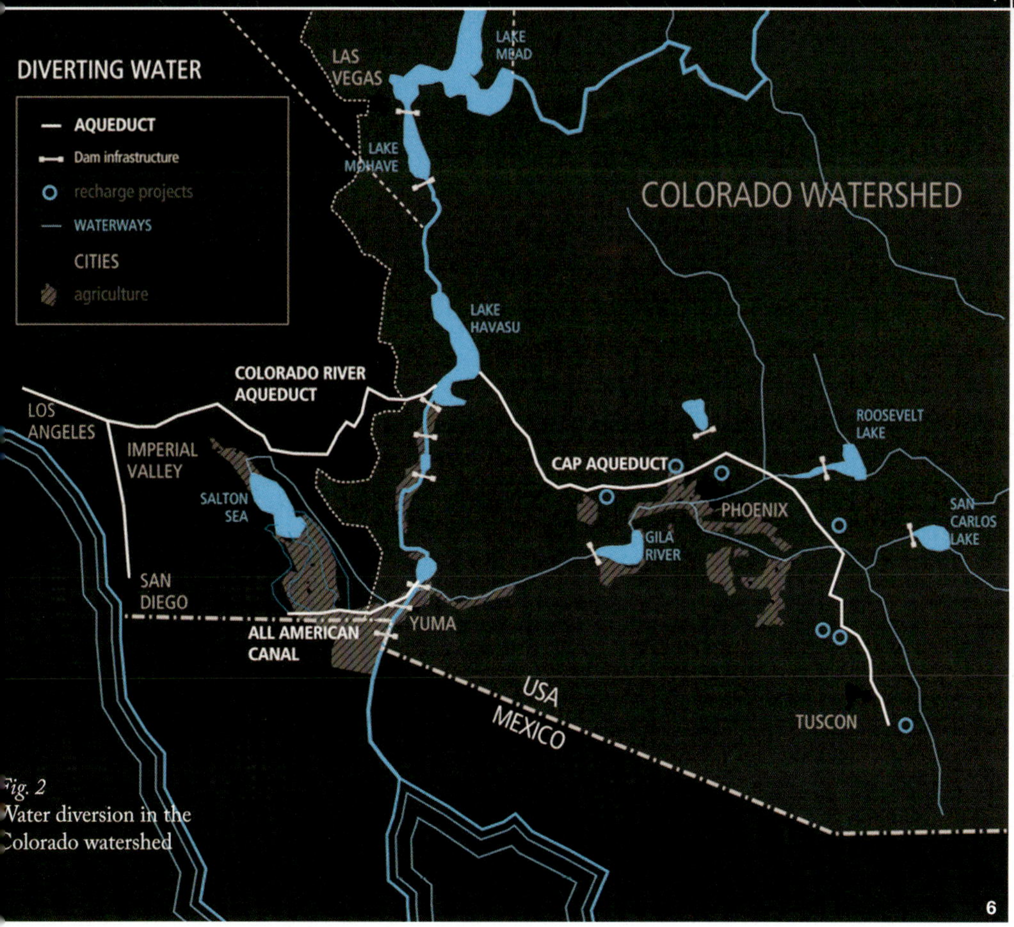

6

2 Die am schnellsten wachsenden Städte Amerikas liegen in den Gebieten mit dem größten Wassermangel.

3 Der Saltonsee ist ein extremer Salzsee, der durch das Wasser aus dem Imperial Valley, einem der größten landwirtschaftlichen Regionen Amerikas, gespeist wird.

4 Phasendiagramm der landschaftlichen Entwicklung.

5 Neue Ökonomien und Ökologien: Verlagerung der wirtschaftlichen Aktivitäten vom Imperial Valley zum Salton.

6 Nirgendwo gibt es komplexere und aufwändigere Eingriffe in den Wasserhaushalt als im Südwesten Amerikas.

2 Fastest-growing cities in the U.S. are in the areas of greatest water shortage.

3 The Salton Sea is an extreme saline lake, fed by water run-off of the Imperial Valley, one of the large agricultural regions in the U.S.

4 Phasing diagram of evolving landscape.

5 New economies and ecologies: shifting economic activity from the Imperial Valley to the Salton.

6 Nowhere is the manipulation of hydrology more complex and extensive than in the American Southwest.

the capacities of infrastructure. Rather than confined within the group, architecture could be seen to exist at the ambiguous intersection of these disciplines.

Sanford Kwinter, in his "Notes on a Third Ecology," suggests one can no longer understand urbanism and ecology as distinct/parallel practices, nor can we understand sustainability uniquely in traditional terms.[3] For many of our cities and built environments have capacities for complex social and economic self-organization, allowing them to behave as robust ecologies. Picking up the argument of the Deep Ecology movement of the 1970s, which sought to understand humans as fundamental constituents of our ecosphere, rather than independent agents, Kwinter argues that the "existential ecologies of cities are intended to comprise everything that is required for the creative and dynamic inhabitation and utilization of the contemporary environment."[4] In other words, we must begin integrating cultural and social dimensions of our environment in our understanding of the natural.

Much as the New Deal infrastructure projects and the federal highway system fundamentally reconfigured the North American landscape in the 1950s and '60s, so will the infrastructurally augmented landscapes of the American Southwest redefine our notion of natural landscapes in the early 21st century. However, the urgent need for these infrastructural landscapes also indicates that there is little room for visions of a nostalgic premodern natural condition. As our natural systems, and constructed ones, reach the end of their lifespan, new models will need to be embraced. There is no turning back; if these ecosystems and habitats are to be maintained, and agricultural productivity to continue, the landscape must exist in a more mutant condition—augmented and amplified. Infrastructure will need to learn from ecosystems: as complex systems that are able to negotiate hierarchies and scales, they will need to be economically self-sustaining, as well as environmentally adaptable, responsive and temporal.

Water Infrastructures in the Southwest. The United States has 6.5 percent of the world's fresh water within its borders, yet, despite this abundance the country is entering a period of crippling water shortages. Making the problem more acute, the driest states are also the fastest growing: six of the ten fastest growing cities in the U.S. are located in water-strapped regions of the Southwest. The constant drive for urban growth in the face of water scarcity has necessitated ever more elaborate infrastructure to transport water from wet regions to dry ones

The Colorado River is the site of ambitious feats of American engineering, many initiated during the 1930s as part of the New Deal. Man-made water networks have successfully enabled cities to grow and prosper in the desert conditions of the Southwest, but impending water shortages mean that increasingly complex regional water infrastructure is urgently needed, especially in the Colorado River basin, subverting or at least converting the natural hydrological order of the region.

3 Sanford Kwinter, "Notes on a Third Ecology," in: Mohsen Mostafavi, Gareth Doherty (eds.), *Ecological Urbanism*. Cambridge, MA 2010, pp. 94–105.

4 Ibid.

wird also aus der ursprünglichen Gruppe entfernt und durch Urbanismus ersetzt. Skulptur wird durch einen Begriff ersetzt, der in letzter Zeit ebenso unklar geworden ist wie Skulptur selbst: *Infrastruktur*.

Durch die Markierung des erweiterten Felds der Architektur zeigen sich neue Formate und Funktionen, die Architektur als einen Kreislauf, einen Transportbehälter und eine Oberfläche verstehen, wie sie innerhalb der Kapazitäten von Infrastruktur gefunden werden. Statt auf ihre Gruppe beschränkt zu bleiben, könnte die Architektur an der mehrdeutigen Schnittstelle von Disziplinen angesiedelt werden.

Sanford Kwinter schlägt in seinen „Notes on a Third Ecology" vor, dass Urbanismus und Ökologie nicht länger als abweichende/parallele Praktiken gesehen werden können, noch kann man Nachhaltigkeit allein in traditionellen Begriffen erfassen.[3] Denn viele unserer Städte und gebauten Umgebungen besitzen die Fähigkeit der komplexen und sozialen Selbstorganisation und können sich somit als robuste Ökologien verhalten. Unter Bezugnahme auf das Argument der Deep Ecology Bewegung aus den 1970ern, welche den Menschen als grundlegenden Bestandteil unserer Biosphäre und nicht als einzelnen Akteur verstand, meint Kwinter, dass die „lebenswichtigen Stadtökologien alles umfassen sollten, was für eine kreative und dynamische Bewohnung und Verwendung der zeitgenössischen Umwelt notwendig ist."[4] Anders gesagt, müssen wir damit beginnen, die kulturellen und sozialen Dimensionen unserer Umwelt in unser Verständnis des Natürlichen zu integrieren.

Ähnlich wie die Infrastrukturprojekte des New Deal und das bundesstaatliche Straßensystem die nordamerikanische Landschaft in den 1950er- und 1960er-Jahren grundlegend verändert haben, so werden auch die infrastrukturell erweiterten Landschaften des amerikanischen Südwestens unsere Auffassung von natürlichen Landschaften am Beginn des 21. Jahrhunderts neu definieren. Der dringende Bedarf an diesen infrastrukturellen Landschaften zeigt jedoch auch, dass für die Vision eines nostalgischen, prämodernen, natürlichen Zustands wenig Raum bleibt. Sobald unsere natürlichen und gebauten Systeme das Ende ihres Lebenszyklus erreichen, werden neue Modelle entwickelt werden müssen. Es gibt kein Zurück mehr; wenn diese Ökosysteme und Lebensräume erhalten bleiben sollen, und die landwirtschaftliche Produktivität andauern soll, muss die Landschaft in einen wandlungsfähigeren Zustand wechseln – erweitert und verstärkt. Die Infrastruktur wird von den Ökosystemen lernen müssen: als komplexe Systeme, die mit Hierarchien und Maßstäben umgehen können, wird sie wirt-

3 Vgl. Sanford Kwinter, „Notes on a Third Ecology", in: Mohsen Mostafavi, Gareth Doherty (Hg.), *Ecological Urbanism*. Cambridge, MA 2010, S. 94–105.

4 Ebd.

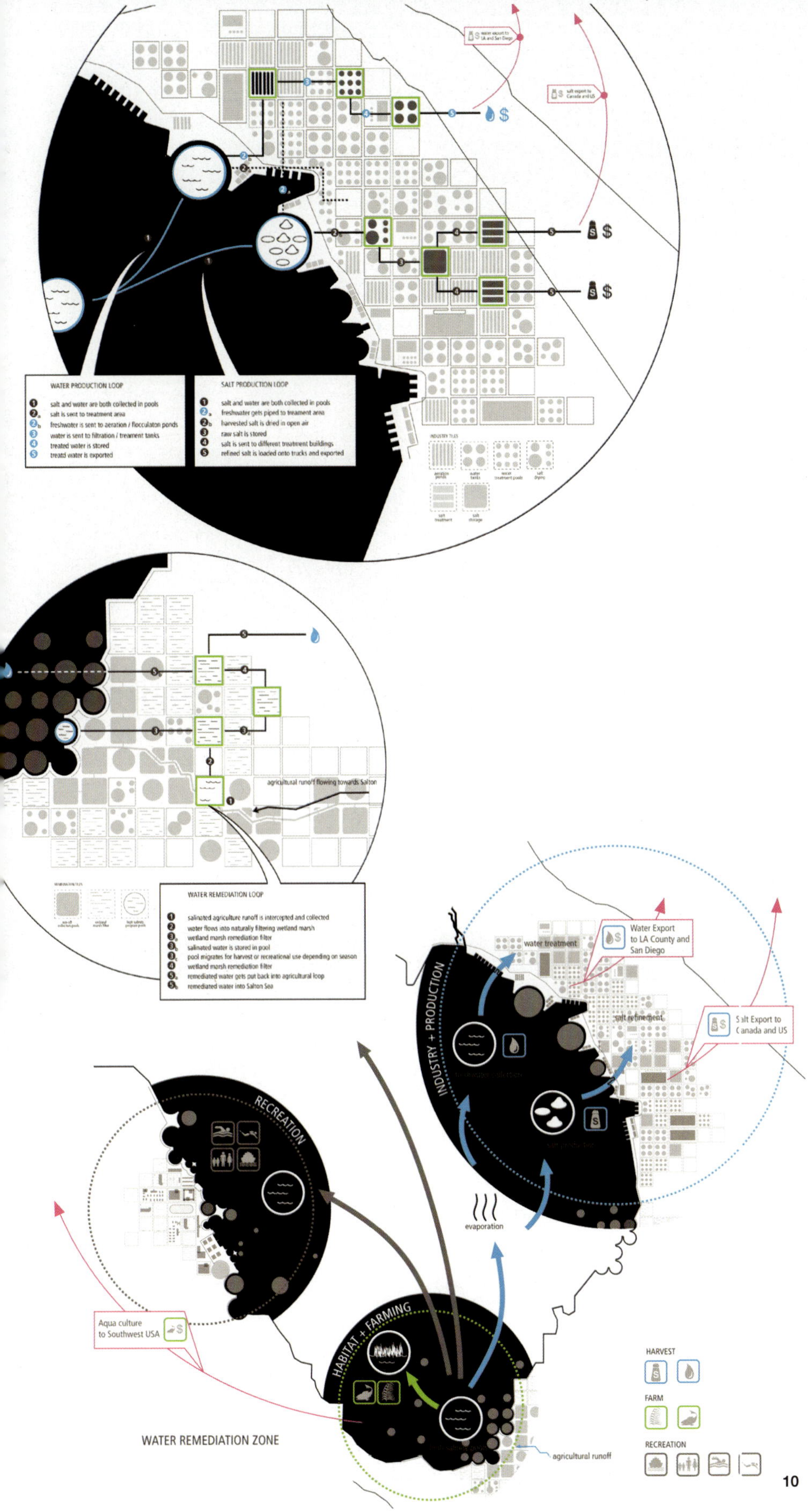

10

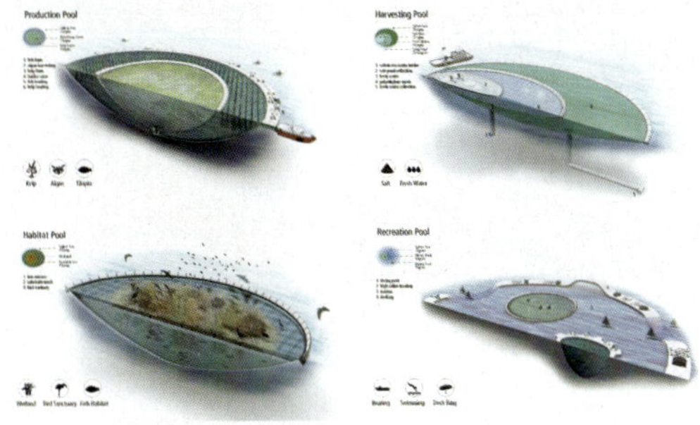

7

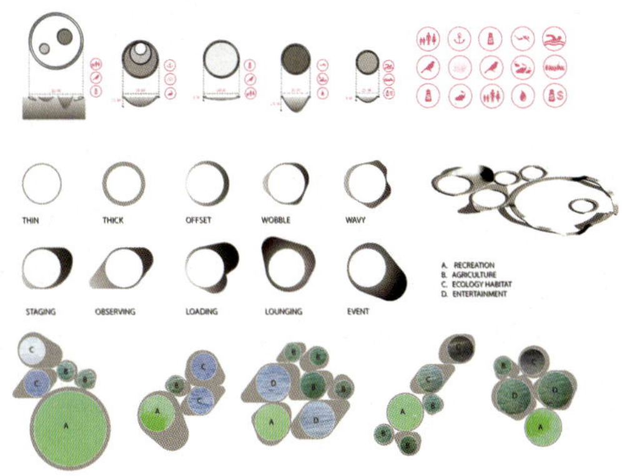

8

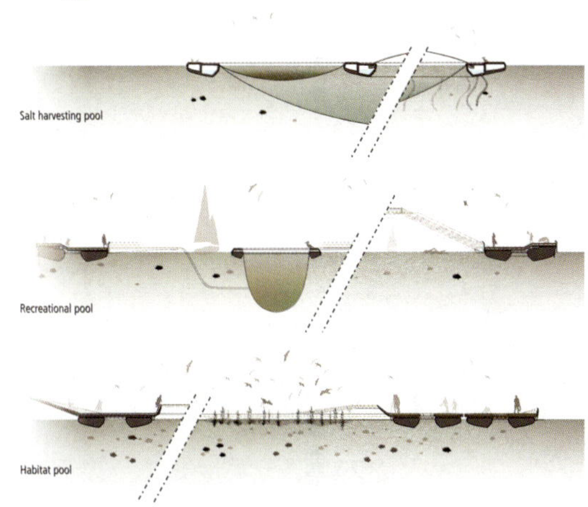

9

7 Unterschiedliche Beckentypen – Produktions-, Ernte-, Habitat- und Ruhebecken – etablieren eine neue produktive Landschaft für Salton.

8 Unterschiedliche Beckentiefen und Beckenzusammenschlüsse ermöglichen neue Ökologien innerhalb des Saltonsees.

9 Unterschiedliche Beckentiefen ermöglichen verschiedene hydroponische Aktivitäten und Ökologien.

10 Das Ernten von Wasser und Salz im neuen Salton schuf neue Industrien, Ökologien und Entspannung.

7 Various pool types—Production Pool, Harvesting Pool, Habitat Pool, and Recreation Pool—establish a new productive landscape for the Salton.

8 Varying Pool depths and aggregation of pools enable new ecologies within the Salton Sea.

9 Varying pool depths enable different hydroponic activities and ecologies.

10 Harvesting water and salt in the new Salton generated new industries, ecologies, and recreation.

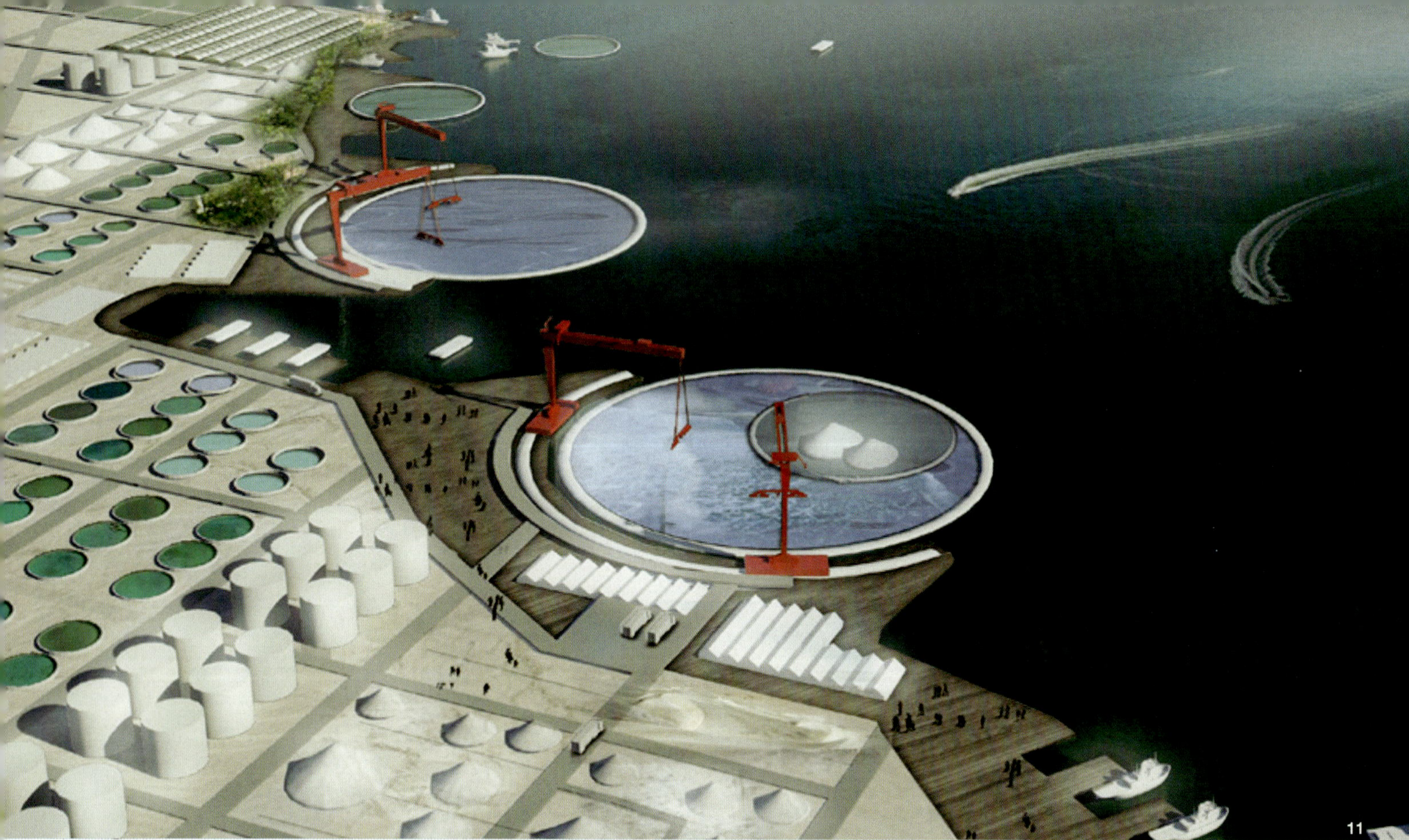

11 Blick auf den Industriebereich.
12 Blick auf die Entspannungspools.
13 Blick auf den Erholungsbereich; unterschiedliche Salinenbecken fördern verschiedene Freizeitaktivitäten.
14 Eine neue durch das Wasser ermöglichte agrarwirtschaftliche Landschaft entsteht.
11 View of industry area.
12 View of recreation pools.
13 View of recreation area; varying salinity pools encourage different leisure activities.
14 A new, water-enabled agricultural landscape emerges.

schaftlich tragfähig sein müssen, ebenso wie anpassungsfähig an die Umwelt, reaktiv und temporär.

Wasserinfrastrukturen im Südwesten. Die Vereinigten Staaten von Amerika verfügen innerhalb ihrer Grenzen über 6,5 Prozent des weltweiten Süßwasservorkommens, dennoch geht das Land trotz dieses Reichtums auf eine Periode lähmender Wasserknappheit zu. Was das Problem noch akuter macht ist die Tatsache, dass die trockensten Staaten auch die am schnellsten Wachsenden sind: sechs von zehn der am schnellsten wachsenden Städte in den USA befinden sich in wasserarmen Regionen des Südwestens. Der ständige Drang nach urbanem Wachstum im Angesicht der Wasserknappheit hat immer aufwendigere Infrastrukturen für den Wassertransport von Regionen mit häufigen Niederschlägen in Trockengebiete erforderlich gemacht.

Der Colorado River ist Schauplatz von ambitionierten Meisterleistungen der amerikanischen Technik, von denen viele als Teil des *New Deal* während der 1930er-Jahre gestartet wurden. Künstliche Wassernetzwerke haben es den Städten ermöglicht, in den wüstenartigen Bedingungen des Südwestens zu wachsen und zu Wohlstand zu kommen, jedoch bedeutet die bevorstehende Wasserknappheit, dass zunehmend komplexe regionale Wasserinfrastrukturen, vor allem im Flussbecken des Colorado River, dringend benötigt werden, was die natürliche hydrologische Ordnung der Region umstürzt oder zumindest wandelt.

In den Jahren zwischen 1935 und 1993 wurde nahezu jede Meile des Colorado River auf irgendeine Weise von diesem System aus Dämmen, Speicherseen, Wasserleitungen und Pumpstationen modifiziert. Ein Großteil der Wassermenge des Flusses in normalen hydrologischen Jahren wird heute für die landwirtschaftliche und kommunale Wasserversorgung umgeleitet, wodurch nur wenig Wasser die Mündung am Pazifik erreicht. In seiner jetzigen Form hat sich das Wassermanagementsystem des Beckens zu einem symbiotischen Netzwerk zwischen den Städten, landschaftlichen Ökologien und infrastrukturellen Technologien entwickelt.

Zusätzlich zur urbanen Nachfrage werden 15 Prozent von Amerikas Feldfrüchten und 13 Prozent des Viehbestands auf den 1,5 Millionen Hektar Ackerland erzeugt, die vom Colorado River bewässert werden; 80 bis 90 Prozent des aus dem Fluss entnommenen Wassers werden von der Landwirtschaft verbraucht.[5] Yuma in Arizona und das Imperial Valley in Kalifornien sind zwei der wichtigsten landwirtschaftlichen Regionen des Landes. Die Landwirtschaft ist dort eine Milliarden-Dollar-Industrie. Als eine der produktivsten landwirtschaftlichen Regionen der Welt konsumiert das Valley den Großteil der kalifornischen Wasserverteilung aus dem Colorado River, wie es im Vertrag von 1922 vereinbart wurde.

5 Vgl. Redlands Institute (Hg.), *Salton Sea Atlas*. Redlands, CA 2002.

In the years between 1935 and 1993 almost every mile of the Colorado River was modified in some way by this system of dams, reservoirs, aqueducts and pumping stations. Most of the flow of the river in normal hydrologic years is now diverted for agricultural and municipal water supply, leaving very little to reach its mouth in the Pacific. In its present form, the water management system of the basin has evolved into a symbiotic network between cities, landscape ecologies, and infrastructure technologies.

In addition to urban demands, 15 percent of America's crops and 13 percent of its livestock are produced on the 1.5 million hectares of farmland fed by the Colorado River; 80 to 90 percent of the water taken from the river is consumed by agriculture.[5] Yuma, Arizona, and California's Imperial Valley are two of the nation's most important agricultural regions. Farming here is a billion dollar industry. Considered one of the most productive agricultural regions in the world, the Valley consumes the vast majority of California's Colorado water allocation, as agreed upon in the 1922 compact.

The local water distribution network—the Imperial Irrigation District (IID)—comprises more than a hundred canal and pipeline branches. The system also includes check dams, spillways, pumping stations, and water reservoirs, all computer monitored. The water infrastructure that has extended, and in some cases supplanted, the Colorado River is not only constructed, it is highly automated.

Accelerated Landscapes. In this context, perhaps the most striking aspect of the water infrastructure sustaining the Southwest is the accelerated rate at which landscapes and ecologies are created, erased, and redefined. An extreme example of this environmental impact is the Salton Sea. During a season of heavy rain in 1905, the Colorado River breached its canal, flooding the Imperial Valley and refilling an ancient inland sea bed. The Salton is endorheic, or terminal, and has high evaporation rates. Officially designated as an agricultural sump or aqueous "dump" for the Imperial Valley, its highly salinated water levels are sustained by agricultural run-off.

> One of the major problems with all of the Colorado River's water, and exacerbated in the Salton Sea, is salinity, from soils and rocks, as well as from agro fertilizers.

Development around the Salton began in the 1920s and peaked in the 1950s and 1960s. The Salton had become a California Riviera, with luxury resorts, country clubs, marinas, and golf courses. In the 1950s the Salton was artificially stocked with a variety of fish species, making it a significant destination for fishing, camping, hiking, bird watching, and boating. Then, from the 1960s to the 1990s, the Salton suffered massive fish and bird die-offs, as agri-chemical pollutants entered the lower food chain species.[6]

5 See Redlands Institute (ed.), *Salton Sea Atlas*. Redlands, CA 2002.

6 Ibid.

Slowly species have begun to reestablish, and with large numbers of fish come large numbers of migrating birds (nearly 400 species), for whom the Salton represents a key stop-over along a Pacific flyway.

One of the major problems with all of the Colorado River's water, and exacerbated in the Salton Sea, is salinity, from soils and rocks, as well as from agro fertilizers. Currently, the Salton Sea is 25 percent more saline than the ocean and increasing by a rate of approximately 1 percent annually, due largely to evaporation. In 2003 a federally mandated requirement to transfer over 10 percent of the Imperial Valley's water allocation to San Diego threatened the Salton's future.

Massive infrastructure projects are proposed to preserve the ecological stability of the sea. Without a long-term plan, the sea will decline rapidly, losing roughly 60 percent of its volume, tripling its salinity, and exposing nearly 300 km^2 of lake bed within a dozen years, leaving it to a fate not dissimilar to Owens Lake, the emblem of water mismanagement in the south.[7] Most proposals for mitigating the collapse of the Salton Sea rely on old technological fixes: piping water from the Pacific Gulf and desalinating, building huge barrier dams, pumping stations, and canals, to partition the sea into northern and southern ecosystems. Most projects suggest that maintaining the sea in its current form is impossible, and take the current environmental problems as a liability to be accepted and accommodated.[8]

The legacy of civil engineering in the American Southwest is one of large-scale infrastructures that seek to control and harness the landscape—as water resource, as energy source, or as cultivatable land.

The legacy of civil engineering in the American Southwest is one of large-scale infrastructures that seek to control and harness the landscape—as water resource, as energy source, or as cultivatable land. *Water Economies & Ecologies* asks: How can water infrastructure be interactive, public, and adaptable, and perform more symbiotically with landscapes, such that they act as "augmenters of ecologies" rather than overhauls?

The Salton Sea's extreme salinity and threatened ecosystems offer an opportunity for economic, social, and ecological innovation. Our proposal establishes the Salton Sea as a site for water harvesting. No longer serving as an hydrological sump or supporting a monoagricultural landscape, the Salton would also offer new forms of leisure, protected habitats, and new industries—harvesting fish, kelp, water, and (in a return to its namesake) salt.

The project proposes three zones of coastal development: an ecology zone, an industry zone and a recreational zone. The project populates the

7 Joel Bourne Jr., "Salton Sea," in: *National Geographic Magazine* (February 2005).

8 Brendan McCarthy, "Restoring the Salton Sea," in: *The Legislative Analyst's Office*, January 24, 2008.

Das lokale Wasserverteilungsnetzwerk – das Imperial Irrigation District (IID) – umfasst mehr als hundert Kanäle und Leitungsverzweigungen. Das System enthält zudem Rückhaltedämme, Überläufe, Pumpstationen und Wasserspeicher – alle von Computern überwacht. Die Wasserinfrastruktur, die den Colorado River erweitert und in einigen Fällen verdrängt hat, ist nicht nur konstruiert, sie ist auch in hohem Maße automatisiert.

Angereicherte Landschaften. In diesem Kontext ist der vermutlich bemerkenswerteste Aspekt der Wasserinfrastrukturen, die den Südwesten versorgen, die beschleunigte Frequenz, in der Landschaften und Ökologien gebildet, zerstört und neu definiert werden. Ein extremes Beispiel dieser ökologischen Auswirkung stellt der Saltonsee dar. Während einer starken Regenzeit im Jahr 1905 verließ der Colorado River sein Bett, überflutete das Imperial Valley und füllte einen ehemaligen Binnensee wieder mit Wasser. Der Salton ist endorheisch, oder abgeschlossen, und hat hohe Verdunstungsraten. Offiziell als landwirtschaftliche Sickergrube oder wasserhaltiger Entsorgungsplatz für das Imperial Valley vorgesehen, wird sein äußerst salzhaltiges Wasser vom landwirtschaftlichen Zufluss gespeist.

Die Entwicklung rund um den Salton begann in den 1920ern und erreichte ihren Höhepunkt in den 1950er- und 1960er-Jahren. Der Salton war zu einer kalifornischen Riviera geworden, mit Luxusressorts, Country Clubs, Jachthäfen und Golfplätzen. In den 1950ern wurde der Salton künstlich mit zahlreichen Fischarten bestückt, was ihn zu einem beliebten Ziel für Fischer, Camper, Wanderer, Vögelbeobachter und Bootsfahrer machte. Später, von den 1960ern bis zu den 1990ern, litt der Salton unter einem massiven Fisch- und Vogelsterben, da agrochemische Verunreinigungen die Lebewesen am unteren Ende der Nahrungskette erreichten.[6] Langsam siedelten sich die Arten wieder an und mit den vielen Fischen kamen auch die Zugvögel (fast 400 Arten), für die der Salton eine wichtige Zwischenstation auf der pazifischen Zugstraße darstellt.

Eines der größten Probleme mit all dem Wasser aus dem Colorado River, ist die Salzhaltigkeit der Böden und Felsen, sowie der landwirtschaftlichen Dünger – was sich im Saltonsee noch verschlimmert. Im Moment ist der See um 25 Prozent salzhaltiger als der Ozean, was sich jährlich um etwa ein Prozent steigert, hauptsächlich aufgrund von Verdunstung. Im Jahr 2003 bedrohte eine Bundesverordnung, die über 10 Prozent des Wassers für das Imperial Valley nach San Diego umleiten wollte, die Zukunft des Salton.

Riesige Infrastrukturprojekte werden zum Erhalt der ökologischen Stabilität des Sees vorgeschlagen. Ohne einen langfristigen Plan wird der See rasch kleiner werden und etwa 60 Prozent seines Volumens verlieren, was seinen Salzgehalt verdrei-

6 Ebd.

15 Luftbild des Saltonsees.
16 Blick auf das Industriegebiet mit Fischzucht, Algenanbau, Wasserentsalzung und Salzernte.
17 Blick auf das Ökologiegebiet mit Feuchtgebieten und Vogelreservat.
15 Aerial view of Salton Sea.
16 View of industry area, with fish-farming, algae farming, water desalination and salt harvesting.
17 View of ecology area supporting wetlands and bird habitats.

Salton with floating pools of various sizes and salinities. These pools serve as salinity regulation devices as well as harvest plots, habitats, and recreational destinations. There are four pool types, varying in scale and complexity, dedicated to production, harvesting, recreation, and habitat. These micro-ecologies are partially moored in place but can also migrate within a territorial range of the Salton. Pool types vary in depth to control evaporation rates; and in width to suggest different uses. Pools can aggregate to establish intensified habitats or harvest.

Regulating the salinity levels of the water, salt water pools separate salt and fresh water. This is done using passive solar desalination, where freshwater condenses on a transparent fabric and collects in the hollow structural ring of the pool. Briny by-product fosters high saline habitats. Salt meanwhile is harvested, shifting a previous ecological liability into an economic asset.

Soft Infrastructures, Mutant Natures. Large infrastructure projects in America in the 1930s, such as those of the Works Progress Administration (WPA) created jobs during their construction that ceased once the projects were built. The Tennessee Valley Authority (TVA) provides perhaps the most interesting model. It too was a major employer during the Depression, on the construction phase of projects. However, it continues its relevance today through economic development, job creation, education, and research. Rather than simply providing an energy resource, its role is more diverse, tentacular and long-term.

Projects such as *Farming the Salton* argue that infrastructure (and architecture) should be entrepreneurial. Current proposals for the Salton Sea are engineered, cost-intensive and serve merely as mitigators of environmental imbalances. *Farming the Salton* projects a system that could be built incrementally, allowing new ways to think about investment. But more importantly, it seeks to generate ongoing economic benefits, through new industries that might dovetail into the infrastructure, and through restored ecologies that in turn reinvigorate recreation and tourism (once the lifeblood of the region).

Current proposals for the Salton Sea are engineered, cost-intensive and serve merely as mitigators of environmental imbalances. *Farming the Salton* projects a system that could be built incrementally, allowing new ways to think about investment.

Farming the Salton seeks to capitalize on existing hybrid conditions between landscape, farming, and water infrastructure in the region. Rather than a New Deal approach of massive engineering or iconic infrastructure, *Farming the Salton* employs adaptable, responsive, small-scale interventions. Easily replaced or upgraded, these infrastructures double as landscape life support, creating new sites for production or recreation. The ambition

fachen und fast 300 km^2 des Seebodens innerhalb weniger Jahre freilegen würde. Damit droht ihm ein ähnliches Schicksal wie dem Owens Lake, der zum Sinnbild für Wassermisswirtschaft im Süden geworden ist.[7] Die meisten Vorschläge zur Verhinderung des Zusammenbruchs des Saltonsees vertrauen auf alte technologische Lösungen: Wasser aus dem Pazifischen Golf zu pumpen und zu entsalzen, riesige Staudämme, Pumpstationen und Kanäle zu bauen, den See in nördliche und südliche Ökosysteme aufzuteilen. Die meisten Projekte vermitteln, dass es unmöglich sei, den See in seiner derzeitigen Form zu erhalten und nehmen die derzeitigen Umweltprobleme als Bürde an, die akzeptiert werden und auf die man sich einstellen muss.[8]

Das Vermächtnis des Hoch- und Tiefbaus im amerikanischen Südwesten ist von großformatigen Infrastrukturen geprägt, welche die Landschaft kontrollieren und sie sich nutzbar machen wollen – als Wasserressource, Energieressource oder als Ackerland. *Ökonomie und Ökologie des Wassers* fragt danach, wie Wasserinfrastruktur interaktiv, öffentlich und anpassungsfähig sein und symbiotischer mit Landschaften zusammenarbeiten kann, so dass sie eher als „Verstärker der Ökologie", statt als deren Reparaturwerkzeug auftritt.

Der extreme Salzgehalt und die bedrohten Ökosysteme des Saltonsees bieten die Möglichkeit einer ökonomischen, sozialen und ökologischen Erneuerung. Unser Vorschlag entwickelt den Saltonsee als einen Standort des Wasserertrags. Dient dieser nicht länger als hydrologischer Sumpf oder unterstützt eine monokulturelle Landschaft, würde der Saltonsee auch neue Formen des Freizeitangebots, geschützter Lebensräume und neuer Industrien anbieten – die ihre Erträge mit Fisch, Seetang, Wasser und (als Rückbesinnung auf seine Namensgebung) Salz erzielen.

Das Projekt schlägt drei Bereiche der Küstenentwicklung vor: einen ökologischen Bereich, einen industriellen Bereich und ein Erholungsgebiet. Das Projekt besiedelt den Salton mit schwimmenden Becken variabler Größe und Salzhaltigkeit. Diese Becken dienen der Salzregulierung wie als Ertragsfelder, Lebensräume und Erholungsziele. Es gibt vier Beckenarten, die in Größe und Komplexität variieren, und die der Produktion, dem Ertrag, der Erholung und dem Lebensraum gewidmet sind. Diese Mikro-Ökologien sind teilweise an einer Stelle festgemacht, können aber auch innerhalb eines territorialen Abschnitts des Saltons umherwandern. Die Beckenarten variieren in ihrer Tiefe, um die Verdunstungsraten zu kontrollieren; und in ihrer Breite, um verschiedene Verwendungen zu ermöglichen. Die Becken können auch verbunden werden, um die Intensitäten von Lebensräumen oder Ertragsfeldern zu erhöhen.

Um den Salzgehalt des Wassers zu regulieren, trennen Salzwasserbecken Salz von Süßwasser. Dies geschieht durch Ver-

7 Vgl. Joel Bourne Jr., „Salton Sea", in: *National Geographic Magazine* (Februar 2005).

8 Vgl. Brendan McCarthy, „Restoring the Salton Sea", in: *The Legislative Analyst's Office*, 24.1.2008.

dunstung, wobei das Süßwasser auf einem transparenten Stoff kondensiert und sich in dem hohlen strukturellen Ring des Beckens sammelt. Solehaltige Nebenprodukte fördern hochgradig salzhaltige Lebensräume. Nebenbei wird Salz geerntet, was eine vormals ökologische Belastung in eine ökonomische Bereicherung verwandelt.

Entstehende Infrastrukturen, wandelbare Naturen. In den 1930ern schufen große Infrastrukturprojekte in Amerika, wie jene der Works Progress Administration (WPA), Arbeitsplätze während ihrer Ausführung, die verschwanden, sobald die Projekte fertiggestellt waren. Die Tennessee Valley Authority (TVA) stellt das vielleicht interessanteste Modell dar. Sie war während der Depression ebenfalls ein bedeutender Arbeitgeber in der Bauphase von Projekten. Dennoch hat sie ihre Bedeutung bis heute durch wirtschaftliche Entwicklung, Arbeitsplatzschaffung, Ausbildung und Forschung aufrechterhalten. Statt schlicht ein Anbieter für Energie zu sein, ist ihre Rolle vielfältiger, verzweigter und langfristiger.

Projekte wie *Farming the Salton* argumentieren, dass Infrastruktur (und Architektur) unternehmerisch vorgehen müssen. Derzeitige Vorschläge für den Saltonsee sind technisiert, kostenintensiv und dienen nur der Abschwächung von ökologischen Unausgewogenheiten. *Farming the Salton* projektiert ein System, das schrittweise verwirklicht werden könnte und somit neue Denkweisen über Investitionen erlaubt. Noch wichtiger ist jedoch, dass es andauernde wirtschaftliche Vorteile generieren will, durch neue Industrien, die sich mit der Infrastruktur verzahnen können, und durch wiederhergestellte Ökologien, die im Gegenzug die Erholung und den Tourismus (einstmals das Herzblut der Region) stärken.

Farming the Salton will aus den existierenden hybriden Bedingungen, die zwischen Landschaft, Bewirtschaftung und Wasserinfrastruktur in der Region herrschen, Kapital schlagen. Statt eines New Deal-Ansatzes mit enormer Technik oder ikonenhafter Infrastruktur, vertraut *Farming the Salton* auf anpassungsfähige, gut reagierende und kleinformatige Eingriffe. Durch ihre leichte Austauschbarkeit oder Erneuerung verdoppeln sich diese Infrastrukturen zu Lebenserhaltungssystemen in und für die Landschaft, was wiederum neue Orte der Produktion und Erholung erzeugt. Der Anspruch besteht darin, gefährdete Landschaften zu ergänzen, anstatt sie zu reparieren. Das Projekt ist bemüht, existierende Landschaften mit entstehenden Systemen zu kombinieren, um ein Netzwerk von Ökologien und Ökonomien innerhalb eines neuen öffentlichen Raums zu erzeugen.[9]

Übersetzung Claudia Wrumnig

9 *Farming the Salton* ist ein diskursives Projekt von Lola Sheppard und Mason White, LeiterInnen des Lateral Office mit Sitz in Toronto, Kalifornien.

is to supplement landscapes at risk rather than overhaul them. The project strives to combine existing landscapes with emergent systems to catalyze a network of ecologies and economies in a new public realm.[9]

9 *Farming the Salton* is a discursive project by Lateral Office, of principals Lola Sheppard and Mason White, based in Toronto, California.

1 *Folding Water*: durchlässige, belüftete Ufermauer zur Regulierung des Meeresspiegels. *Folding Water*: permeable ventilated seawall for regulation rising sea levels.

Fluid Machines

Folding Water designed by Kuth/Ranieri Architects is a permeable ventilated seawall intended to wrap the coastal regions of San Francisco most vulnerable to flooding.[1] Their strategy, which attempts to mitigate dramatic global and climatic transformations by regulating rising sea levels, is a more complex response to the need for urban containment that acknowledges, and draws from, the ever-changing fluctuations of the natural environment.

Flüssige Maschinen. Das von Kuth/Ranieri Architects entworfene Projekt *Folding Water* basiert auf einer durchlässigen, belüfteten Ufermauer, die jene Küstenregionen von San Francisco umschließen soll, welche am stärksten von Hochwasser bedroht sind.[1] Die Strategie der Architekten, die dramatische globale und klimatische Veränderungen durch die Regulierung des steigenden Meeresspiegels entschärfen will, ist eine komplexere Antwort auf die Notwendigkeit einer urbanen Eindämmung, welche die ständigen Veränderungen der natürlichen Umgebung wahrnimmt und aus ihnen schöpft.

ILA BERMAN

2

3

4

Folding Water

2 Schnittansicht
3 Frontalansicht
4 Schnitt
2 sectional view
3 front elevation
4 section

Als Teil einer neuen Art von experimentellen, „bahnbrechenden“ Infrastrukturprojekten, besetzt *Folding Water* die amphibische Zone zwischen Land und Wasser, während es aus den Möglichkeiten Kapital zu schlagen versucht, die von der dynamischen Hydrogeografie angeboten werden, in welche es eingebettet ist.

In dem Projekt wird der traditionelle Gegensatz zwischen Damm und Wasser durch die Erzeugung eines flüssigen Wellenbrechers – buchstäblich eine massive „Wasserfalte“ – aufgelöst, der auf künstliche Weise den Stadtrand beschützt, während er die Ökologie der Mündung erhält, die von dem Fluss der Gezeitenbewegung abhängig ist. Statt einfach eine große Staumauer um die Stadt zu bauen und damit deren Gebäude anzuheben und die Stabilität und Quantität des urbanen Bodens dramatisch zu erhöhen (eine Taktik, die bereits für die Schaffung vieler wachsender, künstlicher Inseln in den Niederlanden verwendet wird), nimmt dieses Projekt kalkulierte Mischungen aus Strömung und Stillstand in seine Entwurfsparameter auf, um eine synthetischere Beziehung zwischen der künstlichen Eindämmung einer Stadt und dem Fluss ihrer natürlichen, flüssigen Umgebung zu fördern. Die Notwendigkeit, den Anstieg der Küstengewässer beizubehalten und zu regulieren, während gleichzeitig der Anstieg des Meeresspiegels und unvorhersehbare ozeanische Veränderungen berücksichtigt werden, wird durch eine strategische Krümmung und Aufspaltung der Wasseroberfläche bewältigt, die ermöglicht, dass die Gewässer zwischen dem Ozean und der Bucht getrennt, verteilt und vermittelt werden können und doch ununterbrochen bleiben. Diese Falte erzeugt einen dynamischen, flexiblen Anschluss auf einer nahtlosen Oberfläche – eine entscheidende Antwort auf unser Bedürfnis sowohl nach Trennung als auch nach Verbundenheit mit der veränderlichen Natur, die uns umgibt.

Die gefaltete Wassermauer, welche die bedrohende Wellenfront der Sturmflut sonderbar nachahmt, der sie standhalten soll, wiederholt sowohl theatralisch die überlappenden, flüssigen Wellenmuster als sie sich auch von ihnen unterscheidet und belebt somit die Meeresoberfläche. Belebt ohne beweglich zu sein, ist sie paradoxerweise eine flüssige Wassermauer, welche die weniger vorhersehbaren Bewegungen des Wassers regeln soll. Das System versteckt seinen raffinierten Mechanismus camouflage-artig hinter einer Mauer aus Wasser, die vielleicht dazu dient, seine künstliche Implementierung eher zu verbergen als zu zeigen, vergleichbar mit der heimlichen Anpassung an die umgebende Oberfläche sowohl von Raubtieren als auch von Beutetieren in der Wildnis.

Als räumliche Strategie, die sich in den Mustern der Gezeiten auf der Meeresoberfläche und den komplizierten topo-

1 Das Projekt wurde ursprünglich für den *City of the Future*-Wettbewerb in San Francisco entworfen, der von History Channel, Infinity und IBM im Januar 2008 organisiert worden war. Es wurde später neu entwickelt und war im Juli 2009 im *Rising Tides*-Wettbewerb ein siegreicher Beitrag.

Part of a new breed of experimental “ground-breaking” infrastructural projects, *Folding Water* occupies that amphibious zone between land and water while attempting to capitalize on the opportunities proffered by the dynamic hydro-geography in which it is immersed.

In the project the traditional opposition of levee and water is dissolved through the creation of a fluid breakwater system—literally a massive “fold of water”—that artificially protects the edge of the city, while preserving the estuarine ecologies that are dependent on the flows of tidal movement. Rather than simply constructing a large levee wall around the city, elevating its buildings, or dramatically increasing the stability and quantity of urban ground (a tactic already used for the creation of many expanded artificial islands in the Netherlands), this project incorporates calculated mixtures of flow and stasis into its design parameters to encourage a more synthetic relationship between the artificial containment of the city and the flux of its natural fluid environs. The necessity of maintaining and regulating coastal water elevations, while accommodating sea level rise and unpredictable oceanic fluctuations, is managed by a strategic inflection and bifurcation of the surface of the water that enables the waters between ocean and bay to be divided, spaced, and mediated, yet still remain continuous. This fold produces a dynamic flexible joint in a seamless surface, a critical response to our need for both separation from and connectivity to the mutable nature that surrounds us.

The folded wall of water, which is strangely mimetic to the threatening wavefront of the storm surge that it is meant to withstand, both theatrically repeats and differentiates itself from the overlapping fluid wave patterns animating the oceanic surface. Animated without being ambulatory, it is, paradoxically, a liquid water wall meant to modulate the less predictable movements of water. Operating through a form of camouflage, the system hides its sophisticated mechanism behind a wall of water, intended perhaps, as with the surreptitious surface transformations of both predators and prey in the wilderness, to conceal rather than reveal its artificial implantation.

The folded wall of water, which is strangely mimetic to the threatening wavefront of the storm surge that it is meant to withstand, both theatrically repeats and differentiates itself from the overlapping fluid wave patterns animating the oceanic surface.

The fold as a spatial strategy, evident in the tidal patterns of the oceanic surface and the intricate topological undulations of coastal and subsurface topographies, draws its logic from operative traits of the real—continuities intrinsic to natural matter that, through its variable forms, both index and

1 This project was initially designed for the *City of the Future* competition in San Francisco organized by the History Channel, Infinity and IBM in San Francisco in January 2008, and was later redeveloped and was a winning entry for the *Rising Tides* competition in July 2009.

reveal the evolutionary forces and material processes responsible for their very genesis.[2] Folds in nature are less distinct as determinate forms than evidence of matter-energy in flux and the confluence of forces responsible for the continuous formations and deformations of the environmental landscape. Modern flood-control systems, often governed by our cultural obsession with stasis and permanence, have traditionally perceived these forces only as threatening and have therefore responded with infrastructures that function solely through resistance, constraint and control, with the intention of neutralizing rather than strategically *enfolding* (and thereby making use of) nature's vital (per)formative energy.

As an alternative to the static and solid levee wall, *Folding Water* is a fluidal perforated surface that depends upon natural tidal movement to manage alluvial and biotic flows across the variable depth of the wall. Solid and liquid, defensive and permeable, the sea wall is therefore both barrier and instrument for fluvial exchange, a flexible system generated from blending mobile and static attributes that coalesce to create a new bio-technological ecological infrastructure. Rather than a rigid and solid protective levee wall, *Folding Water* is a thick porous surface, intermittently filled with a cellular stack of pump ventilators: a supple sponge-like aggregate structure that manages the flow of sediment, salinity and biota across its variable depth. Natural sponges are inherently open systems of variation and flexibility. They are continuous layered cellular organizations that allow for complex and heterogeneous modes of connectivity, while consisting of differentiated degrees of material density and porosity—important attributes of adaptable living systems in constant fluid exchange with their environments. They are also systems, akin to the lungs in our own bodies, whose expanded internal surface areas (the space-filling surface folds that diminish the difference between boundary and fill) exponentially increase their capacity for locally mediated material transfers—a mechanism deployed for storm mitigation and sea level management in this project.

As an alternative to the static and solid levee wall, *Folding Water* is a fluidal perforated surface that depends upon natural tidal movement to manage alluvial and biotic flows across the variable depth of the wall.

The operative functions of *Folding Water* are dependent on the natural movements of the tides, generating an interactive network that not only takes advantage of the dynamic flux of this liquid environment, but also integrates its forces into the programmatic design parameters of the project, invoking a "material model" that capitalizes on the inherent continuities and inexhaustible animation of nature's matter-energy matrix. Here, the

2 The concept of the trait as an operative function of matter, and the fold as a material inflection that conjoins differing material organizations, is drawn from Gilles Deleuze, *The Fold: Leibniz and the Baroque*. Minneapolis 1993.

logischen Wogen der Küsten- und Unterwasserlandschaften zeigt, schöpft die Falte ihre Logik aus operativen Eigenschaften der Realität – immanenten Kontinuitäten der natürlichen Materie, die aufgrund ihrer veränderlichen Form die evolutionären Kräfte und materiellen Prozesse, die gerade für ihre Entstehung verantwortlich sind, gleichermaßen verzeichnen und aufzeigen.[2] Falten sind in der Natur weniger deutlich eindeutige Formen als eher ein Beweis für den Fluss von Materie und Energie und den Zusammenfluss von Kräften, die für die ständige Formung und Verformung der umgebenden Landschaft verantwortlich sind. Moderne Hochwasserschutzsysteme, die oft von unserer kulturellen Besessenheit von Stillstand und Beständigkeit beherrscht werden, haben diese Kräfte traditionell nur als bedrohend wahrgenommen und deshalb mit Infrastrukturen geantwortet, die rein durch Widerstand, Einschränkung und Kontrolle funktionieren – mit der Absicht, die lebenswichtige (per)formative Energie der Natur eher zu neutralisieren, als sie strategisch zu *entfalten* (und sich damit zu Nutze zu machen).

Als Alternative zu der statischen und massiven Dammmauer besteht *Folding Water* aus einer flüssigen, perforierten Oberfläche, die von der natürlichen Gezeitenbewegung abhängig ist, um ablagernde und biotische Strömungen entlang der variablen Tiefe der Mauer zu steuern. Die Ufermauer ist somit gleichermaßen Hindernis und Mittel des fluvialen Austausches – massiv und flüssig, abwehrend und durchlässig –, ein flexibles System, erzeugt durch die Vermischung von beweglichen und statischen Attributen, die ineinanderfließen, um eine neue biotechnologische und ökologische Infrastruktur zu erzeugen. Anstatt einer starren und massiven Schutzmauer ist *Folding Water* eine dicke, poröse Oberfläche, die periodisch mit einer zellulären Schicht aus pumpenden Luftlöchern gefüllt ist: eine geschmeidige, schwammartige Gesamtstruktur, welche die Strömung von Ablagerungen, Salzgehalt und Organismen über ihre variable Tiefe steuert. Natürliche Schwämme sind grundsätzlich offene Systeme mit Variation und Flexibilität. Sie sind durchgängige, geschichtete und zelluläre Organisationen, die komplexe und heterogene Verbindungsarten ermöglichen, während sie gleichzeitig aus differenzierten Graden an materieller Dichte und Porosität bestehen – wichtige Eigenschaften von anpassungsfähigen Lebenssystemen, die in ständigem fließenden Austausch mit ihrer Umgebung stehen. Sie sind außerdem Systeme, ähnlich den Lungen in unseren eigenen Körpern, deren erweiterte innere Oberflächenbereiche (die raumfüllenden Oberflächenfalten, die den Unterschied zwischen Rand und Füllung reduzieren) exponentiell ihre Leistungsstärke für lokal vermittelten Materialfluss erhöhen – ein Mechanismus, der in diesem Projekt für die

2 Das Konzept der Eigenschaft als einer operativen Funktion der Materie und der Falte als einer materiellen Krümmung, die abweichende materielle Organisationen verbindet, bezieht sich auf Gilles Deleuze, *Die Falte. Leibniz und der Barock*. Frankfurt/M. 2000.

5

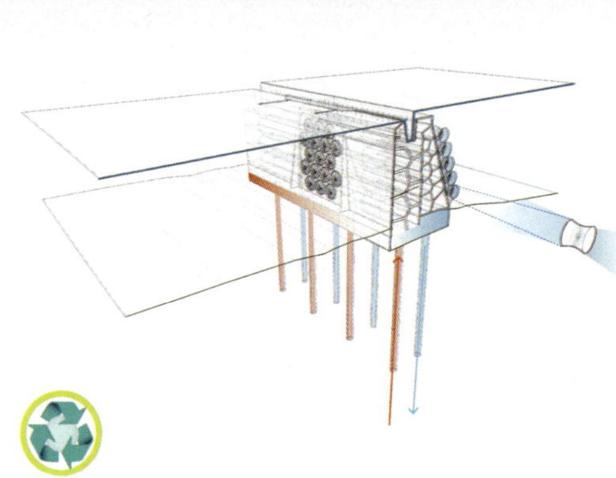

6

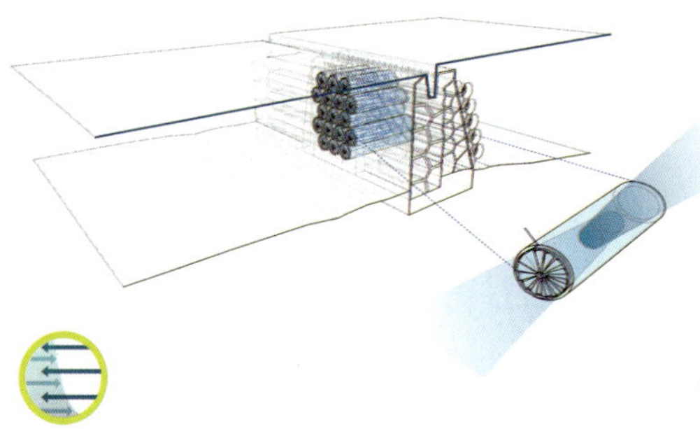

7

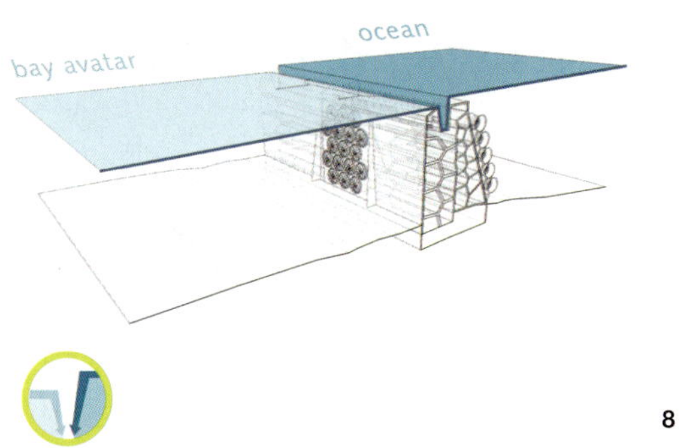

8

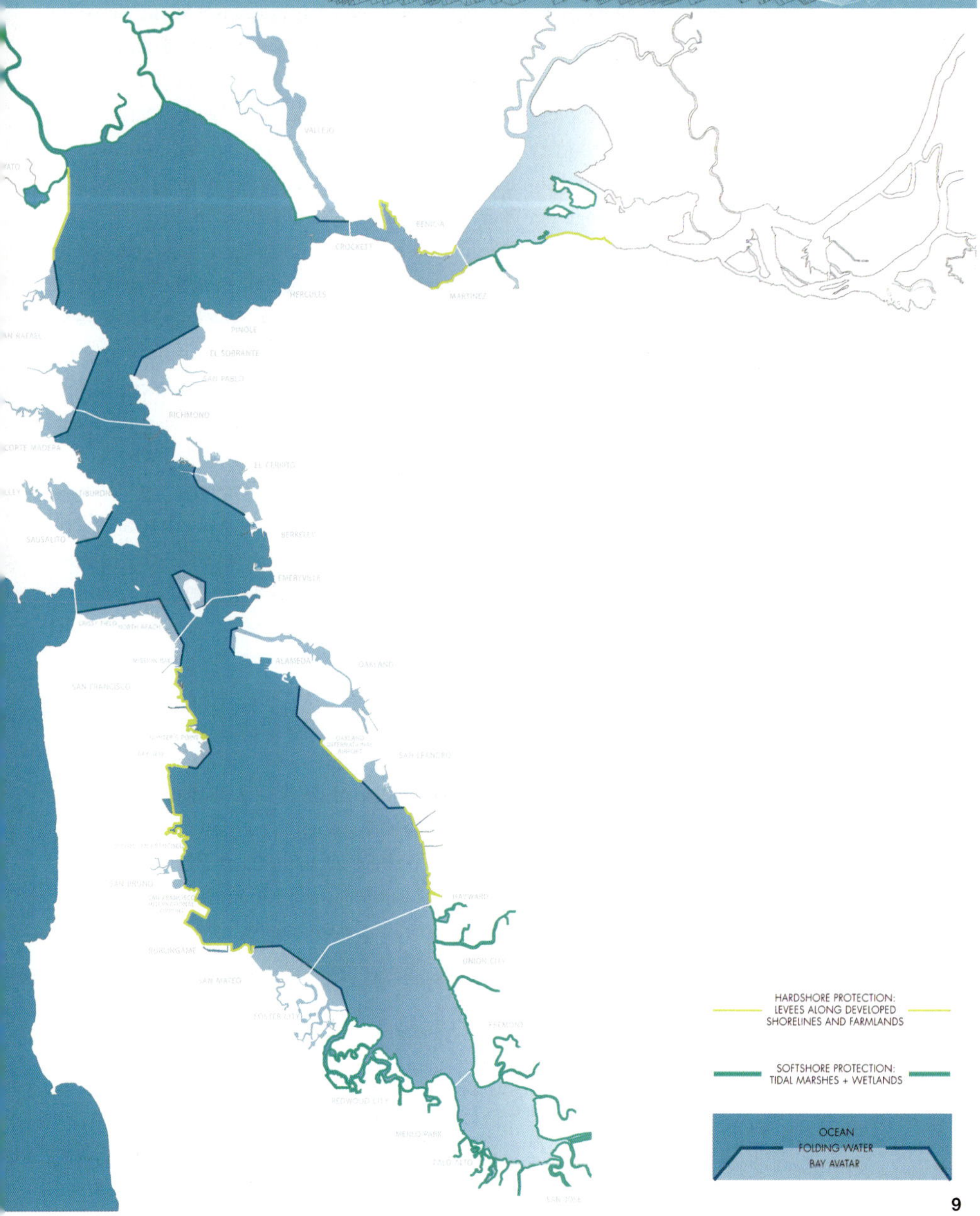

9

Fold ng Water

5 Landmasse und Topografie der Mündung
6 Autarke Energie durch Geothermie und Gezeiten
7 Gezeitenmanagement – der Ventilator
8 Wasserstandsmanagement – die Faltung
9 San Francisco Mündungs- und Deltaplan
5 landmass and estuary topography
6 self-sustaining energy geothermal and tidal
7 tidal management—the ventilator
8 water level management—the fold
9 San Francisco Estuary and Delta Map

One of the definitions of nature is that it encompasses all things and processes specifically not made by, or dependent on, human artifice.

Abschwächung von Stürmen und die Steuerung des Meeresspiegels verwendet wird.

Die operativen Funktionen von *Folding Water* sind von den natürlichen Gezeitenbewegungen abhängig und generieren ein interaktives Netzwerk, das nicht nur einen Vorteil aus dem dynamischen Fluss dieser flüssigen Umgebung zieht, sondern auch seine Kräfte in die programmatischen Entwurfsparameter des Projekts integriert. Es aktiviert ein „materielles Modell", das aus den inhärenten Kontinuitäten und der unerschöpflichen Lebendigkeit der Materie-Energie-Matrix der Natur Kapital schlägt. Die Falte wird hier als ein strategisches Mittel eingesetzt, um die Bewegungen von Wasser und Energie, Sedimenten und lebenden Organismen simultan einzufangen, zu regulieren und zirkulieren zu lassen, während sie gleichzeitig eine abgeschwächte Grenze darstellt, die als erweiterte Oberfläche der Vermittlung und dem Austausch dient. Sowohl durch ihr belüftetes Gezeitenmanagementsystem als auch durch ihre beabsichtigte Verwendung als von den Gezeiten abhängige Turbine erweitert die perforierte Ufermauer zudem das potenzielle produktive „Ressourcing" von ungenutzten ozeanischen und geologischen Kräften und versucht gleichzeitig die Bewegungen größerer Infrastruktursysteme zu integrieren.[3]

In der Theorie ist die Falte ein Begriff, der verwendet wurde, um gleichzeitig trennende und verbindende Vorgänge[4] zu klassifizieren, was den Unterschied zwischen kulturellen und natürlichen Anordnungen verwischt, während es die Verknüpfung von hochgradig künstlichen Organisationsstrategien, wie der planimetrischen und partikulären Ausarbeitung der Ufermauer – ein Verbund aus industriell erzeugten, gereihten, diskreten Gesamtelementen – mit beständigeren natürlichen und ökologischen Prozessen erleichtert. Sowohl in der Entwicklung wie auch in der Ausführung des Entwurfs wird die taktische Verklammerung von Natur und Kunstgriff in *Folding Water* auf mehreren Ebenen wiederholt, unter Verwendung von hybriden Methoden, die jene Syntheseleistung nachahmen, welche am häufigsten im Kontext der materiellen Realität auftritt. Solche kombinierten Umwelttechniken – eine Mischung aus natürlichen und maschinellen Prozessen – verlangen von uns, die doppelseitige Pattsituation zu überdenken, die wir geerbt haben und welcher wir uns oft verschreiben: indem wir entweder weiter blind dem Bewegungsablauf folgen, der durch die Verbindung zwischen modernem Kapitalismus und Industrialisierung definiert wird – worin die Natur, umgeformt nach ihrem funktionellen Verwendungswert (zum Beispiel als „na-

3 In seiner früheren Form für den *City of the Future*-Wettbewerb umfasste der Entwurf für *Folding Water* auch ein regionales Netzwerk infrastruktureller Transportsysteme für Luft, Wasser und raschen Umstieg, sowie größere Einrichtungen zur Verwaltung, Behandlung und Entsalzung von Wasser.

4 Für eine nähere Ausführung über Prozesse mit verbindender und trennender Synthese entlang des Natur-Kultur-Kontinuums vgl. Brian Massumi, *A User's Guide to Capitalism and Schizophrenia. Deviations from Deleuze and Guattari*. Cambridge, MA 1992, S. 48–50.

türliche Ressource"), rein als Rohmaterie angesehen wird, die für die Kulturproduktion beschlagnahmt und instrumentalisiert wird (bis zur unausweichlichen Zerstörung unserer lebenserhaltenden Umwelt); oder umgekehrt glauben, dass wir das Konzept einer idealisierten Natur erhalten müssen, die vollkommen frei von menschlichen Prozessen ist und zu der wir vielleicht zurückkehren – eine paradiesische Utopie, die im Kontext der urbanen Kultur des 21. Jahrhunderts und deren zugehöriger umgebender Landschaft undenkbar scheint.

Eine der Definitionen von Natur besagt, dass sie speziell alle Dinge und Prozesse umfasst, die nicht auf menschlichen Eingriffen beruhen oder von ihnen abhängig sind. Ungeachtet unserer eigenen Verkörperung von Natur ist es gerade die von uns vorgenommene Entfernung aus dem ungestörten Bereich der realen natürlichen Materie, auf der diese historische Definition von Natur beruht. Dennoch besteht, trotz dieser begrifflichen *de jure*-Unterscheidung, unsere *de facto*-Realität aus einer bereits stark kulturell angeeigneten natürlichen Landschaft mit einer vollkommen anderen Ordnung. Dies beruht auf der Tatsache, dass wir die Natur – das Geologische, das Flüssige und das Biotische – ständig erneuert und transformiert haben – gemäß der vorherrschenden Ideologie, nach der wir in jedem Moment der Geschichte die „reale" Natur in eine kulturelle Realität verwandelt haben. Wir haben die Morphologie von bedeutenden Strömungsarterien umgekehrt und verändert, haben Täler in Seen verwandelt, die Landwirtschaft industrialisiert und künstlichen Boden aus Sumpfgebieten geschaffen, um dadurch wieder ein Exempel für die Überlegenheit der technokratischen und utilitaristischen Beherrschung des 20. Jahrhunderts zu geben. Unsere Handlungen hatten natürlich auch unbeabsichtigte Folgen: verschmutzte Atmosphären und saurer Regen, verunreinigte oder geplünderte Frischwasservorkommen, verlorene Biodiversität, eine vermüllte Erdoberfläche, Erwärmung der Erdatmosphäre und steigende Meeresspiegel, und veränderte Wetterbedingungen, um nur einige zu nennen. Tatsächlich existiert die unberührte „Natur", unbefleckt von menschlichen Eingriffen, wie wir es uns einst vorgestellt haben, im Kontext unserer derzeitigen ökologischen Krise in Wahrheit nicht mehr. Was wir jedoch oft nicht realisieren, ist, dass sie vielleicht nie existiert hat. Unsere starre Symbolik erweist sich in Hinsicht auf den von Natur aus transformativen Materie-Energie-Fluss, von dem die natürliche Welt scheinbar abhängt, als vollkommen unangebracht.

Was unsere Gegenwart von dieser Geschichte unterscheidet sind mindestens zwei Dinge: die Tatsache, dass wir die natürliche Welt in solchem Ausmaß verändert haben, dass wir nun ihre irreversible Erschöpfung und apokalyptische Zerstörung fürchten, während wir gleichzeitig unsere eigene biotische Zerbrechlichkeit und die Abhängigkeit von ihrer Existenz erkennen; und dass diese Erkenntnis nicht nur die Neupositionierung von Natur innerhalb unserer ideologischen Hierarchie

fold is employed as a strategic device to simultaneously capture, regulate, and recircuit the movements of water and energy, sediment and living organisms, while providing an attenuated boundary that acts as an extended surface for mediation and exchange. In addition, through both its ventilated tidal management system and its proposed use of tidal turbines and geothermal energy, this perforated seawall also amplifies the potential productive "resourcing" of untapped oceanic and geological forces, while also attempting to integrate the movements of larger infrastructural systems.[3]

Theoretically, the fold is a term that has been used to classify procedures that are both disjunctive and connective,[4] blurring the distinctions between cultural and natural configurations, while facilitating the intertwining of highly artificial organizational strategies, such as the planimetric and sectional elaboration of the seawall—a composite of industrially produced, arrayed, discrete aggregated elements—with more continuous natural ecological processes. In both its design evolution and operation, tactical enfolding of nature and artifice of *Folding Water* is repeated at multiple scales, employing hybridizing techniques that emulate the synthesizing capacity most often found within the context of the material real. Such crossbred enviro-technologies, a blending of natural and machinic processes, demand that we rethink the double-sided stalemate that we have inherited and to which we often subscribe: either blindly continuing the trajectory defined by the nexus of modern capitalism and industrialization—wherein nature, reframed according to its utilitarian use value (i.e. as "natural resource") is perceived only as raw matter to be appropriated and instrumentalized in the production of culture (to the inevitable devastation of our life-sustaining environment); or, conversely, believing that we must symbolically preserve the concept of an idealized Nature, wholly uncontaminated by human processes, to which we might return—an Eden-like utopia seemingly unthinkable within the context of 21st century urban culture and its corresponding environmental landscape.

One of the definitions of nature is that it encompasses all things and processes specifically not made by, or dependent on, human artifice. Notwithstanding our own embodiment of nature, it is precisely our very self-extraction from the unmediated domain of real natural matter upon which this historical definition of nature depends. Yet, despite this *de jure* conceptual distinction, our *de facto* reality consists of an already highly acculturated natural landscape of an entirely different order, in view of the fact that we have been continuously remaking nature—transforming the geological, the fluvial, and the biotic, according to the dominant ideologies through which we have converted "real" nature into cultural reality at every moment in history. We have reversed and altered the flows and morphologies of major fluid arteries, converted valleys into lakes, industrialized agriculture and constructed artificial terrain from marshland as a re-instantiation of the supremacy of 20th century technocratic utilitarian control. And

3 In its earlier form for the *City of the Future* competition, *Folding Water* also incorporated a regional network of infrastructural transportation systems for air, water, and rapid transit, as well as larger water management, treatment and desalinization facilities into its design.

4 For an elaboration on processes of connective and disjunctive syntheses along the nature-culture continuum see Brian Massumi, *A User's Guide to Capitalism and Schizophrenia: Deviations from Deleuze and Guattari*. Cambridge, MA 1992, pp. 48–50.

of course, our acts have also had unintended consequences: polluted atmospheres and acid rain, contaminated or depleted fresh water sources, biodiversity loss, landfill earthscapes, global warming and rising sea levels, and changing meteorological conditions, to name but a few. In fact, within the context of our current ecological crisis, pristine "nature," untainted by human intervention as we once imagined it, truly no longer exists. What we do not often realize, however, is that perhaps it never did. Our static symbolism proves to be wholly inadequate in consideration of the inherently transformative matter-energy flux upon which the natural world seemingly depends.

Our static symbolism proves to be wholly inadequate in consideration of the inherently transformative matter-energy flux upon which the natural world seemingly depends.

What distinguishes our present from this history are, at minimum, two things: that we have transformed the natural world to such an extent that we now fear its irreversible depletion and apocalyptic destruction while recognizing our own biotic fragility and dependence on its very existence; and that this realization has enabled not only the repositioning of nature within our ideological hierarchy, but has also intensified our cultural obsession with it. As we suspend our own self-imposed alienation, we now want to understand nature's life-sustaining principles, its regenerative potential and capacity for the incessant circulation of matter-energy to ensure both its and our own survival. Nature has provided a new territory for architectural and urban thought and practice that exceeds previous models, if only because the new mixtures that are emerging between nature and culture, the biotic and the mechanistic, are specific to this moment in cultural history—its sciences, technologies, geographies and theoretical milieus. It is only within this milieu that a "cyborgian" enviro-technological device such as *Folding Water* could evolve, a context that could give birth to infrastructures that are simultaneously landscapes and fluid machines.[5]

As this discrete architectural object is stretched to the scale scale of the geographical, a new monumental nature is created—one that is highly articulated and deliberately defined, yet also mobile and material in its evolution, operation, and effects. The water wall of *Folding Water* challenges us to incorpo-

5 Donna Haraway had written that "Nature and culture are reworked; the one can no longer be the resource for appropriation or incorporation by the other." Within the contemporary world, the cyborg is both the most disturbing and the most real and ubiquitous, rendering fragile the constitution of humanity and the threshold of the natural. "Late twentieth-century machines have made thoroughly ambiguous the difference between natural and artificial, mind and body, self-developing and externally designed, and many other distinctions that used to apply to organisms and machines." Yet for Haraway, the cyborg was not a lamentable fact of the postindustrial world, but rather a space of potential political subversion, intended to recall us to an imagined organicism and to integrate our resistance (following Marcuse and Merchant), yet to critically and strategically engage the world of technological mediation as a productive and political imperative, in a way, however, that might rethink and redirect its energies in support of the living. See Donna Haraway, "A Manifesto for Cyborgs," in: *Simians, Cyborgs, and Women: The Reinvention of Nature*. New York 1990, pp. 151f., 154.

ermöglicht, sondern auch unsere kulturelle Besessenheit von ihr verstärkt hat. Da wir unsere selbst verordnete Entfremdung aufheben wollen wir nun die lebenserhaltenden Prinzipien der Natur, ihr regeneratives Potenzial und die Fähigkeit zur ununterbrochenen Zirkulation von Materie und Energie verstehen, um ihr und unser Überleben gleichermaßen zu sichern. Die Natur hat der architektonischen und urbanen Theorie und Praxis ein neues Gebiet zur Verfügung gestellt, das vorherige Modelle übertrifft, wenn auch nur deswegen, weil die neuen Mischungen, die zwischen Natur und Kultur, dem Biotischen und dem Mechanistischen, entstehen, spezifisch sind für diesen Moment der Kulturgeschichte – für deren Wissenschaften, Technologien, Geografien und theoretische Milieus. Nur in diesem Milieu konnte sich ein „cyborgisches" umwelttechnisches Verfahren wie *Folding Water* entwickeln – ein Kontext, der Infrastrukturen erzeugen könnte, die gleichzeitig Landschaften und flüssige Maschinen sind.[5]

Durch die Ausdehnung dieses diskreten architektonischen Objekts auf einen geografischen Maßstab wird eine neue monumentale Natur erzeugt – eine, die stark gegliedert und willkürlich definiert ist, und dennoch in ihrer Entstehung, Funktionsweise und ihren Auswirkungen beweglich und materiell bleibt. Die Wassermauer in *Folding Water* stellt uns vor die Herausforderung, flüssige und poröse Räume in unsere statischen, massiven und wasserdichten Umgebungen einzugliedern, so wie sie uns ebenso zur Imagination von neuen Möglichkeiten für amphibische Infrastrukturen und Architekturen verhilft, die technologische Kunstgriffe und deren diskrete, kulturell angeeignete Systeme mit den flüssigen Geografien und der lebensnotwendigen Ökologie einer beständigen materiellen Natur zu synthetisieren versucht. Trotz der jüngsten Befürchtungen in Bezug auf steigende Gewässer und deren Fähigkeit Urbanität zu zerstören, sind die größtenteils unbewohnbaren ozeanischen Volumina, sowie die an unsere ortsgebundenen urbanen Zentren angrenzenden Buchten, Flüsse und Sumpfgebiete für viele Architekten begrifflich und körperlich unterbesetzt geblieben, mit Ausnahme derer, die sich

5 Bei Donna Haraway heißt es: „Natur und Kultur werden neu definiert. Die eine stellt nicht mehr die Ressource für die Aneignung und Einverleibung durch die andere dar." In der modernen Welt ist der Cyborg sowohl das im höchsten Maße Irritierende, wie auch das Realste und Allgegenwärtigste. Er lässt die Konstitution der Menschheit und die Schwelle des Natürlichen zerbrechlich werden. „Die Maschinen des späten 20. Jahrhunderts haben die Differenz von natürlich und künstlich, Körper und Geist, selbstgelenkter und außengesteuerter Entwicklung sowie viele andere Unterscheidungen, die Organismen und Maschinen zu trennen vermochten, höchst zweideutig werden lassen." Dennoch war der Cyborg für Haraway keine beklagenswerte Tatsache der postindustriellen Welt, sondern eher ein Raum für möglichen politischen Umsturz, der uns als einen imaginierten organischen Körper anrufen und unseren Widerstand (nach Marcuse und Merchant) integrieren und dennoch die Welt der technologischen Vermittlung kritisch und strategisch als eine produktive und politische Verpflichtung engagieren sollte, jedoch auf eine Weise, die ihre Energie zur Unterstützung des Lebendigen überdenken und umlenken könnte. Vgl. Donna Haraway, „Ein Manifest für Cyborgs", in: *Die Neuerfindung der Natur: Primaten, Cyborgs und Frauen*. Frankfurt/M. und New York 1995, S. 35f., 37, 39.

mit Infrastrukturen zur Kontrolle und Einschränkung der Volumina beschäftigen. Für andere jedoch muss die Komplexität und Grenzenlosigkeit dieser flüssigen Landschaft erst noch gänzlich erforscht werden, und zwar aufgrund der dynamischen Möglichkeiten, die sie dem amphibischen Leben in der Stadt bietet, sowie der Bereitstellung eines zukünftigen Grenzgebietes für erweiterte architektonische Interventionen.[6]

Übersetzung Claudia Wrumnig

6 Eine verwandte und längere Version dieses Textes ist erschienen in „Amphibious Territories", in: *Architectural Design Journal* 205 (Mai/Juni 2010).

rate liquid and porous spaces into our static and solid waterproof environments, just as it also enables us to imagine new opportunities for amphibious infrastructures and architectures that attempt to synthesize technological artifice and its discrete acculturated systems with the fluid geographies and vital ecologies of a continuous material nature. Despite recent fears associated with rising waters and their potential for urban destruction, for many architects, the largely uninhabitable oceanic volumes, as well as the bays, rivers and wetlands adjacent to our sedentary urban centers, have remained conceptually and physically underengaged, except by those invested in infrastructures intended to control and restrain them. For others, however, the complexity and boundlessness of this liquid landscape has yet to be fully explored, in terms of the dynamic potential it offers for amphibious urban life as well as its provision of a future territorial frontier for expanded architectural intervention.[6]

6 A related and expanded version of this paper has appeared in "Amphibious Territories," in: *Architectural Design Journal* 205 (May/June 2010).

'CLIMATE INCIDENTS'

AMO Roadmap 2050

Unlike its assumed counterpart and palindrome OMA (Office for Metropolitan Architecture), AMO focuses on architectural projects which have little or nothing to do with construction design; AMO produces studies, events, exhibitions and publications—often for the same clients as its big sister—and is, among others, responsible for Prada's brand identity, be it their catalogue, marketing video or fashion show.

AMO, Palindrom und vermeintliches Gegenstück zu OMA – dem Office for Metropolitan Architecture – beschäftigt sich im Gegensatz zu diesem mit Architekturprojekten abseits des Bauens. So entstehen Studien, Events, Ausstellungen und Publikationen – oft für die selben Kunden wie jene des großen Schwesterbüros. AMO betreut u. a. den Markenauftritt von Prada, sei es deren Katalog, ein Image-Film oder eine Fashion Show.

BERNHARD KÖNIG

Recently, AMO has attracted much attention, primarily with its work on two studies about the energy turnaround towards the era of post-fossil energy sources. The first of the two, *Roadmap 2050: A Practical Guide to a Prosperous Low-Carbon Europe*, which appeared in 2010, was published and distributed free of charge by the European Climate Foundation, a kind of climate lobby which receives a greater part of financial backing from a number of private philanthropic foundations. The most important partners involved in the *Roadmap 2050* project were McKinsey & Company, KEMA, the Imperial College London and Oxford Economics, all of them responsible for the first volume of *Roadmap*; E3G and the Energy Research Center of the Netherlands, who produced Volume 2, *Policy Report*; and AMO/OMA who were responsible for the third volume, the so-called *Graphic Narrative*, which is briefly described below.

Roadmap aims to point out possible ways of cutting 80 percent of greenhouse gas emissions in Europe by 2050 as compared to 1990. As regards the energy sector, this alone would mean a reduction in greenhouse gas emissions of between 95–100 percent. Even though the plan outlined in *Roadmap* demands a phasing-out of nuclear power, it still remains a post-fossil source of energy.

AMO's argumentation strategy begins with a diagram of the alleged direct connection between the annual rise in insurance claims caused by natural forces and global warming, showing climate change as a growing economic risk. The next item is a chronology of technical and cultural "revolutions" which inevitably follow each new form of energy, starting with the steam engine and the industrial revolution, to the question as to which cultural effects the use of renewable forms of energy are likely to have. All of these are described under the heading "History Repeats."

Roadmap aims to point out possible ways of cutting 80 percent of greenhouse gas emissions in Europe by 2050 compared to 1990.

This is followed by a series of iconographical images showing European energy networks; they are based on the required integration of European power supply systems and their "shared tasks" in the exploitation of renewable energy, which would obviously correspond to the geographical dimensions of each respective European region or country. Whilst the countries on the shores of the North and Baltic Seas should be able to produce enough wind energy for their own needs, southern Europe, including the northern Sahara, could generate sufficient solar power for domestic use. Additionally, the so-called Tidal States, especially those along the Atlantic coast, could meet their ever-increasing energy demands with the help of wave and tidal stream plants. The same applies to landlocked countries, which should be able to produce their own supplies through regional concepts such as "Geothermalia" or "Biomassburg." Seasonal and daily fluctuations would be able to be compensated by means of an integrated net-

Zuletzt machte AMO aber vor allem durch zwei Studien zur Energiewende ins postfossile Zeitalter auf sich aufmerksam. Die erste davon ist die 2010 erschienene *Roadmap 2050: A Practical Guide to a Prosperous Low-Carbon Europe*. Sie wurde von der European Climate Foundation herausgegeben und kostenlos vertrieben, einer Art Klimalobby, deren finanzielles Rückgrat eine Reihe philanthropischer Privatstiftungen bilden. Wesentliche Projektpartner bei der *Roadmap 2050* sind McKinsey & Company, KEMA, Imperial College London und Oxford Economics, die alle für den ersten Band der *Roadmap* verantwortlich zeichnen, E3G und das Energy Research Center of the Netherlands, die den Band 2, *Policy Report*, produziert haben, sowie AMO/OMA, von denen der dritte Band, der so genannte *Graphic Narrative*, stammt. Letzterer soll hier kurz vorgestellt werden.

Ziel der *Roadmap* ist es, einen möglichen Weg aufzuzeigen, wie der Ausstoß von Treibhausgasen in Europa bis 2050 um 80 % gegenüber 1990 gesenkt werden kann. Allein für den Energiesektor bedeutet dies eine Reduktion von Treibhausgasen um 95–100 %. Auch wenn der in der *Roadmap* vorgezeichnete Weg einen Rückzug aus der Kernenergie vorsieht, bleibt diese als postfossiler Energieträger vorhanden.

AMO beginnt seine Argumentation mit einer diagrammatischen Darstellung des vermeintlich direkten Zusammenhangs aus jährlich wachsenden Versicherungsschäden durch Naturgewalt und dem globalen Temperaturanstieg. Klimaerwärmung erscheint als wachsendes volkswirtschaftliches Risiko. Es folgt eine Chronologie der technischen und kulturellen „Revolutionen", die unaufhaltsam mit der Nutzung jeweils neuer Energieformen einhergingen, angefangen bei der Dampfmaschine und der folgenden industriellen Revolution bis hin zur offenen Frage, welche kulturellen Auswirkungen die Nutzung erneuerbarer Energien haben wird. Das alles läuft unter der Überschrift „History Repeats".

Es folgt eine Reihe ikonografischer Darstellungen zur energetischen Vernetzung Europas. Hintergrund ist eine geforderte Integration der europäischen Stromnetze und eine „Aufgabenteilung" in der Gewinnung erneuerbarer Energien. Diese soll naheliegender Weise entsprechend der geografischen Stärke der jeweiligen europäischen Region bzw. des jeweiligen Staates erfolgen. Die Nord- und Ostseestaaten sollen sich durch Windenergie versorgen, der Süden Europas bis hinein in die Sahara durch Sonnenenergie. Daneben soll es noch so genannte „Tidal States", Gezeitenstaaten, geben, die besonders entlang der Atlantikküste ihren Energiebedarf mit Gezeitenkraftwerken decken, oder Binnenstaaten, die ihre Versorgung durch regionale Konzepte wie „Geothermalia" und „Biomassburg" sicherstellen sollen. Durch ein kontinental integriertes Leitungsnetzwerk würden die jahreszeitlichen und täglichen Schwankungen abgefangen werden können. So sei z. B. im Sommer der Solarenergieanteil besonders hoch, im Winter

wiederum der von Windenergie. Der Darstellung zufolge soll der europäische Kontinent (zzgl. der nördlichen Sahara) auf diese Weise bis 2050 zu einer Insel erneuerbarer Energien werden.

Entsprechend untermauert wird das scheinbar einfache Konzept durch Fotomontagen, Diagramme und Europakarten sowie einfache Rechenbeispiele. AMO zeigt, dass die Abkehr von fossilen Energieträgern im Verhältnis z. B. zum Irakkrieg vergleichsweise wenig kostet oder dass jeder Haushalt für die Finanzierung des kontinentalen Umbaus zur Klimaneutralität nur auf eine Tankfüllung seines Geländewagens pro Jahr verzichten müsste. Viel mehr müssten die Europäer dann aber nicht entbehren, da der Großteil der Treibhausgase durch technische Möglichkeiten, von der Energiesparlampe bis zum „Zero Carbon Commercial Airplane", reduziert werden könnte. Mit einer entsprechenden fiktiven Chronologie bis 2050 beendet AMO den *Graphic Narrative* und färbt die Europaflagge grün.

work of pipelines on the continent. For instance, solar energy input would be highest in summer and maximum wind energy input would occur in winter. According to this project, the European continent (including the northern Sahara area) will become an island of renewable energy by 2050.

What appears to be a simple concept is supported by appropriate photo montages, diagrams, maps of Europe and basic arithmetic examples. AMO demonstrates that the shift away from fossil fuels would cost much less than, for instance, the war on Iraq, or that the cost of shifting towards climate neutrality on the continent could be compensated if each household with an off-road vehicle would do without just one tank of fuel per year. Europeans would not have to spare much more than that, since most greenhouse gas emissions would be reduced by technical possibilities ranging from the low-energy light bulb to the "zero carbon commercial airplane." AMO ends its *Graphic Narrative* with an according fictional chronology up to 2050 and changes the color of the Flag of Europe to green.

WITH THE COST ESTIMATIONS OF NATURAL DISASTERS EVER INCREASING, FAILURE TO ACKNOWLEDGE THE UNDERLYING CAUSE COULD COME AT A VERY HIGH PRICE.

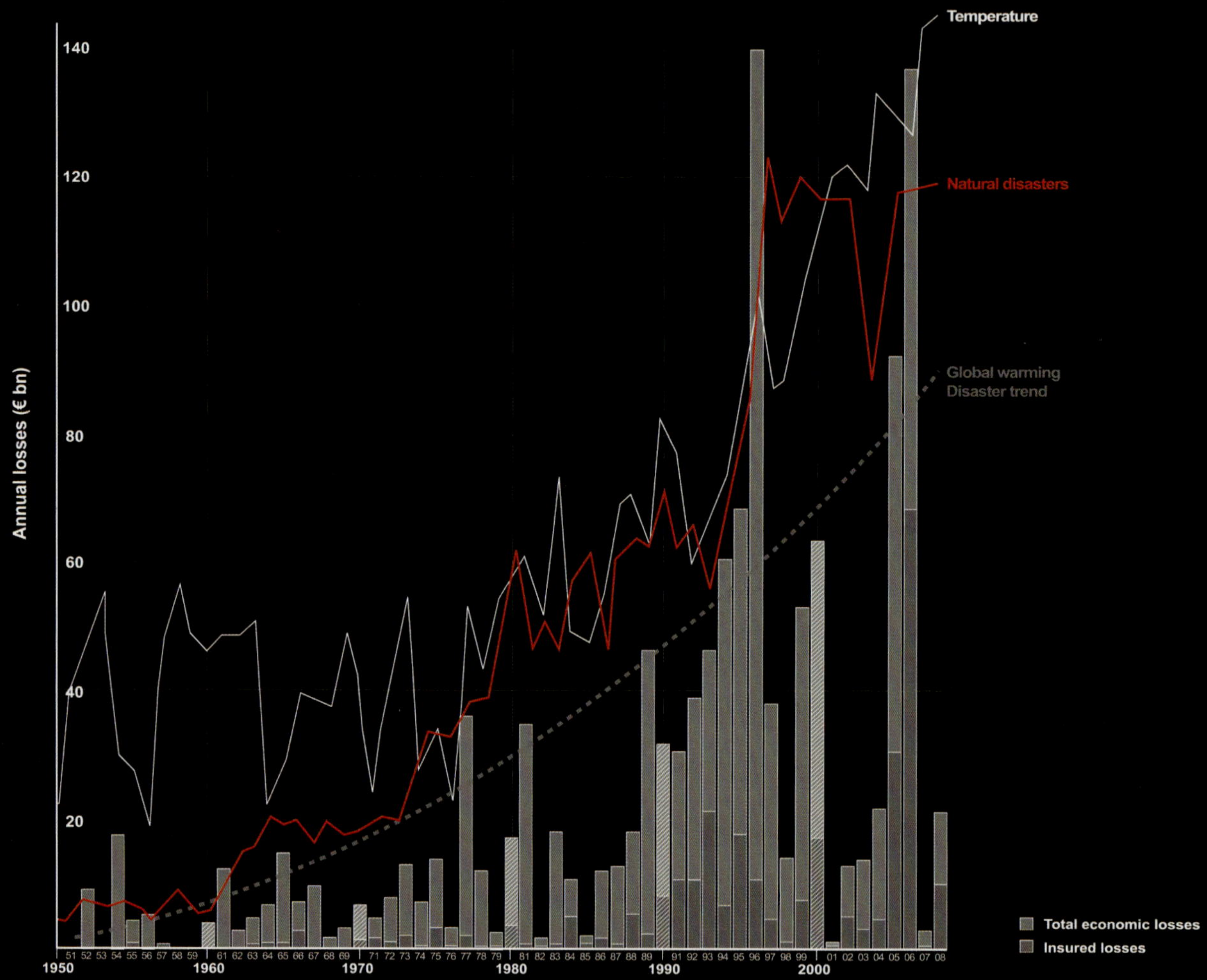

SOURCE: Munich-Re (2009)

COOPERATION AND PLANNING WILL BE CRUCIAL. MEETING THE EMISSIONS REDUCTION TARGET REQUIRES THE MOBILIZATION AND AGREEMENT OF ALL INVOLVED...

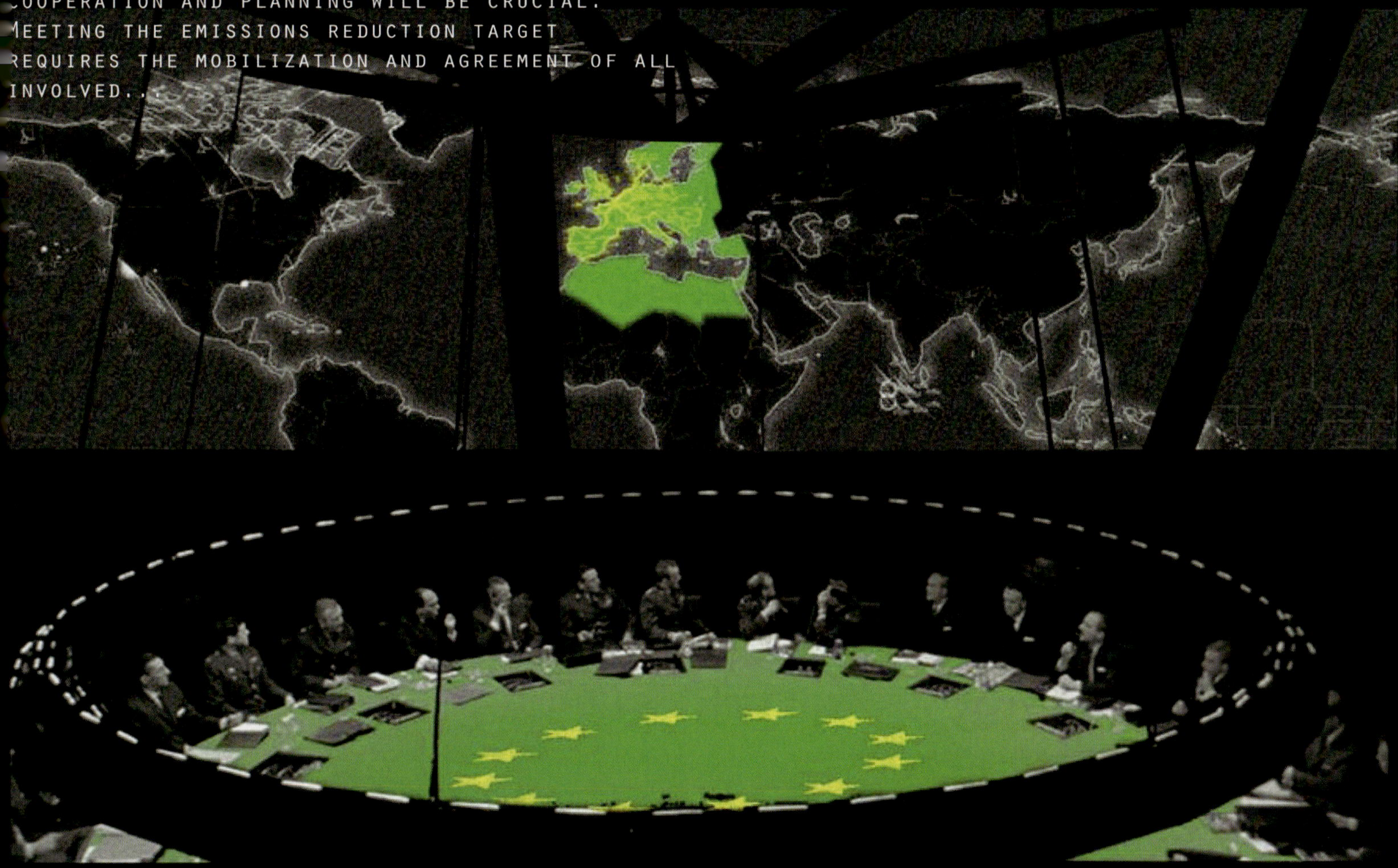

1780 - 1880

The steam revolution began.

Aristocrats lobbied against the change...

But, planning & investment triumphed...

The revolution thrived...

In less than 40 years, the industrial revolution changed the world forever...

1839 - 1890

The railroad revolution began.

Lobbyist tried to scare the public...

But, governments brought stability...

The industry grew beyond expectation...

In less than 50 years, the railroad revolutionized transport.

1899 - 1929

The electric revolution began.

Fear and ignorance confused the public...

But, government vision brought order...

The revolution exploded with innovation...

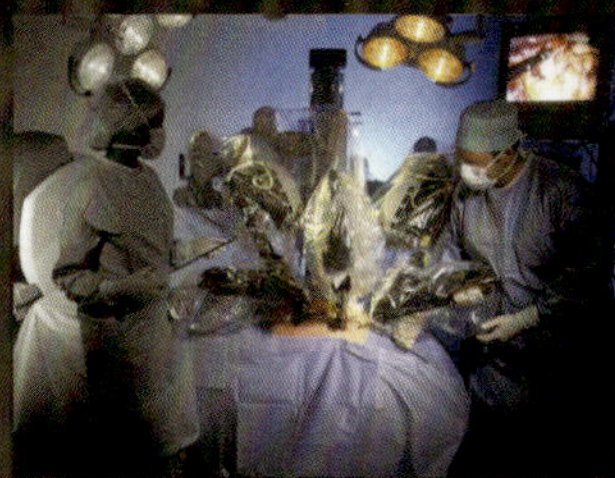

In less than 30 years, the impossible became possible.

1974 - 2000

The technological revolution began.

Fear and distrust soared.

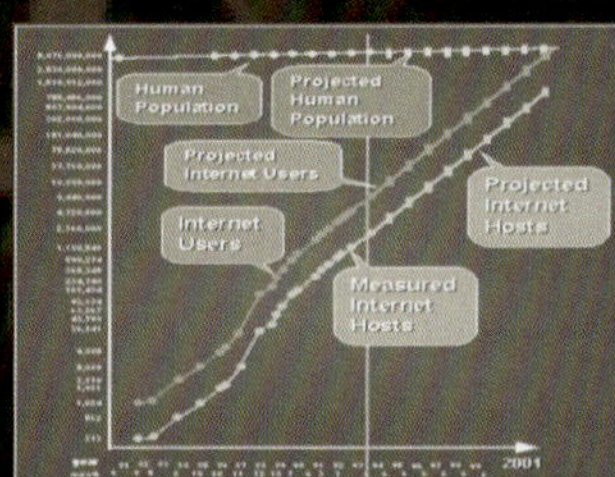

But, users overcame the skeptics...

The revolution created new opportunities...

In less than 25 years, technology changed the way we live.

2010 - 2050

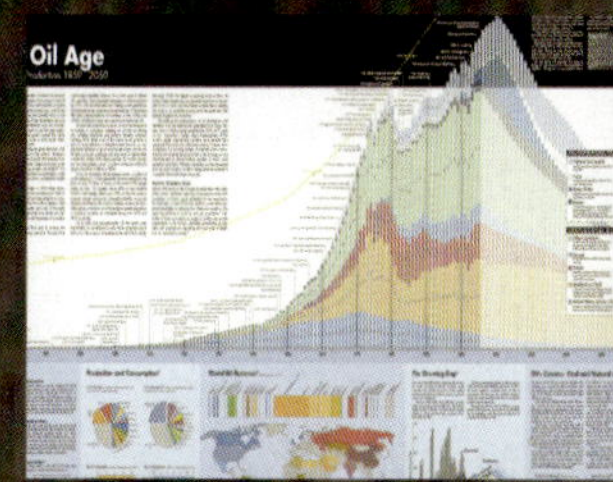

The renewable energy revolution began.

But, ignorance continues to mislead...

Cooperation & planning will be crucial...

The revolutionary potential is endless...

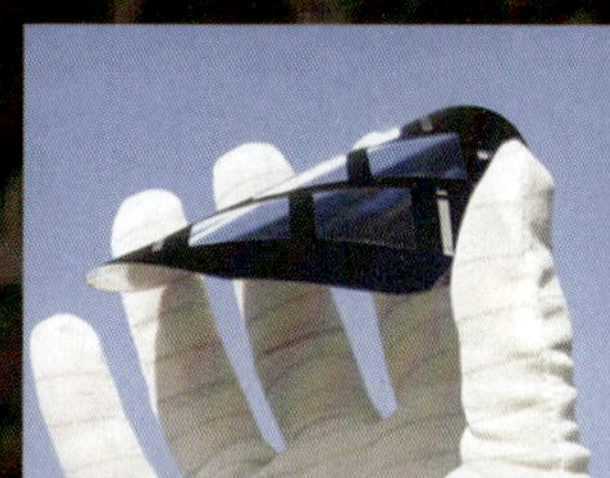

And we have only scratched the surface...

History is about to repeat...

Is the EU ready?

80% CO2 EMISSION REDUCTION

The 80% CO2 reduction overall implies 90-95% reduction in power, road transport and buildings. This could be achieved by maximum abatement within and across sectors. Note: this level of decarbonization is dependent on achieving aggressive 2% year on year energy efficiency savings, without which this level of abatement is not possible in this model.

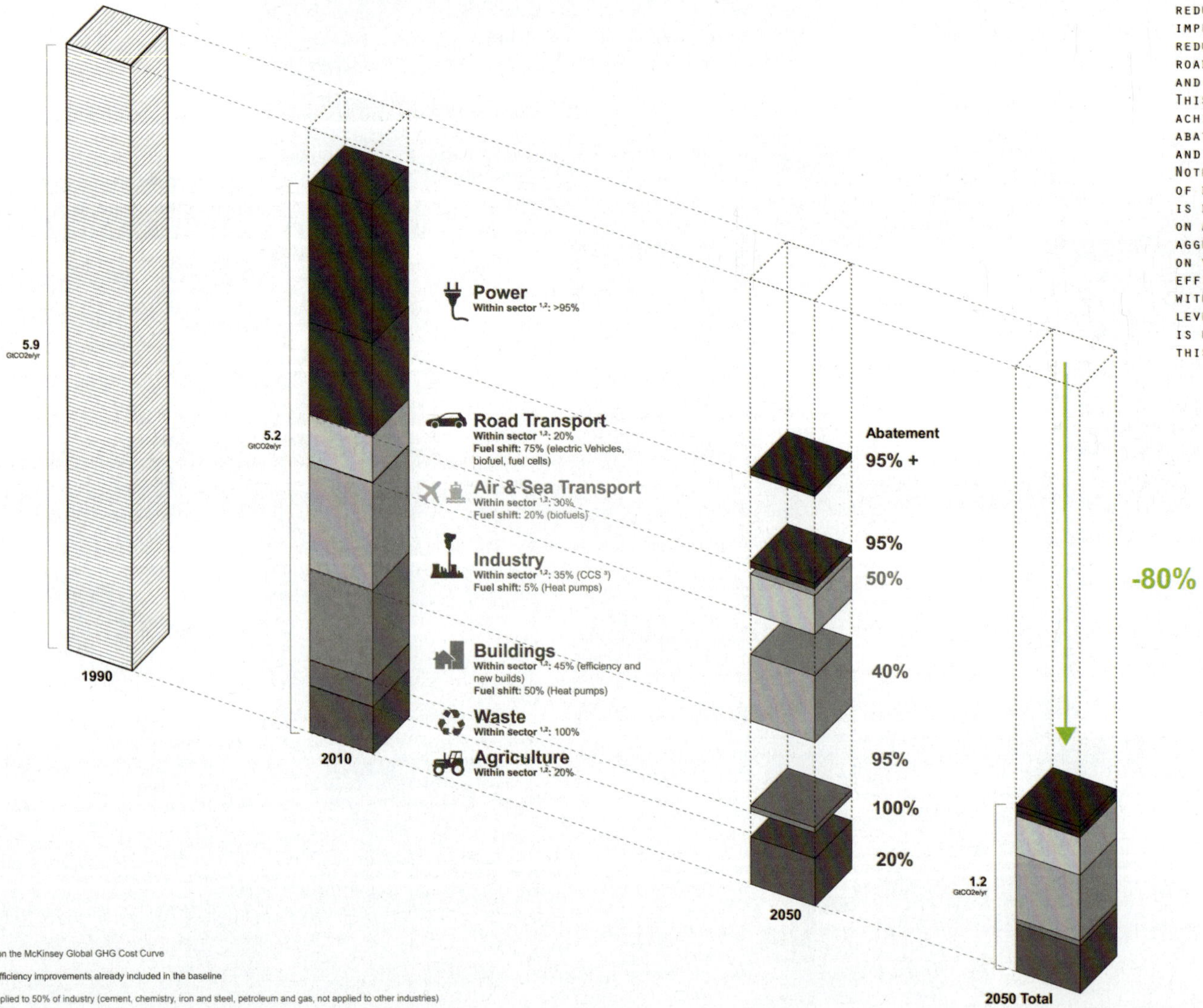

1 Based on the McKinsey Global GHG Cost Curve

2 Large efficiency improvements already included in the baseline

3 CCS applied to 50% of industry (cement, chemistry, iron and steel, petroleum and gas, not applied to other industries)

SOURCE: McKinsey Global GHG Abatement Cost Curve; IEA WEO 2009; US EPA; EEA; Roadmap 2050 Technical Analysis

ENERGY SUPPLY IN 2050 (HIGH RES PATHWAY)

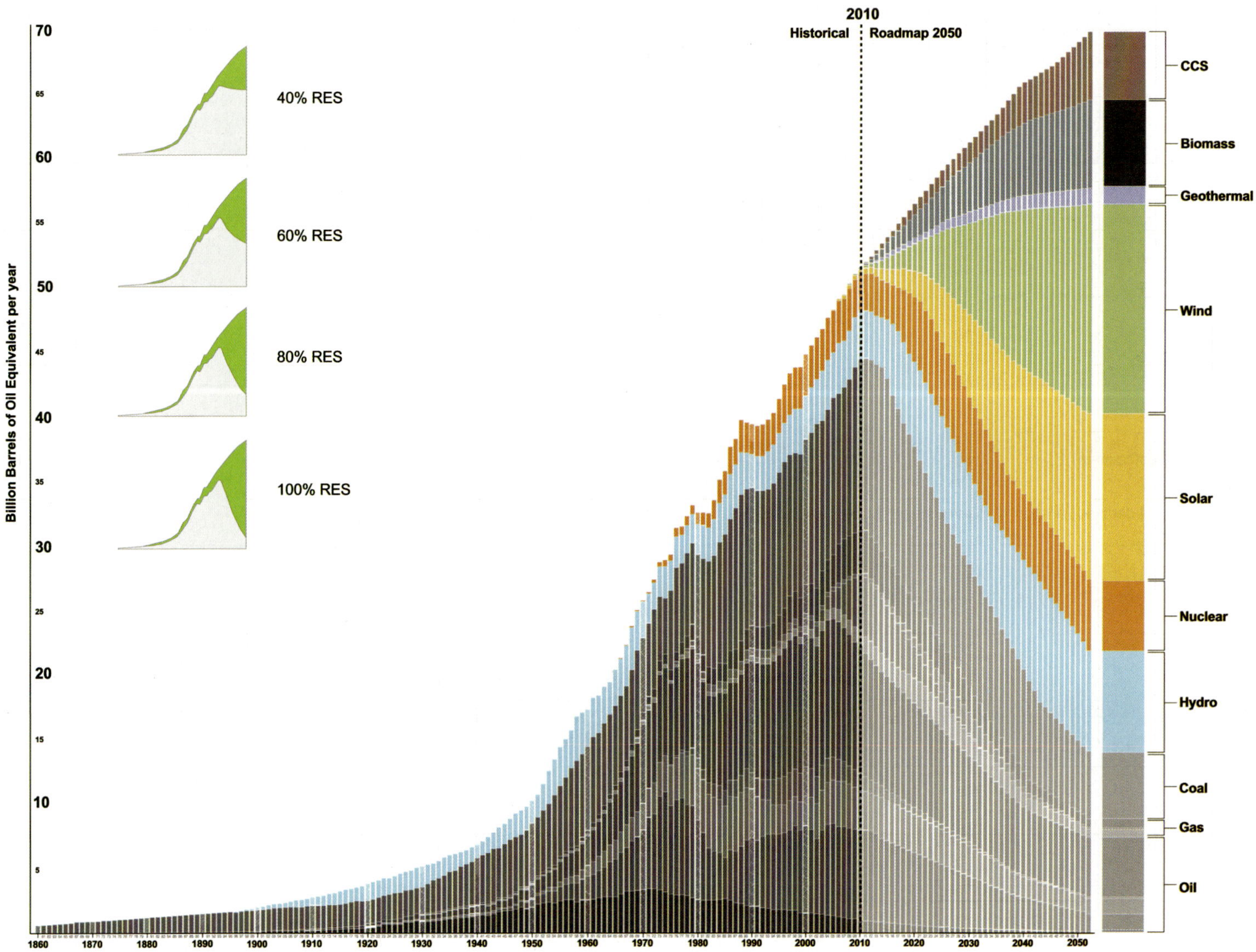

ources: Roadmap 2050 Technical Analysis, McKinsey / Lynn Orr, Changing the World's Energy Systems, Stanford University Global Climate & Energy Project (after John Edwards, American Association of Petroleum eologists); SRI Consulting. / David Rutledge, Professor, California Institute of Technology 2009 / The Oil Age: World Oil Production 1859-2050. San Francisco, CA. Courtesy of San Francisco Informatics. / Dr. Colin Campbell's oil depletion model: The Coming Oil Crisis, by Colin J. Campbell. Independent Publishers Group, April 1, 2004 / The Twenty First Century, The World's Endowment of Conventional Oil and Its Depletion, Dr. Colin Campbell, 1996 / International Energy Agency

COMBINING REGIONAL DEMAND CURVES REDUCES VOLATILITY

Regional demand variation from average over the year

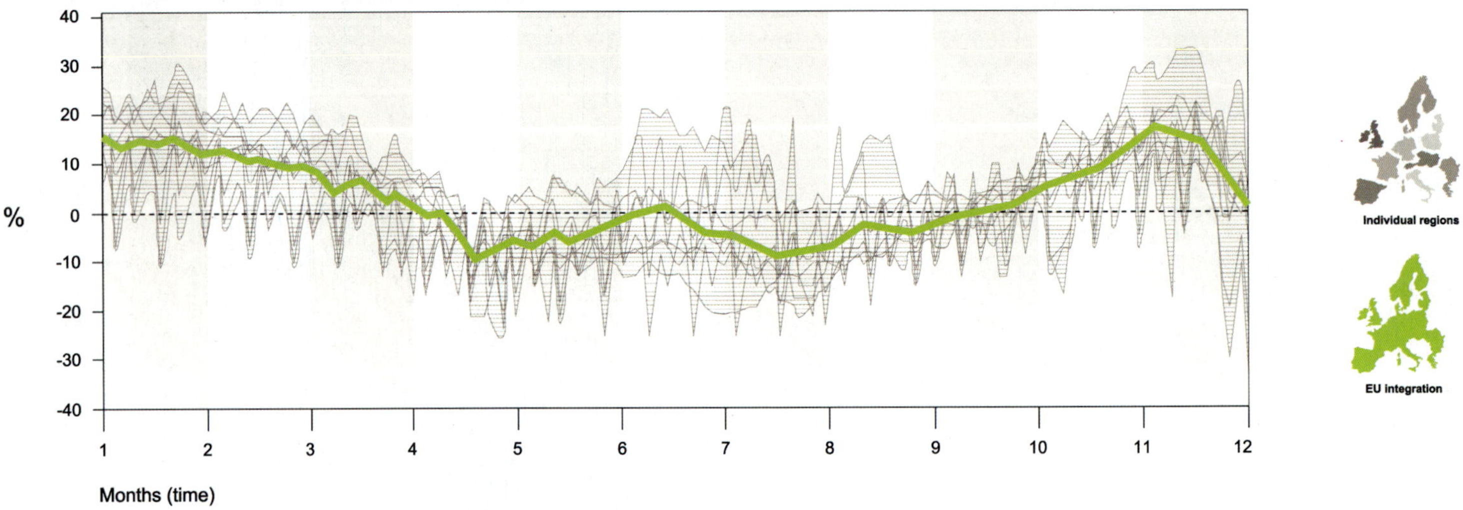

Regional demand variation from average per hour on weekend day

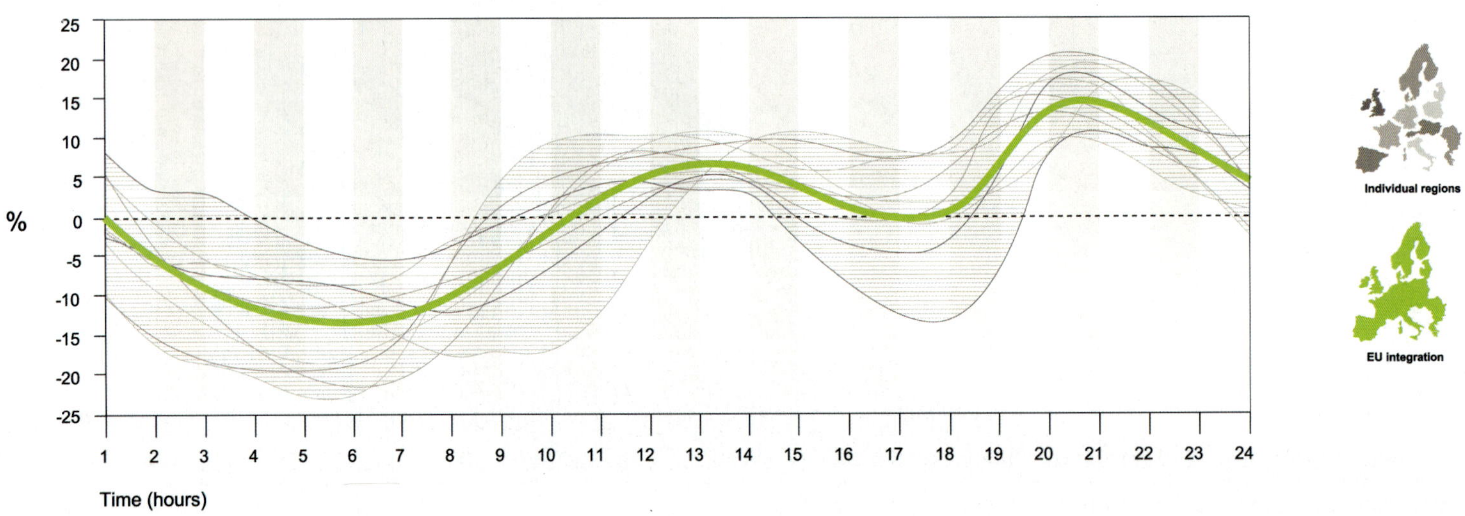

SOURCE: Roadmap 2050 Technical Analysis

ES DIVERSITY CONTRIBUTES TO CONSISTENT SUPPLY

VER THE COURSE F THE YEAR, THE NTEGRATION OF UROPE ALLOWS FOR OME ENERGY SOURCES O COMPENSATE FOR HE LACK OF OTHERS ASED ON SEASONAL VAILABILITY.

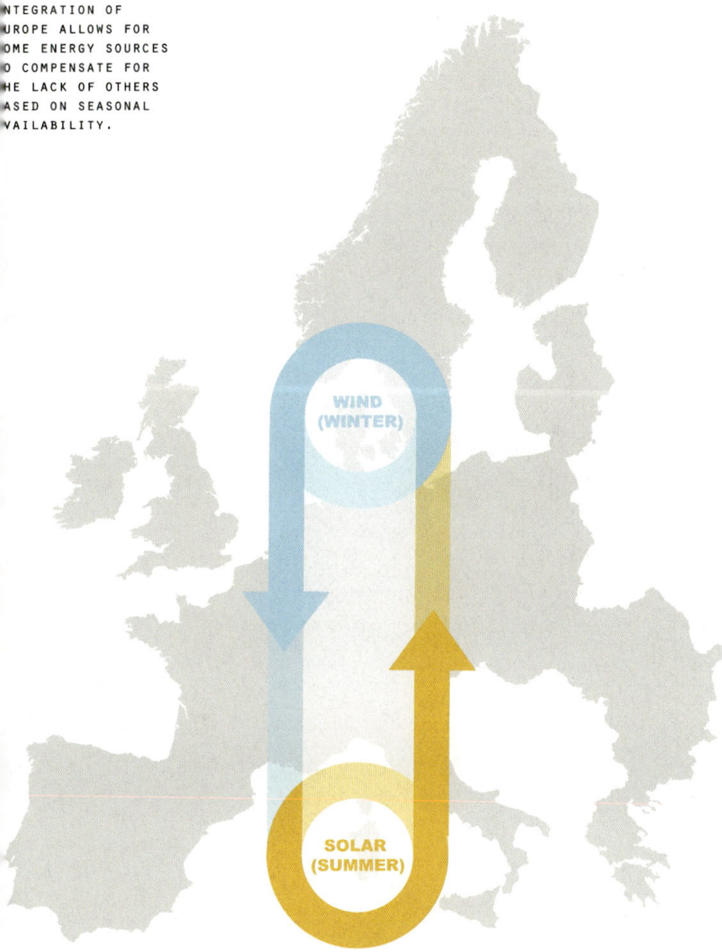

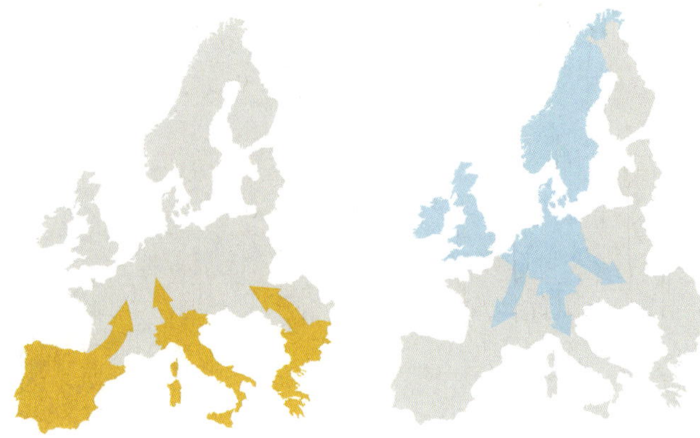

Overview of yearly energy balance, 80% RES pathway (TWh per week)

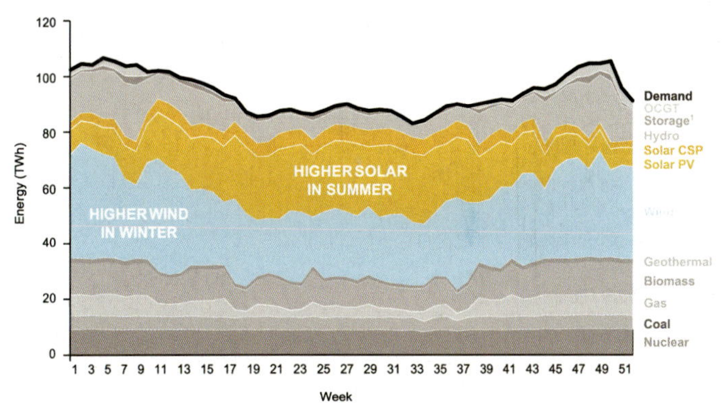

1 Storage included in the model relates to the existing hydro storage available across the regions
SOURCE Imperial College, KEMA. Roadmap 2050 Technical Analysis

EU ENERGY RESOURCE MOSAIC

OVERLAY OF CURRENT
ENERGY USE AND
THOSE REGIONS WITH
THE HIGHEST ENERGY
POTENTIAL.

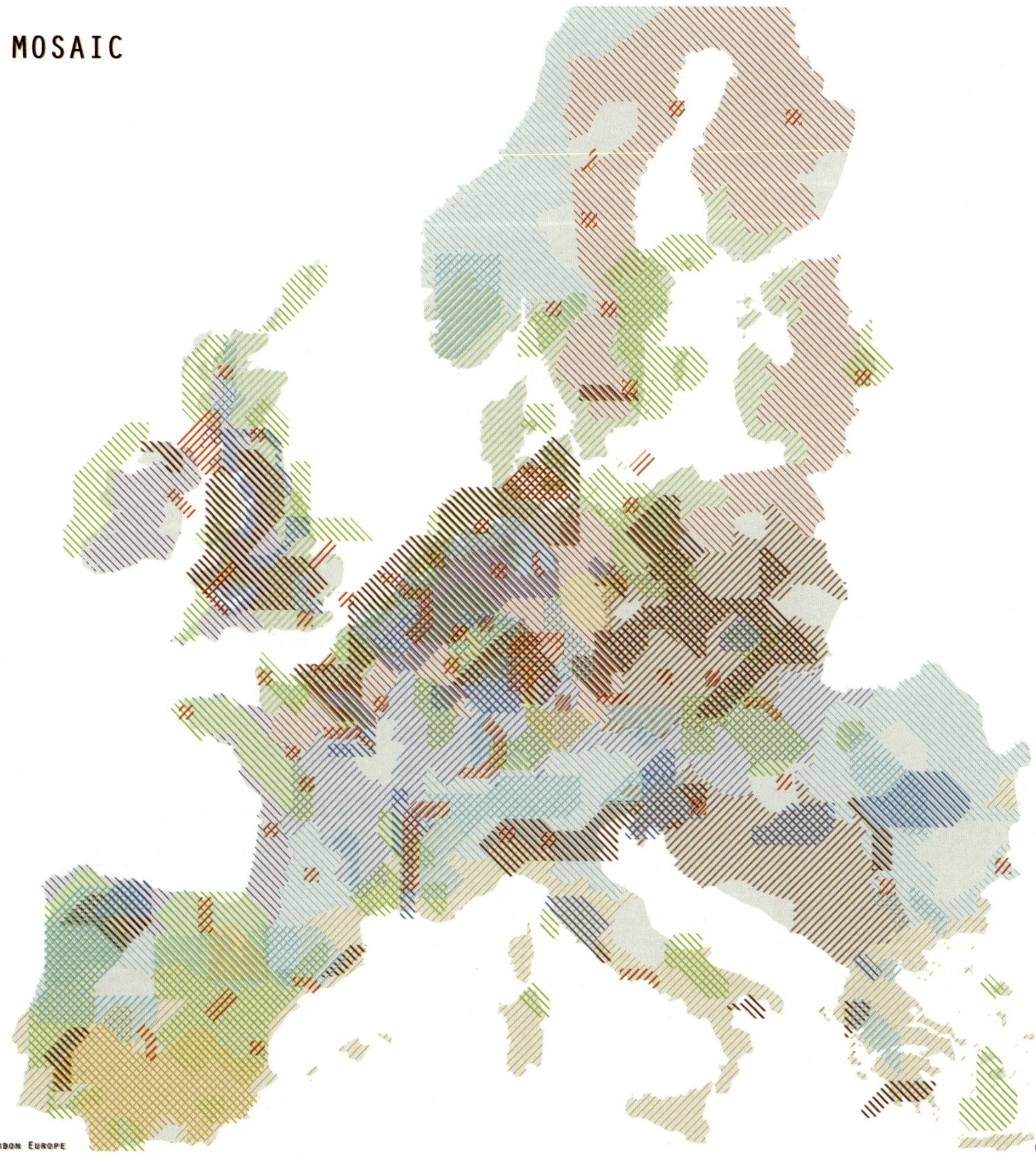

Map of
ENEROPA
Boundaries:
Biomassburg
C.C.S.R. (Carbon Capture & Storage Republic)
Enhanced Geothermalia
Geothermalia
Hydropia
Isles of Wind
Solaria
Tidal States
Vrania
Scale 1 : 20000000
Meridian of Greenwich
NORTH HYDROPIA
ISLES OF WIND
TIDAL STATES
GEOTHERMALIA
C.C.S.R.
VRANIA
ENHANCED GEOTHERMALIA
EAST HYDROPIA
CENTRAL HYDROPIA
BIOMASSBURG
WEST HYDROPIA
SOLARIA

HYDROPIA
ROADMAP 2050: A PRACTICAL GUIDE TO A PROSPEROUS, LOW CARBON EUROPE
OMA

ENHANCED GEOTHERMALIA
OADMAP 2050: A PRACTICAL GUIDE TO A PROSPEROUS, LOW-CARBON EUROPE
OMA/AMO

EUROPEAN ENERGY SECURITY

Today Europe retains a large dependency on other nations for natural gas. A primary incentive for European integration is that it enhances our own energy security and reduces our dependency on others, and especially on politically unstable regions.

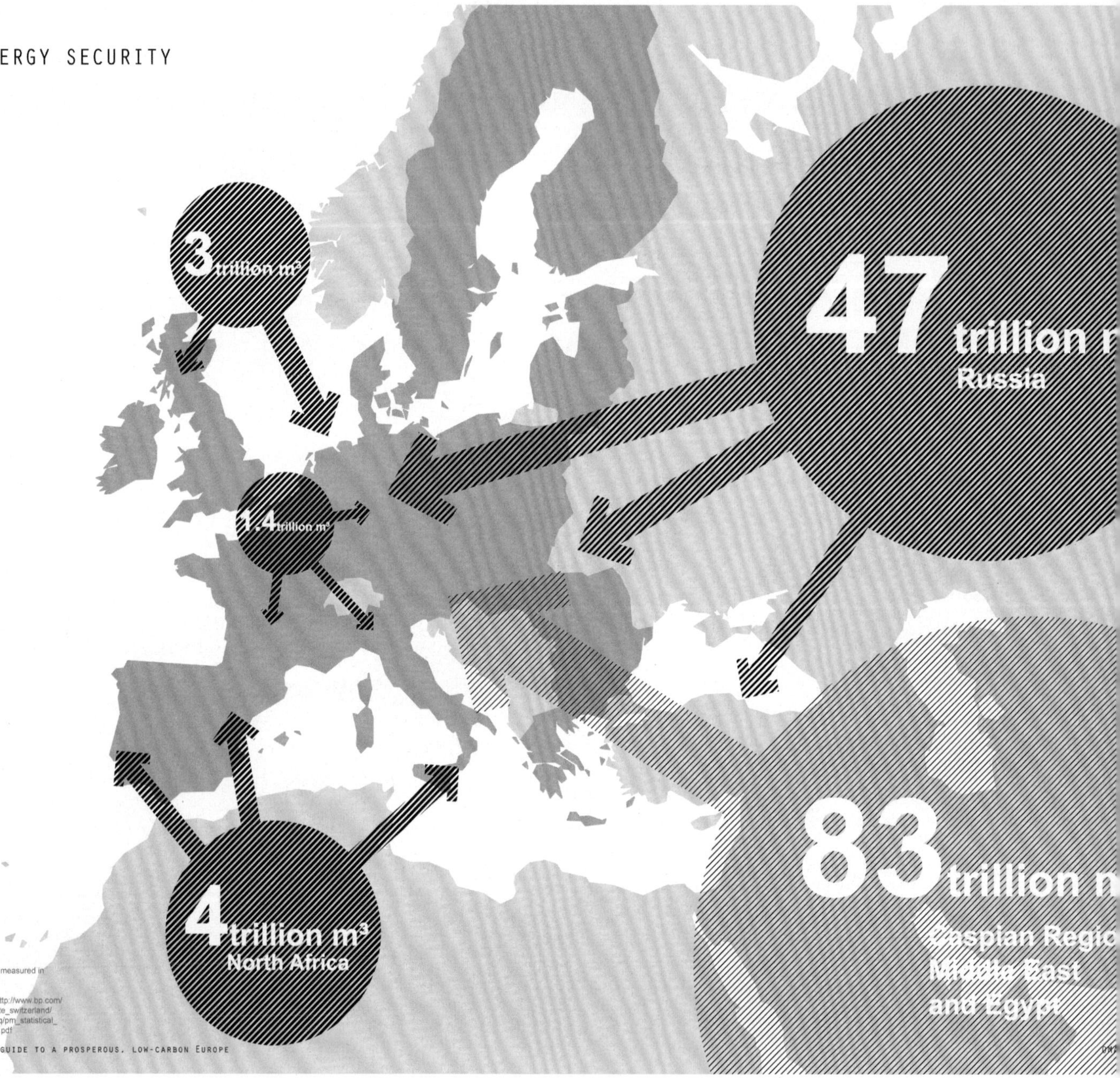

Estimated available Natural Gas deposits measured in Trillion(s) of cubic meters.

SOURCE: BP Statistical Review 6/2006: http://www.bp.com/liveassets/bp_internet/switzerland/corporate_switzerland/STAGING/local_assets/downloads_pdfs/pq/pm_statistical_review_of_world_energy_full_report_2006.pdf

EU ENERGY GRID

Including North Africa in the European Energy grid increases capacity.

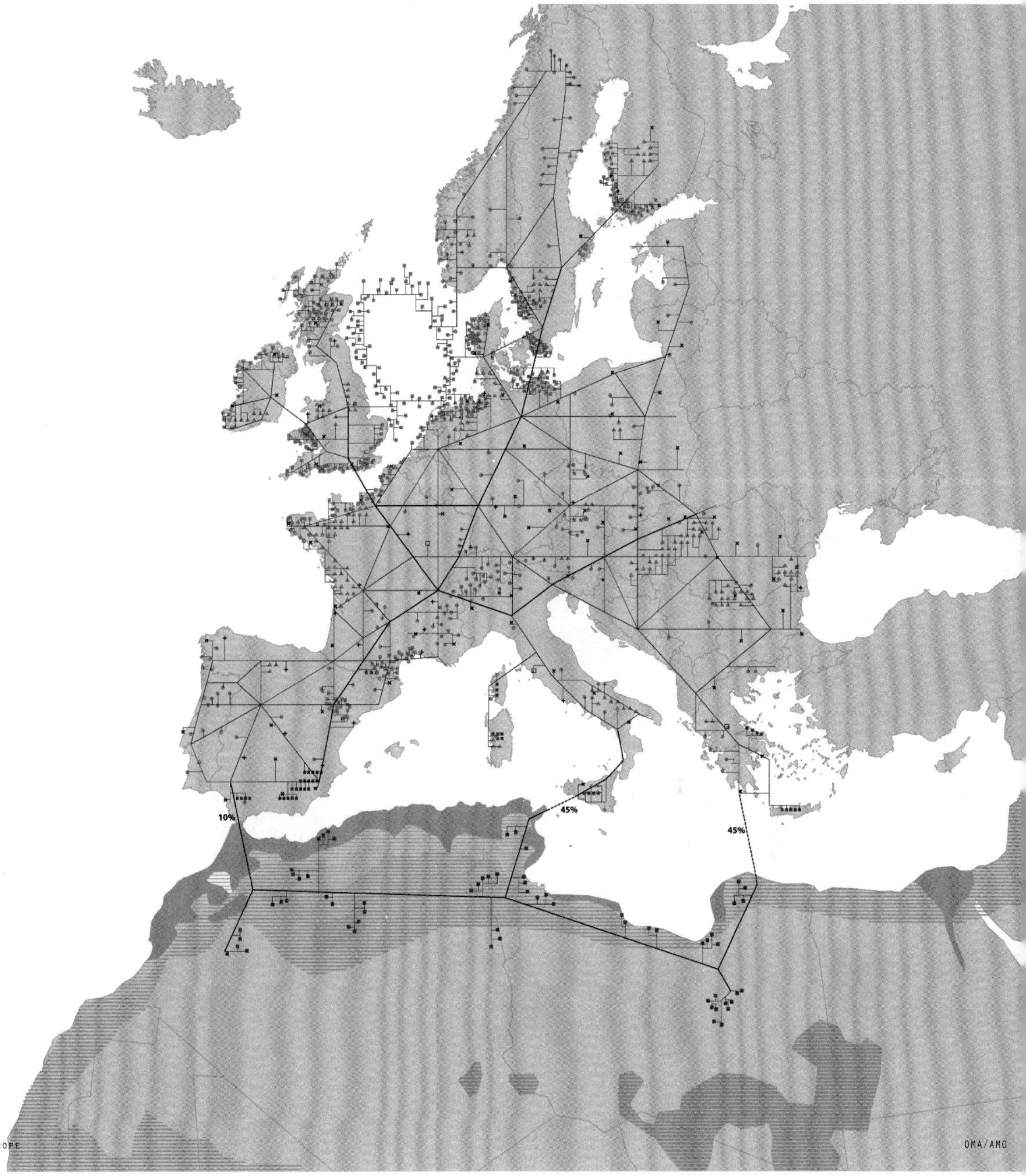

- SOLAR POWER
- WATER POWER PLANTS
- WIND POWER
- BIOMASS PLANTS
- GEOTHERMAL
- COAL-OIL-GAS (CCS)
- NUCLEAR POWER PLANTS

BENEFITS OF NORTH AFRICAN SOLAR

Both the EU-27 and North Africa will benefit from their introduction into the European Energy grid.

EU-27:

- Consistent source of renewable electrical power
- CO_2 — 100% Renewable energy supply

NORTH AFRICA:

- Consistent source of renewable electrical power
- Water from solar powered desalination
- Revenue source that will not run out
- New jobs
- Agriculture from new desalination water supply

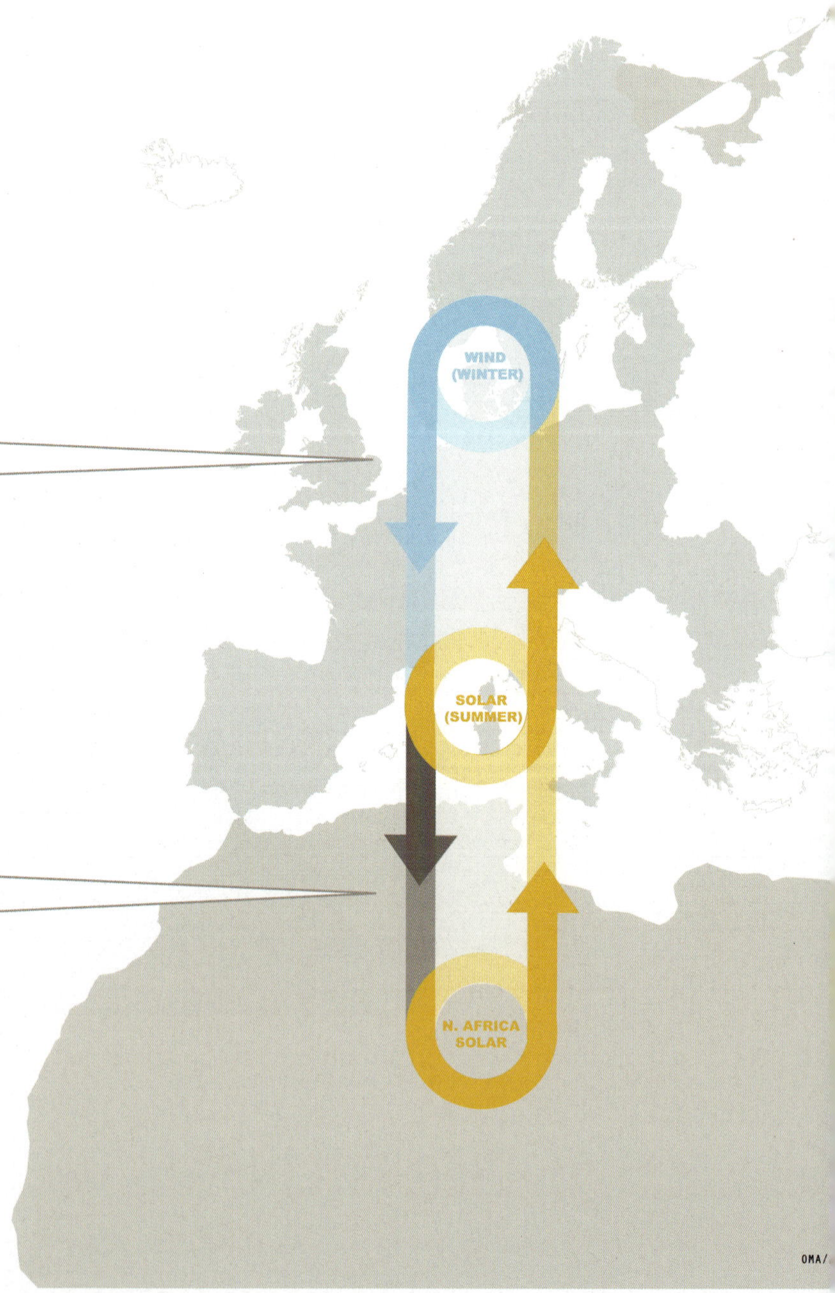

From Landscape as Infrastructure to Landscape as Bioregion

Energy is at the heart of industrial society—but invisibly so. The modern project has taught us to value speed, growth, and control—but not to count the energy costs of those paradigmatic modern values. Modern man is like Icarus: he soars confidently to great heights but lacks one life-critical piece of information: this is that all creation has an energy cost, and no system, or being, can maintain itself in isolation. How else are we to explain a document such as "The Energy Report" as relating to Roadmap 2050?[1]

Von der Landschaft als Infrastruktur zur Landschaft als Bioregion. Energie bildet den – unsichtbaren – Kern unserer Industriegesellschaft. Das Projekt der Moderne hat uns gelehrt, Geschwindigkeit, Wachstum und Kontrolle zu schätzen, die Energiekosten dieser paradigmatischen modernen Werte jedoch zu vernachlässigen. Der moderne Mensch ähnelt Ikarus: Voller Selbstbewusstsein schwingt er sich in ungeahnte Höhen auf, doch ihm fehlt eine lebenswichtige Information – dass nämlich jede produktive Hervorbringung Energie kostet und dass kein System und kein Lebewesen in völliger Isolation überleben kann. Wie sonst ist ein Dokument wie *The Energy Report* in Bezug zur Roadmap 2050 zu erklären?[1]

JOHN THACKARA

This important outcome of Roadmap 2050 takes European energy needs as a given; it adds up how much renewable energy would be required to meet them; and then it ignores the true costs of deploying such an infrastructure. Sweeping, almost weightless visualizations—such as the map of Eneropa—emphasize the Report's central message: the main obstacle to perpetual clean energy is a lack of executive ambition and political will.

The Roadmap suffers from a fatal weakness: the lack of a strategy for social and cultural transformation. It assumes that the same growth-at-all costs global economy that caused today's environmental crisis can be the engine for its resolution. It suggests that the transformation of Europe's entire energy system can be achieved without environmental or social cost. It implies that poor countries will agree to "share" their energy resources without complaint. Above all, Roadmap 2050 "backcasts" from a transformed energy landscape as if this had been primarily a technical, and not a social or cultural, achievement.

The Roadmap suffers from a fatal weakness: the lack of a strategy for social and cultural transformation. It assumes that the same growth-at-all costs global economy that caused today's environmental crisis can be the engine for its resolution.

It is as if Icarus had reached the top of his parabolic ascent. At this brief weightless moment, everything feels possible. He does not yet realize that gravity—in the form of social and environmental constraints—will soon reclaim him. Would it not be a good idea if Roadmap 2050 were to embrace these realities, and thereby help us prepare more realistically for that moment?

An apocalyptic view would be that—in the absence of a strategy for social and cultural transformation, and distracted by the chimera of an effortless transition to a new energy order—industrial civilization will proceed towards "catabolic collapse."[2] This is when a society, by the time it realizes what changes really have to be made, has exhausted the material and cultural energy needed to make them.

At the other extreme are the children of Icarus—technology optimists, such as the cartographers of Roadmap 2050—who are confident that clean energy will emerge, as if from heaven, to save us. Somewhere in-between these two extremes are so-called "soft-landers" [whose number includes this writer]. Soft-landers assume that the ecocidal economy of today will not and should not survive—but they are hopeful that some kind of ecotechnic replacement can be put in place.

1 Stephan Singer, WWF et al., "The Energy Report," 2011, in: http://assets.panda.org/downloads/101223_energy_report_final_print_2.pdf.

2 John Michael Greer, "How Civilizations Fall: A Theory of Catabolic Collapse," 2005, in: http://www.dylan.org.uk/greer_on_collapse.pdf.

Dieses wichtige Resultat der Roadmap 2050 setzt den Energiebedarf der europäischen Staaten als gegeben voraus: Es wird berechnet, wieviel erneuerbare Energie zu seiner Deckung erforderlich wäre, die tatsächlichen Kosten der dafür notwendigen Infrastruktur werden jedoch außer Acht gelassen. Dynamische, fast schwerelos wirkende Bilder und grafische Darstellungen – wie die Eneropa-Karte – unterstreichen die zentrale Botschaft des Berichts: Das Haupthindernis für unbegrenzte saubere Energie ist ein Mangel an unternehmerischem Ehrgeiz und politischem Willen.

Die Roadmap weist einen verhängnisvollen Schwachpunkt auf: Sie entwickelt keinerlei Strategien zur sozialen und kulturellen Transformation. Stattdessen geht sie davon aus, dass dieselbe globale Wirtschaft, die Wachstum um jeden Preis forciert und die heutige Umweltkrise verursacht hat, auch der Motor für die Lösung des Problems sein kann. Gleichzeitig suggeriert sie, dass eine Umgestaltung des kompletten europäischen Energiesystems ohne ökologische bzw. soziale Kosten möglich ist, und impliziert, dass arme Länder ohne weiteres damit einverstanden sein werden, ihre Energieressourcen mit uns „zu teilen". Vor allem aber geht die Roadmap in ihrer Analyse möglicher Strategien von einer bereits transformierten Energielandschaft aus, so als wäre dies eine primär technische und keine soziale oder kulturelle Leistung.

Es kommt einem vor, als hätte Ikarus den Gipfel seines sinnbildlichen Höhenflugs erreicht. In diesem kurzen Moment der Schwerelosigkeit scheint alles möglich. Er hat noch nicht begriffen, dass die Schwerkraft – in Form von sozialen und ökologischen Zwängen – sich seiner gleich wieder bemächtigen wird. Wäre es nicht besser, die Roadmap 2050 würde diese Realität berücksichtigen, so dass wir uns angemessener auf diesen Augenblick vorbereiten können?

Es ist eine apokalyptische Vorstellung, dass sich die industrielle Zivilisation – in Ermangelung einer Strategie für sozialen und kulturellen Wandel und getäuscht von der Chimäre eines mühelosen Übergangs zu einer neuen Energieordnung – auf einen „katabolischen Kollaps" zubewegt.[2] Dazu kommt es, wenn eine Gesellschaft erst dann zur Kenntnis nimmt, welche Änderungen wirklich erforderlich sind, wenn sämtliche dafür notwendigen materiellen und kulturellen Energiequellen bereits erschöpft sind.

Die Kinder des Ikarus verkörpern das andere Extrem – Technikoptimisten wie die Autoren der Roadmap, die fest darauf vertrauen, dass uns saubere Energie wie aus dem Nichts retten wird. Irgendwo zwischen diesen beiden Extremen befinden sich die Verfechter einer „sanften Landung", zu denen sich auch

1 Stephan Singer, WWF et al., „The Energy Report", 2011, in: http://assets.panda.org/downloads/101223_energy_report_final_print_2.pdf.

2 John Michael Greer, „How Civilizations Fall: A Theory of Catabolic Collapse", 2005, in: http://www.dylan.org.uk/greer_on_collapse.pdf.

der Verfasser dieses Beitrags zählt. Sie gehen davon aus, dass die heutige Wirtschaft mit ihrer Umweltzerstörung weder überleben kann noch überleben soll, hoffen aber, dass sie eine Art Öko-Technik-Ersatz finden wird.

Eine Voraussetzung dafür ist jedoch, dass wir aufhören, Landschaft als etwas Abstraktes zu betrachten, und uns wieder mit dem Land selbst verbinden – in wirtschaftlicher, kultureller und sozialer Hinsicht. Eine konventionelle Ökonomie, wie sie der Roadmap 2050 zugrunde liegt, berücksichtigt in ihren Kosten-Nutzen-Analysen keine biophysikalischen und sozialen Systeme. Sie misst sauberer Luft und sauberem Wasser, Artenvielfalt und Gerechtigkeit zwischen sozialen Schichten und verschiedenen Generationen keinen oder nur einen geringen Wert bei. In diesem ökonomischen System errichten wir Infrastrukturen und Städte, für die die Verluste an Ackerland, Wäldern, Feuchtbiotopen oder biologischer Vielfalt bedeutungslos sind. Wir entwerfen Energie-Erzeugungsgeräte, um sie in unbewohnten Gegenden in Gebrauch zu nehmen – wie in den trockenen Gebieten Frankreichs und Spaniens oder in der nordafrikanischen Wüste. Dem zugrunde liegt die Unterstellung, dieses Land sei „leer" oder „nutzlos".

Da die Roadmap 2050 unaufhörliches Wachstum und eine friktionsfreie Wirtschaft als gegeben voraussetzt, könnte man sie als eine späte Spielart jenes Konzepts verstehen, das die Strategien der letzten Jahre geprägt hat und das eine Anpassung an die Umwelt im Sinne eines „Schadensminderungsprogramms" propagiert. Der grüne Unternehmer Gunther Pauli[3] begegnet dieser Selbsttäuschung mit Spott: „Ein Dieb, der vor dem Richter aussagt, er stehle jetzt weniger als zuvor, darf nicht mit Milde rechnen. Warum vergeben wir Umweltpreise an Unternehmen, wenn sie die Umwelt ‚weniger' verschmutzen – obwohl die Verschmutzung nach wie vor stattfindet?" In diesem Sinne ist die Roadmap 2050 eine konservative Strategie, auch wenn sie vorgibt, radikale Wege zu gehen.

Eine ihrer Schwachstellen besteht darin, dass sie das riesige Reservoir an positiver sozialer Energie nicht berücksichtigt – der Übergang von einer Ökonomie der Entnahme („extractive economy") hin zu einer Ökonomie der Wiederherstellung („restorative economy") ist bereits im Gange. So sollte in der Roadmap 2050 das Konzept einer ökologischen Ökonomie, die auf neuen Werten und neuen Messsystemen beruht, zweifellos an prominenter Stelle stehen. Denn wir sprechen hier nicht von irgendwelchen abgehobenen Ideen. Die Veröffentlichung der Stern Review of Climate Change Economics im Jahr 2006 durch einen ehemaligen Chefökonomen der Weltbank leitete einen tiefgreifenden Wandel jener Regeln ein,[4] mit

3 Vgl. Gunther Pauli bei *The Blue Economy*; http://www.blueeconomy.de/.

4 Vgl. „Stern Review on the Economics of Climate Change", 2006, in: http://www.direct.gov.uk/en/Nl1/Newsroom/DG_064854.

A pre-condition for a soft-landing is that we stop thinking abstractly about landscape and reconnect with the land itself—in economic, cultural and social ways. Conventional economics, of the kind that underpins Roadmap 2050, exclude biophysical and social systems from its calculations of cost and benefit. It takes little or no account of the value of clean air and water, species diversity, and social and generational equity. Within this economic framework, we create infrastructures and cities that take no account of losses of farmland, forests, wetlands, or biological diversity. We design energy artifacts to be dumped onto uninhabited spaces—such as the arid lands in Spain and France, or the deserts of North Africa—on the assumption that these lands are "empty" or "useless."

Because Roadmap 2050 takes the perpetual-growth, friction-free economy as a given, it is best understood as a late-flowering of the "do less bad" approach to environmental adaptation that has shaped policy in recent years. The green entrepreneur Gunther Pauli[3] is scornful of this self-deception: "A thief who tells a judge he is stealing less than before will receive no leniency. So why do we give companies environmental awards for polluting 'less'—even though they are still polluting?" In this sense, although Roadmap 2050 strikes a radical pose, it remains a conservative strategy.

Roadmap 2050 is weakened by its omission of huge and positive social energy—the transition from an extractive economy to a restorative economy that is already under way. Ecological economics, based on new values and alternative systems of measurement, should surely be signposted prominently on the Roadmap. We are not talking fringe, here. The publication in 2006 of the Stern Review of Climate Change Economics,[4] by a former World Bank chief economist, marked the beginning of tectonic shifts in the rules by which we measure economic performance. This influential economist did not just question the viability of perpetual growth in a biosphere whose carrying capacity is finite. He also anticipated new rules of competition in which matter and energy flowing through our economic system will be properly counted and paid for at full price—rather than taken for granted as a freebie. Stern paved the way for so-called "external" costs to be counted properly in national- and energy system-accounts for the first time—but Roadmap 2050 has missed this opportunity.

Two years after the Stern Review, another report, *The Economics of Ecosystems and Biodiversity* (TEEB), by Pavan Sukhdev, was published by Deutsche Bank and the European Commission.[5] Building on Stern, TEEB sets out a "comprehensive and compelling economic case for the conservation of biodiversity." TEEB promotes a better understanding of the true economic value of the benefits we receive from nature—but these costs and benefits, too, are missing from Roadmap 2050. If Stern and TEEB are building blocks of new fiscal and regulatory regimes, they are being driven forward politically, and culturally, by new attitudes to land use and, in particular, an appreciation that it's not just empty space out there. This cultural transformation is evident in the growth of the bioregional movement. This nascent regional practice has been stimulated by a wide variety

3 See Gunther Pauli on *The Blue Economy*: http://www.blueeconomy.de/.

4 See "Stern Review on the Economics of Climate Change," 2006, in: http://www.direct.gov.uk/en/Nl1/Newsroom/DG_064854.

5 *The Economics of Ecosystems and Biodiversity* (TEEB): http://www.teebweb.org/.

of grassroots, on-the-ground actions that identify with naturally bounded regions and local communities. There are watershed conservancies, holistic ecosystem management efforts, coordinated resource management plans (CRiMPs), and community-supported agriculture groups.[6] For the writer Robert L. Thayer, bioregions are variously defined "by the geography of watersheds, similar plant and animal ecosystems, and related, identifiable landforms (e.g., particular mountain ranges, prairies, or coastal zones) and by the unique human cultures that grow from natural limits and potentials of the region."[7] Alongside the rediscovery of the bioregion as a cultural frame of reference, a new kind of local self-organization is also growing. Phenomena such as Post-Carbon Cities[8] or Transition Towns[9] are the better-known examples—but there are many more: from dam removers, to seed bankers, from iPhone doctors, to rainwater rescuers. Although these sound like pragmatic, single-issue campaigns, they are different from 1970s-style grassroots campaigns in one important respect: they explicitly embrace culture, economy and ecology as a single space. Local conditions, local trading patterns, local networks, local skills, and local culture are their critical success factor. They focus on resource efficiency at a local level—but not in a parochial way. Around the world there is intensive shared innovation of services and platforms that enable us to share all resources—such as energy, matter, time, skill, software, space, or food.

This powerful interaction of economic and cultural transformation has as its consequence a new design paradigm. This important ingredient, too, is missing from Roadmap 2050. A priority for the new design is the mapping of assets and resources that are already there, in their territory. These assets can be hard or soft: natural assets—such as wind, or sun, with the potential to generate energy; local materials, and the skills needed to use them; abandoned spaces with the potential to be re-purposed; food and systems. These asset maps are being used gradually to replace many of the high-altitude maps used by planners or economists and by Roadmap 2050. The latter tends to focus on hard things, such as roads or buildings.

Restorative economy asset maps take natural biodiversity as their starting point—with special emphasis on the *interconnectedness and interdependence* of social and natural systems. New creative and design skills are emerging, and new forms of representation are being innovated, to communicate energy and nutrient cycles, or biodiversity. These show the different ways that healthy social systems depend upon, and are intertwined with, healthy economies and ecosystems.

The human assets of neighborhoods and communities—people who are engaged in valuable but sometimes invisible innovation at a grassroots level—are also being mapped.

Resource efficiency is at heart a social process, not a technical one. The identification of individuals and groups who are already out there, and active, is therefore key. The role of design is to discover, improve and accelerate

6 See "Coordinated Resource Management: A Voluntary and Collaborative Problem-Solving Process for Resource Management Issues," in: http://www.rangelands.org/education_crm.shtml.

7 Robert L. Thayer, Jr., "LifePlace: Bioregional Thought and Practice," 2003, in: http://www.ucpress.edu/book.php?isbn=9780520236288.

8 See "Post Carbon Cities: Planning for Energy and Climate Uncertainty," in: http://postcarboncities.net/.

9 See *Transition Towns*: http://www.transitionnetwork.org/.

denen wirtschaftliche Leistungen gemessen werden. Nicholas Stern, ein einflussreicher Volkswirtschaftler, stellte nicht nur die Möglichkeit ununterbrochenen Wachstums in einer Biosphäre mit begrenzter Kapazität infrage. Er postulierte auch neue Regeln für den Wettbewerb, mit denen die Material- und Energieströme in unserem Wirtschaftssystem adäquat gemessen und in voller Höhe vergütet – statt wie bisher als selbstverständlich und kostenlos angesehen werden. Stern bereitete den Weg für eine erstmalige, angemessene Berücksichtigung der so genannten „externen Kosten" in der volkswirtschaftlichen Gesamtrechnung und Energiebuchhaltung von Staaten – doch die Roadmap 2050 hat diese Gelegenheit ungenutzt verstreichen lassen.

Zwei Jahre nach dem Stern-Report veröffentlichten die Deutsche Bank und die Europäische Kommission einen Bericht von Pavan Sukhdev mit dem Titel „The Economics of Ecosystems and Biodiversity" (TEEB).[5] Basierend auf den Erkenntnissen von Stern legte TEEB eine „umfassende und überzeugende ökonomische Begründung für den Schutz der Biodiversität" vor. TEEB tritt für ein besseres Verständnis des realen ökonomischen Wertes jener Leistungen ein, die die Natur für uns erbringt – aber auch diese Kosten und Leistungen fehlen in der Roadmap 2050. Wenn Stern und TEEB die Bausteine für ein neues fiskalisches und regulatorisches System sind, so werden ihre Konzepte sowohl in politischer als auch in kultureller Hinsicht von einer neuen Einstellung zur Landnutzung geleitet – sowie insbesondere von der Vorstellung, dass „das da draußen nicht bloß leerer Raum ist". Dieser kulturelle Wandel zeigt sich im Aufkeimen und Wachsen der bioregionalen Bewegung. Diese wurde und wird durch unterschiedlichste Basisaktionen inspiriert, die sich mit den in ihren Ressourcen begrenzten Regionen und lokalen Gemeinschaften identifizieren. Dazu zählen Wasserschutzinitiativen, holistische Ansätze im Bereich Ökosystemmanagement, Programme für das koordinierte Management von Ressourcen und landwirtschaftliche Gruppen, die von der lokalen Gemeinschaft unterstützt werden.[6] Der Autor Robert L. Thayer sieht Bioregionen definiert „durch die Geografie von Wassereinzugsgebieten, gleichartige pflanzliche und tierische Ökosysteme, fest umrissene, ähnliche Landformen (z. B. bestimmte Gebirgszüge, Graslandgebiete oder Küstenzonen) und die einzigartigen menschlichen Kulturformen, die den natürlichen Beschränkungen und Möglichkeiten einer Region entspringen".[7] Neben der Wiederentdeckung der Bioregion als kulturelles Bezugssystem gewinnt

5 *The Economics of Ecosystems and Biodiversity* (TEEB); http://www.teebweb.org/.

6 Vgl. „Coordinated Resource Management: A Voluntary and Collaborative Problem-Solving Process for Resource Management Issues", in: http://www.rangelands.org/education_crm.shtml.

7 Robert L. Thayer, Jr., „LifePlace: Bioregional Thought and Practice", 2003, in: http://www.ucpress.edu/book.php?isbn=9780520236288.

This powerful interaction of economic and cultural transformation has as its consequence a new design paradigm. This important ingredient, too, is missing from Roadmap 2050. A priority for the new design is the mapping of assets and resources that are already there, in their territory.

existing grassroots innovation, not necessarily to create it from scratch—but to add in additional design skills, technology platforms and resources, as and when they were needed. Connecting people to new people, and helping them learn from each other's other experience, is itself a form of innovation in this context.

A restorative economy is about the creation of value without destroying natural and human assets. But it is not about a retreat into an imagined rural idyll. On the contrary, what has also been named regenerative design [as described in 1994 by John Lyle][10] connects city dwellers with soils, trees, animals, landscapes, energy systems, water, renewables and the like. It's about reimagining the urban landscape—itself an ecology with the potential to support us. Regenerative design, restorative design, they are based on a simple principle: leave the world better than you found it.

To Roadmap 2050's authors—"industry players and academia, and a team of recognized experts"—it is axiomatic that fundamental change must be imposed top-down. This belief system explains why "effective permitting and licensing procedures," "socializing the costs between countries," and "investment incentives" figure so prominently. This conclusion may be logical to its authors—but it is at odds with the social and cultural changes that are also under way, that point in a different direction. For every daily-life support system that is unsustainable now—food, health, shelter and clothing—alternatives are being innovated. The keyword here is social innovation, because this movement is about groups of people innovating together. It is not about lone inventors, let alone super-smart engineers and planners, "saving" the planet. The future we are likely to get will not be shaped by one or the other—top-down, or bottom-up. We need both. Unless we embrace that reality, we will not get to the happy future that Roadmap 2050 promises.

The role of design is to discover, improve and accelerate existing grassroots innovation, not necessarily to create it from scratch—but to add in additional design skills, technology platforms and resources, as and when they were needed.

10 See *Centre for Regenerative Studies*: https://www.csupomona.edu/~crs/.

auch eine neue Form der lokalen Selbstorganisation an Bedeutung. Initiativen wie „Post Carbon Cities"[8] oder „Transition Towns"[9] sind bekanntere Beispiele für dieses Phänomen – doch es gibt weitaus mehr: von Staudammbekämpfern über Saatgutbänker und iPhone-Doktoren bis hin zu Regenwasserrettern. Auch wenn diese Beispiele nach pragmatischen Bewegungen klingen, die sich auf ein bestimmtes Thema spezialisiert haben, unterscheiden sie sich von Basisinitiativen à la 1970er-Jahre in einem wichtigen Punkt: Sie verstehen Kultur, Wirtschaft und Ökologie explizit als Einheit. Lokale Gegebenheiten, lokale Handelsformen, lokale Netzwerke, lokale Fähigkeiten und lokale Kultur sind ihre Erfolgsfaktoren. Sie betreiben Ressourceneffizienz auf lokaler Ebene, ohne provinziell zu sein. Überall auf der Welt sind intensive gemeinschaftliche Innovationen an Services und Plattformen zu beobachten, die uns das Teilen von Ressourcen wie Energie, Material, Zeit, Fähigkeiten, Software, Raum oder Nahrung erlauben.

Dieses machtvolle Zusammenspiel von wirtschaftlichem und kulturellem Wandel resultiert in einem neuen Designparadigma. Auch dieser wichtige Faktor fehlt in der Roadmap 2050. Eine Priorität des neuen Designkonzepts ist die Kartierung von Werten und Ressourcen, die in einem bestimmten Gebiet bereits vorhanden sind. Diese Werte können materieller und immaterieller Natur sein: natürliche Grundlagen, die wie Sonne oder Wind als potenzielle Energielieferanten dienen können; lokale Materialien und die zu ihrer Verwendung erforderlichen Fähigkeiten; leerstehende Räume mit neuen Nutzungsmöglichkeiten; Nahrungsmittel und Systeme aller Art. Diese „Asset-Maps" ersetzen zunehmend die von Planern, Ökonomen und den Verfassern der Roadmap 2050 verwendeten Karten, die den Fokus auf materielle Dinge wie Straßen oder Gebäude legen.

Die Asset-Maps innerhalb einer Ökonomie des Wiederherstellens gehen von der natürlichen Biodiversität aus und betonen dabei besonders die *wechselseitigen Beziehungen und Abhängigkeiten* von gesellschaftlichen und natürlichen Systemen. Neue kreative und gestalterische Fähigkeiten entstehen und neue Formen der Repräsentation werden entwickelt, um Informationen über Energiezyklen, biogeochemische Zyklen und Biodiversität zu kommunizieren. Sie zeigen die vielfältigen Abhängigkeiten von und Verflechtungen mit gesunden Ökonomien und Ökosystemen, die für gesunde soziale Systeme typisch sind.

Auch die humanen Faktoren von Nachbarschaften und Gemeinschaften – Menschen, die sich für wertvolle, aber nicht immer sichtbare Innovationsprozesse an der Basis engagieren – sind in den Asset-Maps verzeichnet.

8 Vgl. „Post Carbon Cities: Planning for Energy and Climate Uncertainty", in: http://postcarboncities.net/.

9 Vgl. *Transition Towns*; http://www.transitionnetwork.org/.

Ressourceneffizienz ist im Grunde genommen ein sozialer, kein technischer Prozess. Dem Ausfindigmachen von bereits aktiven, engagierten Personen und Gruppen kommt dabei eine Schlüsselfunktion zu. Die Rolle des Designs liegt dabei nicht unbedingt in der Schaffung neuer Bewegungen, sondern in der Entdeckung, Verbesserung und Beschleunigung bestehender Innovationen an der Basis – durch Bereitstellung zusätzlicher Designfähigkeiten, Technologieplattformen und Ressourcen, wenn es einen Bedarf dafür gibt. Menschen miteinander zu verbinden und ihnen dabei zu helfen, von den Erfahrungen anderer zu lernen, stellt in diesem Kontext selbst eine Form der Innovation dar.

In einer Ökonomie des Wiederherstellens geht es um die Schaffung von Werten, ohne natürliche und humane Ressourcen zu zerstören, nicht aber um den Rückzug in eine imaginäre ländliche Idylle. Ganz im Gegenteil, dieses auch „Regenerative Design" genannte Konzept[10] – im Sinne der Beschreibung von John Lyle aus dem Jahr 1994 – verbindet Stadtbewohner mit Böden, Bäumen, Tieren, Landschaften, Energiesystemen, Gewässern, erneuerbaren Energieformen und Ähnlichem. Es geht darum, die urbane Landschaft neu zu denken, denn diese ist selbst eine Ökologie, die unser Überleben potenziell sichern kann. „Regenerative Design" basiert ebenso wie das Konzept des „Restorative Design" auf einem einfachen Prinzip: Verlasse die Welt in einem besseren Zustand, als du sie vorgefunden hast.

Die Verfasser der Roadmap 2050 – „Vertreter der Industrie, Wissenschafter und ein Team anerkannter Experten" – gehen von dem Prinzip aus, dass ein grundlegender Wandel nur „von oben" angeordnet werden kann. Diese Sichtweise erklärt, warum „effektive Genehmigungs- und Zulassungsverfahren", „die Sozialisierung der Kosten zwischen den Staaten" und „Investitionsanreize" hier eine so große Rolle spielen.

Diese Schlussfolgerung mag den Autoren logisch erscheinen, sie steht jedoch im Konflikt mit den sozialen und kulturellen Veränderungen, die zurzeit stattfinden und die in eine andere Richtung weisen. Für jeden Bereich des täglichen Lebens, der derzeit nicht nachhaltig organisiert ist – Nahrung, Gesundheit, Unterkunft und Kleidung – werden Alternativen entwickelt. Das Schlüsselwort hier lautet *soziale* Innovation, denn bei dieser Bewegung handelt es sich um Gruppen von Menschen, die gemeinsam an Innovationen arbeiten. Hier geht es nicht um die einsamen Erfinder oder gar um die genialen Ingenieure und Planer, die den Planeten „retten". Wahrscheinlich wird unsere Zukunft weder ausschließlich „von oben" noch ausschließlich „von unten" gestaltet werden. Wir brauchen beide Ansätze. Solange wir uns dieser Realität verweigern, wird die schöne Zukunft, die uns die Roadmap 2050 verspricht, ein Traum bleiben.

10 Vgl. *Centre for Regenerative Studies*; https://www.csupomona.edu/~crs/.

1

Nach dem Ende des fossilen Zeitalters

Die bisher einmalige Wachstumsepoche der letzten 200 Jahre in Nordamerika, Europa und Teilen Asiens ist eng mit der Nutzung fossiler Energien verknüpft. Energieressourcen, die über viele Millionen Jahre aus Biomasse entstanden sind, wurden verbraucht und die Vorräte an Erdöl werden bald erschöpft sein. Gravierender ist jedoch, dass das bei der Verbrennung entstehende Kohlendioxid in der Erdatmosphäre einen Treibhauseffekt bewirkt.

After the End of the Fossil Era. The unique period of growth that has lasted for over 200 years in North America, Europe and parts of Asia is closely associated with the use of fossil energy. Energy resources which were formed over millions of years from biomass are coming to an end and our oil reserves will soon be exhausted. However, the greenhouse effect caused by carbon dioxide from combustion processes is an even more serious issue.

PHILIPP OSWALT • ANNE SCHMIDT

Um eine Störung des Klimasystems zu verhindern und die globale Temperaturerhöhung langfristig auf zwei Grad Celsius zu beschränken, muss die Erzeugung von Treibhausgasen in den nächsten Jahrzehnten auf ein bis zwei Tonnen pro Person und Jahr reduziert werden.[1] Dazu müssen wir zum einen den Energieverbrauch massiv reduzieren und zum anderen fossile durch regenerative Energien ersetzen.

Das wird eine Verteuerung der Energie und damit auch der Mobilität zur Folge haben. Der Raumwiderstand wird wachsen: Distanzen werden in Zukunft wieder eine wichtigere Rolle spielen und eine merkliche Re-Regionalisierung bewirken (Abb. 4): Urlaubsfernreisen mit dem Flugzeug werden sich zugunsten eines regionalen Tourismus reduzieren, Baustoffe und andere schwere Güter werden wieder häufiger in der Nähe ihres Verwendungsortes hergestellt, Lebensmittel verstärkt lokal produziert werden. Energieeffizienz kann hier lokal zu neuen Wachstumsprozessen führen.

Die Zukunft unserer Städte und Dörfer wird aber auch zunehmend davon abhängen, wie hoch deren Energiebedarf ist – insbesondere für Gebäudeheizung und die Mobilität der Bewohner. Was nur noch energetisch aufwändig nutzbar ist, wird in Zukunft kaum mehr zu gebrauchen sein.

> Die Zukunft unserer Städte und Dörfer wird aber auch zunehmend davon abhängen, wie hoch deren Energiebedarf ist – insbesondere für Gebäudeheizung und die Mobilität der Bewohner.

Die fossile Energieversorgung wird, soweit nicht ohnehin eingespart, weitgehend durch die verschiedenen Formen erneuerbarer Energien ersetzt werden. Diese werden vor allem durch eine Vielzahl dezentraler Anlagen gewonnen werden. Eine vielfältige Energielandschaft wird sich herausbilden und sekundäre Aktivitäten, die von der jeweiligen Eigenart der Energieproduktion profitieren, die lokalen Spezialisierungen verstärken. Für Sachsen-Anhalt ergibt sich dabei etwa folgendes Bild (Abb. 3): Im Mittelgebirge Harz konzentriert sich die Energiegewinnung aus Wasserkraft, deren Potenzial nach gegenwärtiger Sichtweise schon weitestgehend erschöpft ist. Relevant sind die Möglichkeiten von Pumpspeicherkraftwerken, um das stark schwankende Stromangebot aus Windkraft und Photovoltaik abpuffern zu können. Die Wasserflächen der Stauseen können zugleich für Fischzucht in Aquakultur oder auch den zunehmenden regionalen Tourismus genutzt werden.

Sachsen-Anhalt hat heute den höchsten Anteil an Windenergie im Nettostromverbrauch in Deutschland. Von Vorteil ist dabei insbesondere die geringe Besiedlungsdichte, da Windkraftanlagen nur außerhalb von Siedlungsgebieten errichtet werden dürfen.[2] Im Süden des Landes hat sich mit Solar Valley ein Schwerpunkt für Solarenergie entwickelt, der von der Nähe zu

1 Heute verursacht jeder Einwohner Sachsen-Anhalts durchschnittlich circa 11 Tonnen Treibhausgase im Jahr (globaler Durchschnitt: 4,4 Tonnen).

2 Aufgrund von Geräuschentwicklung, Schattenwurf und Disco-Effekt sind Windräder nur außerhalb besiedelter Gebiete zugelassen.

In order to avoid changes in the climate system and limit the rise of long-term global temperatures to 2° Celsius, the production of greenhouse gas emissions must be reduced to one to two tons per person per year over the next decades.[1] To achieve that goal, we will have to greatly reduce our energy consumption and replace fossil fuels with renewable energy.

As a consequence, energy and therefore mobility will become more expensive. Spatial resistance will also increase, and that means that distances will play a more important role in the future, since they will cause noticeable re-regionalization effects (fig. 4), i.e., long distance holiday travel by plane will decrease in favor of regional tourism, construction materials and other heavy goods will be manufactured nearer to their target location, and more food and foodstuffs will be produced locally. Seen from that angle, energy efficiency can lead to new local growth processes.

But the future of our towns and villages will increasingly depend on how high their energy requirements are—especially with regard to heating buildings and the mobility of the people living in them. In future, everything that costs more to use in terms of energy shall hardly be feasible.

Except for a minimum remainder, fossil energy supplies will be widely replaced by various forms of renewable energy generated by numerous local plants. A multifaceted energy landscape will develop, and secondary activities, which shall benefit from specific types of energy production, will strengthen local forms of specialization. In Saxony-Anhalt, for instance, the energy situation is as follows (fig. 3): most of the energy is produced by hydroelectric power plants in the lower mountain range Harz, whose potential, according to current opinion, is already nearly exhausted. Pumped storage plants could help to compensate high fluctuations in power supplies from wind farms and photovoltaic power plants. The surfaces of water reservoirs could then be used for breeding fish in aquacultures or, alternatively, for the benefit of regional tourism.

Today, Saxony-Anhalt produces the highest percentage of wind power in net power consumption in Germany. Advantageous in this context is especially the low population density, since wind power plants are only allowed to be built away from residential areas.[2] In the south of the state, Solar Valley has developed into a key area for solar energy which benefits from its close vicinity to university and other research institutions. Among others, solar heat and photovoltaics could also be feasible for settlements. Particularly the northern regions and the Magdeburg area have great potential for the exploitation of deep geothermal energy, which has not yet been developed

1 Today, Saxony-Anhalt produces an average of some 11 tons of greenhouse gases per capita per annum (global average is 4.4 tons).

2 Wind farms are not permitted near residential areas because they tend to be noisy and also cause a lot of shade and flickering effects.

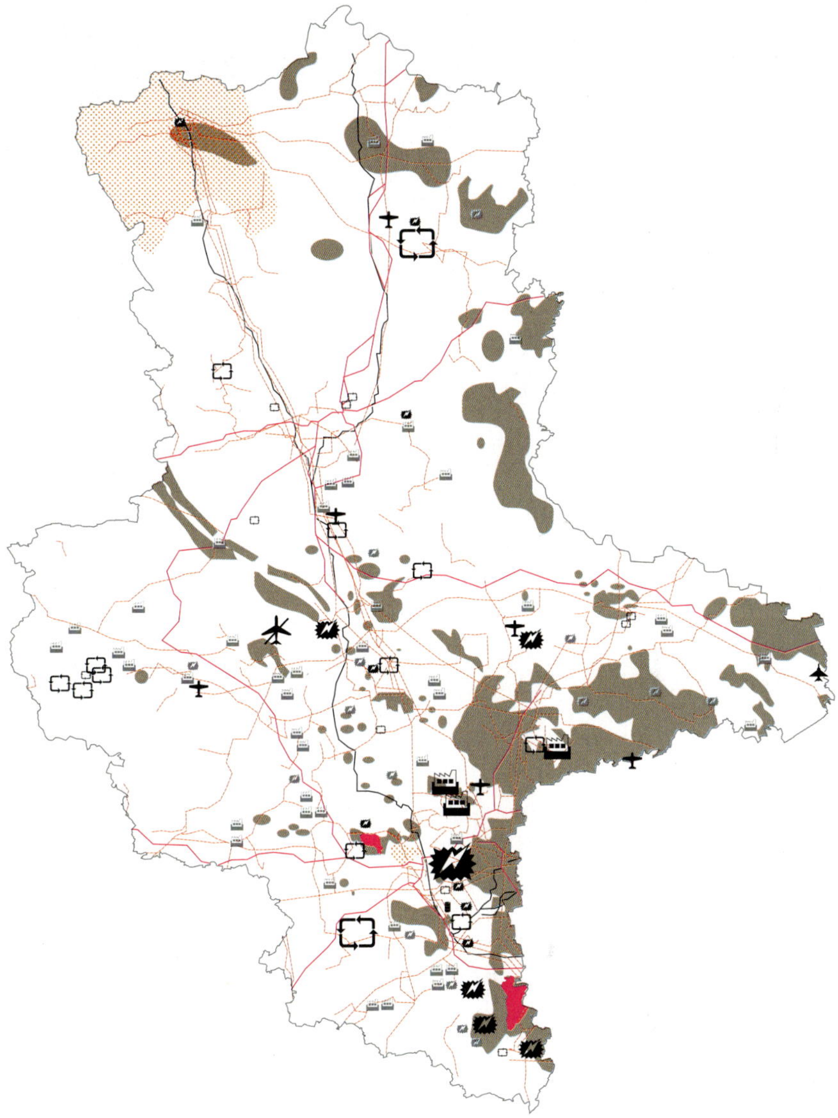

FOSSILE INFRASTRUKTUR 2010, DIE IN DEN KOMMENDEN JAHRZEHNTEN HINFÄLLIG WIRD, WENN SIE NICHT FÜR DEN GEBRAUCH REGENERATIVER ENERGIEN UMGENUTZT WERDEN KANN.

FOSSIL FUEL INFRASTRUCTURE 2010, WHICH WILL BECOME OBSOLETE IN DECADES TO COME UNLESS IT CAN BE CONVERTED FOR THE USE OF RENEWABLE ENERGIES

ERDGAS/NATURAL GAS FIELD
BRAUNKOHLE/LIGNITE DEPOSIT
AKTIVER BERGBAU/ACTIVE MINING AREA
GASVERSORGUNGSLEITUNG/GAS PIPELINE
STROMLEITUNG/POWER LINE
ERDÖLPIPELINE/OIL PIPELINE
KRAFTWERK/POWER PLANT
HEIZKRAFTWERK/COGENERATION PLANT
RAFFINERIE/REFINERY
INDUSTRIEKRAFTWERK/INDUSTRIAL POWER PLANT
FLUGHAFEN/AIRPORT
VERKEHRSLANDEPLATZ/AIRFIELD
MILITÄRFLUGPLATZ/MILITARY AIRPORT

ENERGIEVERBRAUCH 2008 (GJ)/ENERGY CONSUMPTION 2008 (GJ)

› 50.000.000
2.000.000–50.000.000
35.000–2.000.000
VERBRAUCH UNBEKANNT/
CONSUMPTION UNKNOWN

Quellen
Gas-, Stromleitungen, Kraftwerke, Heizkraftwerke, Bergbau
Ministerium für Raumordnung und Verkehr, 2007
Erdgasfelder, Braunkohle Lagerstätten
Landesamt für Geologie und Bergwesen, 2007
Energieverbraucher
Umweltbundesamt, Deutsche Emissionshandelsstelle, 2009

Sources
Gas pipelines, power lines, power plants, cogeneration plants, mining areas
Ministerium für Raumordnung und Verkehr, 2007
Natural gas fields, lignite deposits
Landesamt für Geologie und Bergwesen, 2007
Energy consumers
Umweltbundesamt, Deutsche Emissionshandelsstelle, 2009

2

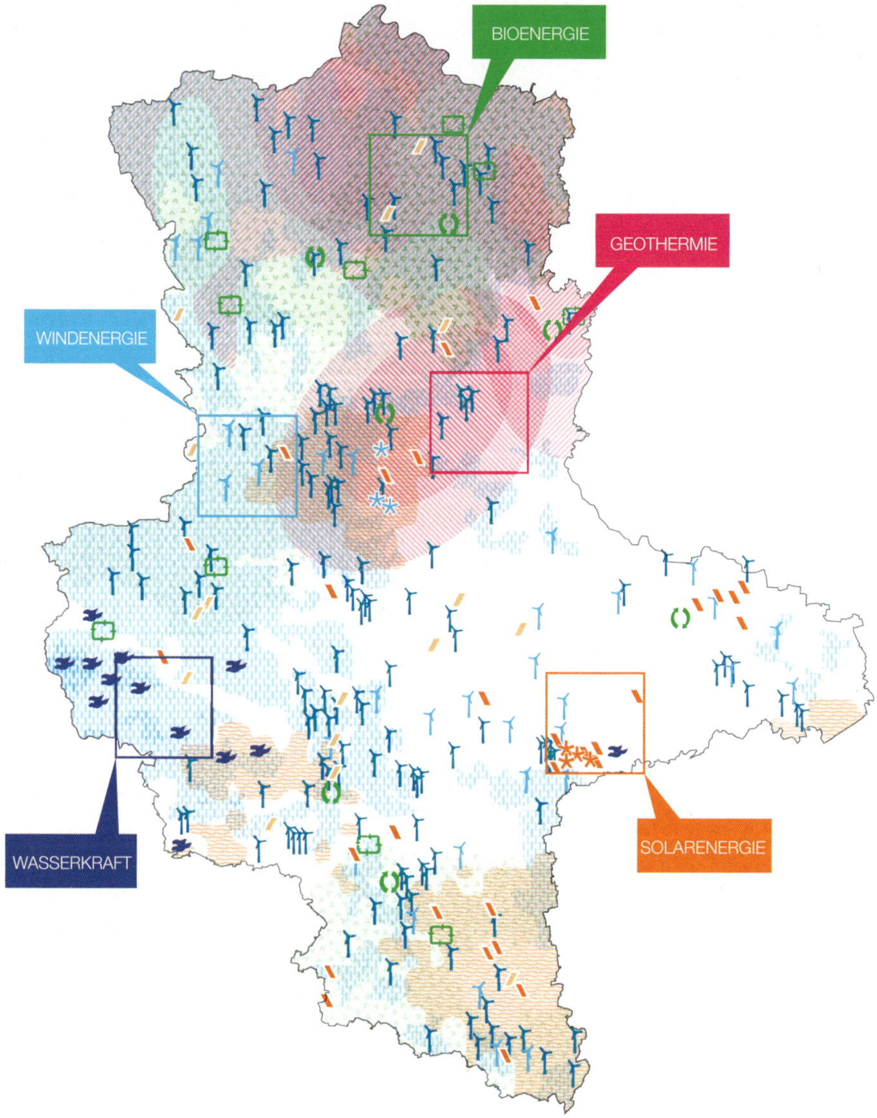

ZENTREN DER REGENERATIVEN ENERGIENGEWINNUNG
CENTERS FOR THE GENERATION OF RENEWABLE ENERGY

- WINDPARK/WIND FARM
- WINDPARK IN PLANUNG/WIND FARM (PLANNED)
- WINDKRAFTANLAGENHERSTELLER/ MANUFACTURER OF WIND ENERGY PLANTS

WINDGESCHWINDIGKEITEN IN 80 m ÜNN (JÄHRLICHER DURCHSCHNITT)/
WIND SPEED AT 80 m ABOVE MEAN SEA LEVEL (ANNUAL MEAN)

- ≤ 4,9 m/s
- 4,9–5,8 m/s
- 5,8–7 m/s
- ≥ 7 m/s

- TALSPERRE/WASSERKRAFTWERK/ DAM, HYDROELECTRIC PLANT
- BIOMASSENANLAGE (RAUMBEDEUTSAM)/ BIOMASS PLANT (LOCAL IMPORTANCE)
- BIOGASANLAGE (RAUMBEDEUTSAM)/ BIOGAS PLANT (LOCAL IMPORTANCE)

THEORETISCHES ENERGIEPOTENZIAL 2006/
THEORETICAL ENERGY POTENTIAL 2006

- + 20 PJ
- 15–20 PJ
- 10–15 PJ

HOHES GEOTHERMISCHES POTENZIAL/
HIGH GEOTHERMIC POTENTIAL

- IN EINER TIEFE VON 2 km/AT DEPTH OF 2 km
- IN EINER TIEFE VON 3–5 km/AT DEPTH OF 3–5 km

- PHOTOVOLTAIKANLAGE/SOLAR POWER PLANT
- PHOTOVOLTAIKANLAGE IN PLANUNG/ SOLAR POWER PLANT (PLANNED)
- PRODUZENTEN VON SOLARANLAGEN/ MANUFACTURER OF SOLAR POWER PLANTS

JÄHRLICHE GLOBALSTRAHLUNGSSUMME/
ANNUAL GLOBAL IRRADIANCE

- 950–1025 kWh/m²
- 1025–1050 kWh/m²

Quellen/Sources
Windparks
Regionale Entwicklungspläne, Raumordnungskataster, LVwA, 2006
Windgeschwindigkeit
Deutscher Wetterdienst, 2004
Talsperren, Wasserkraftwerke
Talsperrenbetrieb Sachsen-Anhalt, 2009
Biomassen-/Biogasanlagen
Ministerium für Raumordnung und Verkehr, 2007
Theoretisches Energiepotenzial
Ministerium für Landwirtschaft und Umwelt, 2006
Geothermisches Potenzial 2 km
Schellschmidt & Rappsilber, 2003 (unveröff.)
Geothermisches Potenzial 3-5 km
Geothermieatlas der DDR
Photovoltaikanlagen
Landesverwaltungsamt, 2008
Jährliche Globalstrahlungssumme
Deutscher Wetterdienst, 2009

in Saxony-Anhalt. Heat from this source could be directly used for heating buildings, for production processes (e.g. dairies) or for operating swimming baths and greenhouses.

The cultivation of biomass for energy production competes in terms of surface area with plant cultivation for food production and is dependent on location and climate conditions. Different processing phases are required for different types of biomass. Energy is generated in form of heat, electricity and fuel; the resulting heat should be used locally and distributed via local power grids.

By expanding renewable energy production and saving energy, fossil energy networks will gradually become obsolete, unless they can be used for other purposes (fig. 2). Every building would then become a potential energy producer, like a small-scale local power station. The electricity grid would comprise a great number of nodes which would be consumers, producers and intermediate accumulators at the same time. It would be an intelligent network, working like an artificial ecosystem of dynamically interwoven and self-monitored energy streams which could respond flexibly to ever-changing environmental conditions and requirements.

Today, consumption and nutrition account for 40 percent per capita emissions; alongside technical and social innovations, it is therefore necessary to rethink our present consumption habits. It is not just a matter of preaching sacrifice, but rather a change in values. Chasing after today's trappings will mean having to do without tomorrow's essentials: peace of mind, children and a future. Studies show that increasing prosperity and wealth does not mean that people are happier. There is more to happiness than consumption. If we developed a culture of "less is more in future," all those who have already had to involuntarily tighten their belts would also be seen in a different, much better light.

The federal state of Saxony-Anhalt, where the decline in population and commercial activity already marks the end of an era of economic growth, has good chances of playing the leading role in the transition to post-fossil civilization. There are hardly any more large-scale fossil energy plants in the region and the proportion of renewable energy in net power production rose to almost 35 percent in 2009.[3]

The motto of IBA Stadtumbau 2010 is "less is more in future," a slogan which primarily points to the decline in population and economic activity. However, both the shift from the fossil era and the adjustment to climate change will have a decisive influence on how our towns and landscapes will develop in the future. The same applies here: less will be more in future.

3 In 2006, only Thuringia was able to boast a larger proportion of renewable energy in power production (Länderarbeitskreis Energiebilanzen, 2010; StaLA Sachsen-Anhalt, 2010).

Universitäts- und anderen Forschungseinrichtungen profitiert. Solarthermie und Photovoltaik sind unter anderem auch im Siedlungskontext nutzbar. Für die tiefe Geothermie, welche bisher in Sachen-Anhalt noch nicht genutzt wird, weist vor allem der Norden und der Magdeburger Raum Potenzial zur Energiegewinnung auf. Die gewonnene Wärme kann direkt zur Gebäudeheizung, für Produktionsprozesse (etwa Molkereien) oder den Betrieb von Schwimmbädern und Gewächshäusern genutzt werden.

Der Anbau von Biomasse zur Energiegewinnung steht in Flächenkonkurrenz zum Anbau von Pflanzen zur Lebensmittelproduktion und ist abhängig von Standort- und Klimabedingungen. Je nach Art der Biomasse sind unterschiedliche Aufbereitungsschritte notwendig. Energie wird dabei in Form von Wärme, Strom und Kraftstoff gewonnen, wobei die entstehende Wärme lokal zu nutzen ist und über Nahwärmenetze verteilt wird.

Mit dem Ausbau der regenerativen Energiegewinnung und durch Energieeinsparung wird die Infrastruktur der fossilen Energienutzung obsolet, soweit sie nicht umgenutzt werden kann (Abb. 2). Potenziell jedes Gebäude wird zu einem Produzenten von Energie, zu einem kleinen, dezentralen Kraftwerk. Das Stromnetzwerk vernetzt jetzt eine Vielzahl von Punkten, die gleichzeitig als Konsumenten, Produzenten und Zwischenspeicher fungieren können. Ein intelligent gesteuertes Netz entsteht, ein künstliches Ökosystem dynamisch miteinander vernetzter und sich selbst steuernder Energieströme, das flexibel auf die sich ändernden Umgebungsbedingungen und Anforderungen reagiert.

Konsum und Ernährung machen heute zusammen 40 Prozent der Pro-Kopf-Emissionen aus. Daher sind neben technischen auch soziale Innovationen und ein Überdenken unserer derzeitigen Konsummuster nötig. Nur auf den ersten Blick wird hier Verzicht gepredigt – vielmehr geht es um einen Wertewandel. Das, worauf die Leute heute nicht verzichten wollen, bedeutet bereits Verzicht: Verzicht auf Ruhe, Verzicht auf Kinder, Verzicht auf Zukunft. Studien zeigen, dass Menschen mit steigendem Wohlstand nicht glücklicher werden. Glück braucht mehr als Konsum. Eine Kultur des „Weniger ist Zukunft" würde auch diejenigen aufwerten, die den Verzicht bereits unfreiwillig proben.

Konsum und Ernährung machen heute zusammen 40 Prozent der Pro-Kopf-Emissionen aus. Daher sind neben technischen auch soziale Innovationen und ein Überdenken unserer derzeitigen Konsummuster nötig.

In Sachsen-Anhalt markiert der Rückgang von Bevölkerung und Wirtschaftsaktivität heute schon das Ende der Wachstumsepoche und das Bundesland hat gute Voraussetzungen, um im Übergang zur postfossilen Zivilisation eine Vorreiterrolle zu spielen. Es befinden sich kaum noch fossile Großkraftwerke im Land und der Anteil regenerativer Energien an der Nettostromerzeugung belief sich bereits 2009 auf knapp 35 Prozent.[3]

3 2006 wies nur Thüringen einen größeren Anteil der erneuerbaren Energien an der Stromerzeugung auf (Länderarbeitskreis Energiebilanzen, 2010; StaLA Sachsen-Anhalt, 2010).

Mit dem Slogan „Weniger ist Zukunft" der IBA Stadtumbau 2010 ist primär der Rückgang von Bevölkerung und Wirtschaftsaktivität gemeint. In Zukunft werden aber auch der Abschied vom fossilen Zeitalter und die Anpassung an den Klimawandel einen prägenden Einfluss darauf haben, wie unsere Städte und Landschaften von morgen aussehen werden. Auch hier gilt: Weniger ist Zukunft.

Das Projekt entstand im Rahmen der Endpräsentation der IBA Stadtumbau 2010 am Bauhaus Dessau. Es ist eines von drei Szenarien zur zukünftigen Entwicklung der Landschaft Sachsen-Anhalts bis 2050. Konzeption: Prof. Philipp Oswalt, Direktor der Stiftung Bauhaus Dessau und Geschäftsführer der IBA-Büro GbR; Projektleitung: Anne Schmidt, wissenschaftliche Mitarbeiterin am ETH-Studio Basel/Studio Stadt der Gegenwart und der Stiftung Bauhaus Dessau.
Wissenschaftliche Beratung: Dr. Klaus Müschen, Abteilungsleiter „Klimaschutz und Energie" im Umweltbundesamt Dessau-Roßlau; Dr. Achim Daschkeit, wissenschaftliche Mitarbeit im Kompetenzzentrum Klimafolgen und Anpassung im Umweltbundesamt, Dessau-Roßlau; Mirjam Neebe, wissenschaftliche Mitarbeit am Potsdam-Institut für Klimafolgenforschung
Fotocollagen: Tobias Steinert, Grafiker, dataholic Leipzig

This project was carried out in the frame of the final presentation of IBA Stadtumbau 2010 at Bauhaus Dessau. It is one of three scenarios on the future development of the landscape of Saxony-Anhalt up to 2050. Conception: Prof. Philipp Oswalt, Director of the Bauhaus Dessau Foundation and Executive Director of the IBA Office GbR; Project Management: Anne Schmidt, scientific assistant at the ETH Studio Basel/Studio Stadt der Gegenwart and the Bauhaus Dessau Foundation. Scientific Consulting: Dr. Klaus Müschen, Head of the Department for "Klimaschutz und Energie (Climate Protection and Energy)" at the Dessau-Roßlau Federal Office; Dr. Achim Daschkeit, scientific collaboration at the Competence Centre Klimafolgen und Anpassung (Climate Impact and Acclimatisation) at the Dessau-Roßlau Federal Office; Mirjam Neebe, scientific collaboration at the Potsdam Institute for Climate Impact Research
Photo collages: Tobias Steinert, graphic artist, dataholic Leipzig

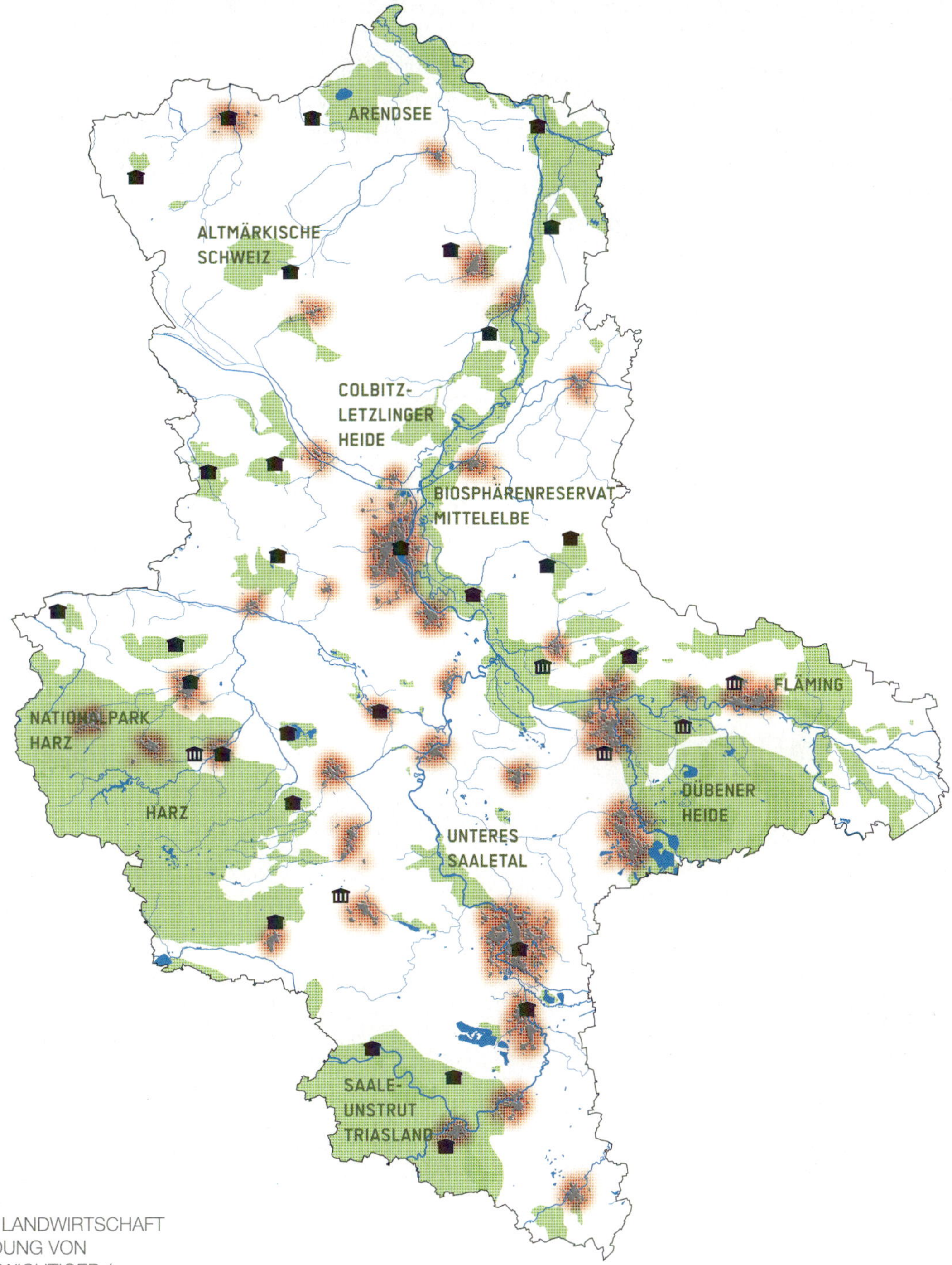

TOURISMUS UND SIEDLUNGSNAHE LANDWIRTSCHAFT WERDEN IN ZUKUNFT ZUR VERMEIDUNG VON TRANSPORTENERGIE ZUNEHMEND WICHTIGER./
TOURISM AND AGRICULTURE NEAR SETTLEMENT AREAS WILL IN FUTURE GAIN IN IMPORTANCE, IN ORDER TO MINIMIZE ENERGY CONSUMPTION FOR TRANSPORT.

SEHENSWÜRDIGKEIT/
PLACE OF INTEREST

UNESCO WELTKULTURERBE/
UNESCO WORLD HERITAGE SITE

TOURISMUS- UND ERHOLUNGSGEBIET, NATURPARK/
TOURISM AND RECREATION AREA, NATURAL RESERVE

URBANE LANDWIRTSCHAFT/
URBAN AGRICULTURE

Quellen/Sources
Sehenswürdigkeit
Investitions- und Marketinggesellschaft LSA mbH, 2010
Unesco Weltkulturerbe
UNESCO, 2010
Tourismus- und Erholungsgebiet
Regionale Entwicklungspläne, Raumordnungskataster, LVwA, 2006
Biosphärenreservat Mittelelbe, Naturparke
Bundesamt für Naturschutz, 2009

Wanzleben
Oschersleben
Magdeburg
-Ottersleben
100
m

Solar Valley
5

1 Blick von den Ruinen *Kafr 'Inans* auf die Obstplantagen der israelischen Siedlungen. View from the *Kafr 'Inan* ruins to the orchards of the Israeli settlements.

Präsenz und Abwesenheit von Landschaft in Israel.

Raumpolitik unter dem Deckmantel der Natur

Seit Anbeginn wird der israelisch-palästinensische Konflikt über die Landschaft, deren Geografie und Grenzen ausgetragen. Enteignung, Inbesitznahme und Rückforderung des Landes stehen dabei im Mittelpunkt einer raumpolitischen Auseinandersetzung, in der die Landschaft neben der Rolle des umkämpften Gegenstandes als eigentliche Waffe des Konflikts agiert.

The Presence and Absence of Landscape in Israel: Spatial Policy under the Guise of Nature. From the outset, the Israeli-Palestinian conflict has been carried out via landscape, its geography and boundaries. Expropriation, dispossession, and reclamation of land are thereby positioned at the heart of a spacio-political struggle, where landscape operates—next to its role as a hotly contested element—as the very weapon of the conflict.

NINA VALERIE KOLOWRATNIK

Die heutige räumliche Realität stellt ein komplexes Wirkungsfeld von Politiken der Landschaft dar, denen die Überschreibung der palästinensischen Vergangenheit durch eine israelische Gegenwart zugrunde liegt. Die Rückkehr palästinensischer Flüchtlinge in das heutige Israel wird auf israelischer Seite tabuisiert – auf palästinensischer Seite ist das Thema der Rückkehr ständiger Begleiter und manifestiert sich im fortwährenden Flüchtlingsstatus von über sieben Millionen Palästinensern. Um die in Friedensgesprächen bislang ausgeklammerte[1] Frage der Rückkehr palästinensischer Flüchtlinge[2] auf die politische Agenda zu bringen, muss die ideologisch festgefahrene Diskussion überwunden und auf eine greifbare Ebene gebracht werden. Eine Möglichkeit, dies zu erreichen, bietet sich dem räumlichen Planer, indem er seine Umgebung mit dem Wiederlesen des Konflikts aus räumlicher Perspektive konfrontiert. Der Maßstab des Architekten dient hierbei nicht der detaillierten Planung, sondern dazu, Diskussionen zu provozieren und eine andere Zukunft vorstellbar zu machen.

Die Intention der Landschaft. Beschäftigt man sich mit der räumlichen Umsetzung der Rückkehr palästinensischer Flüchtlinge, stellt sich zunächst die Frage: Wohin würde man eigentlich zurückkehren? Die Rückkehr nach Israel bedeutet Rückkehr in eine räumlich veränderte Realität und bewusst überschriebene Landschaft (Abb. 1).

> Obwohl die Mechanismen israelischer Raumpolitik heute die Oberfläche der Landschaft bestimmen, sind sie für den Betrachter vor Ort nicht eindeutig als solche erkennbar.

Obwohl die Mechanismen israelischer Raumpolitik heute die Oberfläche der Landschaft bestimmen, sind sie für den Betrachter vor Ort nicht eindeutig als solche erkennbar. Durch die simple Weiterführung der analogen Wiedergabe aktueller und vergangener Verhältnisse und die Abstrahierung des Landschaftsbildes bis hin zu seinem Gerüst wird die Entwicklung und Intention einer rational konstruierten Landschaft jedoch schlagartig sichtbar.

Die Karte, welche sich von der Landschaft, die sie abbildet, emanzipiert hat, operiert laut James Corner in zweierlei Hinsicht. Sie forscht, findet und stellt dar – sie verbindet, stellt Beziehungen her und strukturiert. Somit kann die Karte durch bildhafte Offenlegung komplexe Beziehungen herstellen und aufdecken. Corner unterscheidet in diesem Zusammenhang zwischen *Tracing*, welches sich mit der bloßen Darstellung des Ist-Zustandes abfindet

1 Obwohl die Frage der Rückkehr den Schlüssel jeder gerechten und dauerhaften Lösung des israelisch-palästinensischen Konflikts darstellt, wurde in allen bisherigen Friedensgesprächen die Rückkehr der Flüchtlinge von Seiten der israelischen Politiker, welche die Agenda vorgeben, entweder ausgeklammert oder nur am Rande diskutiert – ohne eine Einigung auf eine praktikable Lösung zu erreichen.

2 1948 wurden 760.000 Palästinenser aus ihrer Heimat vertrieben, 1967 weitere 300.000. Drei Generationen später stellen über sieben Millionen Flüchtlinge mehr als 70% der gesamten palästinensischen Bevölkerung, sowie die größte Flüchtlingsgruppe weltweit dar. Viele von ihnen leben bis heute in stark überbevölkerten Flüchtlingslagern der umliegenden arabischen Staaten, im Westjordanland und Gazastreifen unter prekären Verhältnissen und werden vor allem im Libanon in ihren Grundrechten stark eingeschränkt.

Today's spatial reality represents a complex realm of agency for landscape policies which have come from the Palestinian past having been overwritten by an Israeli present. The return of Palestinian refugees into today's Israel is a tabooed subject on the Israeli end, while on the Palestinian side it is a constant presence, expressed in the enduring refugee status of over seven million Palestinians. If the question of the Palestinian refugees' return,[1] which has to date been factored out of peace talks,[2] is to be brought onto the political agenda, we must break the deadlock on the current ideological discussions and transfer them to a practical level. The spatial planner may do this by confronting the general public with the re-reading of the conflict from a spatial perspective. However, the architect's scale is used not for detailed planning but rather to provoke discussions, and to make a different future imaginable.

The Intention of Landscape. When investigating the practical spatial implementation of the return of Palestinian refugees, a question immediately arises: Where would they actually return to? A return to Israel means a return to a spatially transformed reality and to a consciously overwritten landscape (fig. 1). Although the mechanisms of Israeli spatial planning policy dominate the landscape on the ground today, they are not clearly recognizable as such for observers on site. Yet through a simple continuation of the analogue reproduction of current and past relationships, as well as the abstraction of the notion of landscape right down to its basic structures, the development and intention of a rationally developed landscape becomes abruptly apparent.

The map that has emancipated itself from the landscape it depicts operates in a twofold manner, according to James Corner. It probes, locates, and exposes on the one hand, and connects and structures on the other. Therefore, through pictorial disclosure, the map is able to both set up and unfold complex relationships. In this context, James Corner differentiates between "tracing," which is satisfied with the mere representation of the state-at-hand, and the method of "mapping," which newly formulates the state-at-hand so as to introduce new viewpoints within the perceivedly evident.[3]

1 In 1948, 760,000 Palestinians were expelled from their homeland, and in 1967 so were 300,000 more. Three generations later, over seven million refugees comprise more than 70 percent of the entire Palestinian population, making it the largest group of refugees in the world. Many of them still today live under precarious conditions in significantly overcrowded refugee camps in the surrounding Arab states, in the West Bank, and in the Gaza Strip with their basic rights strongly limited, especially in Lebanon.

2 Although the question of the refugees' return represents the key to a just and sustainable solution to the Israeli-Palestinian conflict, the return of the refugees has either been ruled out by the Israeli politicians specifying the agenda or been only marginally discussed at peace talks to date—without coming to a consensus about a feasible solution.

3 James Corner, "The Agency of Mapping," in: Denis Cosgrove (ed.), *Mappings*. London 1999, pp. 213–252.

2 Straßennetz, gebaute Struktur, Gewässer, politische Geografie, Bewirtschaftete Fläche des Gebiets im Bereich des ehemaligen palästinensischen Dorfes *Kafr 'Inan* im heutigen Norden Israels, 1944 und 2010. Road networks, built-up structures, bodies of water, political geography, farmed areas in the region of the former Palestinian village *Kafr 'Inan* in what is now northern Israel, 1944 and 2010.

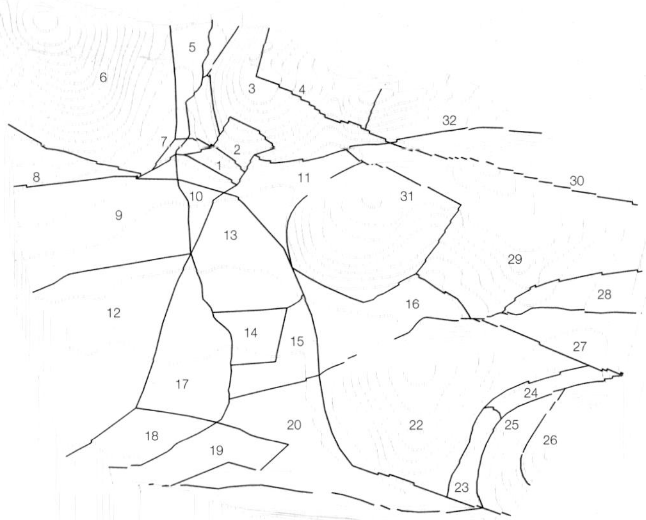

3

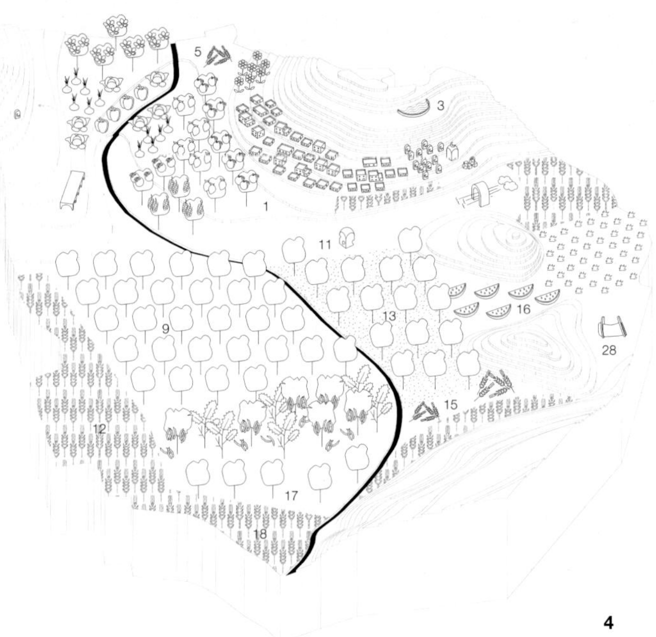

4

1 El Murabba'a – Der Dorfplatz
2 Kafr 'Inan – Dorf Kafr 'Inan
3 El Birka – Die Wassersammelstelle
4 El Jubeil – Der Hügel
5 El Jawabi – Das Lager für Getreide oder Feigen
6 Jabal Abu Esh Shaba – Berg Abu Esh Shaba
7 Nasb Salih – Die Bäume des Salih
8 Wa'ra Abu Esh Shaba – Hang des Berges Abu Esh Shaba
9 Umm El Kadar – Mutter des Kadar
10 El Muquanza
11 Khallat El Kinis – Platz des Tempels
12 El Mirbih – Der fruchtbare Grund
13 El Hariqa – Ort, an dem es einst ein großes Feuer gab
14 El Qausara – Die langen Knochen des Tieres
15 Humat El Jurn – Getreidelager
16 Khallat El Battikh – Wassermelonenfeld
17 Zeitun Es Sidr – Die vorderen Oliven
18 El 'Arqaji – Feld des 'Arqaji
19 Ein 'Atiya – Die Quelle ein 'Atiya
20 Sahl Kafr 'Inan – Flachland von Kafr 'Inan
21 Dheil Hazzur – Ende des Berges Hazzur
22 Jammara – Beginn des Feuers
23 El Marsad – Hoch gelegener Aussichspunkt
24 Khallat Hamdan – Acker des Hamdan
25 Es Sira – Schafstall
26 Karm Zureiq – Hain des Zureiq
27 Marj Abu Diyab – Weide von Abu Diyab
28 Bureidh'a – Sattel des Esels
29 El Mikman – Weide des Mikman
30 El Mikman – Weide des Mikman
31 Jabal Sa'd – Berg Sa'd
32 Umm Es Sunu – Mutter des Sunu

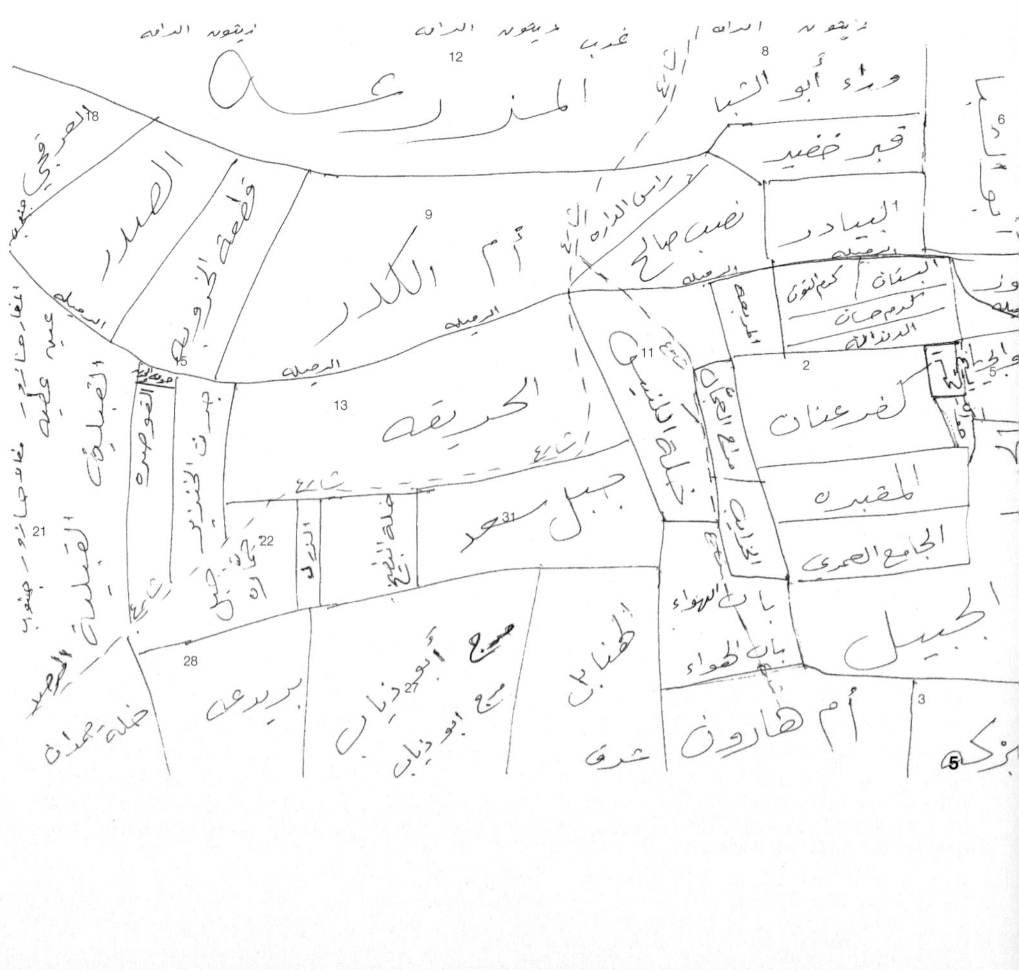

5

3 Grundstücksteilung von *Kafr 'Inan* nach der britischen Landvermessungskarte von 1942, übertragen auf ein dreidimensionales Topografiemodell.
4 *Landschaft der Erinnerung.*
5 Memory Map von Hassan A. Mansour, welche die Teilung des Dorfgrundstückes von *Kafr 'Inan* zeigt, erstellt 2010.

3 Division of land in Kafr 'Inan according the the British land surveying map of 1942, transferred to a three-dimensional topographic model.
4 *Landscape of Memory.*
5 Memory map by Hassan A. Mansour showing the division of land in the village Kafr 'Inan, created in 2010.

The success in uncovering the Israeli landscape through differentiated mapping can surely be traced back to the fact that in this case the map preceded the landscape. The landscape was planned to fit the map, and as a result can be laid bare by using its own constituent practices. The deconstruction of the map—the differentiation of information and the isolated portrayal of the same—makes it possible here to initially align the focus to a single informational plane of cartographic depiction at a time. In the area surrounding the former Palestinian village Kafr 'Inan in the Galilee region (today located in the north of Israel), which is serving as a case study,[4] I liberated elements of physical and political geography as well as of settlement and transport geography from their respective contexts and, in a second step, contrasted these with watercourses, road networks, built-up or populated areas as well as agrarian areas, borderlines and property relations from the years 1944 and 2010 (fig. 2). What at first could be interpreted as a simple temporal development in fact validated, through this superimposition of temporally shifted layers, the strategic-spatial-political intention of the Israeli landscape. The landscape has been deciphered, with those forces that had previously appeared hidden in a conglomerate of multiple details now becoming clearing recognizable. Upon closer consideration of these forces, the role of the landscape has thus been revealed to be not only a product of the conflict but also an actor of the same.

The overwriting of the Palestinian past and its consequences are particularly apparent in the layers of political geography, in the borderlines, property relations, and cultivation structures that have formed between 1944 and today. In comparing these temporally shifted layers, one can hardly detect any correlations. The place was overwritten which detached it from both history and memory. Clearly perceptible here is the idea of the "white map," of the new definition of the landscape for a new state, which Israel set out to effect, for instance by dispossessing Palestinian property and transferring it to Israeli state ownership. Still today, 80 percent of Israel's land is state-owned, while 13 percent is held by the Jewish National Fund (JNF),[5] a private organization whose leitmotifs are anchored in Zionism and whose land is predominantly made up of nature sanctuaries. Likewise whitewashed was the cartographic representation of Israel—Arab land designations as well as numerous Palestinian towns disappeared from the political map.

4 The research phase for the project upon which this essay is based, *Kafr 'Inan—Images of Presence for a Landscape of Absence*, involved two visits to the West Bank and Israel for a total of three months during the winter of 2008 and the summer of 2009, along with collaborative relationships with Sandi Hilal, Alessandro Petti, and Eyal Weizman (project *Decolonizing Architecture*, Bethlehem/London).

5 http://www.jnf.org [accessed July 17, 2010].

und der Methode des *Mapping*, welches den Ist-Zustand neu formuliert, um neue Sichtweisen im vermeintlich Offensichtlichen zu eröffnen.[3]

Der Erfolg in der Enttarnung der israelischen Landschaft durch differenzierte Kartierung ist sicher darauf zurückzuführen, dass in diesem Fall die Karte der Landschaft vorausging. Die Landschaft wurde auf einer Karte geplant – und kann in Folge durch die Anwendung ihrer sie konstituierenden Praktiken offengelegt werden. Die Dekonstruktion der Karte – die Differenzierung der Informationen und isolierte Darstellung derselben – ermöglicht es, hierbei den Fokus zunächst auf eine Informationsebene der kartografischen Abbildung zu richten. Im Gebiet um das ehemalige palästinensische Dorf *Kafr 'Inan* in der Region Galiläa, dem heutigen Norden Israels, welches als Fallstudie dient,[4] befreite ich Elemente der physischen und politischen Geografie sowie der Siedlungs- und Verkehrsgeografie aus ihrem Kontext und stellte Wasserläufe, Straßennetze, gebaute und besiedelte Flächen sowie landwirtschaftlich genutzte Gebiete, Grenzen und Besitzverhältnisse aus dem Jahr 1944 und 2010 in einem zweiten Schritt gegenüber (Abb. 2). Was man vorerst als simple zeitliche Entwicklung deuten könnte, bestätigt in der Übereinanderlegung der zeitversetzten Layer die strategisch-raumpolitische Intention israelischer Landschaft. Diese ist dechiffriert und jene Kräfte, die vormals im Konglomerat vielzähliger Details versteckt wirkten, sind nun deutlich erkennbar. Die genauere Betrachtung dieser Kräfte enthüllt dabei die Rolle der Landschaft nicht nur als Produkt des Konfliktes, sondern als Akteur desselben.

Ähnlich den israelischen Siedlungen in den besetzen Gebieten befinden sich jüdisch-israelische Siedlungen in der Region Galiläa heute häufig auf den höchstgelegenen Stellen der hügeligen Landschaft.

Die Überschreibung palästinensischer Vergangenheit und deren Ausmaße zeigen sich vor allem in den Layern der politischen Geografie, der Grenzen, Besitzverhältnisse und Bewirtschaftungsstrukturen von 1944 und heute. Vergleicht man diese zeitversetzten Layer, ist kaum mehr ein Bezug zueinander feststellbar. Der Ort wurde überschrieben und von seiner Geschichte und Erinnerung gelöst. Die Idee der weißen Karte, der Neudefinition der Landschaft für einen neuen Staat, welche Israel unter anderem mit der Enteignung palästinensischen Besitzes und der Überführung in israelischen Staatsgrund zu verwirklichen suchte, wird hier deutlich sichtbar. Bis heute befinden sich 80 % der Fläche Israels in Staatsbesitz, 13 % sind im Besitz des *Jewish National Fund (JNF)*,[5] einer privaten Organisation, deren Leitmotive im Zionismus

3 James Corner, „The Agency of Mapping", in: Denis Cosgrove (Hg.), *Mappings*. London 1999, S. 213–252.

4 Die Recherchephase zu dem diesem Text zugrunde liegenden Projekt *Kafr 'Inan – Bilder der Präsenz für eine Landschaft der Abwesenheit* beinhaltete zwei Aufenthalte im Westjordanland und Israel von insgesamt drei Monaten im Winter 2008 und Sommer 2009, sowie die Zusammenarbeit mit Sandi Hilal, Alessandro Petti und Eyal Weizman (Projekt *Decolonizing Architecture*, Bethlehem-London).

5 http://www.jnf.org [abgerufen am 17.7.2010].

verankert sind und deren Besitz zum Großteil aus Naturschutzgebieten besteht. Weiß gewaschen wurde auch die kartografische Darstellung Israels – arabische Landbezeichnungen, sowie zahlreiche palästinensische Orte verschwanden von der Landkarte.

Ähnlich den israelischen Siedlungen in den besetzen Gebieten befinden sich jüdisch-israelische Siedlungen in der Region Galiläa heute häufig auf den höchstgelegenen Stellen der hügeligen Landschaft. In der Region mit dem größten Anteil an in Israel verbleibenden Palästinensern oder „arabisch"-israelischer Bevölkerung[6] entscheidet neben der maximalen Ausnutzung landwirtschaftlicher Fläche im ländlichen Gebiet die strategisch günstige Lage über die Standortwahl jüdisch-israelischer Siedlungen. Die Betrachtung der Positionierung von Naturschutzgebieten und Militärzonen wirft ähnlich strategische Gesichtspunkte auf. Auch diese sind im direkten Zusammenhang mit palästinensischen Siedlungsstrukturen in Israel sowie deren Expansionsmöglichkeiten zu lesen. Die Entstehung einer bewaldeten Zone etwa bedeutet, dass diese für Bebauung und landwirtschaftliche Nutzung gesperrt wird. Die Bäume sind rechtlich vor Rodung geschützt und im Falle einer Deklaration des Waldes zum Naturschutzgebiet kann dieser eingezäunt und mit Öffnungszeiten versehen werden. Wälder in Israel werden heute bevorzugt dort gepflanzt, wo eine Ausdehnung palästinensischer gebauter Struktur, Industrie oder Felder verhindert werden soll.[7] Die Instrumentalisierung der Landschaft unter dem Deckmantel des Naturschutzes steht in enger Verbindung mit dem *JNF* und seiner Funktion als Verwalter der israelischen Aufforstungsmission.[8] Ein leitender Vorsitzender des *JNF* erklärt in einem Interview, welches von der israelischen Juristin Irus Braverman geführt worden ist: „Israel understood that it must find a tool for preventing people from occupying lands […]. And this tool was afforestation. When you have trees, you first have to cut them down if you want to take over territory. But since there is a law that protects trees, you can't easily do that."[9] Das Aufforstungsprojekt des *JNF* kann demnach als physische und rechtliche Besetzung des Landes durch die Pflanzung von Bäumen definiert werden. Der Baum fungiert als physische Besetzung des Raumes, juristische Normen definieren den Baum und schützen seine räumliche Präsenz. Dass der *JNF* den gezielten

Die Bäume sind rechtlich vor Rodung geschützt und im Falle einer Deklaration des Waldes zum Naturschutzgebiet kann dieser eingezäunt und mit Öffnungszeiten versehen werden.

6 In Israel wurde der Begriff palästinensisch bewusst durch die Bezeichnung arabisch-israelisch ersetzt.

7 *Adalah – The Legal Center for Arab Minority Rights*; http://www.adalah.org [abgerufen am 10.7.2010].

8 Seit 1901 pflanzte der JNF 24 Millionen Bäume auf fast 1.000 km² des heutigen Israel, um, wie es Theodor Herzl beschrieben hatte, die Landschaft von ihrem trostlosen Aussehen zu befreien.

9 Amikan Riklin, Chefinspektor des JNF, zit. in: Irus Braverman, *Planted Flags. Trees, Land and Law in Israel/Palestine*. New York 2009, S. 29.

Similar to the Israeli settlements in the occupied territories, Jewish-Israeli settlements in the Galilee region are today frequently situated upon the highest points of the hilly landscape. In the region with the largest number of Palestinians remaining in Israel, or "Arab"-Israeli population,[6] along with the issue of maximal productive efficiency in using the agricultural land in rural areas, a strategically favorable location is decisive for the siting of Jewish-Israeli settlements. Reflection on the positioning of nature sanctuaries and military zones raises similarly strategic issues. These, too, are to be interpreted in direct relation to Palestinian settlement structures in Israel and how these might expand. The development of a forested zone, for example, implies that this land will be closed to construction and agricultural usage. The trees would be legally protected from clearing, and should the forest be declared a nature sanctuary, it may be fenced in and assigned opening hours. Today, forests in Israel are preferably planted in places where the enlargement of Palestinian-built structures, industry, or fields is to be impeded.[7] The instrumentalization of the landscape under the guise of environmental protection stands in close correlation with the JNF and its function as administrator of the Israeli re-afforestation mission.[8] As a chairperson of JNF has explained in an interview conducted by Israeli solicitor Irus Braverman: "Israel understood that it must find a tool for preventing people from occupying lands … And this tool was afforestation. When you have trees, you first have to cut them down if you want to take over the landscape. But since there is a law that protects trees, you can't easily do that."[9] Thus, the JNF re-afforestation project can be defined as physical and legal occupation of the country effected by the planting of trees; the tree occupies the land physically, while legal norms define the tree and protect its presence in place. The following statement by JNF's chief inspector makes clear how JNF uses the targeted implementation of designed landscape as a means for safeguarding the Jewish identity of the country: "Tree planting was not perceived as an ecological practice, but rather as a way to physically freeze undeveloped land for future Jewish development. The moment that development is requested, the state will just take down the trees, in full compliance with the law."[10]

6 In Israel the term "Palestinian" has been purposefully replaced by the designation "Arab-Israeli."

7 Adalah—The Legal Center for Arab Minority Rights, http://www.adalah.org [accessed July 10, 2010].

8 Since 1901 the JNF has planted twenty-four million trees on close to one-thousand square kilometers of land in present-day Israel with an aim to free the landscape from its bleak appearance, as Theodor Herzl once described it.

9 Interview: Amikan Riklin, chief inspector of the JNF, in: Irus Braverman, *Planted Flags: Trees, Land and Law in Israel/Palestine*. Cambridge 2009, p. 29.

10 Ibid., p. 96.

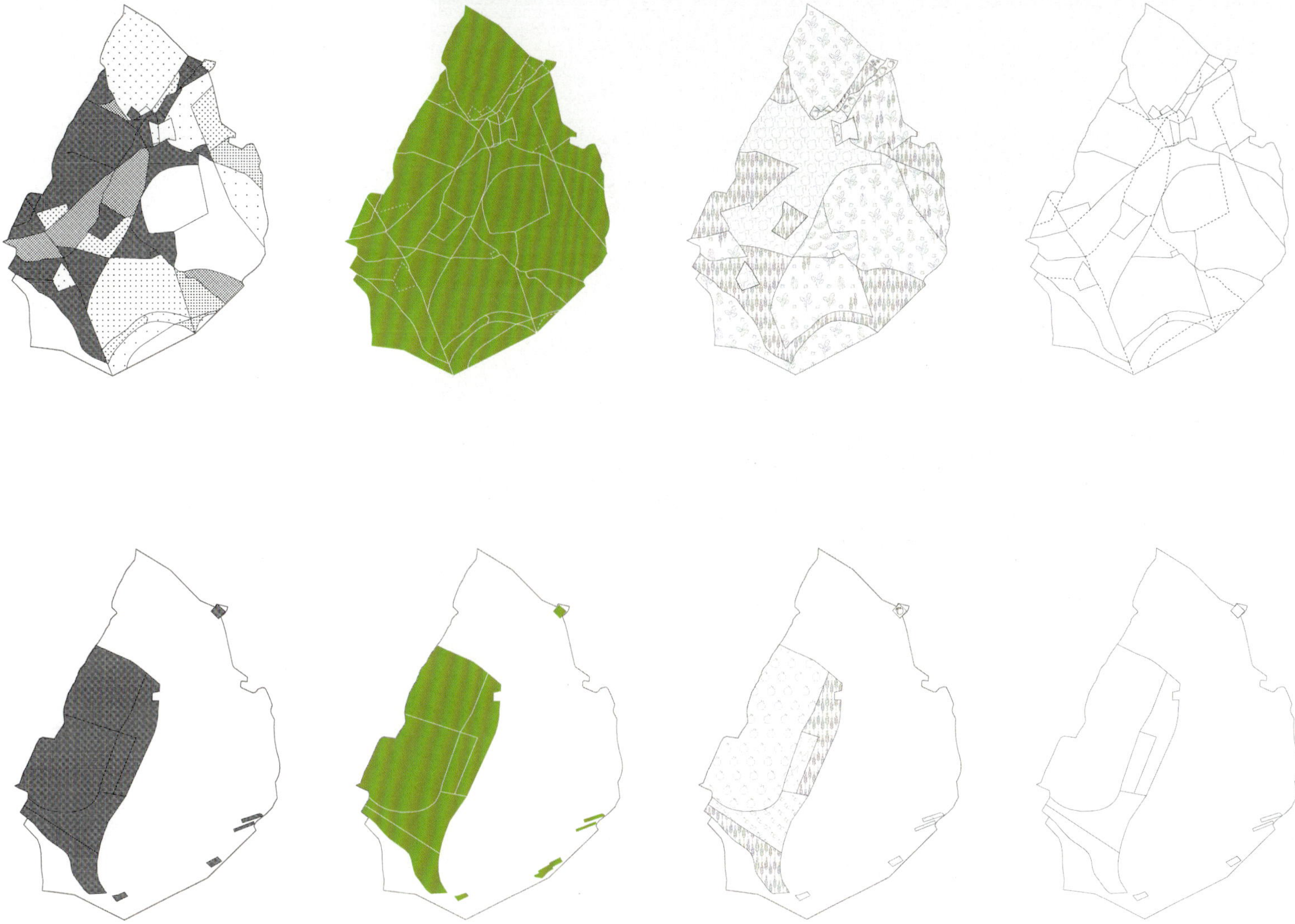

6

6 Ehemaliges Dorfgrundstück *Kafr 'Inans* mit vergleichender Gegenüberstellung von Kultivierungsgrad; Feldteilung; Feldnutzung; Feldnutzung und Feldteilung, 1944 und 2010.

6 Former *Kafr 'Inan* village land with a comparative juxtaposition of cultivation level; division of fields; field usage; division of fields and field usage, 1944 and 2010.

7

8

9

10

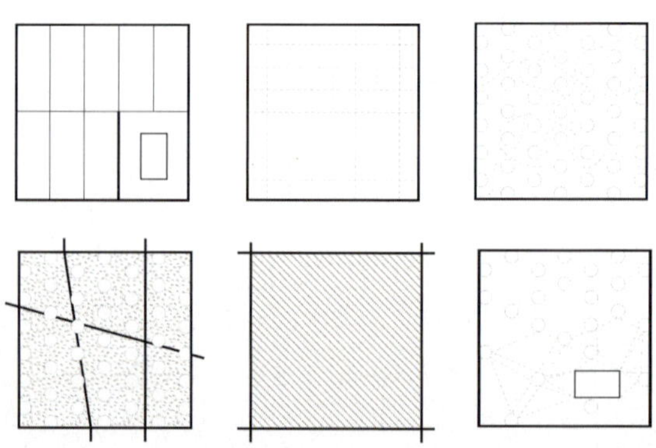

11

7 Britische Landvermessungskarte, 1942, und *Ghostly Presence*, 2010.
8 Vergangenheitsreferenzen.
9 Nutzungsschema produktiver Landschaft.
10 Wegesystem.
11 Typologien der produktiven Landschaft: *Vollzeitgemüsegarten, Wochenendgemüsegarten, Obst- und Olivenhain für Kleinbauern, Feld für Kleinbauern, Gemeinschaftliche Freifläche, Gemeinschaftlicher Selbstpflück-Obsthain.*

7 British land surveying map, 1942, and *Ghostly Presence*, 2010.
8 Past references.
9 Utilization scheme for productive landscape.
10 Route system.
11 Typologies of productive landscape: full-time vegetable garden, weekend vegetable garden, fruit and olive groves for small-scale farmers, shared open space, shared self-harvested fruit orchard.

The feigned innocence of nature in connection with its propagandized necessity in this case disguises spatial-political processes with greenness. Considering how environmental protection is generally understood to foster the protection of an existing natural landscape, and noting how in Israel, however, newly planted forests are placed under nature conservancy measures, and also how another of the JNF's declared central aims is to make the Negev desert bloom, rather than "protecting" nature the reality is one of "creating" nature (in this case: Israeli nature).

Absent Landscape. In the eye of the beholder on site, the Israeli landscape today may well impart an impression of profane normality. Yet in viewing the manifestations of this reality from a cartographic distance it becomes clear which mechanisms undermine the apparent normality, associating it with a negated, Palestinian past. The disavowal of Palestinian history, and also of the present-day situation in which Palestinian refugees find themselves, goes hand in hand with the obliteration of its memory. The endeavors on the part of Israel to liberate the landscape from its Palestinian history are characterized by Israeli historian Ilan Pappe as "memoricide."[11] If the connection between place and memory is severed through the superimposition of the place with a newly constructed landscape, then the Palestinian past stops being visible for the beholders on site, turning the Palestinian question into a unseen, or not visible, issue.

Once the place has been overwritten by a newly constructed landscape, the connection between place and memory is cut off and the observer can no longer grasp the relationship of place to past.

Following the depopulation of Palestinian villages and the displacement of refugees from Israeli national territory, it seemed necessary to liberate the landscape from all visible traces of an unwanted past. This was accomplished, for one, by the demolition of Palestinian-built structures and, subsequently, by the camouflaging of related ruins. Of the 418 Palestinian villages that had been forcefully evacuated and demolished in 1948, today 182 of these are covered by parks, forests, and nature sanctuaries. JNF forests have been planted atop 86 Palestinian villages[12] and are for the most part comprised of pine trees, a quickly growing and deeply rooted tree: "In no time, the moment of the pine's planting becomes invisible. What seems wild [pine trees] takes over, as if it was always there."[13] Hence, the strategic landscape planning in

11 Ilan Pappe, *The Ethnic Cleansing of Palestine*. London, New York 2006, pp. 225–235.

12 Noga Kagman, *Erased from Space and Consciousness: Depopulated Palestinian Villages in the Israeli-Zionist Discourse*. Jerusalem 2008, pp. 68–69.

13 Braverman 2009 (fn. 9), p. 88.

Einsatz von konstruierter Landschaft als Mittel, verwendet um die jüdische Identität des Landes zu wahren, wird in folgendem Ausspruch des leitenden Vorsitzenden des *JNF* klar: „Tree planting was not perceived as an ecological practice, but rather as a way to physically freeze undeveloped land for future Jewish development. The moment that development is requested, the state will just take down the trees, in full compliance with the law."[10]

Die scheinbare Unschuld der Natur im Zusammenhang mit ihrer propagierten Notwendigkeit hüllt hier raumpolitische Vorgänge in Grün. Wenn man bedenkt, dass man allgemein unter Naturschutz versteht, eine bestehende natürliche Landschaft zu schützen, in Israel jedoch neu gepflanzte Wälder unter Naturschutz gestellt werden und ein weiteres Hauptanliegen des *JNF* darin besteht, die Wüste Negev zum Blühen zu bringen, müsste es statt „Natur schützen" eher heißen – „Natur schaffen" (in diesem Fall israelische).

Abwesende Landschaft. Dem Auge des Betrachters vor Ort vermag die israelische Landschaft heute den Eindruck profaner Normalität zu vermitteln. Durch die Betrachtung der Manifestationen dieser Realität aus kartografischer Distanz wird aber deutlich, welche Mechanismen die scheinbare Normalität untergraben und sie mit einer negierten palästinensischen Vergangenheit in Verbindung bringen. Die Verleugnung der palästinensischen Vergangenheit und der heutigen Situation palästinensischer Flüchtlinge geht mit der Auslöschung der Erinnerung an sie einher. Die Bestrebungen Israels, die Landschaft von ihrer palästinensischen Geschichte zu befreien, bezeichnet der israelische Historiker Ilan Pappe als „Memorizid".[11] Wird die Verbindung zwischen Ort und Erinnerung durch die Überschreibung des Ortes mit einer neu konstruierten Landschaft getrennt, so ist die palästinensische Vergangenheit für den Betrachter vor Ort nicht mehr sichtbar und die palästinensische Frage wird zur ungesehenen oder nicht sichtbaren Frage.

Nach der Entvölkerung der palästinensischen Dörfer und Vertreibung der Flüchtlinge aus dem israelischen Staatsgebiet erschien es notwendig, die Landschaft von den sichtbaren Spuren einer unerwünschten Vergangenheit zu befreien.

Nach der Entvölkerung der palästinensischen Dörfer und Vertreibung der Flüchtlinge aus dem israelischen Staatsgebiet erschien es notwendig, die Landschaft von den sichtbaren Spuren einer unerwünschten Vergangenheit zu befreien. Dies geschah einerseits durch die Zerstörung der gebauten palästinensischen Strukturen und anschließend meist durch die Camouflage ihrer Ruinen. Von 418 palästinensischen Dörfern, die 1948 zwangsgeräumt und zerstört wurden, befinden sich heute 182 unter Parks, Wäldern und

10 Ebd., S. 96.

11 Ilan Pappe, *Die ethnische Säuberung Palästinas*. Frankfurt/M. 2007, S. 294–305.

Naturschutzgebieten. *JNF*-Wälder wurden auf 86 palästinensischen Dörfern gepflanzt[12] und bestehen zum Großteil aus Pinien, einem schnell wachsenden und tief wurzelnden Baum: „In no time, the moment of the pine's planting becomes invisible. What seems wild [pine trees] takes over, as if it was always there."[13] Die strategische Landschaftsplanung Israels reicht demzufolge bis zur Wahl der Baumgattung in den Aufforstungsprojekten des *JNF*.

Wie weit die Verdrängung der Vergangenheit bereits fortgeschritten ist, kann man erkennen, wenn der *JNF* einen Park oder Wanderweg ohne Bedenken als besonders romantische Landschaft mit Terrassen „alter" Gärten und blühender Mandelbäume[14] beschreibt, die Informationstafeln, welche sich in jedem Park des *JNF* befinden und die Geschichte des Ortes erläutern, jedoch nie von einer palästinensischen Vergangenheit erzählen. Das Attribut „alt" wird vom *JNF* entweder ohne Zeitangabe oder in Verbindung mit biblischer Vorzeit verwendet. Wenn sichtbare Ruinen palästinensischer Dörfer als natürlich idyllische Landschaft betrachtet werden, scheinen die Mechanismen kollektiver Verleugnung zu greifen.[15] „Locals were transformed from villages into landscape. From life into symbol. While the moment of transition between these conditions – i.e., the stage of expulsion and the ruin that preceded the landscape's transformation into ‚beautiful' – is forgotten and erased from consciousness."[16] Im Gegensatz zur Verleugnung einer palästinensischen Vergangenheit durch die Gegenwart der „schönen" Landschaft steht die heutige palästinensische Realität, welche durch die Präsenz der Erinnerung in Abwesenheit des Ortes gekennzeichnet ist. Das Herkunftsdorf und dessen Grundbesitz sind für Flüchtlinge in der Diaspora sowohl durch ihre räumliche Distanz, als auch durch das Fehlen ihrer Erinnerungsbilder abwesend. Seit der Vertreibung vor 60 Jahren ist es den Flüchtlingen nicht mehr erlaubt, in das heutige Israel einzureisen. Heute sind einzig der ältesten Generation von Flüchtlingen Bilder ihrer Heimat geblieben.

Nach 1948 wurden nahezu alle palästinensischen Dörfer bis auf die Grundmauern zerstört, der landwirtschaftliche Grund enteignet und in israelischen Staatsgrund überführt.

Für Flüchtlinge, die innerhalb der heutigen Grenzen Israels geblieben sind,[17] ist die Abwesenheit des Dorfes und dessen Besitz unmittelbar. Nach

12 Noga Kadman, *Erased from Space and Consciousness: Depopulated Palestinian Villages in the Israeli-Zionist Discourse*. Jerusalem 2008, S. 68f.

13 Braverman 2009 (Anm. 9), S. 88.

14 Mandelbäume stellen oft die einzig verbleibenden sichtbaren Zeichen eines palästinensischen Dorfes dar und sind in ihrer Blütezeit von weitem sichtbar. Von Israelis häufig als „wilde Mandeln" und typischer Bestandteil der natürlichen israelischen Landschaft angesehen, wurden diese Mandelbäume jedoch meist als Nutzbäume von Menschen gepflanzt und gepflegt.

15 Vgl. Pappe 2007 (Anm. 11).

16 Ariel Hirschfeld, „Ha'aretz: Erasing words, names and a way of life", 19.12.2008, in: http://www.palestineremembered.com/Articles/General/Story11869.html [abgerufen am 16.7.2010].

17 Auch Internal Refugees, Internally Displaced Persons.

Israel reaches so far as to influence which tree genus is to be selected for the JNF re-afforestation projects.

It becomes obvious to what extent this suppression of the past has evolved when the Jewish National Fund does not hesitate to describe a park or hiking path as an especially romantic landscape with terraces of "old" gardens and blooming almond trees[14] without, however, ever mentioning a Palestinian past on the information panels situated in every JNF park outlining the history of the site. The attribute "old" is used by the Jewish National Fund either without a designation of date or in relation to biblical antiquity. When visible ruins of Palestinian villages are viewed as a naturally idyllic landscape, it seems that the mechanisms of collective denial have taken hold.[15] "Locals were transformed from villages into landscape. From life into symbol. While the moment of transition between these conditions—i.e., the stage of expulsion and the ruin that preceded the landscape's transformation into 'beautiful'—is forgotten and erased from consciousness."[16] Posited in contrast to the denial of a Palestinian past by way of the presence of "beautiful" landscape is the present-day Palestinian reality, which is characterized by the presence of memory in absence of the site itself. For refugees in the Diaspora, their village of origin and their land are doubly absent—firstly through geographical distance, and secondly due to the absence of images of their home and property. Since the forced displacement sixty years ago, the refugees have been denied access to present-day Israel. So today only the elder generation of refugees have been able to retain images of their homeland.

For refugees who have remained within the present-day borders of Israel,[17] the absence of their respective villages and related property is immediate. After 1948 nearly all Palestinian villages were destroyed down to their foundations, with the agricultural property dispossessed and transferred into Israeli state property. Onetime Palestinian villages are today embodied by fenced-in clusters of rubble, access to which is usually limited, or by ruins overgrown by pine forests. And in cases where even no ruins are left, Israeli settlements or entire neighborhoods have taken over the available space. Olive groves have given way to banana plantations. Refugees living within

14 Almond trees often prove to be the only remaining visible sign of a Palestinian village and when in bloom are easily visible from afar. While Israelis often consider these "wild almonds" a typical feature of the natural Israeli landscape, these trees are nevertheless usually planted and cultivated as trees for human use.

15 See Pappe 2006 (fn. 11).

16 Ariel Hirschfeld, "Ha'aretz: Erasing words, names and a way of life," 2008, in: http://www.palestineremembered.com/Articles/General/Story11869.html [accessed July 16, 2010].

17 Also called internal refugees, internally displaced persons.

Israel, often only a few kilometers from their home village, are constantly confronted with the place which represents their past. However they are not permitted to bring this place from the past into the present.

The Palestinian landscape is absent—ignored by the Israeli population yet ever-present for the Palestinian refugees. The Weekend Walks taken by many internal refugees render a fitting picture. Former villagers and their offspring go picnicking between heaps of stones from onetime houses, their children playing in the greenery slowly covering the site—inconspicuous and undisturbed, since their Jewish-Israeli neighbors do not see this place. So can a place be absent when its residents are present?

Parallel Landscape. If the place can no longer provide the images of its memory, then those images must exist independently, parallel to the place that has been overwritten. The extent at which such images of the past have changed (in absence of the site and through the filter of the present) gains relevance when strategies for the return of Palestinian refugees are to overcome the simple reconstruction of past structures and new approaches to the spatial treatment of the past are sought.

My research on the destroyed Palestinian village Kafr 'Inan in the Galilee region has yielded two maps that set out to convey the same information, yet they illustrate different contents. A land surveying map, which was commissioned in 1942 during the British Mandate rule for the purposes of registration and tax collection, shows the division of village land in Kafr 'Inan (fig. 3). Since the end of the British Mandate, this map has been kept safe in an Israeli national archive which is still today very difficult to publicly access. Without having been aware of this map's existence, internal refugee Hassan Ahmad Mansour, who had lived in Kafr 'Inan until age fifteen as son of the *Mukthar*,[18] drew out this division from memory seventy years later (fig. 5).[19] As a memory map, the map by Mansour makes the site, which only survives in memory, visible again—and thus also communicable. As a personal and intuitive depiction, it visualizes lived experience of a place and its interrelationships, highlighting aspects that are inevitably lost in normative cartographic practice. Furthermore, the depiction by Mansour shows a present-day view of the village landscape of the past, different than the map that has been unchanged and unread for seventy years.

The memory map by Mansour significantly differs from the British map in perspective, scale and proportions, land position-

18 Arabic term for village leader.

19 The fact that H. A. Mansour represents one of the few persons still in a position today to record the village plot in detail was what moved him to put onto paper for the first time the memories which in the refugee community have theretofore only been passed on orally.

1948 wurden nahezu alle palästinensischen Dörfer bis auf die Grundmauern zerstört, der landwirtschaftliche Grund enteignet und in israelischen Staatsgrund überführt. Einstige palästinensische Dörfer stellen heute eingezäunte Schuttansammlungen dar, deren Zugänglichkeit meist eingeschränkt ist, oder Ruinen, die unter Pinienwäldern begraben sind. Wenn selbst keine Ruinen vorhanden sind, haben israelische Siedlungen oder ganze Stadtviertel ihren Platz eingenommen. Olivenhaine sind Bananenplantagen gewichen. Flüchtlinge, welche oft nur einige Kilometer von ihrem Herkunftsdorf entfernt leben, sind ständig mit dem Ort konfrontiert, welcher ihre Vergangenheit darstellt. Diesen Ort von der Vergangenheit in die Gegenwart zu holen, ist ihnen nicht erlaubt.

Die palästinensische Landschaft ist abwesend – von der israelischen Bevölkerung nicht wahrgenommen, für die palästinensischen Flüchtlinge jedoch präsent. Die Spaziergänge am Wochenende vieler interner Flüchtlinge liefern ein eindeutiges Bild. Ehemalige Dorfbewohner und deren Nachkommen picknicken zwischen Steinhäufen einstiger Häuser, Kinder spielen in der alles überwuchernden Natur. Unauffällig und ungestört, denn die jüdisch-israelischen Nachbarn sehen diesen Ort nicht. Kann ein Ort abwesend sein, wenn seine Bewohner präsent sind?

Parallele Landschaft. Wenn der Ort nicht mehr die Bilder seiner Erinnerung wiedergeben kann, müssen die Bilder selbstständig und parallel zum überschriebenen Ort existieren. Inwiefern sich die Bilder der Vergangenheit in Abwesenheit des Ortes und durch den Filter der Gegenwart verändert haben, wird wichtig, wenn Rückkehrstrategien für palästinensische Flüchtlinge vom simplen Wiederaufbau vergangener Strukturen absehen und man nach neuen Zugängen für den räumlichen Umgang mit der Vergangenheit sucht.

Meine Recherche über das zerstörte palästinensische Dorf *Kafr 'Inan* in der Region Galiläa lieferte zwei Karten, welche dasselbe aussagen wollen, jedoch Unterschiedliches darstellen. Eine Landvermessungskarte, die 1942 unter britischer Mandatsherrschaft zum Zwecke der Registrierung und Steuereinhebung erstellt wurde, zeigt die Teilung des Dorfgrundstückes von *Kafr 'Inan* (Abb. 3). Diese Karte wurde seit dem Ende des britischen Mandats in einem staatlich-israelischen Archiv verwahrt, welches bis heute nur erschwert für die Öffentlichkeit zugänglich ist. Ohne Kenntnis dieser Karte zeichnet der interne Flüchtling Hassan Ahmad Mansour, welcher bis zu seinem 15. Lebensjahr als Sohn des *Mukthar*[18] in *Kafr 'Inan* lebte, 70 Jahre später diese Einteilung aus seinem Gedächtnis (Abb. 5).[19] Als *Memory Map* kann Mansours Karte den Ort, der nur mehr in der Erinnerung existiert, wieder sichtbar – und damit auch kommunizierbar machen. Als persönliche und intuitive Darstellung visualisiert sie erlebte Raumbilder und Beziehungen und zeigt Aspekte auf, die in genormten Kartierungen verloren gehen. Weiters zeigt die Mansours Darstellung, anders als jene, welche 70 Jahre ungelesen und unverändert blieb, die heutige Sicht auf die damalige Dorflandschaft.

18 Arabische Bezeichnung für Dorfoberhaupt.

19 Die Tatsache, dass H. A. Mansour einen der wenigen darstellt, die heute noch in der Lage sind das Dorfgrundstück detailliert aufzuzeichnen, bewegten ihn dazu die bisher in der Flüchtlingsgemeinschaft nur mündlich überlieferte Erinnerung erstmals zu Papier zu bringen.

Mansours *Memory Map* unterscheidet sich in Perspektive, Größenverhältnissen, Grundstückslage und Detaillierungsgrad deutlich von der britischen Karte, einzig die Landbezeichnungen stimmen großteils überein. Da aufgrund der unterschiedlichen Natur beider Karten ihre simple Gegenüberstellung keinen sofortigen Vergleich zulässt, wird die Erstellung einer dritten Karte notwendig, um die volle Bedeutung der *Memory Map* zu erfassen. Eine Karte, welche die in der *Memory Map* dargestellten Proportionen und Lage der Grundstücke sowie topografische Angaben in die realen oder britischen Umfassungsgrenzen des Dorfes verlegt und sie zusammen mit den Bildern der Erinnerung, an welchen mich Mansour in mehreren Gesprächen und während der Erläuterung der Karte teilhaben ließ, als Landschaft der Erinnerung visualisiert und interpretiert (Abb. 4). Vergleicht man nun die Information der britischen Karte mit der *Landschaft der Erinnerung*, wird die Selektion und Verschiebung der Erinnerung in Zusammenhang mit ihrer Bedeutung für Mansour deutlich. Viel detaillierter als in der britischen Karte stellt Mansour beispielsweise die Obst-und Gemüsegärten um das ehemalige Dorf, sowie die Gemeinschaftsorte und Treffpunkte dar und verleiht ihnen dadurch mehr Gewicht. Die größten Elemente der *Memory Map* bilden die Olivenhaine, welche teils aus Randbereichen der britischen Karte in das Zentrum von Mansours Karte rücken.

Die subjektive Karte sowie die bildlich dargestellte Interpretation derselben ermöglichen es, näher auf die Erinnerung an den vergangenen Ort und dessen gegenwärtige Wahrnehmung und Dynamik einzugehen. Gleichzeitig wird mit der Karte, welche in der Erinnerung ihren Ausgangspunkt findet und heute Assoziationen innerhalb der Flüchtlingsgemeinschaft hervorruft, ein generatives Instrument der Kommunikation geschaffen. Laut James Corner steht die Karte nicht nur für das, was sie repräsentiert, sondern vor allem dafür, was sie auszulösen vermag. „The function of mapping is less to mirror reality […] than to become a productive and liberating instrument […]. The unfolding agency is most effective when its capacity for description also sets the condition for new eidetic and physical worlds to come."[20] Die provozierende Subjektivität der bildhaften Interpretation einer persönlichen Erinnerung fordert den Leser der *Landschaft der Erinnerung* dazu auf, die Karte und deren Bilder zu hinterfragen, zu verändern oder zu vervollständigen. Sie nimmt somit als wichtiger Schritt in einer räumlichen Rückkehrdiskussion dem Umgang mit heutigen Vergangenheitsbildern seine drücken-

Wegen fehlender politischer Zusagen wurden in bisherigen Rückkehrstrategien nur sehr allgemein ökonomische und organisatorische Abfolgen ausgearbeitet. Zum räumlichen Aspekt und architektonischen Maßstab kam es nie.

20 Corner 1999 (Anm. 3), S. 213–214, Zitat J. B. Harley.

ing, and degree of detail; only the land designations for the most part correspond. Since no immediate comparison is possible through a simple juxtaposition of the two maps due to their distinct natures, the creation of a third map becomes necessary to capture the full meaning of the memory map—a map that shifts the proportions and plot locations depicted in the mind map, along with topographical information, to the real or British outside borders of the village. These—together with images from memory, which Mansour conveyed to me during several conversations and while explaining the map—are visualized and interpreted as *Landscape of Memory* (fig. 4). If one now compares the information on the British map with the *Landscape of Memory*, then the selection and shifting of memory in connection with its meaning for Mansour becomes plain. With much more detail than found in the British map, Mansour depicts, for example, the fruit orchards and vegetable gardens of the former village, and also communal spots and meeting places, thereby lending it heightened significance. The largest elements on the memory map are the olive groves, which at times have been moved from the margins of the British map to central positions in the map by Mansour.

Both the subjective map and the pictorially represented interpretation thereof make it possible to more precisely address the memory of the past site and its present perception and dynamics. At the same time, the map—which has its point of origin in memory and today evokes associations within the refugee community—has fostered a generative instrument of communication. According to Corner, the map stands not only for that which it represents, but most especially for that which it aims to activate: "The function of mapping is less to mirror reality … than to become a productive and liberating instrument … The unfolding agency is most effective when its capacity for description also sets the condition for new eidetic and physical worlds to come."[20] The provocative subjectivity of the pictorial interpretation of a personal memory prompts the reader of *Landscape of Memory* to scrutinize, alter, or complete the map and its images. It thus divests of its oppressive severity, as an important step in a spatial discussion on the return of the refugees, the treatment of today's images of the past—the severity of the seeming necessity of a unified memory to further a homogeneous demand for their return, which today impedes, on the Palestinian end, the step toward a discussion that is tangible rather than symbolic-legal.

Landscape of Return. Due to the absence of any political agreement, strategies for the return of the refugees have sketched out economic and organizational plans in only very general terms. To date, considerations like spatial aspect and architec-

20 Corner 1999 (fn. 3), pp. 213–214, quote by J. B. Harley.

 Ghostly Presence, 2010.

13

13 Schaubild: *Vollzeitgemüsegärten*, *gemeinschaftlicher Selbstpflück-Obsthain* und *Olivenhaine für Kleinbauern*. Chart: full-time vegetable garden, shared self-harvested fruit orchard, and olive groves for small-scale farmers.

tural scale have not yet been addressed. But what if one were nevertheless to begin with what is supposed to be the last step? With a scale that inevitably highlights most explicitly the issues pertaining to possibilities for the refugees' return, one that can be communicated and can likewise contribute to communication. Communicating this topic would have to tentatively be the sole objective of this scale—for the time being, detailed planning is out of the question. Since discussion on the topic of return is currently at a standstill, the primary goal here must be to open spaces of possibility for new ideas, rather than to stipulate the future through design—which would merely hinder any productive discussion, rather then enabling it.

If one considers that the Palestinian refugees' process of return to Israel will take varying forms, and that a mass return after more than sixty years is unlikely,[21] then a broad spectrum of options for their return becomes necessary. Whereby not all options would necessarily have to be tied to the idea of permanent resettlement—which is incidentally the only solution in discussion today, and perhaps also the simplest one, to the issue of the refugees' return. The multilayered significance of the Israeli-Palestinian geography, along with the fact that the refugees would return into a newly designed and spatially transformed reality, necessitates deliberate work on the present-day landscape. The concept touched upon here is not limited to the originally built-up area of the village Kafr 'Inan but rather covers the entire village landscape. Unlike the unambiguous monumentality of a (re)built past, landscape is oftentimes able to more strongly influence one's perception of surroundings through subtle means.

The Kafr 'Inan land is cultivated today by an Israeli kibbutz and two moshavim.[22] Small field divisions and differentiated land use have been replaced by an intensively farmed, large-scale agrarian landscape (fig. 6). Despite the apparent total rewriting of the landscape, it becomes apparent upon closer consideration that numerous present-day field divisions coincide with those from earlier days. All places where no rational, topographical reason for deviations from the strictly orthogonal grid can be found make it necessary to search for the reason in the past. The outside borders of the dispossessed village acreage particularly seem to have been burnt into the landscape. As opposed to political geography, here the landscape may have been severed from memory but not from the past. The signs of the past are visible. Visible, but not seen (figs. 7, 12).

21 Sari Hanafi, "The Sociology of Return: Palestinian Social Capital, Transnational Kinships and the Refugee Repatriation Process," in: Eyal Benevisti, Chaim Gans, and Sari Hanafi (eds.), *Israel and the Palestinian Refugees*. Berlin, Heidelberg, and New York 2007, pp. 3–40.

22 A kibbutz is an Israeli rural collective settlement with jointly owned property and grass-roots democratic structures. A cooperatively organized rural settlement form in Israel whose members own private property is called a moshav (plural: moshavim). While once based upon agriculture, today these settlements also generate revenue from industry and tourism.

de Schwere – die Schwere der scheinbaren Notwendigkeit einer vereinheitlichten Erinnerung für eine homogene Forderung nach Rückkehr, welche heute auf palästinensischer Seite den Schritt von einer symbolisch-rechtlichen zu einer greifbaren Diskussion erschwert.

Landschaft der Rückkehr. Wegen fehlender politischer Zusagen wurden in bisherigen Rückkehrstrategien nur sehr allgemein ökonomische und organisatorische Abfolgen ausgearbeitet. Zum räumlichen Aspekt und architektonischen Maßstab kam es nie. Was, wenn man jedoch mit dem vermeintlich letzten Schritt anfängt? Einem Maßstab, der unweigerlich die Fragen über konkrete Rückkehrmöglichkeiten am deutlichsten aufzeigt, den man kommunizieren kann und der zur Kommunikation beitragen kann? Das Thema zu kommunizieren, muss vorläufig der einzige Zweck dieses Maßstabes sein – an eine detaillierte Planung ist derzeit noch nicht zu denken. Aufgrund der momentanen Pattstellung der Diskussion über die Rückkehr muss es primäres Ziel sein, Möglichkeitsräume für neue Ideen zu eröffnen, anstatt Zukunft durch Gestaltung festzulegen – was eine weiterführende Diskussion verhindern anstatt ermöglichen würde.

Bedenkt man, dass der Prozess der Rückkehr palästinensischer Flüchtlinge nach Israel verschiedenste Muster annehmen wird und eine Massenrückkehr nach über 60 Jahren unwahrscheinlich ist,[21] wird ein breites Spektrum an Rückkehrmöglichkeiten notwendig, die nicht alle zwingend an permanente Rücksiedlung – die heute einzig diskutierte und vielleicht simpelste Antwort auf die Rückkehrfrage – gebunden sind. Die vielschichtige Bedeutung der israelisch-palästinensischen Geografie sowie die Tatsache der Rückkehr in eine neu konstruierte und räumlich veränderte Realität machen die bewusste Arbeit mit der gegenwärtigen Landschaft erforderlich. Das ausgearbeitete Konzept beschränkt sich nicht auf die ursprünglich bebaute Fläche des Dorfes *Kafr 'Inan*, sondern bezieht die gesamte Dorflandschaft mit ein. Denn anders als die eindeutige Monumentalität gebauter Vergangenheit kann Landschaft meist auf subtilere Weise einen größeren Einfluss auf die Wahrnehmung der Umgebung ausüben.

Das Land von *Kafr 'Inan* wird heute von einem israelischen *Kibbutz* und zwei *Moshavim*[22] bewirtschaftet. Die kleinteiligen Feldeinteilungen und differenzierten Feldnutzungen sind von einer intensiv genutzten, großflächigen Agrarlandschaft ersetzt worden (Abb. 6). Trotz der scheinbar vollkommenen Überschreibung der Landschaft stimmen bei genauerer Betrachtung mehrere gegenwärtige Feldeinteilungen noch mit den alten überein. Überall dort, wo kein rationaler, topografischer Grund für die Abweichung vom strengen orthogonalen Raster gefunden werden kann, muss der Grund in der Vergangenheit gesucht werden. Vor allem die Umfassungsgrenze vom enteigneten Dorfgrund scheint wie in die Landschaft eingebrannt. Im Unterschied zur politischen Geografie ist hier die Landschaft zwar von der Erinnerung, nicht aber von ihrer Vergangenheit getrennt wor-

21 Sari Hanafi, „The Sociology of Return: Palestinian Social Capital, Transnational Kinships and the Refugee Repatriation Process", in: Eyal Benevisti, Chaim Gans, Sari Hanafi (Hg.), *Israel and the Palestinian Refugees*. Berlin, Heidelberg, New York 2007, S. 3–40.

22 Ein Kibbutz ist eine israelische ländliche Kollektivsiedlung mit gemeinsamem Eigentum und basisdemokratischen Strukturen. Als Moshav (Plural: Moshavim) wird eine genossenschaftlich organisierte ländliche Siedlungsform bezeichnet, deren Mitglieder Privateigentum besitzen. Ursprünglich auf Landwirtschaft basierend, erwirtschaften diese heute ihr Einkommen auch durch Industrie und Tourismus.

den. Die Zeichen der Vergangenheit sind sichtbar. Sichtbar, aber nicht gesehen (Abb. 7, 12).

Um eine Strategie zu erarbeiten, welche unter Miteinbeziehung vergangener und gegenwärtiger Landschaft mehrere Muster der Rückkehr sowie die erneute Verwebung der Rückkehrenden mit der Landschaft zulässt, entwarf ich ein Umnutzungskonzept der landwirtschaftlichen Flächen. Das Konzept *Landschaft der Rückkehr* vereint unterschiedliche Bewirtschaftungs- und Nutzungsformen, die verschiedene Felddimensionierungen, Anbauprodukte und variierende Frequentierungen der Nutzer ermöglichen. Typologien des Anbaus für den Eigenbedarf, den Gemeinschaftsgebrauch und den kommerziellen Nutzen können mit unterschiedlichem Arbeitsaufwand betrieben werden und begegnen den unterschiedlichen Bedürfnissen, welche durch differenzierte Rückkehrpraktiken entstehen (Abb. 11). Der *Vollzeitgemüsegarten* etwa kann mit 100 m^2 und einem ganzjährigen Anbau den Eigenbedarf einer Familie decken und bedingt aufgrund häufiger Bewässerung und mehrmaliger Ernte- und Anbauperioden eine häufige Anwesenheit der Nutzer. Im *Wochenendgemüsegarten* kann der Benutzer seine Anbaufläche je nach Bedarf erweitern und auch bei geringer Frequentierung eigenes Gemüse ziehen, in *gemeinschaftlichen Selbstpflück-Obsthainen* erlaubt ein großzügiger Baumraster auch eine freizeitliche Nutzung und macht den Obsthain somit zu Blüte-, Reife- und Erntezeit interessant. Die *Oliven- oder Obsthaine für Kleinbauern* werden wie die *Felder für Kleinbauern* von privaten Benutzern betrieben, welche die Ernte am lokalen Markt oder im regionalen Handel verkaufen. Die Freifläche am ehemaligen Dorfplatz bildet zentralen Einstiegspunkt in die produktive Landschaft und zu den alten Dorfruinen, zu welchen man über einen gemeinschaftlichen Mandelhain gelangt (Abb. 13, 14, 15).

Um eine Strategie zu erarbeiten, welche unter Miteinbeziehung vergangener und gegenwärtiger Landschaft mehrere Muster der Rückkehr sowie die erneute Verwebung der Rückkehrenden mit der Landschaft zulässt, entwarf ich ein Umnutzungskonzept der landwirtschaftlichen Flächen.

Mit Layern der Vergangenheit wird dort gearbeitet, wo sie für die Benutzung und Strukturierung der *Landschaft der Rückkehr* von Bedeutung sind (Abb. 8). Durch eine differenzierte Unterteilung und Bewirtschaftung sowie die Ausrichtung an topografischen und strukturellen Aspekten unterscheidet sich die neue Fläche gezielt von umgebenden orthogonalen Monokulturen, deren Lage und Ausrichtung von maximaler Ausbeute und Maschinentauglichkeit der Fläche bestimmt wird. Der gegenwärtigen Konzentration von Aktivitäten auf den höchsten Punkten umliegender Hügel wird mit einer attraktiven, produktiven Landschaft im Tal begegnet (Abb. 9, 10). Der Bruch im Landschaftsbild macht nicht nur eine andere Nutzung, sondern auch eine andere

In order to develop a strategy which would use past and present land use patterns to suggest several possible practices of return, and which would allow the returnees to establish their own authentic and grounded relationship with the land once more, I have developed a concept for the reuse and redevelopment of the agrarian land. The concept of *Landscape of Return* unites various forms of cultivation and usage that make possible fields of various sizes, diverse farming products, and varying frequentation by the users. Farming typologies for personal requirements and for collective and commercial use can be pursued with different levels of effort and thus meet the differing needs arising through differentiated practices for the refugees' return (fig. 11). The "full-time vegetable garden," for instance, can cover the personal needs of a whole family with 100 m^2 and year-round cultivation; it necessitates frequent tending by the user due to frequent irrigating needs and multiple harvesting and planting periods. In the "weekend vegetable garden," the user can enlarge his or her cultivation area according to demand and can harvest vegetables even with scarce frequentation. And in the "shared self-harvested fruit orchard" a generous grid of trees likewise fosters leisure usage, hence making the fruit orchard especially interesting during the blooming, ripening, and harvesting seasons. The "fruit and olive groves for small-scale farmers" along with the "fields for small-scale farmers" are tended by private users who sell the harvested items at the local market or at local businesses. The open spaces at the former village square form a central starting point within the productive landscape and for the old village ruins, which may be reached by strolling along a shared almond grove (figs. 13, 14, 15).

Layers of the past are integrated when they are of significance for the use and structuring of *Landscape of Return* (fig. 8). Through a differentiated division and cultivation as well as an alignment with topographical and structural aspects, the new surface area is specifically distinguished from the surrounding orthogonal monocultures, the location and alignment of which are determined by a maximal yield and machine-suitability of the surface. The present-day concentration of activities at the highest points on the circumjacent hills is encountered by an attractive, productive landscape in the valley (figs. 9, 10). The clear break in the scenery makes visible not only the change in land use visible but also another past (different from the one propagated today). The idea of superimposing the past through protected nature is reversed through making it visible by a productive nature. The new landscape appearance challenges the beholder. It dares the beholder to seek the reason for the otherness while simultaneously allowing him or her to once again view the landscape as a culturally shaped landscape. The concept of *Landscape of Return*, as based upon the example of Kafr 'Inan, associates individual practices of the refugees' return with a productive landscape in order to trans-

14 Schaubild: *Wochenendgemüsegärten*, *Felder für Kleinbauern* und bestehende Plantagen. Chart: weekend vegetable garden, fields for small-scale farmers, and existing plantations.

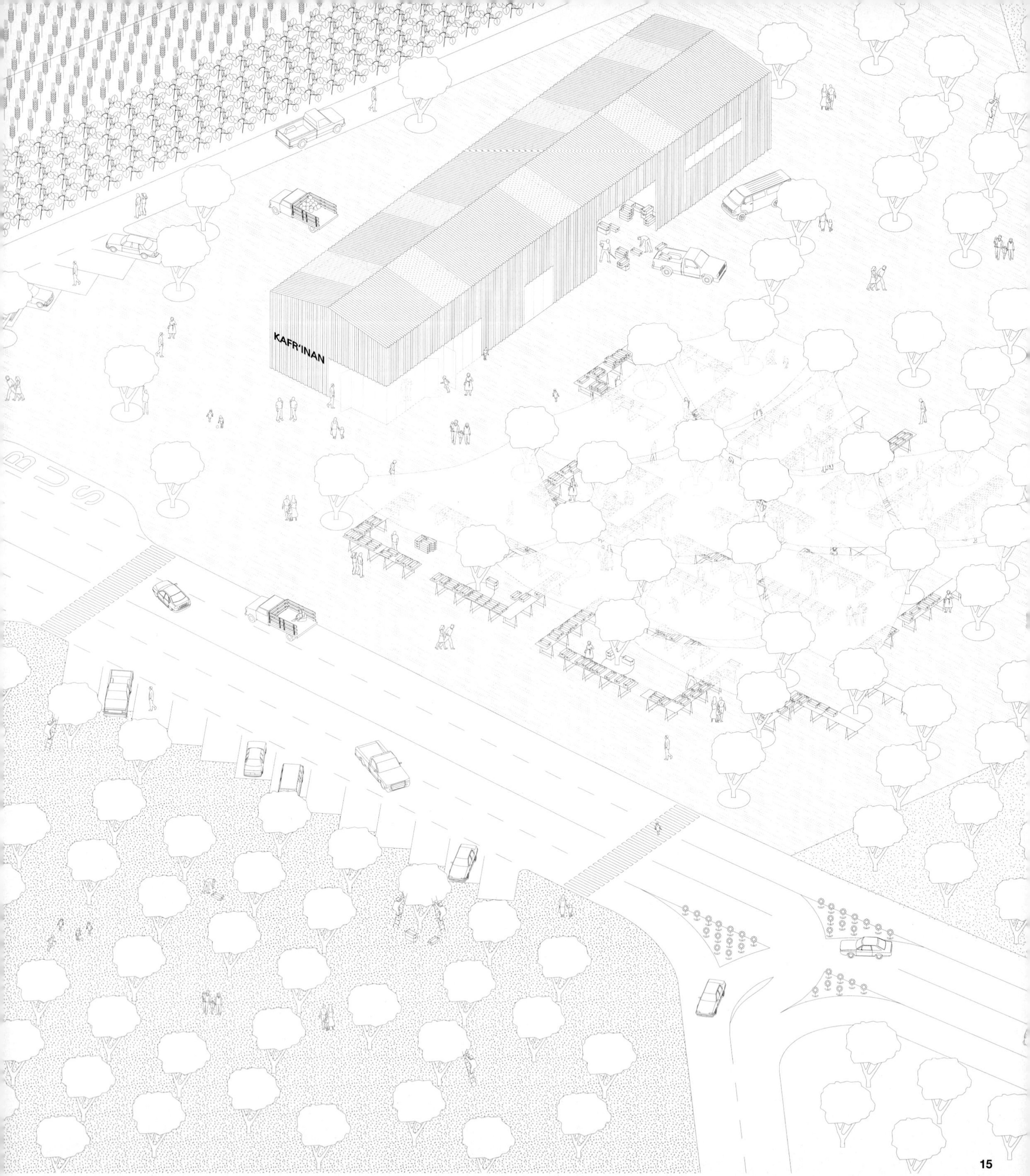

15

15 Schaubild: *Felder für Kleinbauern*, Markt, Information, Lagerhalle, Geräteverleih, *Gemeinschaftlicher Selbstpflück-Obsthain*, Dorfruinen *Kafr 'Inan*. Chart: fields for small-scale farmers, market, information, storehouse, equipment rental, shared self-harvested fruit orchard, Kafr 'Inan village ruins.

fer the enduring reality of absence into a real process of the present, thereby presenting one of many concepts for the refugees' return that needs to be considered. Creating a foundation for a tangible discussion based upon the perception of the present-day landscape is essential in order to further the continued development of the internal discourse as well as the debate on the return of the refugees between Palestinians and Israelis. Only a landscape that not only thematizes the inescapable changes it has experienced over the past seventy years but also reveals its Palestinian inscription and reality can enable a return of the Palestinian refugees to present-day Israel.

Translation Dawn Michelle d'Atri

(als heute propagierte) Vergangenheit sichtbar. Das Konzept der Überschreibung von Vergangenheit durch geschützte Natur wird durch die Sichtbarmachung anhand produktiver Landschaft umgekehrt. Das neue Landschaftsbild fordert den Betrachter. Es fordert ihn heraus, nach dem Grund der Andersartigkeit zu fragen und erlaubt es ihm gleichzeitig, die Landschaft wieder als gewachsene Kulturlandschaft zu sehen. Das Konzept *Landschaft der Rückkehr* am Beispiel *Kafr 'Inan* verbindet individuelle Praktiken der Rückkehr mit einer produktiven Landschaft, um die fortwährende Realität der Abwesenheit in einen realen Prozess der Gegenwart zu überführen und stellt ein Rückkehrkonzept unter vielen dar, die diskutiert werden sollen. Um die Weiterentwicklung des internen Diskurses sowie die Rückkehrdebatte zwischen Palästinensern und Israelis voranzutreiben, muss die Basis für eine greifbare Diskussion anhand der Wahrnehmung der heutigen Landschaft geschaffen werden. Alleine eine Landschaft, die sowohl die zwangsläufige Veränderung, welche sie in 70 Jahren erfahren hat, thematisiert, als auch ihre palästinensische Einschreibung und Realität offenlegt, kann eine Rückkehr der palästinensischen Flüchtlinge in das heutige Israel möglich machen.

CANAL EXCAVATION ALONGSIDE RAISED LAND FOR URBAN DEVELOPMENT

WATER LEVEL 1 IN FLOODABLE AREA

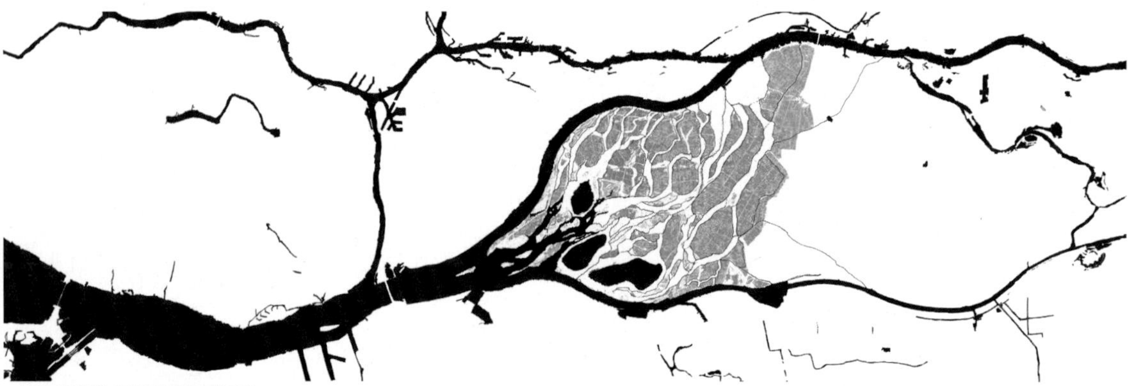

WATER LEVEL 2 IN FLOODABLE AREA

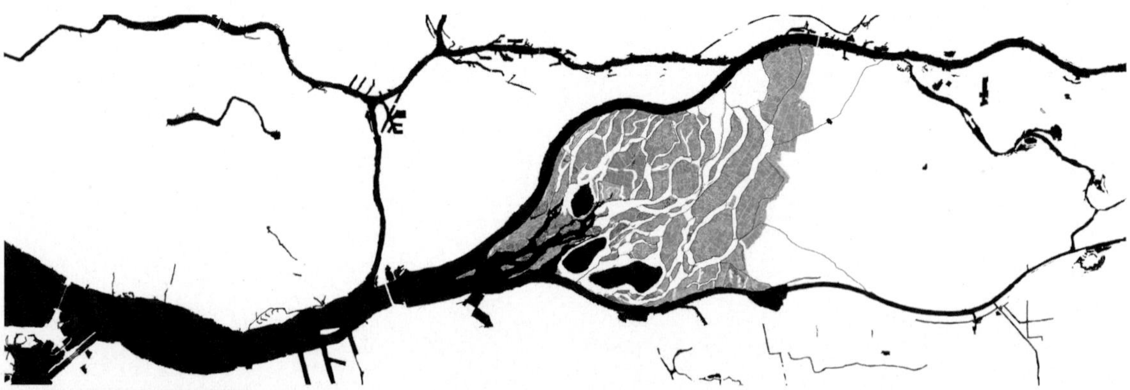

WATER LEVEL 3 IN FLOODABLE AREA

1

1 Wasserprojekt Water project

The Biesbosch

The Biesbosch delta territory in the Netherlands is today a landscape of exceptional natural features with a water landscape to the south, and an agricultural polder to the north, all of this enclosed by a system of dikes. In anticipation of the consequences of climate change, this project conceives a transformation of the current hydraulic mechanical functions to accommodate the high discharge levels of the Rhine and the Meuse, to receive the ebb at high tide, and to resist the possibility of storm flooding.

Der Biesbosch. Das Deltagebiet des niederländischen Biesbosch präsentiert sich heute als eine Landschaft voll außergewöhnlicher natürlicher Charakteristika – von der vom Wasser geprägten Region im Süden bis zum landwirtschaftlich genutzten Polder im Norden, alles umsäumt von einer Reihe von Deichen. Angesichts der zu erwartenden Folgen des Klimawandels zielt das Projekt auf eine Transformation der gegenwärtigen hydraulisch-mechanischen Funktionen ab, um das starke Durchflussvolumen von Rhein und Maas zu bewältigen, den Ebbstrom bei hohem Wasserstand aufzunehmen und der Möglichkeit von Sturmfluten vorzubeugen.

MICHEL DESVIGNE

2

3

2 Rotterdam
3 Zweite Internationale Architekturbiennale Rotterdam, Katalogcover: *the flood*
2 Rotterdam
3 2nd International Architecture Biennale Rotterdam, catalogue cover: *the flood*

Neben der Umgestaltung der Deiche, die eine Aufnahme der Wassermassen im Falle von Überflutungen ermöglicht und steuert, schlagen wir vor, die außergewöhnliche Gestalt der Deltalandschaft spielerisch mit einzubeziehen. Die Prozesse, denen die Region ihre heutige Beschaffenheit verdankt, haben das faszinierende Phänomen der Inversion hervorgebracht: Landwirtschaftlich genutzte Bodenflächen sind durch die Entwässerung abgesunken, während das Sandbett der früheren Flussarme auf dem alten Niveau geblieben ist. Das Resultat ist eine Art Negativ-Landschaft, in der die ehemaligen Flussrinnen als Kämme herausragen.

Wir empfehlen, das Bett der alten Flussarme einzutiefen, um so für einen besseren Wasserdurchfluss bei Überflutungen zu sorgen. Das Grabungsmaterial sollte unserer Meinung nach dazu genutzt werden, um das Phänomen der Inversion noch zu verstärken, indem Teile des alten marinen Flussbetts auf ein Niveau angehoben werden, das auch bei höherem Meeresspiegel nicht überschwemmt wird.

Ausgehend von der natürlichen Geomorphologie des Areals schlagen wir die Schaffung eines Gefüges aus künstlichen Plattformen vor, die für Verkehr und Wohnen genutzt werden können. Die Landschaft stellt ein Negativ-Delta dar, eine Art inverses Bild, eine Manifestation der Kultur in einer langen Tradition von Wechselbeziehungen zwischen Mensch und Wasser. Ihre künstliche Architektur resultiert aus der Umkehrung natürlicher Formen. In diesen Strukturen und Proportionen spiegelt sich die Schönheit der Region wider: in den Konturen, vertrauten Windungen und fließenden Formen ebenso wie in den in Sand eingegrabenen Kanälen und Rinnen.

Zwischen den erhöhten Flussarmen, in den am häufigsten überfluteten Bereichen, kann die Landwirtschaft Platz machen für eine ganz spezifische natürliche Umwelt. Daraus resultiert die Inversion der Landschaft: Die Flussarme verwandeln sich in künstliche Plattformen, die umgebenden Felder werden zu Feuchtgebieten. Die erhöhten Flächen mit ihren Verästelungen bringen eine außergewöhnliche Situation hervor – die Verflechtung und Verschmelzung von natürlichen Dynamiken und künstlichen Eingriffen.

Wir denken, dass die Beschaffenheit des Bodens heute die Errichtung von Siedlungen erlaubt. So könnten Teile der erhöhten Flussarme für urbane Agglomerationen attraktiv sein, die sich in die Landschaft hinein öffnen. Verbunden werden diese neuen Bereiche durch das Gefüge der alten Flussarme.

Die urbanen Agglomerationen und die vorgeschlagene Bebauung sollen zu einem Abdruck, somit zu einer Erinnerung an die natürlichen Prozesse und Formen des Deltas werden. Auf diese Art und Weise bestimmt die inhärente Geografie des Ortes, die natürliche Dynamik des Wassers mit seinen Bewegungen, die urbane Gestalt, ähnlich wie in Stockholm und Sydney, aber auch wie in Boston und Minneapolis, wo es die Parksysteme sind, deren Architektur die ursprüngliche Existenz von Flüssen und Seen sichtbar macht.

In addition to the transformation of the dykes, which will allow and control the storage of water in times of flooding, we propose dealing in a playful manner with the exceptional nature of this delta landscape. The cultural mechanisms that shaped the Biesbosch delta area have created a fascinating phenomenon of inversion. The cultivated areas of polder land behind the dikes have sunk due to drainage, while the sand bed of the old river arm has remained at its original levels. In the west the dikes will partly disappear allowing the sea to reach the new landscape of the creeks. Then progressively, the dikes are less pierced following the chosen levels of the water. By this means the artificial territory of agriculture will be transformed into a natural environment with a decreasing salt content, while the natural traces of the creeks become the dwelling area for the human inhabitants. This results in a delta landscape "in negative," where the furrows of the river movements have become elevated ridges.

As a process, we propose to retract soil as part of the old creek beds, to allow for a greater flow of water in periods of flooding. But we also propose to use the excavated material to exaggerate the inversion phenomenon by raising the height of parts of the old marine riverbed to a level which will not be flooded in times of higher sea level.

In between these raised creeks, in the areas most frequently flooded, agriculture may give way to a specific type of natural environment.

Based on the natural phenomena of geomorphology, we propose the construction of a fabric of artificial platforms on which it will be possible to circulate and live. The landscape is a delta in negative, like an inverse print, a cultural statement in a long tradition of man-water interaction. Its artificial architecture is the result of the transposition of natural forms. Evidence for its beauty is provided in these forms and their proportions: the contours, the familiar convolutions and flows, the gullies and furrows on the sand.

In between these raised creeks, in the areas most frequently flooded, agriculture may give way to a specific type of natural environment. The inversion of the site will take place: the creeks becoming artificial platforms; the surrounding fields wetlands. The ramifications of these platforms create an exceptional situation: interweaving and fusion between natural dynamics and artifice.

We imagine that today the land conditions are favorable for the establishment of settlements. It may be possible for certain parts of these raised creeks to attract agglomeration, which open onto the landscape. All these new areas then are interlinked by the fabric of the old creeks.

Human agglomeration and the proposed constructions should, in turn, become the imprint and thus the memory of the natural processes and forms of the delta. Thus, its inherent geography and the natural dynamics of the moving water determine the urban form, as in Stockholm and Sydney, or also Boston or Minneapolis, where the park systems, which are the architecture of these cities, emphasize the original presence of the rivers and lakes.

04 URBANIZATION

PERMANENT WATER

RAISED CREEKS

CITY DEVELOPMENT ON RAISED CREEKS

FLOODABLE FIELDS BETWEEN RAISED CREEKS

4 Urbanisierung
5 Aktuelles Hochwasserniveau
6 Wasser im flutbaren Bereich
4 Urbanization
5 Current flood water level
6 Water in floodable area

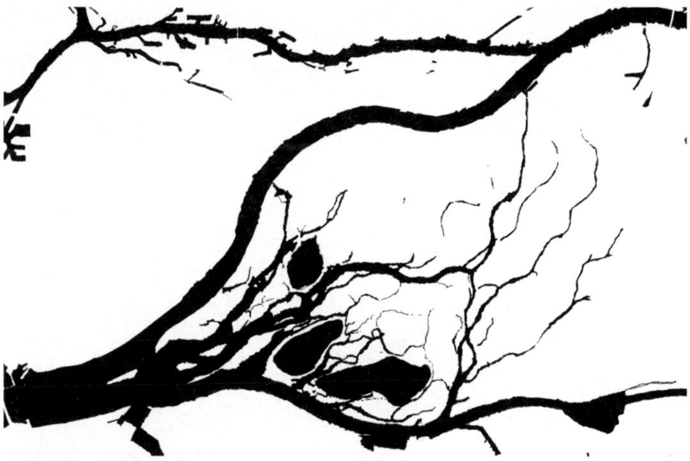

CURRENT FLOOD WATER LEVEL 1

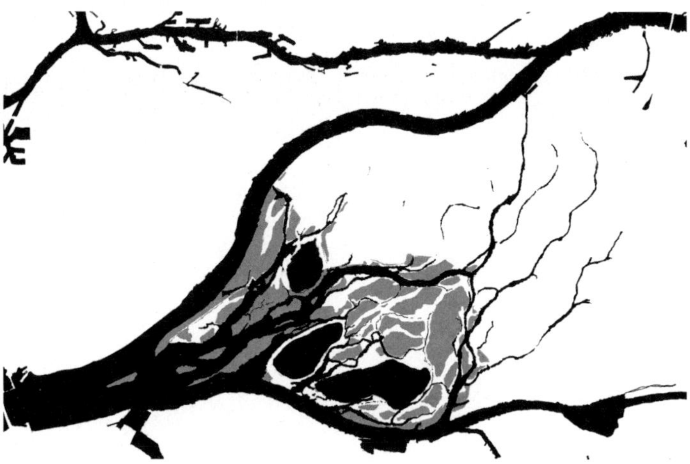

CURRENT FLOOD WATER LEVEL 2

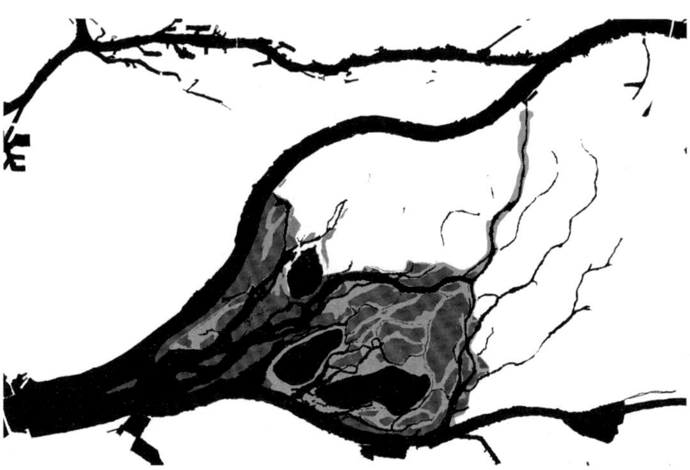

CURRENT FLOOD WATER LEVEL 3

5

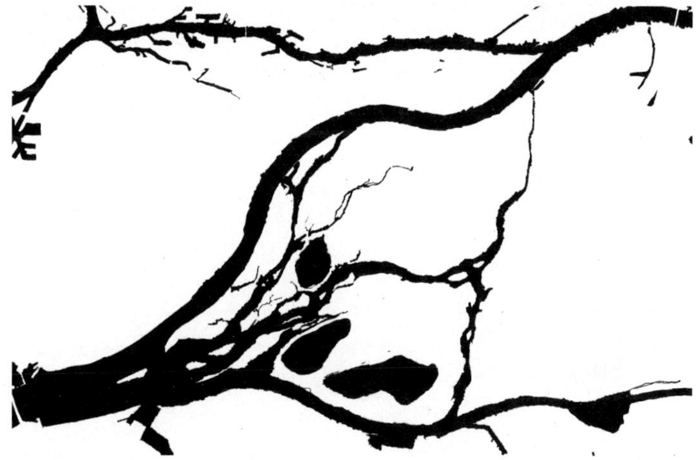

WATER IN FLOODABLE AREA L1

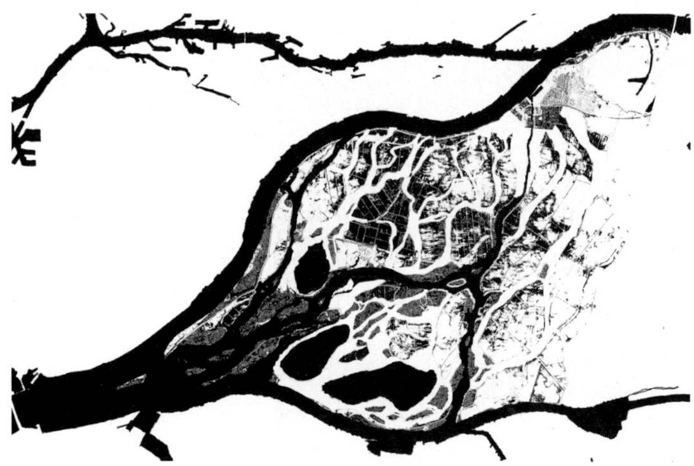

WATER IN FLOODABLE AREA L2

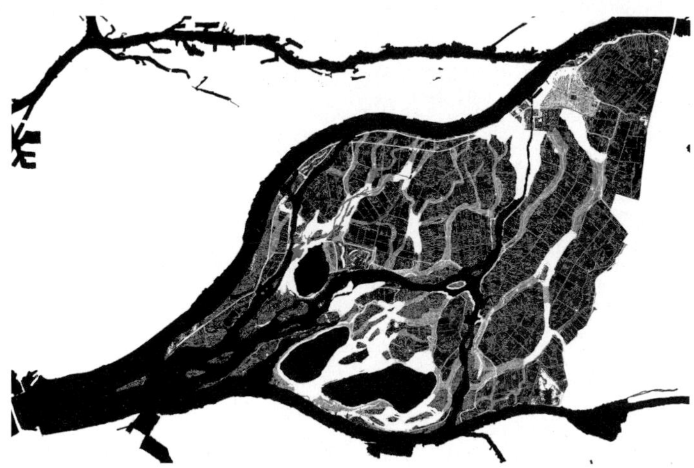

WATER IN FLOODABLE AREA L3

6

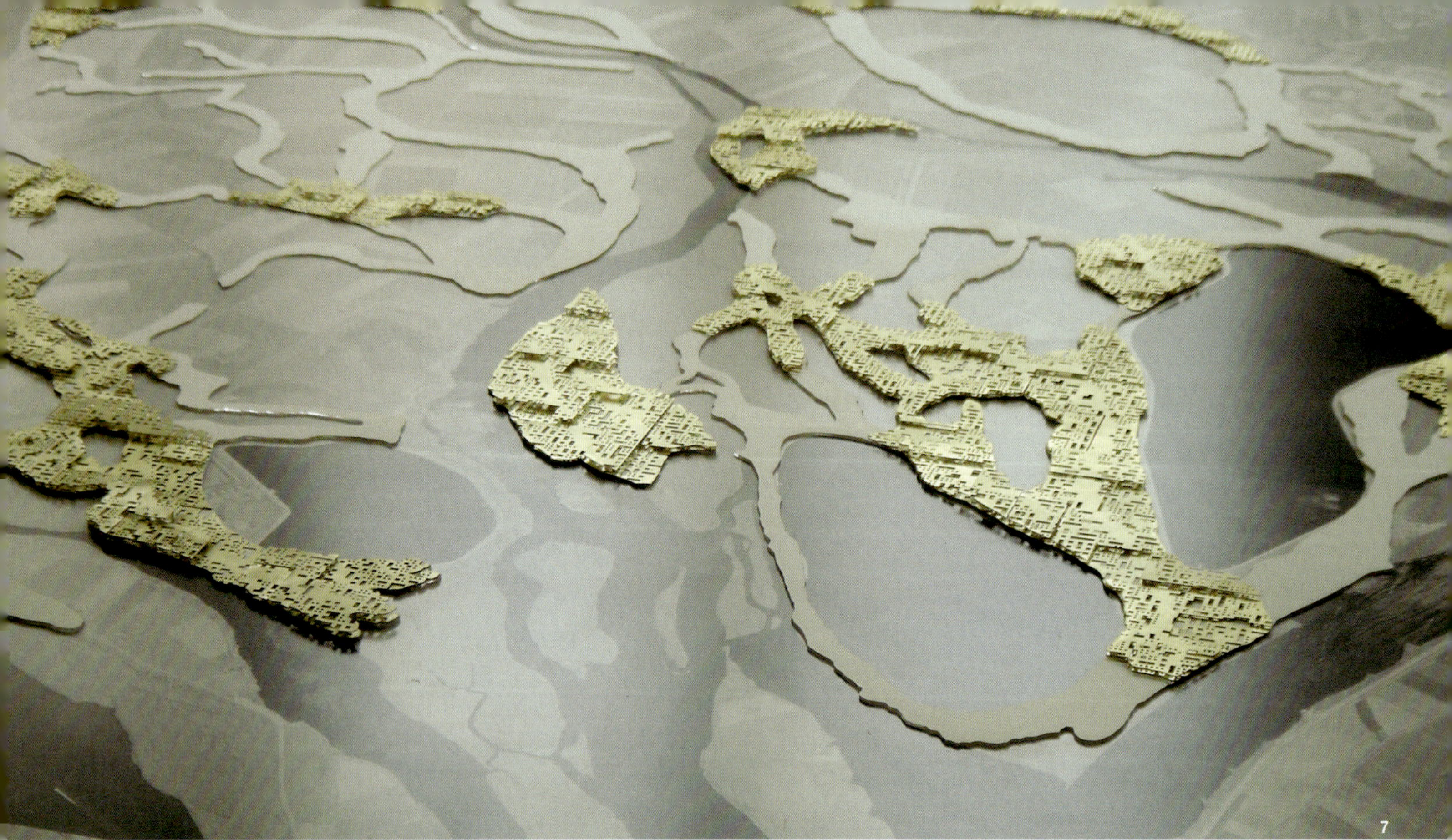

7

8

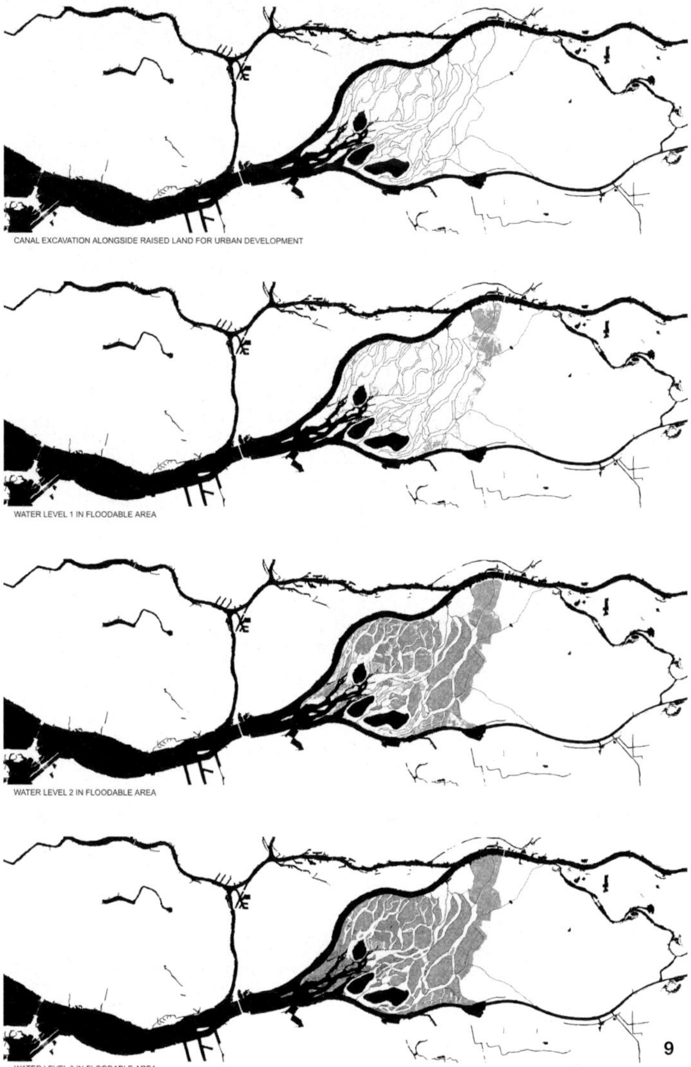

9

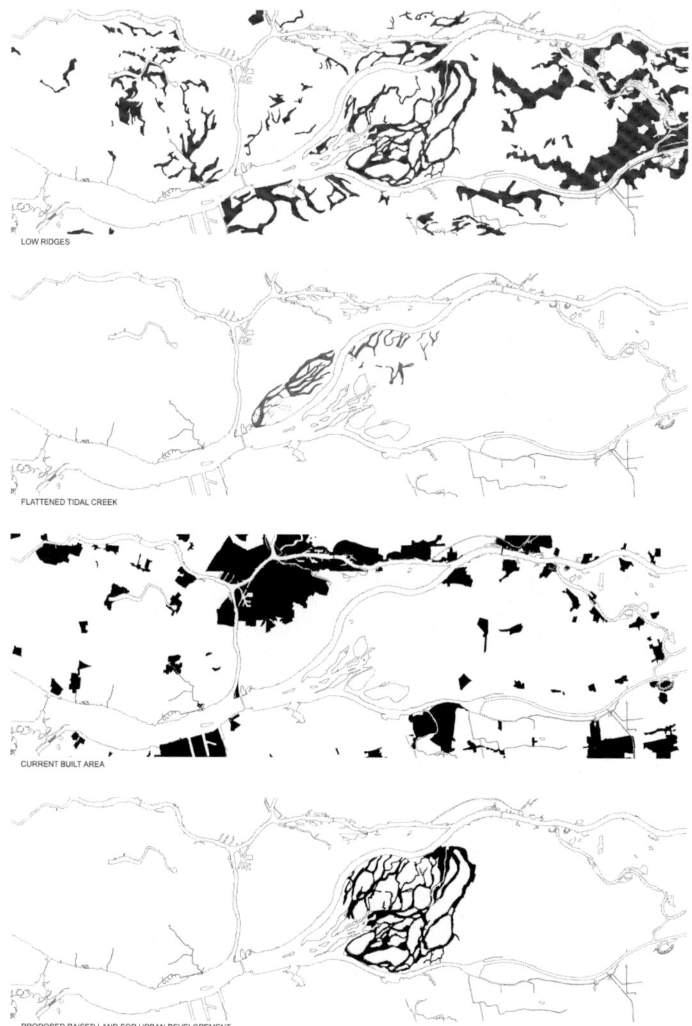

10

7 De Biesbosch, Modellansicht, Foto: © Michel Desvigne.
8 Referenzbild: Barnegat Bay, New Jersey, USA, Foto: © Michel Desvigne.
9 Wasserprojekt
10 Landanalyse und Projekt
7 De Biesbosch, model view, photo: © Michel Desvigne.
8 Reference image: Barnegat Bay, New Jersey, USA, photo: © Michel Desvigne.
9 Water project
10 Land analysis and project

Félix Guattari, *Les trois écologies*. Paris 1989[1]

In seiner kurzen, aber umso tiefgründigeren Untersuchung *Die drei Ökologien*, zuerst im Jahr 1989 veröffentlicht (1), zeigt Félix Guattari, dass sich die ökologische Praxis insgesamt nicht allein auf die Umweltproblematik bezieht, sondern immer auch gesellschaftliche und mentale Umgebungen mit einbezieht. Wir können die besorgniserregende ökologische Krise unseres Planeten solange nicht richtig verstehen, solange wir die Bereiche „Natur" und „Kultur" getrennt halten. Heute mehr denn je ist die Natur von der Kultur ununterscheidbar geworden. Wenn wir also die Interaktionen zwischen Ökosystemen, gesellschaftlichen oder individuellen Bedeutungsuniversen verstehen wollen, dann müssen wir lernen „transversal" zu denken und pseudo-wissenschaftliche Paradigmen hinter uns lassen, die Geist und Materie zu trennen trachten, ebenso wie das Individuelle vom Kollektiven oder das Unbewusste von der gesellschaftlichen Ordnung. Was für die Zukunft gefordert ist, ist viel mehr als bloß die Verteidigung der Natur. Um auf diese Krise zu antworten, müssen wir das Problem auf einer gesellschaftlichen und mentalen Ebene begreifen, ebenso auf einer politischen. In der Tat hängt die Umweltkrise mit dem zusammen, was Guattari „integrierten Weltkapitalismus" nennt. Seit den 1970er-Jahren tendiert der Kapitalismus zunehmend dazu, seine Macht weg von den Produktionsstrukturen von Waren und Dienstleistungen, und hin zur Zeichenproduktion, der Informationskontrolle (Medien, Werbung, Meinungsforschung) und der Subjektivität zu verlagern. Demzufolge hat sich die Kritik des Kapitalismus auf die Produktion neuer Arten der Subjektivität zu konzentrieren.

Wie soll man diese Produktion der Subjektivität nun beschreiben? Mit diesem Problem beschäftigt sich Guattari, das für die gesellschaftspolitische Analyse der Gegenwart von entscheidender Bedeutung ist. Diese Auseinandersetzung soll uns in die Lage versetzen, den schädlichen Effekten des herrschenden Systems entgegenzuwirken, oder aber deren ökologisch günstige Aspekte anzukurbeln. Subjektivität – eine unbewusste kollektive Produktion, für die er den Begriff „kollektives Gefüge" verwendet – muss in jedem Fall als plurale, heterogene und automatische („maschinische") verstanden werden.

Das ganze Problem, worauf der letzte Teil seines Werkes hinausläuft, besteht in der Re-Singularisierung der Subjektivitätsproduktion, der wir unterliegen, ohne dabei aber immer diese korrekt zu entschlüsseln oder umzuwandeln. Die wichtigste Aufgabe besteht hinsichtlich der Analyse der Maschinen, welche die Subjektivität produzieren und den subjektiven Kodierungen, die Guattari „Semiotik" nennt.

Dieses ambitionierte Programm beinhaltet eine gänzlich neue politische Geschichte der sozialen Gefüge, die aus der Perspektive ihrer semiotischen Kodierungen in Angriff genommen wird, mögen sich diese Gefüge auf frühere Formen, kapitalistische oder auch andere, oder auf gegenwärtige Formationen beziehen, deren Mischungen von ökonomischen, rechtlichen, techno-wissenschaftlichen Semiotiken, spezifische Subjekt-

1 Dt.: *Die drei Ökologien*, Wien 1994.

Félix Guattari, *Les trois écologies*. Paris 1989[1]

In his brief yet profound essay *The Three Ecologies*, published in 1989 (1), Félix Guattari shows that ecological praxis as a whole is not only environmental, but always also social and mental. We cannot understand our planet's serious environmental crisis, as long as we think separately the domains of "nature" and "culture." More than ever, today nature has become inseparable from culture. If we want to understand the interactions between ecosystems, social and individual universes of reference, we have to learn to think "transversally" and abandon pseudo-scientific paradigms that separate mind and matter, individual and collective, the unconscious and the social order. What is required for the future is much more than a mere defense of nature. In order to respond to this crisis, we have to understand the problem on a social and mental level, as well as a political one. In fact, the environmental crisis is linked to what Guattari calls "integrated world capitalism." Since the 1970s, capitalism has increasingly tended to move its center of power away from the structures of production of goods and services, toward structures of production of signs, of control of information (media, advertising, opinion polls), of subjectivity. Thus, the critique of capitalism centers on the production of new modes of subjectivation.

How is one to describe these productions of subjectivity? Such is the problem that Guattari deals with, and it is especially valid for the sociopolitical analysis of the present. It is a matter of making oneself capable of countering the harmful effects of the dominant system, or of ecologically stimulating its beneficial aspects. Subjectivity—an unconscious collective production for which he reserved the term "collective assemblage"—must in every case be understood as plural, heterogeneous and automatic ("machinic").

The whole problem towards which the final part of his oeuvre converges is that of a re-singularization of the productions of subjectivity that we undergo, without always decoding or inflecting them correctly. The most urgent task concerns the analysis of machines for the production of subjectivity and of subjective codings, which Guattari called "semiotics."

This ambitious program comprises a whole new political history of social assemblages, undertaken from the point of view of their semiotic codings, as much for what concerns earlier formations, whether capitalist or not, as for contem-

1 Engl. *The Three Ecologies*. London and New Brunswick, NJ 1989.

effekte mit den ihnen jeweils eigenen Werkzeugen hervorbringen. Eine solche Analyse der gegenwärtigen Situation des Kapitalismus veranlasst Guattari dazu, das subjektive und kognitive Kapital von Gesellschaften im Verhältnis zum Planeten Erde, in seiner faktischen und singulären Existenz, zu theoretisieren. Die Menschheitsgeschichte beschäftigt sich nicht mit der spirituellen Odyssee des Geistes, sondern weit mehr mit den Abenteuern des Planeten selbst. Indem er Gregory Bateson folgt, öffnet Guattari das Denken der Ökologie, indem er letztere von ihrem muffigen und rückwärtsgerichteten Beiklang, die Natur schützend zu erhalten, befreit, und mit den *Drei Ökologien* dieses Denken für eine veritable klinische Analyse der Kultur öffnet. Daraus ergibt sich eine Ethik, die der Erde treu bleibt und in der Lage ist, die Ökologie der Gesellschaftskörper mit Bewusstseinszuständen und Umweltschutzvorrichtungen zu verkoppeln.

Um die gegenwärtige Subjektproduktion verstehen zu können, müssen wir die Ergebnisse der Psychoanalyse Freuds und Lacans mit Marx' Analyse des Kapitalismus zusammen denken. Das menschliche Subjekt kann nicht auf der Ebene des Privaten oder Individuellen verstanden werden; in der Tat sollten wir nicht einmal von „Subjekten sprechen, sondern von Komponenten der Subjektivierung". Freud hatte Recht, das Unbewusste als Wunschproduktion zu begreifen, doch diese muss als gesellschaftliche und politische verstanden werden, damit das Unbewusste nicht länger

1

porary formations, with their specific alloy of economic, legal, technico-scientific semiotics, which produced their specific subjective effects with their own tools. This analysis of the current phase of capitalism led Guattari to theorize the subjective and cognitive capital of societies in relation to the Earth, in its factual and singular existence. Human history does not concern the spiritual odyssey of the mind but rather the adventure of the planet. Following Gregory Bateson, Guattari opens thinking onto ecology, freeing the latter of its grumpy and backward-looking connotation of the preservation of nature, to open it up to a veritable clinical analysis of culture, with *The Three Ecologies*, an ethics of the Earth able to arrange the ecology of social bodies with that of mental states and environmental apparatuses.

In order to understand the current production of subjectivities, we have to think the results of Freudian or Lacanian psychoanalysis together with Marx's analysis of capitalism. The human subject cannot be understood on a private and individual level; in fact, "we should not speak of subjects, but rather of components of subjectifications." Freud was right in describing the unconscious as a production of desire, but this production should be understood as a social and political one, so that the unconscious is no longer to be structured only by private symbols of parental figures (such as the Father, the Law …). What Freud decoded as the eternal structure of the human unconscious in general is in fact only a historical-social European mode of subjectivation that is a very particular social semiotics. So that the production of signs cannot be understood as a logical or symbolic one, as if the human conscience was separate from the rest of nature. Guattari proposed to understand signs as rhizomes, that is, no longer in terms of human semantics or a linguistic model, but as "sign regimes," as pragmatic semiotics producing concrete effects: as "machinic assemblages." Such semiotics are social machines, power technology and not men-

in den Schranken privater Symbole väterlicher Figuren (so wie etwa die des Vaters selbst, des Gesetzes ...) verbleibt. Was Freud als die ewige Struktur des Unbewussten im Allgemeinen dekodiert hatte, ist tatsächlich nur der europäische, geschichtliche und gesellschaftliche Modus der Subjektivierung, der auch nur einen speziellen Teil der gesellschaftlichen Semiotik ausmacht. Die Zeichenproduktion kann daher nicht als logische oder symbolische verstanden werden, so als ob das menschliche Bewusstsein vom Rest der Natur abgeschnitten sei. Guattari schlägt hingegen vor, Zeichen als Rhizome zu verstehen, das heißt, sie nicht länger in der Begrifflichkeit menschlicher Semantiken oder linguistischer Modelle zu belassen, sondern sie als „Zeichenregime" zu verstehen, als eine pragmatische Semiotik die konkrete Effekte hervorbringt: etwa „maschinische Gefüge". Solche Semiotiken sind soziale Maschinen, Machttechnologien, und keine mentalen Strukturen. Sie sind nicht aus Gedanken oder mentalen Vorstellungen fabriziert, sondern aus konkreten und materiellen Gefügen. Eine Stadt zum Beispiel, ein Flughafen oder eine Autobahn sind solche konkreten Modi der Subjektivierung, genauso wie historische Architektur oder gesellschaftliche Organisationen.

„Ein Rhizom dagegen verbindet unaufhörlich semiotische Kettenglieder, Machtorganisationen, Ereignisse aus Kunst, Wissenschaften und gesellschaftlichen Kämpfen. Ein semiotisches Kettenglied gleicht einer Wurzelknolle, in der ganz unterschiedliche sprachliche, aber auch perzeptive, mimische, gestische und kognitive Akte zusammengeschlossen sind [...]."[2] Dies ist eine allgemeine Ansammlung von Äußerung, eine Semiotik, die Subjektivität erzeugt.

Wir müssen deshalb das Verhältnis zwischen dem Individuum und der Subjektivität neu befragen. Das Individuum erscheint, in seiner/ihrer aktualen Position, als ein „Verschiebebahnhof" für Prozesse, die sozio-ökonomische Gefüge, Naturabläufe, Daten verarbeitende Maschinen einschließt. Andererseits haben wir immer die Möglichkeit, die Modi der Subjektivität, der wir jeweils angehören, zu verändern, indem wir Singularitäten und neue existenzielle Territorien wieder zurück injizieren und die mentale mit der gesellschaftlichen Ökologie kombinieren. Zum Beispiel können große gesellschaftliche und politische Krisen immer wieder zu einem neuen Gleichgewicht führen.

Es wäre absurd zu hoffen, man könne zu einer Frühform menschlicher Existenz zurückkehren, doch wir können sehr wohl in der Lage sein, Wissenschaft, Technologie und Industrie nach humaneren Zielen auszurichten. Das ist die Aufgabe der sozialen Ökologie. Sie impliziert kollektives Management und Kontrolle, anstatt dem blinden Vertrauen auf die Technokraten der Staatsapparate, die so offensichtlich vom Profitstreben bestimmt werden.

Im Sog von Datenverarbeitung und den Revolutionen in der Robotik, beim Aufstieg der Gentechnologie und der Globalisierung der Märkte wird weder die menschliche Arbeit noch das natürliche Biotop wiederkehren, nicht einmal in dem Zustand, in dem sie sich noch vor ein paar Jahrzehnten befunden haben. Wie Paul Virilio dargelegt hat, zwingt das zunehmende Tempo sowohl der menschlichen als auch der nicht-menschlichen Natur zu einer solchen existenziellen Neuorientierung. Durch die Beschleunigung der technologischen und datenverarbeitenden Umwälzungen, werden wir Zeuge der Entwicklung oder der Entfaltung eines tierischen, pflanzlichen, kosmischen und maschinischen Werdens, das schon

2 Gilles Deleuze, Félix Guattari, *Tausend Plateaus: Kapitalismus und Schizophrenie* Bd. II. Berlin 1992, S. 17.

tal structures; they are not made of thoughts or mental representations, but of concrete and material assemblages. A city, for instance, an airport or a highway are such concrete modes of subjectivation, in the same way as historical architecture or social organizations.

"A rhizome ceaselessly establishes connections between semiotic chains, organizations of power, and circumstances relative to the arts, sciences, and social struggles. A semiotic chain is like a tuber agglomerating very diverse acts, not only linguistic, but also perceptive, mimetic, gestural and cognitive ..."[2] This is a collective assemblage of enunciation, a semiotics producing subjectivity.

Therefore, we have to re-examine the relation between the individual and subjectivity. The individual would appear, in his/her actual position, as a "terminal" for processes involving socioeconomic ensembles, natural processes, data-processing machines. On the other hand, we always have the possibility of transforming the modes of subjectivity we are part of, in re-injecting singularity and new existential territories, combining mental and social ecology. For instance, major social and political crises can always lead to a new equilibrium.

It would be absurd to hope to return to a past form of human existence, but we may be able to orient science, technology and industry towards more human goals. This is the task of a social ecology. It would imply collective management and control, rather than blind reliance on the state apparatuses' technocrats, so clearly dominated by the pursuit of profit.

In the wake of the data-processing and robotics revolutions, the rise of genetic engineering, and the globalization of markets, neither human work nor the natural habitat can return, even to their state of being of a few decades ago. As Paul Virilio has pointed out, the increased speed of temporalities of both human and non-human nature will demand just such an existential reorientation. With the acceleration of the technological and data-processing revolutions, we could witness the deployment or, the unfolding of animal, vegetable, cosmic, and machinic becomings, which are already prefigured by the prodigious expansion of computer-aided subjectivity.

Therefore, ecology can no longer be understood as a return to the past, or a search for ancestral roots. We have to move forward to a mental and social ecology, if we want to solve the environmental crisis. In order to understand the mechanisms on which integrated world capitalism is founded, Guattari suggests grouping them into four main semiotic regimes:

- Economic semiotics (monetary, financial and accountancy mechanisms);
- Juridical semiotics (property deeds, various legislative measures and regulations);
- Technical-scientific semiotics (plans, diagrams, programs, studies, research);

2 Gilles Deleuze, Félix Guattari, *A Thousand Plateaus: Capitalism and Schizophrenia* vol. II. London 1987, p. 8.

durch die gewaltige Entwicklung der rechnergestützten Subjektivität vorweggenommen ist.

Aus diesem Grund kann das ökologische Denken nicht mehr als etwas Rückwärtsgewandtes verstanden werden, als etwas, das nach seinen Wurzeln sucht. Wenn wir die Umweltkrise lösen wollen, dann müssen wir uns nach Vorne bewegen, hin zu einer mentalen und gesellschaftlichen Ökonomie. Um die Mechanismen verstehen zu können, die beim integrativen Weltkapitalismus am Werk sind, schlägt Guattari vor, vier primäre semiotische Regime zu unterscheiden:

- Die Semiotik der Ökonomie (monetäre, finanzielle und steuerliche Mechanismen);
- Die Semiotik des Rechtswesens (Eigentumsrecht, verschiedene gesetzgeberische Maßnahmen und Regulative);
- Die Semiotik der Techno-Wissenschaft (Pläne, Diagramme, Programme, Studien, Forschung);
- Die Semiotik der Subjektivierung, von der schon etwas in die oben aufgelisteten drei anderen Semiotiken eingeflossen ist: Darunter fallen aber auch einige andere Bereiche, wie etwa Architektur, Stadtplanung oder öffentliche Einrichtungen („équipments collectifs").

Der Kapitalismus akkumuliert die subjektive Macht, zum einen auf der Ebene der kapitalistischen Eliten und zum anderen auch innerhalb der Reihen des Proletariats. Der Marxismus, abgesehen vom herausragenden Wert der marxschen Theorie, hat die Neigung, die ökonomische Semiotik zu isolieren, als ob die Produktion materieller Güter hinsichtlich ihrer Beziehung zur juridischen und dialogischen Semiotik eine infrastrukturelle Stellung einnähme. Doch ein solches hierarchisches Modell besitzt längst keine Relevanz mehr. Die moderne kapitalistische Formation muss in ihrer Gesamtheit betrachtet werden: Sie ist gleichzeitig produktiv, ökonomisch und subjektiv. Eine soziale Ökologie darf niemals die Tatsache aus den Augen verlieren, dass sich die kapitalistische Macht verlagert hat, sie hat sich deterritorialisiert, und zwar hinsichtlich ihres Ausmaßes – sie hat ihren Zugriff auf das ganze soziale, ökonomische und kulturelle Leben des Planeten ausgeweitet – und hinsichtlich ihrer Intensität – indem sie sogar die unbewussten Niveaus der Subjektivitäten infiltriert. Deshalb müssen wir der Einflussnahme der kapitalistischen Machtausübung auf die mentale Ökologie des Alltagslebens Widerstand leisten, geschähe dies nun individuell, nachbarschaftlich, kreativ oder personal-ethisch. Die soziale Ökologie kann nicht einfach eine Außenposition einnehmen, so wie das Gewerkschaften und andere politische Praxen tun. Für Guattari besteht die Aufgabe, der wir uns in Zukunft zu stellen haben, nicht darin, nach einem bevormundenden Konsens zu suchen, sondern darin, den Zwist zu kultivieren und singuläre Existenzen zu produzieren.

Natürlich hängt die grundsätzliche Schwierigkeit dabei mit der Art und Weise zusammen, mit der Gewerkschaften und politische Parteien, die der Theorie gemäß darum kämpfen sollten, die Interessen der Arbeiter und Unterdrückten zu verteidigen, diese krankmachenden Modelle reproduzieren, so dass die Unterdrückten selbst wiederum unbewusst repressive Macht introjizieren, die dann die Meinungsfreiheit und Entwicklungsmöglichkeiten innerhalb der eigenen Organisation ersticken.

Deshalb wird eine ökologische Praxis sich an miteinander in Verbindung stehenden heterogenen Fronten zum Ausdruck bringen müssen und isolierte und unterdrückte Singularitäten aktivieren, damit neue mikropolitische und mikrosoziale Praktiken, neue Solidaritäten und eine neue Behutsamkeit organisiert werden kann, während im selben Zuge neue ästhetische und analy-

- Semiotics of subjectification, some of which are listed above: we should add a number of others, including architecture, town planning, public amenities ("équipements collectifs").

Capitalism is accumulation of subjective power, both at the level of the capitalist elites, and in the ranks of the proletariat. Marxism, despite the great value of Marx's theory, shows a tendency to isolate economic semiotics, as if the production of material goods occupied an infrastructural position in relation to juridical and dialogical semiotics. But this hierarchical model is no longer relevant. The modernist capitalist formation has to be regarded in its entirety: simultaneously productive, economic, and subjective. Social ecology should never lose sight of the fact that capitalist power has become de-localized, deterritorialized, both in extension—by extending its grasp over the whole social, economic and cultural life of the planet—and intensively—by infiltrating the most unconscious levels of subjectivities. Therefore, we have to confront the effects of capitalist power on the mental ecology of daily life, be it individual, neighborly, creative, or personal-ethical. Social ecology cannot simply assume an external position, as existing trade union and political practices do. For Guattari, the task facing us in the future is not that of seeking an infantilizing consensus, but of cultivating dissension and singular production of existence.

Of course, the principal difficulty relates to the way in which unions and political parties, which in theory should struggle to defend the interests of workers and the oppressed, reproduce pathogenic models, so that the oppressed are themselves unconsciously introjecting repressive power, which stifles freedom of expression and innovation in their own organization.

Therefore, the new ecological praxis will have to articulate themselves across interconnected and heterogeneous fronts, and activate isolated and repressed singularities, in order to organize new micro-political and micro-social practices, new solidarities, a new gentleness, while at the same time applying new aesthetic and analytical practices to the formation of the unconscious. "Our objective should be to nurture individual cultures, while at the same time inventing new contracts of citizenship: to create an order of the state in which singularity, exceptions, and rarity coexist under the least oppressive possible conditions," he writes in *The Three Ecologies*.

Ecological praxis might be defined as a search to identify, in each partial locus of existence, the potential vectors of subjectivation and re-singularization. Our only common future lies in our capacity to sustain the production of singular existences, or to re-singularize serialized ensembles. That is, as Guattari puts it, to draw new existential cartographies. In this program, art and politics should be thought together, within social productive forces. A fundamental reconstruction of social mechanisms is necessary to confront the ravages produced by integrated world capitalism. But this re-

tische Praktiken hinsichtlich der Formationen des Unbewussten zur Anwendung kommen werden. „Unser Ziel sollte es sein, individuelle Kulturen zu fördern, während wir zur selben Zeit neue Gesellschaftsverträge entwerfen: eine Staatsordnung schaffen, in der Singularitäten, Ausnahmen und Seltenes miteinander unter nach Möglichkeit minimalen Unterdrückungsverhältnissen existieren", schreibt Guattari in den *Drei Ökologien*.

Man kann die ökologische Praxis als eine Suche begreifen, die sich darum bemüht, die potenziellen Vektoren der Subjektivierung und Resingularisierung, in jedem Teilgebiet ihres Auftretens, zu identifizieren. Unsere einzige gemeinsame Zukunft verdankt sich der Fähigkeit, die Produktion singulärer Existenzen aufrechtzuerhalten, oder serialisierte Ensembles zu resingularisieren. Das heißt also, mit den Worten Guattaris, neue existenzielle Kartografien zu erstellen. In einem solchen Programm sind Kunst und Politik innerhalb der gesellschaftlichen Produktivkräfte zusammen zu denken. Eine grundsätzliche Rekonstruktion der gesellschaftlichen Mechanismen ist notwendig, um die Verheerungen zu bekämpfen, die der integrative Weltkapitalismus verursacht hat. Doch eine solche Rekonstruktion kann nicht mittels Reformen, Gesetzen, Erlässen oder bürokratischen Programmen von oben herab erfolgen. Sie verlangt die Unterstützung innovativer Praktiken, die Weiterverbreitung alternativer Experimente, welche beständig Singularität und Arbeit in die Produktion der Subjektivität einbringen; in eine Subjektivität, die autonom bleibt und dennoch ein Scharnier zur übrigen Gesellschaft bildet.

Gemeinsam mit der Daten verarbeitenden Revolution, tauchen auch die Biotechnologien, die beschleunigte Fortpflanzung und die neuen Modalitäten der Subjektivierung auf. Wir sollten dabei einige Faktoren nicht außer Acht lassen, welche die Möglichkeit bieten, neue Modi der Subjektivität für unsere gesellschaftlichen Existenzen zu schaffen:

- Das Potenzial, des plötzlichen Aufbrechens einer massenhaften Bewusstwerdung;
- Die Möglichkeit neuer transformatorischer Gefüge des gesellschaftlichen Kampfes, Möglichkeiten also, die sich aus dem progressiven Kollaps des Stalinismus in seinen zahlreichen Verkörperungen ergeben;
- Das Potenzial die Technologie der Massenmedien für nicht-kapitalistische Zwecke zu benutzen, was durch die immer weiter sinkenden Kosten und der technologischen Entwicklung auf diesem Gebiet möglich wird;
- Eine erweitere Produktion, sowohl auf individuellem wie auch auf kollektivem Niveau, einer „kreationistischen" Subjektivität.

Um diese Welten auf andere Weise als durch diese reine abstrakte Information ins Leben zu rufen, muss diese dreifache ökologische Vision der gesellschaftlichen, mentalen und umweltschützerischen Ökologie Referenzuniversen kreieren und existenzielle Territorien schaffen, in denen Singularität und Endlichkeit von der mehrwertigen Logik mentaler Ökologien und sozioökologischer politischer Kämpfe umfangen werden.

Anne Sauvagnargues
(Übersetzung Andreas L. Hofbauer)

construction cannot be achieved by top-down reforms, laws, decrees, or bureaucratic programs. It requires the promotion of innovative practices, proliferation of alternative experiments, which respect singularity and work permanently at the production of a subjectivity which is autonomous, yet articulated with the rest of society.

With the data-processing revolution, the rise of biotechnologies, accelerated creation, new modalities of subjectivization are emerging. We should not underestimate several factors that show the possibility of creating new modes of subjectivity for our social existences:

- the potential for sudden upsurges of mass awareness;
- the possibilities for new transformational assemblages of social struggles, possibilities that arise out of the progressive collapse of Stalinism in its various incarnations;
- the potential use of mass media technology for non-capitalist ends, as a result of declining costs and continuing technological advancement (miniaturization in particular);
- the increased production, both on the individual and collective levels, of a "creationist" subjectivity.

In order to bring into being worlds other than these of pure abstract information, this triple ecological vision of social, mental and environmental ecology has to engender universes of reference and existential territories in which singularity and finitude are embraced by the multivalent logic of mental ecologies and socio-ecological political struggles.

Anne Sauvagnargues

Rezensionen

Wider die Anpassung: Zwischen digitalisierter Macht und zeitloser Hoffnung

Kafkas Raum im Zeitalter seiner digitalen Überwachbarkeit
Sigrid Hauser
Wien: Löcker Verlag, 2009
deutsch, 296 Seiten, 16 Farbabbildungen, broschiert
ISBN: 978-3-85409-519-4
EUR 29,80

Mit Hannah Arendt gesprochen, konstruiert Franz Kafka in seinen Texten Grundrisse der bestehenden Welt. Grundrisse sind etwas Unwirkliches, Artifizielles. Sie nehmen die Interpretation der Realisierung vorweg.

In ihrem Buch *Kafkas Raum im Zeitalter seiner digitalen Überwachbarkeit* (2) konfrontiert die an der TU Wien lehrende Architekturtheoretikerin Sigrid Hauser die heute allgegenwärtige digitale Vernetzung und Überwachung mit Passagen aus Kafkas Romanen. Zwei sehr unterschiedliche Typen von Kapiteln wechseln sich jeweils ab: Ein Abschnitt beschäftigt sich mit einem kafkaesken Thema, der darauffolgende mit einem Stichwort aus der Sicherheits-, Überwachungs- und Medienwelt. Die Autorin bezieht sich dabei auf Walter Benjamins *Das Kunstwerk im Zeitalter seiner technischen Reproduzierbarkeit* und denkt dessen Kritik technischer Medien und deren Einfluss auf die Gesellschaft konsequent in die Gegenwart weiter. Benjamin habe als einer der ersten erkannt, dass Kafkas Werk nicht nur totalitäre Regimes, sondern auch die heutige Informationsgesellschaft mit ihren undurchschaubaren Netzwerken fast prophetisch vorwegnehme. Deren literarische Verarbeitung erweise sich heute als ein Schlüssel, um unsere Realität besser zu verstehen. Damals wie heute passierten einschneidende Veränderungen schneller als begreifbar. Wo die technische und gesellschaftliche Entwicklung hinführe, sei nicht absehbar, „es liegt erst in der Luft, nicht im allgemeinen Befinden".

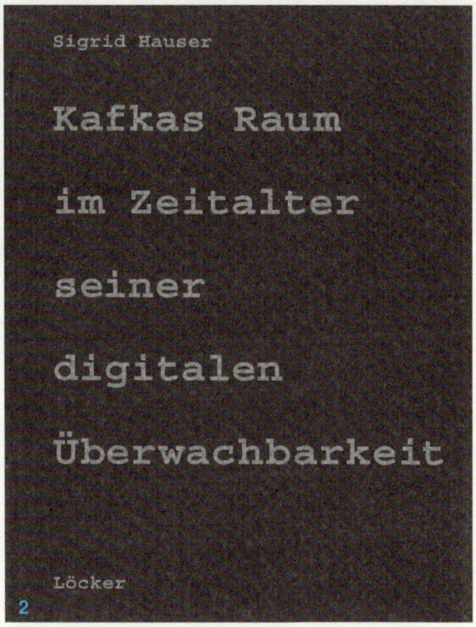

2

So wie Kafka weit über seine Zeit hinaus denkt, betrachtet er auch den Raum über die Grenzen seiner Darstellbarkeit hinaus. Konkrete und abstrakte Architekturen geben der Handlung einen Rahmen, ohne sie dabei zu determinieren: Gänge, Treppen, Lifte, Fluchtwege, eine Portiersloge – ein unzusammenhängendes, nicht überblickbares System von Innenräumen. Die Architektur des Hotels Occidental in *Der Verschollene*

Reviews

Against Conformance: Between Digital Power and Timeless Hope

Kafkas Raum im Zeitalter seiner digitalen Überwachbarkeit
Sigrid Hauser
Vienna: Löcker Verlag, 2009
German, 296 pages, 16 color images, paperback
ISBN: 978-3-85409-519-4
EUR 29.80

To quote Hannah Arendt, Franz Kafka devises the blueprints of the existing world. But blueprints are a bit unreal, artificial. They anticipate the interpretation of the realization.

In *Kafkas Raum im Zeitalter seiner digitalen Überwachbarkeit* [*Kafka's Space in the Age of Digital Surveillance*] (2), Sigrid Hauser, an architecture theorist at the Vienna University of Technology, confronts today's ubiquitous digital networking and monitoring with passages from Kafka's novels. Two fundamentally different kinds of chapters take turns: the first section addresses a Kafkaesque topos the section following it focuses on a keyword in the security, surveillance and media world. Referring to Walter Benjamin's *The Work of Art in the Age of Mechanical Reproduction* the author extends the criticism of technical media and their influence on society consistently to the present. Benjamin was one of the first to recognize that Kafka's work prophetically prefigured not only totalitarian regimes, but also today's information society with its impenetrable networks. Their literary treatment has turned out to be a master key for better grasping our reality. Then, as now, major changes happened too fast for us to understand. Where the technical and social development lead, was not foreseeable, "it is only in the air, not in the general condition."

Just as Kafka thinks far ahead of his time, he also looks at space beyond the limits of its representation. Concrete and abstract architectures provide a framework for action without determining it: corridors, stairways, elevators, emergency exits, a porter lodge—an incoherent, incomprehensible system of interior spaces. The architecture of the Hotel Occidental is in *The Missing Person* another opaque power structure. Kafka provides no visibility from the outside and only describes fragments of the interior. People are interchangeable and take the role of extras; who plays the main protagonist remains undecidable. The function of architecture is to get a person to lose her orientation and forget the goal. It is difficult to find the path of one's own.

Kafka's protagonists are always faced with overwhelming power structures that have built

gibt eine undurchschaubare Machtstruktur wieder. Kafka liefert keinen Überblick von außen, sondern beschreibt nur Fragmente des Inneren. Die Menschen sind austauschbar und übernehmen die Rolle von Statisten; wer in diesem System die Hauptrolle spielt, bleibt im Dunklen. Die Architektur dient dazu, die Orientierung zu verlieren und das Ziel vergessen zu lassen. Die Suche nach dem eigenen Weg wird erschwert.

Kafkas Protagonisten sind stets konfrontiert mit übermächtigen Machtapparaten, die ein unüberblickbares System an Regeln und Abhängigkeiten aufgebaut haben. Die Macht selbst bleibt im Verborgenen und ist nicht lokalisierbar. Ob sie tatsächlich existiert, ist irrelevant, solange ein gefestigtes gesellschaftliches Gefüge auf Basis der Idee dieser Macht besteht.

In den Romanen *Das Schloss*, *Der Prozess* und *Der Verschollene* zeichnet Kafka das Bild dreier kausal verknüpfter gesellschaftlicher Systeme: ein inkompetentes Staatswesen, das es unterstützende Rechtssystem und die davon profitierende Marktwirtschaft. Heute sind diese enger verknüpft als je zuvor und führen zu einer neuen Konzentration von Macht in Form der Global Player. Durch die Digitalisierung konvergieren Schrift, Bild und Ton und ermöglichen eine Bündelung früher getrennter Kommunikationsnetzwerke, wodurch sich ungeahnte Potenziale der Kontrolle und der Manipulation ergeben.

Die Gerichtskanzleien in *Der Prozess* befinden sich auf den Dachböden von Mietshäusern: „Die Wohnhäuser sind die Gerichte". Geht die Macht also vom Volk aus? Oder überwacht hier ein scheindemokratisches System die Masse? Gerade dass sich Kafka nicht auf eine Ideologie konzentriert, sondern sich mit dem Verhältnis des Individuums zur Gesellschaft auseinandersetzt, macht sein Werk so interessant. Jeder seiner Protagonisten muss – und will – sich an die Anforderungen der Gesellschaft anpassen, sucht Anerkennung und Akzeptanz. Die Integration, ja Assimilation, produziert am Ende eigenschaftslose Personen, die ihre Rolle wie Schauspieler spielen.

Hand in Hand mit der Demokratie geht die Demokratisierung der Überwachung. Wurden früher „nur" einzelne Gruppen systematisch überwacht, so heute potenziell jede und jeder. An technischen Methoden mangelt es nicht, wie die Zusammenstellung der Autorin eindrucksvoll demonstriert: Überwachungskameras mit Personenerkennung, Tracking mittels Satelliten oder Funknetzen, RFID-Chips und vor allem eine enorme Menge an personalisierten Daten, die allerorts gesammelt, gespeichert, verknüpft und ausgewertet werden. Mit einem allzu lockeren Umgang mit Google und Facebook nehmen wir den Überwachern sogar einiges an Arbeit ab.

In ihren scharfsichtigen Analysen von Kafkas Texten bedient sich Hauser vieler Metaphern aus dem Theater. So versteht sie seine Raumbeschreibungen als Regieanweisungen, die viel Raum für Imagination lassen. Mit dem Bild des Theaters und durch die Verzerrung von Alltäglichem und Vertrautem ins Absurde erzeuge Kafka eine Künstlichkeit, die das Geschehen wie eine Inszenierung reflektierbar mache.

Als besonders interessant erscheint Hauser das Motiv des Fensters und des Balkons. In der literarischen Darstellung von Architektur stehe das Fenster für Zuschauen, Beobachten und Verfolgen – für soziale Kontrolle. Der Beobachter nehme zwar nicht direkt teil, blicke aber auf eine Welt, die sich nicht so einfach erschließen lasse, die auch nicht jeden einlassen wolle. Der Zuschauer werde durch das Fenster aber auch selbst zum Objekt der Betrachtung. Das Fenster mache aus der Realität jene Inszenierung, die Kafka als artifizielles Konstrukt verwende, um die Wirklichkeit sichtbar zu machen.

up an impossibly complex system of rules and dependencies. The power itself remains hidden and cannot be localized. Whether it exists is actually irrelevant, as long as a consolidated social structure is based on the idea that this power exists.

In the novels *The Castle*, *The Trial* and *The Missing Person*, Kafka draws the picture of three causally linked social systems: an incompetent state, the legal system that supports it, and market economy that draws profits from it. Today these three are more closely linked than ever before and lead to a new concentration of power in the form of a global player. Digitization converges words, images and sound, and connects previously separate communications networks, resulting in unknown potentials of control and manipulation.

The court offices in *The Trial* are situated in the attics of apartment houses: "The houses are the courts." So does the power come from the people? Or is a seemingly democratic system here monitoring the masses? What makes Kafka's work so interesting is precisely that he did not focus on ideology, but rather on the relationship of the individual to society. Each of his protagonists must—and will—adapt to the demands of society, seeking recognition and acceptance. The integration, even assimilation, in the end produced men without qualities who play a role like an actor would.

Hand in hand with democracy proceeds the democratization of surveillance. If in the past "only" certain groups were systematically monitored, today everyone can be under constant surveillance. There is no lack of technological methods, as the author impressively demonstrates: surveillance cameras with personal identification, tracking by satellite or wireless networks, RFID chips, and above all, a tremendous amount of personalized data that is collected, stored, combined and analyzed everywhere. With an all-too-casual use of Google or Facebook, we even do some of the supervisors' work for them.

In her perceptive analyses of Kafka's texts, Hauser makes use of many theatrical metaphors. She understands his spatial descriptions as stage directions, allowing lots of room for imagination. Following the image of the theater and distorting the everyday and familiar into the absurd, Kafka creates an artificiality that lets us reflect on that which is actually happening.

For Hauser, the motive of the window and the balcony is particularly interesting. In literary representations of architecture, the window usually stands for watching, monitoring and tracking—for social control. The observers do not directly take part but instead look at a world that does not open up so easily or let just anyone enter. At the same time, the window also turns the viewer into an object of the gaze. The window turns reality into the kind of *mise-en-scène* that Kafka applied as an artificial construct to make reality visible.

Just like Kafka's texts can be read at different levels, Hauser's book also works on several levels. A good part of it consists of italicized quotes which call the reader's attention to the power of

So wie Kafkas Literatur auf verschiedenen Ebenen gelesen werden kann, funktioniert auch Hausers Buch auf mehreren Ebenen. Es besteht zu einem guten Teil aus kursiv gesetzten Zitaten und führt so dem Leser die Macht der Sprache vor Augen. Die Zitate aus der aktuellen Politik-, Wirtschafts- und Mediensprache verführen, manipulieren und erzeugen fast unbemerkt eine *eben nicht* eigene Meinung. Im Kontrast zur fein gewobenen Sprache Kafkas führt diese sprachliche Authentizität jedoch auch dazu, dass die zwei Teile nie wirklich zusammenfinden und die Doppelconference von Kafkas Texten mit der heutigen digitalen Realität zwar auf der intellektuellen Ebene perfekt, auf der emotionalen aber nur bedingt gelingt.

Kafkas Romane sind Fragmente, die viel Raum für Spekulation lassen. Auch Sigrid Hauser, die sich schon in zahlreichen Publikationen mit der Konzeptions- und Rezeptionsästhetik von Politik, Literatur und Kunst im Zusammenspiel mit Architektur befasst hat, lässt in diesem bemerkenswerten Buch die Reihe der Protagonisten der Überwachung offen; sie schreibt die Zukunft nicht fest. Ganz im Sinne Kafkas wird das letzte Wort nicht gesprochen.

Martin Grabner

Nimbus und Ikone

Clemens Holzmeister.
Architekt zwischen Kunst und Politik
Wilfried Posch
mit einem Werkverzeichnis von Monika Knofler
Salzburg: Müry Salzmann, 2010
deutsch, 414 Seiten, Hardcover
ISBN 978-3-99014-020-8
EUR 29,90

Clemens Holzmeister (1886–1983) zählt zu Österreichs wichtigen Architekten. Seine Kirchen in Deutschland, die Regierungsbauten für die neue türkische Hauptstadt Ankara oder die Gestaltung des Salzburger Festspielbezirks sind ein wesentlicher Beitrag zur Architektur der ersten Hälfte des 20. Jahrhunderts. Als Rektor der Wiener Akademie der bildenden Künste, als Staatsrat des Ständestaates und „Präsident von allem", wie er es selbst nannte, gehörte er zweifellos zu den einflussreichsten Persönlichkeiten im Österreich der 1930er-Jahre. Neben Selbstbiografien von 1937 und 1976, einem umfassenden Werksverzeichnis von Monika Knofler,[1] zahllosen Artikeln zu einzelnen Bauwerken oder Gebäudetypen, einer Ausstellung in Innsbruck[2] und einem Symposion in Istanbul,[3] fehlt bis heute eine kritische Auseinandersetzung mit seinem Gesamtwerk.

Im Sommer 2010 hat Wilfried Posch, Professor emeritus für Städtebau, Raumplanung und Wohnungswesen an der Universität für Gestaltung in Linz, sein Werk *Clemens Holzmeister. Architekt zwischen Kunst und Politik* (3) im Salzburger Verlag Müry Salzmann herausgebracht; ein Buch, das unter dem selben Titel schon vor vier Jahren beim Molden-Verlag angekündigt war.

Laut Eigendefinition handelt es sich um „keine Architekturmonographie im herkömmlichen Sinne, [...] sondern [um] eine ‚politische Biographie' die natürlich auch auf Holzmeisters künstlerische Entwicklung eingeht" (S. 5). Der Klappentext nennt „diese politische Biografie den

1 Monika Knofler, *Clemens Holzmeister. Das architektonische Werk*, Diss. Universität Innsbruck 1976; dies., „Werksverzeichnis", in: *Clemens Holzmeister*. Wiener Akademie-Reihe Bd. 9, Ausst.-Kat. Wien 1982; nunmehr im Anhang auf den neuesten Stand gebracht, S. 382–406.

2 Georg Rigele, Georg Loewit (Hg.), *Clemens Holzmeister*. Innsbruck 2000; die Ausstellung wurde auch in Ankara, Istanbul und Wien gezeigt.

3 *Clemens Holzmeister. Architekt zwischen Tradition und Moderne*, Istanbul, April 2003, publiziert als: Aydan Balamir (Hg.), *Clemens Holzmeister: Çağın Dönümünde Bir Mimar/Architect at the Turn of an Era*. Boyut Yayınevi 2010.

language. Quotations from current political, economic and media language seduce, manipulate and generate almost impercebtibly opinions that are not one's own. In contrast to the finely woven language of Kafka's, this linguistic authenticity results in the two parts never really coming together, so that the conference of Kafka's text with today's digital reality works perfectly on the intellectual level but succeeds only in part on the emotional level.

Kafka's novels are fragments that leave lots of room for speculation. In this remarkable book, Sigrid Hauser—who has already in numerous previous publications addressed the conception and reception aesthetics of politics, literature and art in relation to architecture—also leaves the protagonists of the surveillance undetermined; she does not fix the future. In keeping with Kafka's world, the last word has not yet been spoken.

Martin Grabner

Halo and Icon

Clemens Holzmeister.
Architekt zwischen Kunst und Politik
Wilfried Posch
with a catalogue raisonné by Monika Knofler
Salzburg: Müry Salzmann, 2010
German, 414 pages, hardcover
ISBN 978-3-99014-020-8
EUR 29,90

Clemens Holzmeister (1886–1983) is one of the most important Austrian architects. His churches in Germany, the government buildings for the new Turkish capital of Ankara, or the design of the Salzburg Festival district are significant contributions to the architecture of the first half of the 20th century. As president of the Vienna Academy of Fine Arts, as State Council of the corporate state and as the "President of All Things" as he called himself, he was undoubtedly among the most influential personalities in Austria in the 1930s. Despite two autobiographies (published in 1937 and 1976), a comprehensive catalogue raisonné (compiled by Monika Knofler),[1] numerous essays on individual buildings or building types, an exhibition in Innsbruck[2] and a symposium in Istanbul,[3] until now there has been no critical discussion of his complete oeuvre.

In the summer of 2010, Wilfried Posch, Professor Emeritus of Urban Planning and Housing at the University of Design in Linz, launched his book *Clemens Holzmeister: Architekt zwischen Kunst und Politik* [*Clemens Holzmeister: Archi-*

1 Monika Knofler, *Clemens Holzmeister: Das architektonische Werk*. Doctoral thesis University of Innsbruck 1976; idem, "Werksverzeichnis," in: *Clemens Holzmeister* (Wiener Akademie-Reihe vol. 9). Exhib. Cat. Vienna 1982; now updated in the appendix (pp. 382–406).

2 Georg Rigele, Georg Loewitt, *Clemens Holzmeister*. Innsbruck 2000; the exhibition was also on display in Ankara, Istanbul, and Vienna.

3 *Clemens Holzmeister: Architekt zwischen Tradition und Moderne*, Istanbul, April 2003, published as: Aydan Balamir (ed.), *Clemens Holzmeister: Çağın Dönümünde Bir Mimar/Architect at the Turn of an Era*. Boyut Yayınevi 2010.

Roman eines bewegten Jahrhunderts". In der Unentschiedenheit zwischen politischer oder doch Architekten-Biografie mit akademischem Anspruch einerseits und Roman andererseits ist das Buch entlang einer biografisch-chronologischen Zeitachse angelegt, die von den Vorfahren über Kindheit und Jugend und den Jahren von 1924[4] bis 1938 handelt. Mit der Emigration Holzmeisters in die Türkei in diesem Jahr findet sie schon fast ihr Ende. Von den über 700 Projekten, die Holzmeister in seinem fast hundert Jahre dauernden Leben verfasst hat, wird nur ein kleiner Teil angesprochen, die künstlerische Entwicklung vernachlässigt.

Wilfried Posch beschäftigt sich seit vielen Jahren mit dem Architekten Clemens Holzmeister, hat dazu nicht nur, wie aus Anmerkungen und Bibliografie hervorgeht, ein Forschungsprojekt geleitet, sondern weitere Beiträge verfasst, auf die aber nur teilweise hingewiesen wird.[5] Man hätte dem grafisch schön gestalteten Band mehr Durchgriffe des Lektorats gewünscht, um Doppelgleisigkeiten, Wiederholungen und Ungereimtheiten hintan zu stellen. Holzmeisters eigene Erinnerungen werden entweder unüberprüft übernommen oder als fehlerhaft bezeichnet. Erstaunen rufen verschiedene Behauptungen hervor, so jene, Holzmeister habe Johannes van Acken nie erwähnt (S. 166)[6] und daher sei dessen Einfluss auf Holzmeister erst durch Poschs Forschung belegt. Hier ist auf Holzmeisters Schrift *Pflege des Kirchengrundrisses* von 1929 zu verweisen. Für die Behauptung, Casimir Heinrich Baer, ein bedeutender deutsch-schweizer Architekt und Kunsthistoriker, sei Holzmeisters Mitarbeiter gewesen (S. 103), bleibt Posch leider den Nachweis schuldig. Bislang hieß der Mitarbeiter Bähr.

Vollends unverständlich und abzulehnen ist die Bewertung und Beurteilung respektive die gewählte Sprache des Autors, wenn es um die Zeit von 1933 bzw. 1938 bis 1945 geht. So handelt er im Kapitel „Bewegte Jahre" „Die Judenfrage" ab (S. 247) und verharmlost den späteren Kriegsverbrecher Arthur Seyss-Inquart (S. 257). Die jüngere kunsthistorische Forschung zur unrühmlichen Rolle Hubert Schrades während des Nationalsozialismus und auch zu dessen Buch *Das deutsche Nationaldenkmal*, auf das sich Posch bezieht, wird ignoriert,[7] ja, Schrade erscheint bei Posch als „ein wichtiger Deuter der nationalsozialistischen Architektur" (S. 187).

3

4 1924: Berufung Holzmeisters als Professor an die Akademie der bildenden Künste in Wien.

5 Wilfried Posch, Georg Rigele, „Die Karriere des Clemens Holzmeister zwischen Kunst und Politik", in: *Kunsthistoriker* 12/14 (1997/98), S. 95–105; Wilfried Posch, „An der Wende vieler Zeiten – Clemens Holzmeister zwischen Kunst und Politik", in: Rigele 2000 (Anm. 2), S. 48–66.

6 Johannes van Acken, *Christozentrische Kirchenkunst. Ein Entwurf zum liturgischen Gesamtkunstwerk*, 2. Aufl. Gladbeck 1923.

tect between art and politics] (3), published by Müry Salzmann (although announced under the same title already four years earlier by Molden Verlag).

According to the author, this is "no architectural monograph in the traditional sense, … but a 'political biography' in which Holzmeister's artistic development naturally plays a role" (p. 5). The blurb describes "this political biography" as "the novel of a turbulent century." Without clearly deciding between an academic study (whether a political biography or an architectural monograph) on the one hand and a work of fiction on the other, the book proceeds along a biographical timeline stretching from the architect's ancestors to his childhood and youth and over to the years from 1924[4] to 1938. With Holzmeister's emigration to Turkey in the latter year the book almost reaches its end. Disregarding Holzmeister's artistic development, the author discusses only a small part of the more than 700 projects planned by the architect in his life that lasted almost a century.

As the notes and bibliography of the book show, Posch's long involvement with Holzmeister has not only initiated a research project, but he has also written several articles to which the present work only refers in part.[5] Although the book boasts a beautiful layout, it would have benefited from better editing to remove duplication, repetition and inconsistencies. Holzmeister's own recollections are either uncritically accepted or rejected as erroneous. There are allegations that raise eyebrows, such as the claim that Holzmeister would never have mentioned Johannes van Acken (p. 166)[6] so that the latter's influence on the architect would only have been demonstrated by Posch's research. The claim is easily disproved by Holzmeister's essay *Pflege des Kirchengrundrisses* [*The Care of the Church Plan*] from 1929. Posch's suggestion that Casimir Heinrich Baer, an important German-Swiss architect and art historian, would have been Holzmeister's assistant (p. 103) needs verification; until now the employee has been known as Bähr.

Completely incomprehensible and unacceptable are the author's judgment and language when it comes to the time from 1933 or 1938 to 1945. In the chapter "Turbulent Years," he deals with "the Jewish question" (p. 247) and later plays down the activities of the war criminal, Arthur Seyss-Inquart (p. 257). The author ignores recent art historical research on Hubert Schrade's disreputable role during the Nazi years, and quotes from his book *Das deutsche Nationaldenkmal* [*The German National Monument*],[7] calling Schrade "an important interpreter of National Socialist architecture" (p. 187).

4 In 1924, Holzmeister was appointed full professor at the Academy of Fine Arts in Vienna.

5 Wilfried Posch, Georg Rigele, "Die Karriere des Clemens Holzmeister zwischen Kunst und Politik," in: *Kunsthistoriker* 12/14 (1997/98), pp. 95–105; Wilfried Posch, "An der Wende vieler Zeiten – Clemens Holzmeister zwischen Kunst und Politik," in: Rigele 2000 (fn. 2), pp. 48–66.

6 Johannes van Acken, *Christozentrische Kirchenkunst. Ein Entwurf zum liturgischen Gesamtkunstwerk*, 2nd ed. Gladbeck 1923.

Das Fehlen einer nachvollziehbaren Methode im Bewerten und Auswerten der Fakten, in der Benützung und Auswahl von Quellen und im Analysieren und Gewichten derselben, sowie offensichtliche Begriffsverwirrungen (wie z. B. „Kulturliberalismus" im Zusammenhang mit dem Heimatschutzverein „Deutsche Heimat"; S. 43, 78) sind als Gravamina zu benennen. Dazu kommt das Verwenden klischeehafter Epitheta wie „Nimbus" für Holzmeisters Ruf oder „Ikone" für die Person Peter Behrens.

Zu den Verdiensten des Buches gehört zweifellos, dass Posch im Österreichischen Staatsarchiv die Akten des Staatsrates gesichtet hat und jene Schriftstücke, die Holzmeister betreffen, im Anhang publizierte. Schon zu Lebzeiten, aber vor allem nach seinem Tod wurde Holzmeister in der akademischen Forschung als Gegenpol zu jenen Architekten bewertet, „die links, liberal und jüdisch" waren. Es wäre an der Zeit, diese Gegensätze nicht nur aufzuzeigen, sondern auch zu einer objektiven Bewertung zu kommen. Durch das Heranziehen obskurer Autoren bzw. deren noch obskurerem Umfeld (z. B. Konrad Kurt Brieger und Sig Run, *Pan-Arische Jugendzeitschrift*, S. 191) oder der kritiklosen Überbewertung der „Deutschen Heimat" – einer von vielen Heimatschutzvereinen in Österreich – ist dies sicherlich nicht zu erreichen.

Ein nüchternes Fazit muss diesem Buch zugutehalten, dass es die Bemühungen des Autors wiedergibt, die Person Clemens Holzmeister in einem politischen Kontext während hundert langer Jahre darzustellen. Die gleichzeitige Nutzung von Romanen, Stadtführern, einer selektiven, nicht nachvollziehbaren Auswahl wissenschaftlicher Arbeiten, ist nicht angemessen und macht aus Jahrzehnten Forschung leider nur ein populärwissenschaftliches Werk. Der oben angesprochene Roman liest sich streckenweise spannend, vor allem in jenen Passagen, in denen sich Posch eng an Holzmeisters eigene Erinnerungen hält, zeichnet die komplexen Vorgänge „eines bewegten Jahrhunderts nach", kann aber mit bedeutenden biografischen Romanen schwerlich mithalten.

„Zukünftige Forschungen", meint der Autor bereits in der Einleitung, „werden wohl noch neue Einzelheiten hinzufügen, das Gesamtbild aber nicht mehr entscheidend verändern" (S. 5). Georg Rigele hat Clemens Holzmeister schon 1997 „den Herrn seiner Biografie" genannt.[8] Wilfried Posch scheint daran anzuschließen. Es ist zu hoffen, dass das Gesamtbild durch neue Fragenstellungen sehr wohl noch verändert wird.

Marena Marquet

7 Heinrich Dilly, *Deutsche Kunsthistoriker. 1933–1945*. München und Berlin, 1988; Dietrich Schubert, „Heidelberger Kunstgeschichte unterm Hakenkreuz: Professoren im Übergang zur NS Diktatur und nach 1933", in: *Kunstgeschichte im „Dritten Reich": Theorien, Methoden, Praktiken*. Berlin 2008, S. 65–86.

8 Rigele 2000 (Anm. 2), S. 96.

Von der Schwierigkeit, Nietzsche-Leser zu lesen

Der philosophische Flaneur – Nietzsche und die Architektur (4)
Jörg H. Gleiter
Würzburg: Königshausen & Neumann, 2009
(Habilitationsschrift an der Architekturfakultät der Bauhaus Universität Weimar, 2007)
deutsch, 193 Seiten, Illustrationen, broschiert
ISBN 978-3-8260-3758-0
EUR 24,80

Jörg Gleiter hat bei verschiedenen Gelegenheiten den Versuch unternommen,[1] neben der klassischen Architekturgeschichtsschreibung und der seit den 1970er-Jahren etablierten Architektur-

Other problems include the lack of any detectable method as regards the use of sources or the analysis and weighing of factual evidence, as well as conceptual confusions (as in the author's reference to "cultural liberalism" in connection with the heritage society *Deutsche Heimat* [German Homeland]; pp. 43, 78). Unfortunate are also the clichés, such as describing Holzmeister's reputation as a "halo" or calling Peter Behrens an "icon."

Among the merits of the book is certainly that Posch has examined the files of the State Council in the Austrian State Archives and includes the documents that pertain to Holzmeister in the appendix. Already when he was still alive, but especially after his death, Holzmeister has been viewed by academic researchers as a counterpoint to "left-wing, liberal and Jewish" architects. Now it would be time not only to identify such oppositions, but to evaluate them objectively. This cannot be attained by references to obscure writers, or their even more obscure circles (e.g., Konrad Kurt Brieger and Sig Run, *Pan-Arische Jugendzeitschrift* [*Pan-Aryan youth magazine*], p. 191) or by the uncritical overvaluation of the *Deutsche Heimat* which was just one of many heritage societies in Austria.

One has to give the book credit for reflecting the efforts of the author to present the person Clemens Holzmeister in a political context over a period of a long hundred years. The simultaneous use of novels, city guides and a random selection of scientific studies is inappropriate and extracts, unfortunately, only a popular essay from decades of research. Posch's "novel of the century" gets exciting in those passages where the author adheres closely to Holzmeister's own memories and traces the complexities of a turbulent period, but it does not really compare with important biographical novels.

"Future research," states the author in the introduction, "will probably be able to add some new details, but it will not change the overall picture decisively" (p. 5). Already in 1997, Georg Rigele called Clemens Holzmeister "the master of his own biography."[8] Wilfried Posch seems to agree with this assessment. One can only hope that truly new questions will eventually change the overall picture.

Marena Marquet

7 Heinrich Dilly, *Deutsche Kunsthistoriker: 1933–1945*. Munich, Berlin 1988; Dietrich Schubert, "Heidelberger Kunstgeschichte unterm Hakenkreuz: Professoren im Übergang zur NS Diktatur und nach 1933," in: *Kunstgeschichte im "Dritten Reich": Theorien, Methoden, Praktiken*. Berlin 2008, pp. 65–86.

8 Rigele 2000 (fn. 2), p. 96.

theorie eine weitere Plattform für das Nachdenken über Architektur zu begründen, die sich am besten als Architekturphilosophie beschreiben ließe. Nietzsche passt hervorragend in dieses Programm einer Ausweitung des Faches, gerade weil es sich bei der Befragung seiner Architekturvorstellungen um ein relativ junges Forschungsthema handelt, das erst vor knapp 15 Jahren aufs Tapet kam.[2] Gleiter ergänzt bisherige Interpretationen, die mal den „bauenden Geist" eines griechisch-klassischen Nietzsche proklamieren,[3] ein andermal Nietzsche italienisch-historistisch und ebenso anti-modern auslegen, der die Architektur zur Kur gegen die „dekadente" Musik Richard Wagners in Stellung gebracht habe.[4] Doch auch der Rekonstruktion von Nietzsches italienischen Aufenthaltsorten und deren Nachhall im Werk möchte Gleiter nicht folgen, zumindest nicht bis zu dem Punkt, an dem der Philosoph als proto-modern vorgestellt wird, da sein Denken zu Peter Behrens (bzw. Louis Sullivan) hinführe.[5]

Gleiter zeigt einen anderen Nietzsche, der weniger eindeutig als vielmehr ironisch, ambivalent und französisch ist: Dazu kehrt er zu denselben Textstellen im Werk wie die anderen Autoren zurück, um sie vom Spätwerk einer alternativen Perspektive zu unterziehen. Zum Ausgangspunkt nimmt er dafür 1888, das letzte Schaffensjahr Nietzsches vor dem Wahnsinn, um dessen Schritt von einer Kritik an der klassisch-idealistischen zu einer physiologischen Ästhetik nachzuzeichnen, und weiter von der künstlerischen Reflexion zu einer neuen Kunstpraxis: einer sinnlich-leiblichen Kunst, für die, so Gleiter, beispielhaft nicht mehr wie bisher die Musik stehe, sondern nun die Architektur.

So weist Gleiter auf den Zusammenhang zwischen Nietzsches begeisterter Aneignung der Stadt Turin und seiner Rezeption der zeitgenössischen französischen Décadence-Bewegung hin: Dort habe der Philosoph ein Modell für das Zusammendenken der Extreme und der Widersprüche der Moderne gefunden. Zudem habe er auch französische neurologisch-psychologische Fachliteratur gelesen und als Bestätigung für seine früh geäußerte These von der Kunst als gesteigerten körperlichen Zustand verstanden.

Methodisch destilliert Gleiter diesen frankophilen, modernen und dekadenten Nietzsche als „Flaneur" aus einer kontextuellen Lektüre der Schriften des Jahres 1888, unter Hinzuziehung der Briefe und des Nachlasses. Die Betrachtung eines Aphorismus vor dem Hintergrund des jeweiligen Werkkontextes ist bei Nietzsche unabdingbar, denn viele scheinbare Widersprüche lassen sich als unterschiedliche Positionen zu ein und derselben Frage verstehen, die nur zu unterschiedlichen Zeitpunkten entstanden sind.

Strukturell folgt das Buch zu Dreiviertel diesem größeren Bogen, indem Gleiter nacheinander die Paare „Dekadenz und Moderne", „Mythos und Reflexion", und „Ästhetik und Physiologie" verhandelt. Das letzte Viertel nimmt eine kritische Diskussion der neueren Rezeptionsgeschichte von Nietzsches Architekturaussagen ein, die fremd

1 Z. B. mit der Begründung der Reihe „ArchitekturDenken", deren ersten Band er selbst verfasste (Jörg H. Gleiter, *Architekturtheorie heute*. Bielefeld 2008), oder auch dem philosophischen Stempel, den er 2007 dem 10. Bauhaus-Kolloquium in Weimar, *Die Realität des Imaginären: Architektur und das digitale Bild*, aufdrückte.

2 Alexandre Kostka, Irving Wohlfarth (Hg.), *Nietzsche and „an Architecture of Our Minds"*. Los Angeles 1999 (Publikation der Tagung *Aufbau – Überbau*, Stiftung Weimarer Klassik, 1994); immer noch bahnbrechend für die Nietzsche-Rezeption in den bildenden Künsten ist die Dissertation von Jürgen Krause, *„Märtyrer" und „Prophet": Studien zum Nietzsche-Kult in der bildenden Kunst der Jahrhundertwende*. Berlin und New York 1984.

3 Markus Breitschmid, *Der bauende Geist*. Friedrich Nietzsche und die Architektur. Luzern 2001.

4 Fritz Neumeyer, *Der Klang der Steine*. *Nietzsches Architekturen*. Berlin 2001; 2. Aufl. 2004.

5 Tilmann Buddensieg, *Nietzsches Italien. Städte, Gärten und Paläste*. Berlin 2002.

On the Difficulty of Reading a Reader of Nietzsche

Der philosophische Flaneur – Nietzsche und die Architektur (4)
Jörg H. Gleiter
Würzburg: Königshausen & Neumann, 2009
(Habilitation at the Bauhaus University Weimar, 2007)
German, 193 pages, illustrations, paperback
ISBN 978-3-8260-3758-0
EUR 24.80

Beyond traditional architectural history and theory of architecture, as it was established in the 1970s, Jörg Gleiter has on several occasions made the attempt to establish another platform for architectural thinking, striving for something that might best be described as the philosophy of architecture.[1] Nietzsche fits perfectly into this program of expanding the discipline, precisely because the questioning of his architectural ideas is a relatively new research field that was first put on the table less than fifteen years ago.[2] Gleiter expands previous interpretations that proclaimed either a Greek classical Nietzsche as "a spirit that builds"[3] or discovered an Italianate, historicist anti-modernist who prescribed architecture as cure for the "decadent" music of Richard Wagner.[4] Gleiter also refuses to pursue the reconstruction of Nietzsche's places of residence in Italy and their reverberation in his work to the point where the philosopher is presented as a proto-modernist whose thinking leads to Peter Behrens (or Louis Sullivan).[5]

Gleiter presents another Nietzsche, who is less unambiguous and rather more ironic, ambivalent and French: to this end, he returns to the same passages in the books as all the previous authors but subjects them to an alternative perspective, derived from the later work. As a starting point, he takes the year 1888, the last productive year before Nietzsche's collapse to insanity, in order to retrace his steps from a critique of the classical idealist aesthetics to a vision of physiological aesthetics, and furthermore from the reflection of the art to a new artistic practice: a sensual and physical art that, according to Gleiter, is not any longer represented by music but by architecture.

Thus, Gleiter calls attention to the connection between Nietzsche's enthusiastic appropriation of

1 E.g. by starting the publication "ArchitekturDenken," the first volume of which he wrote himself (Jörg H. Gleiter, *Architekturtheorie heute*. Bielefeld 2008), or the philosophical emphasis he gave to the tenth Bauhaus Colloquium in Weimar in 2007, *Die Realität des Imaginären: Architektur und das digitale Bild*.

2 Alexandre Kostka, Irving Wohlfarth (eds.), *Nietzsche and "an Architecture of Our Minds."* Los Angeles 1999 (publication of the conference *Aufbau – Überbau*, Stiftung Weimarer Klassik, 1994). The PhD dissertation by Jürgen Krause, *"Märtyrer" und "Prophet": Studien zum Nietzsche-Kult in der bildenden Kunst der Jahrhundertwende*. Berlin and New York 1984, continues to hold a central position as regards Nietzsche's relation to the visual arts.

3 Markus Breitschmid, *Der bauende Geist: Friedrich Nietzsche und die Architektur*. Lucerne 2001.

4 Fritz Neumeyer, *Der Klang der Steine: Nietzsches Architekturen*. Berlin 2001.

5 Tilmann Buddensieg, *Nietzsches Italien: Städte, Gärten und Paläste*. Berlin 2002.

gegenüber der Argumentation bleibt und sich nur als „Abgrenzung" im Rahmen der Habilitation verstehen lässt. Zudem enthält das Buch zahlreiche Wiederholungen, die von einzelnen Zitaten über gleichlautende Sätze bis hin zur Wiederholung ganzer Abschnitte reichen. Eine Kritik daran mag kleinlich klingen, aber gerade in der Auseinandersetzung mit einem Stilisten wie Nietzsche bleiben die Redundanzen ärgerlich.

Inhaltlich scheint die Konzentration auf den späten Nietzsche etwas problematisch, da bei ihm nicht unbedingt das chronologisch Späte das „Wichtigere" oder „Wahre" ist, aus dem sich das andere Werk erschließen ließe. Außerdem basiert das ganze Argument Gleiters, dass Nietzsche eher als ein metropolitaner „Flaneur" denn als der bisher bekannte Stadtverächter, einsame Wanderer in der Natur oder antimoderne Verehrer klassischen Ausdrucks zu lesen sei, auf wenigen Textstellen, die zudem mehrheitlich aus Briefen und dem Nachlass stammen, also von Nietzsche nicht als „Werk" konzipiert wurden. Gleiter stellt selbst fest, dass es keinen generellen Schlüssel zu Nietzsche gebe, dass sich keine zentrale Aussage oder Lehre im Werk vorfinde, und auch, dass die Beschäftigung mit der Architektur sporadisch, unsystematisch und oftmals metaphorisch geblieben sei, also keine Architekturtheorie im strengen Sinne bilde. Trotzdem fällt der Autor in die „Heidegger-Falle", indem er versucht, den „wahren" Nietzsche aus dem Nachlass (und den Briefen) zu rekonstruieren.[6] Viele Fragmente im Nachlass sind „Gedankenexperimente", also Versuche einer Position oder einer sprachlichen Formulierung, die gerade nicht den Weg ins Werk gefunden haben, weil Nietzsche sie nach dem Versuch aufgab, nicht (mehr) teilte oder autorisieren wollte. Man sollte den Nachlass nicht mit dem „wahren" (lies: ungefilterten) Werk Nietzsches verwechseln.

Mit der Neuinterpretation einer Schlüsselstelle zu Nietzsches Architekturdenken aus der *Götzen-Dämmerung* zur „Macht-Beredsamkeit in Formen" und dem „grossen Stil"[7] bietet Gleiter einen ebenso erfreulich unkonventionellen wie auch zu diskutierenden Ansatz: Gilt sie wirklich einer Kritik des „Götzen" Architektur als Monumentalbaukunst, der im Dienste der Macht jenseits des dionysischen und apollinischen Zustandes den Bereich der Künste eigentlich verlassen hat? Oder fällt der „Rausch des Willens" nicht ebenso unter Nietzsches erregte Affekte, die zur Kunst treiben? Zudem ist fraglich, ob man

6 Vgl. Martin Heidegger, *Nietzsche*. 2 Bde., Stuttgart 1998, 6. erg. Aufl.

7 Friedrich Nietzsche, „Götzen-Dämmerung oder Wie man mit dem Hammer philosophirt" (1888), Streifzüge eines Unzeitgemässen, §11, in: ders., *Sämtliche Werke. Kritische Studienausgabe*. Bd. 6, hg. von Giorgio Colli, Mazzino Montinari, Berlin 1988, S. 118f.

the city of Turin and his reception of the contemporary French movement of décadence: here, the philosopher found a model for the conceptualization of extremes and contradictions of modernity. Moreover, he read French neuro-psychological literature and understood it as a confirmation of his earlier theory of art as an intensification of bodily conditions.

Through an inspired interpretation of the writings of 1888, including letters and notebooks, Gleiter evokes a Francophile, modern and decadent Nietzsche as a "flaneur." In the case of Nietzsche it is essential to consider each aphorism in the context of the particular work, for many apparent inconsistencies can be understood as different answers to and the same question, simply given at different moments in time.

Structurally, the book follows this basic idea for three quarters of its length, as when Gleiter discusses "Decadence and Modernism," "Myth and Reflection," and "Aesthetics and Physiology." The last fourth of the book, however, does not relate to the general argument. It confronts the recent reception of Nietzsche's architectural statements and only makes sense as the academic drawing of boundaries for the purposes of a *Habilitation*. In addition, the book contains many repetitions, which range from identical quotations to the repetition of whole paragraphs. It may sound petty to criticize a book for such literary problems, but since the focus is on such a stylistic master as Nietzsche makes the redundancies ever more upsetting.

In terms of content, Gleiter's focus on the late Nietzsche seems problematic, since the later works of the philosopher are not necessarily a more "important" or "truthful" foundation from which the earlier statements could be deciphered. Gleiter recognizes himself that there is no master key to Nietzsche, that there is no central message or teaching found in the work, and also that confrontation with architecture remained sporadic, unsystematical and often no more than metaphorical, thus forming no architectural theory in the strict sense. Nevertheless, the author falls into the "Heidegger trap" by attempting to reconstruct the "real" Nietzsche from posthumous notebooks and letters.[6]

Many fragments in the unpublished notebooks are "thought experiments," failed attempts of define a position or a linguistic formulation that was not included in the published books because Nietzsche no longer wanted to authorize them. One should not confuse the posthumous notes with the "real" (that is, un-filtered) work of the thinker.

With his reinterpretation of the key passages relating to Nietzsche's theory of architecture, in particular the section in the *Twilight of the Idols* concerning architecture's relation to power and the grand style,[7] Gleiter makes an attractive but provocative offer: does Nietzsche's thesis really

6 See Martin Heidegger, *Nietzsche*. 2 vols., Stuttgart 1998.

7 Friedrich Nietzsche, "Expeditions of an Untimely Man," § 11, in: *Twilight of the Idols: The Anti-Christ*. Tr. R. J. Hollingdale. Harmondsworth 1968, pp. 73f.

Nietzsches (von Jacob Burckhardt übernommenes) Konzept des „grossen Stils" auf die Architektur der italienischen Renaissance beziehen soll, die sich durch Proportion, Harmonie und Artikulation der Elemente auszeichnet und ideell an der Antike ausrichtet, oder nicht vielmehr auf die barocken Paläste von Genua und Turin, die nach einer beinahe gewaltsamen Überwindung der Antike suchen, nach architektonischem Effekt und Affekt?

Doch gilt es, nicht bei Nietzsche stehen zu bleiben, sondern durch die Rückkehr zu ihm (und den Anfängen einer ambivalenten Moderne) heute weiter zu denken. Frei nach Nietzsche: „Auf die Schiffe, ihr Architekturphilosophen [...]."[8]

Ole W. Fischer

8 Vgl. Friedrich Nietzsche, *Die fröhliche Wissenschaft*. Viertes Buch, § 289, in: ebd., Bd. 3, S. 529f.

Cremige Diagramme

Jenseits des Rasters – Architektur und Informationstechnologie
Anwendungen einer digitalen Architektonik (5)
Ludger Hovestadt
ETH Zürich CAAD
Übersetzung: Tim Danaher
Basel, Boston und Berlin: Birkhäuser Verlag, 2010
deutsch und englisch, 288 Seiten,
84 Farbabbildungen, 50 SW-Abbildungen,
Hardcover
ISBN 978-3-0346-0096-5
EUR 44,90

Wer heute über die Computeranwendung in der Architektur schreibt, muss niemanden mehr überzeugen, dass diese sinnvoll ist. Längst sind die Arbeitsplätze auf den CAD-Betrieb umgerüstet, sind digitalisierte Abläufe in den Büros zum *business as usual* geworden. Dass damit aber längst kein stabiler Endzustand erreicht worden ist, dass es darüber hinaus noch viele weitere Anwendungen der Informationstechnologie in der Architektur gibt, davon handelt das Buch, das Ludger Hovestadt über die ersten zehn Jahre seiner Professur für Architektur und CAAD an der ETH Zürich nun vorgelegt hat. Die Art und Weise, wie der Autor darin die „Anwendungen einer digitalen Architektonik" beschreibt, hebt sich von den meisten einschlägigen Publikationen deutlich ab. Nicht die „Artistik am Rechner", so Hovestadt im Vorwort, habe im Vordergrund gestanden. Statt „Virtual Reality" sei das Motto des Lehrstuhles von Anfang an „Back to Reality" gewesen. Es sei seiner Gruppe um die Nützlichkeit der Computertechnik in realen architektonischen Fragestellungen gegangen.

Die Resultate, die aus diesem Ansatz entstanden sind, werden in *Jenseits des Rasters* vorgestellt. Das Panorama, welches das durchgängig zweisprachig (D/E) verfasste Buch entwickelt, ist breit: vom Städtebau in Holland über das Vogelnest-Stadion der Olympischen Spiele in Beijing bis zur energieoptimierten Monte Rosa-Hütte in den Schweizer Alpen, vom digitalisierten Säulenatlas bis zum intelligenten Strom. Neben Kooperationen mit namhaften Architekten wie Kees Christiaanse, Daniel Libeskind oder Herzog & de Meuron werden auch Projekte aus der Lehre sowie Forschungsarbeiten des Instituts vorgestellt. Viele davon führten zu gebauten Strukturen: mit CAD/CAM in unterschiedlichsten Materialien geplante Pavillons, bei denen keine zwei Teile

function as a critique of the "idol," architecture as the monumental art of building, which has actually left the realm of the arts and the Dionysian or Apollonian condition, in order to serve power? Or does the "intoxication of the will" rather belong to the affects that according to Nietzsche are the driving forces of artistic creation? Moreover, it should be questioned whether Nietzsche's concept of the "grand style" (which he adopted from Jacob Burckhardt) should be seen as referring to the architecture of the Italian Renaissance, characterized by proportion, harmony, and articulation of the elements and indebted to the ancient world, or rather to the baroque palaces in Genoa and Turin that attempt an almost violent overcoming of antiquity, in search of architectural effects and affects?

In the end, one should not dwell on Nietzsche, but return to him (and the beginnings of an ambivalent modernism) in order to think further ahead today. To paraphrase Nietzsche: "Embark, you philosophers of architecture ..."[8]

Ole W. Fischer

8 See Friedrich Nietzsche, *The Gay Science*. Tr. Walter Kauffmann. New York 1974, Fourth book, § 289, pp. 231f.

Creamy Diagrams

Beyond the Grid – Architecture and Information Technology
Applications of a Digital Architectonic (5)
Ludger Hovestadt
ETH Zürich CAAD
Translation: Tim Danaher
Basel, Boston and Berlin: Birkhäuser Verlag, 2010
German and English, 288 pages, 84 color illustrations, 50 b & w illustrations, hardcover
ISBN 978-3-0346-0096-5
EUR 44.90

No one writing about computer applications in architecture today need first convince people that these are purposeful. Workplaces have long been equipped for CAD operation, while digital processes in the offices have become *business as usual*. The fact that a stable final status has by no means been achieved yet, and that there is still an enormous range of information technology applications for architecture left to explore is the subject of this book, which Ludger Hovestadt has presented reviewing his first ten years as Professor for Architecture and CAAD at the ETH Zurich. It is the way this author describes the "Applications of a Digital Architectonic" that sets this book apart from most other works on the subject. The notion of "developing the artistic potential of the computer," as Hovestadt says in his introduction is not what he has in mind. The motto of his chair from the outset has never been "virtual reality" but "back to reality." His working group has been concerned with and examines the utility of computer technology in the real issues of architecture.

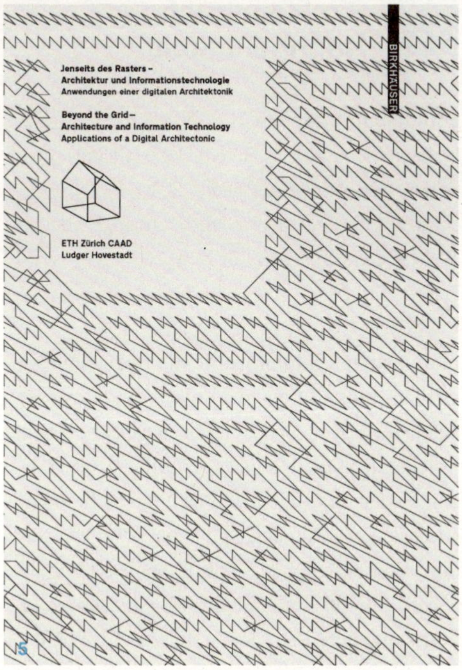

gleich sind, aufblasbare Möbel aus Blech, sogar ein mit Sensoren versehener Flugschirm. Bei den meisten Projekten ist die Software, die notwendig war, um sie umzusetzen, gleich mitentwickelt worden. Trotz Praxis-Nähe also keine Spur von der CAD-Routine, die den Arbeitsalltag in den meisten Architekturbüros heute bestimmt.

Die Projekte sind anschaulich bebildert und in relativ kurzen Texten beschrieben. Erstaunlich, wie wenig technisch diese Beschreibungen daher kommen und wie weitgehend darin auf den einschlägigen Fachjargon verzichtet worden ist. Auch die Grafik wirkt im Vergleich mit ähnlichen Publikationen sehr zurückhaltend und sachlich. Obwohl das Buch viele farbige Illustrationen enthält und man die meisten Projekte nur über diese Bilder verstehen kann, stellt sich nie der Eindruck eines *coffee-table books* ein.

Um die große thematische Breite zu strukturieren, sind inhaltlich verwandte Projekte zusammengefasst und mit Überschriften wie „Muster", „Generische Elemente" oder „Fassaden" versehen. Zudem gliedert sich das Buch durch insgesamt acht eingeschobene Texte in einzelne Blöcke. Diese Texte verknüpfen die einzelnen Abschnitte durch thematische Überleitungen und stellen sie in größere Zusammenhänge.

Hovestadt beschreibt die Aufgabenstellungen der Architektur als „Probleme mittlerer Größe, die weder mit Logik – dafür haben sie zu viele Elemente – noch mit Statistik – dafür haben sie zu wenig Elemente – gelöst werden können." Bei diesen, so Hovestadt, „fängt der Spaß mit der Informationstechnologie an" (S. 17). Immer wieder kommt er auf den Topos des Netzwerks, welches als Organisationsstruktur so anders funktioniert als die „hierarchisch organisierten oder nach dem linearen Ursache-Wirkungsprinzip strukturierten Systeme […]. Beginnt man sich in Netzwerken zu bewegen oder sie gar zweckgerichtet zu entwerfen, sind all jene Gewohnheiten nutzlos, die wir für mechanistisch geprägte Systeme erlernt haben" (S. 81). Auch den Vorwurf des Reduktionismus, der denjenigen, die komplexe Phänomene am Rechner behandeln, oft vorgeworfen wird, will er nicht gelten lassen: „Wir können in weiten Bereichen auf rigide Definitionen und vereinfachende Logiken verzichten und können auch große Reichhaltigkeit algorithmisch abbilden" (S. 17).

Hovestadt spricht von der „Gestaltung des Unvorhersehbaren" (das heißt, „dass wir bis zum Ende der Berechnungen nicht genau wissen, wie ein Gebäude aussehen wird, wir wissen nicht einmal, ‚warum' es so aussieht, wie es aussieht", S. 81), von Ordnungsprinzipien jenseits des Rasters („Klassische Rastersysteme sind klumpig, Voronoi-Diagramme sind cremig", S. 60); er spricht von der neuen Herausforderung für Entwerfer, wenn computergestützte Systeme „eine gewisse emergente Selbständigkeit" aufweisen,

The results of the inquiry pursued by this approach are presented here in *Beyond the Grid*. The panorama, which this dual language book (German and English) develops is a broad one: from urban development in the Netherlands to the Bird's Nest Olympic Stadium in Beijing, or the energy-optimized Monte Rosa Chalet in the Swiss Alps; from a digitalized columns atlas down to intelligent electricity. In addition to cooperations with leading architects such as Kees Christiaanse, Daniel Libeskind or Herzog & de Meuron, projects from the teaching and research work of the Institute are also presented. Many of these have resulted in structures and buildings: Pavilions planned in the most varied materials using CAD/CAM, and in which no two parts are the same, inflatable furniture in sheet metal and even a hang glider fitted with sensors. In most of these projects the software needed for implementation was also developed. So despite proximity to practice there is no trace of the CAD routine that dictates working life in most architectural bureaus today.

The projects are clearly illustrated and described in relatively short texts. It is all the more astonishing how non-technical these descriptions are and how technical jargon has largely been dispensed with. The graphic work too is reserved and professional compared with the material similar publications present. And although the book is full of color illustrations and most of the projects are in fact only understood in reference to these, the volume in no way gives the impression of being a coffee-table book.

The broad spread of subjects is structured by placing related issues together and through the use of headings such as "Patterns," "Generic Elements" or "Facades." Moreover the book is divided up into a total of eight textual insertions in separate blocks. These texts link the separate sections together by means of thematic transitions and place these in broader contexts.

Hovestadt describes the task of architecture as "'middling' problems, those that cannot be tackled using symbolic logic—they contain too many elements—or statistical methods—they contain too few." And Hovestadt says, "that's where the fun with information technology starts" (p. 19). He often returns to the network topos, which functions so very differently as an organizational structure from "hierarchically organized systems, or systems organized along a linear cause-and-effect principle … As one begins working with networks, or tries to develop them in a goal-oriented fashion, all those practices that were learned when dealing with mechanical systems are no longer of any use" (p. 83). The reproach of reductionism too, so often cast in the direction of those who deal with the complex phenomenon of the computer, is one he cannot accept: "In many areas we can dispense with rigid definitions and simplified logics, and we are now, with the help of algorithms, able to map architectural problems on scales that allow for great richness of detail and information" (p. 20).

Hovestadt speaks of "The Design of the Unforeseeable" (his definition: "This means that we

wobei er die Angst um die individuelle Kreativität für unbegründet hält (S. 82).

Die Qualität der im Buch vorgestellten Projekte verleiht diesem ein hohes Maß an Glaubwürdigkeit. Vor allem als Kontrastprogramm zu den ärgerlich oberflächlichen Argumentationen, die derzeit den „Parametrismus" zum neuen Stil erklären, ist das Buch nicht warm genug zu empfehlen. Bei Hovestadt sind die neuen Dimensionen, die sich durch die Informationstechnik eröffnen, ungleich gehaltvoller analysiert und konsequenter durchdacht. Dennoch scheinen auch bei ihm manche der Aussagen etwas überzogen. Wenn er beispielsweise die Trennung von Struktur und Form propagiert und dies als spezifisch schweizerischen Beitrag zur Entwicklung der Architektur bezeichnet (S. 120), möchte man gerne etwas bremsen und nachhaken, ob da die Dinge nicht doch etwas gar einfach dargestellt werden.

Auch kommt der Respekt vor dem, was Architektur neben ihrer technischen Bedingtheit eben auch noch ausmacht – ihre sinnlichen und poetischen Qualitäten –, im Buch kaum vor. Das liegt nicht an den Projekten, welche diese Qualitäten durchaus haben, sondern an der Art, wie die Herangehensweise beschrieben wird. So ist von Architektur-Vollautomaten die Rede, mit denen auf Basis von Programm und Bauplatz ohne weiteres menschliches Zutun Projekte erstellt werden, welche Hovestadts Gruppe bei Architekturwettbewerben einreicht und mit denen er immerhin schon einmal einen vierten Platz belegt hat. Die Beschreibung endet mit den Worten „Es lebe die Architektur" (S. 237), aber man fragt sich nicht nur an dieser Stelle, was genau Hovestadt darunter versteht.

Trotz, oder vielleicht gerade wegen dieser vom Autor bewusst eingesetzten Provokationen ist es ein bemerkenswertes Buch, das eine neue Perspektive auf viele bekannte Sachverhalte anbietet. Man darf, wie sich das der Autor erhofft, „unaufgeregt neugierig" auf das sein, was sich seine Gruppe für die nächsten Jahre vorgenommen hat. Das Motto heißt von jetzt an „Applied Virtuality". Bis dazu die entsprechende Publikation vorliegt, wird wohl die eine oder andere der in *Jenseits des Rasters* beschriebenen Anwendungen einer digitalen Architektonik schon *business as usual* geworden sein. Das Buch selbst wird dazu beitragen. Ich wünsche ihm eine große, kritisch-interessierte Leserschaft.

Urs Hirschberg

Ein Handbuch für Nachhaltigkeit

Ecological Urbanism (6)
Mohsen Mostafavi mit Gareth Doherty (Hg.)
Baden: Lars Müller Publishers, 2010
englisch, 656 Seiten, 1000 Abbildungen, Hardcover
ISBN 978-3-03778-189-0
EUR 40,00

In den letzten Jahren wurde die Bezeichnung „Urbanismus" durch eine Reihe von Adjektiven und in der Folge von Definitionen näher bestimmt, welche die aktuellen und zukünftigen Entwicklungen der städtischen Umgebung beschreiben. Diese neue Terminologie gibt eine Form von Narrativ einer möglichen Stadt für heute oder in der nahen Zukunft vor, eine Darwinistische Evolutionskette, deren Stufen durch Neologismen und ebenso viele Publikationen gekennzeichnet sind.

Der erste, sehr erfolgreiche Neologismus war *Landscape Urbanism*, ein Begriff der Urbanismus, Architektur und Landschaftsarchitektur zu einem hybriden Konzept verband und so eine grundlegende Neuordnung des Fachgebietes schuf. Charles Waldheim prägte diesen Begriff 1997, um die neuen Entwurfspraktiken im Zusammenhang

do not know what the building will look like until the end of the calculation—or even know 'why' it looks like it does," p. 83), using principles of order beyond the classic grid ("Classical grid systems are clotted; Voronoi diagrams are creamy," p. 62); he speaks of the new challenges faced by the designer when computer-supported systems begin to exhibit "a certain emergent independence," and he sees any fears for individual creativity here as entirely without foundation (p. 84).

The quality of the projects presented imparts high credibility to the book. As a contrast program to the irritatingly shallow arguments that have currently declared "parametrism" to be the new style, the book can scarcely be recommended highly enough. The new dimensions that have opened up as a result of information technology are analyzed on a basis that is much richer in content and more thoroughly thought through in the hands of Hovestadt. Nevertheless some of his statements appear to be a little exaggerated. When, for example, he propagates the separation of structure and form and describes this as a specifically Swiss contribution to the development of architecture (p. 122), one might wish to apply the brakes and dig in a little to consider whether this has not been presented in a rather too simplified fashion.

Furthermore the very thing which is the making of architecture, in addition to the fundamental technical conditions—its sensual and poetic qualities—is hardly given a mention in the book. This is not the fault of the projects, which certainly have their qualities, it is that of the manner in which the approach is described. At one point a system for fully automated architecture is discussed, by means of which projects are produced without further human intervention on the basis of the program and the construction site. We are told that Hovestadt's group submitted entries to architecture competitions produced entirely by this system, once even garnering a fourth place. The account ends with the words "Long live architecture!" (p. 237), but not only here do you find yourself asking the question as to what exactly Hovestadt means by that?

Despite, or perhaps precisely because of these intentional provocations made by the author, this is a remarkable book, offering a new perspective for many well-known issues. The author hopes to have "piqued our interest," about the tasks his group intends to implement over the coming years. The motto from now on is "applied virtuality." Until the corresponding publication is available, some of the applications of a digital architectonic described in *Beyond the Grid* will already have become a part of business as usual. This book will itself contribute to this. It deserves a large and critically interested readership.

Urs Hirschberg

mit der nordamerikanischen Stadtplanung wie folgt zu beschreiben: „landscape replaces architecture as the basic building block of contemporary urbanism".[1] 2005 stellte James Corner den Begriff *Botanical Urbanism* vor; bei seinem Projekt für den botanischen Garten der University of Puerto Rico hob Corner hervor, wie wichtig die dynamischen landwirtschaftlichen Prozesse in der städtebaulichen Gestaltung sind.

Die Verbreitung dieses neuen „Urbanismus" war nicht aufzuhalten; sie bewegte sich von *Infrastructural Urbanism* (Stan Allen 1999) zu *Integral Urbanism* (Nan Ellin 2006), *Sustainable Urbanism* (Douglas Farr 2007) und danach zu *Instant Urbanism* (Schweizer Architekturmuseum in Zusammenarbeit mit Francesca Ferguson 2007), *Opportunistic Urbanism* (Diego Ramirez-Lovering 2008) und *Holy Urbanism* (MONU Nr. 10, 2009). Diese Aufzählung ist freilich nur ein Ausschnitt und zeigt, dass die lebhafte Diskussion über die Suche nach neuen Modellen städtischer Formen weiterhin sehr in Mode ist. Sie führt auch vor, dass die Debatte von der gemeinsamen Erkenntnis geprägt ist, dass die Herausforderungen der gegenwärtigen Stadt eine vielschichtige Annäherung über die traditionellen Grenzen des Fachgebiets hinaus verlangen.

Der neueste Beitrag zur Debatte über die Zukunft der Stadt, der eine neue theoretische Annäherung zur Interpretation des urbanen Phänomens darstellt, ist der von Mohsen Mostafavi gemeinsam mit Gareth Doherty herausgegebene Band *Ecological Urbanism*. Dieser jüngste syntaktische Neologismus basiert auf der Überzeugung, dass die Fragilität des Planeten und seiner Ressourcen als eine Gelegenheit zu theoretischen Entwurfsinnovationen verstanden werden kann, die sich nicht darauf beschränken, konventionelle Lösungen durch Planung und Konstruktion einer energieeffizienteren Umgebung zu finden, sondern die über die abstrakten und maßstabsbezogenen Grenzen nachhaltiger Architektur hinausgehen. Diese Innovationen betrachten die städtischen Dimensionen als einen Ort komplexer Beziehungen, wo das Verbinden von Ökologie und Urbanismus nicht nur neue Methoden für die Zukunft aufzeigt, sondern auch der Frage nachgeht, was das Urbane eigentlich sein kann.

6

Das Buch ist das Ergebnis der Konferenz *ECOLOGICAL URBANISM: Alternative and Sustainable Cities of the Future*, die an der Harvard Graduate School of Design (GSD) im Frühling 2009 abgehalten wurde. Bei der Konferenz sollten alternative und nachhaltige Städte der Zukunft diskutiert werden; das ehrgeizige Ziel basierte auf einem multidisziplinären Verständnis von und einer Annäherung an Ökologie und De-

1 Charles Waldheim (Hg.), *The Landscape Urbanism Reader*. New York 2006, S. 11.

A Compendium of Sustainability

Ecological Urbanism (6)
Mohsen Mostafavi with Gareth Doherty (eds.)
Baden: Lars Müller Publishers, 2010
English, 656 pages, 1,000 illustrations, hardcover
ISBN 978-3-03778-189-0
EUR 40.00

In recent years, the term "urbanism" has been qualified by a series of adjectives, which gave origin to a sequence of definitions used to describe recent and future evolutions of the urban environment. This new terminology foreshadowed a kind of narrative of the city possible, now or in the near future; a Darwinian evolutionary chain whose stages have been marked by neologisms coined on the occasion of as many publications.

The first and very successful of these neologisms was "landscape urbanism," dealing with urbanism, architecture and landscape architecture together, a hybrid concept which provoked a thorough disciplinary realignment. The term was conceived in 1997 by Charles Waldheim to describe the emerging design practices—in the context of North American urbanism—in which "landscape replaces architecture as the basic building block of contemporary urbanism."[1] In 2005, James Corner brought out "botanical urbanism"; starting from his project for the University of Puerto Rico's botanical gardens, Corner highlighted how important the dynamic processes of landscape were in structuring urbanity.

The proliferation of these new "urbanisms" proved unstoppable, moving from *Infrastructural Urbanism* (Stan Allen 1999) to *Integral Urbanism* (Nan Ellin 2006), to *Sustainable Urbanism* (Douglas Farr 2007) and then *Instant Urbanism* (Swiss Architecture Museum and Francesca Ferguson 2007), *Opportunistic Urbanism* (Diego Ramirez-Lovering 2008) and *Holy Urbanism* (MONU n. 10, 2009). The list, which is only a partial one, shows how the lively discussion about the search for new models of urban forms continues to be very fashionable. It also shows that the debate is marked by a shared awareness that the challenges of the contemporary city require a multilayered approach, moving beyond the traditional disciplinary boundaries.

The most recent contribution to the debate on the future of the city, a contribution which implies a new theoretical approach to interpreting the urban phenomenon, is a volume edited by Mohsen Mostafavi with Gareth Doherty, and titled *Ecological Urbanism*. This latest syntactic neologism is based on the conviction that the fragility of the planet and its resources can be understood as an opportunity for speculative design innovations, which are not limited to promoting conventional solutions in terms of engineering and constructing a more energy-efficient environment, but that move beyond the mental and scale-related limits

1 Charles Waldheim (ed.), *The Landscape Urbanism Reader*. New York 2006, p. 11.

sign nach dem Motto „new ethics and aesthetics of the urban". Die Konferenz brachte viele verschiedene ExpertInnen zusammen; unter ihnen PraktikerInnen, TheoretikerInnen, Wirtschaftsfachleute, KünstlerInnen und EntscheidungsträgerInnen. Das Buch enthält zahlreiche dieser Beiträge; es ist ein monumentales Handbuch, massiv in Größe und Gewicht mit einer beeindruckenden Liste von 134 AutorInnen und über tausend Illustrationen. Es ist in elf Themen und Abschnitte gegliedert, die Titel wie *Anticipate*, *Collaborate* (drei verschiedene Abschnitte tragen diese identische Überschrift), *Sense*, *Curate*, *Produce*, *Interact*, *Mobilize*, *Measure*, *Adapt*, *Incubate* tragen.

Die Beiträge sind äußerst unterschiedlich und widersprechen einander auch zuweilen. Doch wie könnte es anders sein, wenn man die Weitläufigkeit und Komplexität der Themen bedenkt, worüber die AutorInnen diskutieren und schreiben sollten. Die Bandbreite reicht von detaillierten bis zu gebietsmäßigen Entwürfen, wie der *Eco-City of Agriculture* von Arup; sie reicht von Projekten, die vom ökologischem Bewusstsein und der umweltbezogenen Ethik von Turenscape ausgehen, bis zum Vorschlag von Mitchell Joachim, sich ökologische Städte nach der futuristischen und zugleich fast romantischen Methode vorzustellen, Häuser mithilfe einheimischer Bäume wachsen zu lassen. Das gesamte Werk ist reichhaltig, komplex und mit ungewöhnlichen, interessanten Bildern ausgestattet, die ein faszinierendes Panorama von Forschung und Experimenten rund um die Welt zeigen. Dennoch ist das Buch weit davon entfernt, ein vollständiges Nachschlagewerk für neue Strategien in der Planung der Stadt der Zukunft und der Zukunft unserer Städte zu sein.

Wenn ökologische Themen wie der Klimawandel, die Fragilität der Umwelt, die Nutzung erneuerbarer Ressourcen, nachhaltige Architektur und grüne Technologien in der Diskussion über die Organisation der gegenwärtigen und zukünftigen Stadt immer wichtiger geworden sind, zeigen die jüngsten, zur Modifizierung des Begriffs „Urbanismus" verwendeten Adjektive die Dringlichkeit einer fortlaufenden Erörterung, in der die unterschiedlichen Wege der Beschreibung, des Denkens und des Gestaltens des städtischen Maßstabs auf der Basis einer interdisziplinären Wechselwirkung behandelt werden.

Manchmal beschäftigen sich die neuen Entwürfe eigentlich mit älteren, lang bestehenden Praktiken, die von Landschaftscharakteristika im großen Maßstab ausgehen, ein Zugang, der über Jahrtausende Standard war. Ich glaube zum Beispiel, dass Kaiser Nero einer der ersten war, der mit seiner *Domus Aurea*, wo Weingärten, gepflügte Felder und Wälder die Landschaft seiner imperialen Residenz im Herzen Roms formten, die Theorie des Landscape Urbanism in die Praxis umgesetzt hat.

Auf jeden Fall deutet die Suche nach einer neuen Sprache und einer neuen Zusammenarbeit zwischen den Fachgebieten auf die Notwendigkeit eines ganzheitlichen Zugangs hin, um die Schnittstelle zwischen der Landschaft und dem Urbanen in der Strukturierung der Stadt von heute zu beschreiben. Ein „Ecological Urbanism" tritt dafür ein, dass eine ökologische Annäherung als ein kreativer und praktischer Zugang sowohl für bestehende als auch für neue Städte dringend notwendig ist. Charles Waldheim meinte kürzlich dazu: „the emergent discourse of ecological urbanism has been proposed to more precisely describe the aspirations of an urban practice informed by environmental issues and imbued with the sensibilities associated with landscape".[2]

Landschaftsökologie erscheint als wichtiges Bezugssystem für die urbane Form, und „ökolo-

2 Charles Waldheim, „On Landscape, Ecology and Other Modifiers to Urbanism", in: *Topos* 71 (2010), S. 21.

of sustainable architecture. These innovations are looking at the urban dimension as a site of complex relations, where conjoining ecology and urbanism can provide not only methods for the future, but also insights into what the urban can be.

The book is the fruit of the conference *ECOLOGICAL URBANISM: Alternative and Sustainable Cities of the Future*, held at the Harvard Graduate School of Design (GSD) in the spring of 2009. The conference was set up to discuss alternative and sustainable cities of the future, with the ambitious goal of defining "new ethics and aesthetics of the urban" based on a multi-disciplinary understanding of and approach to ecology and design. The conference brought together a variety of experts; among them were practitioners, theorists, economists, artists, and policymakers. The book contains many of these contributions; it is a monumental compendium, massive in size and weight, with an imposing list of 134 authors and more than a thousand illustrations. It is organized around eleven themes and sections with titles such as Anticipate, Collaborate (three different sections bear this same heading), Sense, Curate, Produce, Interact, Mobilize, Measure, Adapt, Incubate.

The essays are highly diverse and sometimes even contradict one another. But it could not be otherwise, considering the vastness and complexity of the subjects the authors have been asked to discuss and write about. The scale goes from the minute to the territorial, like the *Eco-City of Agriculture* by Arup; from projects based on ecological awareness and environmental ethics by Turenscape to Mitchell Joachim's proposal for envisioning ecological cities, like the futuristic and at the same time vaguely romantic method of growing homes from native trees. The whole work is rich and complex, full of curious and interesting images, showing a fascinating panorama of the research and experimentation going on around the world. Yet the book is far from constituting a complete reference for new strategies in designing the city of the future and the future of our cities.

If ecological issues like climate change, the fragility of the environment, utilization of renewable resources, sustainable architecture, and green technology have become increasingly relevant in the discussion about organization of the contemporary and the future city, the recent adjectives used to modify "urbanism" reveal the urgency of an ongoing discussion on alternative ways of describing, thinking, and designing the urban scale, based on a cross-disciplinary interaction.

It is possible that what these recent formulations really deal with are older, well-established practices based on large-scale landscape features, approaches which have been standard for millennia. For example, I think that the Emperor Nero was one of the first to put landscape urbanism theory into practice with his *Domus Aurea*, where vineyards, ploughed fields, and woods shaped the

2 Charles Waldheim, "On Landscape, Ecology and Other Modifiers to Urbanism," in: *Topos* 71 (2010), p. 21.

gisch“ wird zum wesentlichen Faktor, wie wir über Stadt nachdenken. Doch ist Ökologie nur das neue Opium für das Volk?

Bianca Maria Rinaldi

Ein archäologischer Blick auf *petty apartheid*

Having Words
Denise Scott Brown
AA Words 4, Brett Steele (Hg.)
London: Architectural Association Publications, 2009
englisch, 160 Seiten, broschiert
ISBN 978-1-90290-270-8
EUR 14,99

Mit *Having Words* (7) wird Denise Scott Brown der vierte Band der von Brett Steele herausgegebenen Serie *AA Words* gewidmet, in dem sie mit einer Sammlung von Essays aus knapp vier Jahrzehnten, von 1969 bis 2007, zu Wort kommt. Scott Brown wurde 1931 als Kind jüdischer Emigranten aus England in Südafrika geboren, wo sie ihre Kindheit verbrachte und ihren ersten Universitätsabschluss erwarb, bevor sie in London an der Architectural Association School of Architecture zu Beginn der 1950er-Jahre ihre Ausbildung fortsetzte, um schließlich gemeinsam mit Robert Venturi und seinen Partnern ab 1967 ein Architekturbüro in Philadelphia zu leiten.

In ihrem Architekturverständnis geht Scott Brown von einer *active socioplastic practice* aus, die Planern und Städtebauern trotz vielfältiger ökonomischer und technisch-konstruktiver Rahmenbedingungen stets ihre gesellschaftspolitische Verantwortung vor Augen führt (S. 47). Eine Sensibilisierung für soziale Themen hat sie durch die Verbindung ihrer kulturellen europäischen Wurzeln mit der afrikanischen Lebenswelt in ihren frühen Jahren erfahren. Besonders die intensive Wechselwirkung zwischen natürlicher und gebauter Umgebung kann hier als prägend für ihren späteren künstlerischen Zugang zum Ort und als wesentliche Quelle ihrer Entwürfe gelten. So zeigt sie im Text „Invention and Tradition in the Making of American Place“ (1986) nicht nur die paradoxe Situation von kolonialen Kulturlandschaften auf, sondern sieht die räumliche Struktur als Matrix für die – wie sie es nennt – „Erfindung“, oder eigentlich „Neuerfindung“ Amerikas (S. 8). Gleich Le Corbusiers Aufforderung an die Zeit-

7

genossen, die Ästhetik der industriellen Architekturelemente wie Aufzüge, Schiffe und Flugzeuge als wesentlichen Teil der Entwicklung der moder-

landscape of his imperial residence in the heart of Rome.

In any case, the search for a new language and new disciplinary cooperation suggests the need for a more holistic approach in describing the interface between landscape and the urban in structuring the contemporary city. “Ecological Urbanism” claimed that an ecological approach is urgently needed as an imaginative and practical approach for existing as well as new cities. As Charles Waldheim recently summarized: “the emergent discourse of ecological urbanism has been proposed to more precisely describe the aspirations of an urban practice informed by environmental issues and imbued with the sensibilities associated with landscape.”[2]

Landscape ecology emerges as the basic framework for the urban form, and “ecological” becomes the standard modifier of our way of thinking about the city. But is ecology just the new opiate of the masses?

Bianca Maria Rinaldi

An Archaeological View on *Petty Apartheid*

Having Words
Denise Scott Brown
AA Words 4, Brett Steele (ed.)
London: Architectural Association Publications, 2009
English, 160 pages, paperback
ISBN 978-1-90290-270-8
EUR 14.99

The fourth volume of the *AA Words* series edited by Brett Steele, *Having Words* (7), pays tribute to Denise Scott Brown with a collection of essays from some four decades, from 1969 to 2007. Scott Brown was born in 1931 to Anglo-Jewish parents who had emigrated from England to South Africa, where she spent her childhood and gained her first university degree prior to continuing her studies at the London Architectural Association School in the early 1950s. From 1967 on, she co-managed an architecture firm in Philadelphia together with Robert Venturi and his associates.

Scott Brown’s understanding of architecture is based on active *socioplastic practice*, which permanently confronts planners and urban architects with their socio-political responsibilities, despite multifaceted economic, technical and structural frame conditions (p. 47). Due to her strong ties to both European culture and African life, she had already developed sensitivity towards social issues quite early. It was especially the close interaction between natural and built environments which can be seen as a major source of inspiration for her designs, that would later shape her artistic approach to places. In “Invention and Tradition in the Making of American Place” (1986), she not only unmasks the paradox of colonial landscapes, but also perceives spatial structures as a matrix for what she calls the “discovery,” or perhaps more aptly, the “rediscovery” of America (p. 8). Just as Le Corbusier called on his contemporaries to understand the aesthetics of industrial

nen Architektur zu verstehen, wendet sich Scott Brown der Rhetorik der unterschätzen Elemente des so genannten *sprawl* zu, der oft nur als urbanes Chaos vorstädtischer Zersiedelung charakterisiert wird. Hier bezieht sie sich auf die zentrale Fragestellung ihres eigenen, mit Robert Venturi und Steven Izenour geschriebenen Buches *Learning from Las Vegas*, das viele als Scott Browns wichtigsten Beitrag zur Architekturtheorie der Gegenwart betrachten, und in dem auf durchwegs polemische Art die elektronische Signatur des Las Vegas Strip untersucht wird.[1] Die Kasinostadt in der Wüste, eine Stadtlandschaft der Popästhetik, deren Erscheinung sich durch die Neon-Reklame bei Nacht gänzlich ändert, verwendet Architektur als symbolische Ausdrucksform der Funktion der Gebäude, sodass die Stadt zum System aus Zeichen, Logos, Symbolen und Gesten wird. Der Las Vegas Strip ist jedoch keine Neuerfindung, sondern ein Modell, das Ornament in gleicher Weise wie die historischen Bauwerke von Rom und Paris nutzt – selbst die Hauptfront der Kathedrale von Chartres funktioniert demnach als Schautafel (und Reklameschild) des Bauwerkes.

Die Originalität dieses Ansatzes liegt jedoch nicht nur im kühlen Realismus, eine gleichsam archäologische Bestandsaufnahme der *beauty in ugliness* der banalen, typisch kommerziellen Architektur und städtischen Infrastruktur zu unternehmen, sondern auch darin, die zunehmende Vereinnahmung des öffentlichen Raumes durch Werbebotschaften und Konsumangebote aufzuzeigen. Doch gerade dieser detaillierte, nüchterne und nicht sogleich wertende Blick auf den Ist-Zustand einer amerikanischen Glitzermetropole stößt bis heute auf heftige Kritik – und wird gar als prototypische, vermeintlich unkritische Haltung interpretiert, die von der nächsten Architektengeneration, allen voran Rem Koolhaas, und ihrer „wertneutralen" (gemeint ist „unpolitischen") Weltsicht weitergeführt wird.

Scott Browns Bezugnahme auf soziale Aspekte in der Stadtplanung, sowohl in ihren Entwürfen als auch in den theoretischen Auseinandersetzungen, steht jedoch dieser Kritik entgegen, nicht nur in der Diskussion in *Having Words* über die Wiederaufbaupläne der Post-Katrina Zeit in „What Should New Orleans Do?" (2005), sondern auch beispielsweise in „A Worm's Eye View of Recent Architectural History" (1984), in dem sie die Entwürfe von Architekten wie Alison und Peter Smithson (und Team 10), Cedric Price oder Buckminster Fuller untersucht, inwieweit sie sozial-utopische Ideen aus dem Erbe der Moderne aufgenommen und weiterentwickelt haben.

Gleich zwei Texte in *Having Words* beschreiben Scott Browns Ringen um Anerkennung in einem von männlichen Kollegen dominierten Berufsfeld, da es ihr ein großes Anliegen ist, gerade bei jüngeren Frauen, die oft glauben, keiner Diskriminierung mehr ausgesetzt zu sein, Interesse und Aufmerksamkeit für Genderthemen zu wecken. In „Planning the Powder Room" (1967) analysiert sie Entwürfe von Waschräumen in öffentlichen Bauten wie Konzerthallen und Theatern und stellt sie als architektonische Metapher für die unterschiedliche Wahrnehmung von Männern und Frauen dar. Ihre oft unangenehmen Erlebnisse mit Kunden, Kollegen und Kritikern – die zu wenig gelesen haben oder einfach unwissend und grob sind – führt sie in „Sexism and the Star System in Architecture" (1989) aus: „The scholars whose work we most respect, the clients whose projects intrigue us, and the patrons whose friendship inspires us, have no problem understanding my role. They are the sophisticated. Partly through

1 Robert Venturi, Denise Scott Brown, Steven Izenour, *Learning From Las Vegas: The Forgotten Symbolism of Architectural Form*. Cambridge, MA 1972; dt. *Lernen von Las Vegas. Zur Ikonographie und Architektursymbolik der Geschäftsstadt* (Bauwelt-Fundamente 53). Wiesbaden 1979.

architectural elements, such as elevators, ships and planes, as an essential part of the development of modern architecture, Scott Brown turns to the rhetoric of the underestimated elements of the so-called *sprawl*, which is often characterized as mere suburban chaos. In that context, she relates to the central question of the book she wrote in collaboration with Robert Venturi and Steven Izenour, *Learning from Las Vegas*, in which the electronic signature of the Las Vegas Strip is investigated in an openly polemical manner.[1] It is regarded by many people as Scott Brown's greatest contribution to contemporary architectural theory. The urban landscape of the desert city, with its many gambling halls and pop aesthetics, is completely transformed by night when all the neon illuminations are switched on. It employs architecture as a symbolic means to express the function of buildings, turning the place into a system of signs, logos, symbols and gestures. Still, the Las Vegas Strip is no new invention, but rather a model that uses ornaments in the same way as historical monuments in Rome or Paris do—even the main front of the Cathedral of Chartres works like a display board (and advertisement) on the building.

The originality of this approach, however, does not only lie in the cool realism of doing a quasi archaeological survey on the *beauty in ugliness* of mundane, typically commercial architecture and urban infrastructure, but also in revealing the increasing exploitation of public space through commercial slogans and consumer ads. However, it is exactly that meticulous, sober and tolerant appraisal of the glittering American metropolis, that has met with fierce criticism until today—it is even interpreted as being a prototypical, seemingly uncritical attitude which lives on in the next generation of architects, first and foremost in Rem Koolhaas, and in their "impartial" (or "unpolitical") outlook on the world.

But Scott Brown's references to the social aspects of urban planning, both in her designs and theoretical arguments, contradict that criticism—not only as part of the discussion in *Having Words* on the reconstruction plans of the post-Katrina era in "What Should New Orleans Do?" (2005), but also, for instance, in "A Worm's Eye View of Recent Architectural History" (1984), in which she analyzes designs of architects like Alison and Peter Smithson (and Team 10), Cedric Price or Buckminster Fuller, in order to find out to what extent they had absorbed and further developed utopian social ideas from the heritage of modernity.

Two stories in *Having Words* describe Scott Brown's struggle for recognition in a profession dominated by men. Ever eager to arouse interest for and attention to gender topics, she especially addresses younger women, who often believe they are no longer being discriminated against. In "Planning the Powder Room" (1967), she analyzes the design of powder rooms in public build-

1 Robert Venturi, Denise Scott Brown, Steven Izenour, *Learning From Las Vegas: The Forgotten Symbolism of Architectural Form*. Cambridge, MA 1972.

them I gain heart [...], I have managed to do my work and, despite some sliding, to achieve my own self-respect" (S. 89).

In diesem Zusammenhang gibt Scott Brown bezüglich *Learning from Las Vegas* den interessanten Hinweis, dass die inzwischen sprichwörtlich gewordene Differenz zwischen *decorated shed* und *duck* keineswegs von Robert Venturi, ihrem Firmenpartner und Ehemann, stammt, sondern eindeutig den Ursprung in ihren Kapiteln des Buches hat. In einer *boy's club*-Atmosphäre (oder *petty apartheid*, wie diese Form der sozialen Unterscheidung in Südafrika genannt wird), wird ihre Arbeit allzu oft trotz deutlicher Hinweise falsch zugeschrieben und – schlimmer noch – sie selbst nicht als eigenständige Planerin und Theoretikerin wahrgenommen, es sei denn in Genderfragen, in denen sie rasch als internationale Kapazität anerkannt worden ist (S. 81). Scott Brown stellt in *Having Words* abschließend fest: „I have come to feel like architecture's grandmother, a guardian of its institutional memory who knows the pitfalls and where the bodies are buried" (S. 156). Als 2010 Kazuyo Sejima zusammen mit ihrem Partner Ryue Nishizawa (SANAA) mit dem Pritzker-Preis ausgezeichnet wurde, war Sejima erst die zweite Frau, die diese Auszeichnung bekam – nach Zaha Hadid, die den Pritzker-Preis 2004 erhielt. Der Entschluss der Jury, diesen im Jahre 1991 an Robert Venturi allein zu vergeben, ohne seine Partnerin Denise Scott Brown ebenfalls auszuzeichnen, wird durch die verdienstvolle Publikation von *Having Words* in der Dimension einer historischen Fehlentscheidung lesbar.

Ingrid Böck

Das Gehirn des Architekten

The Architect's Brain.
Neuroscience, Creativity and Architecture
Harry Francis Mallgrave
Chichester: John Wiley & Sons, 2010
(Taschenbuchausgabe 2011)
englisch, 288 Seiten, Hardcover/broschiert
ISBN 978-1405195850/ISBN 978-0470658253
EUR 83,98 (Hardcover)/EUR 24,99 (broschiert)

Der am IIT in Chicago lehrende Architekturhistoriker Harry Francis Mallgrave, der bisher vor allem durch seine theoriegeschichtlichen Arbeiten über Gottfried Semper und Otto Wagner sowie die zweibändige Anthologie *Architecture in Theory: Vitruvius to the Present* (2006 und 2008) bekannt geworden ist, beschäftigt sich in seinen neueren Forschungen mit der Verortung von Architekturtheorie im Spannungsfeld von Ästhetik, Architekturpsychologie, Neurophysiologie, Psychologie und Medientheorie. *The Architect's Brain. Neuroscience, Creativity and Architecture* stellt kunstwissenschaftlich und philosophisch geprägte Wahrnehmungstheorien und empirische Erkenntnisse aus den Neurowissenschaften in zwei Teilen zusammen.

Der erste Teil behandelt historische Positionen aus Architekturtheorie, Kunstgeschichte, Philosophie und Psychologie. Leitendes Interesse bildet die Beantwortung der Frage, wie und warum Architektur auf den menschlichen Körper einwirken kann und umgekehrt, wie körperliche Zustände oder Konzepte zum menschlichen Körper in die Architektur eingeschrieben werden können. Anhand Theorien von z. B. Edmund Burke, Adolf Göller, Gottfried Semper oder Max Wertheimer untersucht Mallgrave den Zusammenhang physiologischer (z. B. Räume, Farben) und psychischer Phänomene (z. B. Gefühle). So stellt etwa Leon

ings, such as concert halls and theaters, which she describes as architectural metaphors for how men and women are differently perceived. In "Sexism and the Star System in Architecture" (1989), she recounts some of her often unpleasant experiences with clients, colleagues and critics, who had not read enough on the subject or who were simply ignorant and crude, as follows: "The scholars whose work we most respect, the clients whose projects intrigue us, and the patrons whose friendship inspires us, have no problem understanding my role. They are the sophisticated. Partly through them I gain heart ..., I have managed to do my work and, despite some sliding, to achieve my own self-respect" (p. 89).

In this context, Scott Brown relates to *Learning from Las Vegas* pointing out that the proverbial difference between *decorated shed* and *duck* does not originate from her husband and associate Robert Venturi, but clearly from her contribution to that book. In the atmosphere of a boy's club (or petty apartheid, as that type of social differentiation is called in South Africa), and despite clear references to the contrary, her work is often wrongly associated and—even worse—she is not even perceived as an independent planner and theorist, except with regard to gender questions in which capacity she quickly gained international repute (p. 81).

Scott Brown's conclusion in *Having Words* is: "I have come to feel like architecture's grandmother, a guardian of its institutional memory who knows the pitfalls and where the bodies are buried" (p. 156). When in 2010 Kazuyo Sejima was awarded the Pritzker Prize together with her associate Ryue Nishizawa (SANAA), Sejima was only the second woman to have received that prize after Zaha Hadid, who won the Pritzker Prize in 2004. In the light of the highly commendable book *Having Words*, the jury's decision back in 1991 to award the Prize solely to Robert Venturi, ignoring his associate Denise Scott Brown, seems to be one of the worst ever.

Ingrid Böck

The Brain of the Architect

The Architect's Brain:
Neuroscience, Creativity and Architecture
Harry Francis Mallgrave
Chichester: John Wiley & Sons, 2010
(paperback 2011)
English, 288 pages, hardcover/paperback
ISBN 978-1405195850/ISBN 978-0470658253
EUR 83.98 (hardcover)
EUR 24.99 (paperback)

The architectural historian Harry Francis Mallgrave, who teaches at the IIT in Chicago, is known primarily for his theoretical and historical monographs on Gottfried Semper and Otto Wagner as well as the two-volume anthology of *Architecture in Theory: Vitruvius to the Present* (2006 and 2008). His new research interest is the positioning of architecture theory in the tension between aesthetics, architectural psychology, neurophysiology, psychology, and media theory. *The Architect's Brain: Neuro-*

8

Battista Alberti mithilfe des universalen Konzepts der *concinnitas* (Ebenmaß) eine Analogie zwischen Körper und Bauwerk her. Karl Friedrich Schinkel diskutiert die Fusion von architektonischer Struktur und Schönheit mit dem Konzept der Zweckmäßigkeit. Bei Wolfgang Köhler ist es schließlich das Konzept der Isomorphie, das die Koppelung neuronaler Strukturen mit distalen Reizen erklärt. Die Metapher des „Gehirns des Architekten" erschließt sich mit fortschreitender Darstellung zusehends, indem Mallgrave anhand der einzelnen Positionen Hypothesen darüber aufstellt, welche spezifischen neurologischen Aspekte beim architektonischen Entwerfen und im besonderen beim Wahrnehmen von Architektur relevant sein könnten.

Der zweite Teil behandelt aktuelle Positionen aus den Neurowissenschaften wie etwa dem Zweig Neuroästhetik. Leitendes Interesse gilt hier der Beantwortung der Frage, welche neurologischen Aktivitäten den kognitiven Fähigkeiten von Architekten zugrunde gelegt werden können. Anhand Theorien von u. a. Bernard J. Baars, Rita Carter, Francis Crick, Susan Greenfield oder Semir Zeki untersucht Mallgrave, ob spezifisch mentale Dispositionen von Architekten feststellbar sind. Konkret werden die Konzepte Plastizität, Mehrdeutigkeit, Metaphorik und Haptizität vorgestellt: Plastizität oder Neuroplastizität bezieht sich auf die Umorganisation neuronaler Zellverbände durch Lernprozesse. Mehrdeutigkeit kann als die Fähigkeit verstanden werden, auf ähnliche distale Reize mit unterschiedlichen neuronalen Aktivitäten zu reagieren. Metaphorik basiert auf dem Konzept der Übertragung und wird häufig zur Erklärung kreativer Prozesse herangezogen. Haptizität kann bei synästhetischen Wahrnehmungen auftreten, wobei die Kombination verschiedener Sinnesempfindungen zu neuen sinnlichen Erfahrungen führen kann.

The Architect's Brain (8) setzt in philosophischer Hinsicht mehr voraus als *Brain Landscape* von John P. Eberhard (2009), wobei sich beide Werke insofern ergänzen, als dass sie zeigen, wie ungreifbar dieses Thema noch ist und wie schwer sich Thesen zur Wahrnehmung empirisch belegen sowie in den architektonischen Entwurfsprozess integrieren lassen. So wird z. B. versucht, Methoden und Erkenntnisse aus den Neurowissenschaften bei der Planung von Ausbildungsstätten, Inkubatoren oder Rehabilitationszentren zu berücksichtigen, um die mentale Entwicklung der Endnutzer zu verbessern. Kritisch ist anzumerken, dass die Aneinanderreihung der einzelnen skizzierten Positionen im ersten Teil ohne eine konzise Zusammenführung erfolgt. So wäre z. B. eine wissenschaftsgeschichtliche oder -psychologische Gegenüberstellung der Funktion und Wirkung der gewonnenen Konzepte in der architektonischen Entwurfshandlung im Speziellen hilf-

science, Creativity and Architecture presents art historical and philosophically oriented theories of perception as well as empirical findings from the neurosciences in two parts.

The first part deals with historical positions of architectural theory, art history, philosophy and psychology. The main interest is the answer to the question as to how and why architecture can affect the human body and inversely how bodily states or concepts of the human body can be inscribed in architecture. Embarking theories of e.g. Edmund Burke, Adolf Göller, Gottfried Semper oder Max Wertheimer, Mallgrave examines how theories of the philosophy of perception describe the amalgamation of physical conditions (such as spaces or colors) with psychological states (e.g. emotions). To this end, Mallgrave studies, for example, the universal concept of *concinnitas* (symmetry), which Leon Battista Alberti defined on the basis of an analogy between the human body and the building. For Karl Friedrich Schinkel, the principle of functionality mediates between architectural structure and beauty. For Wolfgang Köhler, it is ultimately the concept of isomorphism, which explains the coupling of neural structures with distal stimuli. As the argument proceeds, the metaphor of the "brain of the architect" broadens more and more as Mallgrave sets up hypotheses about specific neurological aspects that could be relevant to the design and in particular the perception of architecture.

The second part deals with current positions in the neurosciences, including neuroaesthetics. The central interest examines the question of how neurological activity can be used to describe cognitive architectural skills. He asks, for example, by using the concepts of Bernard J. Baars, Rita Carter, Francis Crick, Susan Greenfield, or Semir Zeki, among others, whether there could be a specific disposition of architects. In particular the concepts of plasticity, ambiguity, metaphor and hapticity are scrutinized: plasticity and neuroplasticity refer to the reorganization of neuronal cell groups through learning. Ambiguity can be understood as the ability to respond to similar distal stimuli with different neural activities. Metaphor or a transfer of concepts is often used to explain the creative process. Hapticity may occur in synaesthetic perception, when the combination of different sensations sometimes produces new sensory experiences.

From a philosophical point of view, *The Architect's Brain* (8) is more demanding than *Brain Landscape* by John P. Eberhard (2009), though the two works complement one another as both show how elusive their subject still is and how difficult it is to prove the perceptual hypotheses or integrate them in the architectural design process. The author attempts to make use of neuroscientific methods and findings in the planning of training centers, incubators or rehabilitation centers to improve the psychological development of end-users. In criticism, it should be pointed out that the theoretical positions are outlined in the first part of *The Architect's Brain* without a sufficient background. It would have been helpful,

reich gewesen. Die Konzepte werden teilweise auf einer sehr allgemeinen philosophischen Ebene und vor allem vor dem biografischen Hintergrund der besprochenen Autoren kontextualisiert, ohne ihre diskursanalytischen Umgebungsbedingungen zu rekonstruieren. Phänomenologische Positionen zur Korrelation von psychischen und physischen Phänomenen sind zwar nur schwache Befunde für eine Theorie, die auf eine empirische Fundierung spezifisch entwerferischer Wahrnehmungs- und Erkenntnisformen mithilfe der Neurowissenschaften hinaus will, können aber zum Verständnis aktueller Hypothesen von z. B. António R. Damásio, Vilayanur S. Ramachandran oder Semir Zeki beitragen. Was im ersten Teil zu viel an Befunden und Beispielen geboten wird, würde im zweiten Teil helfen, den „kreativen Prozess selbst" auf Basis neurowissenschaftlicher Konzepte zu beschreiben. Die beiden exemplarisch besprochenen Bauwerke von Andrea Palladio und Frank Lloyd Wright im Kapitel „Mehrdeutigkeit" schließen nicht bei der Argumentation zur Neuroästhetik an, sondern werden in Form traditioneller Architekturinterpretationen vorgestellt, wobei sich eben nicht der Wert und die Funktion von Mehrdeutigkeit im „kreativen Prozess selbst" erschließt. Mehrdeutigkeit als kognitiver Vorgang, Arbeit mit visuellen Vorstellungen oder Aspektsehen wird durch die formalen Analysen zugunsten ihrer Verwendung in der Bildforschung als Begriff der ikonografischen Bauanalyse entschärft. Denn mittels der Ikonografie ist es schwierig, kognitiv relevante Prozesse beim Entwerfen zu rekonstruieren. Anschlusspunkte zur Erforschung des „Gehirns des Architekten" aus der Perspektive der Kognitionswissenschaften könnten helfen, den Blick mehr auf den architektonischen Entwurfsprozess zu lenken. Aufgrund der Gewichtung philosophisch und künstlerisch geprägter Positionen werden wenig Arbeiten im Spannungsfeld von Neurologie, künstlicher Intelligenz und Kybernetik vorgestellt.

Die vielschichtige Darstellung im zweiten Teil des Buches verdeutlicht die Problematik einer gängigen reduktionistischen Sichtweise von Intelligenz und Bewusstsein. Mit kritischer Distanz zu Computermetaphern des Geistes in den Bereichen Architektur und Design in Hinblick auf die Simulation von Entwurfsprozessen durch die Informatik richten sich die Hauptargumente in diesem Buch gegen Hypothesen einer starken künstlichen Intelligenz. Mallgrave gelangt schließlich zur medientheoretischen und didaktischen Frage nach der Relevanz informationsverarbeitender Entwurfswerkzeuge in der Ausbildung von Architekten. Die Kritik an visuell orientierten digitalen Entwurfswerkzeugen scheint berechtigt, da diese nicht der Schlüssel zur effizienten neuronalen Entwicklung sind und Feingefühl wie synästhetische Wahrnehmung im Entwurfsprozess der Zukunft Berücksichtigung finden müssen.

Gert Hasenhütl

Formfindung jenseits des Marktes

The Function of Form
Farshid Moussavi
Hg. mit Daniel López, Garrick Ambrose, Ben Fortunato, Ryan Ludwig, Ahmadreza Schricker
Barcelona: Actar und Harvard University Graduate School of Design, 2009
englisch, 502 Seiten, Illustrationen, Hardcover
ISBN 978-8496954731
EUR 39,95

Die aus dem Iran stammende britische Architektin Farshid Moussavi ist dem breiteren Architek-

for example, to contrast and compare the function and effect of the various hypotheses, in particular as regards the architectural design process, in historical or psychological terms. In some cases, the concepts are contextualized on a very general philosophical level from a mainly biographical perspective of the authors, without a reconstruction of the relevant discourse analytical conditions. Phenomenological hypotheses about the correlation of mental and physical phenomena only provide weak evidence for a theory that attempts to establish an empirical, neuroscientific foundation for specifically design-related forms of perception and cognition, but they can contribute to the understanding of current hypotheses by e.g. António R. Damásio, Vilayanur S. Ramachandran or Semir Zeki. While the first part brings up too many findings and examples, they would have been helpful in the second part to describe the "creative process" on the basis of neuroscientific concepts. The chapter on "ambiguity," for example, discusses two buildings by Andrea Palladio and Frank Lloyd Wright not in terms of neuroaesthetics but rather as in traditional architectural interpretation, without highlighting the value and function of ambiguity in the "creative process itself." The formal analyses are pertinent to iconography or visual studies but they fail to consider ambiguity in the cognitive process, working with visual images or aspect seeing. Iconography is hardly able to reconstruct the cognitive processes relevant to design. Exploring the "brain of the architect" from the perspective of cognitive science could help draw the eye more on the architectural design process. Stressing of philosophical and artistical positions, the author neglects to discuss studies at the interface of neuroscience, artificial intelligence and cybernetics. The complex presentation in the second part shows how problematic a reductionist view of intelligence and consciousness is. Mallgrave distances himself from the computer analogy of the mind that has been often assumed for the purposes of simulating the design process with a computer; hence the main arguments in his book are directed against hypotheses of a strong artificial intelligence. He ends with the media theoretical and didactic question concerning the relevance of information-processing design tools in architectural education. His critique of only visually oriented digital instruments seems justified, since these are not the key to efficient neural development, and the design process in the future must pay attention to sensitivity and synaesthetic perception.

Gert Hasenhütl

turpublikum spätestens seit ihrem Gewinn des internationalen Wettbewerbs *Yokahama Port Terminal* bekannt. Diesen konnte sie 1996 gemeinsam mit ihrem Partner Alejandro Zaera Polo unter dem Namen F.O.A. (Foreign Office Architects) für sich entscheiden. Der siegreiche Entwurf wurde nach einer intensiven Planungsphase umgesetzt und im November 2002 fertiggestellt. Es handelt sich dabei um ein Passagierterminal im Hafengebiet Yokohamas, der die Bewegungsströme über eine künstliche Landschaft topografisch geformter Flächen organisiert.

„Form follows function" – mit dem bekannten Diktum Louis Sullivans beginnt Moussavi die Einleitung zu ihrem aktuellen Buch *The Function of Form* (9), das sie als Professorin an der Harvard Graduate School of Design nach dem auf Fassaden fokussierten *The Function of Ornament* (2006) herausgegeben hat. Der Begriff „Funktion" besaß für Sullivan immer eine kulturelle und eine soziale Bedeutung. Verschiedene Gebäudetypen waren verbunden mit verschiedenen Materialien. Die Funktion umschloss für Sullivan alle Dinge: organisch und anorganisch, physisch und metaphysisch, menschlich und übermenschlich – „all true manifestations of the head, of the heart, of the soul".[1] Die moderne Architektur des 20. Jahrhunderts adaptierte diesen Funktionsbegriff, indem sie ihn zu einem Aspekt des Gebrauchs verkürzte. Die Funktion wurde als „Hilfsprogramm" einer gebauten Form definiert; eine Interpretation, die bekanntlich bis heute immer wieder Unstimmigkeiten zwischen Architekten und Theoretikern hervorruft.

„But if not function what does form follow?", fragt Moussavi weiters in ihrer Einleitung. Für sie ergeben sich drei wesentliche gemeinsame Bedeutungen aus den Aussagen der Theoretiker der Moderne und den ihnen folgenden Revisionisten: Erstens, dass die Gesellschaft durch eine einheitliche Kultur definiert sei. Zweitens, dass der physischen Form ein Prinzip oder eine Ursache zugrunde liege, die durch eine objektive oder subjektive Einigung entstehe. Und drittens, dass Form einen Eindruck vermittle, indem sie auf eine singuläre Bedeutung – Identität – oder eine Möglichkeit reagiere. Diese konträren Ansichten über die Rolle der Form sind für Moussavi Ausdruck der Fülle an gegensätzlichen Meinungen, welche die Architektur im 20. Jahrhundert dominiert haben.

Der amerikanische Architekturtheoretiker K. Michael Hays umreißt in seinem Essay *Critical Architecture* zwei mögliche Positionen der Architektur gegenüber der Kultur.[2] Entweder sei sie Instrument oder autonome Form. Betrachtet man

1 Louis H. Sullivan, „The Tall Office Building Artistically Considered" [1896], in: ders., *The Public Papers*. Hg. von Robert Twombly. Chicago und London 1988, S. 103–112, hier S. 111.

2 K. Michael Hays, „Critical Architecture: Between Culture and Form", in: *Perspecta 21: The Yale Architectural Journal* (1984), S. 14–29.

Form-Finding Beyond the Market

The Function of Form

Farshid Moussavi
Ed. with Daniel López, Garrick Ambrose, Ben Fortunato, Ryan Ludwig, Ahmadreza Schricker
Barcelona: Actar and Harvard University Graduate School of Design, 2009
English, 502 pages, illustrations, hardcover,
ISBN 978-8496954731
EUR 39.95

Iranian-born British architect Farshid Moussavi has been a household name for a wider architectural audience at least since the international *Yokahama Port Terminal* competition, which she won together with her associate Alejandro Zaera Polo as F.O.A. (Foreign Office Architects) in 1996. The winning design was built following an intensive phase of planning and completed in November 2002. It is a passenger terminal in Yokohama's port area that organizes circulation on the basis of an artificial landscape made up of topographically shaped surfaces.

"Form follows function"—this well-known Louis Sullivan maxim kicks off the introduction to Moussavi's current book *The Function of Form* (9), which she has published as professor at the Harvard Graduate School of Design following *The Function of Ornament* (2006) that focused on façades. The concept of "function" always had a cultural and a social meaning for Sullivan. Different types of building were connected with different materials. For Sullivan, function encompassed all things: organic and inorganic, physical and metaphysical, human and superhuman—"all true manifestations of the head, of the heart, of the soul."[1] Modernist architecture of the 20th century adapted this concept of function by abridging it to an aspect of use. Function was defined as a "utility program" of built form; an interpretation that, as we know, continues to cause differences between architects and theorists to this day.

"But if not function what does form follow?" Moussavi goes on to ask in her introduction. For her, the views stated by modernist theorists and the subsequent revisionists comprise three essential common meanings: firstly, that society is defined by a uniform culture. Secondly, that physical form is founded upon a principle or cause that arises through objective or subjective agreement. And thirdly, that form creates an impression by reacting to a singular meaning—identity—or possibility. These contrary views of the role of form are, to Moussavi, expression of the abundance of contrasting opinions that have dominated architecture in the 20th century.

The American architectural theorist K. Michael Hays outlines in his essay *Critical Architecture* two possible positions of architecture vis-à-vis culture.[2] It is either instrument or autonomous

1 Louis H. Sullivan, "The Tall Office Building Artistically Considered" [1896], in: idem, *The Public Papers*. Ed. by Robert Twombly. Chicago and London 1988, pp. 103–112, here p. 111.

nach Hays die Arbeiten Mies van der Rohes, tue sich eine dritte Möglichkeit auf: „zwischen Kultur und Form" – als Kritik an der vorherrschenden Kultur (der Verdinglichung). Diese Positionen sind nun nach Moussavi nach wie vor gültig. Zudem habe sich die zeitgenössische Architektur zwei wesentlichen Herausforderungen zu stellen: Kultur sei nicht statisch, weshalb Mies' Haltung praktisch nicht mehr einzunehmen sei, und Form sei kein vorab festgelegtes abstraktes Prinzip, welches „der Kultur" Ausdruck und Bedeutung verleihe. Historisch betrachtet sei die physische Form immer an ein Material und dessen Produktionstechniken gebunden gewesen. Zwischen Produktion und Wahrnehmung der Form als solcher habe Unmittelbarkeit geherrscht und Form, anders als heute, nicht weiter vermittelt werden müssen.

Darauf Bezug nehmend unterscheidet Farshid Moussavi drei Arten von Formen im Zusammenspiel mit ihrer kulturellen Rolle: Neben den „unmediated forms" früherer Zeiten die „mediated forms" und so genannten „novel forms". „Mediated" würden Formen als Reaktion auf die moderne Fokussierung auf das Objekt erscheinen, was dazu geführt habe, dass sie oft unter Zuhilfenahme von Metaphern mit Bedeutungen aufgeladen worden seien. Der Symbolismus von Robert Venturi und Denise Scott Brown, aber auch die topografischen Überlagerungen Peter Eisenmans wären dafür bekannte Beispiele. Die „novel forms" schließlich entwickelten sich vor dem Hintergrund eines sich in zunehmendem Maße ausdifferenzierenden Marktes. Konsumgüter aus der Massenproduktion seien über verschiedene Modi der Anpassung individualisierbar. Evolution – nicht Revolution – sei der bestimmende Modus der Entwicklung. Eine existierende Form werde mit einer anderen kombiniert und ergebe eine hybride dritte Form. Die „novel form" sei also niemals eine Kopie von etwas Vorhandenem, aber immer schon in den evolutionären Stammbäumen anderer Formen angelegt. Diese Feststellung ist zugleich mit einer Warnung versehen: Wenn wir nun dem Markt erlauben, die einzige Quelle für neue Formen zu sein, so werde unsere Kultur stagnieren, monotoner und einheitlicher werden. Die Herausforderung aller an der Entstehung von Kultur beteiligten Personen liegt für Moussavi nun in der Durchmischung der Produktion von Form mit einer Vielzahl an Zielformulierungen, die sich nicht ausschließlich an Programmvorgaben des Marktes orientieren und dadurch zu einer Umgebung beitragen können, welche den Individuen eine Vielzahl an entsprechenden Wahlmöglichkeiten offen lässt.

Moussavi erörtert die „novel forms" auch anhand einiger bekannter Beispiele aus der Architekturgeschichte, darunter Moscheen und gotische Kathedralen. Letztere seien, so die Autorin, nicht auf einem idealen geometrischen System aufgebaut, sondern auf einer Art „Proto-Geometrie", die „anexakt" – präzise, aber nicht in genauen Abmessungen festgelegt – sei.[3] Diese „Proto-Geometrie" wäre zu allererst biegsam und elastisch und daher in der Lage gewesen, auf verschiedene Einflüsse zu reagieren: Ob auf unregelmäßig zugeschnittene Grundstücksgrößen, auf die Beteiligung von verschiedenen Baumeistern oder die Änderung der Interessen der Auftraggeber; die Proto-Geometrie habe geholfen, produktiv, ökonomisch oder subjektiv weitgehend flexibel zu reagieren.

Gilles Deleuze gibt uns letztlich einen Hinweis für die Intention des Buches: Nach ihm existiert nichts außerhalb der Welt, in der wir leben. Es gebe keine transzendenten Ideale. Unsere Welt sei aus virtuellen und aktuellen Formen zusam-

3 Gilles Deleuze, Félix Guattari, *Tausend Plateaus. Kapitalismus und Schizophrenie* Bd. II [*Mille Plateaux*. Paris 1980]. Berlin 1992, Kap. 12, S. 504f.

form. Considering the works of Mies van der Rohe from Hays' viewpoint, there is a third possibility: "between culture and form"—as criticism of the predominant culture (of reification). For Moussavi, these positions remain valid. What is more, she says, contemporary architecture must face up to two main challenges: culture is not static, which is why Mies' approach is no longer practicable, and form is not an a priori abstract principle that gives expression and meaning to "culture." Historically, physical form has always been tied to a material and the technologies of its production. There was, she continues, immediacy between the production and perception of form as such, and, unlike today, form needed no further conveyance.

With reference to this, Moussavi distinguishes between three types of form in terms of their cultural role: in addition to the "unmediated forms" of earlier times, these are "mediated forms" and so-called "novel forms." Forms, she maintains, appear "mediated" as a reaction to the modernist focus on the object, which often resulted in them being charged with meanings by employing metaphors. Familiar examples of this are the symbolism of Robert Venturi and Denise Scott Brown, but also the topographic overlappings of Peter Eisenman. "Novel forms," finally, developed against the foil of an increasingly differentiated market. Mass-produced consumer goods, she observes, can be customized by various modes of adaptation. Evolution—not revolution—is the defining mode of the development. An existing form is combined with another so as to create a hybrid third form. "Novel form," then, is never a copy of something that already exists, but has rather always been inherent in the evolutionary pedigrees of other forms. She combines this observation with a warning: if we allow the market to be the sole source of new forms, our culture will stagnate and become more monotonous and uniform. For Moussavi, the challenge for anyone involved in creating culture is to mingle the production of form with a host of formulated targets which are based not only on programmatic goals of the market and which thus may contribute to an environment that leaves a myriad of options open to the individual.

Moussavi also discusses "novel forms" by citing several well-known examples from the history of architecture, including mosques and Gothic cathedrals. The latter, the author says, are not built on an ideal geometric system, but on a kind of "proto-geometry" that is "anexact"—precise but not codified in exact dimensions.[3] This "proto-geometry" was, first and foremost, pliable and elastic and thus capable of reacting to different influences: be it irregular plot sizes, the involvement of different building contractors, or changing client interests; proto-geometry helped

2 K. Michael Hays, "Critical Architecture: Between Culture and Form," in: *Perspecta 21: The Yale Architectural Journal* (1984), pp. 14–29.

3 Gilles Deleuze, Félix Guattari, *A Thousand Plateaus: Capitalism and Schizophrenia*, vol. II [*Mille Plateaux*, Paris 1980]. London, New York 2004, chapter 12, p. 405.

mengesetzt. Virtuelle Formen seien keine Ideale – abgetrennt von der Realität –, sondern abstrakte Ideen, die noch nicht realisiert worden seien. In diesem Sinn erforscht dieses Buch die Idee von Architektur als fortschreitendem Prozess des Produzierens von *novel forms* und als Produktion von Identitäten durch Wiederholung und Differenzierung virtueller Formen. Wobei zwar die Kategorisierung, aber nicht die Auswahlkriterien der auf ca. 450 Seiten geometrisch dargestellten Formen nachvollziehbar sind.

Emilio Hauer

Architekturkritik als Ideologiekritik

From Autos to Architecture.
Fordism and Architectural Aesthetics in the Twentieth Century
David Gartman
New York: Princeton Architectural Press, 2009
englisch, 400 Seiten, Illustrationen, Hardcover
ISBN 978-1-56898-813-9
EUR 47,99

From Autos to Architecture (10): Nicht darum, welche Autos von welchen ArchitektInnen gefahren werden, sondern um den Einfluss der (Auto-)Massenproduktion auf die Architekturgeschichte vom Beginn der Moderne bis zum Dekonstruktivismus geht es in David Gartmans Buch. Durch die Optik der „Auto-Brille" legt der Autor dar, wie Fordismus und Postfordismus – Epochen bzw. Systeme disziplinierter bzw. flexibilisierter Massenproduktion und -konsumtion – ihre Ideologien nicht zuletzt räumlich ausformen.[1]

Industrialisierung ist eng mit Architekturproduktion wie auch -ästhetik verbunden. Dabei beleuchtet Gartman Europa und Amerika separat, so etwa mit der Frage, warum sich gerade in Europa die Neue Sachlichkeit in Anlehnung an die Maschinenästhetik der Industrialisierung so frühzeitig durchsetzte, wo doch Europa im frühen 20. Jahrhundert längst noch nicht „fordisiert" war: „The emergence of a machine aesthetic in Europe rather than the United States must thus be explained by the different class structures and class conflicts of these regions" (S. 17). Basierend auf Pierre Bourdieus Theorie von Habitus und sozialen Feldern verknüpft Gartman die Geschichte von Klassen(bewegungen) mit deren ästhetischem Verständnis von Architektur. So geht es ihm um die soziale Herkunft von Le Corbusier oder Ludwig Mies van der Rohe ebenso wie darum, dass die europäischen Modernen sich der Sozialdemokratie nicht nur aufgrund ihrer politischen Haltung zur Verfügung stellten, sondern auch um von deren öffentlichen Aufträgen zu profitieren.

Gartman, heute Professor für Soziologie an der University of South Alabama, bringt seine eigene Biografie ins Vorwort ein: Er bezeichnet sich als einstigen „working class boy", der in seiner Jugend Autos und Funktionalität schätzen gelernt und sich in seinem Studium „architecture and high culture" erschlossen habe. Er betrachtet sich selbst durch die Bourdieu'sche Optik: Diesem Referenzsystem entsprechend sieht er seine eigene Herkunft und Klassenmobilität als ebenso ausschlaggebend für sein Interesse am Konnex von Auto und Hochkultur wie im weiteren das soziale Feld, in dem die jeweils erörterten Architekten agieren, für deren Ideen und Bauten.

1 Zu eben diesem Zusammenhang siehe auch meinen Text „Vom Herstellen zum Ausstellen – Die Fabriken und Schauräume des Fordismus, Toyotismus und Postfordismus", in: Gabu Heindl (Hg.), *Arbeit Zeit Raum. Bilder und Bauten der Arbeit im Postfordismus*. Wien 2008, S. 138–163.

in being able to react productively, economically or, subjectively, with a large degree of flexibility.

Gilles Deleuze ultimately points to the book's intention: according to him, nothing exists outside of the world in which we live. There are no transcendental ideals. Our world is made up of virtual and actual forms. Virtual forms are not ideals—detached from reality—but rather abstract ideas that have yet to be realized. In this sense, this book explores the idea of architecture as a progressive process of producing novel forms and as the production of identities by repeating and differentiating virtual forms. However, while the categorization of the geometrically presented forms on the roughly four hundred and fifty pages is clear enough, the criteria for their selection are not.

Emilio Hauer

Architectural Criticism as the Critique of Ideology

From Autos to Architecture:
Fordism and Architectural Aesthetics in the Twentieth Century
David Gartman
New York: Princeton Architectural Press, 2009
English, 400 pages, illustrations, hardcover,
ISBN 978-1-56898-813-9
EUR 47.99

From Autos to Architecture (10): David Gartman's book is not about which cars are driven by which architects, but rather about the influence of mass production on the history of architecture from the beginning of modernism to deconstructivism. Looking through "automobile spectacles" the author examines how Fordism and post-Fordism—periods or systems of disciplined or flexible mass production and consumption—unfold their ideologies also spatially.[1]

Industrialization is closely related to the production and aesthetics of architecture. Gartman studies Europe and America separately, stressing the question of why the industrial machine aesthetic took such an early hold in Europe in the form of the New Objectivity even though the continent was not particularly advanced in the Fordian modes of production: "The emergence of a machine aesthetic in Europe rather than the United States must thus be explained by the different class structures and class conflicts of these regions" (p. 7). Applying Pierre Bourdieu's theory of habitus and social fields, Gartman links the history of social classes with their aesthetic understanding of architecture. Consequently, he examines the social background of Le Corbusier or Ludwig Mies van der Rohe, and suggests that

1 On this connection, please also consult my paper, "Vom Herstellen zum Ausstellen: Die Fabriken und Schauräume des Fordismus, Toyotismus und Postfordismus," in: Gabu Heindl (ed.), *Arbeit Zeit Raum: Bilder und Bauten der Arbeit im Postfordismus*. Vienna 2008, pp. 138–163.

10

Neben Bourdieu gibt es einen zweiten durchgängigen Referenzstrang: ein Konzept von „true art", das der Autor von Theodor W. Adornos negativer Dialektik bezieht. Gartman sucht nach einer Architektur, die sich nicht vom Kapital vereinnahmen lässt, sich nicht selbst kommodifiziert oder die Härten des fordistischen Arbeitsregimes vertuscht. Wiederholt kritisiert Gartman die Art, wie Ästhetik dazu dient, einer Konfrontation mit der unschönen Wirklichkeit von Massenproduktion auszuweichen: mit Accessoires und Product-Design in der Auto-Industrie, analog dazu mit fließenden Formen, Applikationen oder Historisierung in architektonischen Stilen. Vergleichbar mit dem Effekt, den privater Autobesitz auf die Beschwichtigung des Unmuts von Massenarbeitern hätte, führe der Besitz des eigenen Häuschens (v. a. in den endlosen Suburbs der USA) zu finanzieller Abhängigkeit und kleinfamiliärer Sozialisierung der Arbeiterschaft: Modernismus als eine Strategie der Segregation. Wenn also die Flucht vor der Stadt nach Suburbia eine Flucht vor dem Fordismus ist, oder die Flucht in Dekorationen bzw. immer neue Stile eine Flucht vor der Ästhetik der Massenproduktion, so münden diese Bewegungen letztlich doch wieder genau in die Abhängigkeit vom industriellen Massenregime. Alles schon oft gehört? Ja, aber selten im Kontext der Architekturkritik.

Ohne in Formenlehre oder Taxonomien zu verfallen, entfaltet der Autor anhand der Ästhetik spezifischer Architekturen Ideologie und soziales Feld sowohl der ProduzentInnen als auch der KonsumentInnen – Blue Collar, White Collar, Capital Bourgeoisie, Cultural Bourgeoisie –, die im ständigen Distinktionsspiel Präferenzen und Geschmäcker wechseln. Die architektonische Form wird so auf das zurückgeführt, worin sie einen Unterschied macht.

Hin und wieder jedoch führt Gartmans Ideologiekritik zu Vereinfachungen, tendenziell zur Mythologisierung. Kapitel 3 über NS-Zeit und -Ästhetik beginnt mit „Ford and the Führer" und neigt dazu, Geschichte und ideologische Systeme auf Einzelpersonen zu reduzieren. Auch romantische Autobahnkonzepte und prämoderne Weltentwürfe stellt Gartman etwas zu sehr als Ideen prägender Männer hin: „[Frank Lloyd] Wright, like Hitler, knew that to create a rural idyll with machines, all the aesthetic markers of the industrial mechanism had to be carefully concealed under an organic veneer of nature" (S. 176f). Hier schrumpfen Systeme und Diskurse zu dem, was ein Wright oder Hitler jeweils „wussten".

Gartman analysiert anhand konkreter Projekte von Louis Kahn, Le Corbusier, Mies van der Rohe, Albert Speer, Robert Venturi, Archigram, Michael Graves und anderen, wie deren jeweiliges Naheverhältnis zum Kapital Ansätze zur Kri-

modern European architects embraced social democracy not only because of their political beliefs but also as a means to get public commissions.

Gartman, who is at present a professor of sociology at the University of South Alabama, refers to his own biography in the preface: he describes himself as a former "working class boy" who in his youth appreciated cars and functionality and only during his college years turned to "architecture and high culture." Looking at himself through Bourdieu's eyes, he acknowledges that his own background and class mobility have shaped his research interest in the connections between cars and high culture as much as the architect's ideas and designs were determined by their social position.

In addition to Bourdieu, the author relies on another frame of reference, a concept of "true art," derived from Theodor W. Adorno's negative dialectics. Gartman is looking for an architecture that resists appropriation by capital, that will not commodify itself nor cover up the harshness of the Fordian regime of work. He repeatedly criticizes the way in which aesthetics is used to avoid a confrontation with the ugly reality of mass production: with accessories and product design in the car industry, and by analogy also with fluid forms or the application of historical styles. Just like having a car of your own appeased the resentment of the workers, the ownership of a small house (especially in the endless suburbs of the U.S.) resulted in their financial dependence and small family socialization: modernism functioned as a strategy of segregation. If, then, the flight from the city to suburbia is nothing but an escape from Fordism, and the flight into decoration and new styles nothing but an escape from the aesthetics of mass production, so these movements ultimately go back full circle to the dependence on the mass industrial regime. Heard it all before so many times? Yes, but rarely in the context of architectural criticism.

Without falling into morphology or taxonomy, the author examines the aesthetics of specific architectures and uncovers the ideology and social fields of both the producers and the consumers—whether blue collar, white collar, capital bourgeoisie or cultural bourgeoisie—who adjust their preferences and tastes in a never-ending game of distinction. Architectural form is thus reduced to the core dimension that makes a difference.

Occasionally, however, Gartner's critique of ideology results in simplifications, even to mythologizing. The third chapter on the Third Reich and Nazi aesthetics begins with the words, "Ford and the Führer," and tends to reduce history and ideology to powerful individuals. Even romantic highway concepts and pre-modern Utopian designs are described too much as the ideas of formative men: "[Frank Lloyd] Wright, like Hitler, knew that to create a rural idyll with machines, all the aesthetic markers of the industrial mechanism had to be carefully concealed under an organic veneer of nature" (pp. 176f.). Here complex social systems and discourses are reduced to what Wright or Hitler "knew."

tikfähigkeit verunmöglichte. Dabei sei die Postmoderne, trotz ihrer lauten Kritik an der Moderne, nicht weniger ideologisch als der Funktionalismus; dasselbe gelte für den New Urbanism oder manche Ausprägungen des Dekonstruktivismus. So sei die dekonstruktive Euphorie in Sachen Globalität und Befreiung von Regulierungen letztlich eine Ideologie der fraglosen Anpassung an veränderte Ansprüche des Kapitalismus. Beispielhaft nennt Gartman *signature architecture* als integralen Teil globaler Konsumkultur: Bauten von Renzo Piano, Bernard Tschumi, Zaha Hadid und, ultimativ exemplarisch, Rem Koolhaas' Prada-Flagship Stores: Das ist so einleuchtend wie wenig überraschend.

Im Dekonstruktivismus als prägnantester Form des Postfordismus findet Gartman aber auch Positionen, die „antagonistische" Züge aufweisen: Als „potentially antagonistic to the economic bourgeosie" sieht er (neben dem International Style) Peter Eisenman. Durch Unterrichts- und Schreibtätigkeit finanziell unabhängig, sei Eisenman fähig, die autonome Position einer „true critical art" zu beziehen, mehr noch: Seine Architektur „would create, in Adorno's words, an ‚emancipated society'", in der die Schönheit eines Versprechens von Versöhnung in Spannung gesetzt sei zur Sichtbarmachung der hässlichen postfordistischen Realität, die diese Versöhnung verweigere. Und: Eisenmans Dekonstruktivismus gäbe dem Protest gegen globalen Kapitalismus eine „formal voice" (S. 388f.). Damit mutet Gartman einmal mehr einer prägenden Einzelperson eine Menge zu.

Solche Momente von Pathos sind umso erstaunlicher, wenn man bedenkt, wie sehr ein Gestus polemischen Insistierens den Großteil des Buchs prägt; dieser Aspekt besticht ebenso wie der Detail- und Materialreichtum der Studie. Nicht zuletzt ist Gartmans Art, kritische Theorie und Soziologie eng mit der Architekturgeschichte zu verknüpfen (und nicht einfach über sie „drüberzustülpen"), in der Architekturdiskussion selten und insofern umso erfreulicher.

Gabu Heindl

Blumen des Bösen, etwas brav

Subnature
Architecture's Other Environments (11)
David Gissen
New York: Princeton Architectural Press, 2009
englisch, 224 Seiten, zahlreiche Farb- und SW-Abbildungen, broschiert
ISBN 978-1-56898-777-4
EUR 27,99

Als George Bataille, Michel Leiris, Carl Einstein & Co. im Jahre 1929 auszogen, dem Bildungsidealismus mit ihrem *Dictionnaire critique* zu Leibe zu rücken,[1] sprachen sie ersterem nicht nur durch betont subjektive Einträge und zufällig wirkende Lemmata Hohn, sondern ließen auch eine Vorliebe für niedere, abseitige oder ekelerregende Themen erkennen. Neben Abhandlungen zu Begriffen wie „Strafarbeit", „Mund" und „Fabrikschornstein" fanden sich auch welche über „Staub", „Spucke", „Reptilien" oder „Formlos". Der provokante *bas matérialisme* des surrealistischen Unternehmens bedurfte aber auch der „zum Abbruch bürgerlicher Ideologien" (so der Titel eines Vorläuferprojekts)[2] geeigneten Feindbilder,

Through analyses of concrete projects by Louis Kahn, Le Corbusier, Mies van der Rohe, Albert Speer, Robert Venturi, Archigram, Michael Graves and others, Gartman shows how their close relationship to capital canceled the possibility of a critical position. In this regard, the postmodernists, despite their loud criticism of modernity, are no less ideological than the functionalists, and the same can be said of New Urbanism and some forms of deconstructivism: the deconstructive euphoria about globalism and freedom from regulations unmasks itself as another ideology of unquestioning adaptation to the changing demands of capitalism. A case in point for Gartman is signature architecture as an integral part of global consumer culture: buildings by Renzo Piano, Bernard Tschumi, Zaha Hadid and, as the prime example, Rem Koolhaas' Prada Flagship Stores: this is as perspicuous as it is unsurprising.

In deconstructivism, which he regards as the most profound reflection of post-Fordism, Gartman also finds "antagonistic" characteristics: along the International Style, he finds Peter Eisenman's work to be "potentially antagonistic to the economic bourgeosie." Because his teaching and writing activities have guaranteed him financial independence, Eisenman was able to reach the autonomous position of truly critical art, and more: his architecture "would create, in Adorno's words, an 'emancipated society'," in which the beauty of the promise of reconciliation is put in tension in order to reveal the ugly post-Fordian reality that refuses any such reconciliation. And Eisenman's deconstructivism is said to furnish the protest against global capitalism with a "formal voice" (pp. 388f.). Again Gartman expects a lot from a dominant individual.

Such moments of bathos are all the more astonishing when one thinks how much the bulk of the book is characterized by a gesture of polemical insistence, as regards the remarkable wealth of both detail and material in the study. After all, Gartman's way of relating critical theory and sociology to the history of architecture so closely (instead of just dabbling with the connections) is very unusual and thus all the more enjoyable.

Gabu Heindl

The Flowers of Evil, Pretty Harmless

Subnature
Architecture's Other Environments (11)
David Gissen
New York: Princeton Architectural Press, 2009
English, 224 pages, illustrations (some colored), paperback
ISBN 978-1-56898-777-4
EUR 27.99

When in 1929 George Bataille, Michel Leiris, Carl Einstein & Co. ventured out to demolish the high ideals of education with their *Dictionnaire cri-*

und dazu gehörte u. a. die Architektur, welcher gleich der erste Eintrag, verfasst von George Bataille, gewidmet war.[3] Architektur verkörpert dort so ziemlich alles, was die Surrealisten verabscheuten: Macht, Gewalt, Hierarchie, Stabilität, Ordnung usw., und das ganze *Dictionnaire* schrieb in den beiden Jahren seiner Existenz dagegen an.

80 Jahre nach dem *Dictionnaire critique* hat sich nun ein Architekt aufgemacht, dem anti-architektonischen *bas matérialisme* eine architekturtheoretische Abhandlung zu widmen. Ironischerweise ist diese selbst ein Abfallprodukt, wie ihr Autor, der am California College of Arts in San Francisco lehrende David Gissen, freimütig in der Einleitung bekennt: Im Zuge der Recherchen zu seiner Dissertation über die Rolle der Natur in New Yorker Bauten der 1970er-Jahre habe er sich nicht nur mit den positiven, von der Architektur traditionell beachteten Aspekten der „reinen" Natur wie Sonne, Bäume, Wind etc. befasst, sondern es habe sich auch zahlreiches Material zu den im Architekturdiskurs marginalisierten, angstbesetzten und als schmutzig und gefährlich geltenden Phänomenen großstädtischer Natur angesammelt. Da er diese in jeder Hinsicht negativen Reste nicht in seiner Dissertation habe verwenden können, sei er zu dem Entschluss gekommen, daraus ein eigenes Buch zu machen. Für den Titel erfand er den Neologismus *Subnature*, weil es sich um eine Art Gegenwelt zum Übernatürlichen handle, die aber in der menschlichen Wahrnehmung weit unterhalb des positiv besetzten Natürlichen rangiere und in der man als Mensch weder sozial noch biologisch existieren könne. Das Ergebnis ist eine lexikonartige Sammlung von Essays zu zwölf Begriffen, deren jeweilige Geschichte Gissen erzählt und die – eine gewisse kanonische Ordnung hat offenbar auch im Subnaturellen zu herrschen – zu drei Vierergruppen zusammengefasst sind: zu den atmosphärischen Gegenständen „Feuchtigkeit", „Rauch", „Gas" und „Abgas", den materiellen „Staub", „Pfützen", „Schlamm" und „Schutt" und den lebendigen „Unkraut", „Insekten", „Tauben" und „(Menschen-)Massen".

Jedes der zwölf Kapitel beginnt mit den frühesten Reflex(ion)en des jeweiligen Phänomens in der Architekturdarstellung und -theorie, die meist mit dem 18. Jh., manchmal auch schon bei Vitruv einsetzt, und führt dann chronologisch bis

1 „Dictionnaire critique", in: *Documents* 2–7 (1929), 1–7 (1930), Reprint Paris 1991, in: http://gallica.bnf.fr/ark:/12148/bpt6k32952s [abgerufen am 10.2.2011]; dt. Übers.: Rainer Maria Kiesow, Henning Schmidgen (Hg.), *Kritisches Wörterbuch. Beiträge von George Bataille, Carl Einstein, Marcel Griaule, Michel Leiris u. a.* Berlin 2005.

2 1917/18 planten Carl Einstein, Carl Sternberg und Gottfried Benn eine *Encyclopädie zum Abbruch bürgerlicher Ideologien*, die aber über zwei Einträge nicht hinauskam; vgl. „Nachwort", in: Kiesow, Schmidgen 2005 (Anm. 1), S. 97–122, hier S. 105.

3 George Bataille, „Architecture", in: *Documents* 1, 2 (1929), S. 117; dt. in: Kiesow, Schmidgen 2005 (Anm. 1), S. 7f.

tique,[1] they sought to express their contempt for the former not only by writing deliberately subjective entries and what seemed like incidental lemmas, but also by demonstrating their preference for primitive, offbeat and even nauseating subjects. Besides dealing with words like "penal labour," "mouth" and "factory chimney," they included some like "dust," "saliva," "reptiles," and "shapeless." However, in order to "demolish bourgeois ideology" (which was the title of a forerunner project),[2] the provocative *bas matérialisme* of that surrealistic enterprise also required suitable enemy concepts, one of them being architecture, which was the subject of the first entry written by George Bataille.[3] Architecture represented almost everything that was detestable to the Surrealists: power, hierarchy, stability, order, etc., against which, in its two years of existence, the *Dictionnaire* revolted with all its might.

Now, 80 years after the *Dictionnaire critique*, one architect has set out to dedicate a collection of essays on architectural theory to the anti-architectural *bas matérialisme*. Ironically, it is a waste product itself, as the author David Gissen, who teaches at the California College of Arts in San Francisco, readily admits in his introduction. During his thesis research on what role nature played in modern buildings in New York in the 1970s, he not only looked into the positive and traditional architectural aspects of "clean" natural phenomena like sun, trees and wind, etc., but also collected lots of material connected to marginalized metropolitan phenomena which were regarded in architectural discourse as threatening, filthy, or hazardous. Since he was not able to use all these—in the true sense of the word—negative leftovers for his thesis, he decided to write a separate book about them. Because his book was about a kind of counterworld of the supernatural world, a world deeply beneath the human perception of a positively connoted natural world, in which people could neither socially nor biologically exist, he invented the neologism *Subnature* as a title. The outcome is a dictionary-like collection of essays on twelve words, whose respective story is told by Gissen and—even the subnatural world seems to be governed by a certain canon of order—which are divided in three groups of four. To atmospheric things he counts "dankness," "smoke," "gas" and "exhaust," to material things "dust," "puddles," "mud" and "debris," and to living things "weeds," "insects," "pigeons" and "crowds."

Each of the twelve chapters begins with the earliest reflexes against (or reflections on) the

1 "Dictionnaire critique," in: *Documents* 2–7 (1929), 1–7 (1930), Reprint Paris 1991, in: http://gallica.bnf.fr/ark:/12148/bpt6k32952s [accessed on February 10, 2011]; English transl.: Georges Bataille (ed.), "Critical Dictionary", transl. by D. Faccini et al., in: Alastair Brotchie (ed.), *Encyclopaedia Acephalica*. London 1995, pp. 29–84.

2 In 1917/18 Carl Einstein, Carl Sternberg and Gottfried Benn planned the *Encyclopädie zum Abbruch bürgerlicher Ideologien* [*Encyclopedia of The Demolition of Bourgeois Ideology*] which never got further than two entries; cf. "Nachwort [Epilogue]," in: Rainer Maria Kiesow, Henning Schmidgen (eds.), *Kritisches Wörterbuch. Beiträge von George Bataille, Carl Einstein, Marcel Griaule, Michel Leiris u. a.* Berlin 2005, pp. 97–122, here p. 105.

3 George Bataille, "Architecture," in: *Brotchie* 1995 (fn. 1), p. 29.

zur Gegenwart. Die Historie beschreibt dabei eine Abfolge unterschiedlicher Haltungen zum Subnaturellen, die meist mit seiner Ästhetisierung in der Ruinenästhetik beginnt, dann mit der Moderne in eine Phase der Ablehnungs-, Vermeidungs- und Bekämpfungsstrategien gelangt, um schließlich bei gegenwärtigen experimentell ausgerichteten ArchitektInnen, welche die „Subnatur" als positiven Planungs- und Gestaltungsfaktor integrieren, die Stufe der (zynischen, phantastischen, zuweilen auch ernst gemeinten) Rehabilitation zu erreichen. Waren z. B. Staub, Schutt und Pfützen in Piranesis Stichen von den Ruinen Roms Zeichen des Verfalls und der versunkenen Größe der Ewigen Stadt, so werden diese Erscheinungen im hygienischen Furor der Moderne aktiv bekämpft – man denke nur an den berühmten Vergleich zwischen „Normaler Stadt" und „Turmstadt" in Le Corbusiers *Vers une architecture*, worin die „Straßenstaubzone" die traditionellen Häuserblocks dicht umhüllt, während sie von den „mitten im Grünen" (= der positiven „Architektennatur") stehenden „Turmhäusern" auf sichere Distanz gehalten wird;[4] oder an Le Corbusiers Abschaffung des Kellers und Aufständerung der Baukörper, was Gissen als „victory of the rhetoric of light and air over the dark, the tepid, and the dank" interpretiert (S. 34). Ab den 1960ern macht sich dann eine Trendwende in Richtung *dirty realism* bemerkbar.[5] Peter und Alison Smithson etwa ließen ihre Bauten kurz nach starken Regengüssen fotografieren, um sie „far less staged" und „authentic" erscheinen zu lassen (S. 104ff.). In aktuellen (allerdings allesamt unrealisierten oder im Kunstkontext angesiedelten) Architekturprojekten wird dann aktiv und integrativ mit *subnature* gearbeitet, wie etwa R&Sie(n) bei ihrem Museum in Bangkok (*B_mu Tower*, 2002), dessen Außenhülle aus dem elektrostatisch angezogen Staub der versmogten Metropole gebildet werden soll.

So materialreich und ambitioniert Gissens Unternehmen daherkommt und so politisch sympathisch es wirkt, dass jemand dem dominierenden neoliberalen, Natur nur zu Produktivitätszwecken instrumentalisierenden Diskurs des „flow" (S. 23) entgegenwirken möchte: Spätestens nach dem dritten oder vierten Kapitel, wenn das Grundmuster klar geworden ist, beginnt die Lektüre zu ermüden. Das unverbundene Nebeneinander, das den Schockeffekt und die Komik der völlig heterogenen Artikel des *Dictionnaire critique* hervorruft, wirkt bei einem homogenen und traditionellen wissenschaftlichen Text wie *Subnature* schlicht langatmig. Gemeinsame Schlussfolgerungen oder Querbezüge werden, wenn man vom allzu summarisch gehaltenen Epilog (S. 210–214) mal absieht, keine gemacht bzw. dem Leser überlassen. Man vermisst eine übergreifende Interpretation der historischen Zusammenhänge, insbesondere eine Kontextualisierung in der Geschichte der Hygiene und der Kunst (bei letzterer würde man z. B. sehen, wie sehr gegenwärtige „Subnature"-Architektur Vorbilder des Surrealismus, des Nouveau Réalisme, der Land Art und der Body Art der 1920er- bis 1970er-Jahre verarbeitet).[6] Gerade bei einem so stark kultur- und naturgeschichtlich angelegten, förmlich nach Interdisziplinarität schreienden Thema verwundert die Beschränkung auf die reine Architekturgeschichte und -theorie. In gewisser Weise ist das Buch jene Materialsamm-

4 Le Corbusier, *1922. Ausblick auf eine Architektur* (Bauwelt Fundamente 2). 4. Aufl. Gütersloh 1982, S. 56.

5 Vgl. Liane Lefaivre, „Dirty Realism in European Architecture Today", in: *Design Book Review* 17 (Winter 1989), S. 17–20; dies., „‚Dirty Realism' in der Architektur. Den Stein steinern machen!", in: *Archithese* 1 (1990), S. 14–21.

6 Aus der umfangreichen Literatur sei stellvertretend nur eine sich auf Bataille beziehende Publikation genannt: Yves-Alain Bois, Rosalind Krauss (Hg.), *L'informe: Mode d'emploi*. Ausst.-Kat. Centre Georges Pompidou, Paris 1996.

respective phenomenon in the description of architecture and architectural theory, most of them conceived in the 18th century, but some as early as Vitruvius, leading chronologically from the past to the present day. This history recounts a sequence of different attitudes towards the subnatural which mostly begin with an aesthetization in ruin aesthetics, moving to a phase of Modernism in which strategies of refusal, prevention and combat were developed, ending with today's experimentally oriented architects, who, by integrating "subnature" as a positive element of planning and design, achieve the final level of (cynical, fantastic, sometimes even seriously meant) rehabilitation. If the dust, debris and puddles in Piranesi's engravings once represented the decay and fall of the Eternal City, they are now fought against in the name of the hygienic rage of Modernism just as the famous comparison between "towns of today" and "city of towers" in Le Corbusier's *Towards a New Architecture* suggests, where the "zone of street dust" envelopes the rows of houses whilst they are kept at a safe distance by "tower houses" standing "amidst trees and grass" (= part of the positive "Architects' nature");[4] or Le Corbusier's abolition of the cellar and elevation of structures, which Gissen interprets as the "victory of the rhetoric of light and air over the dark, the tepid, and the dank" (p. 34). From the 1960s on, a change of trend towards dirty realism started to emerge.[5] For instance, Peter und Alison Smithson took photos of their buildings shortly after heavy rainfall in order to make them appear "far less staged" and "authentic" (pp. 104ff.). Current architectural projects (all of which have not yet been realized or are set in an artistic context) have involved active and integrative work with *Subnature*, such as R&Sie(n) planned their Museum in Bangkok (*B_mu Tower*, 2002), whose outer skin would be formed out of electrostatically loaded dust from the metropolitan smog.

No matter how detailed and ambitioned Gissen's work presents itself and however politically pleasing it may seem, even perhaps tempting the desire to challenge that dominating neoliberal "flow" of discourse which exploits nature solely in the name of productivity (p. 23), when its basic pattern becomes clear in the third or fourth chapters at the latest, reading starts getting tedious. Maybe the random coexistence of the heterogeneous entries, which makes the *Dictionnaire critique* so shocking and funny at the same time, is simply too long-winded for a homogenous and traditionally scientific text like *Subnature*. Apart from the short epilogue (pp. 210–214), which is of a rather general nature, mutual conclusions or cross-references are altogether lacking or are left for the reader to draw. One misses an overall interpretation of various historical contexts,

4 Le Corbusier, *Towards A New Architecture*. Transl. by Frederick Etchells, 5th ed. New York 1970, p. 54.

5 See Liane Lefaivre, "Dirty Realism in European Architecture Today," in: *Design Book Review* 17 (Winter 1989), pp. 17–20; idem, "'Dirty Realism' in der Architektur. Den Stein steinern machen!" in: *Archithese* 1 (1990), pp. 14–21.

lung geblieben, die sie an ihrem Ausgangspunkt war. Für künftige Auseinandersetzungen mit der unerschöpflichen Thematik wird *Subnature* wohl als eine Art Steinbruch dienen. Aber das ist ja auch kein schlechter Dienst.

Anselm Wagner

Publikationen/ Forschung

Anna Margaretha Hohmann-Vogrin 1946–2009 Forschung und Lehre. Scientific Research and Teaching, Hermann J. Hendrich (Hg.)
Graz: Verlag der Technischen Universität Graz, 2010
deutsch/englisch, 334 Seiten, Hardcover
ISBN 978-3851251203, EUR 58,00

Raumdenken. Thinking Space, Irmgard Frank
Sulgen: Niggli, 2010
englisch, 199 Seiten, Hardcover
ISBN 978-3721207682, EUR 48,00

Bruchstücke. Jüdische Friedhöfe in der Steiermark, Antje Senarclens des Grancy, Gertrude Maria Grossegger, Petra Sterry
Graz: Leykam, 2010
deutsch, 130 Seiten, Hardcover
ISBN 978-3-7011-7700-4, EUR 24,20

especially a contextualization of the history of hygiene and art (the latter would reveal just how many ideas from Surrealism, Nouveau Réalisme, Land Art and Body Art from the 1920s to the 1970s have affected contemporary "subnature"-architecture).[6] It is surprising that this subject of all things, with its strong orientation towards cultural and natural history and literally begging for an interdisciplinary approach, is merely limited to the history of architecture and architectural theory. Thus, in certain aspects this book remains exactly what it was at the beginning, namely a collection of material. And that is exactly the role Subnature is likely to play in future discourse on this inexhaustible subject. But that is, presumably, no bad thing.

Anselm Wagner

6 One representative example of the comprehensive collection of literature with references to Bataille is: Yves-Alain Bois, Rosalind Krauss (eds.), *L'informe: Mode d'emploi*. Exhib. cat. Centre Georges Pompidou, Paris 1996.

Publications/ Research

Anna Margaretha Hohmann-Vogrin 1946–2009 Forschung und Lehre: Scientific Research and Teaching, Hermann J. Hendrich (ed.)
Graz: Verlag der Technischen Universität Graz, 2010
German/English, 334 pages, hardcover
ISBN 978-3851251203, EUR 58.00

Raumdenken: Thinking Space, Irmgard Frank
Sulgen: Niggli, 2010
English, 199 pages, hardcover
ISBN 978-3721207682, EUR 48.00

Kunststoffe in Architektur und Konstruktion
Stephan Engelsmann, Valerie Spalding, Stefan Peters
Basel: Birkhäuser, 2010
deutsch, 168 Seiten, Hardcover
ISBN 978-3034603218, EUR 49,90

Abfallmoderne. Zu den Schmutzrändern der Kultur, Anselm Wagner (Hg.)
Wien-Berlin: LIT Verlag, 2010
deutsch, 336 Seiten, Hardcover
ISBN 978-3-643-501172, EUR 29,90

Preise

GAD Awards 2010

Architektur will Verantwortung

Die Jury des diesjährigen GAD Awards vertrat die Auffassung, dass das Diplom den Absolventen die einmalige Chance bietet, gesellschaftsrelevante Themen aufzugreifen und Architektur als Teil der Diskussion zu verstehen. Bewusst wurden daher keine Arbeiten prämiert, deren einziges Augenmerk auf die Form gerichtet ist, sondern Projekte, die aussagekräftige Statements liefern, mit dem Willen Verantwortung zu übernehmen: *Johannes Pointl* bezieht in seiner Abschlussarbeit differenziert zum Schlagwort „Europa“ Position, und *Nina Kolowratnik* sieht in der Perspektive der ArchitektInnen die Chance einer nicht-ideologischen Diskussion im Konflikt der palästinensischen Flüchtlingsthematik. *Stefan Fink* zeigt den wissenschaftlichen Blick auf einen Vertreter des Correalismus, des ganzheitlichen Entwerfens, während *Michael Englputzeder* für ein „Offenes Museum“ mitten in Zürich plädiert.

Prämierte Projekte

1. Preis: Johannes Pointl: *(B)XL – Megalomanie und der politische Raum in der europäischen Hauptstadt Brüssel*. **2. Preis**: Stefan Fink: *Im endlosen Raum des Wissens*. **3. Preis**: Nina Valeria Kolowratnik: *Kafr 'Inan* – Bilder der Präsenz für eine Landschaft der Abwesenheit. Ein räumliches Wiederlesen der palästinensischen Flüchtlingsfrage. **Sonderpreis**: Michael Englputzeder: *Kunsthaus Zürich – Versuch einer Standortbestimmung der Institution Museum anhand des Realisierungswettbewerbes zur Erweiterung des Kunsthauses Zürich*. **Sonderpreis**: Johannes Schlattau: *Tabacalera.Sur*. **Tschom-Wohnbaupreis**: Oliver Wildpaner: *Solitaire*. **Hollomey Reisestipendium**: Eva Maria Hierzer: *Untersuchung von Hausbesetzungen in drei spanischen Städten*.
http://gad-award.tugraz.at bzw.
http://curry.tugraz.at

Gottfried Prasenc

Bruchstücke: Jüdische Friedhöfe in der Steiermark, Antje Senarclens des Grancy, Gertrude Maria Grossegger, Petra Sterry
Graz: Leykam, 2010
German, 130 pages, hardcover
ISBN 978-3-7011-7700-4, EUR 24.20

Kunststoffe in Architektur und Konstruktion
Stephan Engelsmann, Valerie Spalding, Stefan Peters
Basel: Birkhäuser, 2010
German, 168 pages, hardcover
ISBN 978-3034603218, EUR 49.90

Abfallmoderne: Zu den Schmutzrändern der Kultur
Anselm Wagner (ed.)
Vienna-Berlin: LIT Verlag, 2010
German, 336 pages, paperback
ISBN 978-3-643-501172, EUR 29.90

Awards

GAD Awards 2010

Architecture Wants Responsibility

The judging panel of this year's GAD Awards took the view that the diploma offers graduates the unique opportunity to focus on socially relevant topics and to see architecture as part of the discussion. Therefore, no works were awarded a prize whose only focus was on form, but rather works which make meaningful statements with the intention of assuming responsibility: *Johannes Pointl* states his differentiated view on "Europe" in his final project, while *Nina Kolowratnik* sees the architect's perspective as an opportunity for non-ideological discussion in the conflict of the Palestinian refugee issue. *Stefan Fink* presents the scientific view of an exponent of Correalism integrated design, while *Michael Englputzeder* argues for an "Open Museum" in the heart of Zurich.

Award-winning projects: 1st prize: Johannes Pointl: *(B)XL – Megalomania and the political space in the European capital Brussels*. **2nd prize**: Stefan Fink: *In the endless space of knowledge*. **3rd prize**: Nina Valeria Kolowratnik: *Kafr 'Inan*—Images of presence for a landscape of absence. A spatial rereading of the Palestinian refugee question. **Special prize**: Michael Englputzeder: *Kunsthaus Zürich – Attempt to analyze the position of the museum institution based on the competition for extension of Kunsthaus Zurich*. **Special prize**: Johannes Schlattau: *Tabacalera.Sur*. **Tschom Housing Prize**: Oliver Wildpaner: *Solitaire*. **Hollomey travel grant**: Eva Maria Hierzer: *Study of squats in three Spanish cities*.
http://gad-award.tugraz.at and http://curry.tugraz.at

Gottfried Prasenc

EUROPAN 10 GRAZ

http://europan.at/E11/

Das aktuelle Siegerprojekt von EUROPAN 10 am Standort Graz „European Agriculture & Energy Park Graz" (Andreas Lechner (12), Emilio Hauer, Robert Zawodnik & Christoph Simschitz) formulierte Strategien zur vielschichtigen Aktivierung von suburbanen Landschaften/Agglomerationen. Es wird ein Modell für den *zwischenstädtischen* Raum vorgeschlagen, das die ubiquitäre Mischung aus Industrie- und Gewerbegebieten, Wohneinsprengseln und Restflächen sowie potenzielle Freizeit- und Naherholungsgebiete gliedert, indem architektonische Interventionen durch *Framing* (als rahmender Bildausschnitt, als visuelles Dispositiv) eine „Landschaftsaktivierung" erzeugen.

Das Projekt verknüpft nach Auffassung der Jury überzeugend regionale Landschafts-Ressourcen als Energieträger und als lokale Agrar- und Landwirtschaftsflächen mit architektonisch-kulturellen Faktoren: „The project has to be seen as a seed of potential development on the level of territory; this allows for a programmatical freedom in the concrete choice of uses, the installment of infrastructures, and the treatment of the landscape-productivity of the landscape also includes aesthetic values inasmuch the pleasures of the views and panoramas develop and structure the territory, demonstrating a convincing work on atmospherical values".

Andreas Lechner

12

EUROPAN 10 GRAZ

http://europan.at/E11/

The current winning project of EUROPAN 10 in Graz, *European Agriculture & Energy Park Graz* (Andreas Lechner (12), Emilio Hauer, Robert Zawodnik & Christoph Simschitz), formulated strategies for a complex activation of suburban landscapes/agglomerations. It proposes a model for the inter-urban space that divides the ubiquitous mix of industrial and commercial areas, residential sprinklings and residual areas, and potential leisure and local recreational areas by having architectural interventions generate an "activation of the landscape" by means of framing (as an enframing detail, as a visual device).

According to the panel of judges, the project convincingly combines regional landscape resources as energy carriers and as local agrarian and farming areas with architectural, cultural factors: "The project has to be seen as a seed of potential development on the level of territory; this allows for a programmatical freedom in the concrete choice of uses, the instalment of infrastructures, and the treatment of the landscape-productivity of the landscape also includes aesthetic values inasmuch the pleasures of the views and panoramas develop and structure the territory, demonstrating a convincing work on atmospherical values."

Andreas Lechner

Herbert Eichholzer 1903–1943

Förderungspreis für Architektur 2009
Studierendenwettbewerb *kunst.uni.graz*

Der Herbert Eichholzer Förderungspreis für Architektur, der alle zwei Jahre im Auftrag des Kulturamtes der Stadt Graz an begabte ArchitekturstudentInnen an der Technischen Universität Graz vergeben wird, wurde als Ideenwettbewerb zum Thema Kunstuniversität Graz ausgeschrieben: zur Schließung der (Ausbildungs-)Lücke eines Studiums für Kunst (Malerei, Bildhauerei, Neue Medien) wurde als Bauplatz für einen Neubau der Kunstuniversität im Sinne der Bildung einer „Kunst-Achse" entlang der Leonhardstraße, zwischen der Universität für Musik und darstellende Kunst, MUMUTH und dem Neubau der KUG in

Herbert Eichholzer 1903–1943

2009 Scholarship for Architecture
Student competition *kunst.uni.graz*

The Herbert Eichholzer Scholarship for Architecture, awarded by the City of Graz, on behalf of the Kulturamt der Stadt Graz, every two years to talented students of architecture at Graz University of Technology, was published as an idea competition on the subject of Graz University of Art: in order to close the (educational) gap of an art course (painting, sculpture, New Media), the corner plot of Leonhardstraße/Merangasse was elected as the construction site for a new art university building with the aim of forming an "axis of art" along Leonhardstraße, between the University of Music and Performing Arts, MUMUTH, and the new KUG building at Reiterkaserne.

The judges recommended two of the ten entrant teams to receive the prize totalling EUR 6,600:
Ulrike Tinnacher, Oliver Wildpanner (1st prize)

der Reiterkaserne das Eckgrundstück Leonhardstraße/Merangasse herangezogen.

Die Jury hat unter zehn eingereichten Arbeiten zwei Teams zur Preisvergabe im Gesamtwert von EUR 6.600,00 empfohlen: **Ulrike Tinnacher, Oliver Wildpanner** (1. Preis) und **Ahmed Ibrahimpašić, Ana Glavaš, Boško Marušić** (2. Preis). Der Preisverleihung am 27. Jänner 2010 im Haus der Architektur Graz folgte eine zweiwöchige, vom Institut für Architekturtechnologie organisierte und Kulturamt der Stadt Graz, sowie Kulturvermittlung Steiermark unterstützte Ausstellung (13) aller eingereichten Wettbewerbsbeiträge.

Erika Petric

13

Projekte/ Ausstellungen/ Öffentliche Veranstaltungen

Der israelitische Friedhof Graz 1865–2010: eine Annäherung

Eine Ausstellungskooperation (14) des IStBau, Institut für Stadt- und Baugeschichte, TU Graz und des stadtmuseumgraz, 30. Juni–12. September 2010

„Bejt haChaim", Haus des Lebens, lautet die hebräische Bezeichnung für Friedhof. Studierende der Architekturfakultät der TU Graz haben sich im Wintersemester 2009/2010 diesem Thema angenähert und ihr Wissen im Sommersemester 2010 vertieft. Friedhöfe legen Zeugnis einer Zeit ab und hinterlassen architektonische Spuren. Sie sind Orte der Kultur und ihres Wandels, des Gedächtnisses und der Geschichte, Orte der Ruhe, des Glaubens

14

und der Toleranz, der Trauer und der Hoffnung. Die Dokumentation des israelitischen Friedhofes in Graz in Modell, Bild und Schrift ermöglicht vielschichtige Lesarten dieses einzigartigen Ortes in Graz.

Ausstellungskonzept und Umsetzung: Ute Angeringer-Mmadu, Ninela Holtin, Oliver Jungwirth, **Mitarbeit**: Lola Seibt

Ute Angeringer-Mmadu

and **Ahmed Ibrahimpašić, Ana Glavaš, Boško Marušić** (2nd prize). The prize ceremony at Haus der Architektur Graz on January 27, 2010 was followed by a two-week exhibition of all competition entries (13) organized by the Institute for Architectural Technology and supported by Kulturamt der Stadt Graz and Kulturvermittlung Steiermark.

Erika Petric

Projects/Exhibitions/ Public Events

The Israelite Cemetery of Graz 1865–2010: An Exploration

An exhibition co-operation (14) of IStBau, Institute for Urban and Building History, Graz University of Technology, and stadtmuseumgraz, June 30–September 12, 2010

"Beit chaim," House of Life, is the Hebrew word for cemetery. Students of the Faculty of Architecture at Graz University of Technology explored this topic in winter semester 2009/2010, deepening their knowledge in summer semester 2010. Cemeteries testify to a particular time and leave behind architectural traces. They are places of culture and its change, of memory and history, places of quiet, faith and tolerance, of mourning and hope. The documentation of the Israelite Cemetery of Graz in the form of a model, images and texts permits complex interpretations of this unique location in Graz.

Exhibition concept and realization: Ute Angeringer-Mmadu, Ninela Holtin, Oliver Jungwirth, **collaboration**: Lola Seibt

Ute Angeringer-Mmadu

Die Stadt trägt Geschichte/ History Collection 2010/01

Realities of Graz c. 1900—Snapshots 1900 : 2009 An exhibition of IStBau, Institute for Urban and Building History, Graz University of Technology and stadtmuseumgraz, January 20–February 28, 2010

Based on snapshots of the everyday world in Graz around 1900 taken from the exhibition

Die Stadt trägt Geschichte/History Collection 2010/11

Wirklichkeiten Graz um 1900 – Momentaufnahmen 1900 : 2009. Eine Ausstellung des IStBau, Institut für Stadt- und Baugeschichte, TU Graz und des stadtmuseumgraz, 20. Jänner–28. Februar 2010

Ausgehend von Momentaufnahmen der Alltagswelt in Graz um 1900 aus der Ausstellung „Wirklichkeiten Graz um 1900" haben Studierende der Architektur im Rahmen der Lehrveranstaltung AK Architekturgeschichte (Leitung Ute Angeringer-Mmadu und Marion Starzacher) ausgewählte Gebäude im Hinblick auf ihren städtebaulichen und architektonischen Kontext und ihrer Entwicklung im Laufe der Zeit erforscht. Neben der Arbeit im Archiv stand auch die Auseinandersetzung mit den gegenwärtigen Möglichkeiten der Abbildung und Darstellung von Architektur im Fokus. In Form von Szenarios wurden zudem Geschichten aus der Sicht der Gebäude (re)konstruiert, wie sie stattfinden hätten können: „Zuckernot": Andrang bei den „Brüdern Kunz" am Kaiser-Josef-Platz", „Eisernes Tor", „Südtirolerplatz in der Murvorstadt", „Monturdepot am Fischplatz", „Altes und neues Stadttheater", „Technische Hochschule", „Herz-Jesu-Kirche", „Judentempel und Schule am Grieskai und andere Dispositive der Ausstellung dienten als Vorlage, um ihre Geschichten zurückzuverfolgen.

Ute Angeringer-Mmadu

Studio: Eisenerz. Kulturelles Erbe und sozialer Wandel

Präsentation 10. Juli 2010 in Eisenerz

Ausgehend von einem Zukunftsszenario, dass Eisenerz 2021 aufgrund seiner überregionalen und universellen Bedeutung selbstbewusstes Zentrum der Weltkulturerberegion „Österreichisches Eisenland" sein wird, wurde im Rahmen der Projektübung (Leitung Simone Hain, Oliver Jungwirth, Jürgen Moravi) das Thema „Schrumpfung" mit völlig veränderten disziplinären Prämissen bearbeitet: statt neu zu bauen und konkurrierende Nutzungsansprüche zu koordinieren, begleitet der Planer jahrelange, ergebnisoffene Prozesse. Die 74 Studien für Eisenerz, die in den letzten 40 Jahren erstellt wurden und zum großen Teil ohne Umsetzung in Schubladen verschwanden – ein Grund für die vorhandene Skepsis der BewohnerInnen gegenüber Interventionen von außen – wurden gesichtet und ausgewertet, historische Gebäude vom Keller bis zum Dach untersucht, der Kontakt zu den Eisenerzern gesucht.

Ute Angeringer-Mmadu

Atlas: Zersiedelung Steiermark

Interaktive Visualisierungen großmaßstäblicher, raumplanerischer Fragestellungen und algorithmische, städtebauliche Experimente zur Nachverdichtung

In der Visualisierung von Siedlungsprozessen und allem, was damit in Zusammenhang zu bringen ist, sollte im Rahmen des Masterstudios (Leitung Urs Hirschberg, Richard Dank und Stefan Zedlacher; Mitarbeit Thomas Diewald, Jacob Wegerer) ein digitaler Atlas jenseits der üblichen Geo-Informations-Systeme entstehen: eine Neuvermessung der Steiermark. Auf Basis der 30 Themenkreise rund um die Zersiedelung der Steiermark wurde

Realities of Graz c. 1900, students of architecture examined selected buildings with regard to their context of urban development and architecture and their development over the course of time as part of the course AK History of Architecture (taught by Ute Angeringer-Mmadu and Marion Starzacher). In addition to work in the archives, another focal point was examining contemporary possibilities of depicting and representing architecture. In the form of scenarios, the students also (re)constructed histories from the view of the buildings that may have taken place: "Zuckernot": rush to "Brüder Kunz" in Kaiser-Josef-Platz, "Eisernes Tor," "Südtirolerplatz in der Murvorstadt," "Monturdepot am Fischplatz," "Altes und neues Stadttheater," "Technische Hochschule," "Herz-Jesu-Kirche," "Judentempel und Schule am Grieskai" and other dispositifs of the exhibition served as a template with which to trace back their histories.

Ute Angeringer-Mmadu

Studio: Eisenerz. Cultural Heritage and Social Change

Presentation July 10, 2010 in Eisenerz

Based on a future scenario of Eisenerz as a self-confident center of the world cultural heritage region "Austrian Iron Country" in 2021 thanks to its national and universal importance, as part of the project exercise (supervised by Simone Hain, Oliver Jungwirth, Jürgen Moravi) the students worked on the subject of "shrinkage" with completely changed disciplinary premises: instead of building new buildings and co-ordinating rivalling uses, the planner accompanies open-ended processes lasting several years. The seventy-four studies for Eisenerz drawn up over the past forty years, most of which were filed away without having been carried out—one reason for the inhabitants' scepticism with regard to outside interventions—were inspected and evaluated, historical buildings were examined from the cellar to the roof, and the people of Eisenerz were contacted.

Ute Angeringer-Mmadu

Atlas: Urban Sprawl in Styria

Interactive visualizations of questions of large-scale land planning and algorithmic experiments in urban development for the purpose of densification

In order to visualize settlement processes and all related factors, the aim of the master studio (headed by Urs Hirschberg, Richard Dank and Stefan Zedlacher; collaborators Thomas Diewald, Jacob Wegerer) was to draw up a digital atlas beyond the usual geo-information systems: a new survey of Styria. On the basis of thirty topics pertaining to urban sprawl in Styria, an online database was distilled with more than one million entries. Analytical maps were created for a more in-depth analysis of voluminous existing data with regard to

eine Online-Datenbank mit über einer Million Einträgen destilliert. Es wurden analytische Karten erstellt, welche die umfangreich bereits vorhandenen Datenbestände auf bestimmte thematische Fragestellungen für die gesamte Steiermark genauer untersuchen – wie z. B. Bebauungsdichte, Immissionen (Lärm, Verschmutzung), Erreichbarkeit, Fahrzeiten, Versorgung mit öffentlichen Einrichtungen und Infrastruktur (Schulen, Grünräume etc.). Auf Basis der aus den Analysen gewonnenen Hypothesen wurden Modelle entworfen, und in ihren Auswirkungen prozessual erforscht und dargestellt.

Besonders der interaktive Tisch „Augmented Styria Desk" stand dann auch bei der Ausstellungseröffnung am 30. Juni 2010 mit anschließendem Vortrag „Jenseits des Rasters" von Ludger Hovestadt (ETH Zürich) im Zentrum des Interesses.

http://iam.tugraz.at/studio/s10/
Präsentationsvideo: http://vimeo.com/13934683/

Richard Dank

minimalhousing – PrePaidApartment und die Nutzung freier Ressourcen im Tourismus

Das Projekt *minimalhousing* (15) wurde von einer Studentin der FH Eisenstadt zum Thema einer Bachelorarbeit gemacht: Die Idee, Minimalobjekte durch ihre modulare, mobile Bauweise auch für touristische Zwecke einzusetzen, wurde hier an möglichen Standorten erprobt. Die kleinen, flexiblen Wohneinheiten können für die jeweilige Region ein neues identitätsbildendes *Corporate Design* erzeugen. Am Ort der Aufstellung ist lediglich die Infrastruktur für eine primäre Versorgung herzustellen, obwohl als Alternative der „Hypercube" auch völlig autark funktionieren kann. Die Nutzung von minimal Apartments reichen vom Alpinen Bereich durch Schutzhütten und der Aktivierung bestehender Ressourcen in kleineren Bergdörfern bis hin zum Einsatz am Wasser, wie am Beispiel Burgenland, mit dem Surfworldcup in Podersdorf.

Leitung Peter Schreibmayer; Team Matthias Gumhalter, Christian Reschreiter
http://wgdrei.com

Peter Schreibmayer

El Purgatorio Alto – eine bislang unbekannte vorkolumbische Stadtanlage in Peru

Durch Zufall auf der Suche nach den bekannten Ruinen von *El Purgatorio* wurden die ausgedehnten Grundrisse einer bislang unentdeckten Stadt um *Casma* ca. 12 km südöstlich davon entdeckt. Der Autor besuchte die neu gefundene und von ihm so benannte Stadtanlage *El Purgatorio Alto* (16) im Sommer 2009.

Die meisten vorkolumbischen Bauten werden der Chavin-Kultur zugerechnet. *El Purgatorio* liegt auf einem leicht geneigten riesigen Schotterfeld

certain topics pertaining to Styria as a whole—for example building density, emissions (noise, pollution), accessibility, driving times, local facilities and infrastructure (schools, green spaces, etc.). On the basis of the hypotheses gained from the analyses, models were drawn up and subjected to process-based investigation and visualization of their effects.

The interactive table "Augmented Styria Desk" was a particular focus of interest at the exhibition opening on June 30, 2010 followed by a lecture "Beyond the Grid" by Ludger Hovestadt (ETH Zurich).

http://iam.tugraz.at/studio/s10/
Presentation video: http://vimeo.com/13934683/

Richard Dank

15

minimalhousing—PrePaid-Apartment and the Use of Free Resources in Tourism

The minimalhousing project (15) was the topic of a bachelor thesis by a student at FH Eisenstadt: the idea of using minimal buildings for tourism purposes because of their modular, mobile design was tested at potential locations. The small, flexible dwelling units can create a new identity-building corporate design for the particular region. All that is needed at the place where they are installed is the infrastructure for primary supply, although, alternatively, the "Hypercube" can also function completely self-sufficiently. The use of minimal apartments ranges from Alpine facilities and mountain huts, to activating existing resources in minor mountain villages and deployment on the water, for example in Burgenland, with the Surfing World Cup in Podersdorf.

Headed by Peter Schreibmayer; team Matthias Gumhalter, Christian Reschreiter
http://wgdrei.com

Peter Schreibmayer

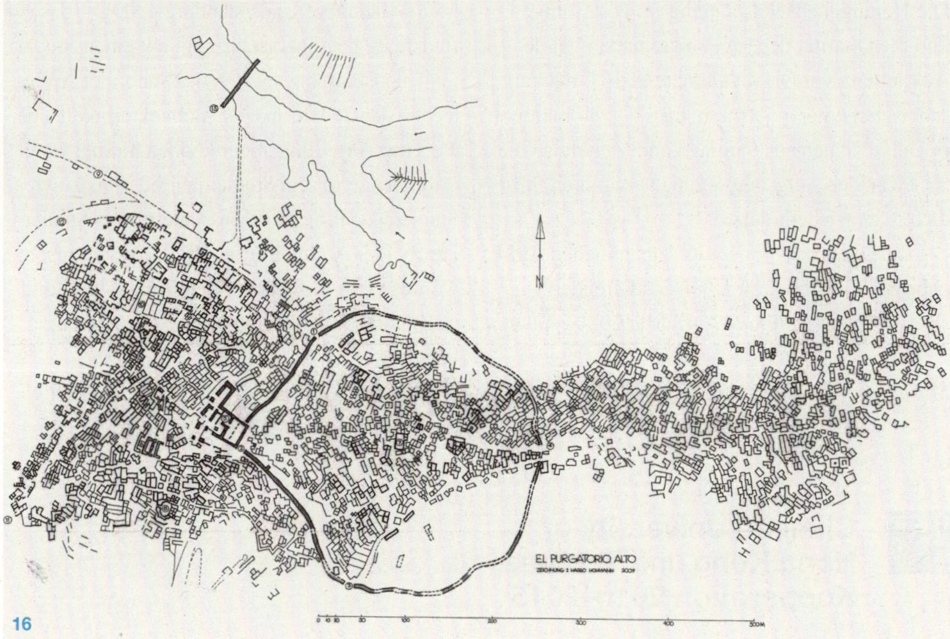

16

am Fuss des Vulkanmassivs *Cerro Mucho Malo*; auf dieses ausgedehnte Kultzentrum hoch auf dem Felsen über dem Pazifik führt geradlinig eine von Steinen flankierte, ca. 55 m breite und etwa 21 km lange Prozessionsstraße aus dem Küstenstreifen zu. *El Purgatorio Alto* war offenbar eine Wohnstadt, zu der *El Purgatorio* als Kultzentrum gehörte. Die ca. 2000 Bauten der Stadt ergeben, bei geschätzten 5 Personen pro Haus, eine Gesamtbevölkerung von ca. 10.000 Einwohnern.

Mehr Information in: *Umrisse*, Zeitschrift für Baukultur 3 (2010), S. 28–31.

Hasso Hohmann

El Purgatorio Alto — An As Yet Unknown Pre-Columbian Town in Peru

While examining the well-known ruins of *El Purgatorio*, the expansive ground plans of an unknown town were discovered approximately twelve kilometers south-east of *Casma*. The author visited the newly found town, which he named *El Purgatorio Alto* (16), in summer 2009.

Most pre-Columbian buildings are attributed to the Chavin culture. *El Purgatorio* is situated on a gently sloping, vast crushed-stone field at the foot of the volcanic massif *Cerro Mucho Malo*; a straight stone-lined 55m-wide and approx. 21km-long procession path leads up to this expansive cultic center high atop the rock above the Pacific. *El Purgatorio Alto* was evidently a residential town that included *El Purgatorio* as a cultic center. Assuming five people per house, the roughly two thousand buildings of the town imply a total population of 10,000.

More information in: *Umrisse*, Zeitschrift für Baukultur 3 (2010), pp. 28–31.

Hasso Hohmann

Students of Graz "contractworld 2010"

The Institute for Architectural Technology presented the results of the "congresscenter dubrovnik" master studio to the public at the annual international "contractworld" platform in Hanover from January 16–19, 2010 (17). The master studio (in co-operation with Krunoslav Ivanisin/Zagreb/ETH Zurich) on the topic of "Structure, space and technology" dealt with the picturesque landscape and the historic downtown of Dubrovnik as a context as well as with the desire for contemporary architectural interventions that are deliberately set in or against this context.

Grazer Studierende – „contractworld 2010"

Das Institut für Architekturtechnologie präsentierte auf der jährlich in Hannover stattfindenden internationalen Plattform „contractworld" vom 16.–19. 1. 2010 die Ergebnisse des Masterstudios „congresscenter dubrovnik" der Öffentlichkeit (17). Das Masterstudio (in Kooperation mit Krunoslav Ivanisin/Zagreb/ETH Zürich) mit der Thematik „Struktur, Raum und Technologie" beschäftigte sich mit der pittoresken Landschaft und der Altstadt Dubrovniks als Kontext sowie dem Wunsch nach zeitgemäßen architektonischen Eingriffen, die sich bewusst in oder gegen den Kontext stellen.

Leitung Roger Riewe, Krunoslav Ivanisin, Till Lensing

Till Lensing

17

Headed by Roger Riewe, Krunoslav Ivanisin, Till Lensing

Till Lensing

Master Studio Valparaíso 2010

The Institute of Building Design
on a visit to the cultural capital of Chile (18)
Workshop in Valparaíso: April 16–May 3, 2010
Exhibition in Graz: June 2010
Exhibition in Valparaiso: October 2010

The Pacific Ocean port city of Valparaíso, with its status as "World Heritage," is with about one million inhabitants the second largest metropolitan high-density area of Chile and the cultural center. During an intensive workshop held on-site the projects of the students were meant to develop

Masterstudio Valparaíso 2010

Das Institut für Gebäudelehre zu Besuch in der kulturellen Hauptstadt Chiles (18)
Workshop in Valparaíso: 16. April–3. Mai 2010
Ausstellung in Graz: Juni 2010
Ausstellung in Valparaiso: Oktober 2010

Die am Pazifischen Ozean gelegene Hafenstadt Valparaíso mit dem Status als „Weltkulturerbe" bildet mit ihrem zirka eine Million Einwohner zählenden Einzugsgebiet den zweitwichtigsten Ballungsraum Chiles und das kulturelle Zentrum. Bei der als Intensivworkshop vor Ort abgehaltenen Projektübung sollen die Planungen der Studierenden an zwei signifikanten Stellen in der Stadt punktuelle Lösungsansätze erarbeiten. Die Lehrveranstaltung wurde in inhaltlicher und organisatorischer Kooperation mit dem Centro de Estudios para el Desarrollo Urbano Contemporaneo (www.duc.cl) und dem Österreichischen Honorarkonsul in Valparaíso, Michael Bier, abgewickelt. Die Herangehensweise an die Fragestellungen und die Qualität der Ergebnisse haben bei der Ausstellung vor Ort im Oktober 2010 ein derart großes Echo hervorgerufen, dass derzeit mehrere Universitäten aus Santiago und Valparaíso die Arbeit an den Aufgabenstellungen mit ihren Studierenden wiederholen.

Eine weitere Kooperation zu ähnlichen Aufgabenstellungen, diesmal mit Studierenden vor Ort, ist für den Zeitraum April/Mai 2011 geplant.

Markus Bogensberger, Ida Pirstinger

Chinese University of Hong Kong und TU Graz Kooperation 2010–2015

Im März 2010 wurde ein Kooperationsabkommen zwischen der TU Graz und der Chinese University of Hong Kong CUHK unterzeichnet. Dieses Memorandum of Understanding – MoU – das auf fünf Jahre begrenzt ist, ermöglicht einen Studierendenaustausch zwischen der School of Architecture der CUHK und der Architekturfakultät der TU Graz. Pro Studienjahr können hierbei zwei Studierende für ein Studienjahr oder bis zu vier Studierende für jeweils ein Semester pro Studienjahr beider Architekturfakultäten ausgetauscht werden. Das MoU kann nach fünf Jahren und nach positivem Verlauf von beiden Seiten verlängert werden.

Hierbei wurde das Thema „residential high rises" bearbeitet. Als kick-off wird dieses Vorhaben von der EPU (Eurasia-Pacific Uninet) finanziell substantiell unterstützt.

Roger Riewe

residential high rises // Graz – Hong Kong – Frankfurt – Madrid – München

In Kooperation den Hochschulen ETSAM (Escuela Tecnica Superior de Arquitectura Madrid), TU

18

specific solutions for two significant places in the city. Concerning both content and organization, the course was conducted in cooperation with the Centro de Estudios para el Desarrollo Urbano Contemporaneo (www.duc.cl) and the Austrian Honorary Consul in Valparaíso, Michael Beer. The specific approach to the topic as well as the quality of the results addressed during the exhibition on-site in October 2010 such a huge audience that several universities in Santiago and Valparaíso are currently repeating work on these tasks with their students.

A further cooperation on similar tasks, this time with students on-site is planned for the period April/May 2011.

Markus Bogensberger, Ida Pirstinger

Chinese University of Hong Kong and Graz University of Technology Co-Operation 2010–2015

Graz University of Technology and the Chinese University of Hong Kong CUHK signed a co-operation agreement in March 2010. This Memorandum of Understanding—MoU—which is limited to five years, permits an exchange of students between the School of Architecture at CUHK and the Faculty of Architecture at Graz University of Technology. Per academic year, two students from both faculties of architecture can be exchanged for one academic year or up to four students for one semester per academic year. If successful, the MoU can be renewed by both faculties after five years.

The focus was on the subject "residential high rises." As a kick-off, this project is substantially funded by the EPU (Eurasia-Pacific Uninet).

Roger Riewe

München und der Chinese University of Hongkong wurde im Sommersemester 2010 das Thema „residential high rises“ im Kontext der Nachverdichtung von Städten bearbeitet. Als Verdichtungsszenarien des Entwurfs wurden leerstehende Bürotürme in Wohnhochhäuser mit einer Höhe von mindestens 150 Metern transformiert.

Im Zuge der Kooperation gab es an den jeweiligen Hochschulen zahlreiche Veranstaltungen, in Form von Vorträgen, Workshops, Präsentationen mit Gastkritiken und Ausstellungen, wodurch ein hohes Maß an Erfahrungsaustausch ermöglicht und nicht zuletzt gute Entwurfsergebnisse erzielt wurden. Die Resultate sind Auslöser einer Diskussion über die Art der Verdichtung von Städten und die Form des zeitgemäßen urbanen Wohnens, die neue Erkenntnisse über Wohntypologien und Wohnhochhausstrukturen hervorgebracht hat.

Autoren des Buches sind die beteiligten Professoren und die jeweiligen Assistenten:
Dietrich Fink und Florian Fischer (Lehrstuhl für Integriertes Bauen, TU München), Juan Hererros, Auxilladora Galves Perez und Lina Toro (Escuela Tecnica Superior de Arquitectura Madrid, ETSAM), Esther Lorenz (Chinese University of Hong Kong, CUHK) und Roger Riewe und Ferdinand Oswald (Institut für Architekturtechnologie, TU Graz). Das Buch wird von Andreas Ruby (Ruby Press) editiert und herausgegeben und soll 2011 im Handel erscheinen.

Ferdinand Oswald

19

GRAZ MASTER LECTURES 2009/2010

07/10/09 | **Stig Mikkelsen + Stehen Savery-Trojaborg** (Kopenhagen) | **DISSING+WEITLING architecture** || 26/11/09 | **Krunoslav Ivanisin** (Zagreb) | **LIQUID CONTEXT** || 14/12/09 | **ppag architects** (Wien) | **WERKVORTRAG** || 11/01/10 | **Gilles Ebersolt** (Paris) | **BALLULES** || 22/03/10 | **Stefan Rettich** (Leibzig) | **RAUM SCHÖN REDEN** || 19/04/10 | **Nicolás Vázquez-Herrmann** (Mexico City) | **WERKVORTRAG** || 10/05/10 | **George Stanishev** (Sofia) | **PROJECTS** || 17/05/10 | **Christiano Toraldo di Francia/SUPERSTUDIO** (Florenz) | **A CRITICAL UTOPIA** || 31/05/10 | **Dietrich Fink** (München) | **PROJECTS** || 09/06/10 | **Esther Lorenz** (Hong Kong) | **ANOTHER CULTURE: PERSPECTIVES ON HONG KONG**

Antrittsvorlesung

Anselm Wagner (Institut für Architekturtheorie, Kunst- und Kulturwissenschaften): „Freundliche Viren. Perspektiven einer kulturwissenschaftlichen Architekturtheorie“, 21.6.2010

residential high rises // Graz—Hong Kong—Frankfurt—Madrid—Munich

In a co-operation of the universities ETSAM (Escuela Tecnica Superior de Arquitectura Madrid), TU Munich and the Chinese University of Hong Kong, the subject “residential high-rises” was studied in the context of densifying cities in summer semester 2010. As densification scenarios for design, vacant office towers were transformed into residential high-rises at least 150 meters high.

In the course of this co-operation there were numerous events at the various universities, in the form of lectures, workshops, presentations with guest critics and exhibitions, thus achieving a substantial exchange of experience and, not least, good design results. The results initiate a discussion on how to densify cities and the form of contemporary urban housing that has revealed new findings with regard to residential typologies and high-rise structures.

The authors of the book are the participating professors and their assistants:
Dietrich Fink and Florian Fischer (Chair of Integrated Building, TU Munich), Juan Hererros, Auxilladora Galves Perez and Lina Toro (Escuela Tecnica Superior de Arquitectura Madrid, ETSAM), Esther Lorenz (Chinese University of Hong Kong, CUHK), and Roger Riewe and Ferdinand Oswald (Institute for Architectural Technology, TU Graz). The book is edited and published by Andreas Ruby (Ruby Press) and is scheduled to appear in 2011.

Ferdinand Oswald

Inaugural Lecture

Anselm Wagner (Institute of Architectural Theory, History of Art and Cultural Studies): “Freundliche Viren. Perspektiven einer kulturwissenschaftlichen Architekturtheorie,” June 21, 2010.

Ausführliche Nachrichten
aus der Fakultätfinden Sie unter
The full length version of
the faculty news is online at
http://architektur.tugraz.at/faculty/gam/07/

GAM.

ARCHITECTURE MAGAZINE **08**

Die 8. Ausgabe von **GAM** widmet sich unter dem Titel „Dense Cities“ dem Themenfeld der „städtischen Dichte“ und dessen Relevanz für die konkrete Architekturproduktion. Der Lebensraum des 21. Jahrhunderts wird aller Voraussicht nach die Stadt sein. Seit dem Jahr 2008 wohnt mehr als die Hälfte der Weltbevölkerung in Städten und der weltweite Anteil der städtischen Bevölkerung wird nach Prognosen der UNO bis zum Jahr 2050 rund 70 % erreichen. Während sich ein Großteil dieser Entwicklung in den Megastädten und megaurbanen Räumen abspielt, die sich in den letzten Jahrzehnten vor allem in Asien und Südamerika mit rasender Geschwindigkeit entwickelt haben, erscheint die offene Entwicklung mittelgroßer Städte, die sich in ihrem Selbstverständnis noch auf die zentral orientierte historische Stadt berufen, als Anstoß für eine Diskussion neuer architektonischer Entwurfs- und Planungsansätze. Werden Städte als urbane Gebiete mit einer bestimmten Dichte aufgefasst, die in historischen Entwicklungsprozessen stehen, so können Entwurfsansätze der „Verdichtung“ und „Nachverdichtung“ auf allen Maßstabsebenen neue Perspektiven ihrer Transformation eröffnen. **GAM.08 Dense Cities** richtet die Aufmerksamkeit auf den architektonischen Zusammenhang zwischen den Prozessen der Urbanisierung und der Entwicklung kompakter städtischer Formen.

Es besteht kein Zweifel, dass die Abkehr vom ungezügelten Landverbrauch und der Verschwendung von Ressourcen angesichts der Bedrohung durch klimatische Veränderungen, aber auch im Sinne eines steigenden Bewusstseins für nachhaltige Lebensweisen, Bedingungen vernünftiger Planungen darstellen müssen. Die Notwendigkeit, höher verdichtete Siedlungsformen zu forcieren, ist daher weithin akzeptiert und hat zu der Entwicklung von zahlreichen Konzepten wie bspw. der Compact City geführt, die sich in Entwicklungsprogrammen der UNO (Agenda 21) und der Europäischen Kommission (Green Paper of Urban Environment) wiederfinden. **GAM.08** geht davon aus, dass es nicht gleichgültig ist, in welcher formalen Art sich das Phänomen „Stadt“ ausdrückt, sondern sieht den Entwurf kompakter städtischer Formen vielmehr im Zusammenhang mit zukunftsweisenden Strategien auf dem Weg zu einer nachhaltigen Stadt. So erfahren das Management von Siedlungsräumen beziehungsweise infrastrukturelle Themen in der Diskussion um nachhaltige räumliche Entwicklungspolitik zwar eine hohe Aufmerksamkeit, inwiefern diese Frage aber mit der Dichte der Stadt zusammenhängt, wird weniger erörtert. Doch wenn der Stopp des Landschaftsverbrauchs ernsthaft diskutiert werden soll, müssen urbane Verdichtungsszenarien auf allen Maßstabsebenen diskutiert werden: Die Dichte von (unterschiedlichen) Infrastrukturen, höhere Bebauungsdichten, die Dichte von unterschiedlichen Nutzungen, die Dichte an Wohn- und Arbeitsangeboten, die Dichte im Sinne der Entwicklung kompakter Gebäude- und Hüllformen bei energetischen Anforderungen, aber auch die Dichte als Frage nach den Grenzen sozialer Verträglichkeit, sobald Menschen zu eng „aufeinander“ leben. In diesem Sinne besitzt quantitative Dichte immer auch einen qualitativen Aspekt, der als „atmosphärische Dichte“ kompakter städtischer Formen für den Ausdruck einer urbanen Lebenswelt verantwortlich ist. Hinsichtlich dieser Frage werden in **GAM.08** die Möglichkeiten und Handlungsspielräume der Architekturproduktion zur Disposition gestellt und neu entworfen. So bildet die Entwicklung und Realisierung intelligenter Gebäudetypologien die Voraussetzung für räumliche Verdichtung auf der Mikroebene, die in Wechselwirkung mit der Vervielfältigung räumlicher Qualitäten im städtischen Raum, mit der Entwicklung neuer Typologien bzw. der Transformation und Erweiterung bestehender Nutzungen steht. Diese beziehen sich immer auf den Gebäudebestand einer Stadt, den die Architektur mit einem Blick auf die historischen Entwicklungsprozesse hinsichtlich der Anforderungen der Zukunft adaptiert und weiterbaut.

GAM.08 stellt die Frage, wie eine aktive Rolle der Architektur bei der Entwicklung von „Dense Cities“ auszugestalten ist. Erklärtes Ziel ist es, architektonische Mittel zu definieren, um den verschiedenen sozialen Gruppen ein hochqualitatives, vielfältiges und anpassungsfähiges urbanes Lebensumfeld zu schaffen. Die Bandbreite der Fragestellung erstreckt sich über alle Maßstabsebenen von der Stadtlandschaft und Agglomeration über das Quartier und den Stadtteil bis zum Block und Einzelobjekt und reicht von der Entwicklung neuer Gebäudetypen über konkrete Interventionen im urbanen Feld bis zu Analysen der Transformation städtischer Dichte. **GAM.08** lädt Sie ein, ein Abstract (max. 500 Wörter) zur Fragestellung einer Neubewertung „städtischer Dichte“ bis zum **30. April 2011** einzureichen. Der Abgabetermin für den fertigen Beitrag (Full Paper) ist der **12. August 2011**.

GAM.08, die nächste Nummer des Grazer Architektur Magazins, erscheint im Frühjahr 2012. GAM ist die offizielle Publikation der Architekturfakultät der Technischen Universität Graz. Der Hauptteil jeder Nummer von GAM ist aber nicht der Selbstdarstellung unserer Universität, sondern dem international offenen Diskurs über ein spezifisches Thema gewidmet. Das Thema von GAM.08 ist „Dense Cities“. GAM versteht sich als Bühne, auf der kontroverse Positionen in der aktuellen Architekturdebatte auf hohem Niveau dargestellt werden und fördert den seriösen Diskurs über Architektur über kulturelle Grenzen, aber auch über die Grenzen des Fachs hinaus.

AutorInnenbeiträge können aus Texten (Deutsch oder Englisch), Bildern und Plänen bestehen. Unser mit internationalen Experten besetzter Redaktionsbeirat unterstützt die Redaktion beim Peer-Review-Verfahren der eingereichten Beiträge und bürgt für deren hohe Qualität.

AutorInnen, die sich mit einem Beitrag zum Thema „Dense Cities“ für die nächste Nummer von GAM bewerben möchten, werden gebeten, schon frühzeitig mit der Redaktion in Verbindung zu treten (gam@tugraz.at). Hinweise zu Layout, Einreichungs- und Copyright-Bestimmungen sind unter http://gam.tugraz.at zu finden.

http://gam.tugraz.at